THE
BATTLE
OF THE
ATLANTIC
1939–1945

The 50th Anniversary
International Naval Conference

EDITED BY STEPHEN HOWARTH
AND DEREK LAW

Greenhill Books, London

Naval Institute Press, Annapolis, Maryland

Printed and bound in Great Britain by
Butler & Tanner, Frome, Somerset.

Contents

Contents

In May 1993 I had the privilege of representing The
Queen, the Lord High Admiral, in HMY Britannia at the
multi-national naval review off Anglesey in commemoration
of the fiftieth anniversary of the culmination of the
Battle of the Atlantic. That was perhaps the most dramatic
event among those memorable celebrations on Merseyside.
Among the others, probably the least publicised was a
specialist conference on this relentless campaign that went
on, principally in the North Atlantic, throughout the
Second World War. It was Winston Churchill who declared it
to be a 'battle' and he saw it as 'the dominating factor
all through the war. Never for one moment could we forget
that everything happening elsewhere, on land, at sea, or in
the air, depended ultimately on its outcome.'

This collection of papers is the result of that
conference. It is probably the most comprehensive and
definitive analysis of an immensely complicated and
constantly evolving struggle to obtain mastery of the
Atlantic shipping lanes. It involved merchant and naval
seamen and growing numbers of airmen from many countries,
but it was the merchant seamen and their ships that the
battle was all about; the allied warships and aircraft were
there to get them and their vital cargoes to their
destinations against the most strenuous and skilful efforts
of the enemy.

As Patron of the Society for Nautical Research, I am
very pleased that the Society played such an important part
in the organisation of the conference and in the
preparation of this volume. I am sure it will have a
prominent place in the history of the war. It is certainly
a worthy monument to the memory of all those who lost their
lives in the homeric battle.

1994

Preface and Acknowledgements

by J. D. Brown

The idea for a Battle of the Atlantic anniversary conference was first proposed in Paris, in the former *École-Polytechnique*, on Thanksgiving Day in November 1986, during an interval in one of a series of excellent conferences organized by the *Service historique de la Marine*. The basic themes were established that evening by an *ad hoc* international 'panel' whose members included Professor Jürgen Rohwer, Eric Grove, Jock Gardner and David K. Brown, all of whom later featured among the speakers. The final programme was remarkably close to the original scheme. The conference would attempt to describe all the principal elements of the campaign from both sides - the command structures and the conduct of the Battle, the shipbuilding and repair organizations, the training and the introduction of new technology, the impact of aviation and the even newer science of operational analysis. Although many of these topics had been aired before, it was believed that all merited re-evaluation in the light of recent research and analysis and from the perspective of 50 years. Some other topics had been insufficiently examined, such as the economics of the Battle and the development of the bases, while the contributions of the merchant navies of the occupied Allies and of the Italian submarines were little known outside those countries.

It was the intention that the conference would be held in mid-1991, to mark the 50th anniversary of the first use of 'code-breaking' by the Royal Navy, but this proved to be over-optimistic. It was not until that year that detailed planning could begin for a conference in May 1993. Agreeing the list of speakers and chairmen (from Britain, the United States, Canada, Australia, Norway, Germany, France and Italy and the former Soviet Union) was a long process, but choosing the venue was simple - where else but Liverpool? It was at this stage that the Society for Nautical Research became the conference's principal sponsor and D. K. Brown, Eric Grove and I were joined by Derek Law and, subsequently, Tony Sainsbury. Invaluable secretarial support was provided by Jean Hollis during these early months. The National Museums and Galleries on Merseyside, which was to be the principal conference venue, sent Alan Scarth as its representative. When he had to leave, to concentrate on his task of organizing the Maritime Museum's splendid Battle of the Atlantic Exhibition, Adrian Jarvis proved to be a most energetic and practical addition to the team, as did Diane Ascott, of the University of Liverpool. We are grateful to Dr Mike Stammers, Director of the Museum, for nominating such capable assistants.

The last member of the organizing team should have been Justin Powell, who came to the Naval Historical Branch in late 1992 to give much-needed administrative assistance. It seemed that this young Lieutenant had no sooner arrived, and made himself indispensable, before the exigencies of the Service took him away to join the UN Protection Force in the Western Sahara. We were extremely fortunate that he was relieved by the equally competent Lieutenant Michael Smith who, with less than four months to go before the conference, took the measure of the job as though he had spent a lifetime at it.

Our thanks are also due to Dr Stammers for allowing the use of the Museum's facilities on the first two days of the conference and for his hospitality; to the cheerful and helpful staff of the Everyman Theatre, where the third day's proceedings took place; to Caroline Griffiths of the Merseyside Tourism Board, who coped with everything that was thrown at her; and to Sandra Sheldrake, the Library Secretary of King's College London, who dealt with the conference bookings and associated queries of the multi-national participants. Financial viability was virtually assured by the good offices of Captain Nigel Hoskin, co-ordinator of the Battle of the Atlantic 50th Anniversary events on the staff of Flag Officer Plymouth, and his successors Captains Hugh May and John Harvey. All generously allocated funds sufficient to cover the running costs of the conference from the money raised, by public appeal under the chairmanship of Lord Stirling, to pay for commemorative events. Assistance and encouragement from the Royal Navy was much appreciated, particularly the keen interest and support shown by the then First Sea Lord, now Admiral of the Fleet, Sir Julian Oswald, and Rear Admiral Mike Gretton, himself the son of the famous Escort Group leader, Vice Admiral Sir Peter Gretton. Finally, I owe a personal debt of gratitude to Commander Tim Sloane, whose heavy responsibility as the 'shore-side' public relations co-ordinator for the huge naval presence in Liverpool did not prevent him from doing everything in his power to promote the image of the conference.

Material sufficient for a 10-day programme was suggested, and rigid self-control was needed to keep within the three-day limit. Like the presenters, the audience, ranging from veterans of the campaign to young researchers, also came from the four corners of the world and provided a broad and informed cross-section of interest which made for stimulating discussion periods. The gathering of academics, professionals and engineers gave a blend of inspired research and hard-won experience which would be difficult to rival and their presentations were of a uniformly high quality. This volume constitutes a body of scholarship which adds immeasurably to the understanding of the Battle and should become, as the organizing team intended, a standard work of reference. Lest this opinion might seem to strike an overly self-congratulatory note, it should be added that the programme did attract criticism at the time, mainly because of its perceived failure to deal adequately with the Merchant Navy or to allow certain topics to be presented in national terms. The organizing team accepts full responsibility for these and any other omissions and will try to rectify them in time for the centenary conference.

David Brown
Head, Ministry of Defence
Naval Historical Branch

Contributors

Thomas A. Adams is a member of the Chartered Institute of Journalists whose interest in shipping stems from his student days at Belfast Nautical College. Since then he has researched and contributed over 100 articles to historical and technical periodicals and books. He has made a particular study of the logisitical support of warships by merchant ships, and is an authority on Royal Fleet Auxiliaries and Hospital Ships. His first book, *Irish Naval Service*, was published in 1982. With David J. Lees, he compiled the *Register of Type VII U-boats*, published in 1991. Since 1988 he has edited the World Ship Society's quarterly naval magazine *Warships*.

Dean C. Allard is Director of Naval History at the Naval Historical Center in Washington DC. Located in the Washington Navy Yard, the Center undertakes historical, museum, library, archival and art programmes for the US Navy. Dr Allard holds advanced degrees from Georgetown University and The George Washington Uniiversity. His publications relate to US Naval history and to the history of American marine science. They include the books *The United States Navy and the Vietnam Conflict* (volume I) and *Spencer Fullerton Baird: A Study in the History of American Science*. His articles have appeared in a number of journals, including the US Naval Institute *Proceedings*, *Military Affairs*, *American Neptune* and *Airpower Journal*.

Horst Boog received his first degree at Middlebury, Vt., USA, and his PhD at the University of Heidelberg. Now retired from the posts of Leitender Wissenschaftlicher Direktor and head of Research Department II (World War II) at the Militärgeschichtliches Forschungsamt, Freiburg, he is the author of *Die Deutsche Luftwaffenführung 1935-1945* (Stuttgart, 1982), and of numerous articles in international journals on the conduct of the air war, Intelligence, historiography, aviation technology and logistics, as well as policy and strategy. He edited *The Conduct of the Air War in the Second World War* (Oxford, 1992), and has co-written three more books: a history of the West German armed forces entitled *Verteidigung im Bündnis* (Munich, 1975), *Der Angriff auf die Sowjetunion* (Stuttgart, 1983) and *Der globale Krieg* (Stuttgart, 1990). He frequently lectures at international conferences.

David K. Brown spent the whole of his career, since leaving Liverpool University, as a member of the Royal Corps of Naval Architects, working on ship design and associated research. He retired in 1988 as Deputy Chief Naval Architect. He is a member of Council of the Royal Institute Architects and has written many technical papers for that Institution and others. His most recent paper attempts to show the relevance of historical studies to future design. He has been on the staff of the Royal Naval College and University College, where he still lectures occasionally. Since retirement he has been a consultant to the Department of Transport on RO-RO ferry safety. He has published four books, contributed to many others and written many historical articles.

Ian L. Buxton, BSc, PhD, CEng, FRINA, FACE, is Reader in Marine Transport in the Department of Marine Technology at the University of Newcastle upon Tyne, where his teaching and research interests are concerned with technical and economic aspects of the design and operation of all types of marine vessel. His naval interests include the design, construction and demolition of British warships. He plays a leading part in the British Shipbuilding History Project, the objective of which is to produce the definitive history of the British shipbuilding, marine engineering and shiprepairing industries.

W. J. R. Gardner, a serving Lieutenant Commander in the Royal Navy, is a specialist in ASW. In 1989 he gained an MPhil degree at Cambridge University, with a thesis on the Soviet submarine-based ballistic missile force. Whilst there he edited the *Cambridge Review of International Affairs*. He has presented several papers and had articles published on 20th-century naval historical topics, both in Britain and abroad. As well as being a regular reviewer of books for several journals, he is currently working on a modern ASW volume in the Brassey's Seapower series.

William Glover, a serving Lieutenant Commander in the Royal Canadian Navy, is currently an Historian with the Directorate General of History, National Defence Headquarters, Ottawa, Canada, where he is researching the RCN in World War II. He has degrees from Queen's University at Kingston, Ontario, and the University of London. He first joined the Canadian naval reserve in 1969, and has also served with the Royal Naval Reserve. Since transferring to the permanent force in 1977 he has held a number of appointments at sea, both in training destroyers, and in ASW frigates and destroyers. Immediately before moving to Ottawa he taught History and Political Science at Royal Roads Military College, Victoria, BC. He has written and lectured on aspects of defence history and policy in Canada.

James Goldrick, a serving Commander in the Royal Australian Navy, was born in 1958 and joined the RAN in 1974. He holds BA and MLitt degrees from Australian universities and is an ASW specialist who has seen sea service with the RAN and on exchange with the Royal Navy. He has served as ADC to the Governor-General of Australia and as a Research Officer to the RAN's Chief of Naval Staff. Command of HMAS *Cessnock* (PTF 210) was followed by a year as an International Research Fellow at the US Naval War College at Newport. He is presently serving at the RAN Surface Warfare School at HMAS *Watson* in Sydney and is in charge of the RAN's Principal Warfare Officer training and Tactical Development Unit. Publications include *The King's Ships Were at Sea* and a variety of edited books, as well as many articles on contemporary and historical naval subjects.

Eric Grove joined the History Department at Britannia RNC, Dartmouth, as a civilian lecturer in 1971. In 1980-81 he was exchange professor at the US Naval Academy, Annapolis. Leaving Dartmouth as Deputy Head of Strategic Studies in 1984, he worked for a year with the Council for Arms Control and then became a freelance defence analyst and naval historian. He taught at the Royal Naval College Greenwich and

Cambridge University, was a research fellow at the University of Southampton and was consultant for the National Maritime Museum's new Sea Power gallery. He also helped set up the Foundation for International Security, and, under its auspices, initiated the Adderbury Talks, annual discussions between the RN, USN and Russian Navy. His many books and articles include *Vanguard to Trident: British Naval Policy since World War II* (Annapolis and London, 1990). Since October 1993 he has been Lecturer in International Politics at the University of Hull, where he is also Deputy Director of the Centre for Security Studies.

Jan G. Heitmann was born in 1960 in Hamburg, Germany, and served in the Federal Armed Forces before going on to study Modern History, Political Sciences, and Social and Economic History at Hamburg University. Following the award of his MA in 1989, he worked in a private company, and then, sponsored by a post-graduate scholarship, started research work for his doctoral dissertation. Since 1990 he has worked as a self-employed historian. In addition, he is a freelance scientific staff member of and author for a British publishing house. He also holds a part-time lectureship at Hamburg University, and, as a Lieutenant in the German Naval Reserve, frequently serves in the Naval Infantry and as Duty Officer Military Diary in the German Maritime Headquarters.

David Hobbs, a serving officer in the RN, entered Britannia RNC in 1964. For his current service in the MoD he was recently appointed MBE. After qualifying as a pilot in 1970, he served in many ships and naval air squadrons world-wide - notably the LCT *Bastion* (Persian Gulf) and six aircraft carriers, including the fourth *Ark Royal* and her successor, as well as 849 Squadron (flying Gannets) and 845 Squadron (flying Wessex). A regular lecturer and contributor to naval publications and a recognized expert in naval aviation, his books include *Aircraft of the Royal Navy since 1945* and *Ark Royal: The Name Lives On*. Now writing a comprehensive book on British aircraft carriers, he lives in Dorset with his wife (a former WRNS officer) and son.

Stephen Howarth, co-editor of the present volume and a retired officer of the Royal Naval Reserve, is the author of several books on naval, maritime and general history. These include *The Koh-i-Noor Diamond, The Knights Templar, Morning Glory: A History of the Imperial Japanese Navy 1895-1945, August '39: The Last Four Weeks of Peace, To Shining Sea: A History of the United States Navy 1775-1991*, and *Sea Shell: The Story of Shell's British Tanker Fleets 1892-1992*. With his late father, the historian David Howarth, he co-wrote *The Story of P&O: The Peninsular and Oriental Steam Navigation Company 1837-1987* and *Nelson: The Immortal Memory*. He was contributing editor of *Men of War: Great Naval Leaders of World War II*, and writes articles, reviews and obituaries for a wide variety of periodicals. Currently writing the centenary history of the "Shell" Transport and Trading Company, he is a Fellow of both the Royal Geographical Society and the Royal Historical Society.

Jean Kessler studied at the *École Navale*, graduated from the *École Supérieure de Guerre Navale*, and is now a rear admiral. He has exercised command both at sea and on land: in the coastal minesweeper *Pegase*, the ocean minesweepers *Narvik* and *Garigliano*, the 2nd Aviso Division and the aviso *Detroyat*, as well as in the *École Fusiliers marins* (Marines College) and as *Commandement des Fusliers marins*. He has often served in Paris as a Naval Staff Officer, and has been Chief of Staff to the French

Navy's Admiral Inspector-General. Since February 1990 he has been Head of the French Navy's Historical Service.

Tony Lane, an ex-merchant seaman, is a senior lecturer in sociology at the University of Liverpool. He is the author of *Grey Dawn Breaking: British Merchant Seafarers in the Late 20th Century* (1986), *Liverpool, Gateway of Empire* (1987) and *The Merchant Seamen's War* (1993).

Derek G. Law, co-editor of the present volume, read history at Glasgow University and trained as a librarian at Strathclyde University. He is now Director of Information Services at King's College London, where he is a Trustee of the Liddell Hart Centre for Military Archives. He is the author of *The Royal Navy in World War II: An Annotated Bibliography* (1988) and has contributed bibliographies to several other works. He is joint editor of the *Annual Bibliography of Maritime History* and Secretary of the Society for Nautical Research.

Philip Lundeberg studied at Duke and Harvard Universities, and is Curator Emeritus of Naval History at the Smithsonian Institution. Surviving the loss of USS *Frederick C. Davis* during Operation Teardrop in April 1945, he subsequently assisted Samuel Eliot Morison in chronicling American anti-submarine operations, 1943-45. Prior to joining the Smithsonian in 1959, he taught naval history at the Naval Academy, where he continued to study undersea warfare. His publications include *Samuel Colt's Submarine Battery*, 'Undersea Warfare and Allied Strategy in World War I' in the *Smithsonian Journal of History*, naval exhibits in the National Museum's Hall of Armed Forces History, and 'By Land and By Sea: Yorktown, 1781'. He is past president of the Society for Military History and the US Commission on Military History.

David J. Lyon read History at Kings College, Cambridge, and has spent his working life at the National Maritime Museum, Greenwich. There he worked on the world's largest collection of ship plans before becoming Curator of Naval Ordnance, then Head of Enquiries, and now Chief of Research at the Maritime Information Centre. He was an officer in the Royal Naval Reserve, where he learned to dive. He was joint founder of both the Ordnance Society and Maritime Archaeological Surveys. He is the author of several books and many articles on ships and naval history, most recently *The Sailing Navy List*. He is married to an EC lawyer with whom he shares the ownership of a 16' sailing boat.

N. V. Naumov was born on 25 May 1936 in Saratov province. He gained his BA from Moscow State University, Department of History, as a student of 19th-century Russia. In 1959, he was awarded the degree of MA for his thesis on *The Russian Goldmining Industry on the Eve of the First World War*. For one year he worked as a guide at the M. I. Kalinin Museum, before becoming a research fellow at the Institute for the Study of Marxism-Leninism (1960-63). He then returned to Moscow State University for four years of post-graduate work, including one year (1965-66) at the Sorbonne, and wrote a dissertation on *French Bourgeois Historiography of the Great October Socialist Revolution 1917-1967*, published in Moscow in 1975. From 1967 to 1972 he was associate professor in Moscow State University's Department of History, Soviet Society section, and since 1972 has been Associate Professor (Docent) in the department's 20th-Century Russia section. He has published more than 30 articles on the Russian revolutionary movement, the Civil War in Russia, the social history of the Soviet Union, the Great Patriotic War 1939-45, and Soviet foreign policy. In addition to his published dissertation, his books include *Essays in the History of the USSR, 1861-1961* (Novosty Press Agency, Moscow, 1965) and chapters for the period 1917-45 in *History of the USSR: A Supplementary Textbook for Higher Educational Institutions* (Moscow, four editions, 1979-88).

Sönke Neitzel served in the Federal German Armed Forces in 1987-88 before studying History at the University of Mainz. His first book, *Die deutschen U-Boot-Bunker und Bunkerwerften*, was published in 1991. He is currently completing his doctoral thesis on the subject of the Air War over the Atlantic and North Sea from the German point of view, 1939-1945.

Axel Niestlé is a geographer by profession, holding a PhD from the Technical University of Berlin. As an amateur historian he has been working for more than a decade on technical and operational aspects of the U-boat campaign of World War II, and has written monographs on the Type VIIC and Type IXC U-boats.

Henry Probert graduated in Modern History from Sidney Sussex College, Cambridge, in 1948. He subsequently joined the Education Branch of the Royal Air Force, in which he served until 1978 when he retired as Director, holding the rank of Air Commodore. He was then appointed Head of the Air Historical Branch, where in addition to his administrative duties he undertook many writing projects, including assisting with the in-house history of the RAF role in the Falklands campaign and publishing 'High Commanders of the RAF.' He now chairs the Programme Committee of the RAF Historical Society, which he helped establish 10 years ago, and is writing a history of the RAF role in the war against Japan, due for publication in 1995.

Philip Pugh was born in 1940 and graduated in mechanical engineering from the University of Leeds in 1960. He conducted research into high-speed flight and the aerodynamics of weapons first at the National Physical Laboratory and then within the MoD. Subsequently, he transferred within the MoD to work on the analysis and cost-forecasting of major weapon systems, becoming Assistant Director, Project Time and Cost Analysis (Weapons and Electronics). Application of similar analyses to historical questions gave rise to his book *The Cost of Seapower*. At present, he is on loan from the MoD to University College London where, as a member of the Defence Engineering Group, he is engaged in teaching and research.

Werner Rahn, a captain in the Federal German Navy, was born in 1939 and joined the FGN in 1960. He holds a PhD in history from Hamburg University and is head of the Second World War Research Department, Military History Research Office of the German Armed Forces, Freiburg-im-Breisgau. He is the author of *Reichsmarine und Landesverteidigung 1919-1928 [German Navy and Defence Policy 1919-1928]* (Munich, 1976) and several articles on German naval history. He is co-editor with Gerhard Schrieber of the facsimile edition of *Kriegstagebuch der Seekriegsleitung 1939-1945 [War Diary of the Naval Staff 1939-1945], Part A*, (Herford and Bonn, 1988-94.)

Graham Rhys-Jones served in the Royal Navy as an aviation and anti-submarine specialist. He has a degree in International Relations from Cambridge. On leaving the

Royal Navy he took up a two-year (SecNav) Research Fellowship at the US Naval War College to pursue studies in 20th-century maritime operations. In 1993 he was awarded the Edward S. Miller naval history prize for an account of the *Bismarck* operation. His other studies have included an examination of Grand Admiral Dönitz's conduct of the U-boat campaign of 1941; a critique of German planning for the invasion of Norway; and a review of British operations in the Arctic 1942-43. He is now working in England as a defence consultant, writing and lecturing on maritime strategy as time allows.

Eberhard Rössler was born in Berlin, Germany, in 1929. Between 1948-51 he studied Mathematics and Physics at the Humboldt University, Berlin. In 1953 he passed the *Staatsexamen* and was awarded the degree of Diplom-Mathematiker at the Free University, Berlin. From 1954 until his retirement in 1991 he taught at various institutions of higher education and the Wirtschaftsakademie Berlin, most recently as Director of Studies. Since 1966 he has published many books and papers on German U-boat development and U-boat construction, German torpedoes and German sonar developments.

Jürgen Rohwer was born in 1924 and served in the German Navy, in destroyers and minesweepers, from 1942 to 1945. From 1948 to 1953 he studied history at Hamburg University before becoming Manager of the Council for Defence Research (1954-59). For the following 30 years (1959-89) he was Director of the Library of Contemporary History in Stuttgart. He was also editor of the journal *Marine-Rundschau* from 1958 to 1987, and since 1985 has been a Vice President of the International Commission on Military History. He is a member of many national and international institutions, and has published many works in Germany and abroad on military and naval history, especially on the Battle of the Atlantic and on Signal Intelligence.

A. B. Sainsbury was born and brought up in Liverpool, and saw Captain Walker go to sea for the last time. He served in the Liverpool Fire Service 1940-42 (at a rather illegally early age) and became a reluctant Bevin boy, allegedly drawn by ballot to carry out his war service in a coal mine. That at least took him to Northumberland. After post-war Oxford (reading PPE and learning to row), he returned there and met his wife; they have two sons and one grandson. He joined Tyne Division RNVR in 1950 and retired after 33 years' service (latterly in London Division, and including three appointments as a Captain), during which time he was awarded the VRD with clasp. In 1992 the second edition of his *Royal Navy Day by Day* was published. Since winning the Julian Corbett Prize in 1963 for an essay on 'The Dardanelles and Admiral Duckworth', he has been writing, spasmodically, the life of that officer; now in retirement from a civilian career in academic administration, he is engaging him more closely. Ceasing to be Chairman of his Bench should help, but he remains a Vice-President of the Navy Records Society and of the Society for Nautical Research, as well as a Trustee of *The Naval Review*.

Alberto Santoni was born in Rome in 1936 and is Professor Docent both in Military History at the University of Pisa and in Naval History and Policy at the Italian Naval Academy in Livorno. Among his many distinguished historical works are three volumes on the Pacific War, three successful books on British cryptography in the World Wars, the official account of the military campaign in Sicily in 1943 (issued by the Historical Department of the Italian Army) and three recent volumes covering the whole of naval history from the discovery of America to the Falklands conflict. He is also a member of the Italian Committee of Military History and a council member of both the Italian Society of Military History and the Historical Office of the Italian Navy.

Alan J. Scarth earned his PhD in Medieval History at Liverpool University, where he had earlier gained his BA (Hons). Since 1982 he has been a curator at the Merseyside Maritime Museum (National Museums and Galleries on Merseyside, Liverpool). As well as being responsible for the museum's internationally important ships models collection, he recently researched and produced its highly acclaimed 'Battle of the Atlantic' gallery, which opened in May 1993.

Paul M. Sutcliffe works for the Ministry of Defence. He spent much of his early career there at the Defence Operational Analysis Establishment, but moved into technical research in 1986 when he transferred to the then Admiralty Research establishment, Portland. He later became Deputy Director Submarines and Underwater, and subsequently Director Underwater Systems in the newly formed Defence Research Agency. He has done much work in the field of Maritime Operational research, covering most aspects of maritime systems and warfare from the design of patrol craft to total force mix issues, and has also worked on such diverse topics as economic warfare, space and missile technical intelligence and underwater weapons and technology. He moved to his present post as Assistant Chief Scientific Adviser (Research) in September 1992.

Atle Thowsen, director of the Bergens Sjøfartsmuseum (Bergen Maritime Museum), was born in 1940, gained his MA from the University of Bergen in 1965 and his PhD from the same institution in 1984. Amongst other publications he is the author of *Growth and Structural Changes in Times of Crisis, 1914-1939* (volume IV of the four-volume work *Bergen and Shipping*, Bergen, 1983), *The History of the Norwegian Shipowners' Mutual War Risks Insurance Association 1935-1985*, vol. I (Bergen, 1988), and *Nortraship: Profit and Patriotism* (volume I of the five-volume work *The Merchant Navy at War 1939-1945*, Oslo, 1992).

Geoffrey Till is Professor and Head of the Department of History and International Affairs at the Royal Naval College Greenwich. He also teaches in the Department of War Studies at King's College London, and before that, was in the Department of Management and Systems at the City University. In addition to many articles on various aspects of defence, he is the author of a number of books including *Air Power and the Royal Navy* (1979), *Maritime Strategy and the Nuclear Age* (2nd edn., Macmillan, London, 1984), *Modern Sea Power* (Brassey's, London, 1987), and, with Bryan Ranft, *The Sea in Soviet Strategy* (2nd edn., Macmillan, London, 1989). He has recently completed, with D. J. Pay, *East-West Relations in the 1990s: The Naval Dimension* (Frances Pinter, London, 1990). Most recently he edited a volume in the Brassey's Seapower series, *Coastal Forces*. Another volume on *Seapower* is currently in preparation for Frank Cass.

Erich Topp was born in 1914 and entered the German Navy shortly before his 20th birthday. He conducted 17 war patrols in the period 1938-42: four as watch officer in U-46, three in command of U-57 and 10 in command of U-552. In 1943-44 he was Chief of the 27th U-boat Flotilla, providing tactical training to all U-boats. In 1944 he became Chief of the Research and Development Group testing the new Types XXI and XXIII, and in 1945, as commanding officer of the Type XXI U-2513, he conducted his final war patrol. He was awarded many decorations, including the Dagger of Honour with Diamonds. Following the war he qualified as an architect and civil engineer at the Technical University, Hanover (1945-50), and over the subsequent eight years was associated with the construction of theatres and administration buildings. In 1958 he joined the Federal German Navy and served for three years as German Liaison Officer with SACLANT and as Head of the Navy Section, German Permanent Military Representative, in NATO's Military Committee. He then commanded Germany's amphibious forces and submarine forces, and was successively Chief of Staff of the Fleet, Assistant Chief of Staff (Plans, Policy and Operations), and Deputy Chief of Naval Operations, Chief of Navy Staff. For his federal naval service he was awarded the Great Service Cross of the Federal Republic. He retired at the end of 1966 in the rank of Rear Admiral (Upper Half). He and his wife Ilse have two sons and two daughters.

Gary E. Weir earned his PhD in modern German history from the University of Tennessee at Knoxville in 1982. After a year of teaching at the US Naval Academy, he joined the the Contemporary History Branch of the US Naval Historical Center in 1987. In this capacity he has written *Building American Submarines, 1914-1940* and *Forged in War: The Naval-Industrial Complex and American Submarine Construction, 1940-1961* (Naval Historical Center, 1991 and 1993). As well as articles in a wide variety of journals, his other publications include *Building the Kaiser's Navy: The Imperial Naval Office and German Industry in the Tirpitz Era, 1890-1919*, the expanded version of his doctoral dissertation (Naval Institute Press, 1992). He holds a part-time Associate Professorship of History at the University of Maryland University College, and is the recipient of fellowships from the McClure Foundation, the Office of Naval Research and the DAAD (German Academic Exchange Service).

H. P. Willmott was educated at the Universities of Liverpool and London, earning his MA in History (1971) and his PhD in War Studies (1991). In 1985 he was elected a Fellow of the Royal Historical Society. He has been a senior lecturer in the Department of War Studies at the Royal Military Academy, Sandhurst (1969-92), and visiting professor at Temple University (1989) and Memphis State University (1989-90). He has written extensively on warfare in general and World War II in particular, his most important books being *The Great Crusade* (a military re-interpretation of World War II), *Empires in the Balance* and *The Barrier and The Javelin*, the latter pair being the first two parts of a four-volume history of the Pacific War for the US Naval Institute Press. In 1983, *The Barrier and The Javelin* won the Lyman Book Award. He has presented papers at numerous distinguished institutions and conferences as well as in world-wide broadcast form, and is now Professor of naval history in the Department of Military Strategy and Operations, National War College, National Defense University, Washington DC.

David Zimmerman is associate professor of military history at the University of Victoria, Victoria, BC, Canada. His major works include *Top Secret Exchange: The Tizard Mission and the Scientific War* (forthcoming), *The Great Naval Battle of Ottawa* and *Coastal Fort: A History of Fort Sullivan Eastport, Maine*. He is currently writing a social history of the RCN in World War II and a study on the development of Britain's air defence system prior to the Battle of Britain.

Maps

drawn by Richard Natkiel

The following six chronologically consecutive maps vividly depict the expansion and alteration of the Battle of the Atlantic in its 68-month course. Each map shows the locations of Allied and neutral merchant ships sunk, and of U-boats sunk; the extent of unescorted and later escorted convoys routes; and the extent of territories under German/Axis control. In addition, maps 1-3 indicate the limit of the Pan-American Neutrality Zone, and maps 3-6 show the ever-growing areas under Allied air cover.

Map 1	September 1939-May 1940
Map 2	June 1940-March 1941
Map 3	April 1941-December 1941
Map 4	January 1942-July 1942
Map 5	August 1942-May 1943
Map 6	June 1943-May 1945

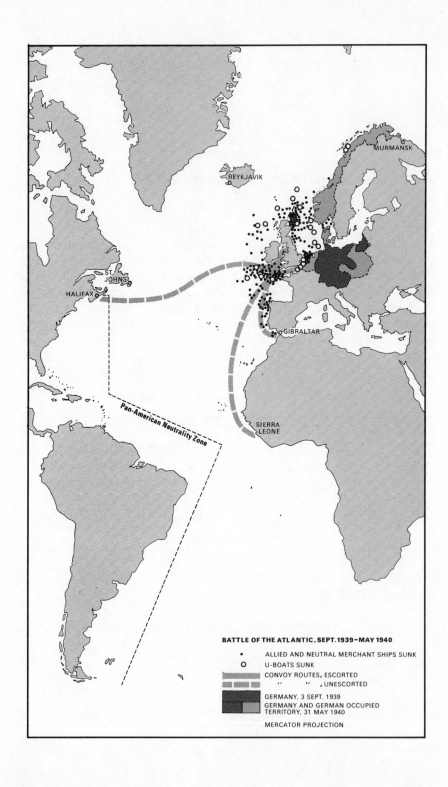

BATTLE OF THE ATLANTIC, SEPT. 1939 – MAY 1940

- •   ALLIED AND NEUTRAL MERCHANT SHIPS SUNK
- ○   U-BOATS SUNK
-     CONVOY ROUTES, ESCORTED
-        "   "   , UNESCORTED
-     GERMANY, 3 SEPT. 1939
-     GERMANY AND GERMAN OCCUPIED TERRITORY, 31 MAY 1940

MERCATOR PROJECTION

MURMANSK

REYKJAVIK

ST. JOHNS

HALIFAX

GIBRALTAR

Pan-American Neutrality Zone

SIERRA LEONE

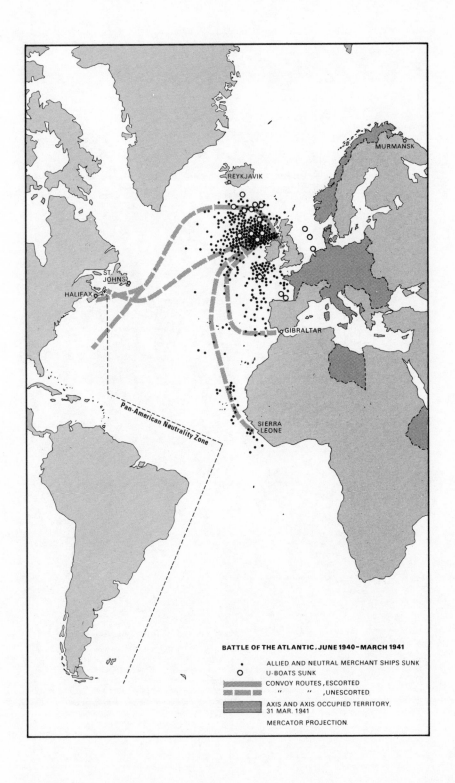

MURMANSK

REYKJAVIK

ST JOHNS

HALIFAX

GIBRALTAR

Pan-American Neutrality Zone

SIERRA LEONE

BATTLE OF THE ATLANTIC, JUNE 1940–MARCH 1941

- •   ALLIED AND NEUTRAL MERCHANT SHIPS SUNK
- ○   U-BOATS SUNK

CONVOY ROUTES, ESCORTED

     "   "   , UNESCORTED

AXIS AND AXIS OCCUPIED TERRITORY,
31 MAR. 1941

MERCATOR PROJECTION

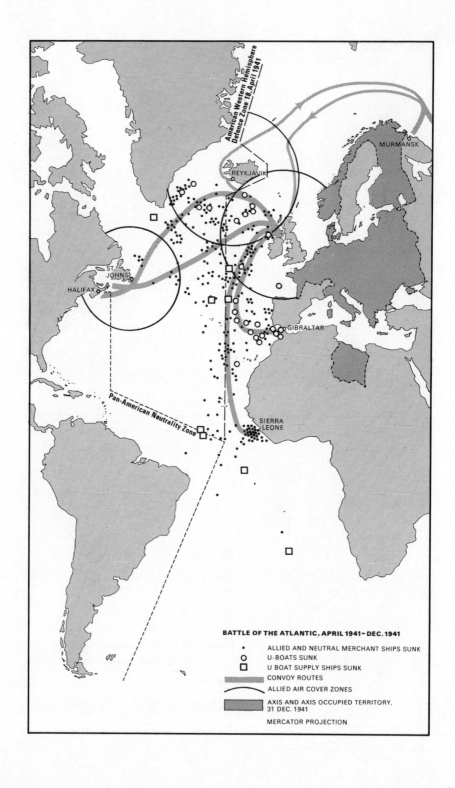

BATTLE OF THE ATLANTIC, APRIL 1941–DEC. 1941

- ALLIED AND NEUTRAL MERCHANT SHIPS SUNK
- ○ U-BOATS SUNK
- □ U BOAT SUPPLY SHIPS SUNK
- CONVOY ROUTES
- ALLIED AIR COVER ZONES
- AXIS AND AXIS OCCUPIED TERRITORY, 31 DEC. 1941

MERCATOR PROJECTION

MURMANSK

REYKJAVIK

ST. JOHNS

HALIFAX

American Western Hemisphere
Defence Zone 18, April 1941

GIBRALTAR

Pan-American Neutrality Zone

SIERRA
LEONE

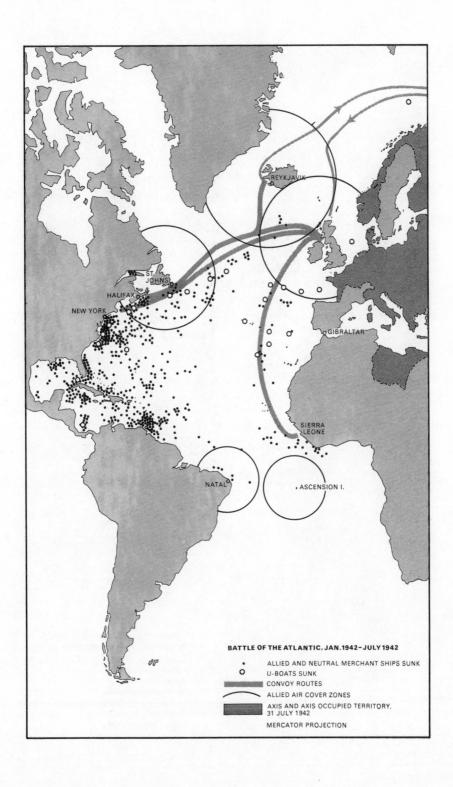

BATTLE OF THE ATLANTIC, JAN.1942–JULY 1942

- ·   ALLIED AND NEUTRAL MERCHANT SHIPS SUNK
- ○   U-BOATS SUNK
- ▬▬   CONVOY ROUTES
- ⌒   ALLIED AIR COVER ZONES
- ▬▬   AXIS AND AXIS OCCUPIED TERRITORY, 31 JULY 1942

MERCATOR PROJECTION

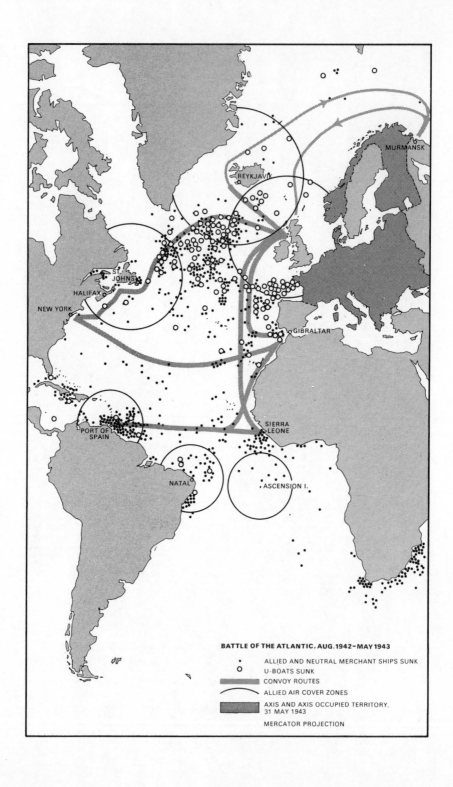

BATTLE OF THE ATLANTIC, AUG. 1942–MAY 1943

- · ALLIED AND NEUTRAL MERCHANT SHIPS SUNK
- ○ U-BOATS SUNK
- ▬ CONVOY ROUTES
- ⌒ ALLIED AIR COVER ZONES
- ▓ AXIS AND AXIS OCCUPIED TERRITORY, 31 MAY 1943

MERCATOR PROJECTION

MURMANSK

REYKJAVIK

ST. JOHNS

HALIFAX

NEW YORK

GIBRALTAR

SIERRA LEONE

PORT OF SPAIN

NATAL

ASCENSION I.

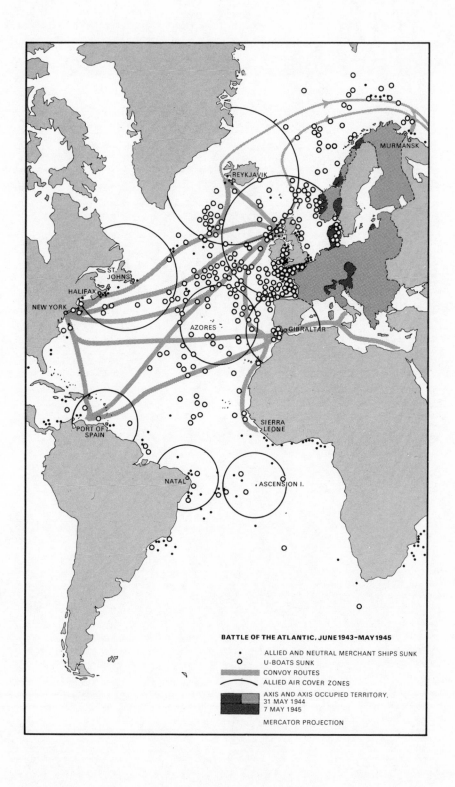

BATTLE OF THE ATLANTIC, JUNE 1943–MAY 1945

- •   ALLIED AND NEUTRAL MERCHANT SHIPS SUNK
- ○   U-BOATS SUNK
- ▬   CONVOY ROUTES
- ⌒   ALLIED AIR COVER ZONES

AXIS AND AXIS OCCUPIED TERRITORY,
31 MAY 1944
7 MAY 1945

MERCATOR PROJECTION

MURMANSK

REYKJAVIK

ST. JOHNS

HALIFAX

NEW YORK

AZORES

GIBRALTAR

PORT OF SPAIN

SIERRA LEONE

NATAL

ASCENSION I.

Introduction

by Stephen Howarth

The Battle of the Atlantic was the longest naval campaign of the 20th Century. Beginning on 3 September 1939, when Great Britain declared war on Nazi Germany, it climaxed in May 1943 and continued until 8 May 1945, when British Prime Minister Winston Churchill and American President Harry Truman proclaimed VE Day, the day of Victory in Europe.

The Battle can be summarized as a six-year struggle between submarines and surface ships, armed or unarmed, with or without air support - a focal contest between two intrinsically opposed systems of economy and politics, the democratic and the dictatorial. In full, the Battle and its attendant issues were so complex that one would be rash to suggest the whole picture could be given in manageable form anywhere, even within the covers of a book as large as this. Nevertheless, *The Battle of the Atlantic 1939-1945* must surely present one of the deepest, broadest, most informative, accurate and thoughtful pictures of the campaign to be found in any single volume.

For those who were not participants, the value of a conference can only be judged by its published proceedings. *The Battle of the Atlantic 1939-1949* will probably stand for many years as an essential reference for all students of the campaign. Co-edited with the stalwart and invaluable aid of Derek Law, the book reflects and dissects the experiences and points of view of France, Germany and Great Britain - the preliminary combatants in the campaign - and of later participants: Australia, Canada, Italy, Norway, the United States and the former Soviet Union. This unusual international breadth is one of the book's great values. Another is the depth given to national views. Overall, *The Battle of the Atlantic 1939-1945* provides and analyses a possibly unique wealth of information and data, much of which would only be otherwise available by working through a world-wide range of archives and other distant sources.

Statistics concerning the Battle are notoriously hard to agree, depending, as they often do, on different definitions and records which are sometimes hard to correlate. Nevertheless, it is generally accepted that in the course of its 68 months, something in the order of 5,140 Allied merchant vessels aggregating over 21.5 million tons were sunk world-wide. Nearly half the ships and more than half the tonnage went down in the North Atlantic. In defending and manning them, approximately 47,000 British and Commonwealth naval seamen and 30,000 merchant seamen were killed.

Britons tend (naturally enough) to think of the Battle in their own national terms, for in Britain, perhaps more than anywhere else, victory at sea was a clearly visible and easily understandable precondition for national survival. To an extent, the same goal was valid for member nations of the British Empire: loyalty to the 'Mother Country' was still an active force. Likewise, France and

Norway could readily see that regaining their own freedom depended upon Allied victory, and under the conditions of occupation they gave all they could to the fight. But among the Allies in World War II there was one nation to which the Battle of the Atlantic was, if not a sideshow, certainly not an essential: the United States of America. Though Hitler rashly declared war upon the USA, and though U-boats ravaged its East Coast shipping during 'the second happy time', it was in practical terms quite impossible for Germany to threaten American nationhood, and for many Americans, shocked into national unity by Japan's assault on Pearl Harbor, the natural sea-war lay in the Pacific. Nevertheless, and despite every temptation to ignore the Atlantic, the USA adhered magnificently to the agreement with Britain - 'Germany first'.

Much as Britons may like to imagine it, the glue which held the Alliance together was not an overwhelming desire to see Britain survive; rather, it was a shared contempt for and disgust with Nazism. Hence came the Soviet Union's part in the campaign. Across the continent of Europe, the USSR (like the USA) viewed the Battle of the Atlantic as secondary in terms of its own survival. Unlike the USA, however, the USSR was one of the Battle's direct beneficiaries, receiving supplies through Arctic convoys without making any direct contribution to the campaign. But the value of its indirect contribution would be hard to measure: Soviet courage and sacrifice were amply demonstrated on land, on the battlefields of Kursk, Stalingrad and elsewhere, and the diversion of Nazi manpower to the east lightened the burden in the west.

Courage was not the prerogative of any one country: on both sides, and from all nations actively involved, there were many individuals who fought throughout with a sense of purpose so urgent that they accepted everything, even self-sacrifice, for what they perceived as the greater good - even if others perceived it as a manifestation of ultimate human evil. Young people are malleable, and young people in armed service perhaps particularly so, especially when their society applauds them. The young men who crewed and officered Nazi Germany's U-boat fleet were indoctrinated in a sinful and repulsive creed, but one must admit that they were often extremely courageous. Recognizing their human courage does not accept the wickedness of the regime they served. Rather, that recognition delivers on a two-edged sword elements of respect - for their professional ability, dedication, loyalty and bravery - along with an element of sadness that in the hands of skilled manipulators, some of the greatest parts of the human spirit can be so exploited.

Something the same may be said of the young men who served in the Italian submarine fleet in World War II. Italy, in many ways the most civilized of European nations, had an odd war - first as a member of the Axis, then as an Ally, without ever really wishing to be involved at all. But Italian Fascism was a different beast from Nazism, and though Italy and its navy may have had no great collective desire to join the Battle, there were many naval units which fought in it to great effect. Their achievements are given suitable record here.

Every participant in and every student of the Battle of the Atlantic has a different perspective, national or individual or both, and everyone is likely to see a different key to it. I see the key as the survival or destruction of Nazism. Throughout the Battle the full extent of Nazi criminality was unknown to others. When rumours of systematically organized death camps began to circulate outside Germany, they were so horrific that even the enemies of Nazism found them hard to believe. However, for most people who fought against Nazi Germany, what they knew of the regime was already quite sufficiently repugnant, driving them to resist it to the utmost of their power. Therein lies the inestimable debt owed by each subsequent generation to the 77,000 Allied sailors, naval or civilian, who died in the Battle.

If it is accepted that the defeat of Nazism was central, then it is clear that Great Britain's contribution to the campaign was critical. The nation might have surrendered in 1941. That it did not, when effectively fighting alone, is remarkable. Every merchant ship lost was one more broken link in its vital chain of supply. Without cargoes of food, fuel and raw materials, the British people would have faced early starvation and virtually certain defeat. Had that occurred (and it came close) then along with the peoples of most of continental Europe, they would have become part of the burgeoning Nazi empire, with a large proportion, perhaps the majority, of the Royal Navy's and Royal Air Force's strength becoming available to the Kriegsmarine and Luftwaffe. This is not a fanciful 'What if?' view of history: as this book makes clear, it was a real and terrible possibility that loomed large in the minds of all Allied governments. British endurance was a pre-requisite for Allied victory in the Battle; Allied victory was a pre-requisite for the liberation of all the Nazi-dominated countries of continental Europe. Enormous quantities of transatlantic supplies and enormous numbers of soldiers were needed for the Allied invasion of Nazi-occupied France on D-Day, 6 June 1944, and for their subsequent advance from the beaches of Normandy all the way to Berlin; and without control of the ocean, the supplies and the soldiers simply could not have been transported with any safety or certainty.

The intellectual tour de force which is *The Battle of the Atlantic 1939-1945* may also be seen as a tribute to those from whom our freedoms stem. Their trials and terrors were infinitely greater than any which most of us need now endure, and, whether for study or relaxation, we can now read of them in peace. If we recognize that privilege, give it its proper value and do all in our power to pass the privilege of peace to our children as our forebears did to us, we go some of the way towards repaying an unrepayable gift.

Stephen Howarth
Shelton, Nottinghamshire
April 1994

1

Military Need and Civil Necessity

by Philip Pugh

Tonnage Sunk and Built

Britain entered World War II uniquely dependent upon sea-borne imports but also predominant in world shipping. Her Merchant Marine of around 20 million gross tons was not just the world's largest such fleet but, of itself, accounted for by far the greater part of all ocean-going carrying capacity. Preparations for defence of this vital asset may have been less than ideal, but were substantial in both quality and quantity. Hence, Britain's ability to feed her population, supply industry and support armies abroad was never in question during the first year of the war. Convoy, introduced immediately, prevented repetition of the U-boat successes of 1917. Damage inflicted by the magnetic mine, first of the weapons new to this war, was neither sufficiently intense (at its worst sinking circa 0.5% of British tonnage per month) nor of sufficient duration (being countered promptly by the double L-sweep and degaussing) to affect greatly the availability of ships. Indeed, the total tonnage under Allied command increased, since ships brought to their cause by German attacks on Denmark, Norway, Netherlands and Belgium exceeded that which the Axis had sunk until then. In particular, Norway contributed around 1 million tons (i.e. an addition of *circa* 5%).

All this changed with the fall of France and the consequently easier access to the Atlantic for German aircraft and U-boats. Like magnetic mines, aircraft were a new weapon causing much concern for a while but soon countered. U-boats were sufficiently checked by convoy, so that sudden collapse of trans-Atlantic shipping was never in prospect; but, on the other hand, there was no prompt means of ending their much increased and continual depredations. Nor did entry of the USA into the war bring any immediate relief, with much of her merchant shipping being lost in the U-boats' second 'happy time', prior to the belated introduction of convoy along the eastern seaboard of the USA. With Germany now dominant throughout Europe, the prospect thus arose of the war becoming so long and the shipping haemorrhage so great that Britain might bleed to death. In the grinding battle of attrition about trans-Atlantic convoys of 1941-43, losses did sufficiently outpace new construction for Allied tonnage to be eroded from its peak back to its pre-war level. But then more and better escorts gained the mastery, while US shipyards got into their stride pouring out new merchant ships at amazing speed. Thereafter, victory seemed assured - a measure of its completeness being that Allied merchant tonnage at the end of the war was about twice what it had been at the start.

This account, so far, has simply reiterated the familiar overall story.

Popular memory of the Battle of the Atlantic holds two other elements: that it was a close run thing, and that the contribution from the US yards was crucial. That both are correct is shown by an approximate balance sheet for 1 March 1943, i.e. at about the turning point of the Battle:

Ocean-Going Shipping at 1 March 1943 (in millions of GRT)

At September 1939		
British	18.5	
Other	1.5	
Total	**20.0**	**20.0**
plus		
Gains from new allies and charter		
USA	3.0	
Norway	1.0	
Others	4.0	
Total	**8.0**	**+8.0**
plus		
New construction		
USA	10.0	
UK	3.5	
Total	**13.5**	**+13.5**
less		
Losses	**18.5**	**-18.5**
At March 1943		**=23.0**

(NB: Differences in definitions and difficulties of attribution make all such figures imprecise; hence, those above have been rounded to nearest 500,000 GRT.)

How close run a victory it was may be appreciated by calculating that in the period July 1940-March 1941 inclusive, some 22 merchant vessels had been lost for every U-boat sunk. If the same exchange rate been maintained until the end of June 1943, then the 215 U-boats lost by then would have accounted for 4,730 Allied merchantmen. This would have wiped out the Allied merchant fleet. Instead, though, the U-boats sank less than half that figure, namely, 1,980 merchantmen. Likewise, by deducting the US contributions, their importance at this turning point in the Battle may be seen: without them, there would have remained a net residual tonnage of about half that the start of the war. That would have been just enough to meet irreducible minimum British needs for imports; but the victory of escort over U-boat would have been made hollow by the inability, for want of shipping, to prosecute the war to any end beyond Britain's survival.

Questions of Priority

As far as these figures go, the popular memory is correct. In one important respect, however, it is deficient. It neglects the demands of other theatres of war and wrongly supposes that the sustenance of Britain always had first call upon Allied shipping. Conflicts of priority arose throughout the war, leading to the U-boats coming close to a great victory not only in 1943 but in 1945 as well - in the latter year, not because of the losses they inflicted then, but because of the ships they had sunk much earlier.

Amongst the Allies, questions of priority arose concerning almost all aspects of the war. This was largely because their alliance did not come from any comprehensive pre-arranged pact but, rather, from them being flung together by the common experience of Axis aggression. Hence, there was ample scope for divergence of interests - a point well exemplified early in the war by the Norwegian and Danish governments-in-exile retaining many of their vessels in the safe and lucrative cross-trades where they provided one of the few sources of revenue remaining to those governments.

Conversely, nations (or individuals) could find particular interests coinciding even when their grand strategies differed. Thus, in Atlantic waters, the reinforcement lent by co-belligerents was matched by that derived via commercial charter from neutral Sweden.

The most important differences of interest were those between Britain and the USA. From the late summer of 1942, these became of increasing consequence, as replacements for ships lost began to come predominantly from US yards. Britain therefore had to argue her case for them against competing priorities. Indeed, for Britain from October 1942 to April 1943, it was not just a matter of making do with less than the maximum reinforcement possible, but of suffering actual inroads into her own capacities. This was partly because, between those dates, British support for US military operations in the Pacific caused net lendings to them of 17% of British merchant tonnage; and partly because Britain had assumed (and carried to the end) most of the burden of transporting and then supporting US troops in Europe. Thereafter, debate centred upon allocation of the 'Liberty' ships by then being poured out of the US shipyards. The policy which emerged was, in effect, that of the first call upon new ships being to make good losses as they occurred (so securing an Atlantic victory already largely won); and beyond that, for the growing surplus to go in support of US military operations in the Pacific theatre.

Allied shipping thus ceased to be predominantly British (or British-controlled). The British share of ocean-going tonnage declined from around 90% in autumn 1942 to about 50% by the end of the war. In absolute terms, British shipping reached a minimum during the summer of 1943, when it was close to its level at the start of the war. Thereafter, it recovered a little, but, though total Allied tonnage doubled, that under British control received only enough to make good losses. It therefore remained much the same at all times during the war.

Why US operations had such a capacity for absorbing most of the huge output of its shipyards gradually became evident, but only began to be tackled with the US Presidential directive of 9 December 1944. This stopped the practice of detaining ships as floating warehouses in lieu of employing storage ashore. However, gross inefficiencies persisted, and wastage was compounded by the fact that US theatre commanders' demands were both unfettered and unquestioned, with US troops consuming stores at twice the British Army's *per capita* rate.

Such profligacy was not unique to US forces. However, the American economy's productive capacity was so great that, given the resulting constant flow of new shipping to the Pacific theatre, the USA never experienced those conflicts between military needs and civil necessity that forced improvement upon British forces.

British Mobilization

To appreciate why the British situation was so different one must turn to the mobilization of its economy. This was central to its strategy from the moment when, recognizing that they had begun re-armament later than Germany, Britain and France elected to stand on the defensive while performing rapid, but ordered, mobilization. Once that had been achieved, then, in a war planned to last three years, and when brought to bear on a Germany already weakened by blockade, their combined economies were expected to prevail. Thus, from the beginning, British victory was not predicated upon arms immediately to hand, but upon a deliberate draw-down of the civilian economy for military purposes. This necessarily implied a successful resolution of the inevitable conflicts between military need and civil necessity.

At the outset, the U-boats struck a substantial blow at this strategy. By forcing the adoption of convoy, they immediately brought about a loss of productivity in ships, since convoyed vessels must move at the speed of the slowest, and since (when ships leave and arrive in groups rather than spaced out individually) there are inevitable delays, whether waiting to assemble or to be given a berth. This loss in shipping capacity was made good only by a complete withdrawal of British shipping from cross-trades - the proportion of British vessels thus employed falling from its pre-war level of about 30% to less than 5%, a constant figure throughout the war.

The resulting loss of revenue was significant for Britain's ability to wage a protracted war. It had been expected that substantial armament would be bought from the USA, but, early in 1940, in order to preserve dollar reserves, expenditure in America was limited to £150 million a year. Efforts to increase exports, and longer voyages to suppliers in the sterling area, further diminished the availability of shipping. However, such economic strains were only to be expected and, even if somewhat more severe than anticipated, they did not invalidate the chosen Allied strategy.

But when France capitulated, such careful long-term management had to go by the board. Instead, at a speed and scale which were then unprecedented (and have never been matched since, except in Soviet Russia), Britain extemporized her economic mobilization. Alone, she sought to out-produce Germany, which now commanded the resources of most of Europe.

Typical of the measures taken was the UK government's 'Emergency Powers Act' of 22 May 1940, giving practically unlimited authority over all British citizens and their property. Typical of the response to these measures was that the 'Essential Work Order' of March 1941 did no more than make British seamen subject to registration and centralized direction of their labour, in return for continuity of employment and entitlement to leave at a rate of two days for every completed month of service in articles. These sound less like conscripting men for dangerous duties in a desperate war, and more like efficiency agreements within a previously ill-organized industry. Nevertheless, notwithstanding the death of one merchant seaman in every six (a casualty rate far higher than the generality of the armed services) and the particular stress of constant danger without being able to fight back, merchant ships continued to be manned. It remained rare for even a day's delay to be suffered for want of crew - all on recruitment, training and usages unchanged (save as just mentioned) from peacetime, and including the acceptance of 16-year-old boys, too young to be conscripted to the armed forces.

By the summer of 1941, 49% of Britain's total occupied population were employed on government work of one kind or another. By early 1942, the strains were beginning to show in, for example, a coal shortage with output having fallen 10% below pre-war levels as 80,000 miners had been taken into the armed forces and yet others diverted to munitions work. By the end of that year, it was apparent that 'all-out' increases in the manufacture of munitions had gone too far with Britain having, by then, rifles for a further 10 years of war and troop carriers for four years. With Britain thus in danger of defeating herself in a war of economic attrition, production of bombs began to be reduced. So many of these (and shells) had been produced that many road-side dumps of them remained unused until the end of the war. In early 1943, production of guns began to be scaled down as well; the manpower budget had reached its limit, with neither men nor women remaining to be mobilized even part-time, and with household stocks having been run down so far as to require some revival of civilian manufacturers to stabilize civilian supplies. Hence, production of tanks - a commodity in which Britain was definitely not over-supplied with the latest and best - began to be reduced from its peak in mid-1943.

When the war began, about 10% of Britain's industrial capacity lay idle. When it finished, all was in use, but output had decreased by some 5%. In other words, about 15% of capacity had been lost - most simply through lack of replacement when worn out, as all efforts were concentrated upon winning the war. In contrast, even with the severity of the Allied bombing campaign, the corresponding figure for Germany was only some 10% of capacity lost.

As Britain's dollar reserves ran out, concerns over financing purchases from the USA were lifted when the Lend-Lease Act came into effect in March

1941. Exhaustion of dollar reserves was a precondition of Lend-Lease to Britain which was not imposed on later beneficiaries. This was because certain elements in the USA were then prone to remember that, in the words of its preamble, the Act was intended 'to promote the defence of the United States' and not to benefit others otherwise. Thus, the proportion of US-originated munitions for British Empire forces grew from 10% in 1941 through 27% in 1943 to 28.7% in 1944. Nevertheless, the achievement of British industry in supplying, right to the end, the great majority of munitions used by British Empire forces (and much of those supplied to governments-in-exile) is perhaps not as well appreciated as it should be. It is as well that it was so, since that which did come via Lend-Lease was a severe drain on shipping. The USA might have become an arsenal to make the world safe for democracy, but its products still had to be brought across an ocean made dangerous by U-boats, the British population still had to be sustained to some minimum standards and British industry supplied with raw materials. From 1940, the best hope of German victory was for her U-boats to effect some irreconcilable conflict between these preconditions of Allied success. Therefore, it is to the deprivations of life in wartime Britain and their management that one must come for any true measure of U-boat effectiveness.

Inland Transport

Indispensable in all this were the docks at which ships were unloaded, and the inland transport by which their cargoes were distributed. Failings in these could, and did, delay shipping, while there would have been little purpose in bringing goods across the Atlantic were they not to reach the right destinations.

Difficulties here arose primarily from the virtual closure of London and other east- and south-coast ports. Magnetic mines first achieved this in November 1939. Scarcely had they been overcome than the German conquests of 1940 exposed traffic to and at these ports to bombing and naval action. As those threats were contained, so traffic and harbourage over much of these coasts were claimed by the needs of Operation Overlord. Hence virtually all ocean-going traffic had to arrive and depart at and from ports on the west coast - notably Liverpool and Glasgow.

Closure of London and adjacent ports by bombing had been anticipated by pre-war planning. This took as representative of wartime restraint the depressed levels of trade experienced in 1931-33, and compared the results of concentrating that upon west and south-west coast ports with the traffic which those ports had handled in the (more prosperous) 1920s. It was deduced that the ports would have to deal with twice that level, but planners calculated a 75% increase could be handled quite readily. This would leave a shortfall of only 15% in total traffic to be coped with by residual use of east-coast ports, reduced consumption etc. Also considered was the extra inland haulage needed to supply the hinterlands of London and near-by ports from more distant points of landing. That, too, was evaluated and thought possible.

In the main, those pre-war calculations were vindicated by events. Where they were found wanting was in matters of detail - small flaws, but ones that were almost fatal under the intense pressure of so radical a change in loading and in patterns of traffic compounded with rapid economic mobilization. The changes in pattern and their effects are exemplified by monthly average steel imports, September-December 1940, being 1,163,000 tons as against a mere 50,000 tons pre-war. Another 1,113,000 tons of haulage might of itself be manageable - with difficulty - but a 22-fold increase in demand for specialized wagons with which to do so was not.

Matters came to a head in the winter of 1940-41 when severe weather and bombing throughout the UK further exacerbated difficulties of inland transport. Production was constrained not by landings in ports but by distribution of these and indigenous cargoes. Failure to clear goods from ports knocked back into delays in unloading, so that between July 1940 and April 1941, congestion at British ports effected an average loss in shipping capacity for dry-cargo imports equal to about 5% of the pre-war British fleet.

Problems at ports were gradually resolved by better organization, including the use of inland sorting depots to which goods were dispatched directly upon landing. This arrangement both cleared quays and minimized the exposure of cargoes to the particularly intense bombing of ports such as Liverpool. However, those changes alone would merely have shifted the bottleneck from one point to another, had not wider improvements been put in hand to inland transport (then predominantly by rail). Most of the main lines of the rail network radiated from London; but the new patterns of distribution required both longer hauls and more intensive use of previously quiet cross-country routes - often ill-equipped to handle heavy traffic. Easing these inland bottlenecks was achieved by centralized control of all railway wagons, construction of some extra wagons of specialized types and modest additions to track at junctions and at crossing loops on single-track lines.

The programme of improvement to railways cost £5 million, rising (with other works, mainly for Overlord) to £11.5 million by the end of the war. Thus aided, compared to pre-war figures, the railways hauled 11% more tonnage of freight over, on average, 32% greater distance - and that was despite enemy bombing, loss of 15% of their staff to the forces and diversion of 25% of their workshop capacity to munitions manufacture. The extra investment in the railways (of about 0.4%, rising to 0.9%, of their capital value) thus provided the nation with the equivalent of almost a million tons of extra shipping. Even if it had been possible for shipyards to build this additional tonnage, the cost would have been three to four times higher - an example of the interdependence of all aspects of the British war effort.

Thereafter, with this interdependence of shipping and inland transport recognized in the unification of their UK Government departments in May 1941, the principal problem for railways and ports became that of continuing their normal tasks while also coping with movements of troops and their supply as Britain was turned into an armed camp, an unsinkable aircraft carrier and the springboard for the invasion of Europe. The special and increasing burden of moving oil was alleviated by the construction in 1942 of a pipeline linking Avonmouth with Stanlow (on the Manchester Ship Canal) and its extension in 1943 to airfields in Eastern England. These were the only completely new wartime additions to the inland transport system. As regards troop movements, Overlord was by far the biggest; but also particularly disruptive was Operation Torch. Preparing for this invasion of North Africa, in the period 7-26 November 1942, 373 troop trains moved soldiers northwards from camps all over southern and midlands England, to embark mainly at Liverpool and Glasgow before sailing back south. Many troops travelled almost 1,000 miles by rail and sea before clearing Land's End - a point which illustrates both the concentration of traffic at those ports at the height of the Battle, and how military and civil needs could conflict for transport and port facilities as well as shipping space.

Military Profligacy

At any one time during the war until July 1940, about 5% of UK dry-cargo ocean-going shipping was in dock for repair. Between July 1940-April 1941, this increased to about 10%, remaining at around that level for the rest of the war. More was tied up by delays in ports, and, as just described, one benefit of the re-organization of Britain's ports and inland transport system was a release of delayed shipping capacity sufficient to offset the increased loss through ships undergoing repairs. With hulls still being in short supply, however, British governmental attention turned to the military's use of this scarce resource.

Supporting British military units was expensive in shipping terms. This was partly because many of the units were stationed overseas, engaged in guarding the Empire, and partly because pre-war British planning included the intention that if Italy joined the war, forces would be exercised (as they built up) by 'knocking away the props' of the Italian Empire. But, when Italy did declare war (10 June 1940), British vessels bound for Egypt, India and the Far East had to travel via the Cape of Good Hope rather than through the Mediterranean and Suez. This forced extension of their passages effectively reduced their productivity. That situation lasted nearly three years, until use of the Mediterranean could be resumed in 1943, with the first through convoy leaving Gibraltar on 17 May and arriving at Alexandria nine days later.

Whatever the inefficiencies of British ports in early 1941, they were soon found to be as nothing compared to those of Middle Eastern ports under unco-ordinated military and Sea Transport Officer control. The worst example was found at Suez where, in May 1941, ships were being unloaded at the rate of one every two days - while 117 more ships waited in the roads. Once identified, such waste was quickly obviated by comprehensive civilian control and reorganization along lines already proven in British ports. In a different climate and almost a century later, the ghost of Balaclava harbour had risen, but was swiftly laid to rest.

Despite these reforms, the demands of British Mid-East forces escalated in

1942 along with those of trooping and naval requisitions. These drew vessels from the carriage of imports to Britain, which fell rapidly until total landings in that year were but 90% of consumption. This itself was around 60% of its level during the first year of the war (i.e. to September 1940) and was incapable of any significant further reduction.

The British government now faced a double threat of scant stocks of imported food and raw materials running down, and of industry lacking even its minimum manpower requirements. In the face of this, nothing could remain sacrosanct. In March 1943, British military demands were subject to their first complete and critical scrutiny. Results were startling. At 1942 rates of loss, British forces in the Middle East had four years' worth of motor transport in reserve, and 14 years' worth of rifles. Similarly, if calculated from the single month that included the Battle of Alamein - notable for an unprecedented use of artillery - there were ammunition reserves sufficient for 16 months of expenditure.

Thus, early 1943 saw the culmination of not one but two battles crucial to Britain's survival. One was that fought in the North Atlantic. The other was fought in Whitehall, as British production and shipping of munitions were reined back to sustainable levels. The reining-in was sharp and decisive - as it had to be. Sailings to the Indian Ocean (including Middle East) area were simply halved, with the military being instructed to match their operations to that limit (which to judge by the stocks which they had accumulated, and given efficient logistics, would impose few, if any, restrictions). Unhappily, this had an unexpected and tragic outcome. In the Indian Ocean area, the halving of sailings there was locally applied across the board, to include residential cross-trades. These were largely irrelevant to the point at issue. When they were adjusted (if they had to be), then rather than being reduced, they should have been increased somewhat, to help make good the loss of food supplies to India from Japanese-occupied Burma. Being unrationed save by price, Indian food distribution was always unstable; the first signs of shortage prompted hoarding and profiteering. Over the preceding century, one of the main claims of the British Raj to prestige and legitimacy had been its ability to manage the food market and avoid famine. Now the authorities lacked the means to check hoarding, and when the Bengal harvest failed in 1943, there was no equality of belt-tightening. Instead, with the Raj helpless, 1.5 million of the poor died from starvation.

This terrible human tragedy rather takes the shine off the fact that at the same time in Britain - all national demands on shipping having been brought under control - an excess of imports over consumption was achieved. But with Britain obliged to concentrate every effort on its own survival, those deaths could well be counted as yet further, albeit indirect, victims of Nazi aggression.

The turn-round in Britain's import-consumption ratio was aided by the surrender of Axis Forces in North Africa during May 1943, ending Operation Torch, which had detained ships in greater number and for longer than anticipated. From then until the invasion of Normandy, the main pressure of military demand upon British shipping came from the transport to and supply in Britain of US forces. On 23 May 1943, during the Washington conference debate on the allocation of shipping, an official US view had tactlessly described the bombed and rationed British as 'living soft'. By D-Day, 1,421,000 Allied troops were stationed in Britain. Most were American, and showed little inclination to share the British life-style. On the contrary, they enjoyed an access to food and luxuries which - being lavish even by pre-war British standards, and all having to be shipped over the Atlantic - added substance to the complaint that they were 'overpaid, over-sexed and over here'. Their sheer numbers constituted a noticeable increase in population (about 3%) and their effect on upon the volume of imports and consumer goods was far greater. Although it has never been precisely calculated, this disparity in living standards must rank with earlier congestion at ports, or even repairs, as a significant drain upon shipping capacity.

Rationing

Given a near-constant tonnage and, despite efforts recounted above, ever-growing military needs, there was no alternative for Britain to cut further and further into civilian consumption.

Here again, it was the use of mines that first hurt Britain. At the outbreak of war, the RN's demands for minesweepers prompted the requisitioning of some 1,300 trawlers and 550 drifters. These constituted about half the fishing fleet and included almost all the big (and productive) trawlers of Hull and Grimsby. The consequent reduction in food supply was significant for its quantity, and later became particularly missed for its contribution to variety.

Immediately war started there came, too, the mass evacuation of children from British cities. The nation-wide programme was astonishingly successful: in less than four days, 1,473,391 evacuees, including escorts and teachers, arrived in their reception areas, carried from 72 stations by 4,000 special trains, without a single accident or casualty. The government paid their train fares, and, almost without realizing it, British people undertook the greatest single migration of population in the history of their kingdom. This affected subsequent events in several important ways, not least the awareness which it spread of low nutritional and general health conditions within inner cities, where rickets and other diseases of malnutrition were endemic. Public opinion was disquieted by seeing for itself how, although average living standards had been adequate, peacetime disparities of income had caused 20% of the population to be clearly undernourished and a further 20% slightly so. Moreover, because poorer, less well-educated people tended to have larger families, half of the nation's children were being raised by one-quarter of its parents. All told, this meant that about 70% of British children lacked in some way a fully adequate diet, with 40% of them being clearly undernourished. Nationwide in 1939, mortality of infants in their first year was 6.2%.

Thus, when rationing of food was introduced on 3 January 1940 it was not because of any immediate shortage but in response to public demands for equity, should sacrifices become necessary. Concern for children, just aroused so acutely, was manifest in priority of access to dairy products, eggs, fruit and meat being given to children and pregnant mothers. That priority was maintained thereafter with the happy result of infant mortality (in the first year of life) falling to 4.5% in 1944. The move towards greater equity amongst the rest of the population had its benefits also with health overall showing an improvement by 1942 - although, here, matters were subsequently to worsen as equity became increasingly a matter of all being levelled downward.

During 1941, when UK consumption of imported dry cargo fell to less than 70% of its level in the first year of war, the primary purpose of rationing began to change from assurance of equity to a means of reducing total consumption. By way of compensation for reduced imports, great efforts were made to increase home production. Four million acres of land were returned from pasture or fallow to the plough between the outbreak of war and the end of 1941. Encouragement of allotments also made an important contribution, especially to the variety and freshness of extra vegetables. Nevertheless, reductions in standard of living were marked. Despite some rise in prices, in 1941 the British population spent some 20% less on food, 38% less on clothes, 43% less on household goods and 76% less on private motoring than they had immediately before the war.

Civilian Austerity

Still further reductions were necessary. Through exhortation and regulation, the British government focused on every possible means of cutting consumption and preventing wastage of hull space. Early in 1942, Stafford Cripps told the House of Commons that 'personal extravagance must be eliminated altogether'. Petrol ceased to be allowed for any pleasure motoring, the clothes ration was reduced and sporting events curtailed. To begin with, these and numerous other measures found general public support, but later, in the face of widespread evasion or protest, there were a few instances of regulations that had to be revoked - notably in connection with the reinstatement of a few special train services, such as those for fresh products from the Scilly Isles, and for day excursions for London's much-bombed inhabitants.

However, just as it would be naive to believe contemporary propaganda showing the British responding to being bombed out of house and home merely with a merry quip or a stiff upper lip (according to social class), so it would be wrong to regard these instances as evidence of any serious weakening of the will to fight on. Rather, they manifest some weariness with as yet unrewarded sacrifices, along with a disinclination to believe that certain necessities (or at worst, modest indulgences) could seriously be regarded as debauching luxuries. Typical of such petty regulation, then and later, was banning the use of sugar for icing cakes and of cakes with more than one layer of jam. These, dictating how a given supply could be used, did little to reduce imports, but showed that presumption (incorrigible amongst many of the British intelligentsia) that lesser mortals cannot manage their affairs competently without detailed interference from the enlightened. Strangely, the lesser mortals disagreed, and in so doing, demonstrated that the British tolerance of sacrifice was great but not limitless. U-boat operations did not approach their ultimate objective of breaking British will, but it was not an unattainable goal. If escorts had been less efficient, merchant seamen less resolute, rationing less equitable, or docks and railways less well and determinedly run, it might have been achieved.

The one excuse for petty regulations was that, in the matter of reducing consumption, Britain had got to scraping the bottom of the barrel. Their ineffectiveness was demonstrated by consumption during 1942 being only a little lower than it had been in 1941. It was accepted then as being at an irreducible minimum of about 60% of what it had been in the first year of war. Thus, when imports failed to match even this level, it had to be military need rather than civil necessity which gave way in the continual clash of priorities. To give a further illustration of how far civil necessity already had been sacrificed, the production of consumer goods in Britain during 1942 was 35% less than pre-war. At the same time in Germany, it had scarcely changed at all.

Nevertheless, as victory came within sight for Britain, so it became possible to consider further temporary reductions in civilian supplies to below this long-term minimum. Continued reductions did take place, notably within Lend-Lease shipments. In 1941 munitions made up 31.7% of Lend-Lease from the USA to Britain; in 1942 they accounted for 53.6%; in 1943, 70.3%; and in 1944 most British civilian supplies from Lend-Lease were cut out altogether. Meanwhile, the fishing industry's contribution to food supplies had been further diminished by the loss to enemy action of many of its remaining boats. In the war as a whole, about 11% of these were sunk; but until respite came with the re-deployment of German air forces against Russia, losses were particularly intense, to the extent that 84% of fishing-boat losses occurred before the end of 1941. Mining off the east coast remained a major hazard thereafter, so many vessels were transferred thence to Fleetwood, with the consequence that in 1943 landings there were double pre-war levels. However, with activity at other centres being much depressed, total landings were only around 40% of pre-war rates, representing a notable diminution of British food supplies.

Added to the fact that their supplies of meat, fruit, sugar and jam were also reduced by large percentages, the loss of fish meant that the British diet had become markedly less varied and palatable. On average, compared to the period 1937-8, weight of food per head fell by 20%. Protein content remained constant, but energy content (calories) fell by 25%. In fact, through reasonably equitable distribution by rationing, and supplemented by the produce of allotments (and, for manual workers, by canteen meals), this was generally adequate. However, being subject to seasonal variation and, as the war dragged on, to further slow deterioration in variety and quality, its later adequacy became questionable.

A similar slow decline, following abrupt reductions in 1941-42, was also visible in British consumer goods production. In 1944, this was down by 45%

from its pre-war level. In comparison, the corresponding reduction for Germany (which only mobilized fully late into the war) was a mere 15%. In contrast to both, wartime expenditures in America, including purchases by Britain prior to 1941, had served primarily to stimulate a huge economy which was still not fully recovered from the depression of the 1930s. Its vast production of munitions then drew upon general economic expansion, so that by 1944 production of consumer goods in the USA had risen some 15% *above* its pre-war level.

Overlord

The great stroke towards which so much preparation and sacrifice had been made was Operation Overlord - the invasion of Normandy and the return of Allied armies to continental Europe. Britain's contribution of two-thirds of the shipping employed in this huge enterprise meant that she abandoned any hope of balancing imports and consumption. Moreover, the devastation by air attacks of the harbours and railways of northern France, which had been a precondition of landing troops, meant that port and railway equipment had to be sent from Britain for the restoration essential to supplying those same troops as they fought their way forward. Some of that sent had been supplied from the USA and some was of British origin; but whether as a loan now reclaimed or a gift, all diminished Britain's ability to handle imports in the face of imperative demands to ship munitions.

The requirements of Overlord, of subsequent fighting in France and of succour to liberated populations all combined to soak up shipping capacity and so again drive UK imports below consumption - despite the already huge reductions in the latter. In effect, Britain gambled all on speedy success of Overlord, with the last year of the war being a race between the Allied advance into Germany and the run-down of slender British stocks of food and other vital supplies. That so desperate a throw was necessary may be traced to the U-boat depredations of 1940-43. Had they not occurred, Britain would have been able to balance her shipping books in 1944. Even with those losses, had German U-boats not kept attacking to the end, convoy could have been relaxed and the shipping productivity thus gained would have gone far to resolve British problems. As it was, a furious urgency, uncharacteristic of its previous conduct, pervaded British military affairs in late 1944. General anxiety to have done with a long and weary war and V-1 and V-2 attacks would have added their share, but the (correct) perception that everything was beginning to run down too fast for comfort may well have been a major motivation in this change of heart. In visible terms, this was epitomized both by Arnhem and by renewed enthusiasm for bombing into dust anything within Germany that might be so treated - however small the contribution that its destruction might make to victory.

When the war did not end in 1944, matters became critical; yet in January 1945 the US Chiefs of Staff argued that with all of two months' worth of rations in store, British food reserves were still too high, and should be further run down. They also refused to divert any US ships from meeting the (unfettered) demands of their forces, even to avoid mass starvation in Europe. For their part, believing that starving people could not wait, Britain found food and ships to alleviate this problem. It was USA generosity that helped later to fund the rebuilding of Europe with the Marshall Plan; but it was Britain's earlier sacrifice which preserved many of its inhabitants to do that work.

Just how highly Britain gambled, and how near she came to disaster, was manifest in many ways. For example, near the end of the war some doctors observed the first signs of general adult malnourishment - notably in extended recovery times from attacks of septicaemia and conjunctivitis. Then, notwithstanding the demands of war having lifted, it only took severe winter weather in 1945-6 to bring the British economy to the point of near-total collapse. Subsequently, the demands of financial and industrial recovery obliged most rationing to be continued for several years more.

U-boats and Grand Strategy

In brief, the impact of U-boat operations on grand strategy was two-fold. In 1941-3, it came close to giving Germany the victory over Britain which she had been denied by the failure of direct assault in 1940. Thereafter, the damage inflicted continued to have profound effects on the Allied war-effort, since earlier shipping losses exacerbated an acute conflict between military need and civil necessity. Within the sphere of British control, that conflict was eventually resolved via due (but not inhibiting) economy in military use of supplies, together with reduction in civilian consumption to the minimum sustainable over the long term.

However, since the USA never experienced a comparable clash over civil and military consumptions, Britain failed to persuade her ally of the need for a similar audit and oversight of the demands of its forces. The Allied war efforts benefited far less than they might have done from the output of US shipyards and, when Allied forces returned to France, Britain had to abandon balancing imports and consumption in meeting new demands upon the shipping at her disposal. The closing stage of the war thus became a race between German military defeat and British economic collapse; and with continuing U-boat warfare maintaining the need for convoy, the losses inflicted by U-boats during the Battle again came close to inflicting a major defeat upon the Allies.

General Lessons

More generally, one may remark upon a feature of war on trade which appears to have remained true throughout the ages. A small effort of this sort imposes disproportionate costs upon the victim, as when the small U-boat fleet active at the start of the war obliged the Allies to institute a convoy system at once, with consequent substantial loss of productivity and, hence, effective shipping capacity. However, such actions (although very cost-effective for the attacker) are not, of themselves, sufficient to win the war. Doing that via blockade requires much larger efforts and brings about major battles, in which costs to attacker and defender can become more evenly balanced. The defender's original fixed costs (of convoy, etc.) become proportionately diluted in importance, as other costs mount on both sides. Hence, war on trade is no cheap road to triumph even over a nation so vulnerable to that form of attack as Britain was in 1939. On the other hand, even if such an attack fails, it can inflict such losses of shipping as to severely constrain the defender's ability to counter-attack by other modes of war.

Finally, Britain's conduct of WWII offers an outstanding example of acute conflict between military needs and civil necessity. That military endeavours must be tempered in peacetime (so as to secure their foundations within a civil economy) is a lesson whose relevance to the present day should need no argument, given the recent collapse of the Soviet Union. The Battle of the Atlantic shows that, so far from being less important in wartime - especially in an all-out war of national survival - finding the right balance between military need and civil necessity can be more important still.

Bibliographical Note

No worthwhile account of wartime shipping can do other than draw heavily upon the comprehensive work of Miss C. B. A. Behrens, *Merchant Shipping and the Demands of War*, just as the statistics of losses reprinted as *British Vessels Lost at Sea, 1939-45* are indispensable to analysis of an unremitting six-year battle. The realities of that Battle are well conveyed in many individual accounts and company histories, of which that by S. D. Waters, *Ordeal at Sea*, is particularly recommended for its celebration, via simple factual recording, by a company of the bravery of the men in its employ. Less familiar to historians of maritime affairs, but, as argued earlier, essential to full appreciation of the Battle of the Atlantic are histories of industry and inland transport such as that by O. S. Nock, *Britain's Railways at War*. As for the 'home front', much insight is to be gained by taking official, statistical and scientific reckonings together with collections of individual reminiscences and contemporary publications. Of these, Sir John Russel's *Britain's Food in Wartime* and R. Minns' *Bombers and Mash* are excellent examples of the respective genres. Concerning how these matters were influenced by, and influenced, grand strategy, the general history by A. J. P. Taylor, *English History 1914-1945* remains, to this author's mind, still the best, notwithstanding many subsequent worthy accounts. These are offered as a small selection of the numerous works consulted during the preparation of the chapter and as useful starting points for any reader wishing to take further a study of particular aspects of a large subject necessarily sketched here only in bare outline.

2

The Human Economy of the British Merchant Navy

by Tony Lane

It is axiomatic for social historians of war that the 20th Century is the century of total war. This means that in modern societies, war is usually waged to maintain the political and territorial integrity of the nation state, and that in doing so, the state reaches deep into the texture of institutional and daily life, to ensure the optimal mobilization of economic, political and social resources.[1]

Mobilization proceeds at two basic levels. In the first instance, the state takes on many of the characteristics of a command economy, in which the allocation of resources and the production and distribution of goods are undertaken by specially-formed Ministries and agencies. In the second instance, the state seeks to secure the allegiance of an actively participant civilian population, by delivering social reforms and by celebrating the contributions of persons of lowly status. By its significant actions in these two spheres, a state engaged in total war brings into high relief the two dominant, if often contradictory, spheres of modern societies.

The defining characteristics of modern societies are the large, bureaucratically structured organizations of national and regional economic and political life and, in profound contrast, the face-to-face social networks of personalized contacts and associations of private life. In the former, purpose and design is centrally conceived and co-ordinated by small cadres of high status while execution is delegated down through a long, extended chain of personnel of dwindling status whose separate functions are fractions of the whole. In the case of the latter, the domain of the citizens' private lives, there are the lived-in and small-scale networks of familiars, in the household, the neighbourhood and localized organizations of leisure and citizen activity. In these milieux, persons are known and recognized by their personal qualities rather than by role and status as in the bureaucratic organization.

War makes more prominent the existence of these two spheres of modern society by rapidly expanding the extent of bureaucratic organization while simultaneously bringing into public prominence the lives of 'ordinary citizens'. This chapter explores this theme through an examination of the structures of experience available to two groups of personnel in the wartime shipping industry.

First to be considered is an élite group of planners in the Ministry of Shipping War Transport whose constant preoccupation was with finding sufficient ships to ensure supplies to the armed forces in the field and the civilian population at home. The second group consists of merchant seafarers whose ships were sunk and whose preoccupations were with survival. Given the relative poverty of evidence concerning the world of the planning élite and the abundance of evidence on the society of survivors, the chapter has more to say about seafarers than about planners.

In war as in peace, the shipping industry's population consisted of two specialized communities whose lives glancingly touched but rarely intersected, except administratively. On the one hand were the managers and their subordinates who organized ships' itineraries, arranged maintenance and overhaul in port, found the crews and counted the costs. On the other hand were the seafarers, who, in more or less good order, delivered the ships and their cargoes from port to port. Unless chance factors of weather or engine failure provided exceptional tests of skill, the life of the peacetime seafarer was routine and mentally undemanding for everyone, including the technically educated and experienced officers. The frequent experience of risk and exercise of significant initiative was reserved for those managers whose decisions could affect the financial success or failure of the voyages of handfuls, or even fleets, of ships.

However, the war at sea in general - and the Battle of the Atlantic in particular - equalized the balance of performance opportunities as between seafarers and ship operators. If the demands on the shipping industry's directors and senior managers were often more onerous than in peacetime, seafarers were now regularly encountering life-threatening risks which provided ultimate tests of human capacity.

Merchant ships were requisitioned by the government for the duration of the war. This meant that the Ministry of Shipping and its successor, the Ministry of War Transport, decided where ships would go and, in consultation with other Ministries, determined what cargoes should be carried to which destinations. A number of senior managers and directors from shipping companies were recruited by the Ministry of War Transport for the duration of the war. Together with established civil servants, they formed a new élite group of central planners responsible for the allocation of ships to different trades and routes. Other shipping industry shore-staffs continued in their normal work of organizing the crewing, provisioning and maintenance of the ships. This was a neat and effective way of absorbing an industry into the machinery of government with minimal disturbance where it mattered most - at the level of the voyage-management of ships themselves. Ships were no longer fixed for voyages according to finely tuned considerations of covering costs and a margin for profit, but according to the often competing demands of the army and civilians. The general direction and management of shipping remained in the hands of those who had run the industry of pre-war years. This was a sensible decision, for, as Charlotte Behrens has said in her official history of wartime merchant shipping:

> To get the best use out of a fleet of cargo-liners in peace is a very complicated undertaking; to get the best use out of all British ships combined and amidst the confusions and hazards of war, is a great deal more complicated still.[2]

Despite the fact that in pre-war years, British owners and managers had shown themselves to be excessively cautious and conservative in the types of ship they built, shipping management was nevertheless a highly skilled task and their experience and expertise were indispensable. The newly formed élite of planners and their immediate subordinates found their skills as regularly tested as any pre-war tramp-owner, trying to keep his ships at sea and paying their way. One member of this élite, J. Gibson Graham, in charge of merchant shipping operations in the Mediterranean after the Allied invasion of North Africa late in 1942, subsequently wrote of the ingenuity needed to get ships turned round and to supply an army and an air force constantly on the move. Graham's sense of achievement was securely caught in the following passage:

> Looking back now I feel some pride in having been associated with the plans made in North Africa for the advance to Sicily and Italy. I can recall the long and weary meeting we had at the St. George Hotel [in Algiers] when every detail was dealt with to the minutest extent. Our little organization had to see that every ship was fit to make the journey across the Mediterranean and deliver its load of troops, shells or tanks and have a sufficiency of bunkers, water and stores aboard to stand the inevitable delays. For the information of those who have not been in this I can tell you now that the Commander-in-Chief's staff had a note of every ship's cargo. Now, a C.-in-C. does not know how his battle will go - whether he will want guns first or tanks, or what size of shell and so on. He, therefore, calls for them as the battle goes on. This means that what we thought would be the first ships discharged and sent back for more were often the last and were kept waiting days, aye, even weeks. As a ship burns five tons of bunkers a day and uses two tons of water, I sometimes exploded with wrath and also dreamt at nights of ships roaming around the seas with no fuel and water. But it didn't happen.[3]

Underlining the magnitude of this successful operation, Graham then quoted from an ironic doggerel verse which apocryphally described the administrative tangle to be unknotted after two convoys had met and intermingled:

> They chanced to meet, as convoys do,
> Just seawards of Cap Matifou,
> Ignoring previous instructions,
> Slowed for mutual introductions.
> And having slowed (as sailors say)
> They naturally lost their weigh
> And intermingled willy-nilly,
> Which, though polite, was rather silly.
> Thus ships, perhaps for Suez bound,
> In Bone were subsequently found,
> Others steamed for Gib, or further,

Popped up strangely in Bizerta.
Some that were to Sousse directed
Called on Dakar unexpected.
One or two for Casablanca
Back in Philippeville dropped anchor.[4]

Shortages of ships in some world regions and gluts in others, chaotic ports and over-full anchorages, strident yet competing simultaneous demands from the Ministries of Food, Production and Supply, not to mention the War Office - altogether, these provided the small group of MOWT planners with endless intellectual, political and administrative challenges, with far-reaching consequences on the overall conduct of the war.

Exactly similar sorts of challenges were presented to Gibson Graham in the Mediterranean - although his memoir, perhaps revealingly, is devoted as much to reports of encounters with the great men of the period as to sketches of problems presented and ingeniously overcome. King George VI and General Eisenhower are met at dinner, Field Marshal Alexander is encountered in the course of work, Admiral Sir Andrew Cunningham becomes a familiar figure at meetings. Even the Pope makes an entrance. While these sketches are presented with a note of deference, the author's account of the words exchanged with these figures suggests that if he was aware of their rank, he could nevertheless engage with them as a familiar, as a fellow member of the same élite of power. This consciousness of membership of the collegiality of power is signalled in Gibson Graham's preface where he describes himself as one 'who has "enjoyed" the experience of "history-making" in the Mediterranean'. It is signalled even more powerfully when he recalls asking Admiral Cunningham if he might go out on a destroyer for a submarine chase. The admiral refused, 'but softened the blow by saying "Graham, the best seats in any war are high up and at the back."'[5] The force of this is amply and regularly confirmed by Graham and innocently symbolized in his recall of his first billet in Algiers:

> War is never a happy experience. To us often came a homesickness for London and our friends, but we had taken up this and had to see it through. 127 [Rue Michelet] made it bearable - that lovely view with the morning sun, the blue Mediterranean and the comparative comfort of good beds and good linen were palliatives, at least. The wine merchant gave of his best and my mouth waters to this day when I think of the Perrier, VSOP, and the best Algerian wine, which is far different from what one drinks at home today under the same label.[6]

War was not a happy experience for the crews of ships at sea either. But then they were low down and at the front.

Some inkling of what might be involved in survival at sea was commonly reported in the press, and can briefly be seen in the following news items from 1941. Under the headline CRAZED MEN DIED IN 18-DAY HELL OF

ATLANTIC, the *Daily Mirror* reported in January: 'Sixteen men in an open boat drifted in an Atlantic Hell. Man after man died. Two friends, as death came on them, rose and clasped each other. Five men went mad.'[7]

In July, the shipping industry daily newspaper, *The Journal of Commerce*, reported that of 25 men who had taken to boats when their ship had been sunk 1,000 miles out in the Atlantic, only six were left alive after a 10-day voyage. A 20-year old Liverpool seaman whose frostbitten legs had been amputated said that after making a landfall on the Hebridean island of Barra, the survivors had walked for two miles before finding a house.[8] Among the more harrowing tales, one or two could be humorous, such as this from *The Times*, in September:

Gambling "debts" running into "thousands of pounds" were accumulated by 23 sailors and ship's officers who played cards for mythical stakes while sailing for 15 days in an open lifeboat after their ship had been sunk... The "school" was formed to relieve the monotony. The cards were made by tearing up a white vest and making the pips with an indelible pencil. Poker was the most popular game, the two winners, an officer and a sailor, having about £5,000 of their comrades "IOU's" to divide between them.[9]

Newspaper stories rarely had humour to report, but when they did it simply provided an alternative means of celebrating stoicism. Seafarers, whether mutilated and tormented, dying or surviving, were all publicly summonsed to become icons and exemplars of ordinary citizens doing their bit. Unnoticed and undiscovered was the immense human significance of the mutuality of the survival experience itself.

Whether they were aware of it or not (and typically they were not), survivors, once their ships were sunk, were obliged to acknowledge that their very existence was predicated upon mutual support. The same lesson was being learned elsewhere in WWII, in the infinitely more threatening but nonetheless comparable circumstances of the German concentration camps. In his famous study of survivors in the death camps, Terrence Des Pres robustly makes the point about the necessity of co-operation:

The assumption that there was no moral or social order in the concentration camps is wrong. Except peripherally and for brief periods similar to the "initial collapse" of individuals, the general condition we call chaos or anomie - what philosophers designate as the "state of nature" - did not exist. Certainly it did not prevail. Through innumerable small acts of humanness, most of them covert but everywhere in evidence, survivors were able to maintain societal structures workable enough to keep themselves alive and morally sane. The "state of nature", it turns out, is not natural.[10]

The experiences of merchant seamen survivors provide no less telling evidence of an intuitive understanding of the need for co-operation as a condition of survival. Survival chances after merchant ships were sunk by enemy action have been estimated at almost 50%. Since there were approximately 28,000 deaths due to enemy action, we may assume that similar numbers had some first-hand survival experience.[11] The most important and detailed data source on seamen survivors is the Medical Research Council's report, *The Hazards to Men in Ships Lost at Sea, 1940-44*. Although the study was not published until 1956, the research was conducted during the war and was derived from interviews and depositions from the survivors of 448 sinkings. The total population of seafarers and passengers at risk in the study was 27,000.[12]

The key variable determining chances of survival was the time elapsed and nature of the circumstances separating the initial attack on the ship from the subsequent re-assembly of survivors in boats or rafts. Of all those at risk in the MRC study, 26% died in the period between the attack on the ship and subsequent reassembly, 6% died later in boats or rafts and 68% were rescued.[13] The phase between leaving the ship and finding a place in boat or raft was the most dangerous. The MRC reported of this interval:

> ...it seems likely that relatively few men were killed by the explosion or lost their lives by being trapped in the parent ship. Failure of survival equipment was probably the cause of most of the deaths in [the initial phase].[14]

The chances of survival during and immediately after sinking were a function of the time the ship took to sink, the sea-water temperature, sea conditions and the time of day. In general, survival chances were optimal when the ship sank slowly in a warm climate, calm sea and in daylight. One-third of deaths in the immediate aftermath of sinking occurred in sea-water temperature between 5-20°C, compared with less than one-fifth in temperatures more than 20°C, while the death rate in rough sea at night was double that in daylight and calm seas.[15]

Once into boats or rafts, the chances of survival (if in general high) were conditional not merely upon such things as adequate clothing and water supply but also, and perhaps critically, on the maintenance of good social order. Regarding the latter, the MRC in its advice to shipwrecked seamen in 1943 said: 'Experience has shown time and again that the comfort, and indeed the chances of survival, of those adrift depend upon the frame of mind of the boat's company.'[16] This assumption was left untested by the MRC study. Although data on morale was collected, it was not presented systematically in the report.

Except in calm conditions and with a slowly sinking ship, the first phase of survival, which involved leaving the ship, was the point at which the customary shipboard order became stressed, ragged and sometimes incoherent. Boats might be damaged or otherwise unlaunchable; their crews might no longer be the persons assigned to them in boat drill training sessions. Roles would therefore become confused, with confusion compounded by the fact that the persons best suited for the moment in terms of personality and training were not necessarily where they could be most effective. What the moment required for optimal survival was a well-rehearsed and 'lived-in' division of labour - but these were precisely the conditions that could not ordinarily be met. Something of what might ensue in those circumstances can be seen in the case of the *Arletta*'s survivors after their ship was sunk in August 1942, 300 miles ESE of Halifax, Nova Scotia. The ship was a straggler, having three days earlier been involved in a collision with another ship and dropped out of her convoy. The ship's Mate, W. M. Duncan, gave the following account of his experience:

> By the time I had grabbed my lifejacket and gone on deck the crew had started lowering my boat, but one of the falls slipped and the boat crashed into the sea and was smashed. I rushed round to the other side and found the starboard boat had jammed on the ships side owing to the heavy list, but after a great deal of effort it was cleared and lowered. The ship was under water by this time and I found myself floating in the sea, with the 2nd steward and a sailor also swimming near me. After a short time an upturned boat came drifting past so we clambered on it... We remained on this upturned boat for two and a half days, being unable to right it with only three men. The weather abated so we rigged a line through the grab lines and all got over to the lee side and waited a suitable chance, we eventually turned her over.[17]

In the following account of escape from an unknown ship, brilliantly painted by Michael Page, there is more evidence of social order although it was plainly extremely fragile. The account is so vivid it is worth quoting *in extenso*:

> One minute we had been on watch on deck or in the engine-room, or sleeping snugly in our bunks; the next we were engaged in a frenzied scramble through the dense, shrieking blackness which assailed us with squalls of freezing spray, and slipped and fell on the wet iron decks which canted faster and faster into the hungry sea with every passing second... 'What's happening? What's happening?' someone kept demanding in a high-pitched wailing cry, full of agonized bewilderment; it was a question which no-one could answer because no-one knew. We struggled with the stiff reluctant ropes and bulky gear of the boat in a kind of automatic frenzy... The boat was lowered somehow, and we scrambled down the ladder, or the boat-net, or the life-lines towards it.
>
> Some of us got there, some did not - misjudging their distance as they jumped towards it, as it bucked and swooped on the pounding waves; smashed by it against the ship's side, as the sea flung it back... 'Cast off!' bawled someone when the boat seemed crowded; a cry echoed by several others, but answered at once by yells and screams above us - 'No, no -

wait! Wait a second!'

A darker body hurtled through the darkness and hit the waves with a tremendous splash, reappearing to struggle towards the boat and grab at her gunwhale. She tipped as he strove to scramble aboard, and at the same instance a wave broke fully into the boat, drenching and swamping us completely; we gasped and spluttered with the icy shock, yelling viciously at each other to cast off before it was too late; someone immediately slipped the painter... Whether every one who could be was in the boat, God knows; we were swirled away in an instant...

When daylight broke more confusion and argument followed until, at last, a young AB 'suddenly began giving us orders, and we obeyed them almost with relief'.[18]

Even in the early moments of Michael Page's account we can see a social order of sorts: there had to be some minimal level of co-operation for the men to have got away from the ship at all. Yet it is revealing that some hours elapsed before a familiar, consensual structure re-emerged, headed by the 'young AB'.

Except in optimal conditions, the formal hierarchy of the ship which had previously been the instrument of social order was apt to be reduced. Although a new order invariably emerged, it tended to do so hesitantly, even when a person with a formal position of authority from the ship was present and capable of acting as a focal point for a rapid re-creation of social cohesion. In these new circumstances, a rank derived from the formal hierarchy of the ship would be unlikely to count for much unless the person with the rank could invest it with qualities appropriate to the moment. The next example shows in its sub-text something of the ambiguity of rank in changed circumstances. The ship *Harpagon* sank within minutes, 150 miles NNW of Bermuda in April 1942. No boats were launched and nine of the 49-strong crew survived 34 days adrift on a raft. Chief Officer R. D. Creser reported events in the immediate aftermath:

A few minutes after the ship disappeared I heard the 2nd Officer shouting, I replied and he swam over to me and helped me into my lifejacket, we then had a drink of brandy which I kept for emergencies in my mackintosh pocket... at last after what seemed an eternity we sighted a small raft... and clambering aboard we found J. McBride (a sailor) on it. We sat on the raft huddled together to try and keep warm, taking it in turns to sit in the middle where there was less draught. Every few minutes we shouted in unison in the hope of collecting other survivors. After about one-and-a-half hours a voice answered our shout... and after a short time the 3rd Wireless Officer loomed in sight, seated on a bag of kapok and using driftwood for a paddle. He was completely exhausted and we had to drag him aboard. He told us the Chief Steward was in the water nearby supporting himself on the inner-tubes of motor tyres. We shouted loudly... and after one hour's searching we found this man who had been in the water for four hours and was now delirious. We took him aboard and took his brandy flask from him but it was many hours before he resumed a normal mental condition.[19]

In this case we find a detailed but simple and even-voiced account of the reassembly of the crew. But it is a careful account, for although the narrator is the chief officer, he does not claim or imply that his role was dominant. The activity, aimed at re-grouping the survivors, is in each instance presented as a collective activity. This does not mean of course that the authority associated with the person holding the rank was necessarily reduced, but it does at least suggest the possibility that in these conditions the rank itself might not be enough to command allegiance.

In the far more extreme conditions of the example which follows, the narrator is again a chief officer. Here, we see the person acting his rank in the process of abandoning ship but, once on a raft, he moves between the first person singular and first person plural. This use of 'I' and 'we' interchangeably seems to show that he regards himself solely as one among equals. The occasion was the sinking, in January, 1942, of the *Dayrose*, just 12 miles from the Canadian coast. It was eight o'clock at night, the wind was from the west, force 6, and there were frequent squalls of snow and hail. On his return to Britain in April, Chief Officer E. W. Bushen gave this account to the Admiralty :

We lowered the port jolly boat but the confused sea turned it over and several men were drowned. There were about 18 men amidships when this boat turned over. The Second Mate and myself each ran to the forward deck and released two rafts from the forward rigging. We cleared everybody in sight off the fore part of the ship, but Captain Newman would not leave. He refused to leave until everybody was off. I asked him to make haste and come with us but he stayed too long and I believe he went down with his ship. Neither would the Second Wireless Operator leave as he refused to jump into the water, and, realizing that there was no time to argue with him, I jumped overboard and decided to swim to one of the rafts. I scrambled aboard and found that three men had already reached it. Forty minutes after the ship sank our raft turned over and we all managed to struggle back to it. About an hour later the raft turned over again and this time we lost three of them. The rest of us managed to scramble back, but it again turned over and this time only four men managed to scramble back. It was bitterly cold - the temperature of the water being 33 F. It was snowing with the wind force 6-7 all that night. We could just manage to sit on the raft, but as one side of it was completely submerged our feet were constantly in the water. One of the men was very weak and ill; I tried to keep him warm with my coat but was unsuccessful. The raft again turned over and we lost this man as he was too weak to get back. Another of the men died soon after daylight and shortly afterwards yet another. There now remained only two men left alive - an Ordinary Seaman and myself.

One of the bodies slipped off, but the other remained jammed on the raft. We had this man's body with us throughout the day.

The following day at 1600 we were picked up by the American destroyer *Stack*. We had been on the raft for 20 hours. I suffered from frostbite all over when rescued, but later only my legs were affected. The other survivor - the Ordinary Seaman - suffered badly from frostbite and nearly contracted gangrene.[20]

Instances of apparently small gestures of solidarity, as of a man being warmed by another's coat, constantly recur in survivors' reports, but almost as asides. The writing of these incidents as asides underlines both the ubiquity of the acts and the assumption that they would not be exceptional, but well within the range of normal expectation.

It should be remembered, however, that these reports were not written by the survivors themselves but from notes taken at interviews. The accounts we have are therefore tidied-up and jointly authored versions, in which the interviewer appears as a privileged spectator to the reporting survivor's reconstruction of the original event. Interviewer and survivor probably both knew what would be normatively required in the most dangerous moments of initial survival. In other words, both the actor and the audience would have a view of how the situation *ought* to have been and (spontaneously and without fabrication) jointly constructed an account that could be made to conform.

These observations are not as critical as they might at first sound. What is at issue is the relationship between the event as it was and the event as reported. On the assumption that these reports are not actually fabricated (even if they do inevitably consist of selections of observations from everything that was notionally available to be reported by a 'fly on the wall'), we can accept that they were made in good faith. To admit this is of course to acknowledge that any report will be filtered through a mental membrane of normative expectation and principle; but it is also to acknowledge that those same expectations and principles of behaviour would equally be operative in the survival situation itself. If this is the case, then we can be confident that although reports cannot be read literally, they can be read indicatively. This discussion needs to be rehearsed at this point because reports of the second phase of survival (in boats and on rafts) are in all cases extremely condensed and only offer oblique and brief glimpses of social order.

The overwhelming majority of the survival reports collected by the Trade Division of the Admiralty fall into three broad categories regarding social order. In a sample of 40 ships whose survivors undertook boat or raft voyages of 5-37 days' duration, 24 reports make no comment on crew behaviour, 15 reports said little more than that everyone had behaved well, and a single one differentiated between the behaviour of the European and 'coloured' seamen. In this, the 3rd Officer of the *Sylvia de Larrinaga* said:

There were 23 men in the boat, 11 white and 12 coloured men. Two of the Malayans and 1 Arab became rather downhearted but they did not influence any of the rest of the crew, all of whom behaved very well indeed.[21]

This last phrase, 'all of whom behaved very well indeed', appears either in identical or very similar form so repetitiously as to be formulaic. Once again, therefore, one might suspect the hand of the interviewer. This is not necessarily true - or if so, perhaps only to the extent that the participants were influenced by their time and culture, both of which were special, at least in comparison to the daily life of a modern-day non-maritime civilian. Before proceeding further, it is worth spending a moment considering these elements.

First is the fact that for the second time in one generation, the nation was a war for its survival - an obvious fact, but one which (for those of us who have had the privilege of growing up in peace) might need re-stating, in order to emphasize the imaginative leap we must make when discussing those days. These men had experienced at first hand, or knew from their own parents' experience, the horrors of the Great War, and had hoped they would never be repeated. Few of us can tell how we would react under comparable circumstances, but most would accept that - as for our forebears - individual, group and national survival would be paramount. Having survived sinking and understood at least some of the reasons for survival - which included 'everyone behaving well' - we would seek to communicate those lessons to others.

Second is the maritime culture in which these apparently formulaic phrases were born. With all respect to their professional skills, sailors of any nation are not commonly extremely articulate, at least in writing. Words are not their stock in trade, and when required to write something they often tend to resort to set examples. This is especially true when the writing is for the record. No doubt, in these examples, one question asked by the interviewer would have been, 'And how did the men behave?' Faced with a quizzical look, his prompt might have been, 'Badly? Well? Very well?' To say one's men behaved badly reflects upon one's self. To say they behaved as models of perfection might be incredible. To say they behaved well, or perhaps very well, satisfied all requirements - personal record, professional record, and if necessary, the propaganda record too.

Third was the more general cultural expectations of the time. Obedience, co-operation, respect were all more widely expected then as a norm, and more widely given, than today. Respect was not only more widely exercised upwards, but downwards too, and so tended to encourage co-operation and obedience.

All these factors should be borne in mind when we today attempt to analyse the factual accuracy of survivors' reports. Even if it may seem surprising, it nonetheless remains perfectly possible that all these men actually did behave 'very well'. Time and culture inevitably played their part then, as they do with us today; and perhaps today we should be sufficiently humble to recognize one further notable element of these examples, namely, their remarks about non-European sailors, the 'Lascars'. Generally in Britain at that time, attitudes to non-whites were expressed in terms which most people today would find profoundly racist; but, while it is true that these reports did distinguish between Lascars and the rest, it is notable that the terminology was not discriminatory - except insofar as, if a white man behaved badly, it was considered more reprehensible.

All that having been said, it remains true that 'all the men behaved well' was a very common statement. The master of the *Larpool*, for example, reporting an eight-day voyage to Newfoundland in November 1941, said that his crew had '...behaved well throughout, the men in my boat did everything possible and although they suffered from the cold, they never gave up hope.'[22] In similar vein the 3rd Officer of the tanker *San Arcadio*, sunk some 400 miles NNE of Bermuda, in January 1942, reported that '...the men in the boat behaved very well and did all they could to help. There was no sign of despondency throughout the whole of the whole of the 11 days 6 hours which was spent in the boat.'[23] The master of the *Medon* was almost euphoric in his report of an 9-day boat voyage in August 1942:

> All the [mostly Chinese] men behaved magnificently and kept remarkably fit. We were a very happy crowd in the boat and I made the men do their exercises every day, and organized a "sing-song" during each evening and on the whole we really enjoyed ourselves.[24]

No less positive was the chief officer of the *Athelknight*, reporting on a 26-day boat voyage:

> There were no arguments, the men being in very good spirits, particularly when we were sailing, and when the boat was becalmed the swimming exercise was most useful in cheering the men up. During the nights the men lay down under the awning, and as most of the weight was forward it became difficult to steer. When I called to them to move aft to help the boat to be steered more easily they did so at once and never argued about it, in fact throughout the 26 days everybody behaved remarkably well, and were a thoroughly good crowd of men.[25]

Some few reports offered a low-key portrayal of a social order that had almost collapsed. After a 19-day boat voyage in the North Atlantic, the chief officer of the *Empire Endurance* was one of five out of an original 28 survivors. He reported:

> There was only the 3rd Officer and myself to do any bailing out or steer the boat, and we took it in turns to steer, four-hour watches at a time. We were thirsty more than hungry, but I made the 3rd Officer swallow some powdered biscuits each day, as I did. I was determined that I would get the boat home and I wanted to be sure that the 3rd Officer kept himself in a condition to help me.

The boat was adequately provisioned and had a full hood which covered the whole boat and kept the men dry, but after they had twice been sighted by aircraft and messages sent promising help (which did not materialize), the chief officer believed the men lost heart, could not be trusted to steer the boat and took no interest in their surroundings.[26]

Another note is sometimes struck in the survivors' reports wherein the theme of 'everyone behaved well' is the entry recording the final balance, but where earlier dissonance is also heard. The chief officer of the *Auditor* said of his boat's crew after a 13-day voyage to the Cape Verde Islands:

There were 7 white men and 16 [Lascars] in my boat....The natives in the boat behaved very well, mainly through the efforts of the Officer's Mess Boy, Abdul Rahman, who maintained the morale of the natives and inspired confidence in all of us... He was the first to volunteer for any job of work and would not allow anyone to help him with the bailing of water. The men were at times despondent and had small arguments, but I consider that these slight disagreements were good for them.[27]

Captain Foulkes of the *California Star* recorded a little more difficulty with some of his crew during an 11-day boat voyage to the Azores:

...most of the crew behaved very well, there were four men, however, who refused to do anything, they would not bail or look-out, and even stole the fresh water from the forward tank.[28]

The master of the *Holmpark*, for his part, had difficulties with one of his crew during a 16-day boat passage to St Lucia, in the West Indies:

I would mention that all my crew behaved extremely well throughout, with the exception of a Gunner....Amongst my crew there were ten Arabs, all the time we were in the boat these men were very helpful, bailing etc., and keeping together as closely as possible in order to make room for the others. Gunner Hunt was agitating these Arabs all the time, under the impression, I think, that they were not doing enough work whilst he was doing too much, whereas it was very much the other way round. Several times I told him to 'shut up', and on one occasion it became necessary to threaten him with an axe.[29]

Ralph Barker's outstandingly good reconstruction of the survival experiences of the crew and passengers from the *City of Cairo* emphasizes the conflicts among the boat's crews, but plainly regards this as the normal condition of the social order of the boat.[30] Dissent, however, is not a common feature of survivors' reports in the Admiralty collection, although it is almost impossible to imagine the absence of friction among boat crews. This lacuna in the evidence is probably not of great importance. The presence of conflicts is hardly an indication that a social order is in the throes is disintegration.

In the fullest and most nuanced account of boat survivors in the Battle of the Atlantic, there are references to heated quarrels and arguments verging on violence - but the No.7 lifeboat from the Anchor Line's *Britannia* safely landed on a remote part of the Brazilian coast after sailing some 1,400 miles in 23 days. When the 28-foot boat began its voyage, 82 men were packed into a space designed for 50. Of these, 38 survived.[31] Such a feat could not have been accomplished without a generalized understanding among the crew of the need to maintain co-operative social relations. If the necessity of social order was most obviously asserted in the rules of rationing provisions and a hierarchy lacking coercive powers ('What threats could we use?', asked William McVicar, the 3rd Officer in charge of the boat. 'We were all in the same boat.'), it was also shown in actions which in other circumstances could be passed over as insignificant. When the boat finally found a bottom to the ocean and the survivors got out to walk the last 100 yards through the shallows to the beach, they found they could scarcely keep upright and so, recalled McVicar, 'We held hands and walked ashore; people were falling down and you'd pick them up.' Likewise, some days previously, when it seemed that West, an RNVR Lieutenant and passenger in the *Britannia*, might die and when McVicar and another young naval officer were themselves extremely weak, they kept West alive. 'West nearly died', said McVicar, 'and one night for half the night I held him in my arms in the bottom of the boat and McIntosh did the other half. I think we saved his life with the heat of our own bodies.'[32]

In this as in other boat and raft voyages, the truth was that, if they were often distinguished for their competencies in seamanship and navigation, these professional skills were secondary to the ability to create a collective discipline which could then sustain the fortitude necessary for survival. When merchant seafarers and others in their charge showed their ability to survive, they simultaneously learned and demonstrated that co-operation is the existential precondition for the continuity of all human life. Very few persons ever have the opportunity to live out and reaffirm such deeply fundamental principles. It is instructive as well as salutary to note that they were rediscovered, not by the cadres of strategic decision-makers with seats high up and at the back, but by small groups of ordinary citizens living at the very edge of existence, far removed from the experience of 'making history' as it is conventionally understood.

Notes

1. See Marwick, *War and Social Change in the Twentieth Century*, Shaw, *The Dialectics of War*, Calvacoressi & Wint, *Total War*.
2. Behrens, *Merchant Shipping and the Demands of War*, p. 19.
3. Graham, *A M.O.W.T. in the "Med"*, p. 50.
4. *Ibid.*, p. 51.
5. *Ibid.*, p. 16.
6. *Ibid.*, p. 37.
7. *Daily Mirror*, 9 September 1941.
8. *Journal of Commerce*, 12 July 1941.
9. *The Times*, 9 September 1941.
10. Des Pres, *The Survivor*, NY, 1976, p. 142.
11. The average was 46.3%. See Behrens, *op.cit.*, p. 178.
12. McCance, *The Hazards to Men Lost as Sea, 1940-44*, p. 13.
13. *Ibid.*, p. 12.
14. *Ibid.*
15. *Ibid.*
16. Medical Research Council War Memorandum No. 8, *A Guide to the Preservation of Life at Sea After Shipwreck*, 1943, p. 4.
17. PRO ADM 199/2142, *Arletta*.
18. Page, `All in the Same Boat', in Kerr, *Touching the Adventures of Merchantmen in the Second World War*, pp. 175-9.
19. PRO, ADM 199/2140, *Harpagon*.
20. PRO, ADM 199/2139, *Dayrose*.
21. PRO, ADM 199/2142, *Sylvia de Larrinaga*.
22. PRO, ADM 199/2139, *Larpool*.
23. PRO, ADM 199/2139, *San Arcadio*.
24. PRO, ADM 199/2142, *Medon*.
25. PRO, ADM 199/2140, *Athelknight*.
26. PRO, ADM 199/2136, *Empire Endurance*.
27. PRO, ADM 199/2137, *Auditor*.
28. PRO, ADM 199/2144, *California Star*.
29. PRO, ADM 199/2142, *Holmpar*.
30. Barker, *Goodnight, Sorry for Sinking You*.
31. West, *Lifeboat Number Seven*.
32. Imperial War Museum, transcript of interview between the author and Captain William McVicar, pp. 7-8.

3

The Norwegian Merchant Navy in Allied War Transport

by Atle Thowsen

Introduction

World War II is generally considered as a conflict between two different political systems, that is, between a totalitarian and a mainly democratic one. From this angle, to the Battle of the Atlantic is just one amongst many important battles of the war. But World War II may also be seen as a conflict between two different *economic* systems: between the closed German system, based mainly on a policy of self-sufficiency, and the open British system, based to a large degree upon free exchange of goods within a world-wide area. While Germany became less dependent upon imports, Great Britain's survival depended totally on such supplies. By relying on a trade system based on imperial preferences within the vast sterling area, Britain had (in the words of Hancock and Gowing) 'chosen to live dangerously.'[1] Seen within such an economic context, it is clear that in World War II the transatlantic trade routes were a life-line for Britain, not merely valuable but vital to fight for.

The term 'the Battle of the Atlantic' was coined on 6 March 1941 when Churchill stated that 'In view of various German statements, we must assume that the Battle of the Atlantic has begun.'[2] The Prime Minister's speech to the House of Commons a few months later shows, however, that he alluded more to the sharp escalation of the naval battle caused by the intensified German submarine offensive, rather than to the beginning of Allied efforts to secure the vital supply lines across the Atlantic. These efforts were as old as the war itself.

From the war's first day until its last, the merchant navy suffered heavy losses. On 3 September 1939 the passenger steamer *Athenia* was torpedoed some 250 miles north-west of Ireland, and 112 persons lost their lives.[3] On 7 May 1945, three days after Admiral Dönitz had given the order to surrender, a German submarine sank the Norwegian steamer *Sneland* and the British freighter *Avondale Park*, off the Firth of Forth on the east coast of Scotland. Nine seamen from the two vessels were killed.[4]

In the five years, eight months and four days following the loss of *Athenia*, 2,232 Allied and neutral merchant ships aggregating nearly 12 million grt were sunk in the North Atlantic.[5] A further 174 ships aggregating more than 1 million grt were sunk in the South Atlantic. These Atlantic losses - more than 2,400 vessels totalling almost 13 million grt - represented 46.6% of all merchant ships and 60% of all tonnage lost world-wide during World War II.

It is worth noting that while the loss of Allied and neutral tonnage during the Atlantic campaign has been painstakingly computed, we still lack accurate data for the total loss of lives.

Status of Research

It is a great disadvantage that we still lack a comprehensive comparative study, acceptable from a research point of view, of the Allied and neutral merchant navies during the Atlantic campaign. However, a few national surveys have been written. Many of the volumes in the official History of the Second World War, United Kingdom civil series, deal with the British merchant navy.[6] In the military series, Roskill's three-volume work is a standard reference work.[7] Both the Netherlands and Denmark have quite recently published comprehensive studies of their merchant navies in World War II.[8] In Norway a five-volume work is under way, of which three volumes have been published.[9]

The Problem Defined

In 1942 the Battle of the Atlantic swung steadily in favour of the Germans. In that year alone, the Allies lost 7.8 million tons, while their shipyards only managed to produce 7 million tons. In 1943 the situation seemed to become even worse. In March 1943 a climax was reached: in the first 20 days of the month, more than half a million tons of shipping were sunk. The Allies were on the verge of losing the Battle. In May the same year, however, the U-boats started to withdraw from the main convoy routes in the Atlantic. The crisis passed, and the scales proved to have tilted definitely in favour of the Allies.

The crux of the whole Battle of the Atlantic was a shortage of shipping, a shortage creating a crisis in both the civil and military provisioning of Great Britain.[10] I have chosen to concentrate on one small, but still important theme: Norway's role in relation to the Allied supply and demand of merchant shipping during the Battle. I intend to show that the Battle was fought not only at sea, but also at the negotiating table, and that Britain's adversaries did not always seem to be the Germans.

Years of Miscalculations

In order to understand fully the Allied shipping situation during the Battle, it is necessary to review shipping policies of the inter-war period. During that time, the relative decline of British merchant shipping was a dominant feature in international shipping.[11] In 1919, more than one-third of world tonnage was British. By 1939, the British share had decreased to 26%. In the same period, Britain's maritime transport demand increased strongly, and the nation became increasingly dependent upon chartered foreign tonnage.

In the 1930s, representatives of the British shipping industry argued persistently that the government should help in turning this negative trend. In spring 1938, national safety was used as an argument when the president of the

Chamber of Shipping claimed that the British merchant navy 'had been allowed to decline to a level incompatible with the safety in time of war.'[12] The warning was not taken seriously, but was merely regarded as just another attempt by shipowners to promote the interests of their industry at national expense in a difficult economic climate.

Countering the pessimistic statements about insufficient British shipping resources in the event of war, the Board of Trade that same year drew up a much more optimistic report on the subject.[13] The report (which dealt only with dry cargo imports) concluded that Britain alone had ample tonnage to meet the nation's import needs during the first year of a possible war.[14]

It was also in 1938 that attempts were made to calculate Britain's possible need for oil imports in wartime, with the purpose, *inter alia*, of ascertaining whether Britain had sufficient tanker tonnage to carry the necessary oil.[15] The report was based upon the assumption that 1940 would be the first year of the war and that Japan and Germany would be Britain's opponents.[16] The appraisal of the British tanker situation was marked by optimism, although less so than in the case of dry cargo. While the British realized that their tanker tonnage was insufficient to meet national transport demands in wartime, they found comfort in the firm conviction that 150 large tankers from neutral nations would be available.[17] If all of these were chartered, then even if the Mediterranean was closed for the transport of oil from the Middle East and the ships had to sail around the Cape, Britain would have a surplus of tanker tonnage. The way the British analysts saw it, there was only one problem: America's policy of neutrality. Because of this, there was a risk that the US might stop supplying European belligerents with oil. If that happened, a shortage of tanker tonnage *would* occur, and another six large tankers would be needed.

With the benefit of hindsight, it is clear that British prognoses of wartime tonnage demand, both for dry cargo and tankers, were based on false premises and were far too optimistic. In the planning, the difficulties the war would bring upon shipping were under-rated, whereas Britain's own resources were over-estimated. The planners were also far too hopeful about the possibilities of chartering neutral tonnage.

Following the Munich crisis of 1938, British war planning was intensified and made more effective, but the misjudgement of the tonnage situation continued. As late as February 1939, the Sea Transport Department claimed that if war broke out in 1940, there would be a surplus of about 300 neutral tankers in the world, and that these would be available to the Allies.[18]

By and large, the responsible authorities accepted the tonnage prognoses until the very outbreak of war. Consequently, little was done by the government to stimulate growth in the British shipping industry. The few measures that were taken came too late and seldom achieved the intended effect. In April 1939 the British government proposed to subsidize newbuilding.[19] However, the

Merchant Shipping Assistance Act, which was passed in July the same year, only covered dry cargo vessels.[20] Regarding tankers, the government only decided to extend plans previously approved in 1938 to buy second-hand ships from abroad. Even tankers offered for scrapping should now be bought, on condition that there was 'some economic life left in them'.[21] However, the price the government was willing to pay for second-hand tankers was so low that not a single one had been purchased when war broke out.

The situation in Britain's shipbuilding industry then offered little or no comfort. The industry had suffered serious setbacks in the 1930s. In 1930, an organization named National Shipbuilders Security Ltd. was established.[22] The goal of this institution was to improve newbuilding prices by reducing the yards' output. In the period 1930-37 the capacity of British yards was reduced to from 3½ million to only 2½ million tons.[23]

The Hunt for Neutral Shipping

After the outbreak of war in September 1939, the weak foundation of British planning for wartime tonnage gradually became evident. Britain's own dry cargo tonnage was far from sufficient to meet the transport demand.[24] The tanker situation gave rise to even greater concern. In spite of a drastic fall in the domestic oil consumption in the first nine months of the war, the national stock of oil and oil products was dramatically reduced, solely because of the shortage of tankers.[25] The number of neutral tankers offered for British charter had been much lower than expected. At the same time, higher than expected numbers of ships lost and lower numbers of newbuildings resulted in a net decline of British tanker tonnage.

Thus the British import and tonnage prognoses failed to come true. The outbreak of war brought an unforeseen acute demand for tonnage, especially tanker tonnage,[26] and not only in Britain: the French needed further tonnage too. In order to solve the maritime transport problem, the Allies, led by the British, plunged headlong into an intensive and hectic hunt for neutral tonnage. However, there were fewer possibilities than might have been thought of acquiring such tonnage, especially tankers.

With a merchant navy of nearly nine million grt, the US was by far the most important neutral shipping nation,[27] but, seen from an Allied point of view, the importance of the American merchant navy was strictly limited. In 1937 Congress had passed the Neutrality Act, forbidding export of weapons and ammunition and denying the extension of credit to belligerent nations.[28] In November 1939, President Roosevelt managed to get Congress to lift the weapons embargo, but Congress made it a condition that the sale of war material was effected in accordance with the Cash-and-Carry principle. In other words, Britain and France were only allowed to buy war material in the US for cash, and they had to transport the goods in their own ships. In order to get Congress to make these concessions, Roosevelt in turn had to declare the waters outside the belligerent nations as war zones, areas which were forbidden for American vessels to enter. Consequently ships owned and/or manned by American citizens could not call at ports in France, United Kingdom, Germany, Ireland, Sweden, Denmark, the Netherlands, Belgium, the Baltic countries, or Norway south of Bergen.[29] With the US thus excluded from the list of potential suppliers of maritime transport services, Britain turned to Norway.

Space prevents me from giving more than a short outline of the history of the Norwegian merchant navy in allied war transport. I have therefore concentrated on three major subjects with impact upon Norwegian shipping:

1. The Problems of Neutrality - Norwegian Shipping Policy during the 'Phoney War'.

2. Norway's transition from neutral to Ally, and its consequences for Norwegian shipping and the Allied war transport.

3. The relationship between the American, the British and the Norwegian maritime authorities.

The Problems of Neutrality - Norwegian Shipping Policy during the 'Phoney War'

From the outbreak of World War II until 9 April 1940, Norway's major political desire was to keep the country out of the war.[30] To achieve this goal, the national policy, under the Ministry of Foreign Affairs, was one of strict neutrality policy. However, two main factors complicated and endangered the continuing success of this policy: the large Norwegian merchant marine, and the country's dependence upon supplies from abroad. The Norwegian merchant fleet was far greater than the country's own demand for tonnage, and the majority of it was chartered by other nations. After the outbreak of war, chartering of too large a portion of Norwegian tonnage to one belligerent could be interpreted by the other as a breach of neutrality. Therefore, in order to control chartering, the Norwegian government made it dependent upon the approval of an official body (the *Fraktkontrollen*) set up with governmental consent by the Norwegian Shipowners' Association (NSA).[31]

The main dilemma facing neutral Norway at this early stage of the war was the duality of its relationship with Britain. In their efforts to have their considerably increased tonnage demands met, the British looked to Norway. Partly because Britain was a major supplier of goods to Norway, and partly because Norwegian shipping was a free enterprise and unlikely to be amenable to governmental wishes and orders, it seemed almost impossible to prevent Britain from chartering tonnage on a large scale; but that could provoke Germany. However, the dilemma was temporarily resolved by the Norwegian shipowners themselves, for because of the great risks involved and the steep rise in war insurance premiums, Norwegian ships immediately after the outbreak of war stopped calling at British ports.

The consequences could have been fatal for Britain. As in World War I, the British pressed hard for an Anglo-Norwegian Tonnage Agreement, making Norwegian tonnage available to the Allies. Knowing that there was more money to earn on a steadily rising freight market, both the Norwegian government and the NSA tried to bargain for time. British pressure increased: Norwegian ships ceased being supplied with bunker coal, and it was hinted that British exports to Norway might have to be curtailed. Faced with this, Norway had to give in.

An Ally in Disguise - The Memorandum of Arrangement, 11 November 1939

The first Anglo-Norwegian shipping negotiations in September 1939 failed, mainly because the Norwegians tried to get a war trade agreement in exchange for a tonnage agreement.[32] The British attitude towards the Norwegian negotiators did not help to ease the atmosphere. The British delegation had been instructed by their government 'to deal somewhat stiffly with the Norwegian representatives', especially with regard to the question of chartering Norwegian tankers, and to 'avoid being what is called blackmailed.'[33] For their own part, the Norwegian delegation found both the rates and conditions offered by the British to be unacceptable.[34] One of the Norwegian delegates, a representative from the NSA, stated that no laws prevented Norwegian ships from sailing to Britain, but the 'decisive factors were simply rates and conditions offered.' Other countries offered a better price and it was only 'just and right that these offers were accepted.' Clearly, at this stage of the war, the Norwegian shipowners intended to let their policy be governed by the laws of supply and demand. The British, on the other hand, wanted by every means to avoid conditions similar to those of World War I, when the freight levels were more or less decided by what they considered to be war profiteers.

After the failure of this opening round, however, the Norwegians were soon forced back to the negotiating table, where the basis for new talks became the British desiderata presented during the first session.[35] In principle Britain wanted all the tonnage she could get, with the chartering of 150 large Norwegian tankers as the primary objective. In the period 8-18 October 1939, negotiations went on in London between representatives of the British government and the NSA. The Norwegian government took no official part in these negotiations, but tried to foster the impression of the talks being conducted strictly on a business footing. In practice, though, the Norwegian delegation acted in full accordance with instructions from their government, and on 11 November 1939, the final agreement, called a 'Memorandum of Arrangement' had to receive governmental approval before the chief negotiator could initial it. The agreement later came to be referred to as 'the Scheme', and the vessels chartered under its terms as 'Scheme vessels'.

At this time, still acting on instructions from their government, the Norwegian negotiators tried once again to use the tonnage agreement as a lever to reach a trade agreement, in order to secure British supplies to Norway; and once again they failed. An Anglo-Norwegian Trade Agreement was not signed until 11 March 1940.

The negotiations had been tough. To a large extent, the British delegation had followed the advice of the First Lord of the Admiralty, Winston Churchill, to use 'both the bait of any price under twenty shillings, combined with the maximum threat of all retaliatory measures, to force prompt agreement.'[36] The Anglo-Norwegian Shipping Agreement implied that before February 1940, Britain could charter almost half Norway's tonnage. From the British point of view it was perhaps even more important that this tonnage included 150 large and modern tankers.

In the beginning the shipping agreement seemed, from an economic point of view, favourable to the Norwegian shipowners. But as freight rates on the open market rose, the agreement's economic advantages diminished to the level where they complained of having to 'subsidize British warfare'. Britain feared that in a given situation Norway could be tempted to break the agreement.

Such a situation came in the beginning of April 1940 when the British War Cabinet decided to put into effect Operation Wilfred and mine Norwegian territorial waters. The purpose of the operation was to force ships sailing to Germany to keep out of neutral Norwegian waters and remain in international waters where the Royal Navy could reach them. The plan would be an obvious breach of Norwegian neutrality. The British assumed that the operation would be met by Norwegian countermoves and that the termination of the Anglo-Norwegian Shipping Agreement would be the most likely one. Therefore, on 4 April 1940, with the War Cabinet's consent, the Admiralty started to make plans for a: 'forcible possession of Norwegian shipping....in the event of the Norwegian Shipping Agreement being denounced.'[37] The British requisitioning of the Norwegian merchant fleet would be enforced in accordance with a much disputed principle in international law, the right of angary.[38]

From Neutral to Ally - 9 April 1940

The German invasion of Denmark and Norway on 9 April 1940 changed the situation in every way. Neither Norwegian nor Danish tonnage could now be requisitioned by the British with reference to the right of angary. In the case of the Danish fleet the problem was relatively simple. The Danish government had capitulated on the day the invasion began. Danish ships were thus defined as enemy property by the War Cabinet and were 'put into Prize Court and requisitioned for the duration of the war.'[39] Regarding Norwegian tonnage, though, the situation was much less clear. The Norwegian government had avoided falling into the hands of the Germans and had instead managed to put up a fight against the invaders, but the British doubted Norway's ability to hold out for very long against a superior enemy. If the Norwegian government capitulated the War Cabinet decided that 'the decision taken in regard to Danish Shipping should apply *mutatis mutandis* to Norwegian vessels.'[40] In the meantime all Norwegian ships should be sent into Allied ports 'on some pretext or other. All Norwegian ships in British ports or arriving, or sent in, [were] subsequently to be detained until further orders.'

After the invasion of Norway, there were thus four parties struggling to gain or retain control over the Norwegian merchant fleet: the Norwegian government in flight from the Germans; Quisling and the German invaders; the British government; and representatives abroad (primarily in London and New York) of the Norwegian government and Norwegian shipping interests.

During the first days the struggle was fought over the radio, as the different parties tried to contact Norwegian ships and order them about. From broadcasting stations in Norway and in other German-controlled areas the vessels were ordered, in the name of the NSA, to go to Norwegian or neutral ports.[41] The British on the other hand warned Norwegian ships that these messages were dictated by the Germans and should be ignored;.vessels should instead proceed to the nearest British or Allied port.[42] On 13 April, this radio-fight was won by the British, when (with the full agreement of Ingolf Hysing Olsen, representative of the NSA in London and Erik Colban, the Norwegian minister in London) they transmitted a message to all Norwegian masters, stating: 'Your ship is held covered by the British Government against War and Marine risks on the values and conditions under which she is at present insured.'[43] The condition was that the ships at once proceeded to the nearest British or allied port. Given the choice between sailing with or without insurance of vessel and cargo, the decision for Norwegian masters was an easy one. All of them chose to follow the directives from London. The question was, however, what to do with the Norwegian ships after they had reached their destination? Their owners were in occupied territory and could consequently give them no directives or orders; but what about the Norwegian government?

The Establishment of Nortraship -
the Norwegian Shipping and Trade Mission

As they had no radio-contact with the surrounding world, the Norwegian government could at first take no part in the struggle for control of their national tonnage. This communication failure also complicated efforts made towards a more permanent solution regarding the administration of the ships. British proposals - to put the whole Norwegian merchant fleet under British flag for the duration of the war - were turned down by both Colban and Hysing Olsen.[44] Instead, acting in co-operation with Norwegian shipping-people in Britain, they began to set up a body to administer the Norwegian merchant marine from London. A few days later, as a result of the combined efforts of the Norwegian consul-general in New York and representatives of Norwegian shipping interests in the US, a similar body was established in New York.

Britain now gave up the idea of hoisting the British flag on Norwegian vessels and instead proposed that the Norwegian government itself should requisition the merchant fleet.[45] When they finally managed to get in touch with the Norwegian government, via the Norwegian legation in Stockholm, this proposal was accepted.

On 22 April 1940, by Provisional Order in Council, the Norwegian merchant marine was brought under government control for the duration of the war.[46] Simultaneously, Øivind Lorentzen, who had been appointed director of Norwegian Shipping at the outbreak, was given power of attorney to 'act as Director of the Norwegian Shipping Directorate to be established in London.'

Lorentzen set off for London at once, but when he arrived there on 25 April, he found to his great surprise that, under the auspices of the British Ministry of Shipping, an organization to administer Norwegian merchantmen had already been established under Hysing Olsen. This organization - the Norwegian Shipping and Trade Mission, known by its telegraphic address as Nortraship - had opened its offices at 144 Leadenhall Street only a few hours before Lorentzen's arrival.[47] In accordance with his power of attorney Lorentzen took it over, and for a short period Hysing Olsen was relegated to the background. In June 1940, however, it was decided, much to the dismay of the British, that Nortraship should establish a new main office in New York in addition to the one in London. Lorentzen became manager of the new office, whereas Hysing Olsen now took over in London. Lorentzen was still to be the formal leader of the whole organization, but as the Norwegian government had their offices in London, Nortraship's London office, at least at this stage of the war, became the most important one, with Hysing Olsen being regarded in many ways as the organization's real leader. To understand its management and assess its importance to the Allied cause, let us begin by looking at the number and types of ships and the total tonnage of the Nortraship fleet.

The Nortraship Fleet

At the time of the German invasion the Norwegian merchant navy (ships above 500grt) consisted of 1,172 vessels aggregating more than 4.4 million grt. Of these, 252 were tankers aggregating almost 2 million grt. In addition came over 100 whalers and 13 whale factory ships.

In accordance with the Anglo-Norwegian tonnage agreement, with later addenda, the British Ministry of Shipping had already chartered or achieved an option to charter 1.8 million grt, i.e. almost 40% of the total Norwegian tonnage. 160 tankers totalling about 1.2 million grt, i.e. about 60% of the total Norwegian tanker fleet, were sailing on time-charter for Britain.

Nortraship did not control the entire Norwegian merchant navy. On 9 April 1940 its ships were scattered all over the world, with about 15% of the total in Norwegian or German-controlled waters at the time of the invasion. However, it did control over 1,000 vessels, aggregating somewhat more than four million grt and employing 25,000 seamen, and including 241 tankers totalling 1.9 million grt. It thus became the largest shipowning firm in the world.

Both from an economic and a political perspective, Nortraship proved to be the most valuable asset of the Norwegian government-in-exile, with profits making it economically independent, and able to pay for its navy, army and air force. The assistance to the Allies also brought much political good will.

Division of Management
and Anglo-Norwegian Controversies

In November 1940 the management of the Nortraship fleet was divided between London and New York. Roughly speaking, the London office controlled all ships sailing on Scheme for Britain, and most of the tramps engaged in the Far East. The New York office was left with most of the liners and the so-called 'free' tankers and tramps. Though the majority of Nortraship hulls were run by the London office, the dollar-earning part of the fleet was managed from New York. This division between pound- and dollar-earning ships created conflicts within Nortraship itself, between Nortraship and the Norwegian government-in-exile, but first and foremost between the Norwegians and the British.

Before Pearl Harbor, British demands for additional tonnage for the 'war-effort' were met with reluctance by the Norwegians. Their argument was that the transfer of 'free' tonnage to Britain would lead to a reduction of Norwegian dollar-income, an income needed for the payment of interests on Norwegian debts in the US and to build up a reserve for post-war rebuilding of the country and the shipping industry. The Norwegians had little or no confidence in the value of the pound after the war and preferred to stick to convertible currencies.

The first serious crisis occurred late in 1940 and in early spring 1941. Britain demanded more Norwegian tonnage and complained of Norway's seeming unwillingness to contribute to the war effort.[48] Meeting the British demand would mean giving up dollar-earning liners managed by Nortraship New York. Nortraship London was partly willing to meet the demands, but in New York Lorentzen put his foot down.[49] He had already rejected British accusations of Norway not contributing enough to the war-effort,[50] saying that Norway's real economic contribution to the war-effort was 'concealed by the policy of Nortraship in London and by accepting Scheme-rates far below actual market-rates'. In order to make clear the magnitude of Norway's contribution, Lorentzen suggested that in the future Nortraship should demand full market-freights in dollars from Britain. The difference between Scheme- and market-rates could then be put at the disposal of Britain, either as a gift or a loan.

TABLE 1: Management of the Nortraship fleet divided between London and New York *(As at 21 November 1940)*		
	London	New York
Liners	27	88
Free tramps	80	126
Tankers on neutral charter	-	54
Tankers on British charter (Scheme)	151	10
Dry-cargo ships on British charter (Scheme)	241	-
Ships in the service of the Norwegian or British government	5	1
Ships detained in French ports	23	3
Ships in Sweden and Finland	43	-
Totals	**570**	**282**

Lorentzen could not have picked a worse moment to put forward such a proposal - British dollar reserves were at their lowest. Nevertheless, in March 1941, Britain and Norway concluded a new tonnage agreement.[51]

The controversies led William Weston in the Ministry of Shipping to analyse Britain's shipping relations with Norway.[52] In March 1941 he concluded that Lorentzen had no idea whatsoever about the Allies' shipping situation. Nor was the Norwegian government's attitude totally satisfactory to Britain. In the Ministry of Shipping the feeling was that only the Norwegian foreign minister, Trygve Lie, stood for a 'whole-hearted co-operation with us.'

The gist of the problem, however, was the two different attitudes represented by Hysing Olsen and Lorentzen. Hysing Olsen did stand for whole-hearted, but not unconditional, co-operation, whereas Lorentzen in New York was more interested in dollars and in protecting the post-war interests of the Norwegian shipowners. Weston decided it would be for the good of the British cause if the Prime Minister found time to meet with members of the Norwegian government and make clear to them 'the gravity of the present shipping situation and how greatly we depend upon their full co-operation at whatever sacrifice of immediate shipping interests.'

Britain Demands the Rest of the Norwegian Merchant Navy

At the end of April 1941, Sir Kingsley Wood, the Chancellor of the Exchequer, demanded that the rest of the Nortraship fleet be put at Britain's disposal to benefit the war effort.[53] The high-handed sound of this must be understood in relation to Britain's desperate need for tonnage in the Battle of the Atlantic. On 8 March, two days after Churchill gave the Battle its name, the US Senate had passed the Lend-Lease Act, making it possible for Britain to meet the Norwegian demand for dollars. The Norwegian argument - that transferring tonnage from New York to London management would lead to a loss of dollar income - could no longer be sustained.

Politically it was impossible for both the Norwegian government and Nortraship to refuse to negotiate with the British. The Norwegians were, however, still reluctant to place more tonnage, especially American-chartered tonnage, at the disposal of the Ministry of War Transport. Both they and the British knew that this would mean 'sacrificing their liner interests in America and other trades',[54] and that years of hard labour could be wasted, since American and British competitors could take the place of Norwegian operators. Withdrawing liners from American trades could also lead to maritime transport problems for the US and thus create problems for the relations between Britain and the US.

In discussions with the Ministry of War Transport in May 1941, the Norwegian government pointed out that two-thirds of its merchant navy had already been chartered to the British.[55] The merchant navy was their only means of income and a further chartering to the British would weaken the political and economical situation of the Norwegian government-in-exile. Recognizing Britain's desperate supply situation, Norway was prepared to contribute 'for the benefit of the common war effort.' The Norwegian government declared its willingness to discuss any proposal put forward by the British, and supported their suggestion of establishing an Anglo-Norwegian Shipping Committee. The ships Britain wanted most were mainly navigating in American waters. It was thus necessary to bring the Americans, i.e. the US Maritime Commission into the discussions.

The news that the government-in-exile and Nortraship London had agreed to negotiate with Britain about further transfers of ships was received with shock in Nortraship New York.[56] Acceding to the British demands would ruin the future of Norwegian shipping.

Britain consented to tripartite negotiations. From May until October 1941, negotiations went on in Washington between the newly-established British Merchant Shipping Mission, the US Maritime Commission and Nortraship. The Norwegians had pressed for American participation, hoping for American support in their efforts to limit the transfer of their American-chartered tankers and liners to an absolute minimum. This hope proved to be futile. After the re-election of President Roosevelt in December 1940, it became more and more clear that the US was willing to support Britain by 'all means short of war'. Moreover, under the leadership of Sir Arthur Salter, the British Merchant Shipping Mission in Washington had successfully created a pro-British atmosphere in the American capital. The first thing Sir Arthur had asked for and had been promised after his arrival in March was massive and immediate tanker assistance. During the summer and autumn of 1941, the British negotiators could with satisfaction report home that nearly all their demands had been met. The predictions of a Treasury spokesman in May, that the Norwegians 'are going to be tough nuts to crack', did not come true. The combination of Sir Arthur Salter's Shipping Mission and the US Maritime Commission proved too strong for the Norwegians, even when some of the American charterers of Norwegian vessels tried to come to their aid. In the summer of 1941 the power of the US Maritime Commission was greatly increased with the passing of the Ship Warrant Act and Ships Requisitioning Act.[57] In practical terms, it became impossible to navigate in American waters without a warrant from the US Maritime Commission. If Nortraship or the charterers did not voluntarily give up the ships in question, then the Commission had the powers to force them.

The October Agreement and the Establishment of the Anglo-Norwegian Shipping Committee

On 10 October 1941, the British Minister of War Transport, Lord Leathers, and the Norwegian Minister of Shipping, Arne Sunde, signed the October Agreement, which the British hoped to be 'an agreement to end all agreements',[58] wrapping everything up. They proved to be wrong.

In the future use of their tonnage, the October Agreement committed the Norwegians to giving 'absolute priority to the transport of vital war supplies'. An Anglo-Norwegian Shipping Committee was established to function in an advisory capacity in questions dealing with the allocation of Norwegian vessels. Ships coming under the new agreement were called Plan-ships to distinguish them from the Scheme-ships.

In accordance with the so-called Tripartite Agreement, 80% of the hire for the Plan-ships was paid in dollars and the rest in pounds. The dollars were supplied by the Lend-Lease administration. Lend-Lease could not just hand over the money to Britain, so the Plan-ships were chartered by the US Maritime Commission who in turn let the British have them.

Most of the tankers that Britain had demanded were sailing on long-term charters for American oil companies. The companies were brought into the negotiations with Nortraship, British Merchant Shipping Mission and US Maritime Commission and a so-called Quadruple Agreement was signed. Under this agreement the oil companies transferred their charters to the Ministry of War Transport and the Norwegians received a 100% dollar payment.

The British could look back on the Anglo-Norwegian tonnage agreements concluded in 1941 with satisfaction. At the end of the year almost three-quarters of Norwegian tonnage was sailing for the British. The Norwegians, however, could also claim to have been partly successful. Britain had accepted that the Norwegian demand for payment in dollars was a just one and should not be mistaken for greed and war-profiteering.

The Squeeze - Nortraship between the British Ministry of War Transport and the American War Shipping Administration

Before Pearl Harbor, the Norwegian government and Nortraship negotiated with Britain on tonnage matters. After the US entered the war, American interest in the Norwegian merchant navy increased considerably, and American control over foreign shipping in American waters was strengthened. At the beginning of February 1942, the War Shipping Administration was established under the leadership of Admiral Emory Land, a man whose chief ambition was to make the US the world's greatest maritime nation.

The British and Americans differed on the best use of Norwegian vessels. From time to time the Norwegians were able to take advantage of the conflicting views to promote their own interests. After Churchill and Roosevelt had agreed to the establishment of the Combined Shipping Adjustment Board, Anglo-American co-operation on shipping matters improved.[59] The Board had one division in London led by Lord Leathers and Averell Harriman, and one in Washington headed by Sir Arthur Salter and Admiral Land.

The Norwegians tried in vain to get a seat on the Board, but only received assurances that Norway would be represented when the Board discussed matters concerning Norwegian interests. The sole time they were called in was on 6 August 1942, and then they were confronted with an Anglo-American demand that the rest of their merchant navy should be chartered to the Ministry of War Transport. The Norwegians protested and demanded negotiations.

Nortraship New York had already proposed, in January 1942, that its government should enter into tonnage negotiations with the US, hoping to benefit from the increased American tonnage demand, to strengthen the Norse-American maritime relations, and thereby to diminish the British pressure for more tonnage. However, this plan was frustrated by the British, who rightly feared that bilateral negotiations would result in their losing control over Norwegian shipping in American waters. Instead Britain suggested, and in November 1942 the Americans approved, that tripartite negotiations should take place in Washington.

The basis of negotiations was the disposal of the remainder of the Norwegian merchant navy. The outcome was that a group of 53 ships was time-chartered to the British Ministry of War Transport, which in turn re-let them to the War Shipping Administration. Freights were paid in dollars. Another group of 63 ships was allowed to sail in American waters, but under the control of the War Shipping Administration. As a result of these negotiations an American-British-Norwegian Shipping Committee was established in Washington.

Concluded on New Year's Eve 1942, this agreement was named the 'Hogmanay Agreement' by the Norwegians and Americans, Hogmanay being the Scottish term for New Year's Eve. The British (or perhaps more exactly the

English) reaction to the christening can best be illustrated by a telegram from one of their negotiators:

> ...attempt agree official name deplorable failure. Other two parents only exerted brains utmost destructively or worse. Nortraship suggested Washington....but WSA considered inappropriate. Hogmanay now being freely used not only by US and believing squatter's rights well established suggest you consider adopted.[60]

This was the last agreement to be concluded involving Norwegian tonnage. The atmosphere of the negotiations may best be described by the eyewitness reports of two of the chief negotiators, Erling Dekke Næss from Nortraship, and William Weston from the British Merchant Shipping Mission. First Næss:

> The men I had to negotiate with on behalf of Nortraship were William Weston, of the British Ministry of War Shipping, and David Scoll of the US Maritime Commission. Bill Weston was a lean, red-haired British civil servant. Dave Scoll was a lawyer with little or no shipping experience. They were a strange pair. Bill Weston, diabolically clever and astute in international shipping and finance, was determined at all cost to advance the British interests. In spite of the United States controlling everything from money bags to military hardware, the British member dominated the team.
>
> My obvious strategy was to appeal to Dave Scoll's basically kind feelings. Were we not both confronted by this wily and cunning Englishman? If we did not oppose his Machiavellian plots would not Dave himself be his next target? It worked.[61]

Secondly Weston:

> Our discussions with the Norwegian Shipping Delegation have proceeded in two hectic bursts lasting for about seventy-two hours almost without a break in each case. The battle has been fast and furious and not without vituperation. I caused a diplomatic incident by a personal remark to Naess....on a private occasion after our second lengthy bout of negotiations. It was late and Naess was arguing that the ships we wished to charter are already completely serving the war effort. This is an affirmation which has been made by every Norwegian I have met in this country, both diplomatic and commercial, until I am tired of hearing it. I replied to Naess, 'Yes, provided the cargo is going in the right direction and the dollar freight is enough'. The Norwegian Embassy, to whom Naess reported this remark, displayed great irritation and it took me a lunch and two visits to the Embassy to calm them down. This incident illustrates the touchiness of the Norwegians here and their great distance from the reality of this war.[62]

The Costs

Norway's considerable merchant naval contribution to the Allied cause was achieved at a terrible human cost. From September 1939 to 9 April 1940, 120,000 tons of shipping were sunk and nearly 400 people were killed. Thereafter, in the period from the German invasion of Norway to the end of the war, nearly two million tons of the Nortraship fleet were sunk, and more than 3,200 sailors and passengers in Norwegian ships lost their lives.

Concluding Remarks

The Battle of the Atlantic started from day one of World War II and lasted throughout the whole war. It climaxed, however, in the spring of 1943. The underlying causes of the battle were Britain's dependence on provisions from the US and Canada and the shortage of shipping to carry these supplies. The British scarcity of tonnage, which due to faulty planning to a large degree was self-inflicted, led to a constant British hunt for ships. This hunt brought Norway into focus, first as a neutral nation, later as one of the Allied nations. In both capacities Norway showed a certain degree of reluctance to meet the British demands, but was forced to give in.

This chapter has focused on some of the economic aspects of Britain's chartering of Norwegian tonnage in World War II. There have been many references to dollars and pounds, to chartering-conditions and hard bargaining, and the impression may have been given that Nortraship and the Norwegian government-in-exile were filled with money-grubbers. To talk about business in connection with war sometimes leaves a bad taste in the mouth; the concept of business seems so inconsistent with war. If business tries to keep the wheels turning in times when a nation has been occupied, it is sometimes referred to as collaboration. When business takes an active part in warfare and demands to be paid for it, it runs the risk of being characterized as war-profiteering.

To give a precise distinction between economic resistance and collaboration in an occupied territory is a subject full of pitfalls. In trying to describe the role of the Norwegian shipping industry in World War II, the same goes for the distinction between profit and patriotism.

The shipping industry of neutral Norway was forced into the war in 1939, and in return it demanded what was considered a fair economic compensation for risks and wear and tear. The shipping industry of belligerent Norway went to war in 1940 with two goals: to win the war together with Norway's Allies, and to survive as a business capable of rebuilding itself and its nation. The second goal could only be reached with the help of money, preferably convertible currency which could be used for the contracting of new tonnage to replace the lost. It was also important for Norwegians to maintain the established international shipping system and their part of it (the liner trades, the long term charters with the international oil companies etc.) which they had managed to build up through years of hard work and heavy investments.

In judging the behaviour of the Norwegians when shipping is concerned, we must also keep in mind that there were mixed motives on the British and American sides as well. It was not only the Norwegians who had to man their war-time shipping administration with people from the shipping industry itself: to a large degree, the American War Shipping Administration depended on the services of the so-called 'dollar-a-year-men', executives put at the disposal of the WSA by the shipping division of oil companies and firms like United Fruit. One influential group in the War Shipping Administration was referred to as the 'banana boys' because of their United Fruit background. The real professional bureaucrats were to be found on the British side. Based on the experiences from World War I, the British were also able to establish a smoothly-running shipping machinery, based on highly developed shipping expertise.

Keeping its shipping industry alive was also an important goal for the Norwegian government-in-exile during World War II. The British and American economies were less dependent on their shipping industry; when peace was restored, both those nations had a much more diversified economy to lean back on. Norway's economy was highly dependent upon the currency-earning ability of its shipping industry, which is why, after the war, the Norwegian government resolved that a large proportion of the nation's scanty stocks of foreign currency should be reserved for the rebuilding of the merchant fleet to its pre-war capacity. Thus the merchant fleet would be able to resume its position as the nation's principal earner of foreign currency and would in turn be able to finance the reconstruction of other sectors of the Norwegian economy.

Sources

Primary

Public Record Office (PRO) Kew

Admiralty	ADM 116	(Operational Records)
	ADM 199	(Operational Records)
Foreign Office	FO 371	(General correspondence: political)
Ministry of Transport	MT 59	(Shipping control and operation

Norwegian National Archives (NAA) Oslo

    Ministry of Foreign Affairs:

        Archives of the Norwegian Legation in London

        Archives of the Norwegian Legation in Stockholm

    Ministry of Trade and Shipping:

        Department of Shipping 1940-1960

Secondary

Basberg, Bjørn L.   *Nortraship. Alliert og konkurrent, Handelsflåten i krig.* Vol 2
                      (Oslo 1944)

Bezemer, K.W.L.   *Gescheidenis van de Nederlandse Koopvardij in de Tweede*

Wereldoorlog. Vol 1-3 (Amsterdam/Brussels, 1987-90)

Dahl, Hans Frederik *"Dette er London" NRK i krig 1940-1945* (Oslo,1978)

Huseklepp, Per   *Kapteinane og 9. april* - unpublished MA thesis in history,
University of Oslo 1970.

Pettersen, Lauritz   *Hjemmeflåten. Mellom venn og fiende, Handelsflåten i krig.*
Vol. 5 (Oslo, 1992)

Thowsen, Atle   *Nortraship. Profitt og patriotisme, Handelsflåten i krig.*
Vol. 1 (Oslo, 1992)

Tortzen, Christian   *Søfolk og skibe 1939-1945. Den danske handelsflådes
historie under den anden verdenskrig,* Vol. 1 'Ind i krigen'
(Tønder,1981)

Vogt, Benjamin   *Vår ære og vår avmakt* (Oslo,1967)

Ørvik, Nils   *Norge i brennpunkt. Fra forhistorien til 9. april 1940,* Vol. 1,
Handelskrigen 1939-1940 (Oslo,1953)

Other English language sources are listed in the Consolidated Bibliography.

Notes

1. Hancock and Gowing, *British War Economy*, p. 102.
2. The Prime Minister informed the House of Commons about the directive in secret session speech held 25 June 1941, Eade, *Secret Session Speeches*, pp. 24-45.
3. *Lloyd's War Losses*, vol. I, p.2. The number of casualties varies in different sources. According to Van der Vat, *Battle of the Atlantic* (p. 4), 118 sailors and passengers lost their lives.
4. *Lloyd's War Losses*, vol. I, p. 807.
5. Roskill, *War at Sea*, vol. III, part II, table I, p. 479.
6. See for instance Behrens, *Merchant Shipping and the Demands of War*, Hancock and Gowing, *British War Economy*; Payton-Smith, *Oil*; Medlicott, *The Economic Blockade*.
7. Roskill, *War at Sea*.
8. Bezemer, *Gescheidenis van de Nederlandse Koopvardij in de Tweede Wereldoorlog* and Tortzen, *Søfolk og skibe 1939-1945*.
9. Thowsen, *Nortraship*; Pettersen, *Hjemmeflåten;* and Basberg, *Nortraship.*
10. Calvocoressi, *Total War*, p. 459.
11. Behrens, *Merchant Shipping*, p. 34. Cf. Sturmey, *British Shipping*, chap. IV, 'The Troubled Years: The Inter-War Period.'
12. Hancock and Gowing, *British War Economy*, p. 122.
13. The report was drawn up by the Mercantile Marine Department in Board of Trade, cf. Hancock and Gowing, *British War Economy*, p. 122f.
14. In the report it was calculated that the British import demand in the first 12 war months would be 47 million tons of dry cargo. The British merchant navy would in the same period be able to transport 48 million tons. This would leave the nation with a margin of safety of 1 million tons. Hancock and Gowing, *British War Economy*, p. 123.
15. The survey was made by The Oil Board, one of the permanent sub-committees of

The Committee of Imperial Defence. Cf. Payton-Smith, *Oil*, p. 39.

16.   Payton-Smith, *Oil*, p. 52.

17.   *Ibid.*, p. 57.

18.   *Ibid.*, p. 104.

19.   *Ibid.*, p. 60.

20.   *Ibid.*, p. 107. Cf. also Jones, *Shipbuilding in Britain*, p. 156.

21.   Payton-Smith, *Oil*, p. 60.

22.   Jones, *Shipbuilding in Britain*, p. 135.

23.   *Ibid.*, p. 136.

24.   In the beginning of the war new estimates were made as regards the British demand for dry cargo tonnage. These showed that British and neutral tonnage together could possibly meet the demand. When the account for the first year of the war was settled, it showed that neutral and British ships together had transported 44.3 million tons of dry cargo to Britain. Prewar prognoses had stated that British ships alone should carry 48 million tons. Hancock and Gowing, *British War Economy*, p. 123.

25.   Payton-Smith, *Oil*, p.104.

26.   Behrens, *Merchant Shipping*, p.55.

27.   Sturmey, *British Shipping*, p. 139.

28.   American neutrality in relation to Allied supply problems is treated at length in Hall, *North American Supply*, cf. especially chap. III, "The American Potential: The coming of War in Europe" and in Hancock and Gowing, *British War Economy*, chap. IV, "Cash and Carry". Difficulties in connection with European oil supplies are treated in Payton-Smith *Oil*, chap. IV, "Imports". See also Larson, *New Horizons*, ch. 13, "Jersey's Involvement in World War II, 1939-1941", especially the passage "Oil and tankers for Great Britain and its Allies", p. 391.

29.   Hall, *North American Supply*, p. 53.

30.   Ørvik, *Norge i brennpunkt*.

31.   *Ibid.*, p. 76.

32.   Minutes of departmental meeting held on 26 September 1939 to consider the plan for Norwegian negotiations for a war trade agreement, MT 59/1405, PRO.

33.   The urgency of chartering neutral tonnage. Memo. by the First Lord of the Admiralty, 16.10.39, MT 59/1541, PRO.

34.   Norwegian tonnage negotiations, 29.9. and 2.10.39, MT 59/1405, PRO.

35.   General paper no. 2, from Board of Trade to the Norwegian delegation, 4.10.39, MT 59/1405, PRO.

36.   Memo. by the First Lord of the Admiralty, 16.10.39, MT 59/1541, PRO.

37.   Notes from a meeting at the Admiralty, 7.4.40, ADM 116/4251 and extract from Conclusions of a meeting of the War Cabinet, 8.4.40, ADM 116/4251, PRO.

38.   In international law the **right of angary** is defined as a belligerent nation's right to requisition neutral material which may be used against it in warfare.

39.   Present position with regard to Danish and Norwegian Merchant Shipping, 12.4.40, FO 371/25180, fol. 18, PRO.

40.   From War Cabinet Conclusions 87 (40), 10.4.40, FO 371/25180, fol. 440, PRO.

41.   Huseklepp, *Kapteinane og 9. april*, p. 23.

42.   Dahl, *"Dette er London"*, p. 117.

43.   ADM 199/495, fol. 23, PRO.

44.   Note on the proceedings of the first meeting of the Inter-Departmental Co-
      ordination Committee to deal with Scandinavian and Danish shipping, 12.4.40, M
      59/1661, PRO.

45.   Telegram from Colban, Norwegian minister in London, to the Norwegian legation
      in Stockholm, 13.4.40, archives of the Norwegian legation in London, box 317,
      K1B3 (I) 1940, Norwegian National Archives.

46.   Provisional Order in Council 22 April 1940, published in *Samling av provisoriske
      anordninger, kgl. res. m. v. 1940-1945*, published by the Kgl. Justis- og
      Politidepartement, London.

47.   Vogt, *Vår ære og vår avmakt*, p. 23.

48.   Memo, 3.12.40, concerning Hysing Olsen's discussions with Weston, Ministry of
      Shipping, 26, 29.11 and 2.12.40, HD, Skipsfartsavd. 1940-1960, box 548,
      22.03/2, Norwegian National Archives.

49.   Telegram from Nortraship, New York to Nortraship, London, HD, Skipsfartsavd.
      1940-1960, box 548, 22.03/2, Norwegian National Archives.

50.   Telegram from Lorentzen to Sunde, 20.12.40, copy in HD, Skipsfartsavd. 1940-
      1960, box 548, 22.03/2, Norwegian National Archives.

51.   Second Memorandum of Agreement regarding chartering of additional Norwegian
      tonnage, HD, Skipsfartsavd. 1940-1960, box 548, 22.03/2, Norwegian National
      Archives.

52.   Minute Sheet with notes on Norwegian Shipping, Weston, 22.3.41, MT 59/1736,
      PRO.

53.   Letter from Sir Kingsley Wood to Torp, 29.4.41, MT 59/1736, PRO.

54.   Note on Norwegian dollar earnings from its ships, 20.3.41, MT 59/1736, PRO.

55.   4th Anglo-Norwegian Shipping Negotiations, Summary of Discussions on 21 May
      1941, 22.5.41, HD, Skipsfartsavd. 1940-1960, box 548, 22.03/3, Norwegian
      National Archives. See also Weston's note on Norwegian Negotiations, Minute
      Sheet, 23.5.41, MT 59/1736 and UK Document no. 5, "Flag discrimination", no.
      6, "Norwegian Contribution to the War Effort" and no. 7, "Proposed Anglo-
      Norwegian Shipping Committee", all dated 20.5.41, MT 59/1879, PRO.

56.   Telegram from Gogstad to Lorentzen, 25.5.41, HD, Skipsfartsavd. 1940-1960,
      box 548, 22.03/3, Norwegian National Archives.

57.   US Maritime Commission, Report 1941, p. 6, and Payton-Smith, 1971, p 201.

58.   Hampden's memo on Norwegian Shipping Agreements, 31.3.42, MT59/1529,
      PRO.

59.   Rosen, *Combined Boards*.

60.   Telegram from Anderson to Weston, 2.4.43, MT 59/596, PRO.

61.   Næss, *Autobiography*, p.98.

62.   Letter from Weston to Hampden, 17.12.42, MT 59/1436, PRO.

4

British Warship Building and Repair

by Ian L. Buxton

Introduction

Britain entered World War II with a shipbuilding and shiprepairing industry much weaker than at the outbreak of World War I. During the inter-war economic slumps, some 30 shipyards had closed. The Admiralty had done what it could to preserve key facilities for warship construction by judicious placing of orders, but inevitably had had to give a significant share to the Royal Dockyards. It was not only hull construction that had felt the cold blast; marine engine builders had suffered similarly, while the three major armaments companies of 1914 had been reduced to only one in 1939, namely Vickers-Armstrong. Equally serious was the loss of skilled manpower during the slump, particularly that of the early 1930s, and the lack of recruitment of apprentices. However, to put the picture in some perspective, Britain's shipbuilding industry still led the world, with some 60 shipyards, and more than double the merchant ship output of each of the next two largest producers, Germany and Japan.

The naval orders of the 1936-39 re-armament period were vital in restoring some of the industry's capabilities and profitability. After the Washington and London Treaties, the recommencement of battleship building (with the laying down of *King George V* and *Prince of Wales* on 1 January 1937) was a boost. Although few of the vessels ordered had been delivered by September 1939, at that stage the major elements of the proposed building programme comprised 101 vessels - nine battleships; six aircraft carriers; 19 cruisers; 44 destroyers; 11 fast minelayers, sloops and fleet minesweepers; and 12 submarines.

The importance of the convoy system and the provision of escorts was recognized in 1939, even if the number and capability required was underestimated. Admiralty committees had reviewed the types likely to be required, given that mass production of turbine-engined sloops like the *Bittern* class would not be possible, which were best suited to the facilities of the major warship builders. There were 13 builders on the Admiralty list. In decreasing order of shipbuilding value output between September 1939-June 1943, they were: Vickers-Armstrong; Harland & Wolff; Swan Hunter & Wigham Richardson; Cammell Laird; John Brown; Hawthorn Leslie; Fairfield; Scotts; Stephen; Denny; Yarrow; White; and Thornycroft. These builders were all heavily committed to the vessels ordered under the re-armament programme, now including 'fast escort vessels' - the first 20 *Hunt*-class destroyers having been ordered in March 1939. It was essential to develop another design which could be built by the large number of shipyards that normally concentrated on merchant ships, and by engine builders who normally supplied such ships with steam reciprocating machinery and cylindrical (Scotch) boilers - and a few diesel engines. Smith's Dock of Middlesbrough had long experience of building whale-catchers, and during World War I had also built simple escort vessels like gunboats and trawlers. In the spring of 1939, their managing director, William Reed, pointed out to the Admiralty that their recent whaler *Southern Pride* was larger, faster, more seaworthy and more manoeuvrable than a trawler, yet much simpler, cheaper and quicker to build than a sloop. The company was asked to develop the design of what was originally called a whaler, later a *Flower*-class corvette. Thirty feet were added to the length, making 205 ft overall. This resulted in a loaded displacement of 1,170 tons. Armed with one 4-inch BL Mark IX gun, Type 123A asdic and 40 depth charges, this 16-knot vessel was considered entirely suitable as a coastal convoy escort which could be built in large numbers.[1] At that time, close escort was not considered necessary for ocean waters, which were thought too far out of range of German submarines or aircraft. Thus in July and August 1939, orders were placed for 60 corvettes (including 10 for France) with 16 shipbuilders who had little experience of warship building. At the same time, some 150 large commercial trawlers were requisitioned for conversion as anti-submarine (A/S) escorts. Work was put in hand with shiprepairers during August and September.

So began a programme which would see the development of a fleet of around 1,000 vessels capable of A/S operations, ranging from fleet destroyers down to trawlers. While some 270 were already in the 1939 fleet[2] and others were obtained from overseas (including the United States and Canada), nearly 900 were completed in the UK during the war.

Shipbuilding Programmes

In peacetime, the First Lord of the Admiralty would submit a proposed shipbuilding programme in the Navy Estimates to Parliament each February. After funds were voted, orders were placed over the following 12 months with suitable shipbuilders, after tenders had been sought and evaluated. Generally a contract for both hull and machinery was placed with one of the 13 warship builders, who all had both shipyards and engine works. However, there were two specialist marine engine builders, namely Parsons Marine Steam Turbine Co. Ltd. (who typically sub-contracted the hull to Vickers-Armstrong's Tyneside shipyard), and Wallsend Slipway Engineering Co. Ltd., who were a subsidiary of shipbuilder Swan Hunter & Wigham Richardson. The former regularly bid directly for warship contracts, bearing in mind that the value of the machinery could exceed that of the hull. The Admiralty would order guns and mountings and armour plate directly with specialist manufacturers, and then allocate them to the appropriate shipbuilder as Admiralty supply items (ASI). Thus the shipbuilder's contract value was significantly less than the finished cost of the ship to the Admiralty, which would also include dockyard-furnished items and headquarters services. This meant that the larger the ship, the greater the difference between shipbuilder's contract value and the eventual cost to the Admiralty. With, for example, a battleship costing £7 million, the hull and machinery contract amounted to just over 50% of total cost, whereas with a destroyer costing £0.5 million, hull and machinery were nearer 80%.

As war loomed, this established pattern changed. In both 1938 and 1939, Supplementary Estimates were put forward, the funds being largely devoted to new construction. The formal 1939 Programme included two battleships (*Conqueror* and *Temeraire*), one aircraft carrier (*Indefatigable*), two cruisers, the 60 corvettes and 20 *Hunt*-class escort destroyers noted above, plus two sloops and 20 *Bangor*-class minesweepers (which were also capable of A/S work). The War Programme of September 1939 put the emphasis firmly on escort vessels, including a further 60 destroyers (fleet and escort), 60 more corvettes (of which 10 were ordered in Canada) and 42 minesweeper/escorts (including 20 ordered for the Royal Australian Navy), plus a host of smaller vessels. By early 1940, contracts had been placed for all these vessels.[3]

After the outbreak of war, formal Programmes existed for administrative purposes, as listed by Roskill,[4] but in practice procurement procedures reflected the immediate priorities and available resources, so that some ships nominally in Programmes were never actually ordered from shipbuilders, e.g. the 1940 *Admiral* class of 8-inch-gun cruisers. By this time, it was clear that the British shipbuilding industry would be very hard pressed to cope with this huge new programme simultaneously with its backlog of naval orders, going back to 1936. Given the way the war at sea was developing, the Admiralty agreed in March 1940 to sacrifice the whole of its 1940 share of the 'long term' programme of naval construction and to concentrate on escort vessels.[5] Thus construction of the new *Lion*-class battleships was 'suspended' - never to be resumed - while work on aircraft carriers like *Implacable* and cruisers like *Black Prince* was deferred.[6] In some cases, progress would have been held up anyway, with large quantities of armour plate being diverted to tank manufacture, and by delays in producing new designs of gun mounting like the dual-purpose 5.25-inch (see Section 10, below). The 1940 Programme also concentrated on escort vessels with some 280 ships down to trawlers, but did include the battleship *Vanguard* and the monitor *Roberts* (both of which used existing 15-inch turrets which only needed modernization) as well as 54 submarines. Such was the shortage of shipbuilding labour and materials that in March 1941, Churchill instructed that building should continue only for merchantmen which could be completed by the end of 1941 and warships which could be completed by the end of 1942.

The 1941 Programme continued the emphasis on escort vessels, but the 1942 and 1943 Programmes recognized the military importance of aircraft carriers, now clearly apparent after Taranto, Pearl Harbor and Midway. No fewer than 31 were ordered (excluding the 38 escort carriers provided from the United States), mostly of the light fleet-carrier type. Six of the latter were completed just before the war against Japan ended, with 15 of the remainder being completed postwar for the Royal or Commonwealth navies. The other 10 were cancelled.

Although not formally part of the Programmes, the need for tank landing craft (LCTs) for amphibious operations had been recognized following the evacuation at Dunkirk. Work on the first design (the LCT Mark 1) started in June 1940, while separate building arrangements were instituted (see Section 11, below). These were given priority from October 1943, so that the maximum number would be available for the forthcoming invasion of France. By now, the urgent need for convoy escorts was beginning to diminish as U-boat losses climbed and merchant ship losses fell. Indeed of the 105 *Loch*-class frigates ordered early in 1943, about half (55) were cancelled in November that year. Similarly 52 *Castle*-class corvettes were cancelled, releasing resources which could be better employed on landing vessel output; 45 tank landing ships (LSTs) being ordered from December 1943.

The 1944 Programme included 22 destroyers, but otherwise the main elements were 74 more LSTs and 21 maintenance ships, all to be built in Canada. No 1945 Programme was necessary, given the backlog of vessels already on order and the end of the war in sight. However, a substantia' effort was put into converting vessels for service with the Fleet Train supporting the British Pacific Fleet, which then became the shipbuilding and shiprepairing priority. Immediately after the defeat of Japan, a large number of vessels was cancelled, including 47 destroyers and over 50 LSTs. A few of these were taken to the launching stage to clear their slipways for merchant ships, now more urgently needed for postwar reconstruction. The naval hulls were then towed away either for mercantile conversion or for scrap.

Figure 1 shows the timing of the 1,029 orders placed in British yards between 1939-1945 for vessels potentially capable of A/S operations (destroyers to trawlers). It shows clearly the two peaks. Approximately 141 of these orders were cancelled by the end of 1945.

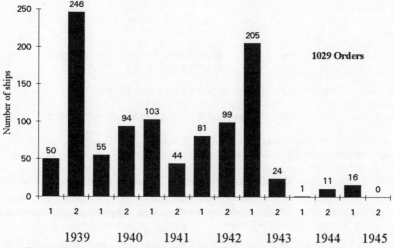

Fig.1: Orders for Escort Type Vessels Placed in Each Six Months

Output Statistics

Table 1 summarizes the naval vessels built in the UK in the years 1939-45. Completions peaked in 1943 with 2,021 vessels of 499,300 standard displacement tons. Up to 89% by number were small craft, constructed largely by non-shipbuilding firms, so a better measure of shipbuilding output is the Total Ships line, which shows a peak by tonnage of 364,600 in 1941, although over 40% of this is made up of large vessels ordered before the war.

TABLE 1: BRITISH WARSHIP BUILDING OUTPUT 1939-45
Number of vessels completed with standard displacements in '000 tons

	1939	1940	1941	1942	1943	1944	1945	TOTAL 9/39-9/45	TOTAL 1939-45
Battleships, carriers,	3	10	11	8	10	6	7	50	55
cruisers	29.6	126.9	161.5	110.4	84.9	88.3	84.3	636.0	685.9
Destroyers	22	27	39	73	37	31	22	229	251
	38.6	31.3	50.6	99.5	61.6	53.7	41.9	337.3	377.2
Frigates	5	49	74	30	57	73	28	311	316
sloops, corvettes	4.2	48.8	75.4	35.0	73.1	88.2	32.9	356.4	363.8
Submarines	7	15	20	33	39	39	17	164	170
	8.1	12.0	14.1	24.0	27.7	29.0	15.0	123.3	129.9
Minelayers,	20	47	92	95	79	39	28	380	400
sweepers, trawlers, BDV's etc.	13.2	27.3	63.0	58.1	56.4	28.8	18.4	251.8	265.2
Total	**57**	**148**	**236**	**239**	**222**	**188**	**102**	**1134**	**1192**
'ships'	**93.7**	**246.3**	**364.6**	**327.0**	**303.7**	**288.0**	**198.7**	**1704.8**	**1822**
Mosquito	14	121	395	403	337	234	103	1575	1607
craft MTB's,MLs, MMSs etc)	0.3	6.9	37.7	46.1	44.4	24.5	12.0	169.7	171.9
Landing	4	158	246	521	1462	1306	739	4324	4436
ships and craft	0.1	5.6	19.5	60.6	151.2	152.7	138.9	507.6	528.6
Total	**18**	**279**	**641**	**924**	**1799**	**1540**	**842**	**5899**	**6043**
'craft'	**0.4**	**12.5**	**57.2**	**106.7**	**195.6**	**177.2**	**150.9**	**677.3**	**700.5**
Total vessels Number	**75**	**427**	**877**	**1163**	**2021**	**1728**	**944**	**7033**	**7235**
Displace- ment	94.1	258.8	421.8	433.7	499.3	465.2	249.6	2382.1	2522.5

Source: Ref. 7. *Author's estimates for final quarter of 1945. War load displacement of landing craft converted to standard displacement by multiplying by 0.56.*

Figure 2 shows the rate of completions of 947 escort type vessels, which was comparatively steady once production had built up and before the need for escorts had declined. Thus over six years of war, approximately 7,000 naval vessels were completed in the UK, aggregating about 2.4 million tons, or at the 'ship' level about 1,130 of about 1.7 million tons. This compares with a Royal Navy strength at the outbreak of war of about 1.5 million tons, and at the end of about 4.5 million. In between, losses of over 1.1 million tons of naval vessels were sustained,[7] excluding naval auxiliaries whose tonnage was measured as gross registered tons (GRT), whilst additions of an uncalculated tonnage of vessels built abroad or merchant ships converted for naval purposes were made.

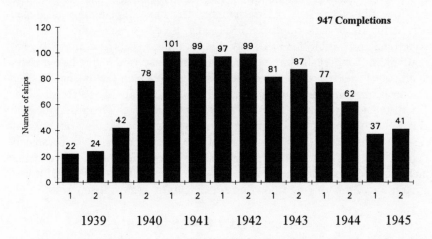

Fig.2: Completions of Escort Type Vessels in Each Six Months

Over the six calendar years 1940-45, 1,576 merchant ships were launched totalling 6.25 million GRT, a similar annual rate to the years immediately preceding the war. Different sources give different figures for merchant ship output, owing to different scope, dates, or completions rather than launchings, but are all of a similar magnitude, e.g. 6.0 million GRT completed January 1940 to August 1945.[8, 9] Since GRT is a measure of internal volume and standard displacement a measure of mass (full load minus fuel and reserve feed water), it is not possible to add the two sets of figure together directly. However as a rough guide, one ton of warship standard displacement was estimated as the equivalent of five GRT, in terms of shipbuilding and engineering work content. On this basis, an equivalent average annual output during World War II was about 3.0 million gross tons, or about double a good year's output between the wars.

Organization

The Admiralty had long been responsible for warship procurement, under the Controller or Third Sea Lord (Rear-Admiral Bruce [later RAdm Sir Bruce] Fraser in 1939). The Director of Naval Construction (Sir Stanley Goodall) was responsible for the design and construction of the ships, the Engineer-in-Chief (Vice-Admiral Sir George Preece) for main and auxiliary machinery, and the Director of Electrical Engineering (James [later Sir James] Pringle) for most electrical equipment. The Director of Naval Contracts placed production orders with British companies.[10]

In peacetime, merchant shipowners were of course free to place orders for new vessels with shipbuilders either at home or abroad. In 1937, a Shipbuilding Consultative Committee including prominent ship-builders was established to review the national shipbuilding, marine engineering and shiprepairing facilities. In October 1939, a Directorate of Merchant Shipbuilding and Repairs was set up in the new Ministry of Shipping, headed by shipbuilder Sir Amos Ayre, and responsible for assessing merchant ship needs and allocating both newbuilding and repair work to the most appropriate yard. To reduce potential conflicts of priority between naval and merchant ship needs for the same resources, the Directorate was transferred to the Admiralty on 1 February 1940. On that date Sir James Lithgow, another prominent shipbuilder, joined the Board of Admiralty as Controller of Merchant Shipbuilding and Repair, essentially as a counterpart to the Controller of the Navy. Ayre became his deputy. Regional offices provided day-to-day liaison with individual companies and granted licences for repair work.[11] On the naval side, local Flag Officers in Charge and Warship Production Superintendents oversaw warship work.

Escort Vessel Construction

Construction of the *Flower*-class corvettes was given high priority. Smith's Dock provided working plans to the other builders, not only for the hull but also for the machinery. The latter was based on their own design of triple-expansion engine, but with two low-pressure cylinders to improve balance, uprated from *Southern Pride*'s 2,300 indicated horsepower to 2,750 with higher r.p.m. First-class mercantile standards were applied to hull, propulsion and auxiliary machinery. This widened the range of potential suppliers beyond those normally used on Admiralty contracts. It also made possible the use of (mercantile) British Corporation and Lloyds Register surveyors to oversee much of the construction, relieving the hard-pressed Admiralty overseers for the more specialized major warship work

Smith's Dock were used to building whalers in batches in less than a year. Nevertheless, to deliver *Gladiolus,* the first of the class, in April 1940 - 8½ months from the date of order - was a notable achievement, which Harland & Wolff matched with their first 'Flower', *Arabis*. By the final quarter of 1940, corvettes were being delivered at the rate of one a week, ready for working up.

With bases now available to German forces on the French Atlantic coast, convoys had to be escorted further west, so that the *Flower*s had perforce to be used as deep-sea escorts, a role for which they had never been designed. Changes were made in successive batches of orders (and some retro-fitting), including a lengthened forecastle, new hull lines forward and increased depth-charge capacity. But by the autumn of 1940, it was clear that a larger A/S escort was needed, much more capable of withstanding Atlantic conditions, as well as being appreciably faster than a surfaced U-boat. Initially called 'twin-screw corvettes', a new design was evolved by the Admiralty and Smith's Dock, using two of the by now standard engines. With a longer 301-ft hull, watertube boilers and scantlings to Admiralty rather than to mercantile practice, a speed of 20 knots could be achieved.

The first of these contracts were placed with six shipbuilders in March 1941, who then ordered the machinery, usually from engine works with which they had a close association. The name 'frigate' was resurrected for these new escorts, which were named after British rivers. Smith's Dock delivered *Rother*, first of the class, in April 1942, less than 14 months after contract-placing. The bulk of the class of 57 British-built *Rivers* was delivered in 1943, while 71 more were built in Canada and 12 in Australia.[12] 1943 also saw the completion of almost all of the later batches of *Flowers*.

Allied merchant ship losses continued to mount during 1942. Although the United States had now entered the war, its navy was desperately short of escorts. Some of the Canadian escort production destined for the RN and RCN was therefore diverted to the USN, until the latter's building programme got under way. A new design of A/S frigate was consequently prepared late in 1942, carrying two ahead-throwing mortars and improved Type 144/147 asdics. These vessels were planned to use the resources of structural engineers to prefabricate much of the welded steel hulls, as was already being done with the landing craft programme. The same twin 2,750 ihp steam reciprocators were used, but with production expanded by bringing in some land-based engineering companies. Orders for machinery and major items of equipment like steering gear were placed by a special Admiralty drawing office set up in Glasgow, which were then allocated to shipyards as necessary to keep pace with hull construction. These *Loch*-class frigates were ordered from January 1943, as before almost all from non-warship builders. *Loch Fada* was ordered from John Brown at Clydebank, essentially as a prototype to iron out teething problems associated with what was more an assembly rather than a shipbuilding operation; over 80% of the structure was prefabricated.[13]

As the war progressed, increasing quantities of weapons and equipment were being fitted, from close-range anti-aircraft guns to radar. The merchant-turned-warship building yards had insufficient outfit workers for the altered mix of structural and fitting-out work. To ease the problem, two facilities were financed by the Admiralty from March 1943 to undertake outfitting of the steel hulls of frigates after launch. One was at Hendon Dock, Sunderland, managed by the North Eastern Marine Engineering Co. Ltd.; the other was at the former Beardmore shipyard fitting-out basin at Dalmuir on the Clyde, managed by John Brown.

Since the *Lochs*, at 307ft, were too long for many of the *Flower*-class builders' berths, a smaller non-prefabricated design was prepared: the *Castle*-class corvettes. At 252ft, these were longer than the *Flowers*, but could be handled by the *Flower* builders. They proved to be not only more seaworthy than the *Flowers*, but could make ½ knot more with the same machinery. With extra oil fuel capacity, their endurance was about double that of the *Flowers*. Starting in December 1942, orders for 59 were placed in UK yards, with a further 37 in Canada.

However, neither programme had made much progress before the priority was shifted from escorts to landing craft. This brought about the cancellations of November 1943. Smith's Dock again completed the first of class, *Hadleigh Castle*, in September 1943 after only nine months, while John Brown delivered *Loch Fada* in April 1944 after 14 months. While *Lochs* and *Castles* were both very effective ships with their improved A/S weapons, the reduction of U-boat operations in the North Atlantic gave them less chance to demonstrate their capability. Thus, 19 *Lochs* were modified into anti-aircraft *Bay*-class frigates more suited to the war in the Pacific (for which their 7,000-mile endurance would be useful), while six *Castles* were completed as convoy rescue ships.

Seven *Bays* were completed before the war ended, but too late for active service in the Pacific War. The semi-centralized production arrangements were never required to deliver the planned maximum of 12 vessels per month, but did confirm the American experience of increasing shipbuilding output by standardization, prefabrication and widespread use of sub-contractors, often far inland.

Merchant Shipbuilding

During the war, it was not reasonable to expect private shipowners to order a mix of ships which entirely matched the nation's needs, or indeed to order any at all, given the low controlled freight rates. Control and financing of merchant shipbuilding orders thus became a government interest. The emphasis was on production of a limited range of vessel types and sizes, best suited to the shipbuilders' normal peacetime work, although with a greater degree of standardization of machinery. Most of the tramp ship builders typical of the North East Coast of England concentrated on only one or two types, such as Doxford on the River Wear with diesel-engined 10,000-ton deadweight cargo ships. From the same river, J. L. Thompson's *Dorington Court* and North Eastern Marine's reciprocating machinery was used as the basis design for the Canadian and American standard cargo vessels, culminating in the series of 2,580 'Liberty' ships.

Smaller vessels such as coasters, colliers and coastal tankers were also built by some of the escort builders, like Pickersgill on the Wear and Burntisland Shipbuilding on the Forth. Most vessels were ordered directly by the Ministry of War Transport (as the successor to the Ministry of Shipping) through the Director of Merchant Shipbuilding and Repairs, given a licence number in the AMS series (believed to stand for Admiralty Merchant Ship). They were given 'Empire' names and allocated to existing shipowners to manage.[14] Shipowners were only permitted to order ships for their own account which fitted into the overall needs, such as tankers, fast cargo liners and refrigerated ships.

Contrary to the general belief that closures of shipyards by National Shipbuilders Security Ltd in the 1930s had reduced Britain's shipbuilding potential, the limitations on output during the war were due rather to shortages of labour and materials than of shipbuilding berths.[15] Thus the laying out of new shipyards (as happened in the United States) was neither necessary nor a realistic option, since there was not the capacity in British industry to equip major new facilities, with all manufacturing resources overstretched.

Existing plant was made more effective by judicious re-equipping with better cranes, more welding equipment and new machine tools. After the years of depression, few shipbuilders had the financial resources for such re-equipment, so most was provided by the Admiralty - particularly from 1942 - at a cost of about £10 million (about £200 million in 1993 money values).[16] However, two shipyards which had closed in the 1930s were re-opened and operated by the Shipbuilding Corporation: the former Swan Hunter & Wigham Richardson yard at Southwick on the Wear, and Armstrong-Whitworth's Low Walker yard on the Tyne. But they diverted skilled labour from existing yards, and only added 17 cargo vessels to wartime production, at high unit cost. Much higher productivity was achieved in traditional yards, with Ayre estimating that output per man in 1941-43 was 50-75% higher than in 1917-18.[17]

Marine Engineering

The provision of propulsion and auxiliary machinery was just as important as hulls, although getting less publicity and with fewer records available. The major warship building programme was limited by the capacity of the 14 turbine builders on the Admiralty list, so that such propulsion machinery was generally restricted to higher powered vessels requiring over 4,000 shp. As steam turbines also required gearing to obtain optimum propeller revolutions, gear-cutting capacity was also a significant bottleneck. Better equipped companies like Parsons Marine Steam Turbine frequently supplied gearing to other engine builders, for example to Thornycroft for *Hunt*-class destroyers. Land turbine builders used to power station work supplemented output by engining a few turbine powered escorts, including C. A. Parsons of Newcastle, but they could not provide gearing or the full machinery installation.

Diesel engine manufacturing was limited to relatively few builders, mostly with licences for Continental designs of direct-drive engines like Sulzer. Of the larger diesel engines, the only significant British design to survive between the wars was the Doxford, whose engine works concentrated on building these opposed-piston engines during the war. Unlike in the US, there was no locomotive diesel building industry to supply medium power engines for escorts, whether by mechanical transmission or electric. A variety of diesel types was installed in submarines: Vickers, Admiralty, Paxman, MAN and Sulzer. Lower-powered diesels (up to about 500 bhp) were eventually produced in large numbers for smaller vessels like landing craft (e.g. Paxman engines) and motor minesweepers (e.g. Crossley and Gardner). But following the cutting off of imports of Italian Isotta-Fraschini engines in 1940, British motor torpedo boats and gunboats were largely powered by American Packard petrol engines.

Fortunately there were still some 35 marine engine-builders producing steam reciprocating engines for medium- and low-powered merchantmen. These builders could be partly switched to naval production. Such works were either part of a shipbuilding company like Smith's Dock, or an independent producer like Richardsons Westgarth. Most of the boilers that these companies produced were simple Scotch boilers, either coal- or oil-fired. Thousands of seagoing personnel were familiar with these - hence their use in naval trawlers and the early corvettes. As the boiler-making industry expanded, later vessels could be equipped with watertube boilers, which were not only more responsive to naval steaming patterns, but were also lighter.

Drawings and patterns for the Smith's Dock 2,750 ihp engine were sent to all the escort engine-builders and even some land-based engineers such as Fawcett Preston of Merseyside, who had been one of the first to produce marine engines in the 1820s, but had subsequently left that market. For the *Loch*s and *Castle*s, the Admiralty ordered centrally the appropriate number of engines direct with the manufacturers, and allocated output according to whichever shipbuilder needed them next. Thus engines built by Plenty of Newbury were fitted in *Loch Katrine*'s hull, built 400 miles away by Robb at Leith.

Unfortunately no comprehensive statistics exist for marine engineering output during WWII, but it probably approached four million hp annually - double that of even the better pre-war years. Between September 1939-December 1945, 880 sets of turbine machinery totalling 12,658,500 shp were produced for the RN, plus 942 reciprocating engines totalling 1,800,700 ihp.[18]

Shiprepairing

British shiprepairing had suffered relatively less during the depression than shipbuilding - orders for new construction could be postponed, but repairs and drydocking could not. The British shiprepairing industry came under central control on 4 September 1939. It was essential to bring into the system the 256 privately-owned drydocks to supplement the 52 government-owned drydocks in the Royal Dockyards. As with shipbuilding contracts, both naval and merchant repair jobs were controlled by the Admiralty. The Director of Merchant Shipbuilding and Repair allocated repair work through regional offices to commercial yards according to the urgency and scope of the job, and the availability of capacity and drydocks. Licensing officers who were often former Board of Trade surveyors agreed the extent of the work to be done.[19] The Director of Merchant Ship Repairs was Lawrie (later Sir Lawrie) Edwards, formerly of Middle Docks on the Tyne. His naval counterpart throughout the war was Vice-Admiral Cecil P Talbot, Director of Dockyards. Both had to work closely together, reconciling priorities; an advantage since both were Admiralty departments.

The demands on shiprepairers in wartime were vastly higher than in peacetime. In addition to the regular drydocking and overhaul of ships, there was the need to repair damage, not only from enemy action, but from the increased amount of accidental damage through collisions and groundings resulting from the black-out both of ships and navigational aids. Conversion work added a huge extra load. At the outbreak of war, 56 liners were converted to armed merchant cruisers (AMCs), while several hundred commercial trawlers were converted to anti-submarine, minesweeping and auxiliary patrol roles. Such work could be very extensive: fruit carriers were converted to anti-aircraft ships, cargo ships to minelayers, passenger liners to depot ships for destroyers or submarines. By the end of 1941, some 2,000 conversions had been completed, mostly of trawlers.[20]

The industry found it difficult to keep pace with demands, particularly after the fall of France. Britain was coping alone with large numbers of damaged vessels resulting from intensified attacks by U-boats, surface ships, mines and aircraft. A heavy backlog of ships awaiting repair built up, reducing the effective tonnage available. Additional men were released from building new ships, as many of the trades were common, and some companies like Cammell Laird had both newbuilding and repair facilities, simplifying the transfer.

Public drydocks in major ports were usually poorly equipped, compared with those in commercial repair yards or the naval dockyards, so the Admiralty had to spend money on supplying them with cranage and welding plant. Shiprepair facilities abandoned during the Depression were re-instated, such as the yard at Londonderry to service North Atlantic escort vessels, which was put under Harland & Wolff management. On the Tyne, a 75-year old dry-dock at Jarrow was re-opened by Palmers-Hebburn. Additional facilities were required on the west coast in order to service escorts without having to withdraw them to regular repair yards. The Admiralty set up organizations at Greenock on the Clyde, at Liverpool and at Pembroke Dock. In August 1941, an Admiralty floating dock (AFD 4) capable of lifting 32,000 tons was towed from Devonport to the Clyde to increase docking capacity for large vessels.[21] The following year, two new destroyer-size dockyard-built floating docks were moored near Oban (AFD 18) and Fort William (AFD 19), manned largely by Special Repair Ratings (Dockyard), as volunteer civilian labour was in short supply.

In 1943 a special repair base was set up at Belfast with the 2,750-ton lift AFD 21, particularly to service the American-built diesel-electric and turbo-electric destroyer escorts (DEs) which were then being delivered under Lend-Lease to the RN. Little expertise existed in the civilian repair industry for such relatively unusual power plants.[22] Lesser facilities including slipways for landing craft were also set up at strategic locations. The workload per ship continued to increase throughout the war, as more elaborate fittings were installed on both merchant and warships: defensive weapons, degaussing, radar, heavy derricks for tanks, arcticization for Russian convoys, followed later by tropicalization for the Indian Ocean and Pacific. Many also required more accommodation for additional crew members. The refit period for cruisers nearly trebled during the war.[23] Particularly large jobs included the conversion of nine Shell tankers to merchant aircraft carriers (MACs) in 1943-44.[24]

For the first time, statistics of shiprepairing (a notoriously difficult industry for which to produce meaningful output figures) were collated on a national basis to assist overall monitoring and control. Examples of figures published after the war included an average of 728,000 tons gross of merchant vessels repaired and returned to service *each week* throughout 1942-43.[25] At any given time, there might be two million GRT undergoing repair, of which about half - excluding naval vessels and conversions - were immobilized in repair berths, the others being repaired whilst still working their cargoes. The proportion under repair as a result of enemy action fell from a peak of 30% in mid-1942 to only 4% in 1945.

Repairs to naval vessels also constituted a continuing workload throughout the war. With the demand for auxiliary vessels to support the British Pacific Fleet, additional priority was given to such conversion work in 1944. Major jobs included four Cunarders turned into repair ships, and cargo vessels into aircraft repair vessels and amenities ships. Severely damaged vessels (such as escorts hit aft by homing torpedoes) were often not considered worth the effort of repair, as was the case with eight *Captain*-class destroyer escorts between June 1944-April 1945. Similarly, some elderly vessels requiring excessive maintenance effort (like the *Town*-class four-stackers and V- and W-class destroyers) were laid up from 1944; this also released their crews for vessels then more urgently needed, such as landing craft.

A total of 52,377 naval vessels was repaired in commercial yards during six years of war, the majority being small craft, but still including 1,959 destroyers.[26] Even more impressive was the rise in the value of ship repairs by contract (i.e. outside the dockyards) from a paltry £340,000 in 1938 to £42 million in financial year 1944.[27] The payment system was broadly similar to that for newbuilding, with the contractor being repaid materials, labour and overhead costs, plus a 5% margin for profit.[28]

Shipbuilding Contracts and Prices

While the pre-war system of seeking fixed-price tenders for shipbuilding contracts survived into the early months of the war, it was soon recognized that the pace of development and the urgency of construction called for a different system. A review showed that the previous system had resulted in high profit rates on naval contracts placed between 1936 and 1939, as shipbuilders sought compensation for their years of losses. For a sample of 32 ships, the profit averaged 27% of actual cost, and, in the case of three submarines, over 70%.[29] These were contracts for hull and machinery placed with shipbuilders and marine engine-builders, but the final cost of the vessel also included ASIs such as guns, mountings, armour, fire control and later radar. After 1941, a new system was substituted. The hull and machinery contractor would receive reimbursement of agreed costs for material, labour and establishment charges, plus a profit margin of 6½-7½% of these costs. This corresponded roughly to a 13% rate of return on capital.[30] This was not quite 'cost-plus', because for a group of similar ships, the profit margin was based on the average cost for the group, resulting in less than 6½% profit on cost to a high-cost builder.

Despite the inflation during the war in which prices rose by about 50%, the price of warship hull and machinery increased relatively modestly. J- and K-class destroyers delivered in 1939 each cost around £390,000 (54% of which was for machinery), while the similar size and horsepower Ca class completed in 1944 each cost about £450,000 (49% machinery). The learning curve and 'austerity' was partly responsible, as well as the lower profit margin, but the higher utilization of facilities contributed lower overheads per ship.

Escort vessel prices escalated more rapidly as larger, faster and better equipped vessels entered service. Typical ship prices including ASIs were:[31]

Type	£000/unit	Std Displacement	£/ton
Flower corvettes	90	950	95
Castle corvettes	190	1,060	179
River frigates	240	1,370	175
Loch frigates	300	1,435	209
Black Swan sloops	320	1,470	217

Even after inflating the costs by about 20 to equate the then value of the pound roughly to 1993 values, the *Loch* frigates cost only about £4,000 per ton. Today's frigates cost approximately £40,000 per ton - vivid confirmation of how the real costs of warships have risen.[32] The machinery proportion of escort hull and machinery was around one-third, reflecting the lower power per ton compared with destroyers.

There are no detailed published statistics on the value of naval shipbuilding output during the war. Naval Appropriation Accounts for 1939-45 were published after the war, giving aggregate figures for expenditure under Vote 8 (Shipbuilding, Repairs Maintenance). It is possible to extract some figures from Section II (Material) and Section III (Contract Work).[33] The latter relate to vessels built in commercial yards and therefore exclude dockyard-built ships, which were however only a tiny fraction of the total during WWII. Four of the published categories probably cover the bulk of the hull and machinery costs of naval production. As the figures cover financial years April to March, I have added half of FY1939 and FY1945 to the full years 1940-44 to represent wartime totals. Figures are in millions of pounds.

Hulls of ships building by contract	294.9
Propelling machinery for HM ships	182.3
Auxiliary machinery for HM ships	55.5
Fairmile patrol boats	23.1
Estimated hull and machinery total	555.8

To give an indication of the total construction cost, certain ASIs can be extracted some from Vote 9 (Naval Armaments) which were mainly installed in ships:

Armour for HM ships	15.2
Gun mountings and	
air compressing machinery	100.6
Guns and ordnance stores	43.9
Electrical and scientific apparatus	201.0
Estimated Admiralty Supply Items total	360.7

Of course some of the latter will have been installed in existing ships being refitted, but even so, the figures suggest that ASIs add about another 50% to the basic vessel cost - and though it is probably too simplistic, it may be helpful to describe this as payload added to platform. A different approach is to use known hull and machinery costs for representative ships to give average costs per ton, and apply these to output figures as in Table 1. My estimate for the major categories for the period September 1939-September 1945 is:

	£M	%
Battleships, carriers and cruisers	102	23
Destroyers	88	20
Escorts	53	12
Mine ships, trawlers and boom defence	38	8
Submarines	27	6
Sub-total 'ships'	**308**	**69**
Mosquito craft	85	19
Landing vessels	55	12
Total	**448**	**100**

The total monetary value is of the same order of magnitude as the previous estimate for hulls and machinery. Although escort vessels appear to be only about 12% of the total, many of the other vessels in the categories above and below were involved in the anti-submarine campaign - say one-third of the cost, or, excluding small craft, about one-half. The annual rate so calculated is thus about £75 million, which compares with a figure of around £5 million for new construction hulls and machinery in the early 1930s. Prewar figures were published in considerable detail.[34]

Manpower and Materials
Between the wars, shipbuilding industry employment in Britain fluctuated with the fortunes of the industry, from a peak of about 300,000 in 1920 to a trough of about 66,000 in 1932. In the latter year, over 60% of the industry's 182,000 insured workers were unemployed.[35] By 1939, the number of workers in shipbuilding and shiprepairing had increased to about 140,000. This included about 30,000 on such work in the Royal Dockyards, but excluded about 58,000 in machinery manufacture. Given the low recruitment during the 1930s and the high levels of specialized skills required, it was not easy to expand the number of shipbuilding workers to meet the demands of increased wartime output. Despite publicity attending the training and employment of women in trades

such as welding, the trade unions were reluctant to accept 'dilutees', fearful of their position postwar.

The Central Statistical Office published figures of employment in shipbuilding and repair, usefully broken down between naval and merchant work, newbuilding and repair.[36] Employment figures in thousands for the first and last dates published and the peak quarter of September 1943 show:

	June 1940	Sept 1943	June 1945
Naval Vessels			
Private yards, new work	62.4	89.3	73.9
repair and conversion	41.5	44.1	38.8
Dockyards	26.4	36.7	35.7
Total naval	**130.3**	**170.1**	**148.4**
Merchant vessels			
Private yards, new work	28.8	42.9	42.5
repair and conversion	44.0	59.5	61.4
Total merchant	**72.8**	**102.4**	**103.9**
Grand Total	**203.1**	**272.5**	**252.3**
Total new work*	93.8	135.9	120.0
Total repair	109.3	136.6	132.3

* Assumes 90% of dockyards on repair work.

Thus, approximately 60% of the quarter million or so were employed on naval work; just under 50% on newbuilding. Employment of women peaked in 1944 with 27,500. Marine engineering employment rose from 58,000 prewar to 88,900 in June 1943 (of which 13,100 were women), falling slightly to 80,500 in June 1945.[37]

The total industrial workforce associated with Admiralty work was estimated at 918,000 in December 1943, including those producing all types of naval equipment and stores.[38] By comparison, the naval personnel strength at that time of the war was 756,000 men plus 65,000 women, six times the size of the pre-war Navy.[39]

Air raids caused some disruption to production, especially in 1941; partly from damage to yards such as Scotts of Greenock, and partly due to restrictions such as blackouts and air raid alerts. Contrary to the propagandist line that all shipyard workers contributed enthusiastically to maximize output, strikes were not infrequent.[40] Although the shipbuilding figures are aggregated with 'Metals and Manufacturing', in 1944 1.048 million working days were lost, over three times the 1939 figure.[41] They tended to be concentrated in the larger firms and associated with the usual causes: demarcation, bonuses and overtime. Naval personnel standing by ships under construction were disgusted at such conduct; when at sea, they were risking their lives for far lower pay and longer hours - and they were not permitted any industrial action.

Between 1938 and 1944-45, average weekly earnings in engineering and shipbuilding approximately doubled from about £3.50 per week to nearly £7.00.[42] By comparison, a naval petty officer in 1939 received a weekly pay of about £2.50 in 1939; which even by 1946 had only risen to £3.50.[43]

As the war progressed, the mix of skills required in the shipbuilding workforce changed. Demand for welders increased substantially - for example by about 80% in the two years to 1944 in 27 yards building naval vessels.[44] This was the technique that made possible the mass production of landing craft, and later of frigates. But it was not possible for British yards to adopt the near-100% welding of US yards. Existing skills and equipment could not lightly be discarded when replacements were in limited supply, especially in the case of riveters and their robust and reliable equipment. Although welders needed less training than riveters, they also needed much extra capital investment to function most effectively: in welding plant, new electrical supplies, fabrication shops and new cranage. None of these were in plentiful supply from heavily overstretched British industry, so it was a case of judicious additions, and making the most effective use of existing plant. The shipbuilding industry was not alone in this situation, with the steel industry also having to make the best use of existing plant, rather than laying down brand-new facilities. Those would not help the short term, and the longer term would have to wait for better days.

Demand for electricians continued to rise as more and more electrical equipment was fitted in ships. Degaussing, radar, improved heating, ventilating and air conditioning all made heavy demands on electrical capacity. More and larger generators had to be installed to meet high-power needs, while low-power systems like fire-control circuits and communications added substantially to cable installations.

The specialized nature of British shipbuilding and staff resulted in high productivity, so maximizing output from the limited labour force and plant capacity. Although building times were not shorter than in US yards constructing comparable vessels, typically only about half the actual manhours were required, while final ship cost was also much less. For example, early American destroyer escorts needed about one million manhours each, reducing to about 600,000 after production had built up.[45] By contrast, the British *Rivers* required about 350-400,000 manhours apiece. The average cost of an American *Liberty* was $1.78 million (then about £450,000) while a similar British 10,000-ton deadweight *Empire* vessel cost about £180,000.

Materials for shipbuilding were almost always in short supply, with steel being one of the biggest bottlenecks. Home supplies were supplemented with imports from the US, Australia and even India, so priorities had to be carefully allocated. But special steels, particularly armour plate, were a still greater problem. The 1936 and 1937 battleship programmes had required the Admiralty to finance new armour-making plant at the three major makers (English Steel, Firth-Brown and Beardmore), since there was no civilian market for such a product.[46] Meanwhile, some orders for non-cemented armour (the more ductile material used for deck armour) for cruisers and carriers were placed in Czechoslovakia. However, much of the new capacity was diverted early in the war to armoured vehicle production, delaying part of the naval programme. Steel forgings were in continual demand, with additional supplies ordered on the Continent. After the fall of France, shortages limited the output of items such as large diesel engines, which in turn restricted the construction of diesel-powered tankers. Alternatives, such as welded fabricated shaft brackets, were used where possible.

The centralization of ordering of much equipment for vessels like the *Lochs* did ensure that supplies were directed in line with immediate production needs, rather than to those firms having the largest commercial influence with sub-contractors.

After 15 years of low demand, gun-mounting manufacture could not be rapidly expanded. This slow expansion reduced the availability of both plant and skilled labour. It proved impossible to produce both 16-inch and 14-inch battleship turrets, both 8-inch and 6-inch cruiser turrets - hence the ultimate cancellation of those planned ships. Despite bringing back into production the former Coventry Ordnance Works at Scotstoun, Glasgow (now owned by Harland & Wolff), twin 5.25-inch mountings were in particularly short supply. Several *Dido*-class cruisers designed to carry five such turrets were completed either with only four, or like *Scylla,* with four twin 4.5-inch mounts - barely more than the secondary armament of a 6-inch cruiser. Despite harnessing non-specialist firms like Molins for anti-aircraft equipment, who normally manufactured cigarette-making machinery, precision-engineered gun mountings large and small were always a bottleneck. This lack of capacity also meant that obsolescent equipment like the 2-pdr multiple pom-pom continued in production long after it should have been superseded by multiple 40mm mounts.

Specialist Vessels

Although designs for landing craft, and what would post-war be called fast patrol boats (then often termed 'mosquito' craft in official parlance), were soon developed by regular shipbuilders like Thornycroft, large scale production had to rely on less conventional builders. As is well known, the majority of tank landing craft were fabricated by steel construction firms and bridge-builders, who also erected them on sites of former shipyards on the Tees, Forth and Clyde. There is not space here to recount the story; indeed any adequate telling of their story has yet to be written.

In much the same way, many motor torpedo boats and motor launches were produced by the Fairmile Marine Co. Ltd. This Admiralty-financed organization was given responsibility for design, planning, ordering and supply of materials and equipment to the 45 small boatbuilders who actually assembled such wooden craft.

Table 1 shows the impressive number of such small craft that were built, of which only a small proportion came from regular shipbuilders. Since most of vessels were essentially 'hostilities only' types, such manufacturing organizations were disbanded shortly after the war. Indeed, many of their products were sold for civilian use, and in Britain's backwaters today, it is still possible to find today former LCTs, MTBs or even motor minesweepers.

Britain's Allies

The resources of the countries of the British Empire were essential to winning the war at sea, as well as, of course, those of the USA. Canada took an early responsibility to build escort vessels; indeed the Royal Canadian Navy made anti-submarine warfare its speciality. Canada rapidly expanded its previously modest shipbuilding industry, producing (in addition to escorts and minesweepers) cargo ships and later LSTs, both for Britain and itself. Australia too built up a significant shipbuilding industry, producing escorts, minesweepers and small craft for the Royal Australian Navy. Modest numbers of vessels were also built for the RN in India, New Zealand, Hong Kong and Portugal.

But it was the vast resources of the USA that ultimately had the greatest influence on the war at sea, particularly in the Pacific. From the shipbuilding angle, the story has been well documented.[47] The broad pattern as it affected the RN is also well known: the 50 four-stacker WWI destroyers exchanged for bases in 1940, then orders for 60 Ocean-class freighters delivered in 1941 (later the basis for the 'Liberty' programme). After US entry into the war came the first escort carriers - albeit requiring significant modifications in Canada and the UK to meet British operational practices. 1943-44 saw the delivery of 99 Lend-Lease escorts of the Colony-class (derived from the Rivers) and Captain-class DEs. Britain had ambitiously planned no fewer than 520 DEs in the US, but the great majority were either diverted to the USN or cancelled.[48] Tank landing ships Mark 2 were produced only by the US, to avoid disrupting merchant ship output in the UK; large numbers were operated both by the RN and USN in the Mediterranean and north European operations from 1943 onwards.

All these programmes provided vessels that an overstretched British shipbuilding industry could not have produced in addition to its existing commitments. But, given that repair work in British yards required more men than newbuilding (see Section 10, above), together with the shortage of larger drydocks, significant relief was provided by the United States undertaking repair of damaged RN ships even before she entered the war. Early in 1941 arrangements were made to carry out repair work in US Navy Yards. The first vessel was the battleship Resolution. Torpedoed at Dakar, she arrived at Philadelphia Navy Yard on 22 April 1941. From then until the end of the war, 180 vessels underwent refits at both US Navy and commercial yards, some requiring very substantial damage repairs such as the battleships Queen Elizabeth and Warspite.[49]

Conclusions

The British shipbuilding industry, together with its close associates marine engineering and shiprepairing, was a key contributor to victory not only in the

Battle of the Atlantic but also in the entire war against Nazi Germany. It expanded rapidly in 1940-41 when Britain stood alone, and could have been starved into surrender had supplies not got through by sea.

Performance records were broken, not by vast new investment (which was simply not an option in wartime Britain), but by making best use of existing labour and facilities. The contribution of central control of shipbuilding and repair in allocating workload and resources has been somewhat overlooked, much assisted by the presence of forceful and knowledgeable shipbuilders like Lithgow and Ayre in high positions. Many key personnel remained in the same post throughout the war.

The contribution of shiprepairing has been under-rated. Often seen to be something of a Cinderella industry, it nevertheless employed over half of the industry's manpower, and greatly increased the availability of ships, whose normal productivity inevitably suffered from the delays inherent in the convoy system. There are few signs visible today of this frantic activity. Photographs of the same areas today show hardly a ship to be seen. Only seven of the British shipyards turning out corvettes and larger vessels are still building ships today, of which only four are using the same berths, albeit re-equipped: Swan Hunter at Wallsend, Fairfield (now Kvaerner-Govan), Thornycroft (now Vosper-Thornycroft at Southampton) and Ferguson at Port Glasgow. None of the engine builders works is now producing marine machinery, but a few of the major repair docks are still in operation on the Tyne, Tees, Clyde, Mersey, Falmouth and Southampton. Of the naval dockyards, only Devonport and Rosyth are still in full operation at the time of writing, although there are plans to reduce their activities further, while there are plans to close Portsmouth's repair facilities altogether, and possibly the base itself. So, even though physical reminders have all but disappeared - and unlike in America, Canada or Australia, no British escort vessel has been preserved - at least this book has demonstrated the interest of those achievements, and the desire to put them on record.

Notes

1. Preston & Raven, *Flower Class Corvettes.*
2. Roskill, *The War at Sea,* I, p. 583.
3. Naval Estimates and Building Programmes 1919-1945. *Warships* Supplement Nos. 55, 57, 58. World Ship Society 1978-79.
4 . Roskill, *op. cit.,* p. 588.
5. Postan, *British War Production,* p. 52.
6. Moss & Hume, *Shipbuilders to the World,* p. 326
7. *Ships of the Royal Navy*
8. *Statistical Tables.* Lloyds Register of Shipping. Postwar Years.
9. *Statistical Digest of the War,op. cit.,* Table 113.
10. Scott & Hughes, *Administration of War Production,* p. 89.
11. Ayre Sir A. L., 'Merchant Shipbuilding during the War', *Trans Institution of Naval Architects* 1945, p. 4.

12.   Elliott, *Allied Escort Ships of World War II*, pp. 211, 357, 380.
13.   Watson, A.W., *'Corvettes and Frigates' Trans Institution of Naval Architects* 1947, p. 167.
14.   Mitchell & Sawyer, *The Empire Ships,* 2nd ed.
15.   Ayre, *op. cit.,* p. 4.
16.   Postan, *op. cit.,* p. 204.
17.   Ayre, *op. cit.,* p. 19.
18.   Bean, C.W.C., 'The Production of Naval Machinery from 1935 to 1945', *Journal of Naval Engineering* Vol 7, No 2, 1954, p. 184.
19.   Edwards, Sir L., 'The War Effort and Organisation of British Shiprepairing', *Trans North East Coast Institution of Engineers and Shipbuilders* 1946-47, p. 195.
20.   Postan, *op. cit.,* p. 65.
21.   Buxton, I. L., 'Admiralty Floating Docks'. *Warships* Supplement Nos. 77, 78. World Ship Society 1984.
22.   Wildish, Sir H. W., 'Some Maintenance Aspects of the Western Approaches Command in the Second World War' *Journal of Naval Engineering* Vol 4, No 1 1950, p. 53.
23.   Bassett, G. A., 'The Repair and Upkeep of HM Ships and Vessels in War' *Trans Inst of Naval Architects* 1946, p. 22.
24.   Howarth, *Sea Shell,* pp. 114-119.
25.   *Statistical Digest of the War, op. cit.,* Table 116.
26.   Bassett, *op. cit.,* p. 22.
27.   Appropriation Account, Navy Services 1938; 1939-43; 1944; 1945-46.
28.   Ashworth, W., *Contracts and Finance,* HMSO 1953, p. 139.
29.   Ashworth, *op. cit.,* p. 108.
30.   *Ibid.,* p.112.
31.   Brown, *A Century of Naval Construction*, p. 172.
32.   Pugh, *The Cost of Seapower.*
33.   Appropriation Account, *op. cit.*
34.   Navy Estimates 1932. HMSO.
35.   Ayre, *op. cit.,* p. 2.
36.   *Statistical Digest of the War, op. cit.,* Table 21.
37.   *Shipbuilding and Shipping Record* 21 February 1946, p. 205.
38.   Postan, *op. cit.,* p. 295.
39.   *Statistical Digest of the War, op. cit.,* Table 10.
40.   *Build the Ships*
41.   *Statistical Digest of the War, op. cit.,* Table 36.
42.   *Ibid.,* Table 189
43.   Navy Estimates 1939; 1946. HMSO.
44.   Goodall, Sir S. V., 'Some Recent Technical Developments in Naval Construction' *Trans North East Coast Institution of Engineers and Shipbuilders* 1944-45, p. 32.
45.   Fassett, H. G., 'The Shipbuilding Business in the USA' *Society of Naval Architects and Marine Engineers,* 1948. Vol 1, p. 101.
46.   Gordon, *British Seapower and Procurement between the Wars*, p. 212.
47.   Fassett, *op. cit.,* 2 vols.
48.   Elliott, *op. cit.,* p. 245.
49.   Bassett, *op. cit.,* p. 26.

5

A Truly Allied Undertaking:
The Progeny of Britain's *Empire Liberty*,
1931-43

by Gary E. Weir

Introduction

While we regularly describe major wartime undertakings such as Operation Torch or the Normandy invasion in terms of an Allied effort, we rarely think of ships in the same way. As both a symbol of Allied determination and a means of sustaining European resistance to Hitler, the *Ocean*, *Fort* and *Liberty* ships demonstrated the potent industrial power of Great Britain, Canada, and the United States. From preliminary design to actual production, building these vessels displayed very early a high degree of effective collaboration between actual and potential Allies.

These ships were truly a co-operative venture. They began as a single British design, modified in co-operation with American and Canadian builders, and produced in various forms and in great numbers by Canadian, British and American shipyards.[1] Thus from the outset the British prototype, christened *Empire Liberty*, represented a truly Allied collaboration to produce quickly built, standard cargo ships of approximately 10,000 tons displacement capable of 11-12 knots.

Declining Inter-War Fortunes in the Shipbuilding Industry

The pressing need to replace the disturbingly high number of U-boat victims sparked the co-operation between the United States and Great Britain that first conceived these ships in 1940. In spite of this grim incentive, the building programmes instituted in Canada, Britain and the United States were welcome. The shipbuilding industry on both sides of the north Atlantic had shared the same misery and declining prospects during the inter-war period. With the onset of the Great Depression in 1929 each country took rather drastic measures to ensure the survival of its construction capacity.

During the first decade after the Great War the shipbuilding concerns of the major western powers suffered terribly both from the wartime over-expansion and the general decline in ship construction during peacetime. Major British shipyards operated from 1919 to 1931 at only 50% capacity, surviving by accepting a very small margin of profit. Rather than waiting for 'natural selection' to cull out the weaker firms and reduce total capacity in the industry over the long term, the Bank of England sponsored a programme that began to break up the most inefficient companies. This process brought construction capacity in line with demand.

In 1931, after approval from the Securities Management Trust, the newly formed Bankers' Industrial Development Company obtained a £1 million loan on behalf of National Shipbuilders Security Limited, a company created the previous year. National Shipbuilders immediately began using its new resources to purchase 'redundant and obsolete shipyards' for disposal or resale to financially stable shipbuilding companies. When a sale took place, the proceeds were used to repay the Bank of England which had devised the rationalization scheme and helped obtain the loan to make it work. All the major shipbuilding companies agreed to co-operate with National Shipbuilders Security Limited, for most of them had little to lose and everything to gain. Fewer firms and a redistribution of assets meant relatively steady work for those who survived the rationalization process. Every participating company also agreed to pay 1% of the contract or sale price of any ship built thereafter, to offset the debt incurred in creating the Bankers' Industrial Development Company.

Even with this plan, the industry desperately needed new contracts. During the first quarter of 1931 British shipyards received orders totalling only 326,000 gross tons, by far the lowest amount in three years. Only 17% of the available berths were occupied with construction projects.

Prospects for new construction remained bleak until the naval build-up began in 1936-1937 in response to German rearmament and Italian activities in North Africa. Merchant shipbuilders then confronted a very different problem. Prices increased rapidly with every new warship contract, and skilled labour as well as shipyard space was almost completely absorbed by naval rearmament.[2] In the midst of a renewed commitment to shipbuilding, merchant construction became a poor step-child in an economy preparing for war. By 1939 the reduced number of shipyards and the priority given to naval construction ensured that building the necessary numbers of merchant vessels to keep British sea-lanes open would require some degree of international collaboration.

Britain naturally looked across the Atlantic for allies in the effort to supplement its shipbuilding. Unfortunately, by 1939 the improved merchant shipbuilding capability developed in Canada during the Great War had decayed significantly. In 1914-18, new Canadian shipyards and industrial facilities completed 26 steamships for Britain and 63 for the new Canadian Government Merchant Marine, operated by the Canadian National Railway.[3] By 1920 merchant tonnage had reached a total of 164,074 tons, only to decline precipitously over the next 15 years to a mere 4,306 tons. The industry retained its workforce by specializing in overhaul and repair. In 1939 this type of activity occupied 70% of Canadian shipyards.[4]

Like Great Britain, the United States took measures to protect its merchant shipbuilding capacity. Ships such as the French passenger liner *Normandie* challenged American designers and engineers to match her speed and luxury. The British Cunard 'Queens' and the French newcomer threatened to exclude Americans from the lucrative transatlantic luxury passenger market. Furthermore, in this and other categories of commercial transport, construction costs placed American industry in a poor competitive position. In 1931 the US

Naval Attaché in London reported that American companies paid $135 per deadweight ton for ships costing $80-86 in Europe.[5]

Five years later this unfavourable balance had not changed much. With the Merchant Marine Act of 1936, Congress created the US Maritime Commission, empowering it to distribute government subsidies 'among shipbuilders and shipping companies'. These measures both sustained American presence on important shipping routes and provided incentives to allow shipbuilders to compete for construction contracts world-wide. Congress created the Maritime Commission to help the American shipping and shipbuilding industries survive under these conditions.

The Maritime Commission formulated an emergency long-range shipbuilding programme under the chairmanship of Joseph P. Kennedy, who, on his departure for the Court of St James as American Ambassador, was succeeded by retired Vice Admiral Emory S. Land. When the Commission awarded the first construction contracts in 1938, the plan called for 50 ships per year over the next decade. With the outbreak of war in September 1939, Land and his colleagues on the Commission revised these plans, anticipating the need for a larger merchant marine to meet the demands of the conflict. They set a construction programme goal of 200 new ship contract awards between 27 August 1940 and the end of July 1941.

From the beginning the new American programme exceeded all expectations. By the end of October 1940, 47 ships were delivered and the Commission had already awarded contracts for 130 more.[6] In selecting the shipyards, the Maritime Commission distributed the construction of its vessels among seven shipyards scattered along all three American coasts, from the huge Bethlehem-Fairfield Shipyard in Baltimore, Maryland, to the Delta Shipbuilding Company in New Orleans, to the Oregon Shipbuilding Company in Portland. The effort that would soon occupy every worker and strain every shipbuilding facility to its limits had begun.[7]

The British Foundation: *Empire Liberty* and the *Ocean* Class

Confronted by a disturbingly effective U-boat offensive, the British came to North America in the final months of 1940 looking for the additional construction capacity they lacked at home. The British Technical Merchant Shipbuilding Mission, authorized by the Ministry of Shipping and led by engineers Robert C. Thompson and Harry Hunter,[8] sailed from Britain on 21 September 1940 to select Canadian and American shipyards for the construction of 86 new cargo ships based on a design developed by the Admiralty's Director of Merchant Shipping, Sir Amos L. Ayre.[9] Ayre designed a standard cargo ship of just over 441 feet long, with a beam of 57 feet two inches and a deadweight capacity of 9,300-10,100 tons. The propulsion system consisted of a reciprocating saturated steam plant fed by Scotch boilers. According to the British trade publication *Marine Engineering and Shipping Review*, the designer sought cargo-carrying efficiency, economical operation, and swift construction.[10] The North Sands Shipbuilding Yard of Joseph L. Thompson and Sons Ltd. in Sunderland built the first ship of this design: *Empire Liberty*.[11]

After their arrival in New York, the British mission soon departed on a whirlwind two-week tour of American and Canadian shipyards and manufacturing centres from New Orleans to Vancouver, British Columbia, ending on 1 November. In the process they saw 21 facilities in the United States and 10 in Canada. After extensive negotiations, the leaders of the mission signed an agreement on 20 December 1940 in the United States with Todd Shipbuilding Company for the construction of new yards in South Portland, Maine and Richmond, California and the construction of 60 ships. On the same day the mission leaders signed Canadian contracts with Burrards, Canadian-Vickers, and Davie Shipbuilding Company for 26 more vessels of the same design. The latter agreements pumped about $30 million into the Canadian shipbuilding industry.[12]

Construction of the American yards by Todd and the organization known as the Six Companies under the leadership of Henry J. Kaiser went equally well on both coasts in spite of challenging site conditions. The wild card was the weather. Immediately after completing the Grand Coulee Dam in Washington, Kaiser's construction crews hurled themselves into the shipyard project in Richmond California - the first of three the company would eventually build in that area, because the temperature permitted the work to begin immediately. While the construction team at Richmond drove piles in at the rate of 700 per day, the ground in Portland, Maine, was still frozen.[13]

Both sites received seven construction berths, the Richmond yard had normal slipways built on piles and Portland's rock foundation made the construction of dry-docks or basins more efficient. The latter would take longer to build, but this alternative saved more costs because it permitted the company to float the hulls rather than spending extra money on launching. From the beginning, the Richmond yard demonstrated greater speed in ship construction, delivering all 30 vessels by July 1942, a construction time of 19 months. Portland followed, with a 30 November delivery, well within contract limits.

The Maritime Commission worked as hard as the British to ensure the successful completion of these yards and their effective operation. For when Todd finished its 60 *Empire Liberty*s, the Commission planned to purchase both British-financed yards - Richmond Number One, as the Californian site became known, and the Portland yard, Todd-Bath Iron Shipbuilding Company. Both locations contracted with the Maritime Commission for the production of cargo ships on 16 January 1942 as their work for the British ended. Negotiations for their purchase began soon thereafter.[14]

Problems of site selection and construction did not plague the early Canadian effort. The contractors working with the British already had their facilities in place. However, some construction techniques suggested by the Americans posed possible obstacles to the pace of construction. Like many American companies after 1940, Todd welded its hulls and abandoned riveting for welding in other phases of construction when the new process suited the task. Shipbuilders in the United States readily admitted the higher cost of welding. This assembly technique required a greater number of expensive skilled workers. In spite of the expense, American builders argued that welding offset the increased labour costs by saving a great deal of expensive steel in a time of increased production and materials shortages. Todd and other companies also found it easier to keep total ship tonnage under control. For the Canadian yards to follow suit would have required a revised set of plans from the United States and very substantial modifications at the construction sites. Rather than introduce upheaval, and for the sake of rapid production, the British agreed to purchase from Canada versions of the *Empire Liberty* which were mostly riveted.[15]

Ottawa then stepped in to streamline the entire production process. On 18 April 1941, the Canadian government created a company to oversee the merchant ship construction effort. Wartime Merchant Shipping Ltd., as it was called, took over the job of co-ordinating procurement of every sort, labour supply, the distribution of contracts among the bidders, the supervision of manufacture and construction, and the creation of factories around the country to supply the shipbuilding effort. Harvey R. MacMillan, an executive of considerable ability who had already demonstrated his talents as a private businessman, Timber Controller, and the Chairman of the War Requirements Board, took over the new company along with a board of six.[16]

MacMillan and his colleagues rejected the highly centralized approach to mass production adopted by the United States at Philadelphia's Hog Island Shipyard during the emergency shipbuilding programme of World War I. Hog Island had 50 slipways on 900 acres and produced 122 ships between August 1918 and January 1921, in spite of considerable logistical and supply problems. Drawing conclusions from that experience, MacMillan pursued a decentralized scheme, utilizing the plants and yards already in place as opposed to building a single giant shipyard and supplying it from every corner of the country.[17]

Within one year, Canadian industry had fully adapted to fast, mass-production techniques. The shipyard of Marine Industries Ltd. of Sorel, Quebec, for example, favourably impressed the American naval attaché in Canada, Commander Edmund W. Strother. He admired its ability to fabricate much of the ship in enclosed shops in a way similar to that employed by Manitowoc Shipbuilding Company in Wisconsin when building American submarines on the Great Lakes during the war. Strother observed that:

the ships are built up in sections where it is at all possible. All joints are riveted in the keel, shell, keelson and part of the double bottom. In the double bottom the transverse seams are welded and the longitudinal seams are riveted. This gives a continuous two sea joint, standardises the size of the rivets, eliminates hundreds of liners, and the many joggled joints, thereby making for greater speed in production and for reduction in costs.[18]

Indeed, both the Canadians and the Americans not only used all available shipyards and factory facilities searching for quick and maximum output, but also filled the weekend and holiday time of many smaller contractors whose physical plant lay idle during those hours. Many of these small machine shops had precision machinery and tools that served the war effort well after hours.

From the beginning, the construction of the *Empire Liberty* design crossed borders and covered a considerable geographic expanse. These two factors alone called for a common design, in spite of varying construction techniques, and a tightly co-ordinated procurement system. The Canadian yards and Todd Shipbuilding agreed that Gibbs and Cox would provide the standard plans for the *Empire Liberty*s built in the United States and Canada. These ships eventually became known as the *Ocean* class, or 'North Sands-type' after the company of their origin, North Sands Shipbuilding Yard of Joseph L. Thompson and Sons. Gibbs and Cox drew more comprehensive plans for Canadian use and, across the border, composed drawings that took the American preference for welding into consideration. The company's staff swelled to over 900 to provide comprehensive design services as well as a centralized organization for the acquisition of systems and materials for both the Canadian and American yards.

Gibbs and Cox performed an extraordinary feat of organization in responding to British, American and Canadian demand. According to Thompson and Hunter of the British mission:

> Gibbs and Cox were to purchase all the major items - main engines, boilers, shafting, propellers, auxiliaries, steering gears; windlasses, joiner work, plates, sections, rivets, welding rods, stem frames, rudders, electrical installations, sidelights, boats, davits, upholstery, to name a few, to be delivered at the shipyard at the right time.

The company's success in co-ordinating the British project later led Emory Land and the US Maritime Commission to copy the system in the creation of the first American *Liberty* ships, known early in their distinguished career as the EC-2 Emergency Cargo Ship. *Ocean Vanguard*, first of the American-built *Ocean* class to come down the ways, left Richmond and passed its final trials in summer 1941 before entering service on 15 October.[19]

Birth of the *Liberty* Ship

As Gibbs and Cox, Todd, and the Canadian yards began work on the *Ocean*-class cargo vessels, the Maritime Commission sought a new design for the first 200 ships of the emergency programme initiated by President Franklin D. Roosevelt on 3 January 1941. Reacting to European events, the President decided to embark on a far more ambitious programme than that envisioned by the Maritime Commission in the autumn of the previous year.

Originally doubtful as to the suitability of the British *Ocean* type, the Commission briefly considered imitating two World War I veterans, *Hog*

Islanders built in Philadelphia and the *Los Angeles*-class cargo vessels built by the US Shipping Board. The former measured 380 feet overall with a 54-foot beam, sporting 2,500hp steam turbines. Variations on this design, longer by 58 feet and more powerful, could generate 6,000hp. *Hog Islanders* converted 3,500 IHP into more than 10.5 knots at full speed. The *Los Angeles* design carried water-tube boilers and triple expansion engines, and in the opinion of some engineers and architects represented the best American merchant vessel of that era. This vessel could surpass the speed of a *Hog Islander* by half a knot.[20]

When Maritime Commission engineers examined more closely the plans and performance record of the *Los Angeles* type, they discovered three major faults. The skeg would break if the ship sat on the bottom, an air pump that served as part of the propulsion system caused unacceptable vibration, and the engine foundations lacked the necessary rigidity. This ship would require a great deal of new design work and testing before the Commission could declare it suitable.

On the recommendation of fellow Maritime Commissioner and retired Vice Admiral Howard L. Vickery, who led and reported on the design debate, Emory Land decided to use the Gibbs and Cox version of the British *Ocean* class as a prototype, adjustable to American needs.[21] The transition from the British project would not pose any great difficulty. While Maritime Commission engineers made some significant changes, they tampered very little with the original plans as amended for Todd by Gibbs and Cox. Substantive design differences between the *Ocean* type and the future American *Liberty* ships were limited to the propulsion system and the location of all crew accommodations amidships in the EC-2, rather than separating the officers from the crew and housing the latter aft as in the original *Empire Liberty*. As opposed to the *Ocean*s, the first 200 *Liberty* ships would have welded hulls, oil-fired watertube boilers, fathometers, contra-rudders, and Kingsbury thrust bearings.

Convenience and the need for rapid production dictated some of these changes. While American industry could not produce Scotch boilers in sufficient numbers to permit following the British lead, Babcock and Wilcox could manufacture watertube boilers aplenty. Other design alterations also sought to exploit practical advantages. The American shipbuilding industry naturally preferred the more plentiful domestic oil as fuel. The fathometer and new rudder added greater manoeuvrability and better navigation. A contra-rudder made the ship more agile in the face of attacking U-boats and the fathometer provided greater safety when degaussing interfered with the effectiveness of the magnetic compass. Adopting all-welded hulls merely conformed to preferred American shipbuilding practice and the Commission also mandated extra ballast to ensure a deeper draft and greater stability underway. Maritime Commission engineers placed deep tanks within the hull that could easily carry cargo, fuel oil or ballast water depending upon the ship's needs. By early April 1941 the adaptation from *Ocean*-class merchantman to *Liberty* ship neared completion and the material orders were placed to permit construction to begin.[22]

These changes proceeded quickly and with remarkable efficiency because of the very close relationship established between the Maritime Commission and Gibbs and Cox. For the latter, this was second nature after its experience with the British merchant ship construction project. While Gibbs and Cox drew the working plans for the EC-2s, the Commission created a new division from the components and personnel of its old Technical Division. The new Division of Emergency Ship Construction set up shop at the same New York address as Gibbs and Cox to provide 'bedside approval' of drawings and specifications as the draughtsmen finished them. This did not eliminate every obstacle to quick design and procurement, but it did reduce paperwork and accelerate the implementation of design and plans. William G. Esmond and John E. P. Grant, the directors respectively of the former Technical Division's Hull Plan Approval and Engineering Plan Approval Sections, now took over these same functions in the new organization but on a more ambitious scale, reflecting the Commission's new mandate.

With Gibbs and Cox acting as a central procurement agency, creating a network of qualified contractors presented only minimal difficulty. The company not only knew what to order and when, but its working plans took advantage of standardization and particularly able companies to ensure a quality product quickly built. This intimate knowledge of the design and the company's familiarity with naval technology made it easier to identify the best contractors for the various major on board systems. In addition the Maritime Commission met frequently with all the principals on the project, including Harry Hunter of the British Merchant Ship Mission, to ensure thorough standardization.

After Gibbs and Cox expanded the 80 working plans provided by the British for the steam propulsion system to the 550 necessary for American construction, the Maritime Commission approved the company's selection of General Machinery Corporation of Hamilton Ohio as the lead manufacturer for the engines and other propulsion components. General Machinery produced the engines for the 60 British *Ocean*-class ships and joined 10 other contractors on the expanded American programme that included the *Liberty*s. Babcock and Wilcox designed a standard water tube boiler for the EC-2s that differed significantly from the British Scotch boilers. As Maritime Commission historian Frederic Lane pointed out, they were 'placed athwartship with the firing aisle fore-and-aft instead of transversely as in the case of the British coal-fired Scotch boilers'. The designers placed all valves in the same location and the boilers did not differ at all from ship to ship. Standardization ruled the day. Along with Babcock and Wilcox, Combustion Engineering and Foster Wheeler manufactured all of the boilers for Roosevelt's 200-ship emergency programme.[23]

During the first half of 1941, the expectations placed on the American shipbuilding industry increased dramatically. With approval of the Defence Aid Supplemental Appropriations Act of 27 March 1941, the Roosevelt Administration both initiated the Lend-Lease Programme and authorized Admiral Land to build more merchant ships. On the heels of this legislation the

Office of Production Management (OPM), in charge of the wartime production effort, approved a measure that cleared the way for the construction of 106 additional ships by the Maritime Commission. Thus the latter's 17 April 1941 construction programme included plans for 306 new ships. Although 112 of them were standard Maritime Commission C-series cargo ships, the 306-ship total also included 72 badly needed tankers and 112 *Liberty* ships.[24]

With Congressional approval and the allocation of funds, the Commission quickly acted to select yards for the construction of these new vessels. The emergency programme would certainly consume available shipyard space and talent, would require an expansion of the industrial base, and make agreements with the Navy about the use of existing berths absolutely necessary. Years before, President Roosevelt had also strongly suggested developing the shipyard industry in the south, along the Gulf coast.

The Commission now took stock of its shipyard resources. In June 1941, Land sent an incentive letter to each yard and requested that his words appear on the shop floor for everyone to read. Near the end of the letter he drove home the extent of the emergency:

> The Commission seriously and urgently requests that you and your organization resurvey your activities with the idea of doing everything possible to expedite the construction of vessels at your yard. The shipping situation is serious to desperate.[25]

When the programme called for only 200 American and 60 British ships, the Commission found their nine major yards and 60 berths adequate. Besides the Todd shipyards working on the British *Ocean* class in Maine and California, the Commission also employed Bethlehem-Fairfield, North Carolina Shipbuilding Company (Wilmington), Alabama Drydock and Shipbuilding Company (Mobile), Delta Shipbuilding Company (New Orleans), Houston Shipbuilding Company, California Shipbuilding Company (Terminal Island, Los Angeles), and the Oregon Shipbuilding Company in Portland.

With 306 ships on order as of spring 1941, Land and the other Commissioners frantically sought new yards and more berths, only to find the US Navy in direct opposition to merchant ship construction at any yard with warship contracts. The Navy even opposed the Maritime Commission effort to let contracts in regions predominantly engaged in Navy work because *Liberty* construction might draw skilled workers away from the warship effort!

Changing these circumstances proved nearly impossible. For the next few months Land and his colleagues worked to convince major American yards of the dire need for cargo ships. The Commission tried to lure various companies into taking additional merchant ship contracts. Major shipbuilding firms were asked to consider managing new government-financed yards that might extend their capacity, thus making *Liberty*-ship construction possible. Shipbuilding companies, already over-committed, did not reply to the Commission's appeals in an encouraging manner.

In spite of the struggle and an uncertain future, the first EC-2s began coming down the ways. The SS *Patrick Henry*, first of the 'Liberty Fleet', as Maritime Commissioner John J. Dempsey called it, was launched by Bethlehem-Fairfield on 27 September 1941. The builders averaged a quick 250 days with this first round of *Liberty*s and the contracts for a second round specified 150 days. 'First round' referred to the initial ship launched from each berth or slipway at every shipyard. The pomp and ceremony surrounding the first launch both helped the 'Liberty' name stick and made America very aware that these ships, built and operated by private companies, formed part of a giant emergency public project driven by the Roosevelt Administration and tax dollars.

Just as Land's effort to find additional yard space began to prove frustrating, the attack on Pearl Harbor changed everything. Initially, the Commission accelerated production roughly 25%. Given the nature of the emergency, the Roosevelt Administration felt the need for a more ambitious plan. During January 1942, at the height of the devastation wrought by Admiral Karl Dönitz's execution of Operation Drumbeat along the North American coast, Roosevelt - in spite of the scarcity of shipyard space - authorized a further increase, raising the pace of construction beyond 25% to a full one-third.

To provide the additional production capacity, the Maritime Commission urged the expansion of the shipyard industrial base. Henry Kaiser, up to this point only a shipyard-builder and Todd-partner, agreed to construct two new yards on the west coast that his company would also operate. He built the first near the Richmond California shipyard, already engaged in producing the British *Ocean* class. The new yard took the name Richmond Number Three. He quickly erected the other facility at Vancouver Washington, near the Oregon Shipbuilding Company directed by his brother Edgar Kaiser. Bethlehem also joined the effort by developing an old repair yard in San Francisco Bay at Alameda into a construction site. The only other additions came from the Maritime Commission itself, completing a yard already started at Savannah and convincing the Navy to permit merchant construction at Federal Shipbuilding Company's Kearney Plant in New Jersey.

Even with these additions the Commission and private industry effected only a modest increase in capacity. The number of berths increased by only 22, from 199 to 221. Thus, to achieve the goals set by the Roosevelt Administration, the Maritime Commission looked to each yard to increase its output by about 25%.[26]

On 19 February 1942, just when Admiral Land was sure the industry could stand no more, the President called him to the White House and made an extraordinary request. Roosevelt desperately wanted nine million tons of ships in 1942 and another 15 million in 1943.[27] Although Land and Vickery knew these goals severely tested the limits of American industrial capacity, and might represent the impossible, once again they began expanding the number of ways at existing shipyards and creating new yards at other sites. The Commission augmented the capability of Sun Shipbuilding, the Kaiser-built facility in

Vancouver, and Richmond Number Two, a yard built in 1941 adjacent to Todd in California. New sites included a Maritime Commission yard managed by Kaiser at Swan Island in Portland, Oregon; Marinship, built by California Shipbuilding Company in Sausalito, California; and a yard in Providence, Rhode Island managed by the Rheem Manufacturing Company. With the approval of another facility at New Orleans with 41 ways, as well as construction of three smaller sites at Brunswick, Georgia, Panama City and Jacksonville, Florida, the Maritime Commission's astounding pace of expansion truly matched the spirit of the President's extraordinary construction request.

Canada and the *Fort*-Type Cargo Ship

Although more modest in scope than the American effort, the Canadians quickly responded to the demand for new merchant vessels with the construction of the *Fort*-class cargo ships, their version of the basic British design that gave birth to the *Liberty*. In autumn 1941, Wartime Merchant Shipping Ltd. expanded its shipbuilding programme by 50%, awarding new contracts and drawing new yards into the effort. Marine Industries Ltd., Davie Shipbuilding and Repairing Ltd., and two other Quebec shipyards went to work on cargo ships, as did the Montreal Plant of Canadian Vickers. The latter received orders for six freighters as well as $1 million from Wartime Merchant Shipping for a boiler and allied equipment plant to support the entire national ship construction effort.

During the final months of 1941, the total cost of the programme approached $250 million and the demands on Canadian industry increased considerably. Viewing the situation in a broad perspective, the American naval attaché in Ottawa commented that:

> the stepping up of Wartime Merchant Shipping's total programme now being put into effect, has increased the number of vessels being constructed under the direction of the Government war company from less than 100 to more than 140.[28]

When building plans soon called for production exceeding that mandated by the British Technical Merchant Shipbuilding Mission, construction sites on Canada's west coast entered the picture. Shipyards in Vancouver and other locations in British Columbia received contracts to build more than 90 freighters, each of 10,000 tons and roughly 9,300 tons deadweight capacity. Of the 140 ships then on order in the Canadian emergency programme, the remaining 50 went not only to Marine Industries, the only yard in eastern Canada to operate a marine railway, but also to Vickers and Davie, two of the eastern yards that signed contracts with the British for *Ocean*-class freighters in 1940. Vickers launched the first of the emergency programme ships, *Fort Ville Marie*, on 10 October 1941 and Vancouver followed one week later.[29]

The rapid expansion of the industrial base for shipbuilding in Canada proceeded at the same frantic pace as in the United States. The companies participating in the Canadian programme constantly demonstrated their adaptability and innovation in wartime emergency conditions. In the early months of the war, for example, Vickers built much-needed corvettes and minesweepers, delivering them months ahead of schedule. At virtually the same time the yard began work on the *Fort*-class cargo ships, manufacturing them year round, assembling components and prefabricated sections inside the protection of their five-slipway enclosed construction shed. Vickers' machine shop manufactured parts and systems on site, saving much time and money.

The smaller yards further demonstrated the innovative use of domestic industrial capacity. United Shipyards Ltd. of Montreal, for example, grew out of wartime need and effective co-operation between Dominion Bridge Company Ltd. and Fraser, Brace Ltd. Built on a swamp near Victoria Bridge, United Shipyards began its work on the *Fort* class ships in May of 1942 and launched its first, the *Fort Longueuil*, in October. For the balance of the war this yard repeatedly set construction records, twice launching two ships in one day. On Thursday 19 August 1943, United found its way into the record books by launching three 10,000-ton cargo ships in 24 hours. The last, *Fort Romaine*, took only 38 days from keel to launching.

Just as the US Maritime Commission depended heavily on the west coast facilities built and operated by Todd and Kaiser, the Canadians also relied on their Pacific coast shipyards. These firms built nearly 70% of Canadian emergency cargo ships. *Fort*-class vessels emerged in startling numbers from West Coast shipbuilders, North Van Ship Repairs, Burrard Drydock Company, Prince Rupert Drydock and Shipyard and other construction facilities along the British Columbia coast.[30]

Commenting on the figures released in the RCN Monthly Review, Commander Strother, American naval attaché in Ottawa, reported on the quickened pace of Canadian shipbuilding to the US Office of Naval Intelligence in July of 1942. In addition to impressive statistics, he noted the reduced Canadian dependence on imported materials and systems:

> At the present time, a 10,000-ton ship is being launched every four days, but it is anticipated that this can be reduced to one ship every three days. Up to the present, the shortest time which has elapsed between laying of the keel and launching of a 10,000-ton ship is 77 days, this record being held by the *Fort Pitt*. Ships have been delivered, ready for sea duty, 35 days after launching... The completed cargo ships are 95% built with Canadian materials and labour, whereas in the last war, a very large proportion of the steel, engines, shafting, propellers, pumps and auxiliaries had to be imported.[31]

The Canadian programme peaked in 1943 and was fuelled by Canadian funds and orders from Great Britain. The Canadians relied on Britain more heavily for designs and ship plans than the United States. However, the British still had to adjust to some construction circumstances and habits unique to the quickly expanding Canadian shipbuilding industry. In one important case, the Canadians decided to switch from coal- to oil-fired 10,000-tonners in March 1943 and the plans were altered accordingly.[32] In November 1944, Captain Glen Howell, the new US naval attaché, reported that:

> Plans for all ships built have been supplied by the British government but certain minor changes have been made locally to allow for the peculiarities of local conditions. Most of the changes were to permit the application of principles of mass production but other improvements were to make the ships more comfortable and convenient for the crews or to utilize existing materials or the output of existing machinery.[33]

Before the war ended, Canadian shipyards built approximately 3.5 million deadweight tons of merchant shipping, most of which remained under Canadian ownership. Ten-thousand-ton *Fort*-class cargo ships represented about 2.79 million tons of the total. By 1944, Great Britain purchased two of these ships and the United States 90. About 100 more went to the British as mutual aid and another 110 to Canadian companies serving the war effort.[34]

Domestic British Merchant Ship Construction

Emergency conditions forced the British to husband their resources, specialize and augment their capability with foreign construction agreements. They left most of the mass-produced merchant shipbuilding to Canada and the United States, producing domestically only about one-sixth of the tonnage built during the war in the United States alone.

In 1939 and 1940, demand for warships and the need to repair and overhaul damaged merchant ships completely consumed the British shipbuilding capability. It came to the point that Prime Minister Winston Churchill ordered a slowdown in the construction of merchant ships in March of 1941 to permit the industry to revise construction priorities, to allow a new distribution of skilled labour, and to determine ways of coping with the pressing need for repair to the existing merchant fleet. His target figure for merchant ship construction in 1942 went from 1.25 million tons down to 1.1 million.

Churchill's decision provided the proper remedy. With British industry finally coming up to speed in the second half of 1941, the supply of marine engines and boilers began to increase dramatically, the necessary repairs to the merchant fleet significantly reduced the backlog of disabled vessels, and the labour supply began to increase with recruits to the industry. All of this was accomplished by an increasingly motivated and co-operative industry under the supervision of the Ministry of Shipping and the Admiralty.

A demanding battle against the U-boats forced the War Office to make hard decisions in spite of the encouraging news from the yards. Before the end of 1941 the industry met and surpassed by 50,000 the production goal of 1.1 million tons, building at an annual rate of 1.4 million tons. This favourable trend continued into 1942, when production approached 1.3 million tons, and the number of workers in the industry reached 43,000, the highest level of any year during the war.

The losses to German submarines during the height of the Battle of the Atlantic in 1942 caused a change in priorities. In October, the Cabinet decided to shift British shipbuilding resources to the construction of escorts for the merchant convoys. Building the merchant hulls did not present a problem. However, supplying propulsion systems for the cargo vessels would have interfered with the corvette production programme.[35] Thus by the end of 1942, Great Britain relied almost completely on North American merchant vessel construction, the *Ocean* class, the Canadian *Fort*s, the American *Liberty*s, and the faster *Victory* ships then in the planning and design stage.

Observations

Months before American entry into the war, merchant ship production demonstrated an early and easy interdependence between Great Britain, Canada, and the United States. In a time that often employs 'jointness' as a watchword in military and Naval operations, logistics specialists and shipbuilders of the 1990s would do well to examine and appreciate the level of co-operation, the speed and remarkable efficiency of the Canadians, Americans and British between 1940-43.

Each *Ocean, Liberty* or *Fort* was the product of British marine architects whose plans were adapted by their American and Canadian colleagues. British investment and demand helped pull the North American shipbuilding industry out of a depression-era slump, and the spreading conflict motivated American and Canadian industry to extraordinary achievements in expansion, organization, procurement, building techniques and construction time. The cargo ships that emerged from Todd's Richmond Number One yard or Canadian Vickers represented the earliest completely Allied or joint effort of the war, and its success went beyond all expectation. In the United States alone, an industry that first experienced the war effort with 60 British *Ocean*-class ships, ended that conflict by building a wide variety of vessels including an astounding 2,500 *Liberty* ships.[36] As much as any other single factor, the Allied merchant ship construction effort helped ensure the defeat of the U-boats in the Battle of the Atlantic.

Notes

1. I realize that my use of 'American' in this paper ignores the fact that the Canadians are just as American as citizens of the United States. Both countries share the geographic region known as North America. This said, I hope my Canadian neighbours will excuse my rather exclusive use of the term 'American' to permit an easy distinction between the two countries and for diversity of style.

2. Gordon, *British Seapower and Procurement Between the Wars*, pp. 172-181; *Cost of Merchant Ships*, by Lt Cdr L. C. Stevens, USN, 15 February 1937, box 309, Naval Attaché Reports, 1886-1939, Naval Intelligence Division (ONI), RG-38, NA.

3. German, *The Sea is at Our Gates*, p. 52.

4. Lt Julius Fleischmann, USNR, Assistant Naval Attaché, Ottawa, ONI Intelligence Report on Canadian Shipbuilding, 18 August 1941, box 320, Naval Attaché Reports, 1940-1946, Naval Intelligence Division (ON1), RG-38, NA.

5. Cdr R. T. Hanson (CC), *Cost of Cargo Vessels and Cargo Passenger Vessels*, 24 March 1931; Cdr G. W. Nelson (CC), *Shipbuilding Costs in Europe*, 10 March 1939, box 309, Naval Attaché Reports, 1886-1939, Naval Intelligence Division (ONI), RG-38, NA.

6. Lane, *Ships for Victory*, pp. 10-13; 22-24.

7. *Ibid.*, p. 51.

8. Thompson was the managing director of Joseph L. Thompson and Sons Ltd., Shipbuilders at Sunderland. Harry Hunter was a marine engineer connected with Swan, Hunter and Wigham Richardson, a shipbuilder and engineering firm located at Wallsend on Tyne, Northumberland. Lane, *op.cit.*, p. 80.

9. Ayre was born at South Shields in 1885. He served as chairman of the Burntisland Shipbuilding Company Ltd., Fife until 1936, when he became Deputy Controller of Merchant Shipping and Repairs and Director of Merchant Shipping, Admiralty, 1940-44. A. Osbourn to W. E. Spofford, 31 January 1946, box 12, Records of the Historian's Office, 1944-1947, Records of the US Maritime Commission, RG-178, NA.

10. Copy British Prototype of the Liberty Ship, *Marine Engineering and Shipping Review* April 1942 (XLII, No 4), box 12, Records of the Historian's Office, 1944-1947, Records of the US Maritime Commission, RG-178, NA.

11. *Empire Liberty* was launched on 23 August 1941; Lane, *op.cit.*, p.81.

12. W. E. Spofford, 'History of the Design, Construction and Operation of the EC-2 Emergency (LIBERTY) Ships', n.d. 1947, box 13; R. C. Thompson and Harry Hunter,'The British Merchant Shipbuilding Programme in North America', part 1, 2 December 1942, box 12, Records of the Historian's Office, 1941-1947, Records of the US Maritime Commission, RG-178, NA; Lane, *op.cit.*, pp.24-48; Captain Oliver M. Read, 'Eighteen merchant vessels for British Government to be built in Canada; contracts let', box 320, Naval Attaché Reports, 1940-1946, Naval Intelligence Division (ONI), RG-38, NA.

13. Lane, *op.cit.*, p. 139.

14. *Ibid.*

15. R.C. Thompson and Harry Hunter, 'The British Merchant Shipbuilding Programme in North America', part 1, 2 December 1942, box 12 Records of the Historian's Office, 1944-1947, Records of the US Maritime Commission, RG-178, NA.

16. R.C. Thompson and Harry Hunter, 'The British Merchant Shipbuilding Programme in North America', part 1, 2 December 1942, box 12, Records of the Historian's Office, 1944-1947, Records of the US Maritime Commission, RG-178; Cdr Edmund W. Strother, 'Wartime Merchant Shipping in Canada', 4 April 1942, box 320, Naval Attaché Reports, 1940-1946, Naval Intelligence Division (ONI), RG-38, NA.

17. Cdr Edmund W. Strother, 'Wartime Merchant Shipping in Canada', 4 April 1942, box 320, Naval Attaché Reports, 1940-1946, Naval Intelligence Division (ONI), RG-38, NA; Bunker, *Liberty Ships*, pp.12-13.

18. Cdr Edmund W. Strother, 'Layout at Marine Industries Ltd., Sorel, Que; production methods; and new addition designed to suit mass production methods', 6 October 1941, box 320, Naval Attaché Reports, 1940-1946, Naval Intelligence Division (ONI), RG-38, NA.

19. R. C. Thompson and Harry Hunter, 'The British Merchant Shipbuilding Programme in North America', part I, 2 December 1942, box 12, Records of the Historian's Office, 1944-1947, Records of the US Maritime Commission, RG-178, NA.

20. IHP stands for indicated horsepower This unit is calculated by an evaluation of the pressure inside the engine cylinders and the displacement of the ship; Lane, *op.cit.*, p. 75; Bunker, *op.cit.*, pp. 8-9.

21. Vickery, an engineer, had extensive interwar experience in ship construction as a supervisor of shipbuilding at Bethlehem Shipbuilding Corporation, Union Plant in San Francisco and during his tour at the Bureau of Construction and Repair in Washington DC. Biography of Vice Admiral Howard L. Vickery, box 6, Records of the Historian's Office, 1944-1947, Records of the US Maritime Commission, RG-178, NA.

22. W. E. Spofford, 'History of the Design, Construction, and Operation of the EC-2 Emergency (LIBERTY) Ships', n.d. 1947, box 13; W. G. Esmond, Chief Hull Section Emergency Ship Construction Division to Director Emergency Ship Construction Division, 21 April 1941, box 12, Records of the Historian's Office, 1944-1947, Records of the US Maritime Commission, RG-178, NA.

23. Lane, *op. cit.*, pp. 94-97; W. E. Spofford, 'History of the Design, Construction and Operation of the EC-2 Emergency (Liberty) Ships', n.d. 1947, box 13 Records of the Historian's Office, 1944-1947, Records of the US Maritime Commission, RG-178, NA.

24. Lane, *op. cit.*, pp. 55-56.

25. Incentive Letter, Admiral Emory S. Land, 14 June 1941, box 12, Records of the Historian's Office, 1944-1947, Records of the US Maritime Commission, RG-178, NA.

26. Lane, *op. cit.*, pp. 51, 68, 139, 140-143; Bunker, *op. cit.*, pp. 3-5.

27. Lane, *op.cit.*, p.29. Cdr Edmund W. Strother, 'Expansion in Quebec Shipbuilding Program', 30 October 1941, box 320, Naval Attaché Reports, 1940-1946, Naval

Intelligence Division (ONI), RG-38, NA.

28. Cdr Edmund W. Strother, 'Expansion in Quebec Shipbuilding Program', 30 October
     1941; *Ibid.*, 'First of Fleet of Cargo Vessels Ready to be Launched', box 320, Naval
     Attaché Reports, 1940-1946, Naval Intelligence Division (ONI), RG-38, NA.

29. Cdr Edmund W. Strother, 'Expansion in Quebec Shipbuilding Program', 30 October
     1941 box 320, Naval Attaché Reports, 1940-1946, Naval Intelligence Division
     (ONI), RG-38, NA.

30. Roberts, *The Canadian Merchant Navy at War,* pp.113-119; Lt George C. Kinnear,
     'Canada - Dry Dock Facilities on the West Coast of British Columbia', 6 December
     1943; Canada - Ship Building Repair and Salvage Facilities - Vancouver Area', 1
     October 1943, box 321, Naval Attaché Reports, 1940-1946, Naval Intelligence
     Division (ONI), RG-38, NA. All of the companies mentioned in the preceding
     paragraph were limited liability companies (Ltd.).

31. Cdr Edmond W. Strother, 'Status and Progress of Merchant Ship Construction in
     Canada', 21 July 1942, box 321, Naval Attaché Reports, 1940-1946, Naval
     Intelligence Division (ONI), RG-38, NA.

32. Captain Glen Howell 'Construction of 10,000-ton freighters in British Columbia', 10
     March 1943, box 321, Naval Attaché Reports, 1940-1946, Naval Intelligence
     Division (ONI), RG-38.

33. Captain Glen Howell, 'Analysis of Shipbuilding in General in the Montreal Area of
     Canada', 17 November 1944, box 324, Naval Attaché Reports, 1940-1946, Naval
     Intelligence Division (ONI), RG-38, NA.

34. Captain Glen Howell, 'Canadian Shipping Board announces more than three million
     tons of merchant shipping constructed in Canada since the start of the war', 12
     October 1944, box 324, Naval Attaché Reports, 1940-1946, Naval Intelligence
     Division (ONI), RG-38, NA.

35. Postan, *British War Production*, pp. 300-303; 'Work in the Shipyards: New
     Difficulties and New Records', Times Record of British War Production 1939-1945
     box 1, Records of the Historian's Office, 1944-1946, Records of the US Maritime
     Commission, RG-178, NA.

36. Bunker, *op. cit*, p. 17.

6

U-boat Development and Building

by Eberhard Rössler

1. German U-boat Planning before World War II

The Reconstruction Programme of 1932

Towards the end of 1932, the German Navy began planning to construct U-boats again. It would be the first time since World War I that the construction of U-boats had taken place on German soil. Because of the ban on possession and production of U-boats under the Peace Treaty of Versailles, all matters concerning U-boats were handled by 'dummy firms' financed by the navy. In 1932 U-boat research was controlled by the Ingenieurburo für Wirtschaft und Technik GmbH (Igewit) at Schelling Str.2 in Berlin W9, not far from the navy offices at the Landwehrkanal. The 'company' was divided into two offices, 'a' and 'b'.

Office 'a' was responsible for military interests. Its chief was retired Obl.z.S. Schottky, a former U-boat officer, who had served under the successful U-boat commander Kptl. Wassner (on UC-69, UB-59 and UB-117 of the U-Flotilla Flanders). Schottky succeeded Konteradmiral Spindler and was also assigned to Fleet Department AII of Naval Command Office A as an AIIU. Matters of construction were dealt with at Igewit's office 'a' by retired Marinebaurat Schürer, who had worked in the Technical Bureau of the U-boat Inspectorate during World War I as a design adviser.

After World War I, the Reichsmarine assisted the Ingenieurskantoor voor Scheepsbouw (IvS), a construction office in Holland where former U-boat designers (mostly of Germaniawerft, Kiel) could evaluate and extend their experience of warship construction. Igewit's main tasks, in close contact with IvS, were to gather information about new U-boat development, to look at the requirements of the German Navy, to take part in tests of U-boats built according to IvS plans in foreign countries and to evaluate these tests.

Because of the transfer of German territories to Poland and France after World War I, those states were earmarked as possible enemies in any later quarrels. Since any such conflicts would be land-based, the reconstruction of a large U-boat fleet was not considered important. Existing plans favoured small and medium-sized U-boats with short building times, as the current ban on possession and production of U-boats would allow the building of U-boats only at a mobilization. This requirement could of course best be met by planning small U-boats. Of special interest in this respect was the Flanders Type UF from 1917 which was mass produced by several smaller German shipyards in 1918. No documents relating to this U-boat type were given to the Allied commissions after the end of the war.

The Flanders-type U-boat of 364 tonnes displacement met the requirements of strength, of a short diving time and of a reliable engine plant (the UC type), with a relatively powerful armament. For Baltic and coastal missions, a smaller version of 250 tonnes was desirable. This was contrived by reducing weight in the engine plant, batteries and armament. It was even possible to increase the surface speed by using a faster-running Diesel engine. The torpedo equipment was reduced to three bow torpedo tubes, and also altered to accommodate torpedoes of 7m length and 53.3cm diameter.

This 250-tonne U-boat development was realized in the 1931-1933 period through the construction in Finland of CV707, following designs by Igewit (Proj. J7) and IvS (Proj. 179). The building of this U-boat was possible due largely to the considerable influence of retired Korv. Kpt. Bartenbach, former chief of the U-boat Acceptance Commission (UAK) and U-boat Flotilla Flanders, who was working as a naval adviser to the Finnish Government. Financial support was again provided by the Reichsmarine.

As a successor to the medium Type UB III, the UG Type was developed by the U-boat Inspectorate in 1918. Its design criteria were similar to those of the UF type, namely, a powerful ocean-going U-boat with a short diving time and a high strength of hull construction (100m design diving depth). The UG Type U-boat did not have fuel tanks on the external structure, and had a greater engine output and a greater range, permitting operations in the North Atlantic and Mediterranean. External tanks were only needed for ballast and compensation water. An average-sized ballast tank was placed in the pressure hull under the central station. The area of the aft pressure hull segment was reduced so as to hold two extra deck torpedo tubes, each inclined aft at an angle of 7°.

In 1927 the opportunity arose to have this type built in Spain. The Head of the Navy (*Marineleitung*, or ML) was willing to bear a large part of the costs, but the Echavarrieta shipyard in Cadiz could only build the submarine with the permission of the Spanish Navy (which would take over this boat later). The Spanish Navy wanted more powerful diesel engines and a greater range than had been planned for the UG type, but from the German point of view it was very important to keep within the Geneva Conference's limit of 600 tonnes standard displacement for small vessels.

It was difficult to create an appropriate design within this limit. As fuel was not included in standard displacement, it could be stored in the external structure. Similarly, the internal ballast tank of the UG-type could be placed outside. By these means it was possible to slightly reduce the pressure hull diameter, but it was still impossible to keep within the 600-tonne limit while using the desired MAN four-stroke cycle Diesel engine M8V 39/45 (later changed to M8V 40/46). However, the London Naval Treaty of 1930 altered this, by applying the 600-tonne limit only to surface ships. In the same Treaty, the major naval powers (Great Britain, the USA and Japan) agreed a total submarine displacement tonnage limit of 52,700.

This 'Spanish U-boat', E1, was built during 1929-31 at Cadiz and later tested by German specialists. The end of the Spanish monarchy made it impossible to sell E1 to Spain, so in 1931 it was sold to Turkey.

On 2 November 1932 Konteradmiral Saalwächter, Head of the Naval Defence Department AI (*Marinewehrabteilung* AI), made a bid to include U-boats in the so-called Reconstruction Programme for modernization and reinforcement of the German Navy up to 1938. Saalwächter, a former commander of the larger Ms U-boats U-46 and U-94, proposed 16 ocean-going U-boats to support the fleet. Kpt.z.S. Guse, Head of the Fleet Department AII, agreed, and on 17 November 1932, in a conference chaired by Admiral Groos, Head of Naval Command Office A (*Marinekommandoamt* A), a plan for fleet reconstruction was devised. This provided for the construction of a small U-boat fleet in three phases. During the first phase, the building plans were to be prepared, and, if possible, the two boats already completed (El and CV707) were to be bought and their crews recruited and trained. If the political situation allowed, building was to commence in the second phase in April 1934.

Five days after that meeting, on 22 November 1932, technical matters relating to the Reconstruction Programme were discussed at a conference in General Naval Office B. The agenda covered the choice of the U-boat types to be built, the selection of the shipyards, shipyard preparations and the preliminary work required (i.e. the ordering of materials and engines), and the installation of the necessary U-boat bases. At this conference the navy wanted the new U-boats E-1 and CV707, in which so much had been invested, to become the prototypes for the Reichsmarine's first two U-boat types I and II. Fleet Department AII asked for a medium U-boat type as well:

An intermediate Type of about 500 tonnes (like that of the former UB III type) would be important: the development of this type, which would replace the Fi[nland]-type, would have to be left to a later time.

Although there are no documents on the subject, it is supposed that this requirement was the cause of the construction of the later Type VII U-boat. Again the starting point was the UG-Type of 1918, but this time the original principles were retained. The external side structure contained saddle tanks for the storage of just one ballast and compensation tank. The surface power was boosted, the armament reduced slightly. This new design (Arb. Nr. 1115) was developed by Schürer and the IvS. Its main feature was that it kept within a 500-tonne standard displacement limit. As early as February 1934, a general plan from the IvS was ready, which was identical to the later Type VII U-boat. However, at the time when Types I and II were still being planned, no decision was made as to how many would be produced.

Hitler's rise to power did not have much influence on the Reconstruction Programme, which aimed mainly at attaining parity with France, but it did cause a slight setback to U-boat planning. For the time being, preparations would be made only for the construction of two Type I and six Type II U-boats.

Future U-boat building was planned by Naval Command Office A. On 28 October 1933, the plans and finance became available for four Type I and 18

Type II U-boats (with a total tonnage of 7,500) to be constructed by 1938. By 19 March 1934, forward planning allowed for 72 U-boats (24 Type I and 48 Type II) totalling 31,200 tonnes to be built by 1949. These plans were quite academic and without a precise schedule.

The Anglo-German Naval Agreement and U-boat Planning

At the beginning of 1934 the Soviet Union had to be taken into account as a potential opponent besides France. On the other hand, Poland was eliminated for the moment because of its non-aggression treaty with Germany. In order to compensate for the more powerful Continental opposition now expected, closer contact and an agreement with Great Britain was desired. The starting point for that arrangement was to be an agreement permitting Germany's naval re-armament to 33% and later to 35% of British tonnage. The head of the German Navy believed that if the planned naval conference at London could be arranged., then 'the Navy chapter of Part V of the Peace Treaty of Versailles would be done with for ever'.

The upper limit of 35% meant 17,500 tonnes for the U-boats. Plans meeting this limit were presented on 4 June 1934 and included seven Type II and 21 Type I U-boats. But the Shipbuilding Replacement Plan of summer 1934 again provided a higher proportion of the small Type II, which could be built more quickly, and proposed the building of 20 Type I and 18 Type II U-boats by 1938. Another plan of this time (mentioned by the German historian Treue) proposed the building of twelve 275-tonne, six 550-tonne and four 900-tonne U-boats in 1935, to be followed in 1936 by another six or eight 550-tonne U-boats. The 900-tonne U-boats (designated Type IV) were a project which stemmed from the Type I design with an additional section inserted for the storage of torpedo-mines.

In accordance with Hitler's orders, the preparations for U-boat building were kept secret, since he did not want an unnecessary confrontation with Britain before the Saar plebiscite and the planned naval agreement had taken place. The start of the building programme was therefore postponed until February 1935. Instead, preparations for another six small 250-tonne U-boats were decided on.

At the end of 1934, the new 500-tonne Type VII was added to U-boat planning. Although no official records exist, it may be supposed that the preference for this type over the 712-tonne Type IA (improved E1 Type I) was also linked to the tonnage limit in the planned Anglo-German naval agreement. After a vote in the Defence Department, future building of the Type IA was abandoned in favour of the Type VII. The U-boat programme of the Shipbuilding Replacement Plan at the beginning of 1935 now planned for the delivery of no more than 24 Type II, 10 Type VII and only two Type IA U-boats by 1938.

It is astonishing that after having planned all of this and without any further discussion, the construction of the Type VII U-boats was ordered. It was inevitable that comparisons would be made with the Type IA, but tactical arguments and the better diving abilities of the Type VII were only brought out after the delivery of the first boat of each class in the middle of 1936.

Naval Office B now had a new U-boat department, 'BU', under the command of Kpt.s.Z. S. Bartenbach. Its influence must be taken into account. BU was set up by the Head of the Navy to ensure speedy completion of the planned U-boats and to unite Igewit and other offices concerned with U-boat preparation, tests and training. In BU, where the non-administrative work of the Head of the Navy was undertaken, those in favour of a medium attack U-boat similar to the Type UB III of World War I were in the ascendant.

The Anglo-German Naval Agreement was signed on 18 June 1935. In this agreement the restriction imposed on U-boats by the Peace Treaty of Versailles was set aside. Anticipating this, the first new U-boat, U-1, had been launched by a floating crane in Kiel Harbour three days earlier. The other 11 Type II U-boats followed in quick succession. While the British public reacted with astonishment and disapproval, their government and the Royal Navy appeared relaxed. After the successful experience of the introduction of the convoy system at the end of World War I, the threat of U-boats seemed to have lost much of its menace. Furthermore, the development of asdic made it possible to detect submerged U-boats. Their threat therefore seemed manageable - a view shared by several German U-boat specialists (including Werner Fürbringer, a famous U-boat commander of World War I, who did much work on the re-organization of German U-boat armament and training), who were also somewhat sceptical as to the importance of U-boats in any confrontation with Great Britain.

Once BU had started U-boat building and the tests of the first boats were complete, its special status was cancelled and its departments integrated with the offices of Naval Forces High Command (*Oberkommando der Kriegsmarine*, or OKM). Bartenbach and Schottky were moved to different tasks and had no further influence on the U-boat reconstruction programme. Military command of the commissioned U-boats was given to the commander of the light cruiser *Emden* and former U-boat commander, Karl Dönitz.

Igewit's Office 'b' was integrated into the Warship Construction Office K. Probably because of space constraints, it was not established in the Naval Forces High Command buildings at Tirpitz Ufer 72-76, but given a home on the other side of the Landwehrkanal at Grossadmiral von Köster Ufer 71. This physical separation from the other departments of the K Office in a way shielded it from the competence dispute in this area. In 1939-40, the expanded Warship Construction Main Office K moved to Shell House at Tirpitz Ufer 60-62. The U-boat construction departments (since 24 January 1939 designated KIU and KIIU) remained in their offices at Grossadmiral von Köster Ufer.

From 1936 the U-boat construction departments took care of the demands of Naval Command Office A (AI: operational planning and AIV: military planning) as well as those of the Naval War Staff and U-boat Command by constructing, preparing for building, planning the necessary tests and undertaking their evaluation. Proven methods were preferred. New U-boat types, which until 1943 were conceived here, were more or less based on existing developments, in other words on WWI submersibles. The revolutionary Walter U-boat, was developed outside the U-boat construction departments and hardly affected them.

The Walter propulsion system was supervised by Ministerialdirigent Brandes, head of the Engineering Department KII of the K Office. From 1932, the mechanical engineer Hellmuth Walter was engaged with great energy and perseverance in research work on a high-speed submarine with thermal single-system propulsion for both surface and submerged operations. The oxygen needed for combustion during submerged operation was to be gained from storage tanks of hydrogen peroxide. In 1934 one of his designs with a steam turbine, intended to reach a maximum speed of 28 knots submerged, was taken onto the duty list of General Naval Office B as U-boat Type V. A smaller experimental submarine (V80), built in 1939-40 with a simplified Walter propulsion outfit, actually reached 26 knots during a diving trial.

U-boat Planning for the Expected Enemies: France and the USSR

At the end of 1935, Office A's main requirement in the U-boat field was to provide a larger boat for Atlantic operations, for instance near the coasts of the French colonies. Other requirements included an extended range and a higher speed than the Type IA (in order to reach remote operational areas) and an increased supply of torpedoes. The remaining 9,550 tonnes allocated from the Anglo-German Naval Agreement were to be used for the construction of these Type IX U-boats.

This new development was based on the Type IA. To compensate for its heavier engine plant, the aft accumulator room and the berths for the Petty Officers were moved to the forepeak. The layout resembled the WWI Mobilization (Ms) U-boats of the Germania shipyard. Tanks for additional fuel and storage containers for more torpedoes were placed in the enlarged external hull. With these changes it was possible to keep the standard displacement at a relatively low level. Officially it was specified as 740 tonnes - that is, just a little above the 712 tonnes of the Type IA.

The Type VII, until then preferred by Igewit and BU, had received strong support from the newly appointed Chief of U-boats (*Führer der U-Boote,* or FdU) Kpt.z.S. Karl Dönitz, after those institutions had been dissolved. Dönitz (commander of UB-68 in WWI) strongly opposed giving the remaining tonnage to the 740-tonne Type IX; rather, he wanted to use it for an improved Type VII. It might be supposed that the U-boat department of K Office sympathized with his wish, because in a relatively short time an improved Type VIIB design with a greater range and torpedo armament was submitted.

Grand Admiral Raeder, commander-in-chief of the navy, deferred his decision until 22 June 1936, when he ordered the building of eight Type IX U-boats. To use the remaining available tonnage (3,630 tonnes), on 27 October 1936 he ordered that seven improved Type VIIB U-boats should be built. The delay in ordering these led to a delivery gap in 1937. When K Office hinted that completion of the new U-boats could take at least two years, Raeder reacted with a declaration ordering 'special and express aid for the U-boat construction programme', but he rejected special organizational measures that could expedite delivery.

In the London Naval Treaty of 26 March 1936, no total tonnage limit was set for the submarine forces of the Great Powers. However, the size of new individual submarines was limited to 2,000 tonnes, and their artillery calibre to 6.1" (15.5mm). These regulations were adopted by Germany after the further Naval Agreement with Great Britain of 17 July 1937.

Larger submarine orders were the consequence. The RN expected to increase its submarine fleet by 70,000 tonnes. That implied a total of 31,500 tonnes available to Germany. This led to further orders of eight 250-tonne Type IICs, four 517-tonne Type VIIBs and two 740-tonne Type IXBs aggregating 5,548 tonnes. Because the Type IICs could be built faster, gaps in the building process would be overcome.

The remaining tonnage was to be used by building two large U-boats, each of 2,000 tonnes, which met the instructions of Naval Command Office A. One of these boats, named Type X, was designated as a mine-laying U-boat for the SMA heavy anchor-mine, while the other (Type XI) would be used for disrupting overseas trade operations. The request for these 'U-cruisers', which were very close to the upper tonnage limit, must be seen in connection with the international intention to ban unrestricted U-boat warfare, that is surprise attacks against merchant ships. On 23 November 1936 Germany signed a U-boat agreement which had been formulated in 1930, demanding warfare within the prize regulations.

The Franco-Soviet treaty of 18 November 1937 led the OKM to propose that the parity of U-boat tonnage agreed to in the Anglo-German agreement of 1935 should be exploited. This had to be done by mutual consent. At the end of 1938, it was discussed at conferences of German and British naval officers and, on the part of the RN, consent was given in principle. It was therefore possible legally to double the U-boat fleet and to exceed French submarine tonnage.

U-boat Planning in Preparing for Conflict with Great Britain (The Z-Plan)

Hitler's politics firstly concentrated on re-integration former German and Austrian territories which had been separated after WWI. After the *Anschluss*, the union with Austria, the next objectives were Czechoslovakia and Poland. It was clear that the occupation of these countries and the annexation of large parts of them would not be accepted by Great Britain without protest. Although Hitler thought that Britain would not risk a global war, the German Navy was to be prepared for that eventuality. From the middle of 1938, a large Fleet plan, including Britain as a possible enemy, was begun. It led to the so-called Z-Plan.

Initially the increase in U-boat armament was to remain within the limits of the German-British Fleet Agreement. On 27 June 1938, in a schedule reaching to the end of 1941, a large number of U-boats (18 Type VIIB and 11 Type IXB) suitable for a trade war with Great Britain, were ordered. Fulfilment of these additional orders would make parity with the British submarine tonnage just possible by 1 January 1942.

The next U-boat schedule for the Z-Plan of 24 November 1938 was substantially above the 100% tonnage limit and provided for a total of 174 U-boats of 103,340 tonnes up to the end of 1943. These included two Type IA, 48 Type II, 10 Type VII, 69 Type VIIB/C, 26 Type IX, four Type XB, seven Type XI and eight Type XII. By the end of 1947, the number of U-boats was to be increased by a further 75. Medium U-boats dominated this plan, but again it was a compromise between different opinions on what constituted the most effective U-boat operation with a well-balanced fleet.

The FdU, Konteradmiral Dönitz, used the Spanish Civil War to test his U-boats in action, especially the hitherto untested Type VII. He thought this medium type was the most suitable weapon in a possible struggle with Great Britain. He uncompromisingly favoured an unlimited U-boat trade war with Great Britain and proposed surface night attack by U-boat packs to defeat British convoys. For a successful blockade of the British Isles, he asked for 300 operational U-boats of types VIIC and IXC (in the proportion 3:1), of which at least 100 should be in action at all times.

On 21 July 1922 this strategy was described by Kptl. Wassner (Schottky's commander in several U-boats in World War I, *supra*):

In my experience in the last years of the war, surface attack by U-boats had been that with most hope of success...In September 1918 during two nights I was able to fire nine times during a surface raid, of which three times were within 20 minutes. ...The detection of a convoy in the open sea will always take a comparatively large amount of time for a U-boat. Therefore the use of a U-boat is not good [uneconomical] for this purpose. In future, therefore, U-boat packs must be used against convoys in the open sea. This could only be achieved after a further improvement in wireless technology...

With regard to the international prize regulations, the Operations Department of Naval Command Office A proposed a trade war which included trade harassment by surface forces. An unbalanced U-boat re-armament such as Dönitz suggested was thought of, according to the former head of the K Office, Admiral Fuchs, as a strategic risk as well as offering additional provocation towards Great Britain.[1] It could lead to an earlier British entrance into the war, at a time when German Naval forces were not yet strong enough.

Germany's attack on Poland led to Britain's declaration of war at a point when the Z-Plan navy existed only on paper. The long-term battleship projects were stopped and the so-called Mob (Mobilization) plan, which was only intended for smaller war ships (from destroyers down) with short building times, was put into action.

2. U-boat Programmes During World War II

At the Outbreak

After the beginning of the war with Poland the Mob-programme of 1 April 1939 was put into action. This provided for the annual delivery of 24 destroyers, 48 torpedo boats, 132 minesweepers and 108 U-boats (24 Type IXC, 48 Type VIIC and 36 Type II). After Great Britain had entered the war, the number of U-boats was increased substantially. On 8 September 1939 a changed Mob-plan was put into action, in which the share of surface warships was drastically reduced in favour of U-boats. Now only seven destroyers, nine torpedo boats and 60 minesweepers were scheduled to be delivered annually, whereas 272 U-boats (68 Type IXC and 204 Type VIIC) were planned.

As there was no alternative but to defeat the now most important enemy, Great Britain, the Naval War Staff (Skl) made use of the U-boat numbers asked for by Dönitz. Assuming certain monthly rates of loss, a calculation was made to establish what increases were needed in order to reach and maintain a stock of 300 operational U-boats. It turned out that even with a monthly loss rate of only 5%, the changed Mob-plan could not achieve this. However, with a monthly delivery rate of 29.3 U-boats from 1942 and an overestimated rate of 10% losses, a stock of 320 U-boats could be reached by October 1943. After that, newly delivered U-boats would balance losses and the Commander-in-Chief U-boats (*Befehlshaber der U-boote*, or BdU) would have approximately 270 U-boats to operate with. This so-called 'Large U-boat Programme' would mean using all Germany's shipyard capacity, including the shipyard expansion allocated for the Z-Plan in 1938, and a reduction in other obligations for armaments. In the initial period of the war the number of U-boats would stagnate, so, in order to raise deliveries a little in the second half of 1940, on 25 September 1939 a series of 16 Type IID boats which could be built quickly, was slotted into the programme.

However, the transition towards the Large U-boat Programme was delayed. During the Führer conference of 23 September 1939, Admiral Schniewind, Chief of Naval War Staff, asked for a vigorous expansion of U-boat building. For political reasons (that is, Hitler's current peace overtures to Great Britain), a decision was postponed for a fortnight. When Britain refused Hitler's offer of peace after the defeat of Poland and seemed set on continuing the war, the Large U-boat Programme was officially put into effect on 6 October 1939. It provided for an annual delivery of six destroyers, 12 torpedo boats, 49 minesweepers, 60 motor torpedo boats, 72 motor minesweepers, 42 patrol boats and 352 U-boats (274 Type VIIC and 78 Type IXC).

As early as 4 October 1939, Hitler had agreed that this programme must be included in the first (priority) stage of armament projects. At that time the main part of Germany's armament programme was led by Reichsmarschall Göring, the representative of the Four Year Programme (*Vierjahresplan*). In the opinion of the High Command of the Armed Forces (OKW) he had the necessary authority to fulfil the navy's wishes for the Large U-boat Programme, so special permission for the Supreme Commander-in-Chief of the Navy was not thought necessary.

In reality the construction of U-boats was not a priority in the armaments programme. On 22 November 1939 the C-in-C, Grossadmiral Raeder, said at a Führer conference that it was only possible to meet the goals of a Large U-boat Programme if its demands in respect of people and materials, and especially shipyards, could be taken care of. The OKW promised to check on the distributions of raw materials for high priority tasks. However, with the needs of the army at the forefront, the navy's large demands could not be met.

The Limited U-boat Programme and its Continuation

With an allocation of raw materials far below the demands required for the Large U-boat Programme, the OKM deemed the programme impractical. The allocation seemed sufficient only for the opening period, to 1 January 1942, so that date was taken as a limit for the Large U-boat Programme. On 1 June 1940 it was to be decided if and how a Limited U-boat Programme could be continued. On 8 March 1940 this Limited Programme was ordered by Raeder.

Here the question arises as to whether this step of limiting the programme was not a pretext for the cancellation of the Large U-boat Programme, which Raeder saw as less important. The shortage of materials, especially of steel and copper, was overemphasized and was only a small fraction of the amount provided. The relatively long slipway times in U-boat building and the small number of U-boat deliveries was mainly a consequence of the shortage of qualified workmen and proper building places.

In the middle of 1940 Denmark, Norway, Holland and Belgium were occupied by the German Army. France's total defeat was at hand. Only Great Britain remained as an enemy. That enhanced the navy's importance, shown by higher material allocation rates.

During the conquest of France, huge supplies of material, especially copper, came into the hands of the German Army. Because of this, Raeder decided to continue the Limited U-boat Programme with a monthly delivery rate of 25 U-boats after 1 January 1942. Of the 25 boats, 18 should be of Type VIIC, 5 of Types IXC and IXD and two of other Types (VIID, XB, XIV). On 31 July 1940 he showed this plan for the continuation of the Limited U-boat Programme to Hitler, who agreed it. With that, the Large U-boat Programme of October 1939 was finally abandoned, since after the planned invasion of Great Britain (Operation Sealion) in 1942-43 there would be no further need to continue a maritime trade war against Great Britain. In the K Office U-boat departments at this time, construction was not planned for long periods either. The aim was to

supply the BdU and the Skl with U-boats as fast as possible, constructed with
the allocated materials. Lengthy projects like the larger U-boat (Types XI and
XII) were cancelled, and the Walter development assigned to a quiet industrial
office (Krupp/Walter, or K/W). The Head of the K Office, Admiral Fuchs,
believed that the new Walter propulsion should prove its qualifications on land
first, before he would interfere with the planning of construction; but no special
priority was given, even for that.

The new U-boat types demanded by Skl - the long-range Type IXD and the
medium-sized Type VIID for large anchor mines - were created from existing
types. The Type XIV supply boat, requested by Dönitz, was also conceived from
existing and proven designs. The only improvement to the most widespread U-
boat (Type VIIC) was made in respect of diving depth and strength of pressure
hull (Types VIIC41 and VIIC42).

The active sonar echo detection equipment (S-Gerät) planned for U-boats,
for which a lot of construction and building had been necessary, proved to be
unfinished and unusable. Measures against detection by radar for U-boats on the
surface did not exist, and did not begin to be developed until 1942, when U-boat
commanders requested assistance. Against the growing danger of air attack,
trust was placed until 1943 in the U-boats' relatively rapid diving times. When
Dutch submarines were captured, complete with air-inlet snorkel tubes, which
permitted the operation of Diesel engines at periscope depth, the snorkels were
removed because they did not seem suitable for use in Atlantic conditions.

Ever since 1938, the use of sound-absorbent material to prevent U-boat
detection by asdic had been under investigation, but trials had met with little
success because a suitable glue could not be found. Thereafter K Office lost
interest in this troublesome corrective measure. Problems with the detonators
and depth-keeping of new torpedoes led to a high concentration of research
effort in this field, which made considerable progress. After the collapse of the
German U-boat war in May 1943, torpedo technology was overstretched to
provide a reliable defensive torpedo for use against destroyers and other fast U-
boat hunters, and for an effective long-range torpedo that could be used without
precise target data.

After the postponement of Operation Sealion (at first temporarily and later
indefinitely), the U-boat trade war was the only option available to defeat Great
Britain. However in 1941, the U-boat delivery quota was far from being
achieved. Shipyards blamed the shortage of skilled workers, but also backlogs in
the delivery of supplies. At the beginning of 1942 supply was also affected by
the very hard winter. Instead of the planned 75 U-boats only 50 were delivered
by the end of the first quarter of 1942. This equalled a monthly rate of 16 U-
boats. The expansion of U-boat operations to American waters and their
enforced operation in the Mediterranean led to a relatively low density of U-
boats on the Atlantic supply routes to Great Britain. Convoy location therefore
remained a problem for the U-boats and necessitated extensive radio contact
with U-boat headquarters and each other. Because of this, U-boat detection was

made relatively easy for the Allies, especially when these radio messages had been deciphered through Ultra.

Despite initial successes, the war against Russia absorbed more and more of the German economy. Another reduction in steel and copper supplies for the navy followed in the first and second quarters of 1942. Raeder reacted with rigorous restrictions in the building of destroyers and predicted detrimental changes for the construction of U-boats in 1943-44, counting only on a delivery rate of 15 U-boats per month. Hitler would not meet Raeder's steel requirements, but part of the copper reduction was overcome through the intervention of the Minister for Armaments, Albert Speer, who provided the navy with copper scrap. At that, Raeder became willing to take all suspended vessels from destroyers downwards back into the building programme.

In spring 1942, following a request from Skl, the K Office researched possibilities for building auxiliary aircraft carriers and for the completion of the unfinished carrier *Graf Zeppelin*. Once the material and labour costs had been calculated for converting passenger vessels and the unfinished cruiser *Seydlitz* into auxiliary aircraft carriers, Raeder informed Hitler of the plans. On 29 June 1942 the subject was discussed in Hitler's headquarters. Hitler opposed all the planned changes and declared that all resources should be used in the U-boat building programme.[2]

Although the projects for the auxiliary aircraft carriers remained alive for some time yet, they were not seriously worked on. The main points of naval discussions at Hitler's headquarters related to the problems of the U-boat war and the development of new U-boats, with the Walter U-boats obtaining a higher priority, thanks to Dönitz's intervention.

Once more a target was set for 25 U-boats of existing designs to be delivered each month. Because labour was likely to remain in short supply, increased U-boat output could only be achieved by simplifying the construction and by reducing the manpower required. In an attempt to streamline and rationalize production, construction of the pressure hull sections was moved inland to suitable steel construction firms and a better management system for shipbuilding and supply was put into effect. Largely because of this, in spring 1942, the Main Committee for Ship Construction (*Hauptausschuss Schiffbau*, or HAS), was set up by Speer under the leadership of the experienced head of the Blohm and Voss shipyard Rudolf Blohm. On 1 December 1942, HAS announced plans to raise the monthly delivery quota to 23 U-boats in 1943, 24 in 1944 and finally 25, the target, in 1945.

The Dönitz Fleet Construction Programme of 1943

After Raeder was replaced by Dönitz as the Supreme Commander-in-Chief of the Navy in spring 1943, a hectic U-boat schedule started. Through his direct contact with Hitler, Dönitz (now Grand Admiral) had finally received the authority to turn a large U-boat programme into a reality. As planned in October 1939, the programme was also to include the auxiliary ships and light naval forces required for protection duties. The first priority for Dönitz was to ensure a better supply of materials and personnel. Although Hitler was more obliging to Dönitz than in his discussions with Raeder, he could not make any concessions even to a Supreme Commander-in-Chief of his choice. The navy was to start the new Fleet Construction Programme as the first step, and after that the matter would be reconsidered. This programme provided for the annual delivery of 360 U-boats, six destroyers, nine torpedo boats, 74 minesweepers, 72 motor torpedo boats, 72 motor minesweepers, 300 patrol boats and boats for protection duties, 35 *Sperrbrecher* (blockade runners), 900 landing craft and 15 torpedo catchers.

In April 1943, HAS worked in close contact with the K Office on a detailed U-boat schedule organized as follows:

Year	VIIC	IXC	IXD	XB	XX	XVII	XIV	Total	Monthly Average
1943	237	45	15	3	-	4	3	307	25.6
1944	270	45	20	-	13	18	7	373	31.1
1945	275	44	20	-	17	6	12	374	31.2
1946	295	52	20	-	-	-	12	379	31.6

Contrary to the plans already in existence, the increased delivery rates would be achieved by the introduction of double shift work, by the enlargement of shipyards and the relocation of pressure hull section construction to inland industries. However, the shortage of skilled workers in the shipyards still remained a problem. Another uncertain factor in U-boat production was the growing danger of air raids.

The Fleet Construction Programme of 1943 included three new U-boat types. The Type VIIC was further developed to become the VIIC42, which included armour-plated steel or stronger shipbuilding steel for improved diving depths (a design diving depth[3] of 200m was made possible). Its planned surface power was also improved. This met a long-standing demand of the Type VIIC commanders, who wanted to reach attack positions faster. The Type XX U-boat was specially designed for transporting badly-needed raw materials from East Asia, since it had become practically impossible for surface blockade runners to get through. The initial design (Type XIX, based on the supply Type XIV but with a new kind of Diesel engine) was cancelled in favour of a larger boat, the frame of which was similar to the mine Type XB but equipped with ordinary Type VIIC Diesel engines. In 1942 the design of the Walter U-boat Type XVII was finalized in the Blohm & Voss and Krupp Germaniawerft shipyards, based on a small Walter U-boat developed at the Walterworks site. The submarine developed to the K/W plan V300 would not be capable of a high underwater speed and was abandoned. In September 1942, after a report to Hitler and personal intervention by Dönitz, the designs of Type XVII and the larger Type XVIII (constructed using similar principles) were finally given the necessary priority by the K Office.

Then, in May 1943, the unexpected took place in the North Atlantic. U-boat losses reached frightening proportions, whilst their success declined. The U-boat battle appeared to be lost. In two important speeches to senior naval officers Dönitz admitted his defeat but justified the continuation of the U-boat war. His speech to the senior commanders of the navy on 3 June 1943 was very informative and is recorded as a series of points which form minutes. The following translation omits some insignificant parts.

Judgement of the General Situation. Because this war at sea is based on economics it will take some time. Comparing 1918 and 1943, the expansion into the larger war area of today has been correct and is important in ensuring our food supply and war materials. It is impossible for the army alone to determine the outcome of the war. Morale, ability and equipment are good, and will stay favourable and get better. Army reserves are not sufficient for war-deciding operations. Forces are just sufficient to shorten the Eastern front line, which is desirable. Otherwise there are adequate forces to protect Europe. Large-scale landings will probably be repelled, in which case the air war remains the biggest doubt.

Military forces are not sufficient to start operations. For instance going to Spain in order to expand the U-boat bases, which would be of importance. So the Army is not sufficient, not even to push Russia out of the war, as is the case for the Air Force. No decision is possible with these forces.

Naval Warfare. The fundamental question: Is naval warfare still offensive? As we do not have naval power in its real sense we could have waged an operational war with U-boats alone right from the beginning. Great Britain attempted to master the U-boat force by abolition at naval conferences. After that, propaganda, which Great Britain might have believed herself, stated that the U-boat force would never again be important, but in three years of war nothing decisive has been achieved against the U-boat forces. In March 1943 the biggest convoy battle occurred. In spite of all the Allied successes (the winter in Russia, Tunisia) the matter of tonnage continues to be the most important one for Great Britain.

From November 1942, the U-boats encountered strong A/S defences which, after a slow start in the last half of the year, became gradually more effective towards May 1943. High aircraft superiority with a ratio of 7:1 and the use of aircraft carriers in convoys closed the air gap in the North Atlantic. But this would not be important if the enemy did not posses a secret detection method. As we do not know what it is, there is no counter offensive. The British discover U-boat patrol areas without our knowledge and go around them. If convoys are still attacked they prevent U-boats from moving forward. At night and in poor visibility there are unexpected attacks on U-boats. Through high frequency detection, loss rates have risen dramatically - prior to May 1943 13% of operating U-boats, now more than 30%.

Counter measures. Remove forces from the main operating area in the North Atlantic to concentrate on areas that are not so closely watched. It is imperative that I make the U-boats more powerful. Although this development could have been foreseen, few weapons have been developed.

This crisis originated in our air force. This is our fault, since we built a strong U-boat force, but not an air force to support it. In spite of this, we have to make up for it now...

According to the German saying: if you beat my Jew I will beat your Jew. That is why you cannot hit the Englishman by using the air force for air raids on cities. His 'Jew' is and remains tonnage. Even if the U-boat war does not sink more than the enemy is building, we have to go on with it...

If naval warfare stops, the impact on the rest of the war would be very dramatic. It is not just our supply lines inside 'Fortress Europe' and its periphery that will be lost, for the enemy will take these with forces now deployed in naval warfare. We will then lose Norway without a fight. We lost Tunisia because we did not manage the question of supply.

The U-boat war crisis did not appear unexpectedly. We would have come out of it far better if we had worked harder on producing sufficient defensive weapons earlier. Then there is the question as to what new countermeasures the enemy will develop, and there is no certainty that we will be able to sink more than they are building. For the reasons given above we have to be offensive as far as we can.

The best way for surfaced U-boats to defend themselves against radar and air attack was to use the snorkel. The idea was proposed by Hellmuth Walter in spring 1943. The first snorkels used by German U-boats were developed at his company and were built at the Deutsche Werke Kiel shipyard.

On 31 May 1943, Dönitz presented the new Fleet Building Programme to Hitler and informed him of the setbacks and high losses in the U-boat war. When Dönitz was asked how to remedy the situation, he requested a monthly delivery of 40 U-boats. Without further discussion, Hitler agreed. Thus, in June 1943, a new schedule had to be worked out by HAS and K Office. Their aim was to make the U-boat schedule larger by one-third if possible. In order to reach a construction rate of 40 U-boats per month, a series of small U-boats was to be included. Similar to the situation at the beginning of the war, these U-boats could also be constructed outside the slipways and would be ready by 1944. As these boats (Types XVII and XXII) were to have Walter propulsion, this was believed to satisfy another of Dönitz's demands. On 6 July 1943 this plan meant delivery quotas for 1944 as follows:

VIIC	IXC	IXD	XIV	XX	XXI	XVII	XXII	total	monthly average
225	38	11	5	9	6	90	50	434	36.2

According to this plan, the target of 40 U-boats each month was to be reached in June 1944.

The Type XXII was a small U-boat developed by Dr Fischer at the Walter Works especially for coastal and Mediterranean operations. It used a smaller Walter engine than the Type XVII and in other respects required less materials and equipment. But it was farcical to start construction of large numbers of Walter U-boats which remained untested and for which the supply of hydrogen peroxide (H_2O_2) had not yet even been assured. Only by the autumn of 1944 had sufficient testing of experimental Walter U-boats reached the stage where training of crews could commence. As things stood, they could not have begun operating before 1945, and even then the limited range of the small Walter Type XVII and XXII U-boats would mean that they could not be used to attack the convoys to the west of Great Britain.

By spring 1943 the Walter Type XVIII U-boat, developed for this purpose, had reached the stage where the construction of two experimental U-boats was possible. Many changes were expected in the design because of the still incomplete tests on the 15,000 hp Walter engine plant. Hence large scale mass production was not considered, since they could not be operational before 1946.

In May 1943, a construction plan for the Walter Type XVIII, designed by the Deutsche Werke Kiel shipyard, landed on the desk of the KIIU consultant, Naval Construction Director Oelfken. He was fascinated by a new hull shape for U-boats which, as a result of towing tests and wind tunnel experiments, had been developed for increased submerged speeds. He considered the kind of characteristics a U-boat like this would have if conventional propulsion was used instead of the H_2O_2 storage. He proposed an enlarged battery, and instead of the Walter turbines, high speed electromotors with additional small electromotors for silent running, which were built in.

On 22 May 1943, Oelfken conceived a first draft design for an electro U-boat in which the pressure hull received a new 8-shaped cross section (due to the attached bowl used for storing an enlarged battery). With the new U-boat type he calculated a maximum submerged speed of 19 knots and a silent running range of 500nm at 2 knots. Assisted by the young Naval Shipbuilding Adviser Grim, he was able to make this plan presentable by 17 June 1943. The Head of K Office, Admiral Fuchs, was enthusiastic about the results and demanded the immediate presentation of the new U-boat Type XXI to Admiral Dönitz. This occurred on 19 June with the two department heads, Shürer and Bröking, present. Dönitz was also impressed by Oelfken's design and decided that the 1,600-tonne Type XXI should be built instead of the Types IXC and IXD.

K Office was asked to make immediate proposals for the mass production of the new type. In this way the Type XXI would show in the HAS's 40 U-boat schedule. It was planned that the AG Weser shipyard in Bremen should become the preliminary construction yard for the type. The Flender Werke in Lübeck, the Navy shipyard in Wilhelmshaven, the Deutsche Werft AG in Hamburg and two shipyards in Danzig were scheduled as additional construction yards, with the first three Type XXIs expected by November 1944. Full series-production of 13 boats per month was expected by July 1945, and operations by these first Type XXIs were to take place in autumn 1945.

U-boat Planning after the Takeover of Naval Armament by the Ministry for Armament and War Economy

Dönitz could not accept the plans made by HAS at the beginning of July 1943. By June he was already sure that he could make neither the preparations for the large fleet construction programme of 1943, nor the new U-boats required with the naval authorities under his command. He therefore decided to entrust the naval armament and shipbuilding programme to Speer, who already controlled and organized most of the German war economy. By bringing an autonomous method into German industry, he had created an instrument which had already shown great efficiency under difficult conditions.

Against strong resistance from his own people, Dönitz agreed to the changes in the naval armament system. The HAS had extensive authority and a new head, the Magirus director Otto Merker. Merker produced an alternative construction plan for the new Type XXI U-boat, which differed from all former navy plans by proposing mass production. Under certain conditions, he promised delivery of the first three Type XXIs by April 1944, with the facilities for mass production. One of his demands was to cease construction of the older Types and to finish the preparations for Type XXI-building by 1 December 1943. After that, full series-production of 38 Type XXIs per month should start by the end of 1944.

In the meantime, as suggested by Oelfken again and supported by Grim, the small Walter Type XXII had been transformed into an electro U-boat. The new Type XXIII U-boat was to be built in a large-scale production run of 120 boats, replacing the Type XXII whose functions it was to take on. However, construction was dependent upon the transportation by rail of the finished sections to the Mediterranean and Black Sea. The Type XXIIIs were later to be not only assembled but also fitted out directly in those regions (Toulon, Genoa, Monfalcone and Nikolaev).

On 13 August 1943, Dönitz decided on a complete switch of the U-boat construction programme to the new Type XXI and XXIII boats. This decision adhered to the principles of a 40-boat programme, although according to the new plan the maximum monthly delivery of 33 Type XXIs (from October 1944) and 21 Type XXIIIs (from May 1944) varied quite a bit around this target.

Technological difficulties, initial organizational problems and the growing destruction of production plants and transport lines all delayed and reduced the extent of the Merker programme. In spite of this, the new U-boat building programme made possible by the autumn of 1944 an output of U-boats much greater than in the far more favourable production conditions of earlier years. These modern boats and new production techniques came too late, however, to make an impression on the course of the war. There is no doubt that those snorkel-equipped electro U-boats could have been designed and constructed years earlier. Then, despite Ultra and HF/DF, they would have caused significant problems to the British U-boat defence.

It is idle to speculate on this. It is unlikely that the result of the war would have been changed by an earlier introduction to service of the new U-boat types. Their use would only have led to more destruction and losses. For the same reason it would also be useless to speculate on the effect of ceasing U-boat construction in the middle of 1943 in favour of producing tanks. It is arguable that in 1944-45 the German Army was not so much lacking in equipment as in aerial superiority, strong command and fuel.

So, in 1944-45, U-boat construction was actually only a symbol of the efficiency of German industry, which was producing the most modern submarines in the world using advanced building methods under extremely difficult conditions. In this way it was more a testbed for Germany's post-war 'economic miracle'. The next U-boat programmes reflected the changing fortunes of the war and delays in material supplies. The most important programmes at the end of the war were as follows:

1.   The Minister Programme of 1 June 1944, which still planned a medium Walter U-boat (Type XXVI), as well as the Type XXI for 1945, and the continuation of the Type XXIII building programme. The delivery plan for the Minister Programme was:

	XXI	XXIII	XXVI	VIIC	IXC/D	XB	XVII	total	monthly average
1944	155	87	-	113	17	1	6	379	31.6
1945	278	149	62	-	-	-	2	491	40.9

2.   The New Shipbuilding Programme of October 1944 took into consideration the halt in production of Type XXIII U-boats in Mediterranean and Black Sea shipyards, and the mass production of midget U-boats (1,000 *Seehund* Type boats):

	XXI	XXIII	XXVI	VIIC	IXC/D	XB	XVII	XX	total	monthly average
1944	90	51	-	11	24	1	3	-	280	23.3*
1945	188	133	38	6	2	-	5	2	375	31.3*

* without midgets

3.   The Restricted Immediate Programme of January 1945, which, after the advance of Allied forces up to the German borders, only planned the assembly of those U-boats for which raw sections and the equipment were already in existence. It limited the whole delivery quota to 336 Type XXI, 140 of the Type XXIII, 20 of the new Walter Type XXVI and 600 *Seehund* midgets.

4.   After the failure of the counter-offensive into Belgium (the Ardennes Offensive) and the advance of the Red Army as far as the Oder river, the Emergency Programme of February 1945 planned only the completion of U-boats already on the slipways or the assembly of finished sections lying ready. Only 170 Type XXI, 70 Type XXIII and four Type XXVI U-boats and 600 midgets were to be delivered according to that schedule. During the last month of the war, U-boats used for training purposes were changed into operational U-boats and more and more repairs were completed. Only when Allied forces occupied the shipyards were these activities stopped.

Appendix 1
Organization of ML (Head of the Navy)

A	Marinekommandoamt	Naval Command Office
AI	Marinewehrabteilung	Naval Defence Department
AII	Flottenabteilung	Fleet Department
AIII	Ausbildungsabteilung	Training Department
B	Allgemeines Marineamt	General Naval Office (material)
BB	Werftabteilung	Shipyard Department
BH	Nautische Abteilung	Nautical Department
BW	Marinewaffenabteilung	Weapons Department
C	Marineverwaltungsamt	Administrative Office
K	Marinekonstruktionsabteilung	Naval Construction Department

From 1935, the *Oberkommando der Wehrmacht* (OKW, Armed Forces High Command), the *Oberkommando des Heeres* (OKH, Army High Command) and the *Oberkommando der Kriegsmarine* (OKM, Navy High Command) were housed in the former Reichsmarine-Amt (Imperial Naval Office) at Königin Augusta Str. 38/42 and in the extended buildings at Bendler Strasse. As tasks and personnel grew, more and more naval offices were located in other buildings. At the beginning of WWII OKM was reorganized. The division into the two Offices 'A' and 'B' was abandoned and their place was taken by Naval War Staff (*Seekriegsleitung*, or Skl). 'A' was assigned to Skl, 'B' was dissolved. The departments of 'B' were integrated into Skl, 'K' and the new Main Office Naval Weapons. On 22 November 1943, the historic building at Tirpitz Ufer 72/76 was badly damaged by an air raid. Most of the OKM offices were destroyed and had to be relocated to different outside quarters.

Appendix 2
Warship Construction Main Office
After the integration of U-boat department 'BU' into the different offices of OKM their construction bureau 'b' was established in a building at Grossadmiral von Köster Ufer 71. In the spring of 1939 the U-boat construction departments covered the following fields of work:

KIU   Head of the shipbuilding department: Min.Rat. Schürer

KIUa   Project calculations, strength matters, towing tests.
Consultant: Dipl.-Ing. Diestelmeier

KIUb   Building of the Torpedo-U-boat types IIC, VIIB/C, IX and XII.
Models for underwater explosion shock. Calculation of cost.
Consultant: Dipl.-Ing. Kurt Fischer

KIUc   Building of the Mine-U-boat Type XB.
Consultant: Marine-Baurat Fritz Hartung

KIUd   Building of the Artillery-U-boat Type XI. Maintenance of the
finished U-boats. Substitute for the Head of Department KIU.
Consultant: Marine-Baurat Aschmoneit

KIIU   Head of the mechanical engineering department: Min.Rat. Bröking

KIIUa   Design, construction, test and maintenance of the engine plants for
the U-boat types IIC, VIIB/C, IX, XI, XII and V80.
Consultant: Ministerialrat Schatzmann

KIIUb   Test results. Test plans. Periscopes. Engine plant of the
Mines-U-boat Type XB.
Consultant: Marine-Baurat Geister

KIIUm   Diesel engine. Consultant: Dipl.-Ing. Rabien

KIIUp   Ship propellors. Calculation of oscillations.
Consultant: Dipl.-Ing. Baumgärtner

KIIUe   Design, construction, test and maintenance of the electric plants.
Consultant: Reg. Baumeister ret. Wirsching, later Marine-Oberbaurat Oelfken.
Main and auxiliary batteries. Driving gears.
Consultant: Reg. Baumeister ret. Hadre

Shell House at the Landwehrkanal was built in 1930-32 by Emil Fahrenkamp as an office building for the Rhenania-Ossag mineral oil works. In 1939-40 the Warship Construction Main Office 'K' moved into Shell House (Tirpitz Ufer 60-62) but without the departments KIU, KIIU and KIV (Ship's engine operation). On 14 April 1945 it was transferred to Eckernförde-Carlshöhe. According to an order of the last Head of the 'K' Office, Vizeadmiral Ruge, a large number of documents and construction plans had already been burnt. The remaining documents fell into the hands of the Red Army, were taken to Leningrad (St Petersburg) and eventually returned to the Military Archive of the DDR in 1988.

Notes

1. Personal communication from Admiral Fuchs to author.
2. Personal communication from Otto Riedel to author.
3. 40% of the collapse depth.

7

The German System: A Staff Perspective

by Graham Rhys-Jones

Introduction

It is easy to see, at least in retrospect, that the outcome of the Battle of the Atlantic was determined not only by the day-to-day decisions of operational commanders, important though they were, but by at least two other major factors: firstly, the ability of Naval High Commands to win the internal strategic debate, thus gaining the resources needed to fight the battle successfully; and secondly, the ability of scientific establishments to grasp the influence of technology on the course of the Battle, and thus to gain and retain the technical initiative. This was a campaign fought not only between admirals, but between systems.

This chapter examines how the German Navy was organized to meet the broad challenge facing it in the Atlantic. It deals with the structure of U-boat Command; with the Naval Staff directorates responsible for the formulation of strategy and for the setting of operational requirements; with the departments responsible for research, design, and production; and with the relationships between them. It is intended as a backdrop against which the strengths and weaknesses of equivalent Allied 'systems' may come into sharper focus.

U-boat Command and the Conduct of Operations

It is necessary, at the outset, to establish the position of U-boat Command within the hierarchy of the German Navy, for the war that broke out in the summer of 1939 - a war with an unexpected maritime dimension - showed scant respect for established chains of authority. From the first deployment of the U-boat flotillas during the period of tension, Karl Dönitz - the assertive but relatively junior Führer der U-boote (FdU) - became *de facto* if not *de jure* an independent commander, taking his orders from, and reporting directly to, Naval Headquarters in Berlin. This direct relationship, product of the political sensitivities attached to a war against commerce, freed U-boat Command from subordination to intermediate headquarters at Fleet and Group level. Flag Officers commanding surface-ship formations reported to Fleet Headquarters and the Fleet Commander, a little grudgingly, to Group. Dönitz did neither. His relationship with superior headquarters was not precisely defined and this led to occasional friction; but in matters connected with the war against shipping he acted independently of both.[1]

The advent of war forced several organizational changes on U-boat Command. Among the first and more important of these was the division of the formerly united FdU staff into distinct Operations and Administrative sections. The first section, under Dönitz's Chief of Staff, Commander (later Rear Admiral) Eberhard Godt, moved as necessary to keep in close touch with the operational flotillas. It maintained its nomadic existence until February 1943 when, on Dönitz's appointment as Commander-in- Chief Navy, it followed him to Berlin and formed the Second Section of the Naval Staff. The second section, under Captain (later Admiral) von Friedeburg (Dönitz's under-study and the man who, in normal times, would have relieved him as FdU in the spring of 1940), moved to Kiel and assumed responsibility for acceptance, training and work-up. The arrangement worked well. Von Friedeburg enjoyed Dönitz's complete confidence and relieved him of much routine work. Nevertheless the FdU (or, from October 1939, the Befehlshaber der U-boote [BdU]), retained ultimate control of the training machine. This enabled him to resist pressures (such as those applied during the planning of Operation Sealion) to transfer training flotillas to operational duties. Dönitz could also ensure that the training schedule reflected the latest lessons of war.[2]

Appendix I shows the composition of U-boat Command Operations Staff after its transfer to Berlin in February 1943. Although a modest increase in numbers had taken place since the early days, it remained in essence the 'half-dozen young U-boat men' that, to the surprise of historians, ran the Battle of the Atlantic.[3]

Under the efficient but self-effacing Godt, the First Staff Officer (Operations) looked after the programming of the operational flotillas and advised on deployment, tactics, and international law. He acted as the point of contact with external headquarters, notably with that of the Fliegerführer Atlantik.[4] The Second Staff Officer dealt with arrivals and departures, and with related matters such as coast defence, minesweeping, and anti-submarine operations. The Third Staff Officer (Intelligence) was responsible for the presentation of the enemy situation and thus for the fusion of Intelligence and reconnaissance data from all sources, U-boat and Luftwaffe sighting reports, and Radio Intelligence information supplied by the B-Dienst. An important part of his duties was the evaluation of U-boat records and the generation of a body of combat experience. The Fourth Staff Officer (Communications) dealt with radio and cryptographic procedures and with evasive and self-protective measures. From November 1941 and as a result of difficulties encountered, he gained the assistance of a Radio Intelligence specialist to help solve the vexed question of whether the Admiralty had foreknowledge of U-boat concentrations and, if so, how. Finally, the Fifth Staff Officer kept what the Command called the 'Museum', the record of sinkings and statistics on U-boat operating cycles from which Dönitz derived 'U-boat potential', his crude measure of effectiveness. The Fifth Staff Officer also dealt with honours and awards.[5]

An administrative staff, just as lean as this, kept an eye on personnel and training, dealt with questions of supply and transport, and advised the BdU on technical matters.

A bland listing of the routine duties of the Operations Staff is hardly sufficient to capture any realistic idea of the load that rested on these men. Two other major tasks fell on them: tactical development and battle management. Pressures arising from the first of these tasks (which must anyway have been considerable) were aggravated by uncertainties surrounding the concept of group or 'wolf-pack' operations which, although an established feature of U-boat doctrine, had not been tested to any serious extent under oceanic conditions. A working balance had to be struck between concentration and dispersal; scouting and reporting procedures had to be perfected, and arrangements for co-operation with the Luftwaffe built almost from scratch. The influence of the enemy's D/F network, of his air patrols, and of his evasion tactics had to be established. The battle was an experiment on the grand scale and, as changes in enemy technology and method undermined established assumptions, it became a continuous one. It was still continuing as the campaign approached its crisis.[6]

Dönitz was not a man who gave way to bouts of pessimism, but there were extended periods during which fainter hearts than his might have concluded that group warfare simply did not work. Through 1941, finding convoys would remain the chief difficulty but, even when this first step had been achieved, the problem of bringing a U-boat group into contact with the target and then of keeping in touch was considerable. A practical solution was only found through close control of the battle from U-boat Headquarters itself. The extent of intervention, particularly during the summer of 1941 when U-boat numbers remained relatively small, has been well described by Hessler.[7] Headquarters took on itself complex procedures for refining target position. It vectored the U-boat group towards an interception point; established the search patterns to be adopted in the event that contact was lost; chose the moment at which attacks should begin, and decided when they should be broken off. Although increases in U-boat numbers would lessen the need for micro-management, group warfare could never be left to look after itself.

The Operations Staff was thus small in number, uniform in make-up, and heavily loaded. But before considering how these factors may have influenced its conduct of the campaign, some general comments must be made on inter-service and, in the case of the Italian flotilla, on inter-Axis relationships in the Battle of the Atlantic.

Air forces co-operating with U-boat Command in the war against shipping retained separate headquarters and separate lines of accountability. The development of any kind of joint command structure was inhibited by Grand Admiral Raeder's desire to break the Luftwaffe monopoly in matters connected with aviation, and by Göring's equal determination to protect it. After a meeting in February 1941, Dönitz reported the Reichsmarschall as saying that Raeder 'would never get the Naval Air Force he so much desired'.[8] The navy's position was equally rigid. In a letter to Hitler protesting against a recent OKW ruling that the Luftwaffe should take responsibility for reconnaissance in coastal areas,

Raeder specifically rejected what he called a 'combined policy between two sections of the Armed Forces' in favour of 'a *single undivided* operational offensive by all naval forces [including air forces] under one direction and command.'[9] In this climate, operational partnerships such as those that developed between the staffs of Commander-in-Chief Western Approaches and Air Officer Commanding 15 Group could hardly flourish. Such co-operation as was achieved between the Kriegsmarine and the Luftwaffe in the maritime arena depended largely on the goodwill established between local commanders.[10] In the Atlantic, despite initial teething-troubles, co-operation between U-boat Command and the Fliegerführer Atlantik developed well.[11] What was missing - and this was far more damaging than any deficiency in local command structures - was unity of purpose at high level and any depth of commitment on the part of the Luftwaffe High Command to the Atlantic campaign.

Relationships between allies were equally cool. Here too it proved difficult to subordinate the forces of one Axis partner to the operational control of another or to form combined or 'coalition' command structures. Admiral Weichold, Naval Commander in Rome 1940-1943 and a rare proponent of such arrangements, saw German policy as preferring 'voluntary co-operation' on the basis of national (i.e. separate) command structures to the stark alternative of 'compulsory subordination'.[12] As a general rule, therefore, unity of effort was sought through the exchange of liaison officers, whose access to sensitive information was often strictly controlled, and through the recognition of distinct areas of geographical (or functional) responsibility.

In the Atlantic, where the Kriegsmarine was worried that debts incurred might have to be repaid in the Mediterranean, some proper degree of distance in Axis relationships had to be maintained. Although the Italian Flotilla was (nominally at least) subject to Dönitz's operational control, the principle that an Italian should command Italians was enshrined in the concordat governing relations between the two parties.[13] No integration of staffs or of sea-going units took place. Given that U-boat numbers would remain a matter of acute concern at least until the summer of 1942, the relationship was a surprisingly reluctant one. Even when the material and operational weaknesses of the Italian group are accepted, Dönitz's desire to be rid of it, rather than to cultivate it as an asset for the longer term, stands in sharp contrast to the policies adopted by Allied naval leaders, and suggests some limit to his strategic horizons.[14]

The chief impressions emerging from an examination of U-boat Command Operations Staff are of its small size, its heavy loading, the uniformity of its composition, and also, perhaps, its isolation from external influences. This was a close-knit group of like-minded men, all products of Dönitz's training machine, dedicated to his methods and fired with his enthusiasm. But it should come as no surprise if its vision was confined largely to the here-and-now and if its forte was the bold executive decision rather than the identification of long-term trends, or the patient analysis of ambiguous and often contradictory data.

That this was in fact so, is suggested by several surprisingly rapid policy changes during the course of the campaign; by, for instance, Dönitz's sudden conversion to an anti-escort policy in August 1941, by the extraordinary shift in his equipment development priorities between May-September 1942, and by the rapid succession of measures to combat the air threat in the Bay of Biscay in early summer 1943.[15] The short-term perspective is to be found too in the tendency of the Operations Staff to swing from sober realism to a mood almost of euphoria on the basis of some isolated event, and to draw sweeping conclusions from single instances.[16]

At the root of these policy changes lay analytical weakness. There was no shortage of hypotheses to explain the many riddles thrown up during the course of the campaign, but the Staff could seldom reach settled conclusions. Those who have cast doubt on the intellectual capabilities of the BdU and his Staff have overstated their case and have done less than justice to the determined efforts made. The problem lay rather in the pressure of work, in an insufficient breadth of experience, and perhaps also in a lack of cold objectivity. That said, a number of key questions remained unresolved for very long periods of time. For instance, the reasons behind the Admiralty's apparent ability to divert convoys clear of U-boat formations, first suspected in April 1941, was still under investigation by Hessler and Kuppisch (Staff Intelligence Officer) nearly two years later.[17]

These defects might not have mattered had some other element in the 'system' supplied the need, or had the responsibilities of the BdU not extended beyond those of operational command.

The Naval Staff and the Battle for Resources

Under Hitler's 1935 reform of the Armed Forces, Admiral Raeder gained control of the strategic direction of the German Navy (a function formerly exercised through the General Staff) while retaining his organizational and administrative responsibilities as head of what had been the Navy Department (*Marineleitung*). Analogies can perhaps be stretched too far, but, in his new and independent role as Commander-in-Chief Navy (*Oberbefehlshaber der Kriegsmarine*), he exercised the range of military, budgetary, and political powers that, in Britain, resided in the Board of Admiralty. He directed the Navy's war effort, determined its strategies, and, through his material departments, provided the means to execute them.

Raeder discharged his military responsibilities through a Chief of Naval Staff supported by the staff directorates known collectively as the Seekriegsleitung (Skl). Originally modelled on the General Staff, the Skl underwent a succession of reforms during the course of the war to meet unforeseen needs and to relieve the Chief of Naval Staff of duties less immediately connected with the conduct of operations. The functions of the directorates most closely connected with the Battle of the Atlantic are described in Appendix II together with the more significant organizational changes.[18]

Many, perhaps most, of the Skl directorates provided a service to operational commanders or offered expert advice in specialist areas. The Communications Service (2, later 4/Skl) was typical of these. Its terms of reference were wide. In addition to its responsibilities for the communications network and for signal security, it assumed control of the B-Dienst in March 1941 and, in its Fourth Section (MND iv), provided a centre of expertise in radar technology, radar and acoustic counter-measures, and in location methods employed by the enemy. Dönitz's contacts with the Communications Service were many. It was closely involved in the series of measures adopted from April 1941 to close loopholes in internal security.[19] Dönitz again turned to it for advice when, in September 1941, he first suspected a compromise of Enigma.[20] Further contact was made in June 1942, when U-boat Command obtained its first clear evidence of night illumination and attack by Allied aircraft.[21] Here, seemingly, was an organization which might have provided the technical and analytical expertise that U-boat Command lacked.

The Intelligence Division (3/Skl) provided both a policy-making and a supporting function. It had two principal sub-sections, the first dealing with Enemy Naval Forces, and the second with Merchant Shipping. This provided U-boat Command with appreciations on the British convoy system, and later became much involved with projections of Allied ship-building capacity in support of Dönitz's tonnage doctrine.[22]

Broad questions of war policy and strategy lay chiefly with the First, or Operations Section of the Skl which, in its sponsorship of future plans and in its oversight of operations in progress, spanned the functions of the Admiralty's Plans and Operations Divisions. Like the Plans Division, it formed the point of contact with equivalent Sections in the other Services and the OKW. Internally, it was organized by area and by arm. It drafted military appreciations for theatres of war (potential and actual) and developed policies for the surface fleet, mining, aviation, economic warfare, and the U-boat arm. All such sections were influential - some, like the Fleet Operations Section (1/Skl I op) particularly so - and while it would be wrong to suggest that, when war came, the department was divided on the importance of the U-boat campaign, the submarine case was represented by a single officer (1/Skl Iu) in a strength of nearly 20. It was inevitable, perhaps, that other priorities and rival ideas on the conduct of operations should occasionally assert themselves. In due course, Dönitz would feel the effects of these competing views.

In making his revolutionary decision in September 1939 to suspend the construction of a balanced fleet and to concentrate resources on the U-boat building programme, Raeder had recognized the need to strengthen the presentation of the U-boat case within the Skl. Characteristically, Dönitz had recommended a 'single authority vested with wide plenipotentiary powers and responsible directly to the C-in-C'. Understandably, his application to head this organization himself had been refused, but, in a concession that seems to place very unusual powers in the hands of a front-line commander, the Chief of Naval Staff (Schniewind) had assured him that the new department would be 'in practice subordinate to the FdU, who would state his requirements, which the U-boat department would have to fulfill as they stood'.[23]

The end product was the formation on 12 September 1939 of the U-boat Division, Amtsgruppe U-bootswesen or Skl U. Its brief was to plan the organization of the U-boat arm, to identify its personnel and training needs, to advise on the strategic employment of U-boats, their tactics, equipment, and weapon requirements, and to provide for the support of the flotlllas. That Schniewind's assurances were more than an attempt to calm an over-zealous subordinate is suggested by the additional title conferred on Dönitz of FdU Seekriegsleitung, and there can be little doubt that Dönitz saw himself as having special authority in matters of U-boat operational and material policy. However, he had always doubted his ability to control events from his position in the field. Disillusion set in early. Hessler seems to have spoken for the whole of U-boat Command when he observed that 'during the first year, it became apparent that he [Chief of Skl U] was merely a Head of Department without executive authority'. Godt would later complain of the influence of surface-ship officers in Headquarters and of a 'lack of insight into the real significance of the war on British shipping'. Dönitz would blame Skl U for the difficulties that befell the building programme.[24] The organization would become an early victim of his 'seal cull' as C-in-C Navy. On 18 February 1943, it disbanded; its duties passed to the BdU Operations Staff (how did they find the time?) now installed as the Second Section of the Skl.

That Dönitz should have become frustrated at the course of events is understandable. He became acutely aware of delays in submarine construction and, at the same time, found skilled manpower, badly needed for his own hard-pressed flotillas, reassigned to the repair of heavy ships; he found operational boats diverted to support the movements of surface raiders that, in his view, had no prospect of recovering opportunities lost. On occasions like these, Dönitz protested to the C-in-C in forthright terms. U-boats were 'indispensable': surface ships were not.[25] In November 1941, he found his Atlantic operations brought virtually to a halt by the transfer, at short notice, of U-boats to the Mediterranean; in the early months of 1942, he found himself unable to take full advantage of opportunities off the East Coast of the United States because of the failure to oppose Hitler's obsession with the threat to Norway.[26] In July 1942, he was forced to go, cap in hand, to Göring to beg a squadron of Ju 88s to oppose Allied air power threatening U-boats in the Bay of Biscay.[27]

While some of these problems were clearly of the navy's own making, the more serious among them stemmed from deficiencies elsewhere. In Raeder's conferences with the Führer, the forum in which the C-in-C set out his strategic vision and claimed the resources needed to achieve it, there is little sign that the navy, as an institution, was divided in its views or that it 'lacked insight' into the significance of the U-boat war. No topic received more regular exposure than the state of the U-boat building programme. While he remained in office, Raeder raised the subject on no fewer than 23 occasions and did not hold back, when necessary, from describing the resources allotted to him as 'totally inadequate'.[28]

Raeder was equally firm in pressing for the strategy that he believed necessary, namely the need to concentrate the maximum of national resources against Britain's shipping capacity. At least while U-boat numbers remained relatively low, he argued that success could only be achieved if the Luftwaffe supported the naval effort by giving priority to the aerial mining campaign, and by shifting the weight of its bombing offensive to British ports and ship-building yards. In February 1941, Hitler had been of 'precisely the same opinion'. Yet the outcome of this conference reveals much about how strategic decisions were reached. Hitler's Directive, 'Basic Principles for the Prosecution of War against the British War Economy', while providing an accurate summary of Raeder's case, gave Göring virtual *carte blanche* to continue as before.[29]

It would be wrong, therefore, to see any genuine parallel between the Führer Conferences and the deliberations of, for example, Churchill's Battle of the Atlantic Committee. That Hitler met his Commanders-in-Chief individually - Field Marshal Keitel, Chief of Staff OKW, was usually present, the Chiefs of the other Services seldom if ever - was one important difference, although not necessarily the most significant one. The conferences did not provide a forum in which interested parties sat down to review the progress of a campaign of self-evident priority. They were occasions for advocacy and part of a wider, though hidden, competition to shape strategy itself. The effects that Dönitz observed were symptoms of the navy's failure to win that competition.

In searching for reasons behind that failure, a number of factors suggest themselves. A majority of senior naval officers (by no means all) would later complain of 'land-mindedness' at high levels and of unequal naval representation in the OKW. In an attempt to remedy these defects, Raeder, from April 1942, had appointed a Permanent Representative to the Führer Headquarters. Vice Admiral Krancke, who filled the post in 1942-43, came to share Raeder's opinion.[30]

It seems that outcomes were more than usually dependent on the personal standing of the C-in-C concerned. The difficulty that Raeder faced during his final months in office in gaining Hitler's support even in comparatively trivial matters - Dönitz would get far weightier changes agreed with apparent ease only a few months later - suggests that some chemistry was missing in his relationship with the Führer.[31]

But the failure had its origins in the limitations of the U-boat strategy itself and, in the early years of war, this factor was the most significant of all. A plan that could not be implemented with any immediate assurance of success and which would have to await the completion of a lengthy building programme, was not inherently attractive when compared with certain beguiling alternatives. As long as Operations *Gelb, Seelöwe,* and *Barbarossa* offered efficient short-cuts to Hitler's objectives, Raeder could never finally succeed in pressing his claims for priority over those of the army.[32] Nor, while the Supreme Command remained addicted to the idea of some short clear-cut decision, could Raeder advance convincing reasons why the Luftwaffe should lay the foundations of a maritime air force.

Ironically, when Hitler came finally to concede Raeder's point that 'the U-boat war will in the end decide the outcome of the war', the scope for shifting priorities between one Service and another that had seemed plausible enough in the heady days of 1940 had largely vanished; and so had any realistic prospect of major change in Luftwaffe programmes or deployments.[33]

Accepting that flawed strategic thinking in the Supreme Command was the prime cause of Raeder's difficulties, were defective institutions also to blame? There can be no doubt that institutional loyalty within the German Armed Forces was exceptionally strong. So was its obverse, exclusiveness. There was automatic resistance to any sign of encroachment and a reluctance to accept solutions which seemed to make one Service dependent on another. Almost all senior naval officers saw defects in the area of aviation policy; few saw any realistic alternative to a *naval* air force.[34]

Yet some, at least, recognized the dangers of Service tribalism and regretted obstacles to the exchange of information between the staffs. A few went further still and, conscious of the failure of Hitler's institutions to weld the competing visions of maritimists, continentalists, and advocates of strategic air power into a single coherent strategy, favoured a Ministry of War or a post equivalent to that of a modern Chief of Defence Staff, provided always that the right of individual access to the Head of State was protected. But such views were by no means universal. According to Heye, Raeder opposed reforms of this kind for fear of meddling in matters of professional detail, while Dönitz was said (by Ciliax) to have rejected proposals for a unified command in Norway on the grounds that the navy would lose its independence.[35]

Surprisingly, the tenor of senior naval opinion appears to have been that, personalities and staff shortages apart, high level institutions were 'fundamentally all right'.[36] Few commented on the influence of palace politics on German decision-making or on the gross inefficiencies resulting from Hitler's practice of dealing with his Service Chiefs individually. This meant that few decisions were taken on the spot and that many were postponed *sine die*. Few, if any, seem to have recognized the possible defects of the OKW as an institution superior to, but entirely separate from, the Service High Commands.

Members of the British Joint Intelligence Staff who examined the workings of the OKW in the immediate post-war period believed that had it confined itself to non-executive functions, weighed the merits of single-service policies and plans, and presented a balanced synthesis to the Supreme Commander, it might have provided the unifying force that was lacking.[37] In practice the OKW had done - and probably could do - none of these things. Hitler had used it to short-circuit the established staff process (he was well aware of its potential for obstruction and delay) and to direct the Service staff machines down courses already largely pre-determined. Thereafter, the OKW had assigned priorities in the light of decisions taken, settled matters of operational jurisdiction, and exercised a loose co-ordination of plans. It did not produce strategic consensus or offer a genuine substitute for close interaction between the Staffs; by supplying a veneer of 'jointness' it had inhibited rather than fostered the process.

That said, it must seem unlikely that any set of institutions could have guaranteed the Kriegsmarine the priorities that it felt necessary, or dealt with Hitler's strategic 'intuitions' while he remained at the height of his confidence.

The Material Departments: Final Thoughts on 'the System'

The material departments responsible to the C-in-C Navy formed part of the closed circle that gave the navy its independence. There were two of them: the Construction Office, Hauptamt für Kriegsschiffbau (K-Amt), responsible for ship-building, dockyards, and harbour construction; and the Armaments Office, Marine Waffenämter (MWa) which, as its name implies, looked after ordnance, torpedoes, mining, and radio systems. Together, they carried out the functions of the departments which, in Britain, reported to the Third Sea Lord (Controller). Their interests ranged from research, development and design - work conducted in their various experimental establishments - to production, some 'in-house', some contracted to established ship-builders and armaments manufacturers. Specialist inspectorates within the departments ensured the quality of the product.

Those who reflected on the performance of these departments in the post-war period suggested, probably rightly, that they had never fully recovered from the restrictions of Versailles and that plans for their development had then been halted by the outbreak of war. Productive capacity had thus been short from the first; it had been further disrupted, according to some 'totally disorganized', by conscription. Indeed, it was suggested that Germany's armaments industry in general had been seriously damaged by Hitler's inexpert meddling.[38]

Research in some important areas (particularly electronics) was weak. Some put this down to the effects of State regulation; others believed that National Socialism itself had stifled creativity, an idea taken up by, among others, Professor Salewski.[39]

Whatever the merits of these ideas, Dönitz had been unable to take so lofty a perspective. Within a few months, lengthening repair times and the accumulation of boats in dockyard hands had revealed critical shortfalls in yard capacity and in skilled labour.[40] The Construction Office could not escape its share of blame for these nor, as war progressed, for delays in the programme of new construction. Where energy and innovation were needed, Dönitz saw only conservatism and caution as, for instance, in the department's attitude to Professor Walter's revolutionary ideas which he had sponsored since 1937.[41] Dönitz would find similar caution when, as C-in-C, he examined the department's proposals for the development and production of the Type XXI. [42]

The Armaments Office would not escape criticism either. The procedures adopted by the Torpedo Experimental Establishment for the testing and acceptance of the G7e torpedo and its magnetic fuse had been, in Dönitz's view, little short of scandalous. Innovative work might have been done on torpedo discharge and propulsion but, where depth keeping and detonation were concerned, performance had, if anything, deteriorated since 1918.[43]

Progress in the field of electronics would also give rise to concern. As it became clear that the enemy had deployed operationally effective radar systems in surface escorts and in aircraft, the work of MWa began to seem distinctly pedestrian, an impression not lessened by the need for U-boat Command to collaborate in a belated programme of data-gathering to discover the characteristics of enemy radars and their modes of operation.[44]

For Dönitz, these were symptoms of a deeper malaise. The fact that MWa had designed, produced, and then accepted the G7e torpedo suggested the absence of an effective customer-supplier relationship. The material departments seemed top-heavy and bureaucratic. Where complex projects involving both departments were concerned, it could be frustratingly difficult to identify who was responsible.[45] Horizons appeared limited. Not only were the navy's experts ignorant of what was happening in Army and Air Force Experimental Establishments (a defect that could be explained by Hitler's rules on the exchange of secret information) but they seemed, on occasion, positively resistant to external ideas.[46] More generally, Dönitz would come to question whether the navy's scientific base was broad enough to meet the test of war, and further, whether the material departments could compete successfully in an industrial sector increasingly dominated by Speer's Ministry of Arms and Munitions.

It is hardly surprising, therefore, that the material departments should have come under scrutiny when Dönitz became C-in-C. He found the problems facing him serious. Skilled ship-yard workers were still subject to call-up by the army; he at once set about stopping this waste.[47] He found steel quotas totally insufficient to meet the 1943 construction programme and obtained Hitler's consent to an interim increase. But a review of the navy's commitments which took account of recent losses and of the higher number of U-boats now calculated as necessary to achieve the sinking rates required, showed that yet further increases in the navy's manpower and material allocations were needed. Dönitz got Hitler's consent to these as well; if the Führer hesitated in the face of these demands, he did so because he feared their impact on vital army and air force programmes and no longer because he questioned the priority of the U-boat campaign.

However, Hitler's blessing did not remove doubts as to whether there was sufficient skill and elasticity in the navy's production sector to meet the challenge. As he records in his memoirs, Dönitz began to investigate 'whether it was sound that the Navy should be engaged...in the production of its own ships and equipment while the greater part of the country's industry was concentrated under the control of the Minister for Arms and Munitions'.[48] Discussions with Speer convinced him that it was not, and the Minister appeared willing to absorb naval construction into his own Department provided that there was no penalty to army or air force programmes - provided,that is, that Hitler would agree to further sacrifices in the civilian sector.

Hitler approved the plan on 31 May 1943. A Ship-building Commission under Dönitz's control would now determine what was built and to what specification, while Speer's Ministry assumed responsibility for production. Opposition within the Navy Department was strong but the Construction Office was reduced to an advisory role and would, in due course, be absorbed into a new and unified material department, the Marinerüstung. The change appears to have brought some of the energy and efficiency that had, in Dönitz's view, been missing. It seems unlikely. for instance, that new initiatives in prefabricated construction would have come to fruition had matters remained in the hands of the K-Amt.

Dönitz's reform of the material departments took place just as the Battle of the Atlantic was reaching its climax, rather less than 12 months after the first intimations of the coming crisis had presented themselves to U-boat Command. An examination of the period May-September 1942 (when Dönitz and Raeder seem first to have grasped the growing threat to their plans) may serve to put the work of the material departments in perspective and to bring the workings of the German 'system' as a whole into sharper focus.

In May 1942, Raeder, conscious that the time was ripe for a reassertion of his strategic views, summoned Dönitz to brief the Führer on progress and plans. At the time, the U-boats were enjoying their second 'happy time' in the Western Hemisphere but the BdU acknowledged that this could not last and that, before long, he would have to renew operations on the Atlantic convoy routes. Losses, he warned, would increase. Although the race was not 'in any way hopeless', the productive capacity of the United States presented him and indeed all Axis partners with a formidable challenge. On the credit side, the large number of U-boats now becoming available would help solve the problem of finding convoys and allow him to renew the offensive in a variety of areas. All in all, the outlook was 'promising'. U-boat Command had 'faith in its equipment and belief in its fighting capability'.[49]

There was no hint in this statement of any need for fundamental change. The battle would be renewed with the proven Type VII U-boat and with established operational techniques. His top development priority was (still) the magnetic fuse which, by sinking merchant ships more efficiently and, incidentally, by increasing mortality among their crews, would have maximum impact on Allied transport capacity.

The picture presented three months later - Dönitz's forecast had been correct and he had now renewed operations on the convoy routes - was subtly different. Raeder now reported heavy losses, 'four submarines sunk in the Bay of Biscay, three damaged, four more damaged in contact with convoys, some badly', and all attributable to 'superior location devices in English aircraft'. He showed on a map how far Allied aircraft were ranging into the Atlantic. A new radar intercept device (FuMB) was showing promise.[50]

At the end of September, four months after his May statement, Dönitz was again called to the Reich Chancellery. He now outlined the defensive tactics employed by the enemy and explained how Allied escorts were making it difficult for U-boats to close their targets. Aircraft, however, were 'the great menace for submarines today'. He showed how the range of Allied aircraft had increased since 1940 and explained how the ocean areas available for his operations were steadily shrinking. He demanded that the Luftwaffe must now contribute to the U-boat war 'to a much greater extent than had been the case up to the present time'.

His material priorities (which he justified as necessary to sustain success rates rather than to avert losses) had changed radically since May. 'Most important of all', he now stated, 'was the demand for underwater speed. This is to be accomplished by the new Walter submarine'. His top weapon priority was the acoustic homing torpedo for use against surface escorts, and he was convinced that the guided rocket had an application in this role as well. At this same meeting, the Head of the Communications Service reported on the development of reflective coatings and on what would now be called 'stealth' technology. The Head of the U-boat Division had prepared briefs on anti-aircraft armament for U-boats, on look-out masts, helicopters, and other means to extend the visual horizon.[51]

Germany was now entering its fourth year of war. For much of that time, Hitler had followed his strategic 'intuitions' unchecked by any concerted military advice. His hopes of a clear-cut solution on land had been disappointed; he was now ready to concede that the Atlantic campaign would 'decide the outcome of the war'.

The navy's building programme, denied priority in the early years, was at last reaching fruition. But there were worrying developments. While favouring Dönitz's tonnage strategy, recent studies by the Intelligence Division of the Skl showed that estimates of Allied ship-building capacity put forward in May were seriously wrong.[52] In addition, a shadow had fallen over U-boat Command's concept of operations. The invidious comparisons now being drawn between Allied maritime air power and the Luftwaffe's modest contribution suggest that Raeder and Dönitz had glimpsed the possibility that, unsupported, the Type VII

U-boat was not enough. So far, air support had been seen primarily in terms of reconnaissance, a requirement that would diminish as U-boat numbers grew larger. Now U-boat operations needed something more akin to air superiority, a demand that the navy had never made definite before. It is hardly surprising that the Führer could make 'no definite promises'.[53]

How had this crisis arisen? Was it, as many in U-boat Command tended to suggest, the fault of the experts, a *trahison des clercs*? Failure to anticipate advances in enemy technology was obviously a significant factor and one which left military commanders fumbling for an antidote. Yet the omens had been there for some time. Dönitz's remarks on enemy defensive tactics were little different from those he had recorded in his War Diary a year before, when he had found defences on the Gibraltar and Sierra Leone routes so strong that 'there seems little chance of our maintaining contact long enough to make an attack possible'.[54] He had wondered then what technologies might be in use. He had noted that aircraft were extending the range of their operations, and that they were making their presence felt by night as well as by day. In December 1941, he had been given a vivid demonstration of the combined effects of sea and air escort in his action against convoy HG76, the first to include an escort carrier. Nevertheless, six months on, he was proposing to renew his operations with his material and his methods essentially unchanged.

There was more behind this crisis of confidence than a failure in technical intelligence. There had been a failure to read the warning signs and to understand the operational mechanisms that were beginning to influence the course of the Battle. As with earlier problems in it, a hard-pressed group of U-boat specialists, preoccupied with the day-to-day conduct of the campaign, had searched for answers but come to no definite conclusions. In Berlin, a Naval Staff, not well endowed with recent submarine experience, had been content to give its confident and persuasive subordinate a free hand and, protective of the navy's independence, had seen no merit in opening his methods to outside scrutiny.

If the September conference was a genuine attempt on the part of the naval leadership to brief their Head of State on the way forward (and there seems little reason to question their good faith), the advice that they gave was surprisingly inept. They showed little awareness of the need to focus scarce development resources on essentials. Some of their proposals (look-out masts and the like) were solutions to yesterday's problems. Others, like anti-aircraft armament, suggest the bold executive decision rather than any systematic attempt to grasp the campaign as a whole. Most surprising of all is that, in defiance of the advice of their material departments, the leadership should have placed the Walter submarine at the very centre of their priorities. A month later, Dönitz would find, in a hastily convened meeting with the designer and with officials of the K-Amt, that the Walter boat was 'nowhere near ready for service'.[55] Had too much faith been placed in the ability of a front-line commander to influence directions in technical development? In the long-run, Schniewind's promise that the FdU 'would state his requirements which the U-boat Department would have to fulfill as they stood' may not have been a wise one.

Dönitz would later refer to this period as his 'general offensive' to re-equip the U-boat Arm. It was scarcely that. Rather, it was an attempt to extend the effectiveness of a concept of operations that was already well past its prime.

Appendix 1
BdU Operations Staff, and Second Section Skl
[based on 'The German Navy, Organization and Functions', Admiralty, Naval Intelligence Division, November 1944.]

Chief of Staff
KA Godt.

A1.	**SO Operations**. KK Hessler. 2 assistants. U-boat deployments and availability. Liaison with external headquarters. Tactics and International Law. Supply at foreign bases.
A2	**Navigation**. KL Eichhain. Arrivals and departures. Return routes. Anti-submarine operations. Mine-sweeping and harbour defence.
A3	**Intelligence**. KL Kuppisch. 1 assistant. Enemy situation. Evaluation of U-boat War Diaries. Combat Experience.
A4	**Communications**. KL Meckel; KL Hoke. Communications and crypto procedures. Evasive and protective measures. Enemy location methods.
A5	**Statistics**. KK Dr Teufer. Records of sinkings and losses. Honours and awards.
Z	**Central Division**. KK Rösing. Also FdU West. U-boat construction. Organization and training. Personnel and discipline.
ZM	**Supply and transport**.
M1	**Section Engineer Officer**. Advice to BdU on all technical matters.

Quarters Officer, Flag Lieutenant, Adjutant.

Appendix 2

German Naval Staff: Organization and Functions[56]
Commander in Chief Navy
Chief of Naval Staff (C/Skl)

1/Skl. Operations Section. Strategic and operational concepts. Military appreciations by theatre. Fleet and Flotilla dispositions. Future plans and the oversight of operations in progress. Policies for Fleet operations, mine warfare, aviation, and the U-boat Arm. International Law. Economic warfare. Liaison with OKH, OKL, and OKW. Press and publicity.

2/Skl. BdU Operations Staff. (from Feb. '43) See Appendix I.

3/Skl. Intelligence. Enemy situation. Foreign Navies. Foreign Merchant Marines. Recipient of U-boat Command sinking reports. Studies of British convoy system. Projections of enemy ship-building capacity. Liaison with Secret Service (Abwehr).

4/Skl. Communications Service. (originally 2/Skl) Naval Communications network. Signal security. Direction-finding stations. From March 1941 assumes control of B-Dienst (formerly subordinate to 3/Skl); radio intelligence and code-breaking.

5/Skl. Location Section. Radar, radar and acoustic counter-measures. Location methods in use by the enemy. Assumes full departmental status May 1944. Formerly Fourth Section of Communications Service.

6/Skl. Hydrography and Meteorology. Skl H until June 1944.
Skl U U-boat Division. (Amtsgruppe U-bootswesen) Formed September 1939 to progress U-boat expansion. Organization of the U-boat Arm. Strategic employment of U-boats, tactics, weapon requirements. Training and personnel. Anti-submarine measures. Flotilla support. Disbanded February 1943; duties assumed by BdU Ops. Support functions re-formed May 1943 as part of Quartermaster Division.

Skl Adm Qu. Quartermaster Division. Assumes full departmental status April 1941. Fleet support. Supply and Transport including shipping space. Fuel supplies. Armament Supply and inspection. Base facilities and defence of naval bases. Mobilization and training. From May 1943 U-boat support (Skl Adm Qu U). Alleged by Schuster to be 'insufficiently organized' and 'entirely understaffed'.

Appendix 3
Primary Sources

Admiralty, Naval Intelligence Division.
History of U-boat Policy, NID 0698/46, Feb 1946.
Report on the German Naval War Effort', NID/24/T/65/45, October 1945.
The German Navy; organization and Functions, Nov 1944.
Reports *The War at Sea* by the following:
    Vice Admiral Heye, NID 1/GP/13, October 1945.
    Rear Admiral Godt, NID 1/GP/17, November 1945.
    General Admiral Ciliax, N1D 1/GP/18, November 1945.
    General Admiral Boehm, NID 1/GP/15, October 1945.
    General Admiral Krancke, NID 1/GP/11, October 1945.
    Admirals Schniewind and Schuster, NID 06437/46, Nov 1946.

Cabinet Office, Chiefs of Staff Committee, (Joint Intelligence Sub-committee).
Some weaknesses in German Strategy and Organization 1933-1945, October 1946.

United States Department of the Navy
U-boat Command War Diary 1939-1945, Wilmington Delaware, Scholarly Resources
Inc, 1984. (particularly volumes covering period January to December 1941.
Naval Staff War Diary 1939-1945 (Part A), Wilmington Delaware, Scholarly Resources
Inc, 1984. (period March to September 1942)
Axis Naval Policy and Operations in the Mediterranean 1940-1943.
Washington, 1951. (the work of Vice Admiral Eberhard Weichold)

Secondary sources are listed in the Consolidated Bibliography.

Notes

1.   Dönitz remained nominally subordinate to Fleet Headquarters and thus to Group
West until a formal revision of command structures in the autumn of 1941.The
relationship between Fleet and Group Commands would remain extremely
sensitive until the amalgamation of Fleet Headquarters with Group Command
(North) in 1943. Boehm, NID 1/GP/15, para.26. Ciliax, NID 1/GP/18, para. 35.
2.   Godt, NID 1/GP/17, para. 17.
3.   Padfield, *Dönitz*, p. 229.
4.   From summer 1941, the post of First Staff Officer was filled by Commander
Gunther Hessler, Dönitz's son-in-law and an experienced U-boat captain.
5.   Admiralty, Naval Intelligence Division, *The German Navy: Organization and
Functions*; November 1944.
6.   For procedural difficulties in sub-air cooperation, see *U-boat Command War
Diary*, 6 March 1941, PG/30284/NID, p. 28. The influence of the British D/F
network would remain a matter of controversy. See opinion of Rear Admiral
Fricke, Head of Operations Section, Naval Staff, in NID 0698/46, History of U-
boat Policy 1939-45, Admiralty, 1946, p.2. For Ciliax's opinion, see NID 1/GP/

18, paras 20-21.

7. Hessler, *U-boat War in the Atlantic*, vol 1, pp. 80-81.
8. Report to Raeder dated 7 February 1942, cited in NID 0698/46, p. 10.
9. *Ibid*. Original emphasis. The role of the Oberkommando der Wehrmacht (OKW), Hitler's personal military staff, is considered later.
10. See for instance Ciliax in NID 1/GP/18, para 29.
11. Godt, NID 1/GP/17, para. 35.
12. Weichold, *Axis Naval Policy and Operations in the Mediterranean 1939-43*, pp. 66-7.
13. For text, see Dönitz, *Memoirs*, p. 145.
14. For Dönitz's relations with his Italian allies, see Hessler, *U-boat War in the Atlantic*, I, pp.60-62. U-boat Command's attitude was shared by the naval authorities in Berlin. See NID 0698/46, p. 11.
15. See *U-boat Command War Diary*, 13 August 1941, PG/3O294/NID, p.137. For development priorities, see *Fuehrer Conferences on Naval Affairs*, p. 283 and pp. 295-6. For events in the Bay, see McCue, *U-boats in the Bay of Biscay*, p. 27.
16. See for instance, *U-boat Command War Diary*, 30 July 1941, following action against Convoy OG 69. PG/3O293/NID, pp. 123-124.
17. *U-boat Command War Diary* 18 April 1941. PG/3O287/NID. p. 54; Dönitz, *Memoirs* pp. 324-5; Hessler, *U-boat War in the Atlantic*, II, p. 88.
18. Sources for the organization and functions of the Skl are NID 24/T/65/45, *Report on the German Naval War Effort*, Admiralty, 1945: Naval Intelligence Division Report, *The German Navy; Organization and Function*, Admiralty, November 1944: *Geschäftsvertielungsplan der OKM*, dated 1 October, 1944.
19. *U-boat Command War Diary*, 18 April 1941, p. 54.
20. Hessler, *U-boat War in the Atlantic*, I, p.97. Rear Admiral Maertens advised the BdU that there was no cause for alarm and that 'the more important cyphers do not appear to have been broken'.
21. Hessler, *U-boat War in the Atlantic*, II, pp. 25-6. The Department had finally divulged that airborne radar was the probable cause. According to Hessler, 'this was the first positive information that the BdU had received from the experts'.
22. NID 0698/46, pp. 12, 28-9.
23. Dönitz, *Memoirs,* p. 44; *U-boat Command War Diary*, 8 September 1939, pp.18-20.
24. Hessler, *U-boat War in the Atlantic*, I, p. 4. Godt, NID 1/17, paras 25 and 45. Dönitz, *Memoirs,* p. 49. Skl U support functions would reappear in May 1942 as a subsection of the Quartermaster Division, Skl Adm Qu U.
25. BdU report to Raeder dated 26 November 1941, NID 0698/46, pp. 16-7.
26. Hessler, *U-boat War in the Atlantic*, II, p. 29. Dönitz calculated that in February and March of 1942, the diversion of boats for the defence of Norway had cost him 300,000 tons of shipping.

27. For a description of this incident, see Hessler, *U-boat War in the Atlantic*, II, p. 26.

28. Report of 27 December 1940, *Fuehrer Conferences*. pp. 160-3. For a summary of Raeder's representations on the U-boat building programme, see Hessler,*U-boat War in the Atlantic*, I, Appendix I.

29. Report of 4 February 1941, and Hitler's Directive No 23. *Fuehrer Conferences*, pp. 177-9.

30.   Krancke, NID 1/GP/11, para 18.

31. For example, Hitler's refusal to support Raeder's request to include a naval representative on Speer's Central Planning Committee. *Fuehrer Conferences*, 22 December 1942, p. 304.

32. For an example of this process at work, see Report of 27 December 1940, *Fuehrer Conferences*, pp 160-163.

33. Report of 15 June 1942. *Fuehrer Conferences*, pp.284-5.

34. Ciliax, NID 1/GP/18, para. 24. Schniewind and Schuster, NID 06437/46 para. 10. Dönitz, pp. 131-2. Krancke, NID l/GP/11 para. 23.

35. Heye, NID 1/GP/13, para. 22; Schniewind and Schuster, NID 06437 pp. 66-7; Ciliax, NID 1/GP/18, para 111.

36. Schniewind and Schuster, *op. cit.,* pp. 66-7.

37. Chiefs of Staff Committee, (Joint Intelligence Sub-committee), *Some weaknesses in German Strategy and Organization 1933-1945*, Cabinet Office, October 1946.

38. Schuster, NID 06437/46, pp. 66-7. Ciliax, NID 1/GP/18, para. 16. Krancke, NID 1/GP/11, para 31.

39. Schuster, NID 06437/46 p. 59. Ciliax, NID 1/GP/18, para 24; Salewski, *The Submarine War;* Buchheim *The U-boat War*.

40. Hessler,*U-boat War in the Atlantic*, I, p. 15.

41. Hessler,*U-boat War in the Atlantic*, II, pp.44-45. Hessler contrasts Dönitz's energetic sponsorship with the caution of the navy's experts. That the K-Amt was undoubtedly right, seems to have escaped him.

42. Dönitz, *Memoirs,* p. 353.

43. Hessler, *U-boat War in the Atlantic*, II, p. 47.

44. Hessler, *U-boat War in the Atlantic*, II, p. 45.

45. Padfield, *Dönitz,* p. 261. On one such occasion, Dönitz had demanded 'a single department, and a single person to be responsible....and the name of that person to be made known.'

46. Hessler, *U-boat War in the Atlantic*, II, p. 88. NID 0698/46, p. 28.

47. *Fuehrer Conferences*, p. 309. Raeder had long protested on this score, but Hitler appears to have delegated the matter to Keitel and nothing had been done.

48. Dönitz, *Memoirs,* p. 350. He calculated that 83.3% of industry was now under Speer's control.

49. Report of 14 May 1942, *Fuehrer Conferences*, pp. 280-3.

50. Report of 26 August 1942, *Fuehrer Conferences*, pp. 290-1.

51. Report of 28 September 1942, *Fuehrer Conferences*, pp. 294-7. NID 0698/46 p. 31. A recent visit to the Army's Experimental Establishment at Peenemunde explains Dönitz's interest in rockets. He had also found work in progress on new Flak armament for surface ships of which he was unaware. He had demanded better co-ordination between departments.

52. Report by 3/Skl dated 9 September 1942, NID 0698/46, p. 31. Dönitz had set the sinking target at 700,000 grt per month. This study suggested that from early 1943 a target of 1,300,000 tons would be needed to have a decisive effect in a 'measurable time'.

53. Report of 26 August 1942, 1: *Fuehrer Conferences*, p. 291.

54. *U-boat Command War Diary*, 12 August 1941, p. 129. See also diary entries for 13 and 14 August, and for 8 September 1941.

55. Dönitz, *Memoirs*, p. 353. Production plans were frozen following this meeting and the Construction Office began work on the more conventional design that would later become the Type XXI.

56. Based on NID 24/T/65/45, *Report on German Naval War Effort*, 22 October 1945. NID Report, *The German Navy; Organization and Functions*, November 1944. *Geschäftsverteilungsplan der OKM*, October 1944.

8

The Control of British Merchant Shipping

by *Thomas A. Adams*

Part One: Historical Summary to 1939

Control: v 1. To check or verify, and hence to regulate. 2. To exercise restraint or direction upon the free action of; to dominate, command.

It is difficult to draw a straight line separating the control of merchant shipping and the protection of merchant shipping. The purpose of this chapter is to explain the control - particularly the civil control - of British merchant shipping during WWII. To understand this, it is necessary to look briefly at two important historical influences. The first is the commercial aspect of British merchant shipping; the second is what was learned from WWI.

Introduction

British merchant shipping was highly important to the nation. It was not generally understood that for centuries, this island nation had depended upon its commercial shipping, no less than upon its naval power. However, British merchant shipping was not a basic industry - it was not a producer. Rather, it was the pipeline from market-place to market-place. As a developing industry it owed little to the state and much to private enterprise. Merchant shipping was provided for by private finance, and was managed by businessmen who were described as shipowners. Through them, it became a significant force in international shipping, running vessels of all types and sizes to international and governmental standards and engaging in many different operations both in home trade and in world-wide waters. It is not possible to define a typical or average type of merchant ship, but there were five main groups of ship owned and registered as British ships - passenger and passenger-cargo liners; cargo liners; tramps; tankers; and coasters and ships on home trade. These ships were owned and managed by a number of different companies, each with interests in particular fields of activity and manned by personnel from all levels of society throughout the British Empire.

Background

At the turn of the century, British merchantmen dominated the globe: Britain was building nearly 1½ million gross tons of new shipping a year, and half of the world's commercial ships flew the distinctive Red Ensign. Shipowning was an accepted business investment in which many people had financial interests, whether in management or operation. These enterprises generally provided a good financial return with, for example, both the Boer War and WWI being particularly profitable times. The period immediately before WWI was also a time of prosperity, but by then competition had intensified as other nations - particularly Germany, Norway and Japan - increased their merchant fleets.

TABLE 1: World-Wide Tonnage in 1914 (100+grt)		
Country	grt	World Tonnage %
British Empire	20,524,000	47.6
Germany	5,135,000	11.9
USA	2,027,000	4.7
Norway	1,957,000	4.5
Japan	1,708,000	4.0
Source: Lloyd's Register of Shipping, Fairplay		

When Britain entered WWI in 1914, around 47% of the world's merchant tonnage was sailing under the Red Ensign. The demand for shipping was insatiable, freight rates rocketed and the government introduced an excess profits levy of up to 80% on the profits that exceeded pre-war figures. However, the aggregated losses amounted to around nine million tons, with terrible casualties amongst the officers and men of the merchant service.

Britain emerged from that war with a significantly smaller fleet, amounting to around 34% of world tonnage. Many shipowners foresaw post-war prosperity and so, with their profits and reserves plus government grants towards repairs and new construction, acquired new tonnage was acquired at inflated prices.

TABLE 2: Number of ships built in UK		
Year	No. of ships	grt
1920	618	2,055,624
1921	426	1,538,052
Source: Official figures		

Accompanying the dismantling of war-time controls, the immediate post-war boom was unsustainable. In the summer of 1920, freight rates collapsed and a long and severe trade depression hit British shipping. Dividends dropped or ceased, and many shipowners went out of business. However, a number of companies amalgamated and consolidated their interests, particularly in the liner trade. Bigger companies took over smaller ones and these powerful businessmen began to diversify into overlapping activities - wharfing, engineering, banking and mining. It is recorded that 13 members of the board of P&O (the Peninsular & Oriental Steam Navigation Company Ltd) held between them over 100 directorships world-wide, while three directors of Ellerman Lines Ltd collectively held more than 50 directorships. Nonetheless, recovery came only with the impending threat of another war.

TABLE 3: World merchant shipping in 1937			
Country	No. of ships	grt	World tonnage %
British Empire	9,084	20,398,157	32.5
USA	3,037	11,880,200	14.9
Japan	2,564	4,475,110	7.1
Norway	1,899	4,346,782	7.0
Germany	2,185	3,927,916	6.2
Source: Lloyd's Register of Shipping, Fairplay			

On the eve of WWII, British merchant shipping consisted of around 300 fleets amounting to 26.1% of the world's commercial tonnage. Approximately 56% of our exports were carried in British shipping and around 9% of our imports. However, it has been estimated that over a third of the world's foreign-to-foreign trade was carried in British ships, and the gross earning from shipping on the trade routes of the world was Britain's largest export - greater than any other industry. Five companies and their associated concerns owned and controlled around six million tons of shipping - over 35% of the British merchant fleet. Nonetheless, between 1919-39, some shipowners found it difficult and a number of companies lapsed. The great depression and its reductions in the volume of world trade had serious repercussions throughout British shipping. Conditions in ships were bad. Seaman worked over 100 hours per week, and in that period suffered three cuts in their pay. On 8 July 1938, Lady Astor stated in the House of Commons: 'There is nothing too strong that can be said about conditions and it applies to most merchant ships'. A medical officer in the Humber area inspected 4,519 British ships and reported that 374 were dirty and unfit for human habitation. In addition he was concerned about a further 105 ships. During the same period, he inspected 2,360 foreign registered ship and reported that only 41 were dirty and that there was concern about only a further 16.

TABLE 4: Principal British shipping companies in 1937		
Company	No. of ships	grt
British India Steam Navigation	110	672,010
Ellerman Lines	140	690,870
Blue Funnel (Alfred Holt)	75	591,530
P&O	37	441,140
Cunard White Star	19	452,500
Source: Lloyd's Register of Shipping		

A summary of the organization of a typical British shipping company is given in Appendix 1.

Civil Control of British Merchant Shipping

Control of merchant shipping is mostly perceived as Naval Control - even more often, simply as the operating of convoys. This is not the actual case. Government control of British merchant shipping dates well back into the 18th century, and by the early 19th Century various government departments were responsible for regulations concerning merchant shipping - for example, the Admiralty for the supply of seaman; the Treasury for Customs; and the Colonial Office and Emigration Commissioners for passengers. There were also regulations on the registration of seamen; steel-hulled ships had to have watertight compartments; passenger ships required half-yearly surveys. Nevertheless, British governmental policy was to develop trade freely, and the repeal of the Navigation Laws in 1849 did away with control of the commercial side of British sea-borne trade. However, despite fierce opposition from shipowners, the then President of the Board of Trade (Henry Labouchere) proposed the establishment of a Mercantile Marine Department and in 1850 the Mercantile Marine Act laid down that the Board of Trade 'shall undertake the general superintendence of matters relating to the British mercantile marine'. The Board was to appoint ex-shipping masters as Superintendents of Mercantile Marine Offices at the principal ports, to be responsible for the register of seamen and for the seamen's fund. The Act also made the examination of masters and mates compulsory.

Board of Trade interest in ships was nearly total, beginning at the building stage when a ship was measured for tonnage before registration. Passenger ships were surveyed, cargo ships given load-line certificates (the Plimsoll Mark) and a system of periodical hull and machinery surveys was instituted. The Board of Trade was generally responsible for the welfare of the country's mariners, including conditions at sea for officers and seamen, discipline and desertion, the prevention of impressment, the supply of medicine and payment of wages. Ship's officers were examined and certificated and crews signed their Articles of Agreement in the presence of the Mercantile Marine Office Superintendent. The Board was notified of accidents at work and had the power to hold formal investigations. After a voyage, the ship's papers were sent to the General Register and Record Office of Shipping and Seamen - part of the Board of Trade.

World War I

During WWI an enormous number of merchant ships of all types performed naval and military tasks. Liners were taken up and commissioned as armed merchant cruisers to patrol the trade lanes and perform many other duties. Passenger liners and many fast cargo ships were employed as hospital ships and transports; cargo ships were taken up to supply the fleets and support the armies with every imaginable necessity. Some fast channel packets carried seaplanes and aircraft, while others were converted into minelayers, minesweepers, transports, hospital carriers, and acted as fleet messengers.

The open market and the unprecedented demands for tonnage caused freight rates to rise rapidly. By October 1914 Blue Book rates, i.e. those paid by the Government for requisitioned tonnage, were fixed so as to prevent what was seen as profiteering. However, it was not until November 1915 that the Ships Licensing Committee was appointed. This was tasked with seeing that all available tonnage was actually employed to the full advantage of the nation. Operating costs had clearly risen but the industry was continuing to make large profits. There are many and varying estimates of the level of profit made by the industry during the first two years of the war. The Official History *Sea-borne Trade* puts the figure at £174 million.

TABLE 5: Example of freight rates
Time charter rate per deadweight ton

Pre-war	3 shillings
1915	18 shillings
Jan-Sept 1916	30 shillings

Source: Fairplay

Late in 1916, Lloyd George's more interventionist government decided that the growing problems finally required a specialized department of state. In December 1916 the Ministry of Shipping, headed by the Shipping Controller, was established with full authority over the whole of the maritime industries as well as the neutral tonnage which was being employed by Britain. This was the first time in history that the British shipping industry, and the shipbuilding industry, had passed completely under the control of the State. When the Prime Minister announced the decision, he said of shipping:

it has never been so vital to the life of the country as it is at present. It is the jugular vein, which, if severed, will destroy the life of the nation, and the Government feel that the time has come for taking over more complete control of all the ships of this country....the prodigious profits made out of freights are contributing in no small measure to the high cost of commodities and I have always found not only that, but they are making it difficult for us in our task with labour...

The Shipping Controller 1917-1921

By regulations made under the Defence of The Realm Consolidation Act 1914 and under clause 39BBB of the Regulations of Defence of The Realm Acts, the Shipping Controller was given five major areas of power:

Ownership and management. The Controller was the owning authority for ships that were built under his control and for those that had became Government-controlled, and he was responsible for operating them by placing them under the management of commercial interests. He also controlled the management of vessels owned by other government departments, except for those naval auxiliaries of the Admiralty's Director of Transports.

Requisition. Excluding the Board of Admiralty, the Controller was given the sole power to requisition or have placed at his disposal, anywhere, any British registered merchant ship, in order that she could be employed in a manner considered best for national needs. He had the power to requisition any cargo or passenger space irrespective of existing rights under charter or any freighting agreement.

Movements. By taking over the power of the Board of Trade relating to the granting of licences to British ships proceeding on any voyage, the Controller had overall authority to regulate and control movements.

Cargoes. The Controller had authority to regulate and control ships with regards to the trades in which they were to be employed and the type of cargoes they carried. He directed them to the port at which their cargoes were to be loaded or discharged and at which their passengers would be embarked or disembarked. He would also direct the consignees of cargoes to the port at which they would take delivery.

Shipbuilding. Here the Controller had complete authority to order, regulate, direct and even restrict the building, repairing, refitting and converting of ships. His authority covered shipyards, docks, dry-docks, marine engine works and any other facilities that could be used. He had the power to determine the manner and priority in which contracts and orders for building, equipping and repairing were to be done and the payments to be made.

Admiralty Control of Shipping 1914-18

When war broke out in August 1914 the Admiralty instituted a system of blockade and patrols to protect our trade routes and a system of evasive routeing was introduced. The intention was to minimize disruption of normal peacetime movements of merchant shipping. All routeing instructions were handled by one officer in Trade Division. These 'instructions' were advisory only and were communicated to owners through the War Risks Clubs and then by mail to the masters of their vessels. However, the grim reality of war eventually forced the Admiralty to pay increasing attention to merchant shipping movements and attempt to direct ships clear of U-boats, minefields and surface raiders. A route-giving organization was gradually built up employing a variety of retired officers and civilian agencies. In January 1917 routeing orders replaced routeing advice and the organization was expanded. By mid-1917 the Admiralty's Route-Giving Organization, later known as the Mercantile Movements Division, was virtually world-wide and, gradually during 1917, the convoy system was introduced.

Inter-War Re-organization and Planning

The role of the Ministry of Shipping was contentious, and on 8 March 1921 the Cabinet decided that one government department should be appointed not only to liquidate all war work, but also to look after all future government shipping work and the general interests of British merchant shipping in peacetime. The Ministry of Shipping and the post of the Shipping Controller were terminated by the Ministries of Munitions and Shipping Cessation Act, 1921. On 1 April 1921 the duties reverted to the Board of Trade and its reformed Mercantile Marine Department. In 1921, the Admiralty's Transport Department was also transferred to the Board of Trade. This Department's duties included the arrangements for transportation by sea of personnel and stores for government departments. The Director of Sea Transport at the Board of Trade was responsible to the Admiralty for those sections of his work concerning the RN.

The Mercantile Marine Department had two main responsibilities: to complete the run-down of the wartime administration, and to administer the Merchant Shipping Acts, Shipping Subsidy Acts and the British Shipping Assistance Act, as well as to conduct, in peacetime, war planning for the shipping industry. The Department's public face was its 'M' Notice system for communicating with the shipping industry. The Department's backrooms, however, undertook a considerable amount of careful pre-war planning in conjunction with the Committee of Imperial Defence. Divisions undertook:

- a review of shipbuilding and ship repair facilities in the UK, with tentative wartime allocations of work;
- representation on the Shipbuilding Consultative Committee;
- a study on the setting up of coasting and short sea committees at the principal ports;
- a study of the world tanker trade and the availability of tankers;
- a scheme for the diversion of deep sea shipping from east to west coast ports, with proposals for unloading into coasters and lighters for dispersal to smaller ports;
- calculation of the import capacity of the Merchant Marine;
- a review and plan of a licensing scheme for British merchant ships;
- a review of the war Risk Insurance scheme;
- the provision of a complete index of British, and certain foreign, merchant shipping, their suitability for wartime service and their daily movements;
- an analysis of the shipping implications of changed sources of supply

of major imported commodities, such as meat, iron ore and timber;
- investigations into the structure of rates of hire for requisitioned shipping.

It is frequently said that WWII was an extension of WWI, and to some extent this is correct. However, regarding the administration and control of British merchant shipping this was simply not the case. The lessons of WWI influenced Government planners, and the extensive pre-1939 planning concluded that upon the outbreak of war the control of all imports and exports and of British merchant shipping would be taken over by the Government. Amongst many vital points, this course of action would ensure that shipping resources were used to the greatest national advantage and that the law of supply and demand should not again force freight rates to the profiteering heights experienced during the 1914-1916 period.

In sum: on the eve of WWII the control of the employment of British merchant shipping was in the hands of the Board of Trade and control over the safety, sailing and routeing of British merchant ships was firmly placed within the Admiralty.

Part Two: Battle of the Atlantic

There are substantial records about British shipping policy and the administration of the Merchant Shipping Acts. However, despite its importance, few official documents relating to the detailed organization of British merchant shipping and the administration of the relevant controlling authorities have survived. Moreover, within the context of the control of merchant shipping, it is not possible to isolate the Battle of the Atlantic. The structures of control were established to cope with Britain's busiest sea lanes - the grain, oil, ore and passenger routes of the North Atlantic - but were equally applied world-wide.

The wartime control of merchant shipping had two main aims: first, to ensure that the cargoes essential for the national war effort were imported and exported in the necessary quantities and that shipping resources were used as efficiently as possible; and second, for the Admiralty to assume control of all sailing and routeing and to ensure the safety of merchant ships during their passages. The loss of a merchant ship is cumulative - not only is the cargo which she was carrying lost, but all future cargoes that she would have carried are forfeited.

The Size of the Task

In illustrating the size of the British merchant navy and of British trade, statistical tables are essential. On the eve of WWII British sea-borne imports were estimated at 65 million tons and the volume of exports at 50 million tons. Records for the last full trading year prior to the start of war show that British shipping carried only 56.9% of exports and 59% of our imports. The size and capacity of the British merchant fleet of ships over 1,600 gross tons is illustrated by the following table.

TABLE 6: Estimated Size of British Merchant Fleet (1939)			
Type of ship	Number of ships	Total Gross Registered Tons	Total Deadweight
Non-tankers	2,520	14,350,000	18,700,000
Tankers	479	3,000,000	5,050,000
Source: Lloyd's Register of Shipping			

The movement of British and foreign flag ships using UK ports is a useful indication of the size of British trade:

TABLE 7: Shipping entering and clearing UK ports (net registered tons)			
September 1939	Entered with cargo/ballast	Cleared with cargo/ballast	Total shipping movements
British ships	2,827,000	3,167,000	5,991,000
Foreign ships	2,156,000	1,724,000	3,880,000
1st Quarter 1943			
British ships	1,302,000	1,351,000	2,652,000
Foreign ships	709,000	760,000	1,469,000
Source: Statistical Digest of the War			

The wartime organization for the administration and control of British merchant shipping reflected a super-bureaucratic and often conflicting jigsaw with responsibilities spread between civil and Service organizations such as:

- the Board of Trade;
- the Ministry of Shipping;
- the Ministry of Transport;
- the Ministry of War Transport;
- the Admiralty Trade Division;
- the Admiralty's Advisory Committee on Merchant Shipbuilding;
- the Ministry of Food;
- the Ministry of Supply;
- the Ministry of Labour;
- the National Maritime Board;
- the Shipping Defence Advisory Committee;
- the Bunker Control Committee;
- the War Risk Insurance Organization; and
- the Ministry of Economic Warfare.

The real administration and control of British merchant shipping rested initially within the Ministry of Shipping (later the Ministry of War Transport) and within the Trade Division of the Admiralty.

Ministry of Shipping

Under the Defence (General) Regulations 1939, many powers relating to merchant shipping were conferred upon the Board of Trade - the general control of navigation, the employment of British ships, transfer of registry of British ships, desertion from ships, the control of rates and charges for transport, safety measures, wireless telegraphy rules and provision of pensions for seafarers. The Mercantile Marine Department had full control of all merchant shipping under the Red Ensign and it began administration of the War Risks' Insurance Act. Overseas voyages were brought under Government control through the issue of licenses and a Ships Licensing Committee was established.

On 13 October 1939, six weeks after the outbreak of war, the Ministry of Shipping was created to provide and control merchant shipping for the benefit of the national war effort (see Appendix 2). This new Department of State was organized around a nucleus formed from the Mercantile Marine Department, including the General Register and Record Office of Shipping and Seamen, the War Risks Insurance Office, the Mercantile Marine Offices, the Marine Survey Service and the Sea Transport Division. For a short while it also had control of merchant shipbuilding and repairs (see Appendix 3). Based in Berkeley Square House, London W1, the Ministry of Shipping was headed by a Director-General and staffed by Civil Servants and by personnel employed directly from the shipping industry for their specialist knowledge and experience.

During the first two months of the war, imports dropped by around 50%. The shipping situation was serious, the effectiveness of the Ship Licensing Scheme came into question and by December 1939 provision for the requisition of all British registered merchant ships on commercial trade was approved by the Minister of Shipping. This was to improve the accuracy of central control and planning. The Ship Licensing Scheme was aborted in January 1940 and the Ministry commenced the requisition of all deep-sea ships. By October 1940, coasting and short-sea vessels were also requisitioned. Negotiations on the detailed conditions of requisitioning were carried out with the Chamber of Shipping and day-to-day management was left to the shipowners - the experts.

Requisitioning did not meet all our needs for tonnage. This was not helped by the unwillingness of many neutral shipowners to charter their vessels. In the summer of 1940, this resulted in the creation of the Ship Warrant Scheme, under which the British Commonwealth's world-wide facilities were actively denied to any merchant ships not engaged on approved voyages. The Warrant Scheme was all embracing: no bunkers, no stores, no repairs and no Admiralty charts. At the same time, arrangements were made for the transfer to Ministry of Shipping control of shipping registered in the occupied countries. One estimate put this total as high as eight million gross tons.

There was a good deal of overlap between the Ministry of Shipping and the Ministry of Transport. Through its Port and Transit Division, the Ministry of Transport was responsible for preparing the ports for war, for handling ships and their cargoes, and for the inland movement of material to and from the ports. The Ministry of Shipping's Director of Shipping in Port was responsible for reducing the amount of time a ship spent in port. With port congestion, delays in discharging and loading and with last-minute diversions, the situation was far from satisfactory. Great difficulties were encountered, and it would appear that the relationship between the two Ministries was failing to the extent that in November 1940 the War Cabinet instructed the Ministers of Shipping and Transport and their senior officials to meet and to collaborate. Records show that there were seven meetings. On 6 March 1941, this system was replaced by a new standing committee consisting of the Assistant Chief of Naval Staff (Trade), the Director of Shipping in Ports (Ministry of Shipping) and the Director of Ports (Ministry of Transport). Their role was to identify and eliminate all obstacles delaying the turn-round of ships.

By spring 1941, shipping performance had dropped and shipping losses had increased. Prime Minister Churchill established and chaired a Battle of the Atlantic Committee (see Appendix 4) with the Ministers of Shipping and Transport as members. Notes of this Committee show that the turn-round of shipping was always on the agenda. Nevertheless, the situation was still too complicated, so the Prime Minister decided to place the control of all British transport (other than Service transport) under the control of one central body. This was done by merging the Ministry of Shipping and Ministry of Transport to form the Ministry of War Transport (MoWT).

Ministry of War Transport

Under the Ministers of the Crown (Emergency Appointments) Act 1939, an Order-in-Council (No. 654, dated 9 May 1941) appointed the Minister of War Transport and transferred to him all the functions of the Ministry of Shipping and Ministry of Transport (see Appendix 5).

Based (as the Ministry of Shipping had been) in Berkeley Square House, the new Ministry was headed by a Director-General, initally with three Deputy Directors-General. A re-organization in 1942 reduced this to two, one covering shipping and one covering inland transport. After the re-organization, the Deputy Director-General (Shipping) had two Assistant Directors-General. Below this level, day-to-day business was conducted by specialist divisions, which, apart from the overlapping areas, remained very much as those of the old Shipping and Transport ministries.

At its peak the MoWT was organized into 26 divisions, of which 16 dealt exclusively with shipping (see Appendix 6). It had inherited the Ministry of Transport's Diversion Room (see Appendix 7) and the Ministry of Shipping's War Risk Insurance Office, along with the City Chartering Office, the General Register and Records Office of Shipping and Seamen and the Mercantile

Marine Survey Service. It was also responsible for the Inter-Departmental Bunker Control Committee (see Appendix 8). Its control of merchant ships fell into a number of distinct areas:

Requisition. The MoWT was the primary power to requisition or have placed at its disposal any merchant ship that came under British influence.

Movements. The MoWT, in co-operation with the Admiralty Trade Division, had overall authority to regulate and control the movements of any merchant ship that came under British influence.

Cargoes. The MoWT had the authority to regulate and control the trade in which ships were employed and the type and amount of cargo that they carried.

Ownership and management. The MoWT was the owning authority for ships that were built or taken under Government control. The Ministry was also responsible for placing them under the management of commercial shipowners.

The Ministry was also responsible for the administration of the Merchant Shipping Acts and their current amendments. It dealt with the National Union of Seamen, was represented on the National Maritime Board, worked closely with Lloyd's and with the owner's organization the Shipping Federation. Through the Mercantile Marine Offices, it had inherited the responsibilities for the registration of seamen and the certification of officers. It had to deal with manning levels and the shortages of skilled seafarers. It liaised with the Ministry of Labour on the Registration of Employment Order and the Essential Work Order both of which were used to mobilize the services of merchant seamen and direct them back to sea.

The Deputy Director-General (Shipping) maintained a tight management of merchant shipping by means of the Shipping (Operations) Control. This comprised a Chairman and the Deputy Director-General (Shipping), with the Directors of the Sea Transport, Ship Management, Port and Transit, Liner, Coasting and Short Sea Divisions.

In addition to the Mercantile Marine Offices and Marine Survey Offices, the Minister of War Transport's control was exercised by an extensive UK and overseas shore-based regional structure with a network of Representatives and Deputy Representatives (see Appendix 9). Their main functions were:

- to collaborate with Port Emergency Committees, port authorities and other interested parties in order to secure the most efficient and economical use of merchant shipping and in particular to ensure rapid turn-rounds: the Regional Port Directors were MoWT representatives;
- to represent the Minister of War Transport in their port area on all commercial shipping matters;

- to monitor, investigate and attempt to remedy local causes of delay;
- to co-ordinate owners' requirements and settle priorities between commercial shippers; and
- to co-operate with Naval Control Service officers in order to 'ensure that a ship's arrival at a port or anchorage is communicated to the necessary agencies without delay and that a ship was ready in time to sail with the appropriate convoy'.

In 1941 the Ministry of War Transport had over 40 Representatives and Deputy Representatives overseas - Africa, Australia, South America, Canada, India and the United States. The most important overseas post was in New York, employing around 80 in 1940 and nearly 2,000 by 1944. The Ministry's Representatives were the main points of contact for information and for the passing on of instructions from London to the ships under Ministry control. Their function was to manage, in co-operation with Sea Transport Officers, the business of the Ministry and to supervise the work of ship and cargo agents to ensure the economical and minimum turn-round of tonnage. They were generally concerned with the management, operation and repair of merchant ships employed on civil or commercial work together with the shipment of government, civil and commercial cargoes. They had the authority to purchase and charter neutral shipping. They had to work closely with local naval authorities and in most port areas under British control there was a War Transport or Port Executive Committee - the MoWT Representative generally was the Chairman.

Director of Sea Transport

The national demands for merchant shipping came from the the civil ministries and from the requirements of the armed services. Again control was exercised centrally by the Director of Sea Transport.

Sea Transport is an old organization that was originally part of the Admiralty. It was transferred to the Shipping Controller in 1917 and remained in the merchant shipping environment ever since. When the powers of the Board of Trade were transferred to the Ministry of Shipping (later Ministry of War Transport) in 1939, the Director of Sea Transport's division was embodied within the new ministry, although for naval planning he was directly responsible to the Admiralty. As the shipping agent for the Service departments (Admiralty, War Office and Air Ministry), it was the Director's role, acting within the Ministry of War Transport, to see that the requirements of the armed forces were met from within the limits of general shipping policy.

Merchant shipping allocated to the armed services came under his direct control and it was here that his main functions lay:

- fitting out and the conversion of merchant ships for service as troopships, hospital ships and carriers and for ships for special duties;

- the supervision of ship management by the owners, their maintenance, provision of crew, victualling and use of agents;
- bunkering and watering;
- co-operation with the armed services on their requirements for movement of troops and cargo and with the Admiralty on convoy escorts and Naval Control;
- the selection, taking-up and manning of Naval Auxiliary vessels;
- the hire of tugs and other small craft for the provision of services at ports and anchorages;
- provision of berths in ports and the payment of port expenses;
- issue of voyage instructions to the Masters of Transports.

The Director was assisted by a Deputy Director, three Assistant Directors, a Naval Assistant (a Rear Admiral), another Rear Admiral responsible for convoys and Naval Control and a Principal Officer Technical Services. The Sea Transport Division had three main branches:

Naval Branch. Dealing with commissioned Naval Auxiliaries - for example, armed merchant cruisers, minesweepers, minelayers and escort carriers; and non-commissioned Naval Auxiliaries, such as supply ships, tankers, blockships, wreck dispersal ships, rescue ships, accommodation ships and cable ships, as well as the purchase of ships.

Military Personnel Branch. Dealing with troopships, individual sea passages for service and government personnel and the transport of stores. In particular, the movement of British troops to and from Canada and America, the movement of Canadian and US troops to the UK and in particular the North Atlantic operation of the two *Queens*.

Military Cargo Branch. Dealing with planning of cargo movements, port handling facilities for fighting stores (such as ammunition, aircraft and tanks), chairing the Military Requirements (Shipping) Committee.

At ports within the UK and overseas the Director of Sea Transport was represented by a network of up to as many as 1,000 Sea Transport Officers (STOs) and Senior Inspecting Officers (SIOs). In the main these officers were ex-RN, RNR, RNVR or Mercantile Marine officers. On appointment they were given temporary naval commissions and then seconded to the Director of Sea Transport. Their duties were wide and variable but always involved close co-operation with civil and military authorities. Senior Inspecting Officers were responsible for specialist technical advice and for surveys.

Ports had a quota of Sea Transport Officers, the number depending upon the work. Officers in charge of a number of ports and areas that were grouped together for administrative purposes were known as Principal STOs

(Commodore's rank); officers in charge of a major port were known as Divisional STOs (Captain's rank); smaller ports came under an STO-in-charge.

Admiralty Trade Division - Naval Control of Shipping

The relationship between the Admiralty and the British merchant shipping industry was quite different to that which the industry had with the Board of Trade and the Ministries of Shipping and War Transport. The Admiralty was not concerned with commercial problems but had mandatory control over the movement of all merchant shipping. It is in this area that the difference between control and protection becomes difficult to separate.

The Trade Division was reconstituted in May 1939 with a staff of five naval officers and four civilians. By February 1943 it was headed by a Captain RN (Director of Trade Division) supported by two Deputy Directors, two Assistant Directors, a Civil Assistant and a staff of 95 naval officers and 275 civilians. Under a Deputy Director of Trade Division was placed the operational front-line of the Division - the Naval Control Service with its network of NCS officers working in the principal Ports of the UK and overseas. Trade Division's functions are manifold:

The protection of British seaborne trade. This was achieved by the control of merchant ship movements and the organization of convoys. The Director of Mercantile Movements, an Assistant Director of Trade Division, was responsible for:

- the supervision of merchant ships not in convoys:
- the issuing of routeing instructions to independent ships and to ships in convoys;
- operating a system of approved routes into major ports;
- arranging for the assembly of convoys and the support of ships waiting to join convoys;
- the issue of sailing instructions to convoys.

The protection of British ships. This was the responsibility of the Defensively Equipped Merchant Ships Section, headed by a Deputy Director, and was achieved by the provision of armament, paravane equipment, darkening ship arrangements, degaussing and other defensive equipment in merchant ships, as well as by the supply and training of service personnel and the provision of special training courses for merchant navy personnel.

Information and Instructions

The control of British merchant shipping could not he achieved without the issue of a wide range of publications and instructions (see Appendix 10).

The Cost

World War II came to the British merchant marine on 3 September 1939 with the sinking of the Donaldson Liner *Athenia* in the North Atlantic and ended with sinking of *Avondale Park* in the Firth of Forth on 7 May 1945. Between these two dates a huge wartime burden fell upon British merchant shipping which led to the whole fleet (which was private property, built by private capital and privately run) being requisitioned and controlled for the benefit of the nation and its war effort.

Losses to enemy action were heavy and suffering unimaginable - in just under six years an estimated 2,627 ships aggregating 11,396,900 gross registered tons of shipping were lost and 29,180 seafarers died. During the course of the war over 6,000 awards were given.

It is interesting to record that at the last of the War Cabinet's regular Battle of Atlantic meetings, the Prime Minister expressed the view that the number of decorations and awards made to the merchant navy was inadequate. He then invited the First Sea Lord and the Minister of War Transport to take a second look.

Appendix 1: Organization of
a typical British shipping company

General Manager: a businessman; unlikely to have had sea-going experience - responsible to the Board of Directors for the successful management of' the company and its ships. Under his direction the following undertake the overall day-to-day commercial. operational and technical responsibilities.

Marine Superintendent: former sea-going officer. Usually his previous appointment would have been as Commodore; heads the shore-based administration that looks after the operational side of the ships and crews: responsible for Port turnaround, refits, liaison with Lloyd's Register and the Board of Trade. Controls all the company's marine staff and the shore boatswain and riggers.

Engineering Superintendent: former sea-going officer. Usually his previous appointment would have been as a senior chief engineer; heads the shore-based administration that looks after the marine engineering and mechanical side of the company's ships.

Superintendent Purser: former sea-going officer. Usually his previous appointment would have been as a senior purser; heads the department of the shipping company that looks after the passengers, he is responsible for the sea-going pursers and chief stewards and for ensuring that the Stores Manager responds to their requests.

Freight Manager: assisted by a Cargo Superintendent, this manager heads the earning side of the shipping company and looks after liability and insurance, bills of lading and customs. The Inward section of his department looks after home bound cargo and the Outward section looks after export cargo.

Stores Manager: heads the stores department and is responsible for ordering and arranging the supply of seaman like, engineering and domestic stores to the fleet.

Bunkering Superintendent: heads the bunkering department and is responsible for arranging supply of adequate and correct fuel to all ships of the fleet.

Chief Accountant: heads the department responsible for arranging the payment of wages and accounts.

Appendix 2: Ministry of Shipping
13 October 1939 - 1 May 1941

Ministers	Date of appointment
Lt-Col Rt Hon Sir John Gilmour MP	13 October 1939
Rt Hon Robert Spear Hudson MP	3 April 1940
Rt Hon Ronald Hibbert Cross MP	14 May 1940
Parliamentary Secretary	
Sir J. Arthur Salter, MP	13 October 1939
Director-General	
Sir Cyril W. Hurcomb	13 October 1939

Appendix 3 : Control of shipbuilding and repair

Under Regulation 55 of the Defence Regulations 1939, restrictions on the repair of ships came into effect on 4 September 1939. No work was allowed to continue or to be undertaken without a licence issued by the Board of Trade. In addition a restriction was placed on the construction of ships. No construction was permitted unless ordered by a Government department or issued with a Board of Trade licence. In February 1940 the Ministry of Shipping's shipbuilding and repair division was transferred to the Admiralty. This enabled naval and merchant ship building and repair to be under a single authority with a regional organization to keep in touch with the shipbuilding and repair companies. The Controller of Merchant Shipbuilding and Repair was given a seat on the Admiralty Board.

Appendix 4 : Battle of the Atlantic Committee

Chaired by the Prime Minister, this was a War Cabinet committee (*see Chapter 29*). The first meeting was held on 19 March 1941 and the 16th meeting was held on 22 October 1941. Two further meetings occurred in February and May 1942 and by November it appears to have been replaced by the PM's Anti-U-boat Committee.

Appendix 5: Ministry of War Transport
1 May 1941-1 April 1946*

Minister	Date of Appointment
Rt Hon Lord Leathers	1 May 1941

Parliamentary Secretaries	
Rt Hon J. J. Llewellin MP	1 May 1941
Rt Hon Sir Arthur Salter MP	29 June 1941
Philip Noel-Baker MP	4 February 1941

Director-General	
Sir Cyril W. Hurcomb	1 May 1941

Deputy Director-General (Shipping I)	
Sir E. Julian Foley	1 May 1941

Director-General (Shipping II)	
T. Gilmour Jenkins	1 May 1941

Director-General (Inland Transport)	
Reginald H. Hill	1 May 1941

* *Under the Ministers of the Crown (Transfer of Functions) Act, the function of the Ministry were transferred to the Minister of Transport with effect from 1 April 1946.*

Appendix 6: Divisions of the Ministry of War Transport

Statistical and Intelligence
Establishment
General
Public Relations
Finance (Inland Transport)
Costs Investigation
Inland Transport (special duties)
Canals
Railways
Road Transport
Coal

Allocation of tonnage
Commercial Services
Sea Transport
Marine A and rates of hire
Marine B
Marine C
Tanker
Ship Repairs
Finance & Accounts (Shipping)
Rates & Charges
Port & Transit Control
Liner
Ship Management
Coasting & Short Sea Shipping
Foreign Shipping Relations

Appendix 7: Diversion (Shipping) Room

The Diversion Room was set up in September 1939 by the Ministry of Transport. It took the form of a living jigsaw of the merchant shipping scene - ships, convoys, cargoes - in order to determine the ports to which ships should be directed for discharge and/or loading.

Appendix 8: Bunker Control Committee

Responsible to the Ministry of Shipping and later the Ministry of War Transport, this inter-departmental committee included the Foreign Office and major ministries. Policy was established by the Ministry of Economic Warfare. The Bunker Control Committee was responsible for the allocation of fuel to ships. ships applied for bunkers through local Customs authorities. The Committee established the White and Black Lists. Shipowners who did not comply with British requirements were placed on the Black List and denied bunkers from any British sources. Shipowners were invited to be placed on the White List by making a suitable undertaking to the British authorities. The White and Black Lists were widely employed after January 1940.

Appendix 9 : Ministry of War Transport
- an example of the UK Regional structure

Bristol Channel Region   Bristol area
                                                Cardiff area
                                                Swansea area
                                                Milford Haven area
Mersey ports from Holyhead to Silloth   Liverpool area
                                                Manchester area
                                                Barrow, Workingham,
                                                Whitehaven, Maryport and
                                                Silloth
Clyde and West Scotland   Glasgow area
                                                Clyde anchorage emergency
                                                    port (overside discharge)
                                                Greenock area
                                                Oban
                                                Loch Ewe
Leith area - Leith, Dundee, Aberdeen, Burntisland and Grangemouth etc
Methil
Tyne area - Blyth, Sunderland, Hartlepool and Middlesborough
Humber area - Hull, Immingham, Grimsby and Goole
Ipswich
London
Belfast

Appendix 10: Example of Some of the Publications and Instructions issued to British Merchant Ships

Board of Trade/ Ministry of Shipping/Ministry of War Transport:
M notices (weekly)

Sea Transport Division:
Sea Transport Instructions

Admiralty:
Admiralty Notices to Mariners
Admiralty Fleet Orders (weekly)
Confidential Admiralty Fleet Orders

In addition there were various OU (Official Use) books and W/T material.

Admiralty Trade Division:
Admiralty Merchant Shipping Instructions (weekly)
Confidential Admiralty Merchant Shipping Instructions
Naval Control Service Instructions
Instructions for Commodores of Convoys
Mercantile Convoy Instructions
DEMS General Instructions
DEMS Temporary Memoranda

Sources

For the most part this study is based on primary source material mainly official records and publications of the period that are held in the Public Record Office, Kew and in the Naval Historical Branch and Ministry of Defence Library (Naval), London.

The three main published sources relevant to British merchant shipping in this period are the daily newspaper *Lloyd's List*, *Lloyd's Register of Shipping* (annual), the trade journal *Fairplay* and *Brassey's Naval Annual*.

Primary sources - official material
Admiralty Fleet Orders (various issues)
Admiralty Merchant Shipping Instructions (various issues)
British Imperial Calendar and Civil Service List (various issues)
Confidential Admiralty Fleet Orders (various issues)
Merchant Shipping Acts (various)
Defence of the Realm Act

Defence (General) Regulations 1939
Hansard (various issues)
King's Regulations and Admiralty Instructions
M Notices (DTp Marine Library)
Ministers of the Crown (Minister of Shipping) Order, 1939, The
Minister of Shipping (Transfer of Functions) Order, 1939, The
Ministers of the Crown (Minister of War Transport) Order, 1941, The
Ministers of the Crown (Transfer of Functions) The Ministry of War Transport (Dissolution) Order, 1946, The
Notes of War Cabinet - Battle of Atlantic Meeting of Ministers (NHB)
Outline of the work of Trade Division (NHB)
Protection of Shipping at Sea CB 01764(39) (Provisional Issue) February 1939, Plan Division, Naval Staff, Admiralty (NHB)
SR&O 1086 of 1939 Emergency Powers (Defence) Repair of Ships
SR&O 1087 of 1939 Emergency Powers (Defence) Construction of Ships
Public Record Office, Kew
ADM1/9501 Convoys at the outset of a war with Germany (1938)
ADM1 16/3128 Naval Control Service, Operational Policy (1926)
CAB4/26 The Protection of Seabome Trade CID 1368(1932)
MT25/22 Powers of Shipping controller: transfer of Admiralty Transport Department
MT23/203 Admiralty Transport Department, duties of
MT23/227 HM Transport Service Regulations
MT25/62 papers on registration of government ships, Ship Management Branch merging with BoT Transport Branch; Naval Sea Transport Branch
MT25/75 papers on the authority and functions of Director of Transport, Director of Naval sea Transport, British Shipping Control, Ministry of Shipping
MT40 Sea Transport, correspondence and papers including general regulations of Admiralty and Board of Trade regarding Sea Transport Duties in peace and war.
MT45 Shipping establishment and organization, correspondence and papers covering Ministry of Transport and formation of Ministry of War Transport
MT59/489 correspondence on control of shipping and on requisition or control by licence
MT59/1069 correspondence on provision of tonnage for the sea conveyance of commodities (1938)
MT59/2255 Comprehensive scheme for bunker control
MT63 Ports & Transit, correspondence and papers

Secondary sources are listed in the Consolidated Bibliography.

9

The Organizations:
The Admiralty and the Western Approaches

by H. P. Willmott

There are some historians who, it would seem, cannot put pen to paper without subtracting from the sum of human understanding. I have always experienced too many difficulties trying to understand what did happen to worry myself about imaginary scenarios. When I was asked to write this chapter, little did I realize the paucity, particularly in Washington, of material concerning the administration of the Admiralty in World War II: as a leading - perhaps *the* leading - naval academic in Britain noted recently, we probably know more about the workings of the Admiralty in the 1740s than the 1940s. Such a situation was somewhat unfortunate for a chapter on Admiralty Organization; but I was forced to recognize that in the past I, like many others, had been occasionally guilty of resorting to historical shorthand. Using a general term such as 'the Admiralty' implies - not necessarily accurately - an understanding of its meaning in points of critical detail. One speaks of 'the Admiralty' with the ruggedly confident sense that everyone knows what one means, and in one sense we do: the Admiralty was that one part of the Royal Navy where *sang froid* was indistinguishable from *rigor mortis*.

I have been instructed to consider the subject of Admiralty Organization under three headings - in reverse order, the workings of the Admiralty in the conduct of the battle of the Atlantic, the organization of the Admiralty in the period 1939-1943, and the position of trade defence in the inter-war navy's scheme of things. With respect to the latter, I have been instructed specifically to consider what, in popular terms, may be defined as 'reasons for the unpreparedness of the RN to meet the U-boat threat' at the outbreak of war. Wondering how best to consider the whole question of the RN's inter-war position towards trade defence, I recalled a remark made on an essay I once wrote - 'For every complicated problem there is a simple solution: neat, plausible and wrong.' Turning then for assistance to *Engage the Enemy More Closely*, I read that Jutland

> befogged the Royal Navy's thinking over the entire horizon of maritime warfare in the years before the Second World War, and not just with regard to the design of destroyers or the relative importance of battleships or carriers. The role of the British submarine service, for its part, was seen merely as ancillary to the operations of the battlefleet....But far more dangerous was the Admiralty's parallel neglect of the potential threat to Britain's own survival posed by *enemy* submarines. The neglect - or rather, minimising - of this was truly

remarkable....the Admiralty in the 1920s and 1930s chose to believe that technical progress in the performance of sonar would 'greatly lessen the effectiveness of the submarine as a weapon against shipping'.[1]

Here one has the conventional view of an assumed Admiralty failure - its belief that sonar and, I would add, convoy would prove the masters of the U-boat. One is inclined to think that this view describes rather than explains. But as a more serious criticism, one is inclined also to think that if indeed the Admiralty believed that sonar and convoy would prove the masters of the U-boat, then the Admiralty was correct. Sonar and convoy *were* the basis of Allied victory in the Battle of the Atlantic. Other elements had to be added: the improved weapons that were developed during the war, radar, aircraft operating in the close support of shipping, and Allied Intelligence superiority. By themselves sonar and convoy would not have brought victory; but they were the bedrock of success.

Conventional wisdom does not lead us very far in understanding this 'underestimation' by the Admiralty of the threat posed by the U-boat. It is therefore worthwhile questioning the conventional wisdom. I would suggest four matters which, properly researched and considered in combination, might provide an explanation rather than a description of events.

The first is perhaps esoteric. The Royal Navy's aversion to cerebral activity is proverbial, and there is little if any doubt that the RN of the inter-war period was institutionally and by the example of its leaders a somewhat inhospitable organization when it came to such matters as the intellectual effort that would have been needed for in-depth operational analysis. One would not suggest that it did not have the individuals capable of analysing the U-boat campaign of WWI and of developing a comprehensive trade defence concept accordingly, but, as the Naval Staff History of trade defence in WWII noted,

the fact remained that in the inter-war period the Royal Navy never undertook any systematic examination and analysis of the *guerre de course* waged against Allied shipping in the course of the First World War. At no time was there any study that related the number of operational U-boats to the number of merchantmen which they sank, and there was no analysis of the role of anti-submarine units at the time when they made kills. There was no attempt to examine the loss of time and tonnage imposed by independent routeing of merchantmen, and there was no attempt to examine the implications of the fact that in the First World War the number of ships sailing in convoys and the number of U-boats sunk both increased at much the same rate, the figures of one quarter excepted.[2]

Many of the individuals concerned with the convoy controversy of 1917 and the post-war historical controversies were men who found themselves off-side professionally and personally on most issues, isolated and lacking influence in a navy unreceptive to the type of academic, critical analysis which was needed to understand and learn from events in the Battle of the Atlantic in WWI. Some, such as Dyer, would have proved difficult colleagues in any walk of life, not just in the naval service; others, such as Henderson, did reach flag rank - but he did so at the end of a career that changed direction into *matériel* after his contribution to ASW. It is very noticeable that of the individuals who made their names in ASW during WWII, none had been an ASW specialist and none had been particularly conspicuous in the inter-war navy. In 1935 less than 1% of naval specialization had been in ASW: it was not the route to a flag.[3] During the inter-war years, there were individuals who might have provided the all-important element of continuity in the examination of the record, but they lacked the personal and institutional authority to influence a service which never greatly valued staff duties and intellectual activity. The point is a serious one: the under-officered inter-war RN was ill-placed to develop a body of ASW doctrine firstly, because it had very few officers from whom to draw for the development of its professional knowledge; secondly, because by the paucity of their numbers those officers were over-worked; and thirdly, and most importantly, because it lacked the institutional structure and the sympathy to accommodate those who might have provided it with a knowledge and understanding of ASW. One may be guilty of reading into the record a significance that was never there, but it is perhaps worth recalling that the Naval Historical Branch was created, at least unofficially, 'to periodically remind Their Lordships of the importance of convoy' - not to explain why it worked. It may be somewhat unkind to say so, but for the leadership, perhaps, the Naval Historical Branch was, like convoy, a substitute for thought rather than the means of encouraging it.

More substantially, the inter-war period was dominated by economy and by the absence of an enemy. These are well-known facts, but it seems that historians seldom recognize their full implications as reasons for the position in which the RN found itself in 1939. For all but two or three years of the inter-war period the RN lacked an enemy. The threats posed by Germany in general and U-boats in particular emerged very late indeed, not until 1938-39. Of the two potential enemies which emerged earlier, both Japan and Italy posed only regional threats, and neither could move against trade vital to Britain's existence and security. Moreover, in the inter-war period, with Britain unable to match the comprehensive re-building of the Japanese and US battle-lines, there most certainly never was the cash for trade defence. Any attempt to have built up British anti-submarine forces before the last couple of years prior to the outbreak of war would have been for both the nation and the navy financially irresponsible and strategically irrelevant. In Britain's straitened inter-war circumstances, any attempt on the part of the RN to have developed anti-submarine forces would have encountered a very predictable response from the Treasury.

Given that the U-boat threat was very late in developing, this points to the possibility that the RN in 1939 was, perhaps, not as badly placed to conduct the defence of shipping as is often assumed. Certainly it was no worse placed to conduct the defence of trade than was the German Navy to conduct an offensive. Until very late before the outbreak, the RN did not have to face the threat posed by a powerful surface force in the North Sea. Nor did it have to face a submarine threat, and there was little in the way of an air threat. In fact, for almost all the inter-war period the RN could have conducted a German war with all the benefits that would have accrued had Jutland proved an annihilating victory: it could have operated in the southern North Sea and mined to the enemy coastline. One claims no originality in this statement, but a consideration of the warships under construction and the deployment of RAF Coastal Command in 1939 is interesting. Suited to short, steep seas, the general-purpose *Hunt*-class escorts, short-range *Flower*-class corvettes and sloops with a main armament of AA guns and fitted for mine warfare were not being built for Atlantic duties; designs for ocean-going frigates were not approved until autumn 1940 and spring 1941. At the outbreak of war, two RAF groups, comprising almost 70% of Coastal Command's frontline strength, were stationed on the east coast and eastern Channel; only one group covered the Western Approaches. RN construction and RAF deployment thus suggest an intention to complete in a new German war what Britain had been unable to do in the Great War: namely, to seal off the North Sea and throttle the U-boat threat at source, thereby leaving a residual high seas threat to wither.

For most of the inter-war period such a strategy would have worked, and, indeed, it is possible to argue that for the first seven or eight months of WWII the strategy was not ineffective. Two-thirds of all shipping losses were incurred by neutrals, not by Britain; half of Germany's ocean-going U-boats were sunk; the high seas threat was neutralized. Of course, the monoplane's entry into widespread service undercut such a concept, but again this was a very late development. The main conventional criticism of Admiralty unpreparedness would seem to be directed not to 1939 but to 1940, arising primarily as a result of the collapse and partial occupation of France - and it beggars belief that the RN can be justly censured for not having plans based upon the premise of the defeat of Britain's only ally.

Turning to matters of organization, an immediate problem arises in seeking to provide an account of the Admiralty's workings. The system evidently functioned because those within it understood its parts; but those parts do not readily translate into wire diagrams for one simple reason - namely that the available record (the files of the Public Record Office's ADM1 series) fails to provide the essential element of continuity in setting down the changes of personnel and duties of various divisions and their subordinate officers[4] and the exact demarcation of duties between the different departments.[5]

However, even an inadequate record can cast evidence on certain matters that are cause for wonder. This author was struck by two views expressed in the first month of the war which quite contradict the argument that the inter-war Admiralty knew what it was it was doing. One of these said there was no need for an ASW division; the other disagreed, but noted that whereas it had taken three years and 41 officers in the ASW division to prevail in WWI, the ACNS did 'not think for a moment that we shall need anything like such a large division now'.[6] Similarly, there might seem nothing surprising about the observation of 'the importance of having some senior representative of the Air Staff engaged with the Trade Division in a continuous and centralized study of convoys, routeing and protective measures generally' - except that the observation was made more than three years after the outbreak of war, in a minute from the Ministry of War Transport to the Admiralty dated 25 December 1942.[7]

On wider issues, it is well known that the Admiralty organization underwent considerable change, but perhaps less well known is the fact that before November 1942, the Trade Division - and, it would seem, the OIC - did not have a single chart combining the positions of both merchantmen and warships.[8] It is likewise little known that the two major organizational changes, in 1941 and 1943, were joined in two ways. Full proposals for change were made in 1940, partly implemented in 1941, and fully implemented in 1943. The rationale behind the partial implementation in 1941 was that the anti-submarine effort was neither world-wide nor combined. By 1943, however, the effort had ceased to be solely British and limited to the North Atlantic; hence the full implementation of the 1940 proposals.[9]

In terms of the day-to-day running of the Battle of the Atlantic, the record (which is not publicly available) suggests that the Admiralty anti-submarine effort lay within the province of five bodies; and again it was an indication of the lateness of the emergence of the German and U-boat threats that on 1 January 1939, none of these bodies had been constituted. Only one, the Trade Division, already existed, but it was merely a section of the Naval Plans Division. The Operational Intelligence Centre and the U-boat Tracking Room were formed under VCNS in February 1939; the Trade Division was constituted under ACNS (Trade) in May. Though the Admiralty took charge of all British shipping on 26 August 1939, it was not until October, in which month the Ministry of Shipping was formed, that the Anti-Submarine Warfare Division was constituted, again under ACNS (Trade), and it was as part of this Division that ASW analysis and ASW operational research sections were formed after August 1940. There were to be various changes of name and parentage of these bodies, particularly in 1942-43,[10] yet such was 'the Admiralty'. Inevitably it took time to shake down this system and to ensure proper liaison between its various parts, but by 1943 a routine had been established whereby summary reports from the Operations and the Trade Divisions were completed by 0930 daily, when the first liaison meeting of the day was held in the U-boat Tracking Room under ACNS (U-boats and Trade).

This was a review meeting; preparation for executive action, such as the diversion of convoys and the fixing of routes for convoys that were to sail, awaited a second meeting at 1030 headed by the Director Operations Division (Home), again in the Tracking Room and again involving the leading Directors. At or about 1500, the Head of the Tracking Room conducted a review of developments attended by ACNS (Home), the senior Directors and the naval liaison officer attached to HQ Coastal Command. This meeting, which was sometimes attended by VCNS and senior RAF officers, dealt with diversions and the allocation of Escort and Support Groups, and would seem to be the real meeting in terms of executive action. The 1030 meeting reconvened at 1800, and at 2300 the day's final review of events and developments was conducted, again by the same parties to the 1030 and 1800 meetings.

The British anti-submarine effort was directed from the Admiralty by this process of consultation and liaison, and, of course, it was the Admiralty that ordered diversions of shipping and redeployments of escort groups through Western Approaches, specifically in the last years of the war via the Western Approaches transmitter at Criggion in north Wales. After its establishment in October 1940, Western Approaches (along with the Home Fleet and ultimately Coastal Command) came under the operational control of the First Sea Lord, and it was Western Approaches - in its move to Liverpool and in its development of a joint headquarters from the very start of its time on Merseyside - that marked the quickening of the British effort in the Atlantic in 1941. Even at a time when the Air Staff insisted that patrolling the U-boat transit routes represented the most effective contribution that Coastal Command could make to the anti-submarine effort, Western Approaches had naval and air officers co-located and working to ensure that shore-based aircraft operated in close support of convoys. To begin with, this must have been somewhat disheartening, for in the initial phase such efforts were not particularly successful. A technical staff monograph notes unhappily that 'half of the long-range sorties failed to find their designated convoy because of bad homing, while inter-communication left much to be desired.' In late 1942 the RAF set up a special training group with Western Approaches, and in 1943 'remarkable improvements' were registered, with a 90% contact rate being achieved.

This was perhaps a case of a slow but successful sideways movement into the Battle, but it is worth noting that by the time such a return was forthcoming, Western Approaches had under its command 24 Allied escort groups, each with between six and eight warships, plus 30 unassigned escorts, half a dozen escort carriers and a minesweeping flotilla. The manning process that permitted the raising, training and administration of such forces from bases in the Mersey, the Clyde, at Londonderry in Ireland and at Tobermory on the isle of Mull, forms the subject of the next chapter. However, to summarize this chapter, it would appear that despite the undoubted mental sclerosis that afflicted the inter-war Admiralty, the conventional view - that with near-criminal and incomprehensible neglect they overlooked any preparation for a renewed U-boat war with Germany - is wrong. Leaving aside the battleship versus carrier debate, the major failure of imagination, scarcely a culpable one, was not to foretell the fall of France. In the light of painful experience, both inter-war plans and organizations were re-shaped to good effect, but before then, both were in fact suited to the perceived enemy, and worked in the first nine months of hostilities.

Appendix: Organization for the Defence of Trade, Autumn 1943

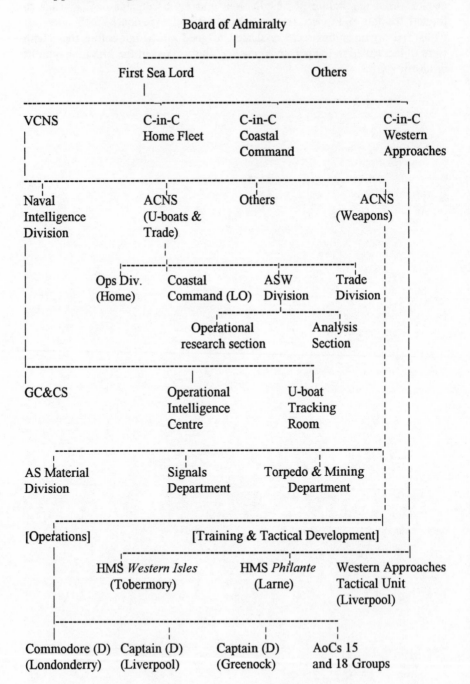

Board of Admiralty

First Sea Lord   Others

VCNS   C-in-C   C-in-C   C-in-C
              Home Fleet   Coastal   Western
                              Command   Approaches

Naval   ACNS   Others   ACNS
Intelligence (U-boats &   (Weapons)
Division   Trade)

              Ops Div.   Coastal   ASW   Trade
              (Home)   Command (LO)   Division   Division

                          Operational   Analysis
                          research section   Section

GC&CS   Operational   U-boat
                  Intelligence   Tracking
                  Centre   Room

AS Material   Signals   Torpedo & Mining
Division   Department   Department

[Operations]   [Training & Tactical Development]

              HMS *Western Isles*   HMS *Philante*   Western Approaches
              (Tobermory)   (Larne)   Tactical Unit
                                                         (Liverpool)

Commodore (D)   Captain (D)   Captain (D)   AoCs 15
(Londonderry)   (Liverpool)   (Greenock)   and 18 Groups

Notes

1. Barnett, *Engage the Enemy More Closely*. pp. 44-5.
2. Naval Staff History, *The Second World War: The Defeat of the Enemy Attack on Shipping 1939-1945 - Volume I: A Study of Policy and Operations*, ch. 1, para 1.
3. This was taken from the Navy List.
4. For example, the Trade Divison was responsible *inter alia* for the routeing of outward convoys (ADM1/12494, Work of the Trade Division) and for liaison with officers abroad concerning certain special shipping and cargoes. Which authority was responsible for the routeing of inward convoys is not clear from the publicly available record consulted by this author. Likewise, it is not clear from ADM1 files which organization bore responsibility for deciding upon and ordering the diversion of convoys at sea. Given the proximity of the various offices within the Citadel, one can only conclude that working practice confounds analysis. Analysis may also be confounded for the opposite reason - an overabundance of information, as in ADM1/9458, List of Admiralty Committees and Committees in which the Admiralty is Interested. This author stopped counting when he reached three figures with 'The Great Barrier Reef Committee', and left unconsidered the committees and sub-committees listed in the remainder of the alphabet. The one that most roused his awe was 'Sub-committee ME/1/1: General Dimensions of Bright Bolts and Nuts', which was part of 'ME/1: Screw Threads, Bolts, Nuts, Set Screws, etc.' One hesitates to consider what was included under the 'etc.'
5. For example, the statement that the Trade Division was responsible for convoy policy with reference to size and that DDOD(H) was responsible for the formulation of escort policy would seem, at the distance of 50 years, to present obvious problems in determining how these two bodies harmonized their respective efforts.
6. Minutes of 25 September 1939 by PAS(A) and ACNS (ADM1, Naval Staff Organization). It is perhaps worth noting that in April 1940, the Treasury remained of the view that the Division was over-staffed, and advised the Admiralty it expected that the latter would be properly alert to the possibilities of economy in its staff establishment.
7. Available in ADM1/14194.
8. This and other matter of administrative detail are to be found in ADM1/10478.
9. References to these matters are to be found in ADM1/14198.
10. For example, in November 1942 ACNS (T) [Trade] was re-hatted as ACNS (UT) [U-boats and Trade]; and in July 1943 the Anti-U-boat Division was from the analysis and operational research sections of the ASW division and transferred to ACNS (UT).

10

Manning and Training the Allied Navies

by William Glover

The accepted wisdoms of how a war at sea might be fought were shattered on 3 September 1939 when the liner *Athenia* was sunk. This, the first U-boat attack of World War II and the opening shot of the Battle of the Atlantic, followed the 'unrestricted' mode of attack established by the Kaiser's navy in the Great War. At once, the Allies had to assume that contrary to international law, all subsequent U-boat attacks would be unrestricted.

To counter this threat - even at the existing level of torpedo and U-boat technology, let alone any developments in those fields - the Allied navies involved in the Battle of the Atlantic had to adopt an entirely new stance. The requirement to protect merchant ships in convoy in turn created demands both for large numbers of escort vessels and for their crews. This specific manpower requirement had to be juggled against other naval tasks and similar calls from the armies and air forces, as well as the continuing need for skilled men in essential industries. The best allocation of national manpower was a decision for each government, but manpower questions also arose within their navies: there, the naval authorities had to arrange the timely provision of trained crews, with the proper balance of rates and trade specialties, to ships as they completed in builders' yards.

This aspect of the rapid wartime growth of navies presented two challenges. First, men had to be trained in numbers and at a speed which the peacetime training establishments could not meet. Second, some had to be trained in skills which were uncommon in civilian society. The physics of wave propagation, in air or water, were still new areas of scientific research, and everyday familiarity with electrical equipment was a development of the post-war years. Hence there was no natural manpower pool of civilians who could easily be trained as radio communicators, radar technicians, or asdic operators. Moreover, the challenge of war required training to a standard that had not been considered in peace.

In the Battle of the Atlantic, these problems affected three Allied navies in particular - the Royal Navy, the Royal Canadian Navy, and the United States Navy, which jointly carried the Battle's major burdens. The history of manning and training ships' companies to serve on convoy escort duty is, in part, the record of how these navies were able to adapt and change while fighting a war.

Before the outbreak of war the RN had been responsible for the training of the RCN, and during the war it trained many members of the British Commonwealth and Empire navies, as well as personnel of some free European navies. In addition, the RN in pre-war years was slightly more concerned about anti-submarine problems than the USN. It is therefore appropriate to begin a discussion of training with a review of A/S in the RN up to 1939, as a benchmark for war developments. A comparison of peace and war training methods and standards then emphasizes the nature and extent of change forced on navies by anti-submarine warfare. Problems of wartime training and manning are most visible in the RCN. Whereas the RN increased approximately six times its pre-war size, and the USN expanded to 10 times its pre-war size, the RCN grew 40-fold.[1] Indeed, it can be argued that over the course of the battle, the RCN, previously a little more than a division of the RN, developed into an independent navy.[2] As will be seen, more stringent standards of acceptable levels of training and efficiency by which actions were judged also evolved during the years 1940-42. Finally, the American response to problems of manning and training, which only developed momentum in 1942, will then be compared with the RN/RCN experience.

The first aspect of the training problem which had to be addressed was that of numbers. How many men with what levels of qualifications would need how much training? Did the facilities and instructors exist to provide it? What was the state of the RN A/S establishment and planning? The pre-war British estimates of 357 escort vessels (of which 200 would be trawlers taken up after mobilization) needed for a European war turned out to be but a small fraction of the total number of ships employed on North Atlantic convoy escort duty. Likewise, the estimated 1,337 Submarine Detector (S/D) ratings[3] thought to be required after mobilization, although nearly double the number available in 1939, were woefully inadequate. In 1939 the anti-submarine branch included 757 S/D ratings, 375 Higher Submarine Detector rates and 73 Submarine Detector Instructors. By 1945 the SDIs had nearly tripled in number, to 204; the HSDs had quadrupled, to 1,492; and the S/D rates had multiplied nearly eight times, to 5,911.[4]

In 1939 'the A/S branch was the cinderella among the specialists' and 'the gunnery branch was accepted as the elite within an elite'.[5] The dominant role of the battleship as 'the backbone of the fleet' was accepted by the naval hierarchy from the First Lord of the Admiralty down.[6] In such a climate of opinion it cannot be surprising that the early fortunes of the A/S branch had been dependent upon the success of the latest piece of new equipment; after the poor results of the Type 115 asdic set in 1928, the Long A/S course had been cancelled.[7] A resurgence in A/S interest had to wait until the decision in 1931 to equip all new destroyers with asdics. (Previously destroyer construction programmes had been alternately fitted with asdics and Twin Speed Destroyer [mine] Sweeping equipment.) This decision was a result of a naval staff paper that examined destroyer needs of the battlefleet and how they could be met under the tonnage limits imposed by the London naval treaty. In practical terms the limit allowed for 13 flotillas of eight destroyers and one leader. In the event of a war in the Far East, the battlefleet in the theatre plus the capital ships remaining in home waters would require 10 destroyer flotillas. The three remaining flotillas would 'be required as destroyer escorts for valuable convoys;

and it is considered that at least 2 of them should be Asdic'.[8] It was concluded that in the event of a Far Eastern war, seven of the permitted 13 destroyer flotillas should be asdic-equipped and six fitted for minesweeping. European war needs would be different. Estimates were more difficult because 'no European power possesses a battlefleet comparable to our own; a fleet action is therefore unlikely, and the battlefleet is more likely to be employed as cover, or support for operations of smaller units'.[9] However, the submarine threat was held to be considerably higher in European waters, and 'attack on British lines of communications by submarine is likely to prove a primary liability'.[10] The conclusion, although reached within the context of the battlefleet needs rather than broader defence requirements, seemed inescapable:

> It would appear therefore that British destroyers should all be fitted with Asdic equipment, and that a proportion of them should have mine-sweeping gear in addition. There is no disadvantage, or loss of efficiency in either capacity, if both are fitted; on the other hand, there are certain very great advantages. The C-in-C would have the assurance that every destroyer was equipped to deal with submarines immediately and effectively; and would not be hampered with question of reliefs for fuelling, refitting, etc. Moreover it is considered that the fact that every destroyer was Asdic fitted, and therefore a potential submarine killer, would have a great morale effect. On the other hand, the ineffectiveness of the non-Asdic fitted destroyer (in anti-submarine work) is well known.[11]

The proposal was approved. The implications for the A/S branch were considerable, and the struggle to expand the branch to meet the increased A/S needs of the fleet was time-consuming.

    The first need was for additional instructors at HMS *Osprey*, the anti-submarine school at Portland. The request, submitted by the Captain A/S (*Osprey*'s Commanding Officer) and forwarded through the Commander-in-Chief Portsmouth, began circulation within the Admiralty on 30 April 1932. Three and a half months later, it was minuted: 'It is very desirable that an early decision should be obtained'.[12] After considerable discussion about the nature of the additional instruction and what sort of background was needed (or the minimum acceptable), whether the increased staff might be a schoolmaster, lieutenant commanders over the promotion zone, or submarine detector instructors, and what the short- and long-term additional costs would be for the various alternatives, at last, on 25 October 1932, somewhat grudging authority to increase the instructional staff was granted. Appointments were to be shown as temporary, and were to be reconsidered in two years.[13] Before that review was made, Captain A/S had submitted a request for a new regulating officer, because of the increased teaching load. However, coming in addition to the review of the previously allowed temporary positions, this request ran headlong into Confidential Admiralty Fleet Order 2677/33 of 9 November 1933.[14] That order had announced the policy of reducing the numbers of lieutenants and lieutenant commanders in the navy, and said in part:

> Proposals involving either:
> (a) An increase to the authorised complements of Lieutenant-Commanders or Lieutenants, or
> (b) an increase in the requirements of executive specialist officers,
> should not be put forward unless of such importance as to justify a departure from the policy laid down above.
> Should an increase in any particular ship or establishment be deemed essential and accordingly asked for, it should, whenever possible be accompanied by proposals for a corresponding or greater reduction elsewhere.[15]

Far from proposing greater reductions elsewhere, Captain A/S had proposed an expansion of the buildings and instructional facilities at the school. The requests received minute examination at the Admiralty. In some quarters the reasons were accepted, but the climate did not easily support expansions. Commenting on a proposed draft reply to Captain A/S, the Naval Assistant to the Second Sea Lord observed, 'no objection is seen to Captain A/S being informed that his proposals for increases in instructional staff are under consideration, but it is considered the word "favourable" should be omitted, as it may create a false impression.'[16]

The A/S branch would have appreciated knowing it stood in anyone's favour. A specialist branch could scarcely have had a lower profile. In 1935, approximately 88% of the lieutenants in the RN specialized in one branch or another, yet only 11 of 1,029 lieutenants and 16 of 972 lieutenant commanders had specialized in A/S.[17] This lack of popularity of A/S cannot be considered surprising. Not only was gunnery the dominant branch of the navy, but it was perfectly possible for a junior officer to go through training up to the rank of lieutenant without any A/S instruction at all. In a 22-page Admiralty Fleet Order outlining junior officers' training, the sole mention of A/S came in the description of training in destroyers. The entry 'Asdic screening, minesweeping' appeared as one of several items included under tactics. But even this brief exposure was not certain, for it was only provided 'on stations where destroyer training can be arranged', and then only for three or four months.[18] With this possible exception, all of a junior officer's sea time while under training was spent in ships of cruiser size or larger. It is interesting to note that notwithstanding the low esteem in which air was widely held, the same order made specific provision for all junior officers, either as midshipmen or as sub-lieutenants, to have a three-week air introductory course.[19] The real difficulty of the A/S branch is emphasized when the provision of officer training in A/S is compared with that for signals. That was an established part of the curriculum for cadets, midshipmen and acting sub-lieutenants, with an examination which counted towards seniority for promotion to lieutenant. Yet even so, the low profile of signals training was blamed for the shortage of officers specializing in signals.[20] Things would not improve for the A/S branch as regards training for junior officers. A 1938 study on the training of junior and specialist officers found that 'the institution of the special course in these subjects [A/S and Mine Sweeping] for Acting Sub-Lieutenants is at present impracticable'.[21]

Regardless of how low a profile the A/S branch might have had, or how unpopular it might have been when compared with other branches of the service, the requests for expansion of *Osprey*'s facilities forwarded by the Captain A/S could not be ignored if the the the battlefleet was to be provided adequate A/S protection. The Defence Requirements Committee, established in the wake of the infamous 'Ten Year Rule', fully recognized the urgent need. The various reports submitted by that committee supported A/S re-equipment as a high spending priority, although the actual sums recommended were the smallest of any of the categories.[22] The rate of growth of the branch was limited not only by the amount of money available in competition with other needs, but by the number of experienced officers and ratings available for appointments. Furthermore, the submarines necessary for S/D instruction were seldom available for training exercises.

Notwithstanding these difficulties, some very useful groundwork for later expansion was completed. In October 1937 the Tactical Division of the naval staff provided a comprehensive paper on 'The Provision and Training of Anti-Submarine Personnel'. Appendices to the paper included a list of the necessary instructional books, an 'outline of minimum requirements for an anti-submarine school for instructing reserve personnel and for periodical training of all S.D. personnel', an 'outline of minimum requirements for an anti-submarine school for instructing A/S officers and all classes of A/S personnel', and nine detailed course outlines varying from a 10-day course for commanding officers and first lieutenants of destroyers, through a 96-day course for Submarine Detector Instructors, to a 14-day course for an RNR Submarine Detector.[23] This level of detail was provided in the hope that 'a Dominion or Colony may desire to possess some less elaborate establishment' (than that at Portland).[24] It was noted that 'to achieve the destruction of the submarine in the ensuing operations, GOOD TEAM WORK IS ESSENTIAL between the Asdic operators and the Officers on the bridge and also between individual ships engaged in operations'.[25] This paper had been prepared with the needs of wartime mobilization firmly in view. It did not stand alone.

War had been presaged by a series of international crises created by the dictators with an increasing frequency and intensity. The first upheavals of the Abyssinian crisis in 1935 led to an examination of the individual training which would be offered after mobilization. Discussion focused on new entry cadets to the RN and specialist training. At first it was proposed that the sub-lieutenants' technical and educational courses and all specialist training should be suspended. Certain courses might be reintroduced when the duration of the conflict and needs could be estimated.[26] Almost immediately it was noted that the A/S branch was already beginning an expansion, the need for which would become even greater in the event of war. A/S specialist training might be shortened, but it could not be cancelled. In the light of future experience, it is interesting to note that the Director of the Tactical Division believed

> it is not considered that RNR Officers can be trained as Lieutenants A/S in peace time. After mobilisation it would probably be possible to select suitable officers and there seems to be no objection to so doing provided they come up to the standard required.[27]

The debate continued long after the immediate tension of the Abyssinian crisis had passed. Perhaps the most controversial suggestion came jointly from the Director of Training and Staff Duties and the Head of the Commissions and Warrants Branch in October 1937. They suggested that 'unless the DSD [Director of the Signals Division] and D of N [Director of Navigation] strongly desire to the contrary it is proposed that Acting Sub-Lieutenants' courses in Signals and Navigation be suspended'.[28] Not surprisingly the two Directors did 'desire to the contrary'. DSD minuted:

> 2. On the outbreak of war the importance of communications cannot be over-emphasised and the need of an officer in every ship with a knowledge of the subject will be strongly felt.
>
> 3. A proposal to lower the standard of knowledge of the officers at a time when the general standard of the personnel must inevitably fall below the normal peace time standard due to the influx of Reserves and 'Hostilities only' ratings, is most undesirable.[29]

The Director of Navigation observed that 'this vitally essential period of training is "but a small price to pay" for the officer's increased efficiency as an Officer of the Watch, and the additional safety to H.M. Ships accorded thereby'.[30] In November 1938 it was finally approved that after mobilization the RN sub-lieutenants' courses would be curtailed. A five-week gunnery course would be given, and torpedo, navigation, and signals would be allowed three weeks each. Additionally, the long gunnery, torpedo, and signals specialist courses would be reduced to six months each, and the long A/S course to 4½ months.[31] These staff papers and discussions had raised the question of what training was essential and how much time could be spared for it. Even though the question was being considered only in the context of limited numbers of RN officers, it was a start. As such it provides a useful point of comparison for the wartime training given the Reserves and 'Hostilities Only' personnel.

The harsh realities of war forced the change of a number of peacetime perceptions. Not merely the existing reserves but civilians joining a volunteer reserve were capable of doing and, of course, were called upon to do much more than might previously have been thought possible. Furthermore, there was less time available to provide them even basic new entry training than had been considered necessary for RN sub-lieutenants. Although it may not have been recognized immediately, the philosophy of the production of officers changed radically. Before the war, when it took the better part of five years to complete the training of a new entry cadet to the standard of a watch-keeping certificate, the young gentlemen had been trained in a manner similar to that of the training of an apprentice. The luxury of learning by seeing and repetition did not exist in war. The opportunity for practical instruction at sea under supervision in a training environment was severely curtailed. It seldom amounted to more than two weeks. Instead volunteer reserve new entry officers had to be educated. Having been taught the theory of a subject, and given some minimal drill in procedures, they had to consolidate and learn to apply their instruction while on active service. Their ability to do that well and quickly was in part a function of the rate of expansion of the particular navy and the likelihood of an individual serving under an officer either of the regular force or from the professional merchant seamen's reserve.

A practical problem of the war was the need for expanded training facilities. As early as 5 August 1939, Hove Marina in Sussex, on England's south coast, had been tentatively identified as the site of the future RNVR officers' training establishment, HMS *King Alfred*. It was commissioned as that on 11 September.[32] The first courses, offered to members of the Royal Naval Volunteer Supplementary Reserve, were three months. Beginning in January 1940, officer candidates were selected from Commissions and Warrants candidates who had first joined the service as ratings. When this became the standard form of officer selection, the course could be shortened to 10 weeks, as elementary seamanship would have already been covered. The 10-week course provided instruction in navigation (52 hours), pilotage (20 hours), gunnery (29 hours), seamanship (38 hours), field training (22 hours), general lectures (23 hours), signals (34 hours), and torpedo (13 hours).[33] Officers appointed to serve in Western Approaches - perhaps as few as 10% of the *King Alfred* graduates - then went on to HMS *Osprey* for an anti-submarine course.[34]

With this British pre-war standard and the example of *King Alfred* as a reference for war expansion, attention should now turn to the Royal Canadian Navy, and its wartime expansion problems of manning and training.

In contrast to the RNVR, the primary focus of officers' training in the Royal Canadian Naval Volunteer Reserve became anti-submarine and convoy escort work for the North Atlantic battle. Before the war, all individual training for the RCN permanent force (beyond basic new entry courses for ordinary seamen) had been done in Britain with the RN. The RCN Barracks on the east and west coasts had limited facilities and a seasonal organization for training the RCNR and RCNVR, both very small. Therefore, after Canada's declaration of war on

10 September 1939, one of the first requirements was the creation of a training system. In the early months of the war, training was conducted on a rather *ad hoc* basis. Reservists who were available were given additional training, following closely the guidelines of existing courses. The first significant step towards creating new training facilities for an expanding service did not occur until January 1940.

HMCS *Stone Frigate* (originally the dockyard building for the early 19th-century RN dockyard on Lake Ontario at Kingston) was commissioned as an officers' training establishment on 3 January 1940. The first group of 33 Supplementary Reserve officers arrived to begin an eight-week introductory course on 8 January. The course content and emphasis were quite different from those of the *King Alfred* course. Pilotage was given 66 hours, and navigation (which included astro-navigation) had 40 hours. Signals received 60 hours (nearly double the *King Alfred* amount), seamanship 56 hours, drill 18 hours, Commanding Officer's and other general service lectures, 24 hours.[35] On graduation the officers went to Halifax where they received a further six weeks of training. This included a three-week gunnery and discipline course, a two-week torpedo course, and a week at sea in *Acadia*, an elderly hydrographic vessel pressed into service as a training ship.[36] Three courses were run along these lines before *Stone Frigate* was paid off. The combination of the *Stone Frigate* courses and the more practical instruction at Halifax provided a very good new entry course indeed. However, not all officers joining the RCNVR received such a solid grounding, and after the Kingston school was closed in late June, there was no proper structured officers' introductory course for almost three months.

Conspicuous by its absence from the early training in Canada was instruction in A/S. Quite simply, until Lieutenant (A/S) James W. White, RN, arrived in Halifax on 17 November 1939, there was no one qualified to run any courses. The RCN had only two specialist A/S officers, both of whom 'had qualified about 1927 and had not been employed in connection with Asdics since that time'.[37] White's first task was to build an Anti-Submarine School. This was ready for operation the following February. The entire range of instruction from basic operation of a trawler asdic set to A/S control officer had to be offered. The longest course was a two-week introduction to A/S for commanding officers.

Before the fall of France, Canada's war policy had been ruled by economic and financial considerations. 'The reign of the dollar' fell with France.[38] After the collapse, the Chief of Naval Staff, Rear Admiral Percy Nelles, made commitments which demanded an immediate expansion of the naval services to provide crews. First, as a result of discussion begun in late July, he confirmed that Canada would provide delivery crews for the first 10 RN corvettes that were being built in Canada.[39] Second, six USN destroyers being given to Britain under the lend-lease arrangement were transferred to Canada.[40] These 16 ships were in addition to the 47 corvettes and minesweepers under construction whose delivery was expected before the spring of 1941[41] and the personnel demands for port services, control of shipping, and other auxiliary and support functions. Naturally this sudden increase caused a manning crisis. Not only were there not enough trained men to go around, but there were neither the instructors nor space at Halifax to train the numbers of men needed. In response to manning concerns raised by the Commanding Officer Atlantic Coast, Commodore H. E. Reid, RCN, a conference to discuss recruiting and training was held at Ottawa in late August. As a result, steps were taken to institute an officers' training programme for all new entry officers, and the gunnery, A/S, torpedo, and signals schools recently established at Halifax were expanded. However, the pressure to put ships to sea as soon as they became available meant that for the first few officers' courses, standards were set aside, on the basis that someone who had failed a course was better trained than someone who had not had it at all. Obviously this had to have an impact on the operational efficiency of the ships.

The word 'efficient' was used to describe what in the 1990s is called the combat readiness of a warship. As standards of individual training changed significantly in the early years of the war, so did the definition of 'efficient'. Again, a useful benchmark to measure the change is found in the pre-war RN, in this instance in the discussion about 'continuous commissions' and the best way to achieve operational efficiency. Until 1936, the normal practice was that the Home Fleet would cruise three times a year - in the spring, summer, and autumn. On each cruise, time was allocated for individual ship training, squadron training, and finally fleet training. However, the fleet cruising schedule was not always synchronized with the availability of all its major units. A ship's refit and/or docking schedule was determined without consideration of the sailing schedule. Further, when a ship went into refit, the entire crew was paid off. On completion of the refit the ship was recommissioned with an entirely new crew, who had to be trained together. The Commander-in-Chief Home Fleet, Admiral William Boyle (who succeeded as the 12th Earl of Cork and Orrery on 13 October 1934), used HMS *Renown* as an unfortunate example of a lost asset.

> The RENOWN recommissioned on 3rd May 1934 but will not finally get away from home ports until 20th August 1934, and a ship could scarely have a worse start for her commission. Add to this the six weeks for 'shaking down' and working up (vide C.A.F.O. 2032/32) and it will be five months after commissioning that this ship will take her place in the fleet.[42]

Even after taking her place in the fleet, *Renown* was not considered 'efficient'. In a later letter, 15 September 1934, Boyle wrote:

> For the purposes of differentiating between the various stages of

efficiency it is assumed that a ship may be classed as follows:-

After two cruises.......EFFICIENT
After three cruises.....FULLY EFFICIENT
After anything less
than two <u>complete</u> cruises
she must be considered......INEFFICIENT.[43]

By this standard, *Renown* could not be considered 'Fully Efficient' until July 1935, 15 months after she had been commissioned.[44] (Boyle noted that cruisers and destroyer flotillas, although affected by the same problem, would not experience it to the same degree.) The example of *Renown* was used to substantiate a case for the Home Fleet adopting a policy of 'continuous commission'. This would mean that periodically, small numbers of a ship's company would be changed, but a nucleus would always remain. Thus the operational efficiency of a ship would never be seriously impaired. The idea was scarcely new. It had been discussed in the columns of the *Naval Review* in its first year of publication, 1913.[45] The idea was finally adopted for implementation in the Home Fleet during the summer leave period of 1936.[46]

The move to the continuous commission raises the important question of what were the acceptable standards of operational training before 1939. In this respect the Confidential Admiralty Fleet Order to which Boyle referred is interesting. It had been issued in the wake of the Invergordon mutiny, and attempted to correct a perceived imbalance in favour of equipment- and armament-oriented training at the expense of training the man. It was 'therefore Their Lordships' desire that for the present the training of the Fleet shall be placed on a policy of giving precedence to the development of the personal qualities of individuals'. As regards ships, the Fleet Order merely required that 'adequate time should be given to newly commissioned ships for "shaking down" (four weeks) as a preliminary to a "working up" period (two weeks)'.[47] This Fleet Order and its training philosophy were still current policy in the months before the outbreak of war.[48] When considered in conjunction with the discussion of continuous commissions and that implied standard of acceptable operational efficiency, it is hard not to conclude that a ship on commissioning was expected only to prove all equipment in proper working order, and to train the ship's company to a basic level of sea safety required by knowledge of the watch and quarter bill. Beyond that, an operational fighting standard of efficiency would be developed within the squadron and fleet to which the ship belonged. Six months would appear to have been considered an acceptable time period over which the demanded standard could be attained for other than captial ships. This peacetime standard of operational efficiency could not long survive the outbreak of war.

In the first months of 1940, the need for some form of refresher training for A/S ships was recognized. However, planning for a joint British-French training base at Quiberon Bay was disrupted by the fall of France.[49] As an alternative location, Scotland was selected. The operations of HMS *Western Isles*, the famous working-up base at Tobermory under the command of the legendary Vice Admiral Sir Gilbert Stephenson, began in the fall of 1940. The time allowed for an escort to attain an acceptable battle-ready standard of efficiency was reduced to a maximum of three weeks.[50]

Stephenson quickly found that the escort vessels, almost all of which had a large number of Volunteer Reserve personnel in their ship's company, required very basic training and drilling to mould them into a team that worked together. Although the base was intended for convoy escort vessels, the scope of the work-up had to extend far beyond A/S work, and included such fundamental matters as cleaning messdecks, book-keeping, and cooking.[51] The reason is obvious. Regardless of the quality and thoroughness of classroom instruction, some practical experience is necessary to gain proficiency at a new task or skill. The expansion of navies to meet the needs of war had swept aside the 'apprentice' system of peacetime training, and simultaneously increased the numbers of men who needed to be shown how to do things. In peace, new recruits were easily assimilated in an experienced, even if new, ship's company. The war expansion effectively reversed the ratio of experienced to new men serving in any navy. However, to maintain the fighting integrity of the more valuable ships, the regular-to-reserve ratio in them remained high, with a corresponding imbalance in smaller ships.[52] Regardless of the proportion, the incorporation of reserves and regulars in the same ship's company was referred to as 'dilution'. It was this problem of dilution, and lack of sufficient experienced leadership at the junior and senior rates, and officer levels, that required Stephenson to take such a broad approach to his training of A/S escorts. The problem Stephenson found in RN escorts would have been more severe in the RCN and USN with their proportionately higher ratio of expansion, and therefore of dilution.

The mushrooming growth of the Canadian navy occuring at this time led in 1941 and 1942 to criticisms about its effectiveness at sea. It is important to remember that the scale of growth of the RCN ultimately was proportionately 3½ times larger than either the RN or the USN. When France fell, the mobilized strength of the RCN and its two reserves was almost three times the combined size just after Canada's declaration of war. Between the fall of France and the August manning conference it grew to four times the September 1939 size. At the time of the conference, the RCNVR component accounted for just over 50% of Canada's total naval service.[53] By December 1940, most Canadian ships smaller than destroyer size had an RCNR officer in command with an RCNVR wardroom. Indeed, one of the first ex-USN lend-lease destroyers was commissioned in the RCN with an RCNR commanding officer.[54] Few RCN officers served in escorts smaller than destroyers. By 1942, the number of ships had outstripped the number of suitable RCNR officers available for command, and the first RCNVR officers were appointed to command convoy escorts.[55]

Regardless of the quality of shore instruction an RCNVR officer might have had, for most of them the opportunity to consolidate classroom theory under an experienced officer simply did not exist. The value of the pre-war 'apprentice' style of training and its experience base was certainly recognized by at least some of the RCNVR graduates of HMCS *Kings* (as the Halifax Officers' Training Establishment of 1940 had become).[56] Nor was the problem of dilution limited to the officer ranks. In HMCS *Chambly,* 33 of 51 ratings were RCNVR; 14 including the coxswain and senior engineroom personnel were RCNR, while two leading stokers, one stoker, and one ordinary seaman were the sole lower deck representatives of the RCN.[57] Dilution on this scale, affecting both practical leadership and training at sea, reduced the operational effectiveness of many of the RCN escorts. The following comment of one of the first RCN corvettes to arrive in Britain is representative: 'The A/S team as a whole is good, but their previous training has been almost entirely theoretical, and the experience of operating under actual sea conditions has been something of a shock to them.' The reporting officer concluded with some observations applicable to most of the Canadian ships.

> This low state of efficiency appears to be evident generally in all Canadian-manned Corvettes, except the first three....and is, I consider, attributable directly to the inexperience and perhaps the age of their Commanding Officers. It is recommended that these officers should be relieved by younger Royal Canadian Navy or Royal Canadian Naval Volunteer Reserve officers who have had war experience in Asdic-fitted ships, although it is realized that there is probably a shortage.[58]

At least the author of this statement understood there might be a shortage of the type of officer he would have preferred in command, even if he did not know what an understatement the suggestion of a shortage was.

The attempt to deal with the shortages both of experienced officers and of ratings who could form the nucleus of a raw ship's company led directly to another problem which was the result of a deliberate manning policy of the Naval Service Headquarters of the RCN at Ottawa. As the ships of the Canadian building programme became available throughout 1941, existing ships' companies, formed perhaps only a few months earlier, but with several months' experience at sea, were 'raided' for key personnel for ships newly commissioning. The result was that it was almost impossible for a ship's company to have the stability necessary to develop into a close-knit team. By August 1941 this had become so serious that Commodore L. W. Murray, RCN, Commodore Commanding Newfoundland, felt compelled to complain to Naval Service Headquarters (NSHQ) at Ottawa.

> ....during a recent visit to Halifax, the ship's company of HMCS "COLLINGWOOD" was reduced again to the standard of that of a

newly commissioned ship by the drafting away, under orders of "STADACONA" [the Halifax naval base], of all three Leading Seamen and nine Able Seamen including the two most reliable S.D. ratings.

2. Removals from the crew of HMCS "NIAGARA" were of a similar nature, though I have not the exact figures available.

3. HMCS "NIAGARA" had returned from seven months service abroad, and it was to be expected that there were a few cases of ratings recommended for courses for higher rating; but the drafting appears to have been very much in excess of that required to replace such men.

4. HMCS "COLLINGWOOD" had been absent only two months, and there cannot have been the same reason for such drastic drafting in her case.

....

7. It is pointed out that the ships' companies of HMC Ships (including our best destroyers) have reached their existing state of efficiency, not through the number of higher non-substantive ratings borne, but almost entirely through having worked together from scratch, through being trained by their own officers whom they learn to appreciate, and by constant work with each other. The resultant efficiency is far above that of any one individual, but it only remains as long as that team is kept together.[59]

The inadequacies of RCN ships had already been brought to the attention of NSHQ. Murray's letter was repeating in a stronger fashion what ought to have been familiar complaints. However, in the short term, despite forwarding equally forceful letters from some of his commanding officers, the problem only got worse. On 6 November, noting that the practice of frequent reliefs continued, Murray provided a lurid example of the consequences of dislocating a ship's team of key personnel.

With a Sub-Lieutenant, RCNVR (Temp.) of two months sea experience as Senior Watchkeeper, backed up by a Sub-Lieutenant, RCNVR (Temp.) with no sea experience, and a Mate, RCNR (Temp.) who has lately risen from apprentice in a merchant ship and has never before been to sea in charge of a watch on the bridge, it will be necessary for the Commanding Officer to spend on the bridge as much of every 24 hours as his constitution will stand.

This, coupled with the necessity of acting as Executive Officer of the ship, A/S Control Officer, Gunnery Officer and cypher staff, is more than the best constitution can be expected to support over a period of 28 days, with only a short break of a few hours in harbour in the middle.

....

Only the desperate operational situation which exists off our coast at the present time persuaded me to allow "ORILLIA" proceed with the unit. She is quite unfitted to meet the enemy, and in no other Service would a unit be placed in the firing line before the officers mastered the use of their weapon. She has been allowed to proceed, however, because her presence will fill a gap in the A/S screen visible to the enemy, and her presence may result in the saving of lives of many merchant seamen, in which case the sacrifice of the health of one Commanding Officer would be jusitified.[60]

When NSHQ finally replied on Christmas Eve, it was clear that the need to keep a ship's company together to promote efficiency had not been fully appreciated. 'To man new construction and at the same time maintain a reasonable proportion of substantive and non-substantive rates in sea-going ships and training establishments, it will be necessary to withdraw approximately 20 percent of ratings from the Fleet per quarter.'[61] This figure was significantly higher than that which Admiral Boyle had considered acceptable when he advanced his proposal for continuous commissions for capital ships with periodic small changes to the ship's company.[62]

To meet the immediate personnel demands of war, both the RN and the RCN had to replace pre-war training systems with wartime schools that could provide trained men for the fleet in a shorter time and in larger numbers than any pre-war staff planning had envisaged. The problem of 'dilution' associated with this expansion naturally had an adverse effect on efficiency of ships. In the RCN, early problems of efficiency were further exacerbated by the two deliberate policies cited above. First, in face of desperate operational necessity, senior commanders had little option but to order ships to sea which were known not to be adequately trained, because the possible benefit of the presence of a ship, regardless of training, outweighed the disadvantages of further weakening a numerically small escort.[63] Second, higher authority deliberately imposed a policy which resulted in crew instability, and therefore contributed to inefficiency, in the hope of widening a small pool of limited experience. It must be noted however that this policy did not extend to what were considered the most valuable ships.

Time would help resolve some of these problems. In 1940 the RCN established the training systems which, when fully functioning, were able to meet the personnel demands. These establishments and schools borrowed heavily from the RN, using personnel, materials, and doctrine. Once the manning crisis of the 1940 exponential expansion had passed, the 'luxury' of imposing the requirement of passing examinations before leaving the shore establishment could be restored. Likewise, after the initial surge of sending men to sea, the pool of available expertise increased naturally. The ships in which these men served were brought to a higher operational standard faster than the pre-war norm by HMS *Western Isles* and other establishments set up in its form.

New methods and standards of basic new entry training and for bringing a ship up to an acceptable level of operational efficiency were not, however, enough to win the Battle of the Atlantic. New tactics and new procedures for team training to drill the ships' companies in the tactics were also needed. These were adopted rather more slowly.

The single most important development in this area was the establishment of the Western Approaches Tactical Unit in January 1942. Prime Minister Churchill was certainly instrumental in its creation.[64] The WATU was the work of Commander (later Captain) Gilbert Roberts, who had been trained as a gunnery officer. His tactical floor was modelled closely on a similar floor at HMS *Excellent*, the RN gunnery school at Whale Island. As the name suggests, the focus of the work was on tactical problems, and at the command level. In addition to being used for training, the floor could also be used for analysis of actual convoy battles. In this respect, it was the first real operational A/S analysis facility that the RN had.[65] Almost the first work of the WATU was also its first important success - an examination of convoy HG76. Working through the battles fought by Captain Walker using his 'Operation Buttercup', in the calm of simulation Roberts realized that U-boats were firing their torpedoes from *inside* the convoy. 'This [was] all against our ideas. Walker's escorts imagined that the U-boat must be a mile or so outside the perimeter of the convoy ships....'[66] When Admiral Sir Percy Noble was briefed by Roberts on his analysis he frankly admitted the error of existing anti-U-boat doctrine. He had a message sent to Churchill saying, 'the first investigations showed a cardinal error in anti-U-boat tactics, and that a new, immediate, and corrected [? semi-legible handwritten original] counterattack would be signalled to the Fleet within 24 hours.'[67] The counterattack was called 'Raspberry'. This was shortly followed by a search plan for a submerged U-boat which had sighted and was believed to be trailing a convoy. This was given the name 'Beta Search', and also worked well. The first time it was tried at sea, the U-boat was sunk with the first depth charge pattern.[68] Analysis of this standard, comparable to the operational research work done in Coastal Command on air search patterns, gave a new sophistication to the evolution of A/S tactics. Until the U-boats' basic tactical methods were understood, escorts could do little more than respond blindly with only limited probability of success. The WATU was also helpful with the formulation of emergency responses such as the development of acoustic torpedo 'step aside' counter measures.[69]

The WATU and its work of operational analysis was a natural and logical development following on new training systems and operational efficiency standards. The work-up base at Tobermory moulded escort vessels, manned in large numbers by 'Hostilities Only' personnel, into ships capable of executing operations expeditiously. However, the necessary doctrine for beating the U-boats could not be thought through by individuals serving in ships amidst the stress and fatigue of convoy duty. That could only be done by people dedicated to the task, with adequate resources at hand. Beginning in January 1942 the WATU was the place where that work was done. It was an essential precondition for victory.

The use of the tactical floor of the WATU both for the analysis and development of tactics, and for the tactical training of commanding officers preceded another important training development - team procedures training. These trainers helped turn a collection of individuals, each trained in a specific task, into a team that worked effectively together to achieve a common purpose - in this instance, sinking a U-boat. As individual members of a team changed, the replacements could be integrated easily into the team by doing several runs in a trainer. Such exercises during lay-overs between convoys also helped prevent teams developing sloppy habits. Finally, it helped keep the teams up to date with the latest tactical developments. In the controlled environment of simulation specific teaching points could be emphasized. This was a valuable addition to the A/S training system.

The introduction of procedures trainers to the Allied navies began in Canada.[70] As Captain Roberts can be identified with the work of the WATU, so Acting Commander (later Rear Admiral) J. C. Hibbard, DSC, RCN, must be given credit for the development of the Night Escort Attack Teacher. He had learned his anti-submarine work as the senior officer of an escort group in the North Atlantic in 1941. Following a reorganization of the operational staff at Halifax, Hibbard became the Training Commander on the staff of Captain (D) on 1 May 1942.[71] He described the purpose and function of the trainer thus.

It is submitted that one of the present outstanding weaknesses that seriously reduces the fighting efficiency of small ships is lack of co-ordination.

2. While each department of the ship may function correctly by itself, it is found that when all departments are required to work together, particularly at night under conditions of stress, the whole fails to function with the requisite precision and effect.

The escort attack teach[er] was evolved to assist in remedying this situation, and plans for its construction were prepared during the latter part of June 1942. The object in view was to provide a means of exercising full night action procedure under the most realistic conditions possible on shore.[72]

The trainer began operation on 10 September, with immediate success. By the end of the month, 53 ships had been exercised in it. A ship's team using the trainer included the captain, the officer of the watch, lookouts, signals officer and signalmen, telegraphists and coders, the gunnery officer, the A/S control officer and his team, and the plotting officer and his personnel.[73] In April 1943, a USN officer from the Bureau of Naval Personnel visited the trainer and wrote a full report about it. He was very favourably impressed, and made a strong recommendation for *several* to be built for training USN personnel.[74]

The success of the Night Escort Attack Trainer marked the introduction of the last component of the new training system that provided the manning for the Atlantic convoy escorts. It had taken three years of war for the RN and RCN to create a system capable of training the large numbers to a high standard of efficiency. This included expanded school capacity for individual training and work-ups training beginning at a sufficiently basic level to address the problems of expansion and dilution of the experience base in a ship's company. The short time allowed and the high standards attained by the new training systems marked a considerable change from the methods of the pre-war RN and RCN. The last new components of the 'new stance' the Allied navies adopted during the Battle of the Atlantic were operational analysis to study tactical problems and develop doctrine, and the use of simulation in team trainers to develop and maintain the final edge of efficiency. It was only in the last year of this process that the United States became a full partner in the Battle of the Atlantic. Having explored these problems of training and manning in the RN and RCN, it is now time to examine, briefly, how the USN adapted to the conditions of anti-submarine war.

In the USN the Battle of the Atlantic never had the primary focus of attention and effort it did in the RCN, and it lacked the life-threatening basic survival quality that it represented to Britain, and therefore the RN. As a consequence, flag officers responsible for the direction of the USN effort in the Atlantic had to compete for attention and resources in Washington with flag officers from other theatres which might have a higher priority. To unravel the full story of the USN participation, some understanding of the bureaucratic and administrative structure of the navy in Washington is necessary.

The USN differed from its allies in one other very important aspect - sheer size. While in December 1941 it was approximately three-quarters the size of the RN, by June 1945 it was four times its size. In raw numbers, the USN expanded by more than 2,700,000 personnel. Less than 20% were involved in the Battle of the Atlantic,[75] but that figure alone nearly equalled the size of the RN. In 1939 the USN was probably less well prepared to protect trade and fight U-boats than the RN had been.[76] Starting from that base, to meet the manning and training challenges of expansion on such a large scale, the USN not only had to create new training systems, but also a new administrative structure in Washington.

One area of significant administrative change was that of responsibility for personnel.[77] Since 1915 this had been vested in the Bureau of Navigation, along with its operational functions. From 1939 to the end of 1941, during which time the navy tripled in size,[78] it had handled the expansion and mobilization of the reserves. Not all of this expansion, at least at the Bureau level, had been orderly. In April 1942 the last remaining navigational responsibilities of the Bureau were transferred to the Office of the Chief of Naval Operations, and it was renamed the Bureau of Naval Personnel. At much the same time the engineering management consultant firm Booz, Fry, Allen and Hamilton of Chicago and New York was engaged to study the structure of the Bureau, and make recommendations.

The Bureau had responsibility for the procurement, performance and distribution of all personnel. As initially set up, these three functions were exercised by two divisions, responsible for officer and for enlisted personnel. Procurement numbers were set by the Bureau's Planning and Control Division, which tried to forecast naval personnel requirements by rank and training level, and the date and location where they would be needed. They produced a document called the Operating Force Plan which was the primary tool used by the navy at the national level of manpower allocation.[79] However, in establishing and reviewing the plan, the USN suffered from the same breakdown of internal communications which hampered RCN personnel planning in 1940.

> ....it is interesting to note that the chart outlining procedure for the consideration of ship construction programs at no point provides for any reference to BuPers, nor, indeed, does it at any point directly charge any agency with responsibility for determining that men will be available to man the ships being planned.[80]

In the early years of American involvement, and certainly until after the crisis of the Battle of the Atlantic, the Operating Force Plan was not constrained by a limit of men available, or budget authorization levels, and the communication problems could be overcome by the generous allowance of a 10% inflation factor.[81]

The responsibility for training was placed in the Training Division under the Director of Special Activities. This included Standards and Curriculum, Field Administration and Quality Control, Training Aids, and the College Training Program. The organization did not function as smoothly as it might appear on paper. It must be remembered that the recommendations of the Booz report, setting up the structure, were being implemented *while* the country was at war, and the navy was expanding. Control was sometimes difficult to exercise.

> Throughout the summer of 1942 the training situation got progressively more and more out of hand. In every naval district schools were mushrooming into being overnight as local pressure made some sort of

incidental training imperative. It was not only that the Bureau did not know what was being taught at the various schools under its nominal cognizance; it actually did not even have a complete and reliable list of what schools were in existence.[82]

The problems the USN experienced in establishing a training system to meet wartime demands in 1942 were rather different from those of the RN or RCN. These had clear lines of control between the training authority and the operational commander, but lacked resources. The USN had resources, but lacked control. However, the USN resolved its problems more quickly. The official American naval historian suggests 'in April and May, 1943, the quantity of escorts and quality of training began to tell'.[83]

The selection of May 1943 as the latest date at which 'the quality of training began to tell' is interesting when compared with certain USN organizational changes. Admiral Ernest King, who, in the office of CominCh, combined the positions of Chief of Naval Operations and Commander in Chief US Fleet, set up Tenth Fleet directly under his control. This was meant to command all USN anti-submarine warfare. However, as it was not set up until May 1943, it could have had no part in the change. Likewise, the creation of the position of Commander, Operational Training, Atlantic (COTCLANT), responsible for work-up and related training, had not been ordered by King until 9 January 1943.[84] The problem it was meant to address - of declining efficiency as a result of expansion and dilution - was exactly the same as that of the RN and RCN. The schools and establishments COTCLANT was to take under his command had been set up on an *ad hoc* basis in the latter part of 1942. It is unlikely that this command alone could have been responsible for the change Morison noted.

Probably the most important contributing factor was the creation, again at King's direction but possibly in response to direct pressure from Captain Wilder D. Baker, USN,[85] of the Anti-Submarine Warfare Operational Research Group (ASWORG) in late March 1942. This grew out of the Atlantic Fleet Anti-Submarine Unit that had been set up in February 1942 under Baker to resolve problems of tactical doctrine. There can be little doubt that work of ASWORG was influenced by the operational research of Professor Blackett and other scientists in Britain.[86] This speedy turn to science only months after formal entry in the war, and following the example of the British at a time when King was still resisting their advice to implement convoys for trade protection, is remarkable. It paralleled the heavy reliance placed upon American universities to provide naval training.[87]

If 'the acute problems of 1942 were probably as much due to equipment as to personnel shortages, with the added element of the time lag for essential training which delayed the visible effects of numbers increase'[88] is correct (and it is not challenged here), credit must also be given to the 'mushrooming' of naval schools. Rather than train men on a broad base, the USN elected to set up schools dedicated to particular classes of ships and tasks. In comparison with the RN and RCN specialized schools, such as HMS *Osprey* or HMCS *Cornwallis* (the ultimate location of the RCN A/S school), two principal differences are evident in this approach. The first is the numbers of the USN establishments. The second is the speed with which they were established. Both were so great that a flow of adequate numbers of trained men became noticeable only 15 or 16 months after America's entry into the war.

In sum, the three major Allied navies responded to the problems of expansion, manning, and training for the Battle of the Atlantic in ways defined by their national circumstances. As might be expected, a greater commonality of method can be found in the RN and RCN approaches than with the USN. However, all three navies were forced to turn to new ways of analysis, and developing tactics that placed emphasis on scientific method. New methods and standards of training, particularly simulation and accepted levels of operational efficiency, were also adopted. These developments in war changed the navies, which in peace had not paid adequate attention to submarine warfare. We now know they were permanent changes. That, perhaps, is the legacy of the Battle.

Notes

1. For figures on the RN see Roskill, *The War At Sea*, vol 1, Appendix C. For the USN, *Administrative History: Bureau of Naval Personnel*, Part IV, 'Training Activity', Volume One, 'Standards and Curriculum Division', p. xxi, World War II Histories and Historical Reports, U.S. Naval History Division. [In the *Guide to United States Naval Administrative Histories of World War II* compiled by William C. Heimdahl and Edward J. Marolda, published by the Naval History Division, Department of the Navy, in 1976, this is Item 83(a)(i). For ease of reference, future citations to these administrative histories, (which are unpublished but available through inter-library loan on microfiche), will provide a long title and guide item number.] For the RCN see Tucker, *The Naval Service of Canada*, vol 2, p. 7 (1939) & p. 478 (1945).

2. See, for example, W. G. D. Lund, 'The Royal Canadian Navy's Quest for Autonomy in the North West Atlantic' in Boutilier, *RCN in Retrospect 1910-1968*.

3. 'Memorandum on Anti-Submarine Policy Regarding the Use of ASDICS', T. D. 1/38, p. 5. Public Record Office, Kew, ADM 1/12140; anticipated 1940 mobilization active service S/D rating estimate by Director of Tactical Division, 31 March 1937, 'S/D Ratings - Requirements. Minute of Conference', P.M. 4267/36, Minute Sheet 10, PRO, ADM 116/3603.

4. *Anti-Submarine Warfare*, vol IV, 'A/S Training', Appendix 1, PRO, ADM 239/248; Roskill, *op. cit.*

5. Whinney, *The U-Boat Peril: An Anti-Submarine Commander's War*, p. 42.

6. Sir Bolton Eyres-Monsell speaking in the House of Commons, 1933, cited in Roskill, *Naval Policy Between the Wars*, vol 2, p. 167.

7. *Anti-Submarine Warfare*, vol IV, p. iv.

8. TD 3637/31 'Tactical Requirements of the Fleet in Asdic and T.S.D.S. fitted Destroyers', para. 4. A copy of this memorandum is on CW 7012/32 'Appointment of Officers to HMS 'Osprey'' Additional'. PRO, ADM 116/3603.

9. *Ibid.*, para. 6.

10. *Ibid.*, para. 9.

11. *Ibid.*, para 10.

12. CW 7012/32, Minute Sheet 1, PRO, ADM 116/3603.

13. CW 7285/32, Minute Sheet 3, PRO, ADM 116/3603.

14. N. 4622/34, Minute Sheet 1, PRO, ADM 116/3603. This comment was made by the Naval Advisor to the Second Sea Lord (who was responsible for personnel).

15. CAFO 2677/33, para. 4.

16. N.5012/34, Minute Sheet 1, NA2SL 19 Dec 1934, PRO, ADM 116/3603.

17. Report of the Committee on Training of Naval Officers for War, (Chairman, Vice Admiral William James), p. 2, PRO, ADM 116/3060; *The Navy List for April 1935 corrected to 18th March 1935*, (London, 1935).

18. AFO 825/35, Section III, 'Midshipmen', para. 25, 'Destroyer Course' & Appendix B, 'Midshipmen - Syllabus of Instruction Afloat', Destroyer Training, para. 5(b), 'Tactics'.

19. *Ibid.*, para. 24.

20. 'The lack of volunteers for "S" is caused primarily by the absence of any thorough instruction in the subject, such as is given in other subjects, to acting sub-lieutenants. ... Consequently, young lieutenants treat "S" as "second rate" specialisation involving a very stiff course, of which very little has been previously taught, and with uncertain intervals of general service to follow specialisation.' Captain H.M. Signal School to C-in-C Portsmouth, 23 Aug 1935, C.W. 7364/35, PRO, ADM 116/3334.

21. 'Interim Report on the Training of Junior and Specialist Officers', para. xiv, (16 July 1938), PRO, ADM 116/3701.

22. Roskill, *Naval Policy Between the Wars*, vol 2, p. 170.

23. T.D. Memo No. 146/37, 'Provision and Training of Anti-Submarine Personnel', PRO, ADM 1/12140.

24. *Ibid.*, para. 32.

25. *Ibid.*, para. 10. Emphasis in original.

26. Comment by Director of Training and Staff Duties, 23.9.35., T.S.D. 2565/35/T, Minute Sheet 2, on CW 9125/35, PRO, ADM 116/3959.

27. *Ibid.*, D. of T.D., 10.10.35, Minute Sheet 5.

28. *Ibid.*, CW 1157/36, minute of D.T.S.D. and H. of C.W. 1 October 1937.

29. *Ibid.*, minute by D.S.D., 4.12.37.
30. *Ibid.*, 5 Jan 38, Minute Sheet 4.
31. *Ibid.*, CW 11011/38, 17 November 1938, 'Action in Connection With Officers' Courses on Mobilisation'.
32. Middleton, *H.M.S. King Alfred 1939-1945*, pp. 5-6.
33. 'H.M.S. King Alfred Training Syllabus', October 1942, National Archives of Canada, Ottawa, RG 24, Acc 83-84/167, vol. 1689, file 4900 - 150/30.
34. *Ibid.*, Minute (probably April 1944) by Lt (a/s) David Macknight, A/S Section Division of Warfare and Training, Naval Service Headquarters, Ottawa. Macknight commented that 'ninety percent of the officers from K.A. go to combined operations or coastal forces. The best - the other 10% go to various commands, however all officers coming from K.A. to Western Approaches go to Osprey for a short A/S course before joining ships'. This would suggest that less than ten percent went to Western Approaches. Whether that figure was accurate, say in 1942, is another matter.
35. 'R.C.N.V.R. Officers' Training Establishment. H.M.C.S. STONE FRIGATE. Kingston, Ontario. Syllabus of Courses', NAC, RG 24, vol 11848, file NE-15-13, vol 1.
36. 'Report on Officers' Training - April 1940', 1 May 1940, Department of National Defence, Directorate of History Archives, National Defence Headquarters, Ottawa, file NS 1000-5-13 vol 1.
37. 'History of Anti-Submarine Measures on the Canadian Atlantic Coast', para. 7, D Hist 81/520/1000-973 vol 1.
38. Stacey, *Arms, Men and Governments: The War Policies of Canada 1939-1945*, pp. 6-17; Granatstein, *Canada's War: The Politics of the Mackenzie King Government*, pp. 97-9.
39. Messages are on NAC, RG 24, vol 5586, file NS 1-24-1, vol 3. The first of the series is from the Second Sea Lord to the CNS, 2031/22/7/40: 'Sheridan [BATM, Ottawa] informs us you are considering helping us with manning of 10 corvettes building in Canada. We are grateful for any assistance you find possible to give.' The final decision to provide the crews was reported in NSHQ 1739/8/8/40. This was also the first message repeated to Halifax, the base which would be responsible for manning the ships. They were: *Arrowhead, Bittersweet, Eyebright, Fennel, Hepatica, Mayflower, Snowberry, Spikenard, Trillium,* and *Windflower.*
40. These were known as the 'Towns'. They were HMC Ships *Annapolis, Columbia, Niagara, St. Clair, St. Croix* and *St. Francis. Buxton* and *Hamilton* were transferred from the RN at later dates.
41. Appendix 1, 'Numbers required for manning new construction' to 'Memorandum of Conference on Manning and Training held at Naval Service Headquarters, August 30th, 1940', NAC, RG 24, vol 4045, file NS 1078-3-5 vol 1.
42. 'Training Policy' (Home Fleet submission No. 1088/H.F.225 of 18th July 1934) para. 49, on CW 6254/34, PRO, ADM 116/3287.
43. Commander-in-Chief Home Fleet to the Secretary of the Admiralty, 15 September

1934, 1445/H.F.225, PRO, ADM 116/3288, para. 5.

44. *Ibid.*, para. 9.

45. Lieutenant A. N. G Firebrace, RN, 'A Plea for Continuous Commissions', *Naval Review*, vol 1, 1913, pp. 270-3.

46. Case 4219, PRO, ADM 116/3288.

47. CAFO 2023/32, paras. 12 & 14 (i). The order was issued 26 August 1932.

48. The last pre-war annual *Admiralty Fleet Order Volume* available to me is that for 1937. The date of the letter of promulgation is 31 August 1938. CAFO 2023/32 is listed as still being effective.

49. Baker, *The Terror of Tobermory*, p. 112.

50. *Anti-Submarine Warfare* vol IV, p. 15.

51. *Ibid.*, p. 16.

52. Although this statement is held to be true in general terms for the RN, RCN and USN, specific evidence is offered only for the RCN. The following ships were among those for which nominal rolls for the ratings of late 1940 or early 1941 were available. The date provided is that of the roll.

HMCS	DATE	RCN	RCNR	RCNVR	TOTAL
Restigouche (RCN, River class, pre-war complement 220.)	21.01.41	102	15	55	172
Assiniboine (River)	24.01.41	92	16	67	175
St. Clair (Town)	Dec. '40	21	35	70	126
Niagara (Town)	Dec. '40	33	29	66	128
Columbia (Town)	Jan. '41	29	42	62	133
Prince David (AMC)	14.01.41	54	61	156	271
Prince Henry (AMC)	14.01.41	52	58	157	267
Collingwood (Flower)	02.06.41	6	14 ·	29	49
Fennel (Flower)	Jan. '41	3	18	30	51
Hepatica (Flower)	21.12.40	4	18	29	51
Mayflower (Flower)	10.02.41	4	16	32	52
Orillia (Flower)	02.06.41	5	23	23	51

Compiled from nominal roles at NAC, RG 24, vol 11,542, file 'Ships' Complement Lists'; ibid., file H-7-7 vol 2; RG 24, vol 5685, file 153-6-1; ibid., file 145-6-1; RG 24, vol 5686, file 163-1-1; RG 24, vol 11,353, file HMCS *Fennel* vol II.

53. The total figures of mobilized strength for all ranks are:

Service	Week ending 23.09.39	27.06.40	29.08.40
RCN	1,990	2,402	2,585
RCNR	145	1,835	2,633
RCNVR	538	3,486	5,348
TOTAL	2,673	7,723	10,566

D Hist, Naval Weekly Reports for dates indicated, file NS 1000-5-7, vol 1.

54. HMCS *St. Clair*, Lt-Cdr D. C. Wallace, RCNR, held command 24 September 1940 to 5 April 1942.

55. The first might have been Lt(n) E. T. Simmons, a member of the second *Stone Frigate* course, appointed to HMCS *Port Arthur* 30 April 1942. The ship commissioned on 26 May, joined the Western Local Escort Force at the end of July, and in September was assigned to the Torch operation.

56. See, for example, the letters home of S/Lt Wilfred Bark, RCNVR, a 1942 graduate of HMCS *Kings,* who was killed in the loss of HMCS *Weyburn* in 1943. In particular, that of 22 October 1942, just after he had completed a two-week A/S course at HMS *Osprey* where he had shared a room with an RN sub-lieutenant. 'Actually their "scholastic" training - such as we had at Kings - isn't much greater, and their marks in most cases are nothing to brag about. Where they do have it over us is in the Midshipman training which is two years and more in a battleship. They can't help but pick up a good deal in that.' The Bark Collection, Marine Museum of the Great Lakes, Kingston Ontario.

57. Nominal Lists, HMCS *Chambly*, 2 June 1941, for ship's company as of 23 May 1941. NAC, RG 24, vol 11, 542, file H-7-7, vol 2, (Ships Complement Lists).

58. 'The Efficiency of Canadian-Manned Corvettes', Captain (D) Greenock to C-in-C Western Approaches, 10 June 1941, forwarded under cover of Captain Commanding Canadian Ships to Naval Secretary, Ottawa, 14 July 1941, NAC, RG 24, vol 11,065, file 41-1-2. The corvette which was subject of the A/S team comments is among those for which the RCN/RCNR/RCNVR rating numbers are provided above. In this instance the four RCN rates were a Leading Seaman Quarters Rating 2, an Able Seaman Quarters Rating 3, a Leading Torpedoman and an Ordinary Seaman S.D.

59. Commodore Commanding Newfoundland to Naval Secretary, NSHQ, 14 August 1941, NAC, RG 24, vol 11929, file 'Operations - Convoy Efficiency of Escorts - 00-220-3-6'.

60. *Ibid.*, Commodore Commanding Newfoundland to Naval Secretary, NSHQ, 6 November 1941.

61. *Ibid.*, 'Training and Manning Policy', 24 December 1941.

62. Boyle described as 'high' a 58% change in HMS *Nelson* over two years and a 31% change in HMS *Hood* over nine months. C-in-C Home Fleet to Secretary of the Admiralty, 15 September 1934, No. 1445/H.F. 225, p. 4, PRO, ADM 116/3288.

63. In addition to the comment by Commodore L. W. Murray at St. John's, Newfoundland, cited above, see also the minute of 12 January 1943 by Commodore H. E. Reid, his successor in that appointment, on Admiral Sir Max Horton's rather scathing comments about Convoy SC107. Reid wrote, 'The Commander-in-Chief Western Approaches' remarks regarding group training are concurred in and such training has been recommended by the Flag Officer Newfoundland Force for the last 18 months. Unfortunately operational necessity and filling various other outside undertakings at the request of the Admiralty have not made it possible to detach groups for this purpose'. NAC, RG 24, vol 11,335, file 8280 - S.C. 107, vol 1.

64. Unpublished MSS, 'The Life and Letters of Gilbert Howland Roberts', pp. 131-2, photocopy in D Hist 88/182.

65. The battle summaries provided by the Anti-Submarine Warfare Division of the Admiralty in the *Monthly Anti-Submarine Report*, (C.B. 04050/[yy (mm)]) had been just that - summaries, with a reconstruction of what had happened, but little useful analysis.

66. Roberts MSS, p. 133.

67. Cited in *ibid.*, p. 134.

68. *Ibid.*, pp. 135-7.

69. *Ibid.*, p. 139.

70. *Anti-Submarine Warfare,* vol IV, p. 18.

71. 'Training Office Monthly Reports', 9 September 1942, NAC, RG 24 D10, vol 11,994, file C-1-6-1.

72. 'Night Escort Attack Teacher', 20 October 1942, NAC, RG 24, vol 11,020, file COAC 7-1-6 vol 2.

73. 'Monthly Report of Proceedings', 6 October 1942, para. 3, NAC, RG 24, vol 11,501, file 'Monthly Reports'.

74. Correspondence and reports of Lt William Exton, Jr, USNR, NAC, RG 24, vol 11,019, file 7-1, vol 1.

75. Morison, *History of United States Naval Operations in World War II*, vol 1, 'The Battle of the Atlantic 1939-1945', p. 205.

76. *Ibid.*, p. 11; Meigs, *Slide Rules and Submarines*, pp. 8-13.

77. Most of this paragraph relies on *Bureau of Naval Personnel: Administrative History*. Part I, 'Structure of the Bureau', [80(a)], pp. 3-15.

78. *Ibid.*, p. 3. The figures are: 30 June 1939, 110,087; 30 June 1941, 244,606; 31 December 1941, 330,821.

79. *Bureau of Naval Personnel: Planning and Control Activity*, [81(a)], p. 12.

80. *Ibid.*, p. 27n.

81. *Ibid.*, p. 38.

82. *Administrative History Bureau of Naval Personnel*, Part IV, 'Training Activity', [83(a)(i)], p. xxiii.

83. Morison, *History of United States Naval Operations in World War II*, vol 1, 'The Battle of the Atlantic 1939-1945', p. 202.

84. *Commander In Chief, Atlantic Fleet*, volume VIII, 'Commander Fleet Operational Training Command', [143], p. 23, (II - 1).

85. Meigs, *Slide Rules and Submarines*, p. 58.

86. Meigs, *Slide Rules and Submarines,* p. 51; Tidman *The Operations Evaluation Group*, pp. 31-2.

87. It was noted above that the College Training Program was a division within the training activity. Faced with the numbers of men who had to be given basic training quickly, not to mention those who also needed specialized training in physics and other scientific programs for work on radar, sonar, and electronics, the USN deliberately turned to the universities. In early 1942 Cornell University, Dartmouth

College, Northwestern University, Princeton University, and the University of
Arizona were among those involved. Neither the RN nor the RCN used the national
academic resources to a comparable extent.

88. *Bureau of Naval Personnel: Planning and Control Activity*, [81(a)], p. 14.

11

Manning and Training the U-boat Fleet

by Erich Topp

Based at Kiel, the 'Higher Command of Submarine Training' was responsible for training several Divisions and Flotillas in all aspects of submarine warfare, including both material and personnel. Learning about the boat as a whole was the premise for developing it into a powerful, combat-ready weapon to be put into the hands of a purposeful commanding officer.

The general training of enlisted men, engineering ratings, petty officers, midshipmen and officers was similar to that of any other navy. For submariners naturally this included diving, surfacing, submerged attack at periscope depth, and surface attack during the night, with torpedoes and gun. Because of the great similarity with other navies, I will confine myself here to saying a few words about the tactical training of U-boat crews, since - to my knowledge - the German submarine service placed a special emphasis on this. Having commanded the Tactical Flotilla in Gotenhafen, I can describe this part of the training from first-hand experience.

The 27th Submarine Flotilla was composed of six or more merchant ships forming a convoy, together with an anti-submarine screen of three auxiliary vessels, four motor torpedo boats and three minesweepers. The convoy was further protected by a squadron of aircraft acting as a combat air patrol.

Every fortnight, 10-14 submarines which had completed their technical and weapons training would assemble with the Tactical Flotilla. Under war conditions, they attacked the convoy, operating in the Baltic Sea between the Danish island of Bornholm and the Swedish island of Gotland. Compared with the convoy scenario in the Atlantic, the training attack operations in the Baltic took place in a relatively small area. Several cases of damage and the loss of two boats occurred in five years of tactical training.

'War conditions' meant under all weather conditions, day and night, but it was not a complete simulation of the Battle of the Atlantic. Radar and sonar on board the escorts was in a rather poor state of development and could not be compared with the electronic equipment of the British escorts. Besides, we did not then know about certain British ASW systems, such as HF/DF and the Leigh Light. These factors clearly imposed some limits on the tactical training we could give our submarines.

As for the training of U-boat personnel, this, in my view, focused on the problem of leadership. The weapon itself - the submarine - made leadership significantly different from the traditional leadership exercised in surface warships. By virtue of their training and experience, submariners are used to three-dimensional thinking. This mode of thinking comes less easily to a surface warfare specialist, who, being used to movement in two dimensions only, considers three-dimensional problems an intellectual exercise.

To trained submariners, three-dimensional thinking is second nature. They live in and are enclosed by the sea in which they operate. Coming from a surface ship, you have to study hard in order to become familiar with and take advantage of this new world. One must develop other human senses, reacting in novel ways to noise and vibration, and to novel phenomena - salinity, temperature-layers, increase or decrease of air pressure, and so on.

Living and working in a submarine, one also has to develop and intensify the ability to co-operate with other members of the crew, because you could need each other simply to survive. Everyone has to know everything on board, and everybody must be able to replace the other, to take charge of another function. More than that: you have to know not only the activities of your neighbour, but his character, his way of thinking, and his strong and weak points, because you are always on the alert. You have to be a psychologist.

When you are leaving harbour, closing the hatch, diving, you and your crew are bidding farewell to a colourful world, to the sun and the stars, the wind and the waves, the smell of the sea. All are living under constant tension, produced by living in a steel tube - a very small, cramped and confined space, with congested compartments, monotony and an unhealthy lifestyle, caused by bad air, the lack of normal rhythms of day and night and the lack of physical exercise.

These conditions can wear down any man quite rapidly, and can only be balanced by discipline for oneself and one's crew, a well organized daily routine, and officers who deal correctly with the individual man and his welfare.

It is, in short, a special way of life, so it is not surprising that all submariners have developed a special spirit, which may be summarized in the words teamwork and solidarity. This is true in the submarine branch of any navy, but perhaps it was particularly so in the U-boats of World War II. During their patrols, in a time of increasing physical and psychological insecurity, the personnel were asked to become a 'band of brothers'. In such a group, human relations can be so strong that they go beyond the natural instinct for self-preservation.

Apart from this general concept of leadership there was a special German situation in the last war. In 1943, the graphical plot of ships sunk fell drastically, and the construction of new ships in the United States was multiplying. At the same time the loss of submarines was increasing. For every three boats leaving for wartime patrol only one returned. In this situation, the internal stress on a commanding officer was extreme. With reduced successes and increasing losses, the life of each crew member was visibly endangered. Yet despite these hazardous conditions, there was never any lack of submariners leaving port on new patrols.

Was there something besides honour and duty that motivated them? I believe on one side of the coin we need to analyse the relationship between training education and leadership, and on the other side, the political environment.

All this culminates in a pertinent question: was leadership sufficient to ensure combat readiness, even under the most difficult wartime conditions? Whereas morale and commitment remained high despite long, unsuccessful patrols, the danger for everybody on board was increasing tremendously - internal stress could not have been more extreme.

To quote Britain's Prime Minister, Winston Churchill: 'There is no reason to suppose that the German submarines would have fought a losing campaign, if the defeat of the German army had not brought collapse and surrender. Their morale was unimpaired to the bitter end.' How was that possible?

A few words on the men in the submarine force. We started World War II with 3,000 well-trained submariners. It was evident that with a normal attrition rate and the construction programme to be accomplished, the calculated necessary replacement of men would not be reached.

By the end of 1941, there was a lack of trained officers, so the navy began a separate recruitment programme with special standards for submariners. Except for volunteers who qualified for 'small boats', non-commissioned officers and officers were drafted.

At the beginning of 1943, the personnel gap was bridged by the overall efforts for total war. By new organizational steps, combined with the set-up of personnel pools in the submarine flotillas, we were able to cover any short-term requirements.

As to volunteers, we had to change our policy by the end of 1941. Extremely high physical fitness had been a decisive criterion in accepting volunteers. This was now reduced to the less demanding level of 'able-bodied personnel'. But very few people had to be drafted in to submarines: many of the crews and practically all of the officers were recruited as volunteers.

I became commanding officer of a small submarine when I was 26. Petty officers achieved rank at the same age. Until 1943, the average age of a U-boat sailor was 23-24 years old. After 1943, the average age of submarine crews dropped to 21 years old, whilst commanding officers were usually 23. The outlook of these late-coming young submariners was shaped decisively by the education and society of the Third Reich. They were, in other words, conditioned by their upbringing in a totalitarian state to accept as natural a philosophy of all-out war, total war.

Germany's then political leaders used every possible means of psychological influence on the population - not only on military personnel, but the entire civilian population as well. An example shows how thoroughly young officers, having passed out of the National Socialist youth organization, were indoctrinated. In 1944, an experienced and rather successful commanding officer, having commissioned a new boat with a young crew, went into his cabin and saw a picture of Hitler on the bulkhead. He asked his officers to remove it, saying, 'There will be no idolatry here.' He was an open-minded man, critical of the political and military situation, and he did not hesitate to voice his opinion to his officers.

Leadership on board German submarines in the last war has to be understood against the background of a special political environment. Young officers such as these were influenced by the political atmosphere prevalent in school and in the youth movement. They swiftly denounced their commanding officer to higher authorities, accusing him of undermining the crew's fighting spirit. He was arrested, and whilst being held prisoner awaiting trial for several months, not one of his senior officers contacted him. He was condemned to death and executed.

This was certainly an exceptional case. However, it shows the influence of the totalitarian regime on military leaders, who did not know at the time that their political masters were already engaged in criminal actions. Here, and in some other cases, the 'band of brothers' was overshadowed by political parameters.

The unconditional power of the National Socialist Party granted a privileged position to the soldier or sailor, as long as he was a reliable follower of the party's principles. Through its propaganda, submariners in particular had a special role in public opinion. This stemmed from the very top. Hitler's charismatic power over the masses is well known. So, too, is his nearly mesmerizing effect on Dönitz, whom he eventually designated as his successor as Führer. Dönitz in turn championed the U-boat arm. His demands on U-boat personnel were high, but his support for them, both personally and politically, was unswerving; and, calling themselves *Freikorps Dönitz*, they responded to him with a depth of respect, even devotion, which has few parallels in naval history. There was always the closest of contact between him and his officers and men. For example, on return from a patrol, commanding officers had to report to him personally in his headquarters. His staff organized special trains to transport crew members to their rest area, at a prepared health resort; and when he addressed submarine crews, he remembered not only the names of most of the crew members, but even any family problems they might have.

With good reason, U-boat personnel were viewed as members of an élite. In national military terms, they were seen to achieve great things in the war at sea; at a more mundane level, they never lacked for specially prepared food for long patrols, nor for coffee, tea or chocolate. Surface crews received such things only in small rations, while the civilian population, of course, never received any of these items at all.

The other end of the spectrum of propaganda was covered by pressure and threats, even capital punishment.

Each submariner obviously enjoyed and profited from the élite image of the U-boat arm. The image also brought a deep sense of obligation. One was profoundly conscious of the privilege of being a member of *Freikorps Dönitz*. This created morale that was strong enough to camouflage or mask the over-riding drive of every human being - to survive. That explains why, even in

March-April 1945, submariners still went on patrol. On 1 May 1945, on board U-2513 and in company with four other boats, I personally sortied from Kiel harbour. Three of them were bombed by British aircraft and sunk; only two arrived in Oslo.

Analysing the question of U-boat leadership during World War II, you must also take an historic lesson into consideration. In 1917-18, Germany's red revolution began in the Imperial Navy. One reason for this mutiny was the lack of leadership in the officer corps. Afterwards, the navy of the Weimar Republic and of the Third Reich was stigmatized by these events. This made the Kriegsmarine of World War II determined to be the most loyal of the loyal, and it is one of the reasons why (with certain notable exceptions, such as Admiral Canaris) naval officers did not participate in the resistance movement. If this was a negative outcome during World War II, on the positive side it resulted in the greatest possible personal and social commitment and inter-relationship of all officers, not only in the lower but in the higher ranks as well. The general care and individual treatment of submariners created a confidence between the higher and lower ranks, that resisted many personal problems. Material and non-material care, acknowledgement and appreciation of personal affairs were important instruments of leadership.

This personal contact between the commanding officer and his crew was the basis of a reliance that culminated in regarding their captain as a kind of life-insurance.

To give an example of psychological care, again from my own experience: sailors are superstitious. Under my command, U-552 was leaving the Norwegian harbour of Bergen. We had already passed the Marsteen lighthouse and were in the open sea, travelling on the surface. My navigator, a petty officer, was on watch. For some reason, perhaps because I had come to know him well over many patrols, it seemed to me that he was not his usual self. He was pale, and seem unable to concentrate. I tried to find out his problem, but he was laconic, taciturn. I questioned him, and finally he told me that he had forgotten his talisman, a myrtle wreath, that people in my country used to store under a dome of glass in memory of their marriage.

I could have told him not to be stupid. Instead, I reversed course. After some hours we re-entered harbour and his myrtle wreath, the symbol of his marriage, was located. We went to sea again with my navigator - a very important man on board - restored to his normal calm. He contributed to a successful patrol.

Another example of individual treatment: obviously most of the punishments prescribed in the disciplinary code cannot be applied to a submarine in wartime. Cells are not available on board, and on shore, having come home after sharing the same dangers and successes, sending an offender to jail or stopping his pay made no sense. On one occasion one of my midshipmen was on the bridge, on watch, looking through his binoculars. For a surfaced submarine and its crew in wartime, to have an effective look-out is neither more nor less than a question of survival, but (apparently because of the last few days and nights in harbour) this young man was tired. I saw him closing his eyes behind the lens of his binoculars, and told him that if he was tired, we could switch the watch with another man. 'No, Captain', he said. 'I am not tired, let me continue the watch'. I agreed. Half an hour later, I returned to the bridge and found him with his eyes closed again. This time he was exchanged. When he was brought before me for sentence on Commanding Officer's report, I told him he was tired and must rest. The punishment I gave him was three days of doing nothing on board, not even assisting the cook. This may sound indulgent, but it was not. What it meant to him is evident. To have no part in an always active crew - to be nothing, when others were always on the alert - carried the necessary message.

This, and other lessons learned on board my boat, remained with him all his life. I know because, after the war, when he was a well-known doctor of medicine, he paid me a visit and told me so.

To summarize: for U-boat personnel during World War II, individual combat readiness could not be secured entirely by selecting able personnel or even through effective training. In common with values, norms, political parameters and social factors, the quality of leadership received the fundamental credit of being successful throughout the war. As such, it contributed to continuing the war, even when it was already lost.

I would like to give you a personal, realistic understanding of leadership in relation to recruitment and training. For me it is like looking through a kaleidoscope, with coloured chips of glass inside. Their positions change, but, although centuries may pass, their meanings never change. The chips of glass symbolize four things.

First is devotion to one's country. An old German proverb expresses this well: 'He who follows the Prussian flag has nothing of his own.' Second is discipline. For that I can do no better than to cite Admiral Nelson's famous words: 'England expects every man to do his duty.' Third is comradeship. To take an English example again, John Jervis called the officers of his fleet 'a band of brothers'. Fourth, but by no means least important, is high morale. I have already mentioned Churchill, who said of the U-boat personnel, 'Their morale was unimpaired to the bitter end.'

When you turn the kaleidoscope, the chips move, and the picture changes. A political regime can exploit the virtues of a soldier or sailor for its own political aims, even criminal ones. Thus, under Nazi rule, with a turn of the kaleidoscope and a movement of the chips, Germany exploited the virtues of its soldiers and sailors.

Primacy of policy is and always has been a rule not only in dictatorships but in all democracies. But this principle can be perverted; and so, in conclusion, I adhere to the poet Franz Werfel, who said: 'The primacy of policy annihilates the spirit, turning a master into a slave.' A civilized world can have one primacy and one alone: the primacy of conscience.

12

Work-Up

by James Goldrick

Introduction

This chapter describes the training systems employed by the Allies during the Battle of the Atlantic to achieve and sustain adequate levels of operational efficiency in the escort vessels involved in the campaign. The focus will remain primarily with the British efforts, although there will be some comments made on both American and Canadian practices.

The basic training processes involved came under two heads - that of preparing a ship for service after its first commissioning, or 'working up' in the traditional sense, and that of continuation training given to units between deployments on escort or support group duty. There were, however, three other inter-related distinctions which affected the nature of training in both areas and whose significance was not fully comprehended until well on into the Battle.

Firstly, training could be *procedural* and intended for the individual ship. Such training was directed at integrating a ship's company with the systems with which the ship was fitted - their maintenance, supply and operation - and with each other. This was 'integration' in the widest sense, since it involved practising every member of a ship's company not only in his own tasks, but in the range of emergencies which a ship might have to face in battle. Second, training could be *tactical*. This work was related to the employment of a unit's sensors and weapons to best effect against the enemy. It was essentially concerned with training the command team - which included sensor and weapon directors - into an appreciation of how an enemy would act in a given situation and in making the most appropriate responses. To give one example of the distinction between the two forms of individual ship training: in the first, a depth-charge party would be exercised in the methods of deploying, setting, firing and reloading depth-charge rails and projectors until its members could perform any conceivable evolution under the most arduous conditions of weather and sea. In tactical training, the ship's captain and control officer would learn the most appropriate depth settings and firing patterns to employ against U-boats under different conditions. Procedural training would naturally need to change as tactics altered - in the example of depth-charges, for example, as patterns became larger and depth settings deeper. But the distinction was clear.

Third, there was *group* training. This could be either procedural or tactical, but it was directed at practising ships which would serve together in the intricacies of operating in company. It concentrated essentially upon inter-ship communications and upon the actions that each ship would take in operational conditions for mutual support. The time required to produce a cohesive force from a collection of individual ships could be greatly shortened - and was - by the introduction of pre-planned responses to contingencies but such training could be neglected only at peril. The difference between a team and a gathering was essentially one of familiarity between the command and communications teams. In 1942, following an action half a world away from the Atlantic, Vice Admiral Pye of the US Navy wrote aptly:

> A Mob of men, without indoctrination and without training in concerted action, does not constitute an army. It can be safely said that a collection of ships, which has never operated together before, and under a strange commander, does not constitute a fleet.[1]

Tobermory - Individual Procedural Training

The genesis of Tobermory came with an Admiralty plan in early 1940 to set up an Anti-Submarine Warfare (ASW) training base to provide continuation training for destroyers and escorts of both British and French navies. In combination with the French Chief of Naval Staff, the First Sea Lord, Admiral Sir Dudley Pound, selected Lorient as the most suitable site and Vice Admiral (retired) Gilbert Stephenson was nominated as the director in the rank of Commodore Second Class.[2]

The fall of France overtook the initial scheme and the site of the proposed training facility was shifted to Tobermory on the Isle of Mull, off the west coast of Scotland. After Stephenson had managed to wrest his headquarters ship, HMS *Western Isles*, from dockyard hands, operations began at Tobermory in July 1940.[3] It was soon apparent to the Commodore that both the nature of the training task and the responses required had changed from the initial conception. While the role of Tobermory was defined as 'giving a refresher course of a week or ten days in new weapons and tactics to vessels of destroyer class and under, after long periods at sea',[4] the ships which were sent for training were new construction, not units which had seen active service, and they were manned by increasingly high proportions of inexperienced and 'Hostilities Only' personnel.

Stephenson realized the implications early and had the right background to set about a solution. He had served in the Mediterranean in World War I, largely concerned with ASW work and much involved with Reserve-manned small craft. This culminated in his appointment as senior officer for the Otranto Barrage operations against German and Austrian submarines in 1917-18. At the peak of activity, there were some 230 ships (largely trawlers and drifters) under his command.[5] His later service included Director of the Anti-Submarine Division in the Admiralty.

Tobermory would be a training facility for ASW units, but one designed to work-up newly commissioned ships from scratch. Stephenson commented:

> I don't think the Admiralty realized how raw many of the ships' companies were. They thought all we had to do was 'work-up' ships already commissioned, with crews who were fully disciplined and

accustomed to working together. But we found this was very rarely the case. So one simply had to *invent* new methods.[6]

He turned the ASW training role into one that reflected a whole-ship approach, concentrating on the basics. His approach was described by one commanding officer as 'violently shaking the lethargy out of ships sent to him.'[7] He relied upon a mixture of exhortation (to create a winning spirit within each ship) and the instillation of strict discipline, initially through the mechanism of close order drill, to ensure that the spirit so engendered could be properly directed.

Perhaps the greatest difference between the time-honoured methods of working up a ship (which continued to be practised for the larger units that belonged to the Home Fleet) and the Tobermory approach was that in the latter, there was no assumption that sufficient expertise resided within the unit concerned to recognize and correct deficiencies. The newly completed escorts did not possess enough experience for that. There was a second difference. Major units worked up under the eye of their squadron or flotilla commanders and staffs, but the Western Approaches lacked equivalent organizations, even after the formal designation of Escort Groups and the development of the organization of Captains (D) within the base ports. Tobermory had therefore to be more than just a provider of facilities.

When a ship arrived at Tobermory, she was immediately subjected to a detailed inspection of her material state and organization. Her captain would be interviewed by Stephenson, in the course of which the aims of the work-up would be explained and the first steps taken towards mapping out a suitable syllabus for the unit concerned. Initially, only eight days were allocated for the programme, but by January 1941 this had been extended to the 14 days which would remain in force for the rest of the war.[8] Although Table 1[9] gives the basic syllabus for each major class of warship and Table 2[10] a break-down of the customary programme of the second work-up base at Stornoway for a *Flower*-class corvette, these were for guidance only. The routines could be and were amended to allow extra time for particular weaknesses. Only rarely did a ship fail outright. The consequences of failure were, in the opinion of most personnel, too awful to contemplate - a repetition of the entire work-up. In reality, Stephenson's most frequently employed 'final solution' was removal of personnel whose performance had proved inadequate. In making such decisions, his criteria seem to have included an officer or rating's attitude and his capacity to improve, rather than the extent of his ignorance. The Commodore was 'equally ruthless with his own ship's officers and instructional personnel - very necessary for the prestige of the working-up base.'[11]

Staff officers were designated from each major specialization to cover particular ships and remain as their 'tutors' for the duration of the work-up. This had obvious advantages. It ensured consistency of doctrine, thus avoiding the complaint of trainees that '...the *other* staff officer said...'. It also allowed *Western Isles* to maintain a comprehensive picture of a ship's progress. To assist with this, written reports were completed after every training exercise, no matter how minor or what its nature, and these reports were discussed with the Commodore on a daily basis. In theory, no specialist evolution would be conducted without the relevant training staff being present. In practise, the numbers of ships passing through sometimes became so great that this connection between staff and individual unit occasionally broke down.

As the flow of new construction increased, steps were taken to establish other work-up establishments to ease the burden on *Western Isles*. HMS *Mentor* began operations at Stornoway in December 1943, dealing primarily with *Flower-* and *Castle*-class corvettes while the more sophisticated units went to Tobermory. *Mentor* was closed later in the war when the rate of new building and refits eased and Tobermory was again sufficient. *Mentor*'s existence did not stop *Western Isles* from achieving the remarkable total of 1,000 escorts worked up by October 1944, which resulted in the famous signal from the Commander-in-Chief Western Approaches comparing Stephenson's performance with that of Helen of Troy - an analogy which the Commodore appreciated, literally at face value.[12]

Stephenson saw little reason to change his approach as the war progressed, despite increasing levels of experience in the ships being worked up. His judgement proved correct, as Captain (then Lt Cdr) Stanley Darling has commented. Of his 1944 work-up in command of HMS *Loch Killin* by comparison with that undertaken in HMS *Inchmarnoch* in 1941, he notes: 'I found it as rewarding. The team went through all the phases with the same thoroughness, but with perhaps a little less apparent panic and rushing about.'[13]

The requirement to provide for American-built escorts resulted in plans being laid in May 1942 for a British work-up facility in the Western Atlantic. At the strong recommendation of the local Commander-in-Chief, it was placed at Bermuda in preference to the Bahamas or the West Indies. The limited facilities of the local dockyard and the need to shelter in the event of hurricanes, constrained this establishment to 12 units at a time, compared with the 20-25 which *Western Isles* could manage or the 10 of HMS *Mentor*.[14]

The Syllabus in Execution

Neither Table 1 nor 2 makes clear the extent to which the training was conducted on a whole-ship basis, or the involvement of the Engineering and the Supply Departments, which were subjected to close examination. Good organization was considered the key to success and 'instruction included advice on such matters as the cleaning of messdecks , stowing of storerooms, keeping books, cooking and dealing with offenders.'[15] If Standing Orders were incomplete or inadequate, they had to be rewritten - a task which did not make the practical elements of the programme any easier to accomplish.[16]

The key element within the programme was the training of the ASW command team and the supporting weapon parties. The emphasis on ASW is not immediately apparent in Tobermory's harbour training syllabus. A frigate received a total of 18 hours on the A/S Attack Teacher, lectures and underwater weapon drills, whereas it was allocated more than twice this (37 hours) for gunnery subjects. But the sea training indicated the real priority - 35 hours of A/S exercises compared with only 8 hours of gunnery firings.

Those 35 hours could comprise the only 'live' training time with a submarine that an escort received before entering operational service. They were spent in a series of progressively more complex and challenging exercises, yet there were limits to what could be achieved. Tobermory and the other work-up bases enjoyed a high priority for target submarines, but even they had to employ artificial targets on occasion.[17] And, despite the utility of the latter, a proportion of live submarine time had to be reserved for basic tracking serials, in order to give operators that essential experience in recognizing the 'real thing' and the quality of performance of which their instruments were capable.

It was this aspect which was one of the hidden strengths of the Tobermory work-up system. The combination of insistence on complete equipment serviceability - and a ship was not allowed to start her work-up until this was achieved - together with the continuous presence of expert staff meant that a ship's personnel could be educated in the levels of performance which they could expect from their systems at sea. It was the absence of this knowledge, particularly in asdic and radar, which prevented a ship which had not been worked up from attaining a real degree of fighting efficiency, however much operational service she endured. This was a fundamental cause of many of the problems of the Canadian escort forces described by Marc Milner in *North Atlantic Run*.[18]

Until the flood of new construction in 1943 allowed Flag Officer Submarines to allocate submarines to A/S training duties for a period as part of their transition to front line service, the 'clockwork mice' tended to be old and only marginally serviceable. This had certain inevitable drawbacks. First, exercises were frequently interrupted or cancelled because the submarine had developed defects. Second (and it was realized, as the war drew on, that because of the U-boats' deep-diving capabilities, this had serious implications), elderly submarines were severely restricted in their ability to go deep. Even diving to 100 feet was beyond the powers of some of the H-class, which were happier at 60-80 feet.[19] It proved necessary to devise a special static 'Triplane Target', which could be positioned at depths of 270 feet or more.[20]

Despite the legends, Tobermory did not attempt to over-work ships' companies during the work-up periods. The Standing Programme for HMS *Mentor* at Stornoway indicates, for example, that a corvette would be expected to anchor each night after its daily sea-training.[21] Ships were generally not interfered with in the silent hours, apart from efforts to ensure that the gangway staff remained alert and the occasional whole-ship 'funny'.[22] In reality, the pressure was carefully judged, but it is hardly surprising that an intensely active schedule which occupied ships' companies every waking minute between 0600 and 2359 for 13 days on end should be regarded in retrospect as even worse than it really was. The approach was one of sustained hard work and relentless attention to detail, in the belief that if a ship's organization and a crew's knowledge of and application of the fundamentals were sound, she would become an efficient fighting unit. The work-up establishments themselves would always emphasize that the limited time available 'could only be devoted to the basic necessities. No attempt was made to teach any but the simplest tactics or carry out any advanced exercises.'[23]

Perhaps most significant was Stephenson's apparently curious insistence that ships' companies should practise close order drill ashore as the first exercise of the programme. The effect could be remarkable, as Cdr Fred Osborne has described. His crew 'went ashore as a bedraggled body, and came back looking like disciplined sailors....it had its effect and it was a very important part of the working up....Men who joined the Navy, whether voluntarily or otherwise, expected to join a service of high tradition and achievement. If they did not get their share of ordered life and routine even in a small ship, they were not getting what they expected.'[24]

The Canadian Approach

The first substantial Canadian efforts to consolidate training activities began in 1941 with the establishment of a work-up base at Pictou, Nova Scotia. An Anti-Submarine School was set up at Digby, NS, in 1943, with ships allocated for training operating in the Bay of Fundy. Apart from a lack of personnel and material in the early years, constant problems beset the RCN through the severity of the winters and the difficult sonar environment off the Canadian coast. Operations moved to Halifax in the winter, but even there, severe conditions hamstrung the training effort, which was in any case restricted by the lack of a local training submarine. Above all, as Marc Milner has suggested, there was a tendency - understandable in the circumstances - 'to batten down the hatches and ride it out. The RCN's approach to training over the winter months reflects this: there was just too little value in it for the effort.'[25]

The RCN had plans to move all or part of the work-up effort to Bermuda in 1943, but RN requirements took priority until the establishment of HMS *Somers Isle* on the island in 1944. At this point, the CO of the new centre took responsibility for post-commissioning sea training from the Captain (D) at Halifax, with an organization directly modelled upon *Western Isles*, and which rapidly built up the same level of support assets.[26]

The American Approach

The United States Navy also took relatively longer than the RN to embrace the concept of dedicated work-up facilities, at least for its larger escorts. Both the material state and the lack of experience in the submarine chasers emerging as new construction in 1942 had brought about the establishment of a 'Subchaser School' at Miami in March 1942, which operated with considerable success for the remainder of the war.[27] But other unit training was conducted in a largely piecemeal fashion, with newly commissioned destroyers and other escorts taking their chances on the availability of facilities in the Atlantic ports. Only in 1943 was the Operational Training Command Atlantic Fleet (COTCLANT) established to integrate the training system. From this, there rapidly emerged the Destroyer Escort Shakedown Task Force, which operated out of Bermuda from April 1943 and, from September that year, included all newly commissioned destroyers.[28]

Continuation Training

It eventually became apparent to Western Approaches Command that the basic work-up centres were not enough. The first measures to improve the situation were to establish facilities for weapon handling drills and A/S Attack Teachers in the major escort ports of Liverpool, Londonderry and Greenock. By late 1944, Londonderry's aids included a Night Escort Attack Teacher - effectively a full-scale night-fighting simulator and a product of Canadian ingenuity - a Tactical School, two A/S Attack Teachers, drillers for all ASW weapons and even a mock-up U-boat conning tower in which boarding parties could practice.[29]

This development had not come easily. There is considerable evidence that the infrastructure did not reach maturity until after the impetus given by Sir Max Horton's efforts to improve training standards had taken effect, following his installation as Commander-in-Chief Western Approaches in November 1942. This was not wholly the fault of his predecessors, particularly Admiral Sir Percy Noble, who had faced shortages of the required material to establish such training aids and sufficient experts to operate them. There was also an inevitable time-lag between the introduction of equipment into operational service and the accumulation of a corpus of expertise in its employment and maintenance which could then be transmitted to newly fitted units. In its first year, for example, Hedgehog's record indicates that there was not only suspicion as to its effectiveness, but uncertainty as to the best methods of use and maintenance.[30]

Group Training

Whilst the absolute requirement for individual ship work-ups had been quickly accepted within the Royal Navy, that of group training took longer. The primary cause of this was initially the sheer lack of escorts and the loss in operational availability implicit in keeping a full group away from convoy work in order to train it. Less obvious, however, was the lack of recognition of the requirement for mutual understanding between escorts as a precondition to effective convoy defence operations. Even the initial proposals to form escort groups at all met with opposition.[31] This derived from the lack of first-hand experience of the problem from authorities ashore, but it was also an inevitable result of the lack of Command-wide pre-planned tactics for use against U-boats. Without such tactics, it was difficult to make clear the efficacy of fully trained groups compared with those which were not, because the former's efforts, however well co-ordinated, were equally likely to be misdirected.

As the Battle went on, the weight of expert opinion in favour of training grew. Captain Donald Macintyre noted of his 5th Escort Group in March 1941:

> it was of vital importance that it should have trained as a team and that each commanding officer should know what was required of him without the necessity for signalled instructions. Lack of these conditions time and again led to unnecessary defeats at the hands of the U-boats.[32]

In November 1941, Commander F. J. Walker was forced to conduct his work-up of the 36th Escort Group while escorting a convoy to Gibraltar.[33] Even a year later, when Acting Commander P. W. Gretton organized exercises before deploying for a group assembled to escort North African invasion convoys, he found that 'many ships had defects to put right and several had not expected to go to sea before the departure of the convoy, and did not approve of all these exercises!'[34]

Horton and the Co-ordinated Approach to Training

The seeds of revolution had, however, already been sown. The first was in the establishment of the Western Approaches Tactical Unit (WATU) at Liverpool, under the direction of Acting Captain Gilbert Roberts. The idea of a Tactical Table for ASW problems had been the December 1941 brainchild of Vice Admiral (retired) C.V. Usborne, the First Sea Lord's Naval Adviser on A/S warfare. It was accepted (albeit with little enthusiasm) by C-in-C Western Approaches, and over the initial objections of the Admiralty Directorate of Anti-Submarine Warfare.[35] Once launched under Roberts' control, WATU rapidly became indispensable both as a training tool and as a means whereby tactics could be developed and disseminated with the Command. By the war's end, more than 5,000 officers of all ranks and from every service involved in the campaign would have completed at least one of the week-long WATU courses.[36] WATU's games made clear the requirement for co-ordinated, pre-planned responses to the U-boat and thus the need for comprehensive group training, of which the Tactical Unit's course marked only the start. By the end of 1942, a second Tactical Unit was operating in Londonderry, followed by another at HMS *Osprey* in 1945.[37]

The second element in the revolution was the arrival of Admiral Sir Max Horton as C-in-C Western Approaches in November 1942. Horton's own instincts and experience as a highly successful submariner naturally pushed him in the direction of raising the standard of training, but he was also prompted by increasing evidence of the importance of the efficiency of surface escorts in convoy defence.[38] Within days of his installation, Horton wrote to the Admiralty to emphasize that

> Until each group is led and manned by competent officers, and until
> it has attained a high degree of group efficiency and is completely
> equipped with the latest devices, heavy losses will continue. The
> immediate problem must therefore be: to raise the standard of the
> less efficient groups to the level of the most efficient ones.[39]

Horton was ruthless in his selection and removal of personnel in an attempt to
raise the standard, particularly of regular RN officers within the Command. He
initially regarded WATU with caution, but was soon converted by Roberts and
personally undertook one of the week-long courses.[40] Horton imported a
number of senior submarine officers, notably Captain G. W. G. Simpson as
Commodore (D) in Londonderry, to instil the professional standards that he
demanded. Equally to the point, regular pre-deployment training programmes
were enforced for each escort group and for the newly formed support groups.

By late January 1943, the routine was in place on the basis of Horton's
assessment that at least 14 days in harbour and seven sea training days were
required in every group's 100-day cycle.[41] In the harbour phase, ships conducted
maintenance and boiler-cleaning, with leave to half the ship's company. The
ships' A/S teams were in one watch for leave purposes and were thus available
for training as a body on alternate stand-offs. If the interval elapsed was too
great, a week was allocated after completion of repairs for whole-ship training
centred on the A/S and the weapons personnel. In any event, the last few days
alongside would be devoted to intensive training, with at least five hours for the
command and A/S personnel in an attack teacher. Their performance would be
assessed and corrected, with written reports going on to the group commander
and Captain (D). Typical reports on A/S training from 1944 are included at
Table 3.[42] Much of this routine had been in place and enforced before 1943, but
Horton's contribution was to make periods in harbour effectively sacrosanct,
something which measurably improved seagoers' attitudes to the prospect of
harbour training. The sea phase followed, leaving vivid memories:

> Before sailing on each convoy passage, harbour training was
> carried out in Derry....Before leaving on each escort duty, two or
> three days and nights were spent exercising off the entrance to the
> River Foyle, working with submarines, firing at targets and
> carrying out the multitude of jobs which might fall to a convoy
> escort. In fact, the men sometimes complained that they felt more
> tired after the pre-convoy exercises than after the convoy passage
> itself![43]

Horton then went a step further. With the establishment of the post of Training
Captain Western Approaches, he overcame a deficiency which he had perceived
as preventing the attainment of high standards within the command. None of

the base Captains (D), he noted, was 'able to give adequate personal attention to the [training problem] in addition to his routine duties.'[44] The Training Captain would also take some of the load from the shoulders of the individual group commanders. Although there were definite advantages to the British approach whereby a senior officer commanded his own ship, the practice did make it more difficult to enforce the required standards in other units. Otherwise a supporter of the RN method, Peter Gretton admitted that without his own ship to command, he could spend more time in other ships of his group during exercise periods; and so by his personal influence he could put across his point of view and his requirements.[45]

Horton's ideas certainly originated in the submarine service's Commanding Officer's Qualifying Course (or 'Perisher'), which put prospective COs through a rigorous and increasingly complex 'pass or fail' course of live attacks on defended ship targets. The Training Captain was assigned the large yacht *Philante* for use as a headquarters ship and as the notional convoy for the ASW exercises conducted by each group. The existing pattern of two to three days sea training before deployment was now replaced or supplemented with an equal period under the direction of the Training Captain.

Depending upon the passage of time since a group's previous session, the first 24 hours were devoted to individual unit serials to ensure that internal organization was satisfactory. The re-assembled group then conducted *Philante* around a pre-planned and pre-timed circuit of the Irish Sea for 36-48 hours. Opposition was provided by two to three submarines and a motor launch with a towed target simulating a surfaced U-boat. Their positioning and attack times were intended to create the maximum tactical challenge for the escort force. In the interests of realism, the standard submarine exercise safety regulations (such as ordering a submarine to remain deep in the presence of manoeuvring A/S escorts)[46] were relaxed to the extent that 'it was necessary ....to employ [only] experienced submarine captains.'[47]

Anti-aircraft shoots were conducted without warning on the unalerted appearance of target-towing aircraft simulating shadowers. As the exercise progressed, these shoots were timed, so far as possible , to coincide with a submarine 'event', thus putting ships to the test of fighting simultaneously in two environments. When escort carriers became available, they were included in the programme and co-operative tactics were practised by escorts with their aircraft and those of Coastal Command. The format provided time for both briefing and debriefing. The latter proved particularly valuable because 'ships could explain their movements',[48] gaining insights into their own and others' thinking which could not otherwise be obtained, short of actual contact with the enemy.

Philante was also used as a sea-going test-bed for new ASW tactics, something in which Horton took a close interest, going 'to sea himself.... for important tactical experiments.'[49] The whole Training Group concept proved a resounding success, and became one of the fundamentals of post-war RN and even NATO training doctrine. The only interruption experienced was a move north to Loch Alsh away from Larne when the Irish Sea itself became a theatre for U-boat operations.[50]

It has to be noted, however, that the priority for this training went to the Support groups rather than the Close Escort groups. The latter 'had very little opportunity to exercise as groups....individual ships exercised their weapons and internal efficiencies at sea when weather and working conditions allowed, which was not very often.'[51]

The need for improvements in co-operation between air and surface forces was met through the establishment of a Joint Anti-U-boat School at Ballykelly in Northern Ireland in April 1943.[52] This combined theoretical instructions and practical exercises to good effect. However, its greatest contribution was not so much in improved tactics as in the greater understanding which was achieved between aircraft and the surface escorts.

Horton Holds the Line on Training

There was a penalty to the enforcement of a rigorous group training programme and its corollary, adequate undisturbed periods for maintenance and harbour training. Under some pressure from Admiralty and Prime Minister to increase the availability of escorts, Horton stood firm. He argued strongly that the apparent reduction in the numbers of units available for escort duties was more than outweighed by the quantum increase in the operational efficiency of the remainder. 'It could not be too often stressed', he noted, 'that the trained group was the basis of protection, not mere numbers of escort vessels.'[53]

Aided by the increased availability of escorts, the weight of evidence to back his claims and the obvious efficacy of his policies, he largely gained his point. By late 1943, Western Approaches units were conscious that they were achieving higher all-round standards of efficiency than ships of the Home Fleet. This was attributed directly to the continuity of training programmes.[54] The victory, however, was never complete. At intervals until the end of the war, Horton had to fight off demands for reductions in training schedules,[55] and despite his extraordinary efforts to prepare ASW forces for the invasion of France, some ships received much abbreviated programmes.[56]

Canada and Group Training

By comparison, the progress achieved by the RCN in group training was mixed. Units in the Western Approaches generally followed the operational cycles of the British ships. However, RCN ships in the western Atlantic never enjoyed the continuation training provided to Western Approaches' escort and support groups and this showed in their results.[57] There were extensive efforts in 1943 to prepare for an inshore campaign and sporadic group exercises were conducted out of Halifax from then on, but these suffered from the tendency (noted earlier) to shut down for the winter. Equally to the point, the shortage of training submarines in Canada forced groups seeking in-contact time to use the three boats based on the Anti-Submarine School at Digby, which cut into basic asdic training for officers and ratings.[58]

Horton himself could go too far. His constant emphasis on improving training was to pay even greater dividends in the shallow water warfare of 1944-45, but with the increased demands this placed on sonar operators and command teams, the pressure was at times excessive:

> His personal interest in training was so intense that he almost defeated his own - and absolutely correct - object. Those responsible for training became so frightened of his insatiable enquiries that they were more interested in sending satisfactory returns than in preparing the ships to fight the enemy. However, when this was pointed out to him, he was - after an extremely tense period - a big enough man to recognize the situation and put it right.[59]

Conclusion

There are two striking aspects to the history of sea training in the Atlantic campaign. The first is the quality, whether by accident or design, of the early British response to the initial work-up requirement, especially by comparison with that of the other navies involved.

The second is the considerable time which elapsed before such a good beginning was built upon in any coherent way. It would be easy to employ hindsight to criticize the failure of the commanders and staffs in appreciating the problem, but the real lesson of this component of the war at sea is the extent to which *useful* training - that is, training which could produce significant operational improvements - was dependent upon the combination of many factors, whose interconnection was by no means apparent. Harbour training requires guaranteed time alongside, dedicated facilities and expert personnel. Sea training requires dedicated exercise periods before deployment, dedicated sea areas, dedicated - and efficient - 'aggressor forces' and a full share of expert personnel as supervisors. It may be a statement of the obvious that both harbour and sea training required agreed and practical tactical doctrine as the meat of their message, but this was the most critical factor of all and one which could not properly operate until WATU and the approaches which the Unit generated could hit their stride.

The unanswerable 'What If?' is what Horton could have achieved had he become Commander-in-Chief Western Approaches two years earlier. Did sufficient doctrine exist? Could the reductions in deployment have been effected? Would the results have been significant? The answers may be 'Yes, possibly' or even 'Yes, probably, at least in the majority', but no one can say for sure. But when he was appointed, Horton was the man with the right idea, in the right place at the right time, and this was enough to make the difference in 1943.

TABLE 1: TOBERMORY WORK UP SYLLABUS

	S	D	F	CC	CF	TO	TC
Working Days	21	20	20	18	14	14	12
Instruction Hours	211	166	160	160	140	118	102
Introduction Film and Talk	1	1	1	1	1	1	1
Sea Time A/S	35	35	35	35	35	28	14
Shoots	20	8	8	8	4	8	8
Gunnery Lecture, Drills,							
Films, etc.	78	37	37	37	33	31	31
A/S Attack Teacher, Films, etc.	14	14	14	14	14	10	10
Harbour Drills, Boat Work,							
Seamanship	17	19	19	17	15	17	15
D.C. Squid, and Hedgehog							
Lectures and Drills	2	4	4	4	4	2	2
Fire Fighting, Damage Control,							
Demolition, Salvus	5	5	5	5	3	-	-
Radar	23	21	15	15	15	8	8
Miscellaneous (CBs, Signals,							
GCX, Dental	12	16	16	19	12	7	7
Field Training	4	6	6	6	4	6	6

NOTES: 1.   7 Working days each week
             2.   7 Instructional hours each working day (seatime hours
                 additional)
             3.   1 Make and mend afternoon after 14 days (progress
                 permitting)
             4.   Instructors 1 day stand down every 14 days

LEGEND: S= Sloop; D= Destroyer; F= Frigate; CC= Castle Class Corvette; CF= Flower Class
Corvette; TO= Ocean Trawler; TC= Coastal Trawler

TABLE 2: TYPICAL SYLLABUS FOR *FLOWER*-CLASS CORVETTE
HARBOUR PHASE (DAYS 01-06)

01   Organization Check
         Departmental Inspections
         Medical Examinations - Radar and Asdic Ratings

02   Drills - Asdic
                  Depth-charge Loading
                  Gunnery
                  Boatwork
                  Radar

                           Damage Control
                           Seamanship
          Working Up Film and Lecture

03   Drills - Asdic
                     Radar
                     Gunnery - Surface
                     Gunnery - AA
                     Boatwork
       Action/Cruising Stations Organization Check

04   A/S Attack Teacher
       Drills - Squad Training
                     Damage Control
                     Close-Range Weapons
                     Ammunition Supply
                     Aiming Rifles (for Major Weapons)

05   A/S Attack Teacher
       Drills - Close-Range Weapons
                     Ahead-Throwing Weapons
                     Depth-charges
                     Aiming Rifles (for Major Weapons)
                     Seamanship
                     Boatwork
                     Gunnery - AA
                     General (introduction)
       Night Action Stations/Darken Ship Check

06   A/S Attack Teacher
       Drills - Close-Range Weapons
                     Loading
                     RYPA
                     Ammunition Supply
                     Ahead-Throwing Weapons
                     Ship's Diving Team
       Action Stations/General Drills

SEA/HARBOUR PHASE(DAYS 07- 14)

07   A/S Exercises - Depth-Charge Attacks only
                                 Visual and Radio Communications Exercises
                                 Anti-Acoustic Torpedo Procedures
           Seamanship - Tow Forward/Tow Aft
                                 Boarding Party

08   A/S Exercises -   Ahead-Throwing Weapons

09   AM: Harbour
          A/S Attack Teacher
          Drills -   Aiming Rifles (for Major Weapons)
          Films -   AA
          PM: Sea
          Gunnery Practices -Surface
                              AA
                              Starshell/Rockets (Night Encounter)
                              Two-Target Night Firing
          Includes: Simulated E-boat attacks by Air
                              Sea Rescue Launches (unalerted)

10   Harbour
          A/S Attack Teacher
          Drills -   Depth-charges
                     Squad Training
                     Boatwork
                     Small Arms Firings
       Action Stations/General Drills
       Maintenance -   Asdic
                        Ahead-Throwing Weapons

11   Harbour: 'Ship Should Now Be a Fighting Unit'
          Action Stations/General Drills
          Maintenance -   Depth-charges
          Lectures -   Night Look Out/Demolitions (Ashore)
          PM: Make and Mend (Granted *if possible* as the only Make
                           and Mend for the period)

12   Sea
          AM: A/S Exercises
          PM: Seamanship Exercises

13   Sea
          AM: A/S Exercises
          PM: Seamanship Exercises

14   Harbour
          AM: Lectures -   A/S Tactics and Policy
                               First Aid
          PM: Final Inspection
                 Includes: Simulated attacks on ship and exercise
                               of casualties, emergency depth-charge attacks,

> damage control procedures and any 'incidents'
> considered appropriate by the inspecting
> officer. Inspection concludes with walk round
> of ship.

Communications
Training conducted every day except Sunday. Includes weekly inter-port HF exercise (arranged by C-in-C Western Approaches). Harbour exercises are independent of the Work-up Harbour Training Programme.

Instruction Hours
0830-1200
1330-1600
1700-1830

Source: ADM 199/1729.

TABLE 3
TYPICAL WEEKLY A/S TRAINING REPORT

Date: 3 June 1944

1. HMS *Tenby*   Hours of Instruction: 4
Runs were carried out on small targets moving at high speeds, giving off plenty of Hydrophone Effect. The A/S Control Officer (Sub Lt RNVR), although not qualified as such, did very well on what knowledge he has. Very keen and quick to learn.

PO	HSD	Average
AB	SD	Average
AB	SD	Average
AB	SD	Average

All ratings are weak on echo pitch reports.

2. HMS *Sidmouth*   Hours of Instruction: 2
A very good all round team who are very A/S minded and can deal with almost any situation. A/S Control Officer - Lt RNVR.

AB	HSD	Very Good
AB	SD	Average
AB	SD	Good

3. HMS *Bridport*   Hours of Instruction: 2
An average team who need more training before they can be classified as an efficient hunting craft. The Commanding Officer always left in the dark, through the lack of information from the operators. The tendency to wait until the range has closed to about 500 yards spoilt almost every attack.

AB	HSD	Good
LS	SD	Average
OD	A/SD	Average
OD	A/SD	Average

All ratings are reluctant to report any changes of echo pitch or bearing. A/S Control Officer - Sub Lt RNVR.

4. HMS *Boston*   Hours of Instruction: 2

An average team, but need a great deal of coaxing on reporting any change of echo pitch. The Commanding Officer has a tendency to nibble at the target instead of giving a good throw off. This was corrected before instruction was completed.

AB	HSD	Good
AB	SD	Average
AB	SD	Average
AB	SD	Average

A/S Control Officer keeps a watchful eye on his operators; very keen. *(Rank and list are not stated in the original.)*

K. R. BAGG
Boatswain, A/S, RN
A/S Training Officer

Key:

A/S	Anti-Submarine
HSD	Higher Submarine Detector
SD	Submarine Detector
A/SD	Acting Submarine Detector
PO	Petty Officer
LS	Leading Seaman
AB	Able Seaman
OD	Ordinary Seaman
	Source: ADM 199/1728

Acknowledgments

The Author is indebted to the A/S Officers' Association of Australia and its members, particularly Ray Worledge, the Society's extraordinarily efficient and helpful Secretary. Ray gave me much material and put me in touch with: Cdr the Hon. Fred Osborne CMG, DSC*, RANVR, (who commanded HM Ships *Gentian, Vanquisher* and *Peacock* as well as serving at WATU), Captain Stanley Darling OBE, DSC**, RANR (who commanded HM Ships *Oskaig, Inchmarnoch, Clarkia, Loch Killin* and *Loch Lomond, Loch Killin* being a member of Capt. F. J. Walker's Support Group) and L. M. Hinchcliffe DSC, RAN, an A/S specialist who served on the staff of *Western Isles* and took part in working up 54 ships. Lt Cdr Max Shean DSO*, RANR, has recently published a most useful book entitled *Corvette and Submarine* detailing his experiences in HMS *Bluebell* before going on to midget submarines. Lt R. P. Hall RNVR and Lt Cdr Denis Rose RAN also gave me valuable information.

The A/S Officers' Association is in the process of producing a history of the Australian A/S School, HMAS *Rushcutter*, and its extremely successful training programme, which was largely initiated by and was under the direction of A/Cdr (later Captain) H. M. Newcomb OBE, RN. A passed-over A/S specialist at the beginning of the war, Newcomb's contribution, to the Allied A/S effort was remarkable and, in its way, deserves comparison with those of Stephenson and Roberts.

Dr Marc Milner of the University of New Brunswick provided much information and guidance on the Canadian work-up effort.

Notes

1.   Warner, *Disaster in the Pacific*, p. vi.
2.   CB 3212D *Anti-Submarine Warfare* Volume IV *A/S Training* p. 14. Public Record Office (PRO) ADM 239/248.
3.   Roskill, *The War at Sea 1939-1945*, I, p. 359.
4.   Baker, *The Terror of Tobermory*, p. 120.
5.   *Ibid.*, p. 68.
6.   *Ibid.*, p. 120.
7.   Whinney, *The U-Boat Peril*, p. 90.
8.   I am indebted to Lt Cdr Denis Rose RAN, of the A/S Officers' Assocation of Australia, who gave me this information from his father's recollections of Tobermory in August 1940 and January 1941.
9.   CB 3212D ADM 239/248.
10.   HMS *Mentor* Standing Orders 1944. ADM 199/1729.
11.   Captain L. M. Hinchcliffe DSC, RAN (former A/S specialist in HMS *Western Isles*). Letter to the author dated 30 March 1993.
12.   See Baker, *Terror of Tobermory*, pp. 170-171. Copies of the signals are contained in ADM 199/1732
13.   Captain Stanley Darling OBE, DSC**, RANR. Letter to the author dated 24 November 1992.
14.   ADM 199/1732.
15.   CB 3212D p.16. ADM 239/248.
16.   Baker, *Terror of Tobermory*,. p. 134.
17.   CB 3212D p.11. ADM 239/248. See also ADM 199/1732 for examples of the complex planning involved in providing sufficient submarines, even late in the war.

18. Milner, *North Atlantic Run,* p. 276.
19. As evidenced by HM Submarine H 43 in 1942 which was not permitted to dive below 100 feet. See Coote, *Submariner,* p. 51.
20. CB 3212D p.13. ADM 239/248
21. ADM 199/1729. PRO.
22. Baker, *Terror of Tobermory,* p. 139.
23. CB 3212D p.15. ADM 239/248
24. Commander the Honourable Fred Osborne CMG, DSC*, RANVR. Letter to the author dated 28 December 1992.
25. Dr Marc Milner. Letter to the Author dated 24 March 1993. I am particularly grateful to Dr Milner for his thoughtful analysis of Canadian activities, which gives particular emphasis to the environmental difficulties which the RCN faced.
26. Milner, *North Atlantic Run,* p. 276.
27. Morison *History of United States Naval Operations in World War II* Volume I *The Battle of the Atlantic September 1939-May 1943,* pp. 229-236.
28. *Ibid.,* Volume X, *The Atlantic Battle Won: May 1943-May 1945,* pp.47-51.
29. *Ibid.,* p.18.
30. Charles M. Sternhell & Alan M. Thorndike *Antisubmarine Warfare in World War II* Operations Evaluation Group Report No. 51, Office of the Chief of Naval Operations, Washington DC, 1946, pp. 124-125. See also Hackmann *Seek and Strike,* p.308.
31. Roskill, *The War at Sea,* I, pp. 358-359.
32. MacIntyre, *U-boat Killer,* p. 37.
33. Robertson, *Walker RN,* p. 39.
34. Gretton, *Convoy Escort Commander,* p.102.
35. Terrell, *Admiralty Brief,* pp. 149-150.
36. Williams, *Captain Gilbert Roberts RN and the Anti-U-boat School,* pp. 100-101.
37. CB 3212D p. 20.
38. Vice Admiral Sir Peter Gretton, 'Why Don't We Learn From History?' *Naval Review* Vol. 46, No.1, January 1958. p. 19.
39. Chalmers, *Max Horton and the Western Approaches,* pp.162-163. Cites C-in-C Western Approaches Letter to Admiralty dated 5 December 1942.
40. Williams, *Captain Gilbert Roberts RN and the Anti-U-boat School,* p. 117.
41. Chalmers, *Max Horton and the Western Approaches,* p. 207.
42. ADM 199/1728.
43. Gretton, *Crisis Convoy,* p. 37.
44. Chalmers, *Max Horton and the Western Approaches,* p. 163.
45. Gretton, *Crisis Convoy,* p. 37.
46. CB 4000(1938).
47. CB 3212D p. 21. ADM 239/248.
48. *Ibid.,* p. 21.
49. Chalmers, *Max Horton and the Western Approaches,* p. 173.
50. CB 3212D. p. 21. ADM 239/248.
51. Cdr Osborne. Letter to the author dated 28 December 1992, *op. cit.*

52.   CB3212D, p. 22.
53.   Roskill, *War at Sea,* II, p. 357.
54.   Whinney, *The U-Boat Peril,* p.115.
55.   Chalmers, *Max Horton and the Western Approaches,* pp. 206-207.
56.   See R. P. Hall (serving as a Sub Lt RANVR in HMS *Kingsmill*), journal entry of
      29 February 1944 for a description of one such abbreviated programme.
57.   See McLean, D. M., *The Last Cruel Winter: RCN Support Groups and the U-boat
      Schnorkel Offensive,* Master of War Studies Thesis, Royal Military College,
      Kingston, 1992; especially pp. 46-7 and 81-3.
58   Dr Marc Milner: Letter to the Author dated 24 March 1993, *op. cit.*
59.   Chalmers, *Max Horton and the Western Approaches,.* p. 183.

13

Liverpool as HQ and Base

by Alan J. Scarth

For over 200 years the port of Liverpool has been one of the world's great seaports, known much more for its commercial activities than its naval importance. In the 20th Century, however, it has played a vital strategic role in two World Wars, of which the second was, undoubtedly, its 'Finest Hour'.[1] This chapter, based primarily on Merseyside sources, is the first detailed account of how the port became not only one of Britain's most important naval bases during World War II, but also the operational headquarters of the nation's Atlantic campaign. The chapter also considers how the port and people of Merseyside responded to this supreme challenge in their history.

*

Early in 1940, when enemy action closed the port of London to ocean convoys, most of the capital's usual sea-traffic was diverted to the 'safer' west coast ports of Liverpool, Glasgow and the Bristol Channel. This involved an enormous re-organization of the country's whole transport and supply system, effectively throwing it into reverse for the duration of the war. Not surprisingly, it also had considerable implications for the Admiralty's arrangements for the defence of trade.

At the start of the war these west coast ports were under the naval operational control of Admiral Sir Martin Dunbar-Nasmith, Commander-in-Chief Western Approaches Command, who was based in Plymouth. As the traffic through the ports concerned steadily increased, however, so did losses of merchant ships due to U-boat attacks in their approach routes. The fall of France in June 1940 brought matters to a head.

From their new bases in French ports, U-boats immediately launched a sustained and highly successful offensive against Britain's Atlantic supply lines.[2] The Royal Navy's understandable preoccupation with the threat of invasion, on the other hand, left Dunbar-Nasmith with too few escort ships and aircraft to protect the convoys using the two main approaches north and south of Ireland. Plymouth had also become too accessible to enemy aircraft based in France, but was too distant for effective control of the vast traffic using the Clyde and Mersey.[3]

It was against this background that the Prime Minister decided that the north of Ireland route should be the only approach and that the headquarters of the C-in-C Western Approaches should be moved to Liverpool, the most central and most important west-coast port. As Chalmers has shown, Churchill had anticipated this need: when he was First Lord of the Admiralty, he directed that the basement of Derby House (a new office block situated behind Liverpool's Town Hall) was to be reconstructed as a massive bomb- and gas-proof citadel, wired and equipped as an operational control centre. Thus, in February 1941, when the building was ready, Admiral Sir Percy Noble was appointed to succeed Nasmith as C-in-C, and took up his post with a large staff at Derby House.[4]

At least a year before Noble's arrival, Liverpool had become established as Britain's most important ocean convoy port, especially for merchant convoys. Its dock system was one of the largest in the world, stretching about seven miles on the Liverpool (north) side of the River Mersey, with extensive additional facilities on the Birkenhead (south) side. But what of the armed fleet presence in the port? Had it grown to a level commensurate with the port's vital importance to the Atlantic lifeline? Before the war, the only notable naval presence within the port of Liverpool was provided by the two drill ships of the thriving Mersey Division of the Royal Naval Volunteer Reserve, namely HMS *Eaglet*, moored in Salthouse Dock, Liverpool and HMS *Irwell*, in Morpeth Dock, Birkenhead.[5] As early as 16 March 1939, however, the Admiralty had informed Sir Rex Hodges, General Manager of the Mersey Docks and Harbour Board, of its intention 'to use the Port of Liverpool as a base, during an emergency, for forty-four auxiliary vessels (Fleetwood trawlers) and eighteen escort vessels'. Berth accommodation was to be identified which would enable these vessels to sail at any state of the tide, together with some 4,000 square feet of accommodation for use as a victualling store. Responding to these instructions, the Dock Board's Harbour Master anticipated no problem in accommodating these vessels in the Wallasey Dock, Birkenhead, without interfering with the use of the dock for general purposes, and earmarked a block at the west end of the Wallasey Dock warehouses for use by the Admiralty as a store. While no permanent berth could be arranged on the Liverpool side of the river, he foresaw no difficulty in finding temporary berthage when required in an emergency.[6]

As war approached, Vice-Admiral L. E. Crabbe was appointed as Flag Officer-in-Charge (FOiC), Liverpool, with an office on the first floor of the Liver Building, a well-known landmark at the city's Pier Head. Crabbe's responsibilities were to supervise all naval aspects of the defence and operation of the port. As a member of the Port Emergency Committee, which was formally established by the Minister of War Transport on 23 August 1939, he and his successor, Vice Admiral J. M. Ritchie, maintained a close liaison with the local port and shipping authorities. The Port Emergency Committee at Liverpool was representative of all the main interests of the port, including, apart from the Flag Officer, the port authority (the Mersey Docks and Harbour Board), shipowners, port labour, warehousing, railways, canals and Customs. Its function was to ensure that all the facilities of the port were used to secure the quickest possible turn-round of ships and the most rapid clearance of their cargoes. Although partly superseded later by the Regional Port Director, the

Committee met regularly throughout the war and had legal powers to control and regulate the traffic of the port.[7]

Among Crabbe's first tasks was to establish, in association with the Dock Board, a network of defences for the port approaches. In this, he was greatly assisted by plans already made by Captain H. V. Hart, the Board's Marine Surveyor and Water Bailiff, in conjunction with the Admiralty, for the darkening of lights on buoys, the closing of subsidiary river channels and for the Examination Service. The purpose of the Examination Service, of which Hart was to have command (as had his predecessor in World War I), was to identify all ships approaching the Mersey Estuary. Ships would be intercepted by armed vessels crewed by civilians, and ordered into the examination anchorage, where they would be boarded and inspected for possible 'Fifth Column activity'.[8] In addition to these measures, Crabbe took steps to organize and control the outer and inner defences of the port, including controlled minefields, shore batteries and signal stations in and around the Mersey Estuary. Within these defences, his staff would work closely with the Board's Harbour Master regarding the allocation of berths, anchorages and other facilities.[9]

Also established on the first floor of the Liver Building, but not responsible to the Flag Officer, was the Liverpool Sub-command, one of six outposts of Western Approaches Command at Plymouth. Under the direction of the Staff Officer, Operations, this sub-command kept a constant watch over a radius of 150 miles to seaward of Liverpool, and covered all ports from Bardsey Island, off Caernarvonshire, to the Scottish coast. Its staff of RN officers and up to 30 Wrens plotted the courses of escort warships operating in the Irish Sea and also kept naval and merchant ships informed of any enemy mines laid or naval units operating within the area. Beyond the areas covered by this and other sub-commands, all shipping between Iceland and Portugal came under the direct control of Western Approaches Command headquarters. This arrangement continued throughout the war.[10]

Completing the RN's triumvirate at the Liver Building was the Senior Naval Control Service Officer (NCSO), Mersey, who was established on the third floor. As in other ports, the NCSO was responsible to the Admiralty Trade Division for the control of all merchant shipping, coastwise and overseas. His main work was in routeing ships to their destinations, and in resolving the multifarious problems associated with the making up and dispatching of convoys. He organized and chaired the Convoy Conferences, and ensured that all masters received their confidential sailing instructions immediately before joining their ships. All masters arriving in the port had to report to him with full details of their ships and cargoes. Subsidiary NCSOs were based at Garston and Eastham, the latter to deal with shipping using the Manchester Ship Canal.[11]

By mid-1939 the naval presence in or near the Mersey Dock Estate was also becoming more pronounced. In August, for example, the Admiralty acquired premises and land near Love Lane, a short distance north of the

Liverpool Pier Head, for the storage of guns and ammunition for distribution to merchant ships.[12] It also obtained the lease of two large casemates or storage units at Herculaneum Dock for the storage of explosives.[13] In the same month money was provided for the supply of fenders, mooring rings, bilge blocks and other fittings to enable HM ships to be docked 'in an emergency' at Gladstone Graving Dock, which, at more than 1,000 feet long and 120 feet wide, was one of the largest docks of its kind in Europe.[14] Soon afterwards a 50-ton travelling crane was installed with over 800 feet of track at the south side of this graving dock, together with 300 bilge blocks for the reception of capital ships.[15] HM battleships *Rodney* and *Barham*, the latter having been seriously damaged by a torpedo attack by U-30 in the Irish Sea, were among the first of many warships of all classes repaired there during the war.[16]

On the outbreak of war, as expected, Wallasey Dock in Birkenhead became the base for a fleet of auxiliary trawlers, sent from Fleetwood for minesweeping and convoy escort work. The dock remained in use for this purpose throughout the war, with training establishments for this work being set up in the vicinity. Eventually, Wallasey Dock was used for ocean-going trawlers involved in convoy escort work, such as the *Northern-*, *Military-* and *Dance*-class boats, while nearby Morpeth Dock housed smaller, minesweeping trawlers and Examination Service vessels. The Birkenhead base itself was named HMS *Irwell*, after the former RNVR drill ship which retained a training function at Morpeth Dock. Over in Liverpool's north docks, on the other hand, a flotilla of old V- and W-class destroyers began to operate regularly out of Gladstone Dock, Bootle. In October 1939 the increasing naval activity on the River Mersey had prompted the appointment of Andrew H. Wilcox, a Mersey Pilot First-Class, as Admiralty Pilot for the Port of Liverpool.[17] In the same month the Admiralty obtained permission to erect a shed containing a workshop, a mess and other facilities alongside the wind screen at the west side of Gladstone Dock for the use of the destroyer flotilla.[18] The shed concerned was a former tennis pavilion purchased from the Liverpool Corporation Parks Department, and was opened as the Flotilla Club by Lord Derby the following Christmas Eve. The club was later extended several times, eventually incorporating a small chapel and reading room as well as other facilities. During the war it never closed, day or night, and catered for no fewer than half a million British and Allied sailors - despite which, it was claimed, 'the beer never ran dry'.[19] The club, which was staffed entirely by civilian volunteers, earned a wide reputation for its hospitality and soon became a part of Merseyside's wartime folklore. In July 1940 the whole of the west wall of Gladstone Dock was formally requisitioned by the Admiralty.[20] Already, this dock and its environs were developing into 'a vast, concentrated hive of naval activity'.[21]

Liverpool rapidly became an important centre for naval recruitment and training. In November 1939 alone, for example, 1,700 naval ratings (presumably new recruits on their way to Portsmouth or other major naval bases) boarded trains at Riverside Station, adjoining Princes Landing Stage.[22]

HMS *Eaglet*, the former RNVR drill ship moored in Salthouse Dock, became one of the RN's main DEMS (Defensively Equipped Merchant Ships) gunnery training schools for Merchant Navy personnel, being equipped with all manually-operated guns from the large six-inch to small anti-aircraft weapons. In all, over 100,000 merchant seamen were trained at this school during the war.[23] *Eaglet*, herself an old fleet minesweeper like *Irwell*, gave her name to the escort base which developed in Liverpool, and from February 1941 also carried the flag of the C-in-C, Western Approaches.[24] From an early stage in the war the old destroyer HMS *Wallace* was attached to the Liverpool base as a gunnery training ship. A DEMS training school for RN personnel was established at HMS *Wellesley*, the former Royal Southern Hospital in Hill Street, Toxteth. The staff and trainees of this traditionally-run establishment soon endeared themselves to local residents by marching up and down Hill Street each morning to a resident Marine Band. *Wellesley*'s gunnery range, mainly consisting of Oerlikon anti-aircraft guns, was sited at Ainsdale, near Southport.[25] Finally, it was in Liverpool that 13,000 merchant seamen from throughout Britain and the Commonwealth registered during the war for naval auxiliary service under naval command T124. A memorial to the 1,390 such men who died while serving under Royal Navy orders was erected at the city's Pier Head in 1952.[26]

For the first year of the war, the small escort force based at Liverpool struggled to cope with the port's growing convoy traffic. Escort numbers, however, were clearly insufficient, and it was not until late 1940 that reinforcements began to arrive. In September, for example, the Admiralty established a set of moorings in the river for berthing trawlers, presumably to allow an overspill from Wallasey Dock.[27]

In October it obtained further berthing facilities 'for destroyers etc.' on the west side of Albert Dock, immediately to the south of Liverpool Pier Head.[28] In practice, however, Albert Dock became an overflow base for many of the small *Flower*-class corvettes which had begun to arrive in force in the Mersey. HM ships *Periwinkle* and *Campanula* were among the first to enter this dock in November.[29] It was to Albert Dock that Nicholas Monsarrat, a young RNVR lieutenant serving in *Campanula* at the time, was referring when he wrote:

> At our usual base there is one small dock, nicknamed 'The Garage',
> that has become Corvette Headquarters. At the end of a convoy it is
> crammed with ships; and this recurrent association, and the chance
> of exchanging visits, is remarkably pleasant, particularly at the end
> of a trip which may have been rough in one way or another.[30]

The corvette crews based at Albert Dock quickly developed a special camaraderie away from the main escort base at Gladstone. This may well have been partly due to the storage in the dock warehouses of the Admiralty's supplies of Navy Rum for the port.[31]

It may have been the arrival in the port of a flotilla of six modern H-class destroyers and several ex-American 'four-stackers' that prompted the Admiralty, in November 1940, to reserve West Langton (Dock) Quay, in Liverpool's north docks, as an additional berth for destroyers. In return for this concession, the Dock Board was assured that fewer ships would be sent to the port for conversion to armed merchant cruisers, hospital ships, transports, and other such auxiliary function.[32] A second Admiralty Pilot, Mr. George Backhouse, was appointed for the port in December.[33]

Merseyside was still recovering from its first serious air raids of the war when, on 17 February 1941, Admiral Sir Percy Noble, 'the best-dressed man in the Navy', arrived at Derby House to take up his post as Commander-in-Chief, Western Approaches. Also transferred to Derby House from Plymouth at this time was the headquarters of No. 15 Group, RAF Coastal Command, under Air Officer Commanding, Air Vice-Marshal J. M. Robb. Noble was to be in overall command of combined naval and air operations.[34]

The 'Area Combined Headquarters' at Derby House eventually housed over 1,000 RAF and RN staff, of whom a large proportion were RN officers and Wrens. It occupied more than 300 rooms on four floors, two of which were underground. But it was within the vast, fortified basement, protected by blast walls and a reinforced concrete 'ceiling', several feet thick, that the 'Fortress' or 'Citadel' was created. Within the 'Dungeon', as it was called by its staff, was the Operations Room with its huge wall maps overlooked by glass-fronted offices. This was to be the nerve centre of Britain's Atlantic campaign. Here, as in U-boat Command Headquarters, the Battle of the Atlantic 'took on the character of a monstrous chess game'.[35]

Derby House possessed a very large communications department, which daily handled over 1,000 messages regarding the conduct of shipping. Staff at the 'Citadel' could communicate directly with ships and aircraft, and had a direct cable link to the US. Each morning at 0900 the C-in-C had a three-way telephone conference with the senior officers of Coastal Command Headquarters at Northwood (North London) and the Admiralty Trade Division Convoy Plot in London. After a full appraisal of the situation, based on up-to-date intelligence and weather reports, his staff would then dispose their sea and air forces to counter the enemy's predicted movements.[36]

Being constantly manned, Derby House was equipped with emergency sleeping quarters and mess facilities, and even had a sun-ray treatment room for the 'cave dwellers' working long hours underground. As a precaution against major air-raid damage, an alternative Command HQ, complete in every detail, was also constructed at 'House X', on Lord Derby's estate at Knowsley, about 10 miles north-east of Liverpool. Despite the destruction caused around Derby House during the blitzes of 1940-41, this facility was never actually used.[37]

At Derby House, Noble created a smooth-running, highly effective organization which, although vast, still managed to retain the personal touch. To escort commanders such as D. E. G. Wemyss, based at Liverpool from mid-

1941, for example, the headquarters staff seemed to 'know all of the seafarers of the command as individuals and was never too busy to listen to their tales'. As he later wrote, 'It was an organisation which inspired every confidence and gave us at sea not only the direction but all the support that we needed.'[38]

On his arrival in Liverpool, Noble had only the promise of ships and men for convoy escort duties. Gradually, however, more of both became available. One of his first recruits as an escort commander was Commander (later Captain) F. J. Walker, who soon became a legendary 'U-boat killer' and one of the RN's most celebrated heroes of the Battle. Describing Walker's arrival in Liverpool in March 1941, his biographer, Terence Robertson, writes that the commander 'at once found himself among strangely-assorted bedfellows. It seemed that by design or accident all the misfits of the Navy had congregated at Liverpool.'[39]

Among Walker's fellow officers at the escort base were many who, like him, had been passed over for promotion during peacetime and had become 'red-tape rebels', consigned to the unglamorous 'backwater job' of convoy escort work. Others were Royal Naval Reservists, usually ex-Merchant Marine officers who, although expert seamen, were often unused and averse to the ways of the Royal Navy. The overwhelming majority, however, were officers of the Royal Naval Volunteer Reserve, rather harshly described by one writer as 'week-end sailors churned out by the recruiting machine, often with inadequate training'.[40] In practice, such men were often well-trained and very capable, and would acquit themselves extremely well in wartime conditions. Even so, they undoubtedly needed time to become fully integrated into the RN at war. As a further complication, several of the Liverpool-based escort ships were, or would soon be, manned by Allied naval crews from Holland, Belgium, Norway, Free France and Poland.

The somewhat varied and cosmopolitan nature of the Liverpool Escort Force was the local background against which Admiral Noble initiated the formation and training of Escort Groups throughout Western Approaches Command. The establishment, in January 1942, of the Western Approaches Tactical Unit (WATU) on the top floor of the Exchange Building, near Derby House, was a further vital step in this direction. Under the extremely able direction of Captain Gilbert Roberts, WATU staff proceeded to develop escort tactics against the U-boats by building on the experiences and ideas of escort commanders like Walker, Macintyre and Gretton. No fewer than 5,000 Allied naval officers, from admirals to midshipmen, took part in the six-day tactical training courses held at WATU during the war. The resultant contribution of the unit to the cohesion and performance of the Atlantic escort forces was considerable.[41]

Between March and early May 1941, Merseyside endured some of its heaviest air-raids of the war. Wide areas were laid waste on both sides of the River Mersey, with the docks being the main targets. Although many merchant ships were sunk or damaged while in port, and many dock facilities were completely destroyed, the work of the port continued. Relatively few escort ships were damaged in the raids, and the escort base, although severely battered, also continued in operation.[42]

By late 1941 the ships of the Liverpool Escort Force were escorting convoys far and wide: north to Iceland and thence to northern Russia, west to Newfoundland and the United States, south to Gibraltar and the South Atlantic. As Monsarrat, among many others, has testified, their work at this stage in the war was relentless, gruelling, and fraught with danger. By January 1942, 60 escort vessels, excluding auxiliary trawlers, were based at Liverpool. These included 22 destroyers, two sloops and 36 corvettes, organized into seven groups. Of the two other main Western Approaches bases, namely Londonderry and Greenock, only Londonderry, with 68 ships, housed more escort vessels at this time. In terms of the number of escorts regularly using the port, Liverpool remained second only to Londonderry among the escort bases of the Command throughout the rest of the war.[43]

In November 1942, Admiral Noble was succeeded as C-in-C, Western Approaches by Admiral Sir Max Horton. Horton's 'quite ruthless and quite selfish' treatment of his staff presented a total contrast in style to that of the suave, tactful Noble.[44] Horton, however, brought Noble's careful preparatory work to fruition by fully developing the Escort Group system and, strongly influenced by Captain F. J. Walker, by introducing the highly successful Support Groups to take the offensive against the U-boats. His leadership proved of vital importance in securing the decisive Allied victories in the North Atlantic in May 1943. Fittingly, it was from Gladstone Dock, Bootle, that Captain 'Johnny' Walker led his Second Support Group to the most successful series of anti-U-boat actions by Allied naval forces in the entire war. From June 1943, his group sank 15 U-boats in just 13 months, accounting for six in one trip alone.[45]

Under Horton, the area controlled by Western Approaches Command Headquarters at Derby House grew substantially, on occasions even straddling the so-called North Atlantic CHOP line which divided the areas of British and Canadian control. By the end of the war the personnel serving within the Command had reached 100,000, only slightly less than the RN's total peace-time strength.[46]

It is clear from the above account that the RN was fully justified in choosing Liverpool as Command Headquarters and as a major escort base in the Battle of the Atlantic. But the tremendous sea and air campaign waged from the city would not have been possible without the enormous contribution of the port and people of Merseyside. Indeed, Merseyside provides one of the most outstanding examples of the wartime co-operation between civilian and military authorities of which Britain, among all the combatant nations, was the prime exponent. This will now be briefly illustrated.

From early 1940 until the end of hostilities, Liverpool was Britain's most important port, handling a large proportion of its ocean-borne traffic. At the hub of Atlantic convoy operations, the port received 1,285 incoming convoys during the war, an average of four every week. A similar amount of convoy traffic also sailed out of the Mersey during the war. Since one convoy might consist of anything up to 60 ships, the amount of shipping and cargo involved often put a severe strain on the port's facilities and workforce, a strain made much greater by the destruction caused in and around the docks by the many German air raids on Merseyside in the early war years. These reached their peak in the seven-night 'May Blitz' of 1941, after which, for a short while, just 12 out of 144 dock berths were still workable. It is an immense tribute to the work of the Port Emergency Committee, the Regional Port Directors (1942 onwards), Dock Board officials, and tens of thousands of port service workers that the port was, for the most part, kept open. During the war it handled more than 75 million tons of cargo, excluding oil imports, and maintained vital coastal traffic of 2½ million tons per year. Over 4½ million troops passed through, of whom more than one million were American. Most of the supplies for the North African landings were sent from the Mersey, and the port also played a vital role in the invasion of Europe.[47]

Deserving of particular praise were the port's 20,000 dock workers, who provided a 24-hour service in the loading and unloading of cargoes. These men often worked under extremely trying conditions caused by the black-out, the number of ships in port and the damage caused by air-raids. Because of losses of younger men to the armed services and other industries, their average age was well over 50.[48] River pilots and tug-boat crews also did sterling service at a time when navigation was particularly difficult and dangerous. Salvage teams from the Mersey Docks and Harbour Board and the Liverpool and Glasgow Salvage Association saved over 200 ships which had been sunk or stranded in the River Mersey and its approaches. These ships were invaluable to Britain later in the war. Cammell Laird Shipbuilders of Birkenhead built more than 100 warships, mainly submarines, and several merchant ships during the war, completing one ship every 20 days. Finally, over 20,000 men and women were employed on Merseyside in the vital work of ship repair. Mostly equipped for small repairs, the yards concerned acted largely as 'hospitals for limping casualties'.[49] As well as repairing 600 naval ships and many more merchant vessels, they also fitted ships of all kinds with guns and other war equipment.[50]

As befitted the wartime 'Home of the Merchant Navy', the merchant ships and seafarers of Merseyside also played a front-line role in the Battle. Liverpool-owned and -managed ships formed a large part of Britain's ocean-going merchant fleet.[51] Whether cargo or passenger liners, many were requisitioned as armed merchant cruisers, troopships, hospital ships, assault ships or for other naval auxiliary service. The rest took their places within the merchant convoys so crucial to Britain's cause. Many of these ships were manned largely by Merseysiders, of whom perhaps at least 10,000 were merchant seamen, amounting to a substantial proportion of all British-born personnel in the ocean-going merchant marine. Losses among these ships and men were heavy. In all, at least 400 Liverpool-registered ships, totalling over three million tons, were lost during the war - more than a quarter of all British tonnage lost.[52] Hundreds of Merseysiders died while serving as merchant seamen, mostly in the Atlantic.

Last, but not least, should be mentioned the inhabitants of Merseyside as a whole. Of them it could truly be said that during the six years of war 'the world's greatest battlefield was on their doorstep'.[53] Even those not directly involved in the work of the port and its ships had family or friends who were, and so took part in the great common cause. This was particularly so during the Merseyside Blitz, which brought the Battle of the Atlantic home to everyone in the area. Between July 1940-January 1942 the Luftwaffe launched at least 68 bombing raids on Merseyside, more than any British city outside London. In all, some 4,000 people were killed and the same number seriously injured. Ten thousand homes were destroyed and almost 200,000 damaged.[54] In the face of this, the people of Merseyside, like those of other blitzed cities, showed remarkable resilience and courage. Indeed, many who visited the port during the war, including Allied seafarers from many nations, have testified to the morale-boosting example set by the unfailing warmth and spirit of the local people. One of the most glowing tributes came from Admiral Sir Max Horton, Commander-in-Chief, Western Approaches from 1942 until 1945, on being granted the Freedom of the City of Liverpool in September 1946. In his words,

> Whilst for nearly six years the swaying battle in the North Atlantic went on, the whole population of this city and port of Liverpool were working for victory at the docks, at the yards, or in the factories, warehouses and shops....The unceasing efforts of its inhabitants with their stern resolve to keep going in every adversity was admirable to observe.[55]

Notes

Unless otherwise stated, all sources cited are available at the Maritime Records Centre, Merseyside Maritime Museum, Liverpool. All newspaper articles referred to are contained in the newscuttings volumes (War series, Book 18, vols. 18-23) of the Mersey Docks and Harbour Board Collection, also at the above repository.

1. See Mountfield, *Western Gateway: A History of the Mersey Docks and Harbour Board*, pp. 126ff., 165ff.
2. Roskill, *The War At Sea, 1939-45*, I, pp. 348ff.
3. Chalmers, *Max Horton and the Western Approaches*, p. 149.
4. *Ibid.*

5.   For *Eaglet* see, e.g., Rayner, *Escort: The Battle of the Atlantic*, pp. 20ff. For *Irwell*, see article in *The Liverpool Echo*, 4 April 1963.

6.   Mersey Docks and Harbour Board, Worked-Up Papers (Bound), No. 112, vol. 3, Docks and Quays Agenda, 22 March 1939. This source will henceforth be referred to as W. U. P.

7.   See Mountfield, *Western Gateway*, pp. 167ff.

8.   *Ibid.*, p. 166; also W. U. P., *op. cit.*, Marine Agenda, 22 December 1939.

9.   See Hurd, *Britain's Merchant Navy* , pp. 85ff.

10. Eglin, G., 'Liverpool At War', in *The Liverpool Echo*, 9 December, 1957; also see *Liverpool Daily Post*, 2 August 1945.

11. Liverpool Steam Ship Owners' Association Miscellaneous Reports, vol. xxiv (1940-41), p. 26. Also see Hurd, *Britain's Merchant Navy*, pp. 89ff.

12. W. U. P., *op. cit..*, Docks and Quays Agenda, August 1939.

13. *Op. cit.*

14 . *Op. cit.*

15. *Op. cit.*, Sept. 1939.

16. See, e.g., *Port At War*.

17. W. U. P., *op. cit.*, Pilotage Committee Agenda, Oct. 1939.

18. *Op. cit.*, Docks and Quays Agenda.

19. Eglin, *art. cit.*

20. W. U. P., *op. cit.*

21. Monsarrat, *The Cruel Sea*, p. 144.

22. W. U. P., *op.cit.*, Marine Agenda, 20 November 1939.

23. *Liverpool Daily Post* article, 21 September 1945.

24. Lennox-Kerr & Grenville, *The R. N. V. R. - A Record of Achievement*, p. 147.

25. Information provided by Mrs. A. Lazo of Wallasey, Merseyside, who was a Wren in *Wellesley* during the war.

26. *Journal of Commerce*, 15 November 1952; *Liverpool Daily Post*, 13 Nov. 1952.

27. W. U. P., *op.cit.*, Sept. 1940.

28. *Op. cit.*, Docks and Quays Agenda, 30 Oct. 1940.

29. For *Periwinkle*, see letter from F. R. Jones in the Supplement to the *Liverpool Daily Post*, 23 March, 1968.

30. Monsarrat, *H. M. Corvette*, p. 29.

31. See W. U. P., *op. cit.*, Warehouse Agenda, 10 July 1940.

32. *Op. cit.*, Docks and Quays Agenda, Nov. 1940.

33. *Op. cit.*, Dec. 1940.

34. Roskill, *The War at Sea*, I, p. 360.

35. Costello & Hughes, *The Battle of the Atlantic*, p. 245; *Liverpool Daily Post*, 14 July 1945.

36. *Ibid.*

37. *Ibid.*

38. Wemyss, *Walker's Groups In the Western Approaches*, pp. 17-18.

39. Robertson, *Walker, R.N.*, p. 36.

40. *Ibid.*

41. Chalmers, *Max Horton and the Western Approaches*, p. 170.

42. The destroyers *Viscount* and *Hurricane* were both badly damaged in West Gladstone Dock during the 'May Blitz' of 1941. This information was supplied by Mr. John Hughes, who provides a detailed account of the 'May Blitz' on Merseyside in his forthcoming book *The Fires of Liverpool*.

43. See Roskill, *The War at Sea*, II, pp. 457ff. Londonderry was unencumbered by merchant convoys, and was better placed than Liverpool for the North Atlantic convoy routes.

44. Chalmers, *Max Horton and the Western Approaches*, pp. 150-1.

45. See Wemyss, *Walker's Group in the Western Approaches*, pp. 73ff.

46. Chalmers, *Max Horton and the Western Approaches*, p. 155; *Liverpool Daily Post* 14 July 1945.

47. Mountfield, *Western Gateway*, pp. 167ff.; *Port At War, op. cit.* By 1942 the Gareloch, near Greenock on the Clyde estuary, had become Britain's Military Port No. 1: *Manchester Guardian*, 20 June 1945.

48. Mr. Robert Letch, Regional Port Director, quoted in the *Liverpool Daily Post*, 18 August 1944.

49. The Port of Liverpool: Moving and Mending Ships, *The Times*, 12 February 1940.

50. Rear Admiral J. W. S. Dorling, District Shipyard Controller for the North-West Area, quoted in the *Liverpool Daily Post*, 24 October 1944.

51. At the end of 1939, the members of the Liverpool Steam Ship Owners' Association owned 18% of the total British steam and motor tonnage afloat, and 26% of the total number of such vessels above 6,000 tons. See *Annual Report for 1939*, The Liverpool Steam Ship Owners' Association, (Liverpool, 1940), p.1.

52. Powell, *History of the Liverpool Steam Ship Owners' Association, 1858-1958*, p. 59.

53. See Lanyard, *Stand By To Ram*, p. v (Foreword).

54. *Port At War.*

55. Chalmers, *Max Horton and the Western Approaches*, p. 246.

14

U-boat Bases in the Bay of Biscay

by Jean Kessler

On 28 August 1939, when war appeared imminent between Great Britain and Germany, Captain Karl Dönitz, commander of the U-boats, wrote a paper entitled *Reflections on the Constitution of the U-boat Fleet* and sent it to his commander-in-chief, Grand Admiral Erich Raeder. Germany then had 57 U-boats. In his paper, Dönitz observed:

> The torpedo-armed U-boat will carry the principal weight of a merchant war in the Atlantic....To assure success it would be necessary to have 100 vessels constantly on operations, which would necessitate a total of at least 300 U-boats....I consider this measure as indispensable to assure success in a war against Great Britain.

At any one time throughout the first 10 months of the war, 12 U-boats were at sea, of which six were solely in sectors upon which the campaign against Britain rested. Dönitz (since 1 October 1939 a rear admiral, and now Flag Officer U-boats) followed the progress of the Wehrmacht in France with close attention. In the event of victory in France, the Kriegsmarine would be able to use the French Atlantic ports and leave the shallow waters and confining dead-end of the North Sea.

He did not have long to wait. In June 1940, the retreat of the French and British armies enabled the creation of U-boat bases much nearer the Atlantic operational sectors, which in turn reduced a U-boat's return journey by 450 nautical miles and allowed an extension of the unrestricted submarine warfare employed in WWI. Brest was occupied on the evening of 19 June 1940, after all vessels there had escaped. Lorient fell on the afternoon of the 21st, after the hopeless but heroic Battle of the 'Cinq Chemins de Guidel' in which the Maritime Prefect, Admiral de Penfentenyo, escaped unhurt, having exposed himself to danger extensively. La Rochelle was occupied on the 22nd. After 25 June, all the French Atlantic coast was in the hands of German forces. As early as 1924, Admiral Wolfgang Wegener had assessed that Germany would be unable to wage war efficiently against Great Britain unless she had use of bases in Norway and northern France at least as far as Brest. His preconditions for an efficient German war against Britain were now more than realized.

Admiral Dönitz did not wait for the Armistice with France to take effect before making his arrangements. While negotiations were still in progress, his train departed for the Atlantic coast with personnel, materials and stores. On 23 June, he made a personal inspection, following which he defined the necessary stages to attain the greatest effectiveness of his vessels using the French Atlantic ports. These were:

1. Establish the feasibility of the supply of fuel, provisions and water.
2. Create the ability to achieve minor repairs.
3. Transfer the Headquarters as soon as the first two stages were realized for the majority of U-boats.
4. Create the ability to achieve all repairs for most U-boats.

At 1100 on 7 July 1940, the citizens of Lorient witnessed the entry of U-30 (Cdr Lemp) into their port - the first U-boat to come into Lorient for the re-supply of fuel and torpedoes. From 2 August, U-boat repairs were started with resources provided by the Military Dockyard. On 29 August, Admiral Dönitz left his headquarters near Wilhelmshaven and established himself provisionally in luxurious quarters on the Boulevard Suchet, Paris, while awaiting the fitting-out of his residence at Kernevel, at the mouth of the Scorff and opposite Port Louis.[1] From 16 October 1940, this became his base. In arriving and departing, the U-boats would parade beneath his windows, close enough to scrape his terrace. Henceforth, U-boats returning from patrol would come not to German ports, but to French ones, and the Battle of the Atlantic would increase in intensity and scope - exactly as anticipated by Flag Officer U-boats.

Five large bases were constructed to receive U-boats on the French Atlantic coast: Lorient, Brest, Saint-Nazaire, La Pallice and Bordeaux. They can be classed in 3 categories:

- Those established directly on the sea, as in the cases of Brest and Lorient.
- Those installed in a basin separated from the sea by a lock, and therefore not subject to the tide./
- Those built entirely ashore. Lorient alone would take care of such establishments.

At Brest and Lorient, the bases were installed in the Naval Dockyard or close by; those at Saint Nazaire, La Pallice and Bordeaux were in the commercial port basins. The first three steps planned by Admiral Dönitz were achieved rapidly. The French dockyards of Lorient and Brest were rapidly restored to a sufficient level under the direction of Vice Admiral Stobwasser, and proved better able to fulfil the maintenance work on U-boats than had Germany's own over-loaded shipyards. In the period before the fall of France (September 1939-July 1940), the Kriegsmarine had had to have 2.35 U-boats undergoing maintenance for every one on operations. Now, because of the facilities offered by French ports to the U-boats alongside, this proportion fell during the summer of 1940 to 1.84 - an improvement of 22% in the U-boats' operational availability.

Lorient became the Headquarters of Flag Officer U-boats and the base port of the 2nd and 10th Flotillas; Brest (which received U-65 on 1 August 1940) had the 1st Flotilla, which arrived from Kiel in June 1941, and the 9th Flotilla, created *in situ* in November of the same year. La Pallice received the 3rd Flotilla in October 1941. Saint-Nazaire, where the first U-boat came to replenish at the end of September, was the base of the 7th Flotilla originating from Kiel, joined in 1942 by the 6th, transferred from Danzig. Bordeaux, the destination of the blockade runners (and where, from July 1940, Italian submarines obtained respite), established an Italian Flotilla, designated BETASOM, in September 1940 under the orders of Admiral Parona, and subsequently received the 12th U-boat Flotilla in October 1942.

To the eight properly designated U-boat flotillas (which represented more than half the effective forces engaged in the Battle of the Atlantic), coastal defence and security forces can also be added - minesweeping flotillas to clear the approach channels, patrol boats, harbour defence launches. They might have been what French sailors call 'naval dust', but they represented no fewer than 11 flotillas of minesweepers, two of *Sperrbrecher* ('blockade runners', i.e. coasters and medium-sized merchantmen equipped to clear channels through magnetic and acoustic minefields), four of patrol boats and one of submarine chasers. In this context, the 8th Destroyer Flotilla, based at Royan, should not be forgotten.

The British responded rapidly. After several bombs on the Dockyard on 2 September, first Brest (25 September) then Lorient (27 September) saw the start of a long series of bombings which marked the war years for the civilian population. Saint-Nazaire, La Pallice and Bordeaux were initially spared, owing to their greater range from the British bases. On 9 December, a U-boat was slightly damaged at No 2 Basin in Lorient. It was agreed to build a shelter for naval personnel and equipment rapidly. Increased anti-aircraft defence and camouflage measures were not sufficient by themselves. Around Lorient, for example, large well-camouflaged barracks were constructed, one of which (Hennebont) could receive up to 1,400 men.

To protect the U-boats themselves effectively, it was necessary to produce solid shelters. Experimental ones had been made at Heligoland. A planning office of the Naval Civil Engineering Service, created by Chief Engineer Triebel, with an area of responsibility from Brest to Bordeaux, was established at Lorient. Whilst Brest, Saint-Nazaire, La Pallice and Bordeaux were able satisfactorily to provide floating pens with bomb-proof overhead protection, the solution adopted at Lorient needed to be different. For reasons relating to the subsoil, a construction at the surface provided a formidable structure for the two main pens which made up the port's U-boat base.

The general configuration of the Atlantic coast U-boat bases is well known; if you visit the five ports in which they were built, it is practically impossible to ignore them. Realized by the Todt Organization, under the direction of the Kriegsmarine, their designs were based on the six experimental pens built from 1940 at the Nordsee Bunker in Heligoland. The huge garage-pens are clearly the most important construction, with a surface area of 15,000-25,000 square metres. To these structures were then added most of the other units - defensive bunkers, workshops, stores, and barracks, distributed over many dozens of hectares of ground. Their construction, especially during wartime, was by any standards a major achievement.

For excavation work (when a building site was situated on partially reclaimed land), abundant labour and powerful tools were necessary. The initial work consisted of establishing a boundary with a screen of watertight timbers, before pumping out the sea water. To obtain a depth of 12 metres below quay-level for the pen entrances, it was necessary to evacuate the rocky seabed using dynamite or drills, and then to remove a considerable amount of rock, sand and mud débris. Once the surface was cemented and the construction of the basins achieved, work started on the superstructure.

Particular care was taken with the application of the concrete roof, as this would make the pens impenetrable against even the most powerful bombs. Initially 3.5 metres thick, they were later modified with inter-crossed anti-detonation beams, increasing the thickness to 7 metres. Designed to explode bombs before they reached the roof itself, this system was very effective, and those bombs that hit the target caused insignificant damage. Finally, 20mm Flak cannon emplacements were installed on the roof against aircraft attacking from low altitude.

As work progressed - and because of the importance of the flooding locks to the floating basins at Saint-Nazaire, La Pallice and Bordeaux - protected locks were constructed in parallel with existing works. Constructed on identical base plans (except Lorient, which we will come to later), these structures consisted of pens built side by side facing the sea, with a technical area at the back of the building. This part comprised many floors where stores, workshops, the generator station and offices were placed. A corridor with a railway traversed the length of the bunker between the rear of the pens and the technical zone. Though electrical power was supplied via the general circuit, the bases used groups of high-capacity batteries. Internal equipment was elaborate: each pen had one or more travelling cranes with a capacity of 1-30 tonnes, the dry-docks being generally better equipped than the floating basins.

Construction was carried out from early 1941 to 1942 for Lorient, Brest and Saint-Nazaire, in 1942-43 for La Pallice and Bordeaux - doubtless because the threat of bombing was less for the last two - but was not fully achieved by the end of hostilities. After the end of 1943, such construction fell to the third level of priority in Reich Fortification work.

To give an idea of the scale of work executed, one should remember that, purely for the production of U-boat shelters, Albert Speer gave the figure of 4 million cubic metres of concrete. This represents about a quarter of the total amount used by the Todt Organization for all the work it had been directed to achieve. It must be frankly admitted that in achieving the construction of substantial fortifications so well and in so little time, the Organization and the Kriegsmarine together accomplished a real technical feat.

Lorient's case merits a brief interruption. Mainly because it was the first in service, all the German aces of the Battle passed through it. Thus, because (at least in the first two years after France's fall) it was the nerve centre of the U-boat war, and because it was the most important and complete, it represented for this type of military architecture the most original solution. The Lorient-Keroman U-boat base was constructed in successive steps. These are worth examining, if only in passing. On settling in the Scorff Dockyard in August 1940, it became rapidly apparent that the three basins and the 10 or so pier positions available in the dockyard would not be enough either for U-boat operations to be carried out to Dönitz's stipulated routine, or to fulfil the intention of putting 25 new units into service each month. But even if there were fewer than he had expected, they allowed him to make appropriate plans.

Two of the six slipways intended for trawler hull-cleaning and which led to the turntable at the fishing port of Keroman were at first protected by bunkers. This was a limited solution, since, being intended for trawlers, the platform (even when reinforced) was unable to accept the small Type IID U-boats. The second phase therefore consisted of the construction of a new installation, using a slipway with 'dry' maintenance, capable of receiving Types VII and IX U-boats. These installations comprised the Keroman I and II projects.

Keroman I included a pen containing the slipway and five sheltered pens, constructed side by side. Keroman II, opposite Keroman I, was divided by an 87-metre-wide platform, on which a carriage (45 metres by 11) was placed laterally. The structure comprised seven pens whose openings were opposite those of Keroman I.

The working principle was simple: the U-boat to be docked was taken from the water on the Keroman I slipway, on a frame fixed to the carriage which was then pulled up the ramp. The frame and carriage were displaced laterally, to move opposite to the pen in which the U-boat was to be sheltered. Disconnected from the main carriage, the frame engaged onto the rails in the pen. The evolution lasted a maximum of two hours. Started in February 1941 and followed three months later by Keroman II, Keroman I received its first U-boat on 1 August 1941, with both bases being fully operational on 20 December that year. Keroman III, comprising seven drainable pens facing the sea, was started in October 1941 and opened in May 1943. It was the largest unit constructed at Lorient.

Lorient could receive a total of 28 U-boats simultaneously under perfect conditions of security, and carried out 492 of the 1,149 dockings achieved in the bases.[2] By comparison, Brest had 15 pens, Saint-Nazaire 14, La Pallice 10 and Bordeaux 11. As may be imagined, these huge structures did not come into being without notably altering the environment. To provide the necessary materials (on average 150,000 tonnes per site monthly), railways were extended, and new lines laid. Two thousand trucks were used at any one time for material transport.[3] Quarries and gravel pits, capable of supplying hundreds of cement mixers, had to be opened. Situated on the coast, the construction sites were sometimes subjected to storms from the sea, and work would stop to repair the damage. Several weeks were lost at Saint-Nazaire following a violent storm.

Construction of these bases required a considerable workforce of all nationalities. Lorient, at the time of the construction site's maximum activity, had a complement of 15,000 men.[4] Mlle. Beauchesne, the Historic Service archivist at Lorient at the time, wrote that the Germans 'had sent for so many different workers from different countries that the comparison with an ant-hill, cliché though it might be, inevitably struck the mind when looking at the yards.' From 1941, this workforce flowed in from all over Europe. First were the Spanish, followed by the Dutch, Belgians, Italians and even North Africans. It should be added that there were numerous German firms, but equally it must be admitted that there were those French construction companies which, in the absence of large French projects, saw there an opportunity to survive. In Morbihan, for example, in September 1943, the management of the Labour and Manpower Department had 8,520 persons at work in French firms working mainly for the Departement's *occupying* authorities.

If most of the workers were conscripted, there were still French volunteers who, from the end of 1942, found in the system a way to avoid being sent to work in Germany under the *Service de Travail Obligatoire* (STO) or living on relief.[5] The salary of a Todt Organization worker (of which there were about 250,000 in 1943) was in the order of 3,000 French francs per month. By comparison, an office worker's monthly salary was around 1,500 francs, whilst a German worker's monthly salary was 2,000-3,000 francs. German workers worked at Lorient and Brest at the Naval Dockyard itself. According to General Fahrmbacher, German personnel at Lorient numbered 33 officers, 137 officials, 300 male employees, 115 female employees and 4,000 labourers. To this number must be added 3,000 dockyard workers under French direction, whose situation was altogether ambiguous.

The French managers and services operating at the Brest and Lorient naval bases began gradually to safeguard, so far as possible, the port installations and knowledge of the naval constructors, for these represented French material capital. On becoming *Industries Navales*, the personnel of the *Service des constructions navales militaires* were thus able to begin the orderly handover of material and of the closed dockyards very soon after the Armistice.

At Brest, the Director of Naval Construction had expressed the intention to refuse all work that could serve military purposes. This led to his early removal. The position of Lorient's director was more qualified. The aim followed there was to work the dockyard to the full, but to the benefit of the French authorities. As Admiral Le Puth wrote in his memoirs, 'Lorient was occupied by the enemy, we wanted to occupy the dockyard'. However, it was evident that there was not sufficient work there for 3,000 labourers; and even though, at the start, they tried to find work of use to the wider community (for example by providing mobile kitchens and charcoal furnaces), nevertheless there had to be some very good reason for keeping qualified naval shipyard workers under French direction. After all, the Kriegsmarine would want them to work for its benefit, not for their own or that of France.

The Dockyard Director, Engineer-General Antoine, managed to oppose them in demanding that if it must be so, the personnel must be supervised by French engineers. This the Germans found hard to accept; but Antoine's prestige was so great that this situation lasted for the duration of his tenure, until August 1942.

The solution was found, oddly enough, in the resumption of the construction of French vessels which were on the slips at the time of the Armistice. The construction of the cruiser *De Grasse*[6] and two dredgers on the large covered slip at Lanester was pursued feverishly, yet artificially - with every appearance of great activity, but with very little actually being done. The dredgers were condemned after British bombing, and *De Grasse* was still on the slip at the Liberation of France in 1945. Thus, with this façade, the alibi was maintained. In his introduction to a report written for the American authorities in 1946, General Fahrmbacher, commander of the 25th Army Corps, described the relationship between occupier and occupied thus:

> The Bretons and German forces had lived side by side for nearly five years and one can say that a good relationship never failed to prevail between one and the other. Thousands of Bretons had earned a living building the Atlantic Wall and working in the German Auxiliary services, gaining an affluence that they had never had before. When a Resistance movement could be seen to develop in Brittany from February 1944, its political origins were imported from elsewhere.

One can only be surprised by such an assessment, even though the General's motive for it is so transparent.

The reason Fahrmbacher had this impression was certainly because the density of the occupying forces in the five Atlantic ports was such that the citizens adopted an apparently generally passive attitude. However, excluding those who through self-interest or ideology deliberately chose the enemy camp, in justice to the citizenry of the area it must be stressed that Fahrmbacher was completely wrong. In making the ports the departure points for all-out U-boat warfare, Hitler and Dönitz marked them out for repeated Allied attack and condemned their people to a long Calvary, which they endured with a stoicism which can only be explained by their support for the Allied cause.

There is direct evidence for this. Although Allied bombardment began in September 1940, on 23 November Lorient's police commissioner signalled in a report to the *Préfet* that public opinion was not anti-government, and that anglophilia was widespread. It was believed in certain circles (and would be for a long time to come) that anglophilia was compatible with support for Marshal Pétain.

On 30 November 1942, the *Préfet* of Morbihan wrote that 'public opinion has welcomed the events in North Africa with a kind of jubilation'. Referring to the raids on Lorient, he said further that 'in spite of the serious risks entailed for the population, they have not led to the least diminution in the obvious sympathy fostered for the Anglo-Americans by the great majority', and finally noted 'that in this region [the matter of Toulon] appears to have tolled the death knell of the policy of Franco-German rapprochement'.[7] Similarly, after the landings in Sicily, and despite Laval's calls for discipline, the *sous-Préfet* of Pontivy noted in a report that 'the Allied victory constitutes the only horizon for most people'.

If the efficiency of the workers under the immediate direction and control of the Germans was satisfactory, those under French management at the dockyard produced work which in contrast was described by Oberbaurat Charton as 'lamentable'. Charton would have preferred the French to be under German control. Those who did not work could then be sacked immediately, he believed, while the threat of being sent to Germany would return certain waverers to a better concept of their duty. However, this belief was not entirely accurate, since the need for manpower was such that at Brest as well as Lorient, the local Todt Organization consistently opposed Sauckel's STO requisitions.

The trouble with the system, according to Admiral Mattiae, was that the French dockyards remained independent organizations whose workers were paid by Vichy 'without anyone concerning themselves whether anyone works there or not'; and he observed that of the 400 French dockyard personnel who were required to work under German supervision, only 100 presented themselves.

This was very far from General Fahrmbacher's 'good relationship' between occupier and occupied.

*

A word should also be said about the attitude of the administrative authorities - prefects, mayors - towards enemy activity in the occupied zone. These authorities were faced with problems whose solutions almost always evaded them. In the eyes of the citizenry, their position often appeared to be more or less favouring collaboration. On the other hand, the German authorities, whom they frequently opposed by silent resistance in administrative affairs, found them suspect and inefficient. Caught between the devil and the deep blue sea, in daily contact with the occupation authorities and having total charge of the population, the administrative authorities had extremely restricted room for manoeuvre. While awaiting Allied intervention, active opposition never transpired, except from the professionals in clandestine operations; but there are numerous examples of administrative obstacles placed by them, notably in the recruitment of manpower, and in the lethargic search for those who evaded recruitment. Thus, in the period 1942-44, when required to provide

Gendarmerie assistance to the Germans in the search for and arrest of evaders, the *Préfet* of Morbihan ordered his subordinates to warn those concerned 48 hours in advance.

Thanks to certain elements who regarded the Armistice as merely a pause in the open struggle, the French Navy was quickly involved in active opposition by clandestine means. For obvious reasons, the archives are not very plentiful on this subject, and, in accordance with French legislation, will remain inaccessible to researchers for a long time to come. However, in chance research, confirmation of eye-witness accounts has been found, although unfortunately it is not possible to supply the references.

Very early on, the *Service des Renseignements Marine* (Naval Intelligence), whose headquarters had moved to Vichy, gave to its German section the objective of Kriegsmarine activity in French ports.[8] Its chief, Lt Cdr (later Captain) Trautmann, was busy in this period establishing a network of agents on the Atlantic coast. The same was true of the Army's *Deuxième Bureau*, which maintained contact with British Intelligence services.

The task was helped by the French Admiralty, which (to safeguard the navy's material inheritance) kept a nucleus of engineers and officers who supervised civil and military elements of maintenance and caretaking. These included Naval Civil Engineering Service personnel, sailors civilianized as boats' crews and working under port direction, maritime police (assimilated by the occupying forces into the civil police), and marine firemen. The responsibilities of these last were not limited to the military zones, but, because of the air raids, extended equally to the civilian ports on the Atlantic coast. Altogether, these groups provided an ideal cadre for an information network.

The *Service des Oeuvres de la Marine* (a welfare institution created to assist military personnel demobilized under the conditions of the Armistice) worked in the occupied ports under the direction of the Vichy central service. Whilst carrying out its primary mission with efficiency, it was also a cover for those whose activities violated the Armistice conventions, notably the *Service des Renseignements'* intelligence-gathering. There is, amongst others, an instance of a naval surgeon appointed to the local *Service des Oeuvres de la Marine* at Rochefort, who had been tasked previously by the *Deuxième Bureau* at Vichy for an information-gathering mission on the U-boat base under construction at La Pallice, work which he subsequently continued at Brest.

Equally noteworthy was the case of Engineer Captain Stosskopf, chief of staff to the Engineer-General, Director of the *Industries Navales* at Lorient. A native of Alsace, he spoke fluent German, and was recruited in September 1940 by Captain Trautmann during a liaison visit to Vichy. His work permitted him to move through the dockyard, which he did daily on the pretext of inspecting the labourers' work. The French did not have access to Keroman, where the U-boats under repair were sheltered, but he was able to go there frequently, thanks to the relationship which he had deliberately established with his German counterparts. From these visits he compiled information and indications, identifying U-boats, in part from work orders which he followed closely via the accounts. Inevitably he was viewed by the workmen as the archetypal collaborator, and endured their loathing until February 1944; but in that month he was arrested by the Germans, and, in September, shot.

It was also from Lorient, via Stosskopf's intermediary, that in March 1942 information on a probable U-boat deployment to the Caribbean was passed. A civilianized Chief Petty Officer Signalman First Class, employed in the chart section, noticed that the Germans had taken a folio of Caribbean charts and received eight more sets a week later. He informed his superior, who then informed Stosskopf. About a month later, U-boats attacked tanker traffic in the Caribbean. The dockyard and town laundries were also closely watched, since, with their meticulously labelled uniforms, the laundry bags gave precious indications on the movements of units. At Brest, baggage was likewise of interest: if it was sent in groups to another port, a change of base could be inferred, while if it was sent to individual families, a U-boat had probably been destroyed. With such clues, in each Atlantic port the U-boat order of battle was patiently worked out and updated.

A more complex question is: How quickly and by whom was this information exploited? Evidence exists that it was passed by naval personnel (doubtless without the knowledge of the higher echelons) to their colleagues in the *Service des Renseignements* and to representatives of the free countries with embassies in Vichy, notably the American naval attachés. The time scale was, however, long; Stosskopf reported on each of his monthly journeys, and neither their frequency nor the 'letterbox system' was adaptable to the transmission of operational information.

The networks controlled by the *Bureau Central de Renseignement et d'Action de la France libre* (the Free French Central Intelligence and Action Bureau, or BCRA) doubtless went differently. Even though, unlike the Intelligence Service professionals, they needed a little time to structure themselves, they had (with the help of the British) radio stations quite early on and the benefit of aerial liaison. Amongst many others, Colonel Remy's network, the *Confrérie de Notre Dame* (Brotherhood of Our Lady) deserves a special mention, because of the importance of its activities. To their great credit they monitored the battlecruisers *Scharnhorst* and *Gneisenau*, using information collected by 'Hilarion' (Lt. Philippon) and transmitted by Leading Radio Operator Anquetil, who was arrested and killed whilst transmitting at Saumur. The contribution of the members of this network to surveillance of the U-boat bases was of considerable importance.

Mention should also be made about information furnished by the personnel of the Naval Civil Engineering Service. In particular, complete plans of five U-boat bases were sent by them to Colonel Remy. A dredging plan established by the Lorient Naval Civil Engineering Service on 11 April 1942, and rediscovered in the port archives, is a good example of what was possible in this area. The inconsistency shown on this occasion by the occupiers in the protection of such sensible and otherwise well-protected installations is striking.

At the end of November 1942, after the invasion of the Free Zone, the *Service des Renseignements* was dismantled. To our knowledge, and from 1943, the only remaining service was the radio communication between the Deputy Naval Attachés at Berne and Algiers.[9] If the books of telegrams showing that U-boat movements were being followed partially, it is well to remember that the distance away of the sites led to delays in forwarding that were incompatible with tactical information. It was on the strong, active Resistance networks and on the British services that the search for information would henceforth rest. Engineer-Captain Stosskopf would link up with the 'Alliance' Network after the disappearance of the Free Zone had dispersed his Vichy contacts.[10] The information was doubtless forwarded faster from that moment on; but only the British records could answer these questions properly, because only they could reveal the assessed value of the information received and the exact uses to which it was put.

*

German activity in the Atlantic ports provided a subject for constant surveillance. Work progress was followed very closely, and the Allies were not ignorant of its main features. The bases were however too well guarded for any actions against them from the land to have any significant results. Except for the remarkable attack on the Saint-Nazaire lock in March 1942, or the Commando raid on the Gironde in December of the same year, such operations were limited to the sabotage of equipment, carried out during transportation between the production site and the bases, or to the deliberate mishandling of material by French dockyard employees.

The Allied response would come only from the air. There is, however, one question: Why did the RAF not interfere with the construction of the bases? Admiral Le Puth, who lived in Lorient during the period, wrote on this subject:

> Since the start of the occupation, Lorient has not been saved from bombardment, although inaccurate. These bombing raids did not give the impression of following a defined programme, to a coherent plan....whilst at the moment when the Germans started construction of the Keroman U-boat base, some well-placed bombs would have stopped work dead - which, according to the technicians, would be very difficult - yet there was no impact in this area. The same situation was found at Brest, where Lieutenant Philippon voiced his concern to Remy, who answered in substance: 'They are waiting for the completion of construction to destroy them.' But each man knew that with their 7-metre-thick concrete roofs, the pens would constitute an invulnerable U-boat shelter against even the most powerful bombs.

The RAF was not against flying over the French ports, despite a strong anti-aircraft defence causing heavy losses: Lorient received 20 raids in 1940, 16 in 1941 and 12 in the first few months of 1942. From November 1942, American Flying Fortresses took over with daylight bombing. There were 10 American raids on Saint-Nazaire between 9 November 1942 and 28 June 1943.

All these were ineffective. The absence of results caused the Allies to adopt another tactic: they no longer concentrated on the U-boat shelters, but struck at the towns to render them uninhabitable. They intended, doubtless, to cause the French as well as the German workers to take refuge, and thus make all work impossible. The Lorient urban area had been wiped off the map by 15 January 1943; Saint-Nazaire was 60% destroyed by incendiary raids on 16 and 28 February, and 5,000 houses were destroyed in Brest in May. However, even though the external base installations had suffered in these huge bombing raids, and despite the agreed losses, the Allies were never able to reduce the practical availability of U-boats.

Life was re-organized once the civilian population was evacuated: those personnel resettled in the neighbouring locality were taken to work by cars, trains, etc. The organization was certainly large and costly, but was eventually proven to be effective. The flow of supplies from Germany to Brest by the coastal railway was not interrupted despite the aerial threat: from 3.6 million tonnes in 1942, it sank to 2.8 million tonnes in 1943, but this was still very important. After an inspection of Lorient and Saint-Nazaire, Admiral Dönitz was able to say, 'Not a cat, nor a dog can subsist at Saint-Nazaire or Lorient. Nothing will stay there, except for the U-boat shelters'.

Even so, at sea the U-boats were never so close to breaking the line of communications between the old and the new worlds as they were in the first few days of March 1943. The Allied decision to commit, with mediocre results, most of their aircraft to the destruction of the U-boats alongside was without doubt a grave error of judgment, and in a certain sense proof of the inadequacies of the strategic bombing doctrine. On the other hand, from April 1943, the U-boat war went against the Kriegsmarine. Many factors are at the origin of this decisive turning point: decryption of German signals, centimetric radar, escort carrier support groups, but most of all the closure of the North Atlantic 'black hole' by the use of long-range 4-engined aircraft, at last available in sufficient numbers. At the same time, after the destruction of Lorient and Saint-Nazaire, the raids decreased in frequency, only to return with increased violence in August 1944, when, following the breakthrough at Avranches, the Allies tried to eliminate once and for all German naval surface and U-boat units in the Bay of Biscay.

'We are facing the greatest crisis of the U-boat war' Dönitz wrote in May 1943, 'because the enemy, with new detection systems, is making combat impossible and is inflicting heavy losses on us'. U-boat losses in that month had more than doubled, reaching 30% of units in the operating sectors. For them, passage across the Bay of Biscay was a real agony. To reach the Atlantic, there was little more than a narrow corridor in the Bay, along the Spanish coast. Although the introduction into service of the Schnorkel was a considerable change, it represented in Dönitz's view only a minor improvement, compared to and pending the anticipated arrival of the new, faster Type XXI and XXIII U-boats. The advantage in holding the Atlantic bases was reduced considerably. When on 24 May 1943 Admiral Dönitz ordered his U-boats to evacuate the North Atlantic, he recognized that he no longer had the upper hand.

In June 1944, when the Allies landed in Normandy, the German flotillas on the French Atlantic coast were exhausted. Nevertheless, they threw all available units from the Biscay bases into the battle - without great success. Despite the *Schnorkel*, U-boats were unable to penetrate the Allied defences. With the Allied armies approaching the ports of Brittany and the Vendée, the flotillas were ordered to withdraw to Norway from 17 August. On the 24th there were still two U-boats at each of Brest, Lorient and Saint-Nazaire, six at La Pallice, and three at Bordeaux, all of which for practical purposes would depart before the end of August. The last to leave Lorient was U-55 on 5 September 1944.

Transformed into entrenched camps which had to be held at all costs in order to deprive the immense Allied supply train of discharge ports, the German bases at Lorient, La Pallice and Saint-Nazaire held out until the surrender in 1945. The only U-boats that would ever stop there were from Norway, entering at night and bringing a little fuel and some spare parts to the besieged. The dissolution of the office of Captain U-boats West, on 29 August 1944, marked the end of activity of the Bay of Biscay U-boat bases.

Gigantic and practically indestructible structures, constructed in record time, the German Atlantic U-boat bases are still in good condition: Brest's today is a minewarfare depot, while that at Lorient, after accommodating a French Atlantic U-boat squadron for 50 years, remains a popular tourist location in the port. The Bordeaux base has become an international boating museum. In the titanic combat that was the Battle of the Atlantic, they played a major role and resisted all bombing without any practical disruption to their activities. Paradoxically, though, from the moment that they had ceased to be a target for the Allied air forces, they had lost a good part of their reason for being.

Bibliography

Aubertin, C. F. (tr. de l'allemand), *Lorient (1940-1945)*.

Brossard (de), M., (CA c.r.), *De Nantes a Saint-Nazaire, l'estuaire de la Loire.* Ed. France-Empire (1982).

Gamelin, P. *Les bases sous-marines allemandes ie l'Atlantique et leurs defenses 1940-1945,* Ed. des Paludiers

Gueriff, F., *Saint-Nazaire sous l'occupation allemande,* Le commando - La Poche, Ed. des Paludiers (1945).

Hilarion, P. (C. V.),. *S. et G.*, Ed. France-Empire.

Leroux, R., *Le Morbihan en guerre (1939-1945)* Imprimeur Editeur Joseph
    Floch - (Rochefort, 1979)

Pallud, J-P., *U-Boote! Les sous-marins allemands, 39/45* Guerres
    contemporaires Magazine, Ed. Heimdal (Brest)

Pallud, J-P., *U. Boote! Les sous-marins allemands: 2 - Les Bases: Brest,
    Lorient, Saint - Nazaire, La Pallice, Bordeaux.* Ed. Heimdal. (Brest)

Peillard, L., *La Bataille de l'Atlantique (1939-1945)*, Ed. Robert Laffont (1987).

Vulliez, A. (C. F.(r)),.*Brest au combat (1939-1944)*. Les Ed. Ozanne.

Notes

1. This is still an Admiral's residence, of the Naval Commander of Lorient; some
    furniture and other articles have been preserved. Admiral Dönitz left there in May
    1942 to return to Paris, the reason appearing to be the vulnerability of the coast to
    Commando attacks, as shown by the raid on Saint-Nazaire.

2. The U-boat command had established the following minimum standards for their
    U-boats: 1/3 of time in the sector, 1/3 en route (coming or going), and 1/3
    undergoing maintenance. This gave an average of 3-4 weeks for maintenance. This
    time limit was never exceeded, rather it was reduced.

3. At Brest, 750 trucks were assigned solely for the transportation of sand.

4. 25,000 were in fact required if the construction of the airfield at Lann-Bihoue is
    taken into account.

5. STO was a working period in Germany that young Frenchmen were forced to do by
    the German authorities.

6. Completed as an Anti-Aircraft Cruiser, she was launched in 1946 and was in
    service from 1956 to 1972.

7. The scuttling of the Fleet, 27 November 1942.

8. Which unfortunately, after the drama of Mers el Kebir, devoted part of its energy
    and means equally to following British activities.

9. Where Captain Trautmann, miraculously appointed to Morocco in August 1941,
    had renewed his activities.

10. Naval Intelligence did not appear to have thought of becoming clandestine in the
    event of a full invasion of the territory, unlike the Army's special services.

15

The British Order of Battle

by David J. Lyon

The problem of accurate statistical analysis of the Battle of the Atlantic has already been touched on in this book. For this chapter, hoping to clarify somewhat rather than confuse further, I have created my own series of statistics. They have been compiled in the main from easily available secondary sources concerned with the escort force under British and Canadian control, and are presented in the form of tables from which I have drawn a number of conclusions. These may be neither original nor profound, no more than 'insights into the obvious', but insights, even into the obvious, should be worth having. Before presenting the tables it will be helpful if I explain their parameters.

Firstly, rather than the *who, how* or *where*, I have been concerned with the *what* and *when* of the escort force - in other words with the rate of growth of the different types of oceanic escort, with their potential and their actual availability, with their losses and their 'kills'.

Secondly, I do not attempt to deal with the geographical organization of that force. However, it is worth noticing the importance of the Atlantic Islands which were taken over from neutral control: the Faeroes, Iceland and the Azores. All, especially Iceland, were essential as refuelling bases. Iceland also became increasingly important as an air base, and in that role (from October 1943, as soon as the Portuguese permitted their use) the Azores became vitally important.

Thirdly, I do not attempt to analyse the development of the administrative, strategic or tactical organization of the force. However, the following chronological outline may be helpful to bear in mind:

Early 1940 Convoys often escorted by a single A/S escort.

Late 1940 First escort groups formed by Western Approaches Command.

April 1941 Fuelling bases in Iceland permit escort of convoys to mid-Atlantic.

June 1942 Introduction of refuelling from tankers in convoys permits escorts to remain in company. By a year later, the number of tankers fitted for this had increased to some 300.

Sept 1942 The first support groups formed to become available for use during the crucial spring of 1943, at the same time as the escort carriers start coming into service in some numbers.

Fourthly, I have omitted the land-based air element - the RCAF and Coastal Command of the RAF, vital though it was, and the largely misdirected strength of Bomber Command. I have purposely ignored the latter since its raids on U-boat bases made no appreciable difference to the Battle and its bombing of Germany only made an impact (though at that stage a very considerable one) on U-boat production in the last year of the war.

As a final disclaimer, I can only mention and then pass over other crucial if less evident elements in British naval strength, such as the Radio Intercept Stations, the Naval Control of Shipping and the Defensively Equipped Merchant Ships organizations, the rescue tugs. The work of net defence and harbour defence should not be entirely forgotten.

Within the field marked out by these parameters, the value of these tables will be readily apparent. The first three tables cover, respectively, the state at the outbreak of war and immediate additions; completions and losses; and cumulative totals. If these three are considered together, they give a clear impression of how, at the end of every three months during the course of the war, the pool of potentially available escort vessels grew. Samples of the actual numbers of escorts involved in the Battle are given in Table 4. Table 5 notes escort losses which occurred in the Battle itself, thus amplifying the loss information given in Table 2. Taken together, these two show the statistical reason for much of what happened in the Battle. Lastly, one yardstick of the escorts' success is given by Table 6, the tally of U-boats sunk.

The low point from which the growth in escort numbers began explains the number of convoys escorted by a single destroyer or sloop at the start of the war. The growth itself is one of the major reasons for success in 1943 and explains why, on New Year's Day 1945, Western Approaches alone had 37 escort groups comprising 26 destroyers, 14 sloops, 123 frigates and 89 corvettes - a total of 252 escorts out of the 426 in all home waters commands.

At the outbreak of war the naval forces available to Britain included a number of purpose-built escorts. There were far too few of these sloops, but no other navy had anything comparable. The French and Italians, for example, had built colonial avisos or torpedo boats. In 1939, the Admiralty was building more ASW escorts in large numbers, intending with them to bottle up the U-boat menace in the narrow seas. It would be unfair to blame the Admiralty Board of the late 1930's for failing to foresee the fall of France or to anticipate a battle in the Atlantic. But they did not, which was why they built the *Hunt*-class escort destroyers and the modified whalecatchers which achieved fame as the *Flower*-class corvettes. The former only played a marginal part in the Battle of the Atlantic, mostly in the Gibraltar convoys. Their short range and strong dual-purpose 4-inch gun armament suited them for the East Coast convoys and the Mediterranean. It was fortunate that the *Flowers* were so sturdy, because they became the workhorses of an oceanic war for which they had not been intended. It is only fair to remark, however, that much the same comments can be made of the main contender on the other side. The Type VIIC U-boat was not intended for an oceanic role either. Those who have heard Klaus Friedland[1] describe the incredible expedients adopted to get these boats across to lie off Cape Hatteras in early 1942 will have an idea of the combination of extreme ingenuity and extreme discomfort involved. The crews of the *Flowers* and of the Type VIICs had, perhaps, more in common than they realized.

The key to most of the forces that fought the Battle through to the victories of 1943 was, in fact, improvization - there were converted destroyers, carriers converted from merchantmen, aircraft which were more or less converted from airliners (Hudsons, Sunderlands and, on the other side, Condors) or bombers (Wellingtons and Liberators). It may be worth pointing out here that with the ships building in 1939, the emphasis had definitely been placed on the anti-aircraft function: the *Black Swan* class was intended primarily intended for anti-aircraft fire,[2] though they proved excellent anti-submarine ships and were the basis for the development of the specialized anti-submarine escorts (for whom the old warship name of 'frigate' was to be somewhat inappropriately revived) of the *River* and *Loch* classes.

The anticipated Battle of the Atlantic (and to an extent the real Battle) was one in which surface raiders played the chief part. This would be a war in which ocean convoys would be escorted by AMCs (armed merchant cruisers) and, when needed or available, cruisers and older battleships. With this aspect of the battle I am not concerned except to note the high casualty rate of the AMCs, 14 of which were lost in the first two years of the war, mostly to U-boats. In the same period, only six major anti-submarine escorts (destroyers, sloops or corvettes) were lost in the Atlantic.

Certainly the list of U-boat losses indicates that the improvised escorts did none so badly. The losses of the escorts themselves were, in the circumstances, surprisingly light compared with those of the merchantmen they escorted and the U-boats they fought. However, those of us who deal with statistics in the context of the history of warfare should be a little wary of talking in such terms when one is dealing with the deaths of human beings. A colleague of mine had only just been born when her father, a leading seaman, died on board the first *Flower*-class corvette lost in the Battle.[3] The result of this was that her mother had to struggle to bring up her family on the pitiful pension provided by the Government. The end result of the Battle in this, and countless other examples, was that a small girl grew up not knowing her father in a 'single parent family' and in straitened circumstances.

What is certain is that as far as losses are concerned, the Battle of the Atlantic belonged on the Allied side to the merchant ships and seamen. In this conference, as is seemingly usual in studies of the Battle, they have received rather less attention than their counterparts in the armed fleets;[4] but their patient endurance is the necessary background to all our accounts of the naval struggle. Without them, the following statistics on their escorts would be meaningless, for the war would have been lost.

The Tables

1: *Potential Atlantic escorts in service in 1939*
    (including RAN/RCN/RIN)

Destroyers and Flotilla Leaders

80 WWI-vintage (V, W and S classes and 1 R class)
81 post-WWI (up to the I class. Later destroyer classes were rarely to be seen in this battle)

= 161 destroyers.

By the beginning of 1943 (which was when the majority of the 'A to I's' were being relegated to escort work) 43, or precisely half the potential pool, had been lost.

Sloops
6 WWI-vintage (*Flower* class)
34 post-WWI (up to *Egret* class)

= 40 sloops (not counting either minesweepers or the *Kingfisher* and *Guillemot* class patrol vessels, of which there were 9).

1A: *Taken into service at beginning of war*

56 Armed Merchant Cruisers

There were also 16 Ocean Boarding Vessels, numerous trawlers, tugs etc., and eight merchantmen converted, to no useful purpose, into Q-ships (special service vessels), two of which were lost to submarine attack.

1B: *Lend-Lease from the USA*

10 coastguard cutters
50 WWI-vintage 'four stacker' destroyers, transferred from September 1940 on.

2: *Wartime Completions of Escort Vessels*
    (RN, Empire and Allied navies. Losses noted in square brackets)

The losses listed here are global figures for the types under consideration. Note that the destroyer losses listed here are *only* those of the pre-war vessels up to the 'I' class and the 'four stackers'; they do not include those of the Fleet destroyers from the *Tribal* class on, nor of the *Hunts* which were not used in the Atlantic. The list excludes the six ex-Brazilian 'H' class destroyers which appear to have completed in 1940 and were very useful members of the North Atlantic escort force. It further excludes the MAC ships (Merchant Aircraft Carriers), of which 19 (six grain ships and 13 tankers) were completed between mid-1943 and mid-1944 (the two Denny-built ones in July 1943 and March 1944 respectively). The comparatively short-ranged *Hunt*-class escort destroyers were not usually employed in the Atlantic, except on Gibraltar convoys, and have therefore been omitted here, as have the minesweepers, trawlers and other smaller escorts. The table also omits those other vital vessels, rescue ships and rescue tugs.

Not all of the vessels noted here would serve in the Atlantic, and those that did would require a period of work-up for both ship and crew; so there would be a built-in delay before they became available for that Battle. For American-built CVEs, that delay was very long, and, as summarized by Professor David Syrett's paper to the BCMH/SNR Kings College London seminar in 1991, caused the Allies considerable high-level problems. It should be added that the majority of these escort carriers were not employed in the Battle of the Atlantic, which had 'turned the corner' before they reached operational status.

The Australian-built *River*-class frigates have been omitted as they never participated in the Battle, as have the *Bay*-class frigates which, unlike their half-sisters the *Loch* class, were neither intended for the Battle nor arrived in time to serve in it. In each case the figures given are those obtaining at the *end* of the quarter of the year concerned.

Key

Slo	sloops (*Black Swan* class)
Cor	corvettes (*Flowers* and *Castles*, including Canadian construction)
Des	destroyers
Fri	Frigates (*Rivers* and *Lochs*, including Canadian construction)
D/P	American-built Destroyer Escorts (DEs, *Captain* class) and PFs (*Colony* class, the American version of the *Rivers*)
CaB	British-built Escort Carriers.
CaA	American-built Escort Carriers.
AMC	Armed Merchant Cruiser.

Year	Slo	Cor	Fri	D/P	CaB	CaA	Other Losses
1939							
4th qtr	1	-	-	-	-	-	[3 Des,1 AMC]
1940							
1st qtr	1	-	-	-	-	-	[3 Des]
2nd qtr	- [1]	10 [1]	-	-	-	-	[15 Des, 3 AMCs]
3rd qtr	- [2]	19 [1]	-	-	-	-	[10 Des, 2AMCs]
4th qtr	-	31	-	-	-	-	[6 Des, 4 AMCs]
1941							
1st qtr	-	31	-	-	-	-	[2 Des]
2nd qtr	4 [2]	40	-	-	1	-	[6 Des, 4 AMCs]
3rd qtr	-	26 [1]	-	-	-	-	[3 Des, 1 AMC]
4th qtr	- [1]	26 [4]	-	-	- [1]	1	[3 Des]

1942

1st qtr	- [1]	10 [3] -	-	-		1	[8 Des,1 coastguard cutter]
2nd qtr	- [1]	14 [3] 3	-	-		1	[5 Des, 1 AMC, 1 catapult ship]
3rd qtr	-	3 [1] 3	-	-		1	[4 Des, 1 catapult ship]
4th qtr	1 [1]	4 [4] 6	-	1		3 [1]	[3 Des, 2 coastguard cutters]

1943

1st qtr	5	2 [4] 4	4	-		3 [1]	[1 Des]
2nd qtr	8	1	15	3	1	5	[1 Des]
3rd qtr	2 [1]	3 [1]	16 [1] 16	-		10	[2 Des]
4th qtr	3	19	4	56	2	8	[2 Des]

1944

1st qtr	1 [1]	12 [1] 11 [1] 23 [1] 1		5			[2 Des]
2nd qtr	4	22	6 [2]	- [2]	-	-	[3 Des]
3rd qtr	- [1]	11 [4] 7	- [1]	-			[1 Des]
4th qtr	-	11 [3] 11	- [2]	-			[1 Des]

1945

1st qtr	- [1]	2 [4] 6	-	-		-	[1 destroyer, ex USN, ex RN, in Russian service]
2nd qtr	1	-	1	- [1]	-	-	

Sources: Elliott, P., *Allied Escort Ships of World War II*; Gardiner & Chesneau, Eds., *Conway's All The World's Fighting Ships 1922-1946;* supplemented by Lyon, D., *The Denny List.* Note the enormous build up of DE and PF deliveries in the second half of 1943.

3: *Cumulative Total*

The lend-lease 'four-stackers' and coastguard cutters (the latter listed under 'Cut') are shown from the end of the first quarter of 1941, though their introduction was more gradual than that. The Brazilian 'H' class are counted into the destroyer total here from the third quarter of 1940, but the other 'A to Is' are not counted into the total of destroyers available until the beginning of 1943.

This is an over-simplification, as some of these ships (notably the Canadian ones) were used earlier as Atlantic escorts, others remained in other service till later, and a few newer destroyers (particularly of the 'O' Class) served in the battle. Moreover, many of the oldest destroyers were converted to 'Wairs' (anti-aircraft escorts) or left in their original configuration for service in the narrow seas. Nevertheless, however arbitrary the figure is, it does give an indication of the *potential* number of Atlantic escorts available. I have not added in the two ex-Turkish 'I' class destroyers.

Year	Des	Slo	Cor	Fri	DE/PF	Cut	CaB	CaA
1939								
4th qtr	80	41	-	-	-	-	-	-
1940								
1st qtr	80	42	-	-	-	-	-	-
2nd qtr	75	41	9	-	-	-	-	-
3rd qtr	79	39	27	-	-	-	-	-
4th qtr	76	39	58	-	-	-	-	-
1941								
1st qtr	126	39	89	-	-	10	-	-
2nd qtr	124	41	129	-	-	10	1	-
3rd qtr	123	41	154	-	-	10	1	-
4th qtr	120	40	176	-	-	10	-	1
1942								
1st qtr	114	39	183	-	-	9	-	2
2nd qtr	111	38	194	3	-	9	-	3
3rd qtr	109	38	196	6	-	9	-	4
4th qtr	108	38	196	12	-	7	1	6
1943								
1st qtr	145	43	194	16	4	7	1	8
2nd qtr	144	51	195	31	7	7	2	13
3rd qtr	142	52	197	46	23	7	2	23
4th qtr	140	55	218	50	79	7	4	31
1944								
1st qtr	138	55	229	60	101	7	5	36
2nd qtr	135	59	251	64	99	7	5	36
3rd qtr	134	58	258	71	98	7	5	36
4th qtr	133	58	266	82	96	7	5	36
1945								
1st qtr	132	57	264	88	96	7	5	36
2nd qtr	132	58	264	89	95	7	5	36

4: *Actually in the Battle area*
(Western Approaches, Gibraltar, Freetown and Western Atlantic)

The designations below are those used by Roskill. It is presumed that the corvettes column will include some of the earliest frigates (originally referred to as 'twin screw corvettes'). The figures include 'special escort groups' (and divisions) which were allocated mainly to Arctic Convoys and Atlantic - nearly all of them destroyers - not counting AA ships for Irish Sea escort force and other such vessels. AMCs all based at Freetown as Ocean Escorts - Freetown also has local escort groups of anti-submarine trawlers. The percentage figure is an approximation to the percentage of the theoretical maximum available total of ships of the type concerned available at the time in question.

Date	Des	Slo	Cor	Cut	AMCs
01.01.42	97 [59%]	25 [62%]	169 [86%]	10 [100%]	12
01.08.42	97 [66%]	26 [68%]	167 [82%]	8 [89%]	7
01.01.43	94 [65%]	31 [82%]	161 [77%]	7 [100%]	6

Note that most sloops and all cutters concentrated at Londonderry were used for South Atlantic convoys.
Source: Roskill, *The War at Sea*

4A: *War-built escort ships (excluding sloops) in the Atlantic sphere of operations* (Londonderry, Liverpool, Greenock, Gibraltar, Freetown, West Atlantic.)

These are January figures for each year listed. They are for RN vessels only, except that figures for 1944 and 1945 figures include RCN ships in square brackets.

Year	1941	1942	1943	1944	1945
Corvettes:	51	99	93	70 [85]	80 [48]
Frigate:	-	-	14	37 [16]	48 [48]
DE/PF:	-	-	-	52	73

Source: Elliott *Allied Escort Ships of World War II*

5: *Battle of the Atlantic Escort Losses of the Royal Navy, Empire navies and Allies under British Control*

This list is only of losses which occurred in the North Atlantic (including Western Approaches).

Year	Des	Slo	Cor	Fri	DE/PF	Others
1939						
3rd qtr	-	-	-	-	-	1 Aircraft carrier (*Courageous*)
4th qtr	-	-	-	-	-	1 AMC
1940						
2nd qtr	-	-	-	-	-	3 AMC
3rd qtr	1	2	1	-	-	2 AMC
4th qtr	1	-	-	-	-	4 AMC
1941						
1st qtr	-	-	1	-	-	-
2nd qtr	-	-	-	-	-	4 AMC
3rd qtr	1	-	3	-	-	1 coastguard cutter

4th qtr	2	-	3	-	-	1 escort carrier (*Audacity*)
1942						
1st qtr	1	-	3	-	-	-
2nd qtr	1	-	1	-	-	-
3rd qtr	2	-	1	-	-	-
4th qtr	1	-	1	-	-	1 escort carrier (*Avenger*)
1943						
1st qtr	1	-	-	-	-	-
2nd qtr	1	-	-	-	-	-
3rd qtr	1	1	1	1	-	-
4th qtr	1	-	-	-	-	-
1944						
1st qtr	1	1	1	1	1	-
2nd qtr	-	-	-	1	-	-
3rd qtr	-	1	-	-	1	-
4th qtr	1	-	2	-	1	-
1945						
1st qtr	-	-	1	-	-	-
Totals	**16**	**5**	**19**	**3**	**3**	**14 AMC, 1 cutter, 2 CVEs**

Source: Roskill, *The War at Sea*, III, pt.2

Losses total 49 escorts, 14 AMCs and one fleet carrier, giving a grand total of 64 larger warships - a small figure compared to the number of merchant ships or U-boats lost. Note the concentration of losses of AMCs in the early years, balanced by very few other losses. Note also the proportionately high number of destroyer losses. One should also perhaps note the following submarines: *P 514* lost in a collision in the North Atlantic; the British *Unbeaten;* the Soviet *B.1* (ex-*Sunfish*); and the French *Perle*, accidentally sunk by British aircraft.

6: U-boats, including Italian, sunk by surface escorts of the RN, RCN and Allies under British Control

Figures are categorized by type of attacker. First figures refer to sinkings in the North Atlantic area, including the Straits of Gibraltar and the West Channel. Figures in square brackets refer to sinkings by similar vessels escorting Arctic convoys. Aircraft involvement in a sinking gives 50% of the credit to the ship(s) involved. Credit is split equally between any ship noted as involved. thus, if three corvettes were concerned in a single sinking, with ships of no other type involved, a score of 1 is given to corvettes. Decimal figures occur if, for example, one sloop and two corvettes are listed as sharing credit. In such a case the score is divided 0.33/0.66 between the sloop and the corvette headings.

Aircraft from escort carriers (including MAC ships)		5			[11.5]
WWI-vintage destroyers		22.72			[2.87]
Four stackers		3			
'A'-'I' class destroyers		27.5			[2.5]
Later destroyers (including Hunts)	6.19			[2.5]	
Sloops		28.88			[2]
Frigates	27.19			[2.33]	
DE/PF (the vast majority by DEs)		28.41			[0.66]
PCE		0.25			
Coastguard cutters		2			
Flower- and *Castle*-class corvettes	30			[1.5]	
Minesweeper		0.86			
Trawler	2.75				
Yacht		0.33			
Submarines		5			[3]

Source: Roskill, *The War at Sea*

Arctic escorts sank one more submarine - the Polish *Jasztrab*, sunk in error by a 'four-stacker' and a minesweeper.

Notes

1. In Professor Friedland's lecture at the combined BCMH/SNR symposium held at King's College London in 1991, he described how the engineer of his boat developed a complex variant of Diesel-electric drive which, by a method somewhat reminiscent of hoisting oneself by one's own bootstraps, stretched the range of the boat until it was just adequate. Food and other supplies were loaded on board to such an extent that neither diving nor use of the heads was possible at the start of the voyage. Having reached Cape Hatteras light, the boat maintained station by lying on the bottom, as there was not enough fuel to do more. Fortunately for the U-boats, the American failure to adopt convoy at the outset of war provided a constant flow of unescorted targets.
2. Alas, their excellent long range armament of 4" guns was not backed up by an adequate close-range armament of automatic cannon.
3. *Picotee,* torpedoed on 12th August 1941.
4. Not a phenomenon restricted to the Allied side. Where are the accounts of the Italian and Japanese merchant seamen who, in the Mediterranean and Pacific, suffered an even more horrifying proportion of losses?

16

The Deployment of the U-boats

by Sönke Neitzel

translated by Klaus Schmider

September 1939-Autumn 1941

On 1 September 1939 the Commanding Officer of the German U-boat arm, Kapitän z.S. Karl Dönitz, drafted a memorandum on the expansion of the U-boat force. In this he demanded 300 U-boats, in order to wage successful commerce warfare against Britain's supply routes. With the 57 U-boats currently available (of which only 26 were of the ocean-going Types I, VII and IX), there could be no hope of achieving any meaningful successes.[1] Two days later the war against Britain and France became reality. For Dönitz the only possible response to this event was, as he later stated in his memoirs, 'to do everything possible within my means to help win this war.'[2] At this time 18 U-boats (17 Type II and one Type VII) were on station in the North Sea, and 21 Type I, VII and IX-boats in the North Atlantic.[3] They started commerce warfare abiding by the Prize Regulations - that is, with the exception of troop transports and convoyed merchantmen, ships had to be searched and the safety of passengers and crew guaranteed before sinking.[4] The locations of the future operational areas of the U-boats were determined by the operational range of the different Types. The small Type IIs operated in the North Sea and off the British east coast, the Types VIIs west of Britain well into the Bay of Biscay, with the Types I and IX penetrating as far as the Gibraltar area. In order to have a second wave of boats on standby for operations in October, 10 were recalled from the Atlantic on 7 September. The remainder were concentrated near the western exit of the Channel, where several trade routes converged. All told, 41 merchantmen (all independent sailing ships but one) and the aircraft carrier *Courageous* were sunk by U-boats in September 1939.[5] Dönitz, however, felt that it would soon be necessary to counter enemy convoys by wolf-pack tactics, which already had been tried out during peacetime manoeuvres. In mid-October, the first attempt at setting a wolf-pack against a convoy was made. Of the projected group of nine, however, only six put to sea and of these three were sunk quickly. The remaining three sank only three ships from HG3.[6] A second attempt in November failed.[7] There were to be no further attempts until the autumn of 1940.

The mining of British ports was a further area of special operations. On 17 September 1939, the Naval Staff decreed that mining operations by destroyers and U-boats should take place in British waters. U-boats were allotted those targets on the West coast which could not be reached either by destroyers or bombers. From October to December 1939, seven mining operations were carried out in Loch Ewe, in the Bristol channel, Swansea, Milford Haven and

The Foreland where the new TMB magnetic mine (Torpedo-Mine B) was used for the first time. Both the battleship *Nelson* (on 4 December 1939 in Loch Ewe) and the cruiser *Belfast* (on 21 November 1939 in the Firth of Forth) were heavily damaged by U-boat-laid mines. The Type IIs also carried out nine mine-laying operations off the English east coast.

A planned thrust into the Mediterranean by U-25, U-53 and U-26 failed. The first two of these were delayed by convoy operations, while the third managed to pass the Gibraltar Strait but found no targets during a short stay in the Mediterranean.[8] Until the beginning of the Norwegian campaign, the main focus of operational effort was on the western entrance of the English Channel. In the period September 1939-February 1940, 701,985 tons were sunk by the U-boats.[9] Obviously a monthly sinking average of about 100,000 tons could not possibly affect the course of the war in any significant way. Greater successes were prevented by the high rate of torpedo failures, the long outward passage through the North Sea (the Dover Strait having been blocked by mine barriers), the delays imposed by the icing of the Baltic and the North Sea, and - most important of all - the small number of U-boats.

From March to mid-May, commerce warfare came to a standstill, due to the operations off the Norwegian coast. The main task of the U-boats was to intercept enemy warships, a mission which (due to the high rate of torpedo failures) they utterly failed to accomplish. Additionally, the U-boat arm was burdened with transport assignments.

The first boat to re-enter the Atlantic was U-37 (15 May), where she accounted for 41,207 tons of shipping.[10] After the anti-climax of the Norwegian campaign the results of this patrol gave an important psychological boost to the U-boat arm. At the same time the fall of France forced British convoys to keep clear of the southern part of the Irish Sea and to enter the West coast harbours via the North Channel. The U-boats had to shift the focus of their operational effort accordingly.

From now on the Battle of the Atlantic would be determined by the new bases in western France, particularly Lorient, which on 21 June 1940 had fallen virtually undamaged to German troops. A fortnight later (5 July), U-30 became the first boat to enter this port for re-supply. Lorient was soon to become a first-rate base for the re-supply and repair of operational boats.[11] The outward passage, which had formerly been a time- and fuel-consuming 3,000 kilometres was shortened by at least 1,000 km, thus saving one week on each sortie.[12] Supported by the new bases at Bergen and Lorient, even the small Type IIs were now able to operate off the North Channel, thus increasing the number of boats which could be deployed at any one time against the main flow of enemy traffic.

All these factors contributed to a greater economy of effort. From September 1939 to July 1940 the average number of operational boats consisted of about 33, of which an average of 14 (42%) were at sea. From August 1940 to July 1941 the average number available was about 30, of which about 16 (53%) were at sea.[13]

However, locating the enemy remained a fundamental problem. Because of the limited scope of vision afforded by a U-boat's conning tower, a surfaced boat could locate convoys or independently-sailing merchantmen only by chance. In order to achieve a meaningful concentration of boats, they had to be deployed at a traffic choke-point such as the North Channel.

Both needs - to keep a certain distance from the British coast and yet to operate as closely as possible to the North Channel - compelled the boats to stay in an operational area between 10°W and 20°W.

The first successful attempt to switch from individual to wolf-pack operations against the weakly escorted convoys occurred between 2-9 September, as five boats sank five ships from convoy SC2. While heavy seas prevented any further successes on this occasion, the subsequent attack on HX72 (11 ships sunk and one damaged) came much closer to corroborating Dönitz's pre-war views. The entry of 22 September in his War Diary reads: 'The action of the past two days has shown the soundness of details, worked out before the war, concerning attacks on convoys and the use of radio when in contact with the enemy.'[14]

Further substantial successes were achieved against convoys SC7 (20 ships sunk, one damaged) and HX79 (12 ships sunk, one damaged). The stormy November weather and the fact that most U-boats were back in Lorient for re-supply, however, precluded comparable successes for the next four weeks. Success came once more on 1 December, when HX90 was intercepted: 10 ships were sunk and one was damaged.

In mid-February 1941, Dönitz assumed that the convoy routes had been shifted to the north. He thus expanded the operational area to include the area south of Iceland.[15] This move yielded the interception of OB288 and OB289, with nine and three sinkings respectively. During the battles of HX112 and OB293 in the following month, however, the boot was on the other foot: four U-boats, amongst them those of the ace commanders Prien, Schepke and Kretschmer were sunk by the escorts. Apparently the area south of Iceland was too strongly guarded, so Dönitz decided to shift his boats further to the west (between 25°W and 30°W), even though this meant renouncing air reconnaissance. Until the middle of April, this area yielded, amongst others, 10 ships from SC26. New evidence, indicating that the heavy March losses had been due to fortuitous circumstances, brought another shift back to the waters south of Iceland from the middle of April.[16]

The frequent switching of convoy routes all over the North Atlantic severely handicapped the systematic location of convoys. Accordingly, from 8 May 1941, Dönitz dispensed with the more or less stationary patrol lines, and re-deployed his boats in wide-ranging search patterns as far afield as the Newfoundland Bank. From mid-June to mid-July, a further re-deployment dispersed the available U-boats over a wide area of the North Atlantic, as the more compact patrol lines had proved too easy to avoid. A much weaker escort presence west of 25°W and the complete lack of air cover gave a promising outlook for future operations in this area.[17] The results, however, were less than satisfactory: only two convoys were successfully intercepted, OB 318 losing seven ships in May and HX 133 six in June. Dönitz reported to the Naval Staff:

> The attempt to intercept traffic in the west, where routes converge, has been fruitless. Fog and bad weather are largely to blame. From 21 July we shall attempt to locate shipping nearer the English coast. In this area the lengthening nights will help the boats to evade pursuit, and renewed attempts at direct co-operation with air reconnaissance will be possible.[18]

During the following southward shift to the Gibraltar route, air reconnaissance and reports from intelligence provided many sightings but few sinkings. Strong escorts prevented any but the most experienced U-boat commanders from coming to grips with the enemy. As a result, sinkings were much less significant than those achieved while fighting the HX and SC convoys. The July tally (22 ships, 94,209 tons) bore no comparison to the sinkings achieved in June (61 ships, 310,143 tons).[19]

As for the patrols in the Freetown area, they only began on a large scale in February 1941, the individual cruises of UA (July 1940), U-65 (November-December 1940) and U-37 (January 1941) having set important precedents. Although a good deal of shipping had been sunk, this was offset by a long and wasteful outward passage, and so it seemed sensible to keep the U-boats in the North Atlantic for the time being. At last, in February 1941, Dönitz sent a group of seven Type IXs to the Freetown area where they proceeded to operate for four months - repeatedly re-supplied with torpedoes, fuel and food - and sank 74 ships.[20] A planned Capetown operation by four boats had to be cancelled due to the sinking of the U-boat supply ship *Phyton* in December 1941.

The decreasing numbers of U-boats left in the North Atlantic kept up a constant surveillance in the area south of Greenland and east of Newfoundland. Their efforts peaked at 202,000 tons in September, but after that the drain imposed by several side-shows and special assignments prevented any consistent level of success. As the last remaining wolf-pack (the Steuben group) took its leave, after 23 November the U-boat war in the North Atlantic came to a complete standstill.

Dispersal of Effort

As we have seen, from autumn 1940 until the summer of 1941, commerce warfare in the North Atlantic remained the focal point of German U-boat warfare. The beginning of the war with Russia on 22 June 1941 and the decline of Axis fortunes in the Mediterranean were, however, to lead to a dispersal of effort which had grave consequences. An attempt at transferring 12 boats into the Baltic was stopped by Dönitz in early June,[21] but between July and

September 1941 he had to part with six training boats and two Type IIs. The gap thus left considerably delayed the training programme.

Acting on Hitler's wish, Grand Admiral Raeder transferred two U-boats to northern Norway, together with the 6th destroyer flotilla, to interdict Russian supply to the Murmansk front.[22] In spite of a query by Admiral Norway as to the Naval Staff's sense of priorities, the U-boats remained on station in the Barents sea.[23] A further reason for the shift was the fear of a British landing in northern Norway, a possibility which had first been raised by the Lofoten raid on 4 March 1941. The Vägsöy raid (27 December 1941) further reinforced Hitler's fears of a large scale landing operation either in northern Norway or Murmansk.[24]

Dönitz opposed any deployments to Norway right from the very beginning:

> ...Hitherto the sinkings by these boats have been of no consequence. This is because their targets were very small ships against which torpedo attacks are not promising....The war will ultimately be decided by attacks on Britain's imports, which are the main objective. The war against Russia will be decided on land and U-boats can only play a secondary role in this campaign...[25]

However, his demand for the return of the Arctic and Baltic boats was refused by the Naval Staff, with references to the relevant Führer directive.[26]

On being asked for a provisional assessment of the Arctic operations by the Naval Staff, Dönitz remained unyielding in his refusal of this new assignment. The few available U-boats could neither hope for any meaningful success nor prevent the British from gaining access to Murmansk should they wish to do so. In his view, these factors made the whole mission an exercise in futility. Still, the Naval Staff proved just as steadfast in its refusal to 're-deploy all boats for the main task':

> The critical situation in the Arctic and the importance of the supply operations to the Polar coast, led to the Führer's unmistakable directive for the deployment of U-boats and called for the engagement of U-boats in the Arctic not just on military grounds, but as in 'honour bound'.[27]

The Naval Staff equally refused the cancellation of escort assignments for U-boats. At the same time, the Naval Staff was inclined to agree with the FO's fundamental assessment of the paramount importance of the Battle of the Atlantic in the fight against the UK. This made a high concentration of U-boats necessary and serves to highlight the Naval Staff's dilemma in this phase of the war. For the duration of the war in the East, the defeat of Russia had priority over England; this fact the Naval Staff could not but acknowledge. Feeling in 'honour bound', while never losing sight of the main task of commerce warfare, they had to deploy U-boats for the direct and indirect support of Operation

Barbarossa.[28] The navy was thus unable to impose its own point of view on the OKW and the other branches of the armed forces. This sad state of affairs was to be repeated time and again in several contentious matters during the first half of the war, such as the Luftwaffe deployment in sea warfare.

However, the Naval Staff's refusal to concentrate all available U-boats in the Atlantic and its espousal of special assignments were only partly due to the pressure by Hitler, the OKW, the Army and the Luftwaffe. In contrast to Dönitz, Raeder had never been an out-and-out advocate of commerce warfare. While Dönitz was willing to stake everything on the sinking of as much Allied shipping as fast as possible, Raeder sometimes lost sight of this potentially war-winning goal. The Naval Staff had been willing enough to send U-81 and U-652 to the Arctic to act as flank guards for the offensive against Murmansk. The deployment of a further two U-boats to the same area at the end of July was equally condoned by them.[29] The same attitude prevailed when allotting Mediterranean or secondary tasks.

At the beginning of October 1941, Hitler once again stressed the need to keep up the attacks on enemy supply to Murmansk and in turn, the supply protection in the Kirkenes area. The Naval Staff proposed on its own initiative the deployment of further U-boats for these tasks,[30] the aim being to keep three U-boats constantly on station in the Arctic.[31] Despite the low rate of sinkings (from July to October 1941 only a 3,487-ton steamer, an A/S trawler, a frigate, and an M/S trawler were sunk),[32] the Naval Staff kept its sights firmly set on the Kola Bay and the entrance to the White Sea.[33] Bearing in mind that at the very same time, much more valuable targets were at hand in the form of the British PQ convoys, it is remarkable that (due to a lack of adequate Intelligence) these did not suffer their first loss until 2 January 1942, when PQ7A lost the 5,135-ton steamer *Waziristan* to U-132.[34]

In the meantime Hitler's conviction that the British would sooner or later land in Norway and cut off the Reich from its all-important mineral supplies from Scandinavia became stronger than ever. On 24 January 1942, he confided to Vice-Admiral Fricke his 'absolute conviction that Britain and the USA are determined to affect the war's course decisively by an attack on northern Norway.' Hitler demanded of the Navy 'the utmost exertions' to thwart the British plans 'at their inception'.[35] On 7 February, he stated his conviction of the imminent transfer of 10 British divisions to the north.[36] Gruppenkommando Nord likewise predicted a British landing in north Norway for 1 April.[37] These assessments led to the transfer not only of all available surface vessels to Norway but also of an increasing number of U boats: by March, 10, and by April, 19 U-boats were operating off the Norwegian coast. Only the high rate of sinkings off the American east coast prevented Hitler from re-deploying all U-boats to Norway.[38] His persistent fear of a landing in Norway also led to the re-deployment of a further eight U-boats in February and March to the area between north Scotland and Iceland. Their task was to locate and attack the incoming invasion fleet at an early stage.[39] In this manner, 20 boats were stuck with the defence of Norway at the very time the U-boat arm was having its second 'happy time' off the American seaboard. Eight boats patrolled the Iceland-Scotland area, six boats operated in the Arctic and two boats each were on stand by in Bergen, Trondheim and Narvik or Tromsö.[40]

The projected transfer of the U-boat training programme from the Baltic to Norway, in order to achieve the number of U-boats necessary for the protection of Norway and thus keep up the level of commerce warfare in the Atlantic, turned out to be unfeasible. In Norway there were no areas sufficiently large or safe for tactical training and convoy attack exercises, while the fjords were unsuitable for torpedo firing practice. Moreover, the northern latitude permitted only day-firing in summer and night-firing in winter.[41]

In Dönitz's view, the successful waging of commerce warfare would in any case make short work of any landing attempt in Norway. The constant reduction of Allied shipping would automatically call into question the feasibility of any large-scale landing operation, with its attendant reliance on merchant shipping. 'The greater our successes in the Atlantic, the less the enemy will be able to even contemplate preparation of such enterprises.'[42]

This long-term calculation could, however, have been proved wrong on a short-term basis. The Naval Staff and Hitler were speculating on an imminent landing operation. It remains open to question whether the additional destruction of not more than 250,000 tons in the months of February and March off the American east coast would have substantially hindered such an operation. The Naval Staff countered Dönitz's objection:

> There can be no doubt that every ton of enemy shipping sunk diminishes the enemy's potential for operations overseas, but the Naval Staff considers that despite losses, the enemy still has sufficient ships for action against Norway. The transportation of 100,000 troops with full equipment would require about 1,250,000 tons of shipping space, and 30,000 to 50,000 tons a month would be needed to keep these troops supplied. The enemy mercantile marine is already fully occupied with civil and military commitments, so that additional demands could only be met by diverting shipping from other tasks....However, if the enemy really wishes to land in Norway, he will probably accept a temporary diminution of non-military imports. If the additional tonnage thus made available is not used for other purposes, such as the reinforcement of the Middle East, then the danger of an attack on Norway persists, despite the recent heavy losses in American waters.[43]

As a matter of fact, at the end of August, Churchill had instructed the Chiefs of Staff to undertake a feasibility study for a landing by four divisions in northern Norway in January or February of the following year. As it turned out, only three brigades and one mountain regiment would have been available for such an operation. Because of the strength of the German defences at Narvik,

Tromsö, Harstadt and Kirkenes and the difficulty of providing air cover, the matter was quietly dropped. A planned move against Trondheim in co-operation with the Swedes was likewise cancelled due to the latter's reluctance to get involved in war with Germany.[44] The enemy attack did not materialize;[45] the U-boats available in this area were used primarily for attacking the Allied supply convoys to Murmansk and Archangel. This new target was seen by the Naval Staff as rewarding. Similarly, until May 1942 the danger of a landing appeared sufficiently strong for the U-boats to remain on station in the Arctic.[46]

The sinkings achieved in fighting the PQ convoys on the Iceland-Murmansk/Archangel run were of a limited nature. In the whole of 1942, the boats sank 235,735 tons of Allied shipping, 102,311 tons of which had been from the scattered PQ17. This rate of 1,000 tons per boat per month could in no way compare with the rate achieved in the Atlantic, which was four times as high. It was the opinion of Dönitz that U-boat attacks against the small, strongly escorted PQ convoys during the polar summer, without the cover of darkness, were of little use. This was made all too clear by the exchange rate achieved during the attack on PQ16: four damaged U-boats had to be set against one steamer sunk. These U-boats moreover remained out of action for a long time, due to the unsatisfactory condition of the Norwegian yards. The situation was further worsened by the navigational problems encountered in these latitudes. Dönitz saw that the deployment of a greater number of boats would only bring about negligible results, while seriously affecting the waging of commerce warfare in the Atlantic.[47]

Meanwhile, escort and reconnaissance assignments continued to sap the strength of the U-boat arm. U-boats were often the only means available to provide any sort of protection for incoming or outgoing blockade runners and raiders. The aim of these missions - so ran the Naval Staff's line of thought - was to provide both wide-ranging reconnaissance and a psychological boost. This the FO U-boats did not dispute, but he did point out that the limited scope of vision from a U-boat's conning tower greatly diminished the value of any reconnaissance, while at the same time there were few, if any, chances to achieve an attack position against an incoming enemy warship from a submerged position.[48] Because of the limited number of U-boats, Dönitz persisted in his opposition to such tasks. Events were to prove him right: only on one occasion did an escorting U-boat achieve a firing position against an attacking enemy cruiser, and that was not exactly a success. On 1 December, while re-supplying UA, the supply ship *Phyton* was surprised by the heavy cruiser *Dorsetshire*. But though torpedoes were fired, they missed their mark and *Phyton* was sunk all the same.[49] The only advantage was the availability of the U-boat for rescuing the crew.

All told, from May to November 1941, 10 U-boats had to be detached just for escort duty.[50] Additionally the Naval Staff requested U-boats for reconnaissance missions in connection with the sorties of surface vessels. The projected Atlantic sortie of the pocket-battleship *Admiral Scheer* at the end of

October 1941 called for four U-boats to be deployed for ice reconnaissance in the Denmark Strait and for patrolling the Faroe-Iceland passage. On 10 November 1941, Group Nord requested a further four boats for weather-reporting duties.[51] This Dönitz refused, as in his mind, the 'sailing of the ship would not mean a relief and a reinforcement of commerce warfare, but to the contrary a weakening of it.' Since the main point of commerce warfare was the location of elusive enemy convoys, the absence of just one boat had a disproportionate effect on the efforts to find a convoy, let alone the achievement of sinkings.[52] In this instance, *Admiral Scheer*'s sortie was cancelled in mid-November, and the U-boats allotted for reconnaissance were able to resume commerce warfare.[53]

The detachment of U-boats to the Mediterranean was soon to become the main reason for the dispersal of the U-boat arm. After the initial successes of the DAK from the summer of 1941, the situation there took a marked turn to the worse. In a conference with Hitler on 10 July 1941, the *Marinereferent im Wehrmachtsführungsstab*, Korvettenkapitän Junge, stated that to prevent the loss of Africa the matter of supply had to be solved, Malta neutralized and Italy compelled to leave her defensive stance.[54] After the matter of the employment of U-boats in the Mediterranean had been repeatedly brought up and rejected, Raeder himself forced the issue at a conference on 19 August:

> In view of the complete failure of the Italians at engaging Britain in the Mediterranean, deployment in the Mediterranean will be unavoidable, no matter how much this affects the waging of commerce warfare in the Atlantic. Naval Staff are considering the matter and estimate that for the time being six to 10 medium-sized boats will have start to operate from Piraeus or a south Italian port.[55]

The Admiral Aegean expected that the planned deployment would bring about 'a considerable improvement of the situation of the Afrika Korps and furthermore have a sizeable effect on the British shipping routes in the eastern Mediterranean.'[56] On 13 September, Hitler ordered the assigned U-boats to be sent into the Mediterranean immediately.[57] The first ones of these passed the Strait of Gibraltar towards the end of September, and were deployed against the Tobruk supply run. Dönitz repeatedly opposed the Mediterranean assignment, which only worsened the considerable dispersal of all available U-boats. At the beginning of October 1941, only 13 U-boats were on station in the North Atlantic. There were in addition nine boats on the inward passage, four on the outward and 12 detached for secondary tasks (three for escort duties, six in the Mediterranean and three in the Arctic). In his War Diary, Dönitz wrote:

> The detachment of U-boats into the Mediterranean and the Arctic works to the detriment of the main task in the Atlantic. It has to be stressed again and again that with a small number of boats the enemy can no

longer be located and successfully attacked.[58]

The much-hoped-for success in the Mediterranean proved to be elusive. The intended victims were often of a shallow draft and as a consequence were often missed by torpedoes which had been set for deeper running.[59] The October sinkings totalled just two lighters, one 758-ton tanker and one 1,208-ton steamer.[60] Despite these small pickings, the Naval Staff never wavered from its stated aim of 'the interdiction of the supply traffic to North African ports, especially Tobruk',[61] but, faced with such a balance sheet, Dönitz tried to convince them not to divert further boats from the Atlantic:

> A change in the operational procedure of the Tobruk run and as a consequence, an improvement of our prospects of success its not to be expected. At the same time a withdrawal of these units from the Atlantic cannot but have the most dire consequences for our position in this main operational area. Therefore, FO U-boats does not think an increase in the number of boats operating in the Mediterranean can be justified. This would only serve to further weaken our operations in the main area, without proportionately increasing our prospects in the Mediterranean.[62]

The Naval Staff, obviously unable to offer an independent assessment, were inclined to agree with Dönitz, but pointed out that a decision by Hitler would be required before the U-boat war could be redirected to the Atlantic.[63] During staff talks the following day, Hitler demanded a fundamental shift to the Mediterranean. Even though the Naval Staff had, in August, also wished for a stronger naval presence in the Mediterranean, the Naval Chief of Staff, Vice-Admiral Fricke, now attempted to dissuade Hitler; but to no avail. The re-deployment of a further 24 U-boats was thus decided upon.[64] For his part, Raeder, who realized the futility of trying to make Hitler see reason, resigned himself to the inevitable. He could still hope that an 'increased employment of boats would in spite of all difficulties achieve successes such as will not only hamper Britain's communications in the Mediterranean, but also affect Britain's overall carrying capacity.'[65] Faced with the Führer's determination virtually to renounce commerce warfare in the Atlantic until a final reckoning had been reached in the Mediterranean, the Naval Staff did not even allow a formal protest to be lodged.[66]

The British Crusader offensive and evidence of British-Gaullist designs on North Africa once again made the Naval Staff see the precariousness of the situation in the Mediterranean. To counter these developments, a further shift to this area was ordered: boats on station both east and west of Gibraltar were to intercept the traffic going to Gibraltar and Malta, respectively. Even so, the struggle against British naval units in the Mediterranean was to remain the paramount mission, with the aim of defeating Britain's sea power in the

Mediterranean.[67]

Although Dönitz no longer dared question the re-deployment to the Mediterranean, he pointed out on 3 November that with so many secondary tasks, commerce warfare in the Atlantic would grind to a halt at the month's end. Though willing by now to acquiesce into sending U-boats into the Mediterranean on political and military grounds, he vigorously opposed all other secondary tasks.[68] However, his objections went unheeded, and on 22 November his prediction became reality when the Steuben group left the Newfoundland area for Gibraltar.[69]

This called into question the very groundwork on which German strategy had hitherto rested. Ever since the beginning of the war in the East, the main effort of both air and land warfare had been in Russia, while the navy's main task had been commerce warfare against Britain. While the shifting of some Luftwaffe squadrons to the Mediterranean did not jeopardize Barbarossa's priority, renouncing the Battle of the Atlantic was a matter of fundamental importance to the navy. As Professor Salewski has put it:

> ...even though the Mediterranean became, by the autumn of 1941, a
> point of critical importance for the Axis powers, meeting this new
> challenge by weakening the two main fronts (Russia and Atlantic) could
> only serve to upset severely the war's whole strategic concept.[70]

With the benefit of hindsight, the shift to the Mediterranean can be seen as a grave miscalculation. In spite of some sinkings, the boats proved incapable of either stopping the British land offensive or neutralizing Malta's striking power. The Atlantic was the only theatre of operations where the fight against Britain's supply routes could in turn bring the relief needed in the Mediterranean and Russia. Sinking tallies like the one achieved during December (nine ships, 33,082 tons) were not sufficient to interdict Malta's supply route. From mid-December to mid-January the island received 42,000 tons of supplies.[71]

As far as the marked improvement in Rommel's supply situation is concerned, this was mainly due to the improved air cover provided by Fliegerkorps II, and not by the U-boats' sinkings. These, in any case, were scattered over the whole length and breadth of the Mediterranean. This is not to say that the successes achieved against enemy warships did not contribute to the stemming of the Allied tide: on 13 November, U-81 sank *Ark Royal*; on 25 November, U-331 sank *Barham*;[72] and on 15 December U-557 sank *Galatea*. But the mining of Force K, the crippling of the battleships *Queen Elizabeth* and *Valiant* in Alexandria, the reinforced Luftwaffe presence and most important of all, the withdrawal of important Allied air and land forces to the Far East, suggest that this situation would have come about in any case.[73]

In the meantime the operations west of Gibraltar also left much to be desired. In trying (with the help of air reconnaissance) to come to grips with several HG convoys, FO U-boats had to put up with serious losses. The battle for

HG76 is a case in point: though the U-boats sank an escort carrier, a destroyer and two merchantmen, they lost five of their own number (among them one commanded by Kapitänleutnant Endrass, previously decorated with the Knight's Cross with Oak Leaves) to the 16-unit strong escort.

On 23 December 1941, Dönitz assessed for the Naval Staff the value of operations in the Gibraltar area, the whole point of which was, as he saw it, to intercept incoming Mediterranean traffic before it passed the Straits. Contrary to general expectations, the size of this traffic had turned out to be small, while the struggle against the strongly escorted HG convoys had meant few sinkings and heavy losses. Dönitz therefore proposed quitting Gibraltar and shifting the boats into an area just off the Azores,[74] while at the same time limiting the number of additional boats to be sent to the Mediterranean to two or three. There, the operational area should shift to the east, where prospects for successes were much greater and the losses smaller than in the Gibraltar area. The heavy losses sustained in running the gauntlet of the Straits formed a further reason to desist from sending a greater number of boats. Since the sinking of *Ark Royal* barely six weeks earlier, a total of 24 boats had been sent to the Mediterranean. Of these, four had been lost in the Straits, while another four had to turn back with heavy damage. That alone meant that a full third of the assigned boats had swiftly become casualties.[75] This time, Dönitz managed to impose his view - although the Naval Staff chose to emphasize a more positive reason. According to them,

...Owing to the recent favourable developments in Libya, the U-boat successes in the Mediterranean, the successful mine laying off Tripoli, the results to be expected from the mines laid by E-boats off Malta, and the intensified German air operations in the south of Italy, the whole situation in the Mediterranean has so improved since last month that it is no longer vital to block the stream of enemy traffic through the Strait of Gibraltar...[76]

Even though the commitment to Gibraltar and the Mediterranean had thus been finally down-rated by the latest Naval Staff decision, the Mediterranean assignment remained a heavy burden for many months to come. FO U-boats had to keep three boats on station west of Gibraltar, while the boats in the Mediterranean were virtually trapped, because of the near-impossibility of attempting an outward passage through the Straits. Dönitz had already written these boats off as far as the Battle of the Atlantic was concerned.[77]

The permanent deployment of 15-20 boats in the Mediterranean during the decisive phase of the Battle of the Atlantic (that is, until April 1943) was the single most serious long-term consequence of the situational changes in the Mediterranean in the autumn of 1941. From mid-September of that year, U-boat warfare in the North Atlantic was increasingly curtailed, and came to a complete halt in November and December. This raises the question as to whether, during the same time-span, greater successes would have been possible in the Atlantic rather than in the Gibraltar area. It has to be borne in mind that in the autumn of 1941, Ultra was having a quite disproportionate effect on the course of the U-boat war - a case in point being the month of October, when 15 Atlantic convoys were successfully re-routed around U-boat patrol lines, with only three of them being located by chance sightings.[78] Accordingly, even though the sinking rate would have been higher than that achieved in the Gibraltar area, it would in all likelihood not have exceeded an additional 100,000 tons.[79] More to the point, even after the Mediterranean situation had markedly improved, the U-boats deployed there could not (and would not) be withdrawn, and thus were unavailable for operations in American waters. It is therefore difficult to assess why, despite his opposition to any dispersal of effort, Dönitz proposed sending a further two or three boats - especially as he knew their assistance in the waging of the main battle would be permanently lost to him. Through 1942, a total of 16 boats were dispatched to the Mediterranean: two in January (U-561, U-73) and the remainder starting in October 1942. Sending this second wave of reinforcements could certainly not have been something Dönitz had in mind originally.

TABLE 1: Sinking Rates					
	Sinking Rate Atlantic	Number of U-boats	*Sinking Rate Med.*	Number of U-boats	*Sinking Rate Arctic*	Number of U-boats
Oct 41	154,000	67	1,966	4	3,487	4
Nov 41	62,000	71	-	6	-	4
Dec 41	117,000	72	33,082	12	-	4
Jan 42	259,000	65	-	21	5,135	4
Feb 42	418,000	76	-	21	11,507	4
Mar 42	447,000	80	2,623	21	18,816	10
Apr 42	342,000	80	7,379	20	12,344	19
May 42	547,000	85	11,754	20	-	19
Jun 42	577,000	88	9,942	17	102,296	21
Jul 42	254,000	99	5,888	16	4,845	23
Aug 42	508,000	110	-	16	40,511	23
Sep 42	379,000	134	-	15	3,770	23
Oct 42	549,000	161	-	15	36,541	19
Nov 42	566,000	162	53,662	17	-	26
Dec 42	281,000	159	25,314	20	5,881	23
Jan 43	176,000	166	19,231	23	7,460	21
Feb 43	294,000	178	20,445	22	18,245	18
Mar 43	482,000	193	46,369	19	-	14
Apr 43	246,000	195	13,934	17	-	21
Total	6,858,000	1299	250,831	322	273,023	300

A conservative estimate of what the U-boats deployed in the Mediterranean and the Arctic might have achieved in the Atlantic may serve to highlight the consequences this dispersal of effort had for commerce warfare.[80]

TABLE 2: Estimated Sinking Rates in Tons			
	Sinking rate per boat/month Atlantic	*Estimated sinking rate by Arctic boats*	*Estimated sinking rate by Med boats*
Oct 41	2,300	9,200	9,200
Nov 41	873	3,492	5,238
Dec 41	1,625	6,400	19,200
Jan 42	3,984	15,936	83,664
Feb 42	5,500	22,000	115,000
Mar 42	5,588	55,880	117,348
Apr 42	4,275	81,225	85,500
May 42	6,435	122,265	128,700
Jun 42	6,557	137,697	111,469
Jul 42	2,556	58,788	41,056
Aug 42	4,618	106,214	73,888
Sep 42	2,828	65,044	42,420
Oct 42	3,410	64,790	51,150
Nov 42	3,494	90,844	59,398
Dec 42	1,767	40,641	35,340
Jan 43	1,060	22,260	24,380
Feb 43	1,652	29,736	36,344
Mar 43	2,497	34,958	47,443
Apr 43	1,262	26,502	21,454
Totals		993,872	1,108,192
Gross total			2,102,064
less Arctic sinkings (Table 1)			273,023
less Mediterranean sinkings (Table 1)			250,831
Net total			**1,578,210**

From these tables it appears that a complete renunciation of the Mediterranean and Arctic side-shows could have yielded nigh on an additional 1.6 million tons of Allied shipping sunk by April 1943. Obviously this calculation presupposes a somewhat artificial linear increase which disregards the sort of Clausewitzian friction usually encountered in war. Still, this computation is, if anything, a low estimate, as it has to be borne in mind that a disproportionate number of ace commanders (who would probably have managed to better their comrades' average in the Atlantic) were sent to the Mediterranean. In addition, the following special assignments further limited the scope of possible sinkings:

    a. deployment of a wolf-pack off the Hebrides
       in January/February 1942   150,000 tons;
    b. losses sustained in the heavily defended
       Gibraltar Strait (both damaged and sunk)   30,000 tons;[81]
    c. escort assignments for surface vessels   20,000 tons;
    d. reconnaissance sorties for surface vessels   10,000 tons;[82]
    e. the limited scope of Operation Paukenschlag
       (five boats instead of the projected 12)   150,000 tons.[83]

These latter figures suggest that a possible 360,000 further tons could have been sunk. All told, therefore, we may surmise a total of some 1.95 million tons of 'missed opportunities'.

Dönitz was well aware of the fact that the deployment of U-boats for all these secondary tasks saved the Allies considerable quantities of tonnage. On 14 May 1942, he reported to Hitler that the Arctic boats would be capable of sinking 120,000 tons per month in the Atlantic.[84] Half a year later Dönitz worked out for Grand Admiral Raeder the sinkings lost due to the deployment of the Arctic boats from 1 January to 30 November 1942. He estimated that had these U-boats been deployed for the same period in the Atlantic, they would have accounted for an additional 650,000 tons.[85] The author's calculations for the same time span are greater by 585,000 tons.

It remains open to question, however, what consequence an overall increase of 25% in the sinking rate would have had. Professor Rohwer has worked out that during autumn 1941 and spring 1943, at least two million tons of shipping were saved by the timely information provided by Ultra - a comparable amount. In his opinion this would have led to a postponement of Operation Overlord. Is it possible to draw a similar conclusion about the tonnage which was not sunk as a result of the Mediterranean and Arctic side-shows?

To begin with, it must be stressed that this amount is only a hypothetical figure which does not include the effect of possible counter-measures such as the withdrawal of anti-U-boat forces from the Mediterranean. Moreover, the conditions pertaining in this case are different from those in the Ultra analysis. An additional 100,000 tons of monthly sinkings would have compelled the Trade Division to take appropriate action immediately. A higher concentration of U-boats could only have yielded decisively higher sinkings during January-April 1943, the first four months of the all-important pre-invasion preparation year. The gains made possible by Ultra, however, were of a different nature. Although at that stage there were few Support Groups and VLR Liberators available for convoy protection, Ultra enabled those few to be concentrated where they were most effective, around and over convoys which had been singled out for attack. Without Ultra, and with additional losses of 500,000 to

1,000,000 tons, the convoy system as a whole would have been called into question and the turning point of the Battle of the Atlantic would have been delayed. A higher sinking rate by the Arctic and Mediterranean boats alone would probably not have achieved disruption on a similar scale.

Deployment of the U-boats, January 1942-End of War

On 11 December 1941, when Germany declared war against the USA, an immediate consequence was that its self-imposed limitations (decreed on political grounds) in the fight against Allied escorts were removed. Moreover, merchant shipping in American waters became a highly attractive target. Accordingly, Dönitz planned Operation Paukenschlag: 12 boats would beat the drum on the US east coast and in the Caribbean. However, because it was still holding boats in the Gibraltar area, the Naval Staff would only allow him six. Yard-imposed delays cut this further, to five Type IXs, which in January 1942 sank 26 ships aggregating 163,021 tons in the New York-Cape Hatteras area.[86] US commercial traffic had not yet been placed on a wartime footing, a circumstance Dönitz was determined to exploit to the utmost. In February the same number of boats was deployed to the Caribbean and achieved considerable success off Aruba, Curaçao and Trinidad.[87] At the same time, the Type VIIs quit the Gibraltar area and were deployed off Nova Scotia. From the end of January 1942 their operational area started a shift to the south. In February they appeared south of Halifax, at the beginning of March off New York and towards the end of the month off Cape Hatteras.[88] The considerable distance separating the French bases from New York (3,000 nautical miles) or Aruba (4,000 n.m.) made the Type IXs especially suited to these operations. The range of the Type VIIC U-boats turned out to be greater than initially estimated, and these boats were also able to operate off the US east coast. But in the phase April-August 1942, the first sorties by the new Type XIV U-tankers, the so-called milch-cows, were of paramount importance.

The concept of replenishing operational U-boats by big supply U-boats had been considered before the war began,[89] and on 14 May 1940 an order was placed for their construction.[90] On 21 March 1942, U-459 - the first of the 10 Type XIVs - sailed on its maiden operational sortie. The milch-cows carried with them 432 tons of fuel, four torpedoes, food and everything else which might be needed by a patrolling U-boat. In this manner, 12 Type VIIs could be put in a position to penetrate the Caribbean, while the Type IXs could now range as far as Capetown: by the time U-459 left base, the modified operational boat UA (originally built for Turkey) had already re-supplied three operational boats. On 20 April U-459 took up station in the west Atlantic supply area, 500 nautical miles north-east of the Bermudas. There, between 22 April and 6 May, it re-supplied 12 Type VIIs and two Type IXs, which proceeded to operate between Cape Hatteras and the Florida Strait.[91]

During the three months from May to July 1942, 37 boats operated in the

Caribbean, of which 20 (eight Type IXCs, three Type IXBs and nine Type VIICs) were re-supplied on the spot. Without the U-tankers U-459, U-460 and U-116 (Type XB), only the Type IXs could have operated in this area. Due to their longer stay in this operational area, the boats were much less sensitive to the erratic progress of the shipping traffic in coastal waters - that is, there was much less chance that after a long and arduous transatlantic voyage, they would reach their hunting ground and find it empty.[92] Now capable of remaining on station for prolonged periods, they had only to wait for the ships to appear. After extremely heavy losses, the US Navy finally imposed the convoy system on East coast traffic. In the Caribbean, however, peacetime conditions - ships sailing singly, with navigation lights burning - prevailed until July 1942. When the convoy system was introduced here too, it led to a rapid decline in merchant losses and on 14 July Dönitz decided to shift the area of main operational effort back to the Atlantic.[93]

Until the Allied landings in North Africa on 8 November 1942, the U-boats remained scattered over almost all of the North Atlantic. In addition, six to eight boats operated continuously off Trinidad, two off Freetown in March and three to six from July to September. From 7 October to 13 November 1942, the Eisbär group operated with four boats off the coast of South Africa and sank 175,616 tons. On its heels came a second wave of four Type IXD2s, which between 8 October and 16 December 1942 sank 141,338 tons.[94] Nevertheless, valuable as these were, they were outside the main operational area, which from July 1942 was once again the North Atlantic. Even before this date, Dönitz had allotted some outgoing boats to Atlantic convoys which happened to be conveniently placed. These achieved several sinkings, such as in the operation against ONS92 (12-13 May 1942), when six boats sank seven ships.[95] They were also able to gather intelligence on convoy routeing and defence measures, which proved important when the majority of the boats were compelled to leave American waters and return to the North Atlantic.

After a weakening of the escort of the Gibraltar convoys had been reported, it was decided to include outgoing boats in an attack on one of the HG convoys at the beginning of June. This was also intended to prevent the enemy from shifting escorts to the American coast. Convoy HG84 was reported several times, both by military Intelligence and air reconnaissance. Of the boats deployed against the convoy, U-552 sank five ships. Having exhausted its stock of torpedoes this U-boat returned to the port of St. Nazaire, while the others continued their passage after re-supplying from U-460 and U-459.[96]

In the meantime operational conditions in the North Atlantic had changed considerably since November 1941. Even though by no means complete, the increased effectiveness of Allied air cover (both in terms of planes available and their range) covered wide areas of the North Atlantic. Surface escorts had both been reinforced and equipped with new technical tools (such as HF/DF). Against these factors, the increasing number of U-boats allowed Dönitz to operate with two or more wolf packs in the North Atlantic, while the big Type

IXs were freed for operations in remote areas.

The 15 convoy operations which took place between July and September of 1942 averaged 13 boats per operation out of a total of 106. In a comparable time span (August-October 1941), seven convoy battles had been fought with an average of eight boats each (out of a total of 97 boats).[97] In other words, a 13% increase in available U-boats resulted in twice as many convoy interceptions, and twice as many boats brought to bear against the enemy during each operation. There were two reasons for this. Firstly, due to the introduction of the M-4 cipher machine and the *Wetterkurzschlüssel*, British radio intelligence suffered a black-out from January to November 1942, which effectively negated all previous gains. Secondly, the U-tankers, which were sometimes able to follow the convoys from a distance of 50-100 miles, allowed a greater economy of effort. Hitherto one U-boat had been able to come to grips with a maximum of two to three convoys during each patrol. The new operational procedures allowed this quota to be raised to four to five interceptions.[98]

However, because of the Allied landings in North Africa, this level of effort could not be sustained. In October (although this move bore no relation to the impending Torch landings), the Naval Staff had already decided to reinforce the Mediterranean U-boats. On 7 November, because of the anticipated small pickings and severe losses, Dönitz questioned this re-deployment. To him it seemed more important to exploit the favourable situation in the Atlantic brought about by the weakening of the convoy escorts and by the increasing number of ships sailing independently.[99] But on the morning of 8 November, learning of the landings, he reacted immediately and re-deployed all fuelled-up boats to the Moroccan coast. He wrote in his War Diary:

> The boats will be too late to interfere with the landings but should be able to interrupt further disembarkation of supplies, and attack shipping bound for the Mediterranean. The prospects must not be overrated in the calm waters of the Mediterranean where the attacker runs big risks, which must however, be accepted.[100]

The importance of supply interdiction demanded (in Dönitz's words) the 'utmost recklessness in this mission'.[101] To his boats he radioed an uncompromising message:

> We must engage ourselves unconditionally with our proven brutal will of attack in this new task ordered to us by the Führer. Even the sinking of one single transport can be of the greatest importance for the American attack and the French defence.[102]

While losing three of their own number and a further eight damaged,[103] the U-boats managed to sink one escort carrier, two destroyers, one depot-ship and 15 transports of 147,270 tons. Once again Dönitz had to concede that in a closely guarded area such as this, the losses sustained bore no relation to the sinkings achieved. The Naval Staff's demands on 16 November for the re-deployment of further U-boats to the Mediterranean, and for a total of 20 to be kept permanently on station west of Gibraltar, brought a strong reaction from Dönitz. As he saw it, this would only entail heavy losses without the possibility of achieving commensurate successes. Given that the main landings had taken place, it was surely better to re-deploy all available boats to the North Atlantic routes.[104] As usual, though, the Naval Staff prevailed, and on 21 November decided that four boats were to be sent to the Mediterranean and a total of 12 were to patrol west of Gibraltar. All Dönitz was able to attain was the transfer of 11 Arctic boats and a temporary shift, starting on 27 November, of the Torch boats to the west.[105] From then until 23 December, these boats passed over the 40th Meridian and back into the area west of Portugal.

In this way, from 16 November, a total of 12 U-boats was unavailable for commerce warfare in the Atlantic.[106] Once again, with the benefit of hindsight, the reaction to the Allied landings in North Africa can be considered as a mistake. During the months of November and December when the Atlantic convoy escorts were weaker, many potential targets were passed up, for which the sinkings of about 150,000 tons achieved in the landing area could be no possible substitute. However, the decision of the Naval Staff and FO U-boats to re-deploy must also be seen from a psychological perspective. The U-boats were the only weapon available to oppose the landings west of Gibraltar. To allow the enemy to proceed without putting up a fight would have made sense from a strictly rational point of view, but would have been militarily unacceptable.

Even so, before the end of the year, the U-boats left in the North Atlantic (five from the Arctic, those which had sailed after 23 November and those which were too low on fuel to reach the Moroccan area) intercepted no fewer than six convoys - ONS144, HX217, HX218, ONS152, ON153 and ONS154.

During the first five months of 1943, the Battle reached its climax. In February, the number of operational boats available for operations in the Atlantic rose to 193. Of these an average of 116 were at sea, 48 being in the immediate operational area.[107] Even though this number was still far from the 100 boats on operations which Dönitz had deemed necessary, it was the highest concentration ever to be achieved by the U-boat arm, and it made feasible the simultaneous interception of North Atlantic convoys and of others west of the Canaries, bound for Gibraltar and North Africa.

Even so, the first convoy battles of 1943 (SC118 and HX224) did not begin until 28 January. In these, 13 ships aggregating 59,765 tons were sunk at the cost of three boats lost and four heavily damaged. During the first 20 days of March (aided by a short-term black-out in Bletchley Park), the U-boats sank 97 ships, two-thirds of them convoyed. However, the concentration of defence measures, the technical superiority and the renewed code-breaking by Bletchley Park could only lead to a turning-point.

On 11 April 1943, HX232 was successfully intercepted, but the operations against HX233 and HX234 were disappointing. The only good results in April were achieved in the Freetown area, especially by U-515. In May, U-boat losses in the North Atlantic became unacceptably high - 31 boats in 22 days. As a consequence, on 23 May, Dönitz withdrew all operational units from the area. Thereafter, only the Seehund group in the Indian Ocean managed to keep up a high sinking rate. The boats withdrawn from the North Atlantic sea lanes were at first shifted to the south-west toward the Azores. While beginning a search pattern aimed at the interception of UGS and GUS convoys, the Trutz group slowly moved to the east towards the Spanish west coast; but on 10 July, having lost five of their own number without sinking any ships, they were recalled.[108]

As the withdrawal from the North and mid-Atlantic was being completed, 43 boats still operated in remote areas such as the US east coast, the Caribbean, off Trinidad, the Brazilian coast and off West Africa including the Gulf of Guinea until 23 August. In these latitudes, especially off the Brazilian coast, it was still possible to achieve the odd sinking, but the defences of these areas had been considerably increased. Of the 43 boats mentioned, 14 were sunk - a loss rate of over 30%. Set against this was the sinking of 28 ships aggregating 170,893 tons.[109] At the same time, the destruction of most of the U-tankers made operations in these latitudes that much harder: by the end of August seven of the 10 Type XIVs and four of the five converted Type XB mine-layers had been sunk. The Indonesian-based Monsun group was the last to enjoy some success after its arrival in the Indian Ocean. These sinkings, however, peaked in August 1943; after this only insignificant successes were achieved.

In September 1943, Dönitz attempted to renew the struggle for the North Atlantic with the aid of new weapons. But even a relatively successful operation against convoys ON202 and ON18 could not disguise the fact that the reinforced flak-armament, the new radar detecting equipment and the new Zaunkönig acoustic torpedo were not enough to counter Allied superiority. The next six operations against convoys between 20°W and 40°W (including the last one, against ONS20 on 17 October 1943) turned out to be costly failures.

On 7 November the boats were concentrated in the eastern part of the Atlantic. On this occasion a new tactical deployment was attempted. The Eisenhart group was subdivided into seven wolf-packs, each three boats strong, which were deployed over a distance of 1,200 km. This was intended to hamper the enemies' attempts at locating the U-boats deployment pattern. This new disposition, however, failed to spot any convoys at all. The group was therefore moved to support the Schill group, which had been operating against the Gibraltar convoys since 3 November. Thus, between November 1943 and March 1944, the U-boats returned to their old operational area of the first half of 1941.

Simultaneously new anti-shipping units of the Luftwaffe became ready for action - for example the Fernaufklärungsgruppe 5 with Ju 290s, and the II. and III./KG 40 with glide-bomb equipped He 177s and Fw 200s. On the whole, though, attempts at direct co-operation with the Luftwaffe on the Gibraltar route and west of Ireland were a failure. To shift his patrol lines during the night, FO

U-boats needed exact convoy positions, but even in the case of a plane finding a convoy, faulty radar or heavy enemy defences usually prevented these from being forthcoming. In March 1944 the co-operation came to an unsatisfactory conclusion.

The invasion of 6 June 1944 and the availability of the snorkel predetermined the U-boats' next course of action. Apart from some patrols in remote areas, the boats once again sought their prey in UK coastal waters. The protection afforded by the new technical device and shallow waters reduced losses to the level of the second half of 1942. Sinkings achieved were, however, of a negligible nature. As losses rose again from February 1945, only the new Type XXIIIs were able to continue operations off the east coast unharmed.

Conclusion

The aim of the U-boat war had been the destruction of the maximum possible enemy tonnage for the minimum possible loss. To Dönitz it was the wholesale attrition of enemy shipping that mattered, not the stress on a specific operational area. As he saw it, each and every ship sunk, no matter where, would have to be replaced by the enemy sooner or later. In accordance with this opportunistic strategy, Dönitz and Konteradmiral Godt kept up a constant search for easy successes so as to achieve the highest possible sinking rate per boat per day. Operations off the US east coast, in the South Atlantic and in the Indian Ocean were all justified on these grounds, even though this temporarily meant renouncing the interdiction of Britain's North Atlantic supply routes.

The U-boats' operational areas had been quickly expanded from the autumn of 1940, to include most of the North Atlantic and the area off Freetown by mid-1941. During 1942, the main operational area shifted first to the American coast and then back again to the North Atlantic. After the attempt to resume the Battle of the Atlantic in September and October 1943 had been defeated, the U-boats returned first to the old operational area of the first half of 1941, and finally, from the summer of 1944, to the coastal waters of the UK, where they had first operated at the beginning of the war.

As FO U-boats, Dönitz had not been in a position to give commerce warfare the priority he had deemed necessary. Time and again he had to divert U-boats to special assignments and side-shows which weakened the main operational effort. Among all operational shifts, it was the deployment of U-boats in the Arctic, the Mediterranean and for the Torch landings that most deeply affected the waging of commerce warfare.

In contrast to this criticism, the strategic background against which these decisions were made has to be borne in mind. Each transport lost by a PQ convoy deprived the Red Army of considerable numbers of planes, tanks or artillery pieces. Each transport lost by a Malta convoy had both graver and more immediate consequences than one sunk in the North Atlantic, the cargo of which would only be of a long-term consequence to the war effort. The sorties of surface raiders had to be preceded by wide-ranging reconnaissance. This the Luftwaffe could only provide in part; the U-boats had to fill the gap. Similarly, the Luftwaffe's reliance on timely weather reports from the Atlantic made the deployment of weather reconnaissance boats inevitable.

The assignment of U-boats to secondary tasks was thus quite often unavoidable. As this chapter has tried to show, the exclusive concentration of the U-boat arm on commerce warfare could have meant the sinking of almost an additional two million tons; but even had that come about, its influence on the course of the war, while significant, would not have been of a decisive nature and cannot be compared with the role played by Ultra.

Notes

1. Salewski, M., *Die deutsche Seekriegsleitung 1935-1945*. Vol. III: *Denkschriften und Lagebetrachtungen 1938-1944*. Frankfurt/Main 1973, pp. 65-9.
2. Dönitz, K., *Zehn Jahre und Zwanzig Tage*, Koblenz 1991, p. 52.
3. Hessler, *The U-boat War in the Atlantic 1939-1945*, Ch. 1, p. 2.
4. The Prize Regulation was abolished in different phases until the German declaration of the total blockade of the UK on 17 August 1940. See Hessler, *The U-boat War in the Atlantic 1939-1945*, Ch. 1, pp. 43ff.
5. Potter, E. B., Nimitz, C. W., Rohwer, J.,: *Seemacht. Eine Seekriegsgesichte von der Antike bis zur Gegenwart*. Herrsching 1982, p. 522.; Roskill *The War at Sea 1939-1945*, I, p. 615.
6. Rohwer & Hümmelchen, *Chronology of the War at Sea*, p. 5.
7. Hessler, *The U-Boat War in the Atlantic 1939-1945*, Ch 1, p. 12.
8. Hessler, *The U-Boat War in the Atlantic 1939-1945*, Ch 1, p. 11.
9 . Roskill, *The War at Sea*, I, p. 615.
10. Rohwer & Hümmelchen, *Chronology of the War at Sea*, p. 20.
11. For further details see Neitzel, Sönke: *Die deutschen U Boot-Bunker und Bunkerwerften*, Koblenz 1991, pp. 51-70, 168-78.
12. Dönitz, *Zehn Jahre und Zwanzig Tage*, p. 110.
13. *Ibid.* See Hessler *The U-boat War in the Atlantic 1939-1945*, Ch. 2, p. 48.
14. Cit. in Hessler, *The U-boat War in the Atlantic 1939-1945*, Ch. 2, p. 50.
15. Dönitz, *Zehn Jahre und Zwanzig Tage*, p. 169.
16. Hessler, *The U-boat War in the Atlantic 1939-1945*, Ch. 2, pp. 69f.
17. Hessler, *The U-Boat War in the Atlantic 1939-1945*, Ch. 3, p. 73.
18. Naval Staff War Diary, Part C IV, p. 116, BA/MA RM 7/846.
19. Roskill, *The War at Sea*, I, p. 616.
20. Dönitz, *Zehn Jahre und Zwanzig Tage*, p. 171.
21. Naval Staff War Diary, Part A, 4.6.41, p. 31.
22. Naval Staff War Diary, Part A, 18.7.41, p. 273.
23. Naval Staff War Diary, Part A, 23.7.41, p. 349.

24. Salewski, I, p. 458ff. See also Naval Staff War Diary, Part A, 7.10.41, pp. 115 ff.

25. Hessler, *The U-boat War in the Atlantic 1939-1945*, Ch 3, p. 89.

26. Naval Staff War Diary, Part A, 5.8.41, p. 75.

27. Naval Staff War Diary, Part A, 2.10.41, p. 35.

28. See Salewski, Vol. I, p. 448.

29. Naval Staff War Diary, Part A, 24.7.41, p. 364.

30. Naval Staff War Diary, Part A, 9.10.41, pp. 146ff., 14.10.41, pp. 228f.

31. Naval Staff War Diary, Part A, 15.10.41, p. 255.

32. Rohwer, *Die U-Booterfolge der Achsenmdchte*, München 1968, p. 196.

33. Naval Staff War Diary, Part A, 31.10.41, p. 547.

34. *Ibid.*

35. Naval Staff War Diary, Part A, 22.1.42, pp. 390ff.

36. Wagner, Gerhard (Ed.): *Lagevortrage des Oberbefehlshabers der Kriegsmarine von Hitler 1939-1945.* München 1972, 7.2.42, p. 352.

37. Naval Staff War Diary, Part A, 6.2.42, p. 109. Two days previously the Admiral Norway had assessed the probability of a Russian land offensive against Finland in combination with a British landing as 'highly likely'. Naval Staff War Diary, Part A, 4.2.42, p. 60.

38. Naval Staff War Diary, Part A, 24.1.42, p. 435.

39. Naval Staff War Diary, Part A, 10.2.42, p. 191, BA/MA, RM87/20.

40. War Diary of FO U-boats, 6.2.42.

41. *Ibid.*

42. War Diary of FO U-boats, 25.2.42, BA/MA, RM87/20.

43. Cit. in Hessler, *The U-boat War in the Atlantic 1939-1945*, Ch. 4, p. 9.

44. Gwyer, J. M. A., *Grand Strategy*, Vol. III, Part I, pp. 204ff.

45. Hitler himself had first doubted the feasibility of such a move on 9 February 1942. In a conference with Raeder and Halder he pointed out that 'in view of England's considerable need of tonnage for the Far East... such a move could by now be called into question.' Naval Staff War Diary, Part A, 9.2.42, p. 161.

46. Naval Staff War Diary, Part A, 9.3.42, pp. 158f, BA/MA, RM87/20.

47. War Diary of FO U-boats, 4.6.42, BA/MA, RM87/21.

48. Naval Staff War Diary, Part A, 2.10.41, p. 34.

49. Jung, Dieter; Maas, Martin; Wenzel, Berndt: *Tanker und Versorger der deutschen Flotte 1900-1980.* Stuttgart 1981, p.406.

50. See War Diary of FO U-boats 2.10.41, BA/MA, RM87/18; Naval Staff War Diary, Part A, 14.10.41, pp. 236f.; 1.11.41, p. 9; Hessler, *The U-boat War in the Atlantic 1939-1945*, Ch. 3, p. 88.

51. Naval Staff War Diary, Part A, 10.11.41, pp. 191f.

52. War Diary of FO U-boats, 10.11.41, BA/MA, RM87/19.

53. Naval Staff War Diary, Part A, 16.11.41.

54. Salewski, Vol. I, p. 470.

55. Naval Staff War Diary, Part A, 19.8.41, p. 306.

56. Salewski, Vol. I., pp. 473f.

57. Reuth, R. G., *Entscheidung Mittelmeer. Die südliche Peripherie Europas in der deutschen Strategie des Zweiten Weltkrieges 1940-1942*. Koblenz 1985, p. 101.
58. War Diary of FO U-boats, 10.10.41, BA/MA, RM87/18.
59. Naval Staff War Diary, Part A, 15.10.41, p. 257.
60. Rohwer, *Die U-Booterfolge*, p. 227.
61. Dönitz proposed wide-ranging operations all over the Mediterranean with an operational focus in the Egypt-Palestine area. Naval Staff War Diary, Part A, 15.10.41, pp. 257f., 18.10.41, p. 313.
62. Naval Staff War Diary, Part A, 26.10.41, p. 448. War Diary of FO U-boats, 1.11.41, BA/MA, RM87/19.
63. *Ibid.*
64. See Naval Staff War Diary, Part A, 29.10.41, pp. 497ff.
65. Naval Staff War Diary, Part A, 28.10.41, pp. 479f.
66. Salewski, Vol. I., p. 478.
67. Naval Staff War Diary, Part A, 15.11.41, pp. 277ff; 17.11.41, p. 307; 22.11.41, pp. 402f.; 29.11.41, p. 516.
68. Naval Staff War Diary, Part A, 3.11.41, pp. 43f. At this juncture the question has to be asked of how strongly Dönitz really opposed the sending of boats into the Mediterranean. In his memoirs he admits to seeing the Mediterranean assignment as inevitable, 'because the danger to the Africa Korps had to be eliminated'. As already pointed out, by the beginning of November he no longer questioned the Mediterranean missions. On the other hand at no time did he speak out in favour of this task in his War Diary. Dönitz, *Zehn Jahre und Zwanzig Tage*, p. 153.
69. Naval Staff War Diary, Part A, 23.11.41, p. 418.
70. *Ibid.*, p. 483.
71. Reuth, *Entscheidung Mittelmeer*, p. 124.
72. *Barham*'s sinking was only confirmed to the Axis side by the interrogation of captured British airmen. Naval Staff War Diary, Part A, 25.11.41, p. 452; 25.1.42, p. 467.
73. See Naval Staff War Diary, Part A, 26.1.42, pp.492f. One of the main reasons for the British advance coming to a halt at the Mara-el-Bregatha position west of El Agheila was the withdrawal of two divisions, one tank-brigade and nearly 300 planes to the Far East. Reuth, *Entscheidung Mittelmeer*, p. 121.
74. War Diary of FO U-boats, 23.12.41.
75. War Diary of FO U-boats, 30.12.41.
76. Cit. in Hessler *The U-Boat War in the Atlantic 1939-1945*, Ch 3, p.92. Further information War Diary of FO U-boats, 2.1.42, Naval Staff War Diary, Part A, 2.1.42, pp. 14f., 9.1.42, pp. 129f., especially 9.1.42, pp. 139ff.
77. War Diary of FO U-boats, 30.12.41. See Dönitz, *Zehn Jahre und Zwanzig Tage*, pp. 155f.
78. Rohwer, J, 'Special Intelligence und die Geleitzugsteuerung im Herbst 1941', in *Marine Rundschau* (75) 1978, Nr. 6, p.719.
79. For this estimate it is possible to compare the sinking rates of October 1941

(202,000 tons) with the sinking rate of November 1941 (62,000 tons) and of December (117,000 tons).

80. Roskill, *The War at Sea*, I, pp. 616ff.; Hessler, *The U-boat War in the Atlantic 1939-1945*, Diagram 32, Plan 59, 60.

81. U-96, U-558, U-569, U-432 and U-202 were damaged in the Strait of Gibraltar and started their next patrol after one month (U-432, 21.1.42) to three months (U-202, 1.3.42) due to the state of the damage. It can be estimated that the damage to the boats cost the U-boat arm 5x30 days at sea.

82. For example: U-430, U-402, U-332, U-105 which were deployed from 4-10.11.41 in the Denmark Strait as reconaissance for the planned sortie of the battleship *Tirpitz*. From 13 November they were sent to Kap Race. Rohwer, *Chronology*, p. 187. Comparable delays were caused by the sorties of *Scharnhorst* and *Gneisenau*, *Admiral Hipper* and *Bismarck* and *Prinz Eugen*.

83. The five boats sank 163,588 tons during Operation Paukenschlag off the US east coast.

84. *Lagevorträge*, 14.5.42, p.394.

85. Dönitz based his calculations on an estimated 910,000 tons these boats would have sunk in the Atlantic. He arrived at the amount of 650,000 tons by subtracting the estimated sinking rate in the Arctic (262,614 tons). War Diary of FO U-boats, 10.12.42.

86. Rohwer & Hümmelchen, *Chronology of the War at Sea*, p. 116.

87. Hessler, *The U-boat War in the Atlantic 1939-1945*, Ch. 4, p. 7.

88. Hessler, *The U-boat War in the Atlantic 1939-1945*, Ch. 4, p. 4.

89. See for further details the memorandum: *Welche Entwicklungsaufgaben und welche operativen Vorbereitungen müssen heute zur Führung eines U Boot-Handelskrieges gegen England in aller erster Linie gesttellt werden*. Mai 1939. Militärische Zwischenarchiv Potsdam WF-0421318.

90. Rössler, E, *Geschichte des deutschen U-bootbaus*. Vol. I. Koblenz 1986, p. 206.

91. Hessler, *The U-boat War in the Atlantic 1939-1945*, Ch. 4, 13; War Diary FO U-boats 2.7.1942, BA/MA, RM87/22.

92. War Diary FO U-boats 10.7.1942, BA/MA, RM87/22.

93. See War Diary of FO U-boats, 19.7.42, BA/MA, RM87/22.

94. Rohwer & Hümmelchen, *Chronology of the War at Sea*, pp. 167, 174.

95. Hessler, *The U-boat War in the Atlantic 1939-1945*, Ch. 4, p. 23.

96. Hessler, *The U-boat War in the Atlantic 1939-1945*, Ch. 4, p. 24.

97. Hessler, *The U-boat War in the Atlantic 1939-1945*, Ch. 5, p. 50.

98. Hessler, *The U-boat War in the Atlantic 1939-1945*, Ch. 5, p. 51.

99. War Diary of FO U-boats, 7.11.42, BA/MA, RM87/24.

100. Cit. in Hessler, *The U-boat War in the Atlantic 1939-1945*, Ch. 5, p. 63.

101. War Diary of FO U-boats, 8.11.42, BA/MA, RM87/24.

102. War Diary of FO U-boats, 9.11.42, BA/MA, RM87/24.

103. Rohwer & Hümmelchen, *Chronology of the War at Sea*, p. 177.

104. U-Bootslage, Beurteilung 18.11.1942 in War Diary of FO U-boats, BA/MA,

    RM87/24.

105. War Diary of FO U-boats, 10.12.42; Lagebeurteilung vom 19.12.42, War Diary of
     FO U-boats, BA/MA, RM87/24.
106. Hessler, *The U-boat War in the Atlantic 1939-1945*, Ch. 5, pp. 60ff.
107. Bekker, C, *Verdammte See. Ein Kriegstagebuch der Deutschen Marine.*
     Frankfurt/Main 1971, p. 377.
108. Hessler, *The U-boat War in the Atlantic 1939-1945*, Ch. 7, pp. 10f.
109. Hessler, *The U-boat War in the Atlantic 1939-1945*, Ch. 7, p. 18.

17

Luftwaffe Support of the German Navy

by Horst Boog

Germany's failure in the Battle of the Atlantic was to a large extent also the failure of Luftwaffe air support for the Kriegsmarine. To understand this, one must look not only at Germany's geostrategic position as a continental power in the middle of Europe; one must also go back in history to the establishment of the German Navy and to German *Weltpolitik* before World War I. As Holger Herwig observed, there was always a

> divergence between the eastern, land-oriented mentality of army officers and the western, maritime-oriented views of the naval hierarchy. During World War I, this conflict came to light most vividly during the Holtzendorff-Ludendorff feud over the future of the Black Sea region, when the navy bluntly declared that the fulcrum of the war was the Atlantic maritime arteries rather than the plains of Russia. In 1940, inter-service differences were also made manifest thanks to the army's (and Hitler's) plans to invade Russia....and because of the navy's Mediterranean programme, which sought to establish Egypt, North Africa, Gibraltar and the Atlantic islands as the pivot of German strategy. There also existed during both world wars an overall lack of co-operation and planning between the two branches of the armed forces.[1]

This is all true, and German inter-service dissension in World War II was aggravated by the fact that Hitler was not a follower of the ideas of Mahan, but of Mackinder's, according to which power does not rest on the control of the sea lanes, but control of continents, with their raw materials, manpower and industries. Hitler wanted to establish a racially-based German-controlled continental empire reaching as far as the Urals. The divergence of views was further aggravated by Göring, the second most influential man in the Third Reich and the Commander-in-Chief of the newly created Luftwaffe, Germany's air force, as well as the top man of the German war economy. Though from 1938 he shared neither Hitler's foreign policy nor his appetite for expansion towards the East and for war, nevertheless he was devoted to him. Göring was, moreover, a vain, covetous and jealous person who wanted to be the master in his own house. Whatever flies, he used to say, belongs to me. In the latter part of the war this attitude was particularly justified by the growing shortage of planes, aircrews and raw materials, which called for a more centralized command, and by the needs of the land fronts (especially in the East) which were of paramount importance to Germany. In addition to the personalities of Hitler and Göring, these necessities and exigencies of the war constituted the third factor determining the relations between the Kriegsmarine and the other services.

Of course, the dissension between Göring and Grand Admiral Raeder, Commander-in-Chief of the Kriegsmarine, were not only due to personalities, but had a long pre-history. In imperial Germany, army and navy possessed air arms of their own. Both were employed in various roles during World War I. In 1915, when the army attempted to establish a unity of command over all German air forces, the navy strongly opposed the plan, believing that only it knew how to build and employ naval aircraft and dirigibles, and how to train air crews for operations over the sea.[2]

This attitude continued from 1919 to 1933, during which period the German armed forces were forbidden by the Treaty of Versailles to maintain an air force. The navy, although clandestinely preparing for a new naval air arm,[3] did not participate in the army's secret aviation training and testing at Lipetsk in the Soviet Union. This was due in part to the memory of the mutiny in 1918, and a fear of being re-infected with communist ideology; but it was also because the navy did not wish to do anything that could lead to army control of a future air force. In 1933-34, opposing the establishment of an independent German Air Force, the Naval Command used the same arguments that had been aired during World War I. This was in vain; the Luftwaffe soon had to be accepted as a political fact.[4] Naval demands for a separate naval air arm ran counter to the principle of economy in personnel, material and finances, an argument which was successfully used by Göring in establishing and defending his new unified and independent service, and which was also supported by the German Armed Forces Supreme Command.

Nevertheless, the navy continued to fight for its own air arm. While Göring stood[5] for the unity of command of the war in the air, Raeder[6] pleaded that the unity of command of the war at sea should include the air units used for reconnaissance, attack and defence. To him, the aircraft was an integral sea-weapon like the mine, the torpedo and the artillery of men-of-war, and belonged to the fleet organically. He further believed that only Kriegsmarine personnel could and should operate aircraft over sea. Göring, in contrast, intended to train a uniform air force officer corps that would be equally capable of carrying out tasks over land and sea.

Actually the two conceptions of unity of command excluded each other. However, during the first years of the establishment of the Luftwaffe, Göring needed the advice and help of the other two services (many of his air force officers were former army or navy officers), and could not dwell too much on conceptual differences.

The years 1935-42 can be looked upon as a period of transition, with the naval air units somewhere between Luftwaffe and Kriegsmarine. When the existence of the Luftwaffe was officially proclaimed in 1935, the naval air units were placed under its overall command, but subordinated to a special Air Administrative Area Command 'Sea' and placed under a Chief of Naval Air Forces.[7] Only in war and during short training periods were the units to be operationally subordinated to the Kriegsmarine.

The Luftwaffe officers commanding naval air units were former naval officers, and the crews of the naval aircraft were taken from Kriegsmarine personnel. But, because the naval air units were part of the Luftwaffe, the Kriegsmarine no longer had a direct influence on the selection of personnel.[8]

It was a strange fact that the German navy - much older than the Luftwaffe and having its own World War I experience, not only in submarine and surface vessel operations but also in naval air war - never produced a basic field manual covering all aspects of the war at sea, to include maritime air war. In contrast, the army had its basic Field Manual No. 300 *Truppenführung* ('Troop Command') and the Luftwaffe its famous L.Dv. 16 *Luftkriegführung* ('Conduct of the Air War'). The latter, written in 1933-4 and issued in 1935, contained a section on 'Co-operation with the Navy' within the chapter on 'Employment of Air Units'. Here a distinction was made between those naval air units which directly supported naval units in battle (and were, therefore, operationally subordinated to the fleet in wartime), and those flying units of the Luftwaffe which co-operated only indirectly with the navy - if the occasion permitted - by attacking naval stations, docks, ports and merchantmen. The latter units were land-based exclusively. The distinction reflected the actual situation of the time.[9]

In the years to come, the Kriegsmarine struggled against the Luftwaffe for more naval air units to be attached to the naval forces in the event of war. Having been the loser in Hitler's decision for an independent air force, the Kriegsmarine wanted the naval air arm eventually under its operational command to be sufficiently strong for all impending missions. But from 1935, the build-up of a strong land-based air force had first priority, because Germany was primarily a land power, taking precautions against the other land powers in her vicinity - at that time France, Poland, and Czechoslovakia. The vital centres of these countries could be reached by the fast medium-range two-engine bomber. These could be built in larger numbers than heavy four-engine bombers, which were in development. Early in May 1936, therefore, the Chief of the Luftwaffe General Staff, Wever, ordered that the two-engined bomber should have priority over the heavy bomber. This decision corresponded with Germany's perceived needs, and was approved in April 1937.[10]

This was the first - and decisive - blow against long-range air support for naval warfare. It had an enduring effect. The idea of eventually building a long-range strategic bomber force was never killed, but was repeatedly postponed to a future time when (it was supposed) Germany would have full control over the continent, which it would then have to defend overseas. Such a time never came, so neither did a long-range naval air force.

In 1936, the Kriegsmarine High Command demanded 800 aircraft.[11] This started a long period of negotiations between the Kriegsmarine and Luftwaffe, aggravated by diverging views between the services in regard to the employment of aircraft over sea. In the course of the talks, Göring managed to gain control of coastal air defence, a responsibility hitherto claimed by the Kriegsmarine.[12] Henceforward, the remit of the Kriegsmarine was limited to anti-aircraft defence of the so-called 'naval fortresses', i.e. naval stations, ports and repair facilities. It was only in spring 1938 that Göring could finally be induced to promise an increase in the number of flying units to be allocated tactically to the Kriegsmarine in wartime from 25 to 62 squadrons - mostly seaplanes - until April 1942.[13]

Meanwhile, Great Britain had entered the German war scenario as a potential enemy, and General Felmy (Commander-in-Chief of 2 Air Fleet, who had been ordered to study the Luftwaffe's chances of success over the RAF) declared that the 62-squadron scheme was too much of an inroad into the development of a land-based operational air force.[14] Thus, in late 1938, Colonel Jeschonnek (Chief of the Operations Department of the Luftwaffe General Staff, and later its Chief of Staff) informed the Kriegsmarine that the Luftwaffe felt fully responsible for the conduct of the air-war at sea and of naval air warfare, but that, due to Hitler's order for the five-fold increase of the Luftwaffe by 1942, it could no longer fulfil its promise to the Kriegsmarine concerning the supply of sea-going planes. On the contrary, a concentration on the production of land-based heavy and fast medium bombers would be necessary. He proposed, however, that in fulfilling the aircraft production programme, 13 out of 58 bomber Geschwader could be assigned to the Kriegsmarine for mine-laying and torpedo missions, and that 30 more bomber Geschwader could be employed against Britain.

Altogether there were to be over 1,100 He-177 four-engined aircraft as bombers and long-range reconnaissance planes.[15] As soon became evident, the programme far exceeded German resources, and in spite of the programme no particular pressure was put on the development of the He-177 long-range aircraft, since it was not required for any specific mission.[16] The use of the term *Piratenflugzeuge* (pirate aircraft) rather indicated, however, that they were planned to be used at sea. In the end, the Kriegsmarine was asked to limit its demands for supporting aircraft to no more than 500 for the time being.[17] The Kriegsmarine's claim for command over the bomber Geschwader to be detailed for co-operation in naval warfare was refused by the Luftwaffe, the number of naval air units reduced to 41 squadrons and its air activities limited to coastal protection.

The results of the negotiation were laid down in an agreement between Göring and Raeder dated 27 January 1939.[18] Air reconnaissance for the purposes of naval warfare was to be the responsibility of the air units tactically assigned to naval units. The air war against Britain and in areas closed to naval warfare was to be the task of the Luftwaffe, which also considered the laying of aerial mines as its own business. The questions of unity of command and of uniform training of air crews for naval warfare, always so important to the Commander-in-Chief of the Kriegsmarine, remained open. A few days later, the ground organization for sea-plane units was re-arranged and placed under the command of the newly established 'General of the Luftwaffe with the Commander-in-Chief' of the Kriegsmarine. He was directly subordinated to Göring, and in the event of war would command all air units to be assigned to the Kriegsmarine as naval. These would be mainly carrier- and ship-based, but included reconnaissance aircraft.[19]

Göring's policy of putting everything that flew under his own command must also be seen in the light of his responsibility for the five-fold increase of Luftwaffe strength, as ordered by Hitler.[20] So, after Raeder had given up his claim for a separate naval air arm on 27 January 1939, Göring even consented to the Kriegsmarine's so-called Z-Plan, which Hitler had approved the same day. This meant that the Kriegsmarine was to get a large battle fleet for global warfare, to be ready in the 1940s.[21] It was not long, however, before the Luftwaffe felt neglected, since raw materials now mostly went into naval armament at the expense of air armament. In order to re-focus Hitler's attention on the Luftwaffe, Göring, on the instigation of his Under-Secretary of State, Milch, staged a big Luftwaffe arms display at Rechlin on 3 July 1939, where the latest models of guns and planes (including the He 178 jet fighter and a rocket bomb for the destruction of warships) were shown to Hitler. Obviously this was a propaganda show, because very little was operational. Hitler is supposed to have derived his own, false, conclusions about the Luftwaffe's readiness for war from this display,[22] but the Kriegsmarine soon lost priority for its Z-Plan.

The war game of 2 Air Fleet of May 1939 had similar disadvantageous results for the Kriegsmarine.[23] The new term *Seekampfverbände* (sea combat air units) denoted flying units of the regular operational Luftwaffe to be used for reconnaissance over sea, laying of aerial mines and the torpedoing and bombing of targets at sea and of naval stations etc. The Luftwaffe was about to take over the tasks that had been the domain of flying units formerly under the tactical command of the Kriegsmarine in wartime. The war game proved, moreover, that the number, the operational radius, the equipment of available aircraft and the training of air crews would not suffice for attacks on the British fleet, or on the western and south-western English ports. The Air Force General Staff therefore suggested attacks on the air armament industry rather than on shipping and ports, and this was to be the task of the Luftwaffe.

It is not astonishing that, despite the demand for close ties between Luftwaffe and Kriegsmarine staff to facilitate combined operations, preconditions were still lacking at the beginning of the war.[24] There had not been many air force-navy exercises. The services used different maps, codes and radio connections. There were differences in reporting terminology, and common communications methods still had to be established. Reconnaissance over sea and air-sea combat were not under unified command. That no larger blunders occurred was due to the merit of the Luftwaffe commanders and front officers who had been naval officers before.

From the very beginning of the war, the Luftwaffe started a policy gradually reassigning the coastal flying units from the tactical command of the Kriegsmarine to the command of the air fleets. The reasons given were manifold, ranging from lack of efficiency of the coastal air units to the shortage of aircraft of the operational Luftwaffe, which became heavily involved in many theatres of war. By late September 1939, the prospective carrier-based fighter and dive-bomber units were transferred to 2 Air Fleet in the West, because the aircraft carrier was still under construction.[25] On 26 September 1939,[26] in a small combined operation using reconnaissance aircraft under the tactical command of the Kriegsmarine and several bombers of the Luftwaffe, the British aircraft carrier *Ark Royal* was erroneously believed to have been sunk. The results of the operation were overrated in favour of the Luftwaffe, and led to the belief that a few bombers could be decisive against warships and deter them from approaching the German coasts.

The combined Luftwaffe-Kriegsmarine operations in October and November 1939,[27] however, had a sobering effect. These revealed that the training of the Luftwaffe crews in combined air-sea operations was so inadequate, and their timing and communications so bad, that even large numbers of bombers proved inefficient. There were heavy losses of aircraft, and on 22 February 1940,[28] the lack of communication between Kriegsmarine and Luftwaffe actually resulted in the loss of two German destroyers caused by friendly aircraft. If nothing else, this proved the impossibility of two commands operating independently and simultaneously in the same area.[29]

Because of these experiences, Göring withdrew 12 multi-purpose squadrons from the tactical command of the Kriegsmarine, who, by the end of 1939 and despite increasing demands for naval air warfare, were left with only 15 squadrons.[30] Quarrels concerning the use of aerial mines and torpedoes further worsened Luftwaffe-Kriegsmarine relations.[31] During the preparations for Operation Sealion (the projected invasion of Britain), there was another controversy between Göring and Raeder. The former believed that, to create a favourable situation for the invasion, British fighter defences and aircraft production plants had to be worn down first. Raeder instead advocated attacks on shipping, ports and the Royal Navy.[32]

Göring steadfastly refused to comply with the Kriegsmarine's request for long-range reconnaissance and bomber aircraft and established his own air-sea commands, for instance X Fliegerkorps (torpedo units) in 1939 and 9 Fliegerdivision/IX Fliegerkorps (mining) in spring 1940.[33] However, on 6 January 1941, when Göring had taken leave to go hunting, Raeder succeeded in persuading Hitler to place the 12 FW-200C long-range reconnaissance planes of the 1st Group of Kampfgeschwader 40 under Kriegsmarine command. Göring was furious and summoned the commander of the U-boats, Admiral Dönitz, to discuss the matter on 7 January and induce him to return the planes to the operational Luftwaffe. Dönitz, Göring said, could 'rest assured that as long as he

[Göring] lived and did not resign from his post, Grand Admiral Raeder would not get his naval air arm'.[34]

Göring, being on better terms with Hitler than was Raeder, soon obtained the Führer's approval for the establishment of the 'Fliegerführer Atlantik' (Air Leader Atlantic), subordinated to 3 Air Fleet. The position was filled by a former naval officer, Lt. Col. Martin Harlinghausen. He ranked relatively low in the military hierarchy, reflecting the value Göring attributed to the new command, which operated from 15 March 1941.[35] Its tasks were (a) reconnaissance for U-boat warfare, (b) air cover and reconnaissance during operations of naval surface forces in the Atlantic and escort duties in the coastal zone, (c) weather reconnaissance and (d) attacking naval targets in areas to be agreed by the Luftwaffe and Kriegsmarine. The command comprised two bomber Gruppen and one bomber Staffel equipped with He-111 and some FW-200 aircraft, and a coastal air Gruppe (Küstenfliegergruppe) with eight Staffeln. These were equipped mainly with He-115, but also with Ar-196 seaplanes and some BV-138 flying boats. One Staffel was to be equipped with Ju-88 aircraft.[36]

By and by, all the flying units were taken away from the Luftwaffe General attached to the Commander-in-Chief of the Kriegsmarine, i.e. from the Kriegsmarine, and by early 1942 there were no more air units under its operational command, excepting some few planes on board ships. General Hans Ritter, Luftwaffe General with the C-in-C of the Kriegsmarine, had already asked March 1941 for the abolition of his command, which he felt to be superfluous,[37] after what Raeder had called the 'pillaging of the naval air arm' by Göring had been so successful.[38] The staff of the General of the Luftwaffe with the Commander-in-Chief of the Kriegsmarine continued to exist until August 1944 as a collecting point for experiences in air-sea warfare, and because of the Kriegsmarine chief's vain hope of eventually getting some air units reassigned to him.[39] In June 1943, the month after the U-boats' defeat in the Atlantic, the Kriegsmarine High Command also planned for the establishment of a special air fleet of over 700 planes for air-sea warfare, to continue anti-shipping operations. This was just a pipe-dream that could not be realized at this stage of the war.[40]

Göring had successfully claimed for the Luftwaffe all naval air activity such as reconnaissance, mine-laying, torpedo and bombing attacks. The Kriegsmarine was already weak when the war started, and, through its losses in the Norwegian campaign and the Atlantic as well as through its inability to bring the weight of its capital ships to bear, was further and fatally weakened. To Hitler, the new Luftwaffe had always seemed more promising, and with his backing Göring defeated the Kriegsmarine. Ranking second only to Hitler in Germany's political and military hierarchy he naturally had a much stronger position than Raeder, whom Hitler in any case did not like particularly. German air-sea warfare never really thrived because, although the two commanders-in-chief agreed that air-sea warfare should be under a unified command, each wanted the command for his own service.

The land-mindedness of Hitler and Göring and the fact that, for Germany, the land fronts were considered to be more decisive than the distant sea have already been mentioned. With the Luftwaffe tied down in Russia, the Mediterranean and in home air defence, there were simply not enough resources and aircraft to fight an air war at sea with equal intensity, and there were hardly any long-range aircraft. Doubtless their lack was one of the main reasons for the failure of the U-boat war, and doubtless the Luftwaffe was not wholly unaware of the necessities of the air war at sea, though it certainly underestimated the numerical air strength needed for control and reconnaissance of the maritime theatre of war. But it cannot be maintained that it was only Göring's hostility against the Kriegsmarine and his greed for power and prestige that induced him to concentrate 'everything that flies' under his command. The Luftwaffe's wide obligations and limited means forced a policy of economizing. In addition, the land-based wheeled airplane proved superior to the seaplane both in speed and range, and unlike a seaplane, could also generally be used in winter. Wheeled planes were the mainstay of the Luftwaffe.

Matching these factors, the Kriegsmarine failed to live up to its own claims of directing the naval air war, taking care of the training of naval air crews and observers, and of manning naval aircraft from its own ranks. Already in early 1941, its commander-in-chief had to admit he did not have enough qualified officer personnel for the U-boats and, therefore, had no naval officers to spare for air reconnaissance training.[41] Nor did the Kriegsmarine have enough surface vessels to justify the allocation of more flying units for co-operation.[42] In short, neither Kriegsmarine nor Luftwaffe had imagined or been ready for the kind of war that developed - a long, inter-continental war of attrition. This joint failure inevitably triggered an intense inter-service fight for resources, a fight which tied in very well with Hitler's and Göring's principle of 'divide and rule'. But there was not enough to be divided with success.

*

Luftwaffe-Kriegsmarine relations were fundamental to the development of the war at sea. Let us now examine in more detail their co-operation in the Battle.

The establishment of *Fliegerführer Atlantik* was, as the name implies, the first manifestation of any Luftwaffe intent to co-operate with the Kriegsmarine on a large scale. There had been co-operation before, of course, as ordered especially by Hitler's Directives Nos. 1 (31 August 1939) and 9 (29 November 1939), with a supplement of 26 May 1940.[43] The Luftwaffe had engaged in attacks on the British fleet, on shipping in the Channel and around Britain, in mine-laying along the British coasts, air-reconnaissance over the North Sea and the approaches to Britain, and in connection with U-boat warfare and in escorting surface vessels - but only haphazardly, and not to the extent the Kriegsmarine would have liked. The Luftwaffe was mainly geared to co-operate with the army, and this it had done quite successfully.

The original Directive No. 9 ordered close navy-air force co-operation in the war against shipping. Much to the Kriegsmarine's annoyance, the Directive's supplement ordered the Luftwaffe to give preference to attacks on the British air armament industry. Similarly, Directive No. 17 (1 August 1940)[44] expressly said that the Luftwaffe's engagement in anti-shipping operations should take second place to the struggle against the RAF and its sources of power. The Luftwaffe was to assist the Kriegsmarine only from time to time, if needed. Thus, by the end of 1940 (as Dönitz noted in his War Diary), Luftwaffe co-operation had become - from the Kriegsmarine point of view - quite unsatisfactory.[45] Although by then Germany had controlled the French Atlantic ports for five months, he wrote that the U-boats had not received sufficient air reconnaissance, and he had been unable to direct the U-boat war in accordance with operational necessities.

This caused complaints from the Kriegsmarine. A controversy with the Luftwaffe[46] was brought to a temporary end by Hitler's Directive No. 23 (6 February 1941),[47] entitled 'Guidelines for Warfare Against the British War Economy'. In this connection Hitler had decided:

> If each service were to obtain all the units needed for carrying out predetermined tasks - even if these units by their nature belong to other services - this might be the simplest and most convenient solution for each service, but for the armed forces in their entirety is, especially in times of great shortage of resources, an uneconomical solution.[48]

In contrast with Directives 9 and 17, he added here that 'contrary to our former conviction, the greatest effect on the British war economy was caused by the high losses in shipping inflicted by sea and air warfare'. It was foreseeable that the U-boat war might lead to the collapse of British resistance, whereas the effects of air operations against the British armament industry were difficult to assess, and an effect on the morale of the British people was not yet recognizable. While the effect on British shipping would presumably increase, the intensity of German air attacks on Britain could not be maintained, because the Luftwaffe would be employed elsewhere in the future; he was already preparing the campaign against the Soviet Union. As far as the Luftwaffe units remaining in the west were concerned, operations had to be concentrated against targets whose destruction was also the goal of German naval operations. Therefore, both land and sea warfare had to be focused on enemy shipping, which was mentioned first, and on the air armament industry. The sinking of merchantmen would be more important than that of men-of-war. Directives Nos. 9 plus supplement, and 17, were rescinded

In spite of the diplomatic wording of the Directive, Hitler clearly gave preference to the employment of the Luftwaffe in land warfare; his new Directive was obviously issued in view of the planned campaigns against Greece and the Soviet Union. There could be no doubt that the focus of future Luftwaffe employment would be the planned offensive in the east, while in the west Hitler wanted to remain on the defensive. For this reason, he repeatedly refused the Kriegsmarine's demand for taking action against the United States,[49] which in practical terms had entered the war at sea against Germany in the Atlantic. He did not need another formal high-intensity theatre of war in the west. There, sea and air defence alone were sufficient for the moment.

Fliegerführer Atlantik was not the only Luftwaffe command created for air-sea co-operation in the war against shipping. The northern parts of the North Sea and of the Atlantic were to be taken care of by *Fliegerführer Nord* under 5 Air Fleet, with the duties of air-sea reconnaissance for the U-boats, escort of German shipping and anti-shipping warfare north of 58° latitude North (and 55° latitude North over Britain). As the third command, *Führer der Seeluftstreitkrafte* (F.d.Luft) remained subordinate to the tactical command of the Luftwaffe General with the Commander-in-Chief of the Kriegsmarine (i.e. under the indirect operational command of the Kriegsmarine). F.d.Luft was charged with air reconnaissance in the North Sea between 52°-58° latitude North and over the approaches to the Baltic, as well as with U-boat protection as far west as Cherbourg. 2 Air Fleet was responsible for air reconnaissance as far as Abbeville, with 3 Air Fleet taking care of air reconnaissance over the western part of the Channel. West of this and over the Atlantic, it was Fliegerführer Atlantik (as the most important co-operation command of the three) who conducted reconnaissance and anti-shipping missions. His forces could also be used against targets in Britain if the needs of the Kriegsmarine permitted. This remained, of course, a matter of interpretation.[50]

The forces of Fliegerführer Nord consisted of two Ju-88 long-range reconnaissance and three Do-18 flying boat Staffeln, plus the staff of a Küstenfliegergruppe. F.d.Luft disposed of two Küstenfliegergruppen staffs with six Staffeln. The strength of the forces of the Fliegerführer Atlantik has been given above.[51] Considering the sea area to be covered, these forces were altogether very small, as were the ranges of the planes. Fliegerführer Atlantik was the strongest command. Some of his long-range planes, the FW-200, could penetrate 1,400-1,700 km into the Atlantic - which was not very far, given that the ocean was 5-6,000 km wide. The range of penetration could be extended if the planes made a stop in Norway for refuelling before returning to base in south-western France. Flights could last 15-20 hours, which was quite a strain on the aircrews.

These three Fliegerführer, plus the higher Luftwaffe headquarters to which they were subordinated and the corresponding Kriegsmarine headquarters (e.g. Marinegruppen West and North), and even High Commands, were Dönitz's partners in his anti-shipping operations. How this rather complicated command system functioned will be dealt with after we have taken a look at the further development of the three air-sea co-operation commands.

In the winter of 1941-42, the forces of F.d.Luft were further depleted in favour of 3 Air Fleet. The question of the disbandment of this staff now arose, because it had no forces left to carry out its tasks.[52] Within the Kriegsmarine, it was especially the Commander-in-Chief of Marinegruppe Nord, Admiral Carls, who protested against this new encroachment of the Luftwaffe on naval interests. He proposed the establishment of a special Fleet Air Arm, made up from the three Fliegerführer which at present were expected to collaborate with the U-boats.[53] The Chief of the Seekriegsleitung himself tried to calm Carls down, in a letter[54] displaying much understanding for the Luftwaffe's tight situation and its endeavour to economize the conduct of the air war, as well as for the fact that it first had to take care of the land fronts. He further pointed out that one of the preconditions of having a large naval air force was a strong navy, which unfortunately did not exist and could not be set up during the war.

On 7 April 1942, F.d.Luft was placed under the command of 3 Air Fleet.[55] Placing all flying units under the command of the Luftwaffe corresponded with Hitler's view that the establishment of a single operational air force would prove the right thing to do, because it enabled the supreme command to form centres of main air effort quickly, as the war's overall situation altered. Even the training of carrier-based aircrews was now to be a Luftwaffe domain.[56]

Fliegerführer Atlantik, a genuine Luftwaffe staff, also gradually lost flying units. A year after its establishment, the forces of this command had been reduced to 87 planes. Only 43 were operational, and only 11 were long-range reconnaissance FW 200, a commercial plane adapted as a reconnaissance bomber aircraft.[57] In March 1944, Fliegerführer Atlantik was disbanded.[58] General-Lieutenant Kessler, the commander, had been requesting the abolition of his staff since September 1942, on the grounds that his organization was already nothing more than a 'living corpse'.[59] Hitler, in fact, believed that the production of tanks was more urgent than anything else; so the revival in 1942 of the idea of completing the aircraft carrier *Graf Zeppelin*, and even of building some more aircraft carriers (which had proved their importance for the Allies both in the Atlantic and Pacific) was very short-lived.[60]

In view of its difficulties in manning the increasing number of U-boats, the Kriegsmarine was no longer in a position to detach naval officers for training as air observers. The results of air reconnaissance by Luftwaffe-trained aircrews consequently deteriorated.[61] This was, however, also a consequence of the short ranges and insufficient numbers of air-sea reconnaissance planes available. On 4 May 1943, Fliegerführer Atlantik informed 3 Air Fleet that in the period 1 March-22 April 1943, his planes had sighted merchant ships aggregating an estimated 3,772,000 tons, plus three aircraft carriers, 12 cruisers, 39 destroyers and 118 escort ships. If all available bombers in the West had been employed against them, at least half a million tons of merchantmen could have been sunk.[62] However, Hitler had just ordered that air reconnaissance and escort duties over sea had precedence over the bombing of vessels.[63]

This leads us to two basic problems: the chain of command, and aircraft availability. The British, living on an island, had always been aware of the importance of their control of the sea lanes for their survival. There, the Battle of the Atlantic Committee - headed by the Prime Minister himself and made up of the War Cabinet, other ministers, the Chiefs of Staff of the Navy and Royal Air Force and some scientific advisors - was established (see Chapter 29) expressly to co-ordinate all efforts in the Atlantic.

In his memoirs,[64] Dönitz contrasted this with the situation in Germany, where nothing similar or equivalent existed. This was not due to a particular disregard for naval affairs. No; under the German system of directing the war, each service pursued its own goals, only co-operating loosely with the others. The Supreme Command of the Armed Forces (Oberkommando der Wehrmacht, or OKW) just did the paper work, with Hitler as the final arbiter in any inter-service quarrel.

The democratic committee system with its principle of discussion before decision was quite different from the German method of conducting the war. This was based on ideology and the military way - that is, without expert civilian advisors, who were separated from the military by a wide social gap. It must be regarded as a gross under-assessment of the Atlantic's importance that Dönitz was left to seek the co-operation of so many different staffs, especially Luftwaffe staffs, on whom he was fully dependent with regard to reconnaissance. Without air reconnaissance, the U-boats were virtually blind; yet he could not order reconnaissance flights according to the necessities of the situation at sea, but had to ask the individual staffs. The same applied to other naval commanders. Thus, Marinegruppe Nord complained to the Chief of Staff of Naval Operations:

> It is an untenable situation that air reconnaissance for current sea operations cannot be ordered by a responsible naval commander, but has to be asked for from a Fliegerführer outside of his command, whose other tasks are not known in detail and who, on account of his education and training, cannot expected to have full understanding for the necessities of naval warfare.[65]

Moreover, the three Fliegerführer (the most important Luftwaffe commands with whom Dönitz could communicate directly) had only limited competencies. Even they frequently had to ask higher authorities for permission or help. Finally, Hitler himself often interfered with naval warfare.

After the incendiary attacks on Lübeck and Rostock in the spring of 1942, Hitler ordered terror attacks against British towns and - much to the consternation of the Kriegsmarine - restricted the laying of aerial mines along the British coast. A year later, the Luftwaffe received orders to drop at least one bomb each night on London in order to render the British population war-weary and divide them from the Americans, unmolested at home. The Luftwaffe Chief of Staff, Jeschonnek, was aware of the nonsense of this order and shared the Kriegsmarine's view that bombs on docks, shipyards and ships were more effective in the struggle against Britain, but he did not think he could disobey and, of course, the planes could not easily be used against shipping.[66] Sometimes Göring too gave general orders for the employment of aircraft which did not conform to the needs of the situation.[67] At another time, the necessary reinforcement of flying units in the northern North Sea was made dependent on Hitler's decision, but this took so long to obtain that it was no use in a rapidly changing situation.[68] Typical of the general situation is a situation report of Marinegruppe Nord:

> The co-operation of Admiral Nordmeer with the Fliegerführer and also between Marinegruppe Nord and 5 Air Fleet is essentially good and without friction. The understanding of the problems of sea warfare exists [in the air commands], as does the intention to match up to them. The effectiveness of the co-operation is, however, suffering from the lack of Luftwaffe forces and the shortage of aviation fuel. As a result, the necessary long-range reconnaissance flights over sea can only be carried through very unsatisfactorily. Also the air reconnaissance requested by the Kriegsmarine for operations against convoys remains insufficient. Moreover, the Luftwaffe High Command has restricted the use of bomber forces in the far North because of lack of forces, which prevents taking full care of the Kriegsmarine's demands. A discussion of these problems between the C-in-C 5 Air Fleet and Marinegruppe Nord could not change the situation.[69]

Sometimes the various Fliegerführer could not act on their own, but had to ask their air fleets to detach escort planes for the protection of German shipping, although this could use up all available planes of the air fleet.[70] The Luftwaffe Operations Staff were once asked to assign fighters to Alta Fjord, but refused because this did not fit with the current needs of the general conduct of the air war, which, at the time, was focused on home air defence.[71] Sometimes the allocation of flying units to the decisive points of the Atlantic battle was refused by the Luftwaffe Operations Staff for economic reasons. According to this reasoning, locating a convoy took much longer in the Atlantic than in the Mediterranean, so it was better to attack Mediterranean shipping than to have air units lying idle for want of an Atlantic target. Operations Staff were also worried that enemy carrier-based fighter escorts might cost too many own losses.[72] For this reason, on 2 April 1944, 5 Air Fleet informed the Kriegsmarine that (for instance) daytime reconnaissance of convoys had to stop.[73]

These sorry examples show clearly that on the German side of the Battle of the Atlantic, there was no unity of command, and that the chain of command was too complicated to be effective. The consequences were of course disastrous.

Much of the confusion, duplicated effort, wasted effort and counter-productivity of the combined German air-sea operations sprang from the inadequate quantity and quality of aircraft and crews supplied to the Luftwaffe.

On 3 November 1941, Luftwaffe Operations Staff received a request for fighter escort of warships. The Staff reported that Hitler had ordered all long-range fighter aircraft to be turned over to the night fighter force. The production of additional aircraft of this type would alter the entire production schedule and, therefore, had to be deliberated on by the Luftwaffe. Meanwhile, the navy was bluntly told to take what the Luftwaffe thought fit.[74]

In April 1942, the Kriegsmarine High Command warned the Luftwaffe Operations Staff that with only one Ju-88 reconnaissance Staffel, one Ju-88 bomber Gruppe, two FW-200 and one ship-based Staffel the coastal sea area could not be protected.[75] When, in summer 1942, the RAF's Coastal Command established an increasingly tight control over the Bay of Biscay (and with the help of Leigh Lights, radar and Ultra, sank a considerable number of in- and outgoing U-boats), Dönitz personally visited Göring and managed to get 24 Ju-88C6 placed with Fliegerführer Atlantik, who had supported his request.[76] In his War Diary, Dönitz reflected gloomily: 'The Bay of Biscay has become the playground of the British Air Force'. They could use even their oldest types of aircraft. 'It is a pity and, for the U-boat crews, a depressing fact that there are none of our own air assets available to protect a helpless U-boat, damaged by aerial bombs and unable to dive, against further air attacks.'[77]

Although the Ju-88 long-range fighters improved the situation in the narrow area of the Bay of Biscay,[78] the overall situation of tight British air control in the wider region remained unaltered, because the range of the German fighters was only about 800 km.[79] The only other available aircraft were a few long-range reconnaissance and combat planes; the FW-200 was no longer considered dependable enough for air combat over the sea, and their depth of penetration was insufficient to challenge Allied Atlantic air control.

In March 1943, Fliegerführer Atlantik reported that he could no longer fulfil his task of combating the enemy air force and protecting the incoming and outgoing German U-boats,[80] and that the Ju-88C6 were inferior to the Beaufighter, from which they had suffered high losses. Their speed and offensive armament was insufficient, the water-cooled engines too vulnerable.[81] Likewise, 3 Air Fleet was forced to give first priority to the rescue of U-boat crews at the expense of air reconnaissance,[82] and - unless it flew in formation - the Ju-88 heavy pursuit aircraft was now hunted itself.[83]

The Battle of the Atlantic was lost by Germany in May 1943 at the very latest, if not much earlier.[84] Even then, though, high hopes were set on the development of new long-range flying boats like the BV-222 and reconnaissance-bombers like the He-177, Ju-290 or Me-264. But these were not yet operational and in any case could not cover the mid-Atlantic gap - the sole remaining area of the ocean where U-boats could operate without tight Allied air control. Sure enough, when brought into service in late 1943, the first three types proved to be of little use. Too few of them were used too late.

Of course, the Luftwaffe had also enjoyed some considerable successes in the Battle of the Atlantic. In the summer of 1942, Kampfgeschwader 26 and 30 had hammered the Murmansk convoys. The former was the Luftwaffe's only aerial torpedo unit, and, ironically, had been created even though the Luftwaffe Chief of Staff, Jeschonnek, at first believed that bombs could sink ships more cheaply than torpedoes. Later, too, in 1944-45, there were some notable victories over Allied shipping in the waters around Iceland;[85] but these alone could not turn the tide any more.

German planning of the air-sea war progressively lost touch with reality. For example, a large naval air fleet was planned, with two air corps - one for coastal defence and attacks on Britain, and one for long-range oceanic reconnaissance and sea combat.[86] Dönitz had always complained that the biggest handicap to the German conduct of the war at sea was 'the absence of any air reconnaissance'.[87] This, as he pointed out in his Memorandum of 8 June 1943,[88] submitted to Hitler, led to 'Germany's war at sea being conducted today practically without the Luftwaffe'. In contrast, he wrote, the Allies assigned strong air support to their naval forces, with crews that were well trained in naval warfare. 'The crisis in the U-boat war', as he euphemistically described the defeat in the Battle of the Atlantic at the time, 'is thus a consequence of the command of the air over the Atlantic by the enemy'.

When, on 31 May and 15 June 1943, Dönitz discussed the critical situation of the war at sea with Hitler, the Führer complained that the Luftwaffe's dive-bombing requirement for big planes had prevented the timely production of sufficient numbers of operational heavy bombers and long-range reconnaissance aircraft (i.e. the He-177), which would have been a great help both to U-boats and surface warships. While the war in the east continued, though, he wished to remain on the defensive in the west; but he did not want the war in the Atlantic to stop, because he preferred to fight there, rather than on the coast of western Europe.

It followed that greater forces would be needed to continue the Atlantic campaign, but when Dönitz described plans for the increase of the Kriegsmarine and the U-boat force and for the creation of a strong naval air arm to compensate for the U-boats' current weakness, Hitler said it could not be done: 'I do not have the personnel. It is necessary to increase the anti-aircraft artillery and night fighter forces for the protection of the German cities. The army needs divisions to protect Europe.'[89]

As for the Luftwaffe, Göring's reaction to the setback in the Battle of the Atlantic was a grotesque Directive as to how Fliegerführer Atlantik was to conduct the air-war over sea in the future.[90] To the man who had described his command as a 'living corpse', he assigned all the duties which, for lack of proper equipment and planes, had been impossible in the past and which, for the same reason, could not be expected to be fulfilled in the future. One gets the distinct impression that he wanted to clear himself from any future blame of not having done everything in his power.

We know to-day that there were many causes, often technological, for Germany's defeat in the Battle of the Atlantic. The British development of centimetric radar; the Allies' increasing availability of very-long-range reconnaissance aircraft and of escort ships after the invasion of Northwest Africa; special anti-U-boat rockets and torpedoes; operations research; Ultra; and, of course, the superior American capacity for shipbuilding - all played their parts. Concerning one of these, Ultra, Dönitz during the war had not the slightest idea of its existence, remaining confident that German naval ciphers were unbreakable; and long after the war, when information about Ultra became publicly available, he appeared not to believe it.[91] But of all the reasons that forced him to break off the U-boat offensive in the North Atlantic, one for him was paramount. As he told Hitler:

> Future historiography will be united in one point: it is simply incomprehensible that the Germans fought the war at sea without air reconnaissance or a naval air force, as if - in the 20th century, the century of flight - aircraft did not exist.[92]

Although he exaggerated his case a little bit, there is no doubt that insufficient air reconnaissance was a major reason for Germany's defeat in the Atlantic.

Notes

1. Herwig, *Politics of Frustration*, pp. 253 ff.
2. Karl Köhler, 'Auf dem Wege zur Luftwaffe. Vor Fünfzig Jahren wurde die Dienststelle "Kommandierender General der Luftstreitkafte" errichtet', in: Wehrwissenschaftliche Rundschau (WWR) 16/1966, No. 10, pp. 353-359; Horst Boog, *Das Problem der Selbstandigkeit der Luftstreitkrafte in Deutschland 1908-1845*, in: Militärgeschichtliche Mitteilungen (MGM), No. 31 (1/1988), p. 35.
3. Karl-Heinz Völker, *Dokumente und Dokumentarfotos zur Geschichte der deutschen Luftwaffe*, Vol. 9 of Beitrage zur Militär- und Kriegsgeschichte, ed. by Militärgeschichtliches Forschungsamt, Stuttgart 1968, pp. 121-130; Karl-Heinz Völker, *Die Entwicklung der militärischen Luftfahrt in Deutschland 1920-1933: Planung und Maßnahmen zur Schaffung einer Fliegertruppe in der Reichswehr*, Stuttgart 1962; Werner Rahn, *Der Anteil der Reichsmarine am Wiederaufbau der deutschen Luftstreitkrafte*, in: MOV-Nachrichten, year 46, 1971, pp. 241-245.
4. Walther Hubatsch, *Der Admiralstab und die obersten Marinebehörden in Deutschland 1848-1945*, Frankfurt am Main 1958, p.204; Walter Gaul, *Die Geschichte des 'F.d.Luft', der 9. Fliegerdivision und IX. Fliegerkorps von der Aufstellung dieser Kommandostellen bis zur Wende der Kriegsjahre 1940/41*, Militärgeschichtliches Forschungsamt (MGFA), Study Lw 9, Part I, p. 1.
5. Gaul, MGFA Study Lw 9, Part I, p. 2.
6. Memorandum of the Commander-in-Chief of the Navy of 3 February 1937, 'Grundsätzliche Gedanken der Seekriegfuhrung', cited in Gerhard Bidlingmaier, *Die

Grundlagen fur die Zusammenarbeit Luftwaffe/Kriegsmarine und ihre Erprobung in den ersten Kriegsmonaten, in: Die Entwicklung des Flottenkommandos, Beiträge zur Wehrforschung, Vol. IV, ed. by Arbeitskreis für Wehrforschung, Darmstadt (1964), pp. 75 f. An indispensable source of information on Luftwaffe-Navy relations is also the *Kriegstagebuch der Seekriegsleitung*, ed. by Werner Rahn and Gerhard Schreiber, Herford-Bonn 1988 ff.

7. *Ibid.*, p 77. Gerhard Hümmelchen, *Die deutschen Seeflieger 1935-1945*, München 1976, pp. 14 f.

8. Bidlingmaier, *Grundlagen*, p. 78.

9. Luftwaffendienstvorschrift No. 16 "Luftkriegführung", paras 135, 142.

10. Horst Boog, *Die deutsche Luftwaffenführung 1935-1945: Führungsprobleme - Spitzengliederung - Generalstabsausbildung*, Stuttgart 1982, pp. 166 f., 180 ff.

11. Hümmelchen, *Seeflieger*, p. 16; Bidlingmaier, *Grundlagen*, p. 78.

12. Gaul, MGFA Study Lw 9, Part I, p. 17; for the strained relations between the Luftwaffe and Navy before the war see also Karl-Heinz Völker, *Die deutsche Luftwaffe 1933-1939: Aufbau, Führung und Rüstung der Luftwaffe sowie die Entwicklung der deutschen Luftkriegstheorie*, Stuttgart 1967, pp. 90 ff.

13. Hümmelchen, *Seeflieger*, p. 16; Bidlingmaier, *Grundlagen*, p. 78.

14. Gundelach, K, *Gedanken über die Führung eines Luftkrieges gegen England bei der Luftflotte 2 in den Jahren 1938/39*, in WWR 1960, pp. 33 f.

15. Völker, *Luftwaffe*, pp. 134 f., 170; Völker, *Dokumente*, pp. 211 f.; Boog, *Luftwaffenführung*, p. 177.

16. Boog, *Luftwaffenführung*, pp. 56 ff.

17. Bidlingmaier, *Grundlagen*, pp. 80 f.; Gaul, MGFA Study Lw 9, Par I, p. 12 ff; Hümmelchen, *Seeflieger*, p. 17.

18. Hümmelchen, *Seeflieger*, p. 18; Bidlingmaier, *Grundlagen*, pp. 18 ff.

19. Hümmelchen, *Seeflieger*, p. 19; Boog, *Luftwaffenführung*, pp. 241 310 ff.

20. Bidlingmaier, *Grundlagen*, pp. 83 f.

21. *Das Deutsche Reich und der Zweite Weltkrieg*, ed. by Militärgeschichtliches Forschungsamt, Vol. I: *Ursachen und Voraussetzungen der deutschen Kriegspolitik*, Stuttgart 1979, pp. 465-473.

22. Boog, *Luftwaffenführung*, p. 45.

23. Bidlingmaier, *Grundlagen*, pp. 84 f.; Gundelach, *Gedanken*, pp. 42 ff.; Völker, *Dokumente*, pp. 460 ff.; Völker, *Luftwaffe*, p. 161; Boog, *Luftwaffenführung*, p. 93.

24. See ltr Oberkommando der Kriegsmarine Nr. 2261 g. 1.Abt. Skl. Iac to Reichsminister der Luftfahrt und Oberbefehlshaber der Luftwaffe of 28 July 1939, subject: Gemeinsame Quadratkarten Luftwaffe/Marine, in: Bundesarchiv-Militärarchiv Freiburg (BA-MA) RL 2/210; Bidlingmaier, *Grundlagen*, p. 90; Hümmelchen, *Seeflieger*, p. 22.

25. Hümmelchen, *Seeflieger*, pp. 49 f.; Bidlingmaier, *Grundlagen*, p. 91; Quellensammlung Bidlingmaier: Zusammenarbeit Kriegsmarine-Luftwaffe, Sept. 1939-Dez. 1940, BA-MA RM 7/169.

26. Gaul, MGFA Study Lw 9, Part II, pp. 7 ff; Hümmelchen, *Seeflieger*, pp. 58 ff.; Bidlingmaier, *Grundlagen*, pp. 92 ff.; Michael Salewski, *Die deutsche Seekriegsleitung 1935-1945, Vol. I: 1935-1941*, Frankfurt/Main 1970, pp. 160 f.

27. Bidlingmaier, *Grundlagen*, pp. 94 ff.; Gaul, MGFA Study Lw9, Part II, pp. 12-29; Hümmelchen, *Seeflieger*, pp. 60 ff.

28. See 'Bericht des Major i.G. Martin Harlingbausen, seinerzeit Chef des Stabes des X. Fliegerkorps, über die Vorgänge und Zusammenhänge am 22. Februar 1940 auf der Doggerbank', in: Rudi Schmidt, *Achtung - Torpedos los!: Der strategische und operative Einsatz des Kampfgeschwaders 26 - Löwengeschwader - Das Torpedogeschwader der deutschen Luftwaffe im Zweiten Weltkrieg*, Koblenz 1991, pp. 305-314.

29. Gaul, MGFA Study Lw 9, Part V, pp. 7 ff.

30. Bidlingmaier, *Grundlagen*, pp. 98 ff.; BA-MA RM 7/169.

31. For this see the documents contained in BA-MA RM 7/168-171, and Gaul, MGFA Study Lw 9, Part II, pp. 29 ff, and Part III, also Salewski, *Seekriegsleitung*, Vol. I, pp. 213 ff.

32. Salewski, *Seekriegsleitung*, Vol. I, pp. 256 f., 435.

33. Gaul, MGFA Study Lw 9, Part IV; Hümmelchen, *Seeflieger*, pp. 126 ff.; BA-MA OKM Case GE 972/PG 32972, pp. 12 f.

34. Karl Dönitz, *10 Jahre und 20 Tage*, München 1977, pp. 132 ff.; Boog, *Luftwaffenführung*, S. 312, Fn 655.

35. Der Reichsminister der Luftfahrt und Oberbefehlshaber der Luftwaffe, Generalstab Gen.Qu.2.Abt. Nr 5437/41 g.Kdos.(IIA) of 5 March 1941, subject: Aufstellung Fliegerführer Atlantik, with 2 enclosures, BA-MA OKM GE 972.

36. Hümmelchen, *Seeflieger*, pp. 126 f.

37. Boog, *Luftwaffenführung*, pp. 311 f.

38. Conference of the General der Luftwaffe beim Oberbefehlshaber der Kriegsmarinerine on 1 Dec. 1941, with marginal note of 2 Dec. 1941, in: BA-MA OKM GE 958, p.295.

39. Oberkommando der Kriegsmarine 1.Skl. IL 6610/43 g.Kdos of 5 March 1943 to Reichsminister der Luftfahrt und Oberbefehlshaber der Luftwaffe, Gen. Qu., 2. Abt., BA-MA RM 7/171, pp. 243 ff.; Boog, *Luftwaffe*, p. 311.

40. BA-MA RM 7/171, pp. 262-287, 295-302; Hümmelchen, *Seeflieger*, p. 129; Salewski, *Seekriegsleitung, Vol. III: Denkschriften und Lagebetrachtungen 1938-1944*, Frankfurt/Main 1973, pp. 358 ff.

41. Der Chef der Seekriegsleitung IL 1.Skl. Nr. 27153/g.Kdos. of 27 November 1941 to Oberbefehlshaber Marinegruppe Nord, BA-MA OKM GE 959, p. 117.

42. Salewski, *Seekriegsleitung*, Vol. I, pp. 256 f.

43. *Hitlers Weisungen für die Kriegführung 1939-1945 Dokumente des Oberkommandos der Wehrmacht*, ed. by Walther Hubatsch, dtv 278/79, München 1965, pp. 23 ff., 46 ff., 50 ff. (see also directives Nos. 2 and 4, ibid., pp. 25 ff., 32 ff.).

44. *Hitlers Weisungen*, pp. 75 ff.

45. Karl Dönitz, *10 Jahre und 20 Tage*, München 1977, pp. 130 f.; see also
    Marinegruppe West, g.Kdos, 1106.41 AL of 3 March 1941, BA-MA RM 7/710, pp.
    59 f.

46. See above p. 308 and BA-MA RM 7/170 pp. 1-34.

47. *Hitlers Weisungen*, pp. 118 ff.

48. Der Führer und Oberste Befehlshaber der Wehrmacht OKW/WFSt/ Abt. L No.
    00354/41 g.Kdos. of 28 February 1941, BA-MA RM 7/170, pp. 52 ff.

49. *Lagevorträge des Oberbefehlshabers der Kriegsmarine vor Hitler 1939-1945*, ed.
    Gerhard Wagner, München 1972, pp. 236, 286.

50. Der Oberbefehlshaber der Luftwaffe, Führungsstab Ia Nr. 600/41 g.Kdos. (op 1) of
    8 March 1941, subject: Abgrenzung der Luftaufklärung ab 15. 3. 41, BA-MA RM
    7/170, pp. 69 ff.

51. Page 308 above.

52. Aktenvermerk der Besprechung des General der Luftwaffe beim Oberbefehlshaber
    der Kriegsmarine of 1 December 1941, 1.Skl. No. 28074/41 g.Kdos., 2 December
    1941, BA-MA RM 7/170, pp. 233 ff.; Aktenvermerk 1. Skl. No. 29294/41 g.Kdos.
    of 22 December 1941, ibid., p. 245. Vermerk, Reduzierung des F.d. Luft-Stabes, IL
    1.Skl. 2367/42 g.Kdos., 30 January 1942, BA-MA RM 7/171, pp. ff; Ltr. Raeder,
    C-in-C of the Navy, to Göring, C-in-C Luftwaffe, 1.Skl. 3447/42 g.Kdos., 19
    February 1942, ibid., pp. 29 ff.

53. Marinegruppenkommando Nord, g.Kdos No. 170/42 A1 of 17 January 1942 to
    Seekriegsleitung, BA-MA RM 7/171, pp. 38 ff.

54. Der Chef der Seekriegsleitung, Neu IL 1.Skl. 27153/41 g.Kdos. of 27 November
    1941 to Oberbefehlshaber Marinegruppe Nord, Generaladmiral Carls, BA-MA
    OKM GE 959, p. 112; Chef d. 1.Skl. No. 1640/42 g.Kdos. to Marinegruppe Nord, 3
    March 1942, BA-MA RM 7/171, pp. 42 ff.

55. Oberbefehlshaber der Luftwaffe, Führungsstab Ia Robinson No. 6919/42 g.Kdos. op
    1 of 7 April 1942, BA-MA RM 7/171, pp. 72 ff.

56. Seekriegsleitung 1.Skl. No. 21435/42 g.Kdos. of 29 August 1942 BA-MA RM
    7/171, p. 178.

57. Hümmelchen, *Seeflieger*, p. 128.

58. *Ibid*, p. 132.

59. Michael Salewski, *Die deutsche Seekriegsleitung 1935-1945, Vol. II: 1942-1945*,
    München 1975, p. 122.

60. Ständiger Vertreter des Oberbefehlshabers der Kriegsmarine beim Führer to
    Oberbefehlshaber der Kriegsmarine und Chef der Seekriegsleitung, 17 January
    1943, BA-MA RM 7/260, p. 55. For the aircraft carrier problem see also BA-MA
    RM 7/171, pp. 25, f., 62, 111 ff., 149-162, 165-172, 200-205.

61. This is the impression one gains from the War Diary of the Befehlshaber der U-
    Boote. See BA-MA RM 87/20-32.

62. Fliegerführer Atlantik Ia No. 1234/43 g.Kdos. 2.Ang. to Luftflottenkommando 3, 4
    May 1943, BA-MA RM 7/171, pp. 251 ff.

63. Cable OKW/WFSt No. 073 of 22 February 1941, excerpt in BA-MA RM 7/170, pp.

1f.; Marinegruppenkommando Nord und Flottenkommando, g.Kdos., Chefs. No. 466/43 AL of 22 April 1943 to Seekriegsleitung, BA-MA RM 35 1/146, pp. 301 ff.

64. Dönitz, *10 Jahre*, p. 114.

65. Cable of Marinegruppe Nord No. 100/41 g.Kdos. Chefsache (copy), 1.Skl. 1op 123/41 of 10 February 1941, BA-MA RM 7/170, pp. 12 f.

66. WFSt/Op(L), 1.Skl. op No. 772/42 g.Kdos. Chefs. of 14 April 1942 to Oberbefehlshaber der Luftwaffe/Führungsstab Ia, BA-MA RM 7/171, p. 78.; Besprechung bei Generaloberst Jeschonnek, 1 May 1943, BA-MA RM 7/260, pp. 176 ff.; Salewskl, *Seekriegsleitung, Vol. II.*, p. 303.

67. So at one time bombers could not be used for reconnaissance, because Göring had ordered attacks against convoys. Annex 5 to War Diary, Marinegruppe Nord, 16-31 March 1943, BA-MA RM 35 1/146, p. 192.

68. *Ibid.*, p. 196.

69. *Ibid.*, p. 278.

70. War Diary Marinegruppe Nord, 1 Aug. - 31 Oct 1943, BA-MA RM 35 1/148, pp. 57 f.

71. War Diary Marinegruppe Nord, 20 March 1944, BA-MA RM 35 1/150.

72. War Diary, 1. Skl., Teil A, BA-MA RM 7/59, pp. 45 ff (3 April 1944), 303 (14 April 1944).

73. War Diary Marinegruppe Nord und Flottenkommando, 1 Apr.-31 Aug. 1944, BA-RM 35 1/151, p. 12.

74. Ergebnis der Besprechung 1. Skl. IL bei Robinson, 3 Nov 1941, BA-MA RM 7/170, p. 177.

75. Oberkommando der Kriegsmarine 1. Skl. No. 8331/42 g.Kdos. of 11 April 1942 to Oberbefehlshaber der Luftwaffe, Führungsstab Ia (Rob), BA-MA RM 7/171, pp. 74 ff.

76. Dönitz, *10 Jahre*, p. 227; War Diary Befehlshaber der U-Boote 1 July-31 Aug. 1942, 2 July, BA-MA RM 87/22, pp. 8 f.

77. War Diary, Befehlshaber der U-Boote, 1 April-30 June 1942, 11 June, BA-MA RM 87/21, p. 195.

78. Oberkommando der Kriegsmarine, 1. Skl. IL No. 5313/43 g. Kdos. of 20 February 1943 to Oberbefehlshaber der Luftwaffe, Führungsstab Rob Ia, BA-MA RM 7/171, pp. 236 f.

79. Eindringsiefen der Flugzeuge des Fliegerführer Atlantik, BA-MA RL 8/187 K.

80. Oberkommando der Kriegsmarine 1. Skl. IL No. 6501/43 g.Kdos. of 5 March 1943 to Oberbefehlshaber der Luftwaffe, Führungsstab Rob. Ia, BA-MA RM 7/171, p. 245; Salewski, *Seekriegsleitung, Vol. II*, p. 271.

81. War Diary, Befehlshaber der U-Boote, BA-MA RM 87/26, pp. 1 16 f. (23 March 1943).

82. Cable Oberbefehlshaber der Luftwaffe Führungsstab Ia (Rob) No. 11611/43 g.Kdos. (op I] of 5 June 1943, BA-MA RM 7/171, p. 258.

83. *Lagevorträge*, p. 509 (31 May 1943).

84. See Werner Rahn, 'Die Seekriegführung im Atlantik und Küstenbereich', in: Horst

Boog et al., *Der globale Krieg: Die Ausweitung zum Weltkrieg und der Wechsel der Initiative 1941-1943*, Stuttgart 1990 (= VoI 6 of *Das Deutsche Reich und der Zweite Weltkrieg*, ed. by Militärgeschichtliches Forschungsamt), pp. 313-425.

85. See Franz Kurowski, *Seekrieg aus der Luft: Die deutsche Seeluftwaffe im Zweiten Weltkrieg*, Herford 1979; Schmidt, *Achtung - Torpedo los!*; Hümmelchen, *Seeflieger*, and Friedrich Ruge, *Im Küstenvorfeld*, München 1974.

86. Der Chef der Seekriegsleitung 1. SkI. IL No. 16977/43 g.Kdos. of 12 June 1943 to Chef des Generalstabes der Luftwaffe, Generaloberst Jeschonnek; Oberbefehlshaber der Luftwaffe, Chef des Generalstabes No. 8542/43 g.Kdos. Chefs. (Ia) of 30 July 1943, all in BA-MA RM 7/171, pp. 267 ff, 295 ff; compare also the illusory project of the navy in expectation of an imminent victory In Russia in October 1942, Oberkommando der Kriegsmarine 1. SkI. No 25222/42 g.Kdos. of 31 Oct 1942, ibid., pp. 189 ff.

87. War Diary Befehlshaber der U-Boote, BA-MA RM 87/25, p. 30 (11 January 1943); the Luftwaffe, on the contrary, even had to ask the Navy High Command and the Commander of U-boats to detach two U-boats for weather reporting needed urgently for the air operations against Britain.

88. Oberkommando der Kriegsmarine 1.Skl. lb No 1629/43 g. Kdos. Chefs., of 8 June 1943, BA-MA RM 7/260, pp. 237 ff (here 242) 247.

89. *Lagevorträge*, pp. 508-512.

90. Hümmelchen, *Seeflieger*, pp. 129 ff.

91. Padfield, P, *Dönitz*, p. 536.

92. Dönitz, *10 Jahre*, p. 127.

18

The Italian Submarine Campaign

by Alberto Santoni

The Birth of *Betasom* and its first engagements

The Italian Navy has seldom established ocean bases for its permanent forces. Before 1940, history's only such examples were at Montevideo (1865-1888), in the colonies of Eritrea (Red Sea) and Somalia (Indian Ocean), and in Chinese waters following the Boxer rebellion.[1]

The first plan detailing the use of Italian submarines in the Atlantic Ocean arose during the Ethiopian crisis of 1935-36. Because of the strained relations with the UK caused by the crisis, this plan was supported by the Fascist navy.[2]

At a meeting in Friedrichshafen on 20-21 June 1939, just a month after the signing of the 'Pact of Steel' between the two Axis powers, Admiral Domenico Cavagnari (Chief of the Italian Naval Staff) reached an agreement with Admiral Erich Raeder (C-in-C of the German Navy) concerning the future use of Italian submarines.[3]

On this occasion, though excluding any operational co-operation or interdependence between the Italian and German U-boats, Raeder asked his colleague to consider the possibility of employing Italian submarines in the central and southern Atlantic, as well as in the Indian Ocean. Cavagnari agreed, confirming that for some years, with the hope of Spanish support, the Italian navy had contemplated the employment of 12 large submarines in the Atlantic, and had also considered basing eight smaller ones in the available Red Sea and Indian Ocean ports of Mesewa, Mogadishu and Kismayu. Cavagnari also stressed the necessity of keeping these submarines under Italian command and was pleased to accept the partitioning of responsibilities in the oceans, which avoided German interference.[4]

Falling in with Raeder's views at that time, this last arrangement was the first signal of the 'parallel war', namely a war without any co-operation between the two Axis powers, which Mussolini and Badoglio (Chief of the Supreme Command) were unfortunately going to impose on Italian strategy. This separatist course lasted till the end of 1940, when Italian losses in Greece, in Libya and at sea persuaded Mussolini to dismiss both Badoglio and Cavagnari, and to ask for German military support.

In fact, in September 1939, Cavagnari had already told two close subordinates, Admirals Somigli and Parona, that he considered the Germans 'encumbering allies' and that he deliberately deceived Raeder at the meeting in Friedrichshafen, by promising him 'everything and nothing', in order to keep the Italian Navy free from any pledge.[5] Cavagnari's behaviour then accorded with the policy of Count Galeazzo Ciano, the enigmatic Italian Foreign

Secretary, who was also Mussolini's son-in-law and whose aim was to loosen, or at least to lessen, the obligations undertaken with Germany.[6]

As we know, Italy finally declared war upon the United Kingdom and France on 10 June 1940, joining Germany on the basis of the previously mentioned strategy aiming for a 'parallel war'. The employment of Italian submarines in the Atlantic was therefore re-examined, at first on 2 June 1940 in a discussion between Rear-Admiral Kurt Fricke (Chief of the Operations Department of the German navy) and Admiral Maraghini (the Italian naval attaché in Berlin), and then in two letters sent on 13 and on 24 July from the Italian Naval High Command (Supermarina) via the German naval liaison officer in Rome, Rear-Admiral Eberhard Weichold, to the Seekriegsleitung.[7]

In these letters, while confirming his willingness to employ up to 40 submarines in the Atlantic, Cavagnari asked the Skl for a suitably large French base, since Italy's hoped-for logistical support in Spain was being hindered by current political problems.

On 25 July 1940, Hitler and Raeder discussed the Italian proposals, accepting them and recognizing the need to maintain two distinct national commands in the Atlantic. This avoided any possibility of Italy requesting tactical command over German air squadrons that might be sent to Sicily and North Africa.[8]

The first Italian submarine operations of the Atlantic war were carried out by *Finzi, Calvi* and *Veniero* in June and July 1940. They completed a round trip to the Italian bases, crossing the dangerous Straits of Gibraltar twice but achieving no success in the ocean. A fourth submarine, *Cappellini*, was forced to abandon its mission owing to British vigilance in the Straits.[9]

In September-November 1940 the same four submarines were sent to the Atlantic once again. This time they did not have to run the Straits on their return, but made port in the new Italian base that had been established at Bordeaux.

In August, an Italian naval commission led by Rear-Admiral Angelo Parona had visited Germany and German-occupied France, and chose Bordeaux near the Bay of Biscay as a permanent base for Italian submarine operations in the Atlantic. From this secure and favourable location, 50 km inland eastwards from the sea, the submarines would access the Bay via a 100-km stretch of the northeastward-flowing river Gironde. From 1 September 1940, the naval base (named Betasom) was placed under the command of Admiral Parona. However, following earlier agreements, it was chiefly equipped and defended by the Germans. Two passenger ships, the French *De Grasse* and the German *Usaramo*, were also converted into floating barracks for Italian personnel.[10]

Regarding operational problems, it is important to remember that while liaison officers were exchanged to benefit co-ordination in technical matters, strategic command remained with the German Admiral Karl Dönitz, C-in-C U-boats (BdU).[11]

Eventually the division between German and Italian hunting-grounds was confirmed. To begin with, Italian submarines were confined to below 42°N. The first three officially assigned to Betasom (*Barbarigo, Malaspina* and *Dandolo*) gained poor results. Managing to sink only two ships (*British Fame* and *Ilvington Court*) during their transfer in August, they claimed there were few targets below 40°N.[12] Supermarina soon asked for a larger hunting-zone with a boundary at the 45th parallel, and a glance at the map shows that this seemed a logical dividing line: lying only 15 km or so north of Bordeaux itself, the 45th parallel bisects the Bay, and would give Italian submarines three degrees - 180 nautical miles - less to travel from base before they could commence operations. However, Raeder rejected the request, because he wanted to avoid any interference with the transfer routes of the German commerce raiders in those waters.

In September 1940, while Betasom was starting its operational life, Maricosom (the Department of the Italian Navy responsible for all submarine warfare) sent a total of 18 boats to Bordeaux. These managed to sink eight merchant vessels in the ocean up to the end of October. But five of the vessels destroyed were neutral ships, namely two Spanish, one Yugoslav, one Swedish and one Greek (the latter sunk 27 days before the Italian attack on Greece), and only two were British: the steamer *Saint Agnes* and the trawler *Kingston Sapphire*.[13]

It was soon apparent that the Italian submarines were technically inferior to the German ones. Their tactics also appeared inadequate, based as they were on the experience gained in the narrow Adriatic sea during World War I. Italian crews were consequently allowed to visit German U-boats, and some Italian submarines were sent to the Baltic Sea for a period of training to German standards. In addition, technical co-operation between the two Axis submarine fleets was hastily improved.

As we now know, the Bay of Biscay was soon to become a bloody battlefield, owing to British Ultra Intelligence.[14] Given that, it was perhaps fortunate that Supermarina did not accept the proposal (emanating from Admirals Parona and Dönitz) for a common training area there.

Of the technical improvements carried out on the Italian submarines, the most important was the lowering and shortening of their large and easily spotted conning-towers. It was not possible, however, to correct all their deficiencies - for example their slow diving time, their low surface speed, their poor manoeuvrability and, last but not least, the age of their captains, who were much older than their German counterparts.[15]

At the end of October 1940, Supermarina asked once again if BdU could extend Betasom's hunting zone. This time the proposal was accepted, and, together with the German U-boats and according to necessities as envisaged by Admiral Dönitz, Italian submarines were allowed to operate off the Western Approaches to the UK. The sector granted to the Italian operations in November 1940 stretched from 51° to 58°20'N and from 17° to 27°W. Here two ships, the Swedish *Vingaland* and the British *Lilian Moller*, were sunk on 9 and 18 November respectively by *Marconi* and *Baracca*, two of the eight Italian submarines then present in the zone.[16]

A better result was achieved in December by the Italian submarines operating in the North Atlantic, when six of them sank as many merchant vessels in that area. For the last three months of that year Betasom employed 19 boats which encountered 10 convoys and 38 independent ships. None of the convoys was attacked, owing either to their strong defence or to the inadequate speed of the submarines involved, while only 19 of the 38 independents were actually attacked, almost always at night. Of those 19, 13 were sunk. In addition, the Canadian destroyer HMCS *Saguenay* was badly damaged on 1 December. Two Italian submarines, *Faa' Di Bruno* and *Tarantini*, were lost in the same period.[17]

Operations in 1941 and 1942

Italian defeats in the Mediterranean and North Africa shattered Mussolini's 'parallel war' strategy, and from the beginning of 1941, German forces were brought into those areas. Italian submarine operations in the North Atlantic zone were still fruitful, however, with *Torelli* (Cdr Primo Longobardo) receiving the lion's share, sinking three merchant ships in two days (15 and 16 January), and a further vessel at the end of the same month.

Bianchi (Lt Cdr Adalberto Giovannini), another well-known Italian submarine, was the only one to sink enemy ships in February 1941, with three British steamers on the 14th, 24th, and 27th of that month. In the whole of March, though, only two English merchant vessels, *Western Chief* and *Agnete Maersk*, were sunk (by *Emo* and *Veniero*).[18]

Decreasing Italian results in the North Atlantic, compared with the much higher figures attained by the German U-boats in the same areas, persuaded Admiral Dönitz in April 1941 to move the Italian zone southward and to offer Betasom greater logistic and technical support. As a matter of fact Supermarina had already stated, at the Naval Conference held in Merano in February, that the Italian contribution to the war efforts should be considered as strictly dependent on German assistance and initiative.[19]

The decision to move the sphere of operations southwards did not appear sufficient to improve results. In April, the submarines *Tazzoli* and *Marconi* sank only one enemy merchant ship and in May three more. In view of these less than encouraging achievements, Supermarina and its Submarine Department (Maricosom) inquired into the organization of Betasom, and concluded that such disappointments could only be attributed to poor materials. The true reason for the Fascist navy's failures in the Battle of the Atlantic was its tactics, which were more inclined to static ambushes than to aggressive cruises.[20] Had it been a more alert armed force, it would have been readier to recognize this.

Similar failures occurred in the Mediterranean, where, in more than three years of war, over 100 Italian submarines managed to sink only 15 enemy merchant vessels and 10 warships. Moreover, not one of the warships was larger than a light cruiser.[21]

Prospects in May 1941 initially seemed to improve, thanks to the arrival at Bordeaux of four submarines which had escaped from the Italian Red Sea station in March, following a British thrust into the Italian colonies there. These were the medium-sized boats *Archimede, Ferraris, Guglielmotti* and *Perla.* Although considered too small for Atlantic operations, they were nonetheless able to avoid the enemy chase brought about by Ultra's information throughout their long voyage.[22]

Their arrival at Bordeaux increased the number of the Italian boats there only for a short time. In the following month, June 1941, Mussolini decided to withdraw 10 of the 27 submarines there, in order to intensify naval operations in the eastern Mediterranean. It was in those circumstances that the *Glauco,* returning home, was sunk by the British destroyer HMS *Wishart* off Gibraltar on 27 June.

Despite the reduction of its submarines and its operational confinement to the less profitable area of the central eastern Atlantic, Betasom made good use of summer 1941; in June, July and August, its boats sank six, seven and two merchant ships respectively. This fruitful season was not to last. In September, Captain Romolo Palacchini succeeded Admiral Parona as Betasom's C-in-C, and during the last four months of the year, there were no further successes to report. Worse, it was Palacchini's sad duty to report the loss (including *Glauco,* already mentioned) of a total of eight Italian submarines in that year.[23] Once again Supermarina became deeply concerned.

Palacchini immediately established an inquiry into his boats' wavering achievements. The verdict, needless to say, was the same as before. It is interesting to note, however, that in the first days of December 1941 four Italian submarines (*Torelli, Tazzoli, Calvi* and *Finzi*) took part in the rescue of the survivors of the famous German commerce raider *Atlantis,* sunk (chiefly thanks to decisive Ultra information) by the British heavy cruiser HMS *Devonshire* on 22 November.[24]

The involvement of the United States in the war from December 1941 led to an enlargement of Italian responsibilities in the Battle of the Atlantic. Betasom was persuaded to move its submarines more westward, up to American waters, so as to operate from the Bahamas to the Brazilian coasts. This left the central ocean almost unattended.

In such a large area, favourably characterized by good weather conditions, isolated and unescorted merchant traffic and a generally poor defensive organisation, the Italian submarines achieved their best results of the whole war. Five boats were initially assigned to those American waters: *Tazzoli* (Lt Cdr Carlo Fecia di Cossato), *Finzi* (Lt Cdr Ugo Giudice), *Da Vinci* (Lt Cdr Luigi Longanesi Cattini), *Torelli* (Lt Cdr Antonio De Giacomo) and *Morosini* (Lt Cdr Athos Fraternale).[25]

These submarines proved to be quite deadly: in the period 20 February-23 March 1942, they sank 16 merchant vessels, most of them independents. Adding to their tally, in the period 29 March-12 April, the southernmost boat,

Calvi (Lt Cdr Emilio Olivieri), destroyed a further five or more enemy merchant ships off the northern coasts of Brazil.

Thus, for the first and last time, six Italian submarines obtained a success rate comparable to that achieved by many German U-boats operating in the central western Atlantic. The six-strong German Neuland group (formed by U-67, U-129, U-156, U-161 and U-502, and flanked by U-126) sank 31 merchant ships aggregating 152,024 gross tons in those waters, remaining at sea for a combined total of 376 days altogether. In comparison, in almost the same area, the six Italian boats sank 21 ships aggregating 125,434 gross tons in a mission lasting 310 boat-days. The resulting ratio was therefore equal, namely 404 gross tons a day.[26]

Italian successes in central American waters continued during summer 1942, thanks especially to *Tazzoli* and the newly joined *Giuliani* (Cdr Giovanni Bruno). This last boat, newly arrived from Gotenhafen, where it had spent a period of training in German tactics, sank three cargoes in August, but was badly damaged by British planes while returning to Bordeaux. *Giuliani*, however, managed to reach the Spanish port of Santander on 3 September and finally Bordeaux on 9 November, showing it to be luckier than *Calvi* (led then by Cdr Primo Longobardo), which was lost off the Azores on 15 July.[27]

Meanwhile *Cappellini* (Lt Marco Revedini) had been employed, together with French warships and three German U-boats, in the rescue of the survivors of the liner *Laconia* which, with 1,800 Italian P.O.W.'s, 248 British soldiers and 80 passengers on board, besides its crew, had been sunk by U-156 off the island of Ascension on 12 September.[28]

The year 1942, which according to every source was the most fruitful year for the Axis submarines, came to a satisfactory end as far as the Italian boats were concerned. In the favourable area north-east of the Brazilian coast, *Da Vinci* (now under the command of Lt Gianfranco Gazzana Priaroggia) and *Tazzoli* (Lt Cdr Carlo Fecia di Cossato) each sank four merchant ships, in November and December respectively. These last successes raised to 47 the number of cargoes sent to the bottom by Italian submarines in the Atlantic during that year, even though Supermarina claimed in its reports many more victories than the actual ones.

In such circumstances it seems appropriate to provide some details about the operational life of the submarine *Da Vinci*. Displacing about 1,100 tons, *Da Vinci* belonged to the *Marconi* class. After commissioning on 7 April 1940 and after the usual dangerous transit of the Gibraltar Straits, it reached Bordeaux on 31 October of the same year. Its first victory came on 28 June 1941, when, commanded by Lt Cdr Ferdinando Calda, it sank the independent British tanker *Auris* west of Gibraltar. Later, under the command of Lt Cdr Luigi Longanesi Cattani, it sank seven cargoes in 1942, first operating in the central western Atlantic and then off the African coast. At the end of 1942, as already noted, this submarine achieved its greatest victories under the command of Lt Gianfranco Gazzana Priaroggia, who was soon promoted to the rank of

Lieutenant Commander, receiving both the German Ritterkreuz 1st class and the Italian gold medal. Unfortunately, this gallant officer was lost together with 63 hands on 23 May 1943, when *Da Vinci* was sunk by the British destroyer HMS *Active* about 300 miles west of Cape Finisterre.[29] Having sunk a total of 17 merchant vessels aggregating 120,243 gross tons, this boat was the most efficient Italian warship of all time, and deserved pride of place among all non-German submarines.[30]

The second highest-scoring Italian submarine was *Tazzoli*, which recorded a total of 96,650 gross tons and remained under the command of the skilful Carlo Fecia di Cossato from 1941 to 1943. This boat made itself conspicuous above all in December 1942, when it was the only Italian submarine to sink enemy ships in the Atlantic - four cargoes off the northern coast of Brazil. *Tazzoli* was lost without warning in May 1943, while it was trying to reach Singapore, as we shall see later.[31]

The *Barbarigo* affair and its consequences

The most debated episodes regarding the whole Italian involvement in the Battle of the Atlantic were the alleged sinkings of two US battleships in May and in October 1942, both ascribed to the submarine *Barbarigo* (Lt Cdr Enzo Grossi). These two events have long received credence in Italy, and are still described with self-satisfaction by the right-wing press.

Barbarigo until then had been an unsuccessful submarine, having sunk only one cargo under Grossi's command. Its crew, however, was naturally anxious to achieve the best results. Nevertheless, on 17 May 1942 when the submarine attacked the Brazilian steamer *Commandante Lyra* off Cape Sao Roque, this hope seemed to be still out of reach: the submarine was unable to sink the merchantman, and only damaged it with gunfire.[32] While under attack, the target managed to signal the event to an approaching American Task Force - TF23, formed of the old light cruisers USS *Milwaukee* and *Omaha* and the destroyers USS *McDougal* and *Moffett*. This American naval group gave assistance to the *Commandante Lyra* and made for the port of Recife, where the damaged cargo ship also arrived later under tow.

At 0245 on the following 20 May, while surfaced at 04°19'S 34°32'W, exactly in between Cape San Roque and the Rocas islands, *Barbarigo* sighted some warships very close by and heading south. Minutes later the submarine carried out an attack, remaining on the surface and firing two stern torpedoes at the short distance of 650 metres. Cdr Grossi declared in his report that his target was 'an American battleship of the *California* or *Maryland* class, easily recognizable by its two high lattice masts'. We shall later dwell on this sentence, asking why two accompanying American destroyers, also sighted by the submarine at the even closer distance of only 600 metres (656 yards), showed a complete lack of concern and according to Grossi's report, did not react aggressively at all.[33]

Every man present on *Barbarigo*'s conning tower, including Grossi himself, believed they had seen the two torpedoes hit the target at 0251. In particular, Grossi gave the following assurance in his report:

> I noticed the escorting destroyers rushing towards the stricken ship, and I saw the giant heeling and plunging its forecastle into the water up to its bridge. I was at a very short distance of about 800 metres.[34]

Neither Supermarina nor Betasom was in any doubt, and the Fascist propaganda machine was therefore pleased to spread the glorious news all over the world.[35] Grossi was rapidly promoted to the rank of commander, and was further rewarded with a gold medal. Then, still commanding *Barbarigo*, he was involved in another war episode very similar to the above.

This second *Barbarigo* affair took place 320 miles south of Freetown (02°05'N 14°23'W) on the night 5-6 October 1942, starting at 0220 on 6 October. At that time, again cruising on the surface, the submarine sighted and then attacked what was once more considered to be an American battleship, this time of the *Mississippi* class. Four torpedoes were fired and, according to Grossi's report, all exploded against the target at 2,000 metres distance, sinking the alleged battleship in six minutes. The Italian Supreme Command therefore received yet another opportunity to extol the Italian crews' ability and bravery, and issued another fanatical announcement.[36]

Thus, Grossi (a fat and unimpressive officer) suddenly became the most celebrated sailor in the Italian Navy. He was once again promoted, reaching the rank of captain, and was awarded a second gold medal. Grossi concluded his career as C-in-C of Betasom - a post he maintained, being a loyal Fascist, even after the Italian armistice.

The Allied navies, of course, at once denied the loss of any warship on those days and at those positions. Nevertheless, the Italian people preferred to think in the most favourable way and, what is worse, they have long maintained their partisan ideas. Many Italian right-wing historians and journalists, as well as some official spokesmen, continued their support for Grossi even in the '50s and '60s, with ridiculous stories of an envious Royal Navy and a jealous US Navy, unwilling to acknowledge defeats caused by the illustrious Italian Navy. These partisan supporters omitted, of course, to remember that by then the British and Americans had already officially recognized all their main losses caused by the three Axis powers. The most active among these charlatans was Antonino Trizzino, a former airman, whose foolish thesis on the *Barbarigo* affair could be trusted only by people equally blinded by a lasting Fascist prejudice.[37]

Eventually, some less biased historians picked up a post-war copy of *Jane's Fighting Ships* and at last 'discovered' that with the exceptions of USS *Arizona* and *Oklahoma*, which had unarguably been destroyed at Pearl Harbor, *all* the American battleships of World War II were still in commission at the end of hostilities. Faced with this straightfoward fact, right-wing elements in Italy came up with a fairy-tale reply. According to them, the US Navy - without a thought for the public coffers, but in order to conceal its losses and thereby demean Italian prestige - had rebuilt *Barbarigo*'s victims during the war, accurately reproducing the old battleships in every detail.

Against this fantastic notion a simple point could have been made. According to the naval almanacs issued in wartime, some American battleships still featured two lattice masts, as noted in Grossi's report on his alleged victims. But these almanacs had failed to report contemporary modifications and improvements in certain classes of US warship, for in May 1942, when Grossi made his attacks, and in contradiction of his report, no American battleship carried two lattice masts.[38]

The controversy was at last solved by two committees of inquiry held by the Italian Navy, which discovered the historical truth in 1962, thanks to careful work on the American, British and national files related to these episodes.[39] Grossi was subsequently discredited and deprived of his two gold medals, raising howls of protest from right-wing circles. The Italian authorities officially recognized that neither battleships nor other warships of any nationality had ever been sunk or even damaged by *Barbarigo*. In particular, it was confirmed that on the first occasion, on 20 May 1942, the Italian submarine had in fact attacked the American light cruiser USS *Milwaukee*, mistaking it for a battleship belonging to the USS *Maryland* or *California* classes. It is difficult to understand exactly how the American cruiser, with its four funnels and no lattice masts, could honestly have been mistaken for a battleship of either type.[40] It is still more difficult to understand why Grossi believed he had sunk his target: *Milwaukee* not only remained untouched, but did not even realize it was under attack! In fact, *Barbarigo*'s two torpedoes fell hopelessly short and off-target, because Grossi miscalculated the speed and bearing for his attack - a fact which also explains why the Italian submarine was not counter-attacked.

Having said that, it remains uncertain whether Grossi and his comrades simply blundered completely or cheated consciously.

The second episode - the attack of 6 October 1942 - showed a greater accuracy of aim, but a yet greater ineptitude on Grossi's part in identifying the target. *Barbarigo*'s second target was the British corvette HMS *Petunia*, unbelievably mistaken for an American battleship of the *Mississippi* class, which actually was 35 times bigger![41] In spite of this blunder, one of the four torpedoes ran just under HMS *Petunia*'s keel, without touching it, which would indicate Grossi's good faith on this occasion, insofar as he certainly fired at the target. But none hit, and since (contrary to what some authors have said) torpedoes did not explode at the end of their run, the four explosions heard from *Barbarigo* must have been imagined. As for sinking the supposed battleship, *Petunia* actually gave chase to *Barbarigo*. If the corvette's asdic had not been temporarily out of action, Grossi might not have survived to make his erroneous report.

In every war and in all armed services, misidentification of targets takes place. What has been unforgivable in these episodes, however, was the persistent and deliberate attempt of some Italian journalists and historians to distort their responsibilities, letting people conceive - even 20 years after the events - of a British-American plot against Italian bravery, and supporting this prejudice with fanciful arguments.

The saddest aspect is that, for those people who have always believed no country can possibly gain maturity while it is lacking in accurate historical perception, the loud cries and complaints in the '60s that followed the government's decision to deprive Grossi of his medals have been simply shaming.

Last Operations of the Italian submarines

As historians usually affirm, the year 1943 signalled the turning point in the Battle of the Atlantic, which became more and more conditioned by the British Ultra information, as well as by Allied technical improvements in anti-submarine warfare. Added to those factors, Betasom decided both to reduce its hunting zone to south of the line and only to allow attacks on independent merchant ships. It is therefore understandable that in that year the Italian submarine force suffered heavy losses, without achieving satisfactory results.[42]

In these circumstances only three Italian submarines made themselves conspicuous. The first one was, again, *Da Vinci* (Lt Cdr Gianfranco Gazzana Priaroggia) which operated fruitfully in the South Atlantic and off Durban, sinking respectively two and four cargoes in March and April 1943. The other two successful boats were *Barbarigo*, which, under the command of Lt Roberto Rigoli, definitely sank three merchant ships off the Brazilian Cape Sao Roque between 24 February-3 March, and *Finzi* (Lt Mario Rossetto) which sent two cargoes to the bottom in as many days at the end of March.

That same month, an agreement was reached between Supermarina and the BdU regarding the employment of Betasom's 10 remaining submarines. It was decided to turn all of these boats, except *Cagni*, into underwater cargo carriers, in order to establish a sea-trade of machinery and raw materials - above all rubber and tin - between Bordeaux and the eastern territories controlled by Japan. In order to replace these Italian submarines, now employed in trading duties, the German Navy offered Betasom nine Type VIIC U-boats. These were delivered to the Italian Navy in August 1943 and were named *S-1* to *S-9*.

Meantime, however, *Archimede* and the famous *Da Vinci* had been sunk by the enemy on 15 April and 23 May respectively. The planned conversion into underwater cargo carriers was therefore carried out on only seven Italian boats (*Bagnolini, Barbarigo, Cappellini, Finzi, Giuliani, Torelli* and *Tazzoli*), which were stripped of all armament, so as to maximize stowage space.[43]

As mentioned already, Italian submarines were generally too big and awkward for effective ocean operations, but such shortcomings turned to be helpful in their new roles. In fact, even before their conversion, these boats with their roomy hulls were able to carry much more cargo than the German ones and could also accommodate larger fuel tanks, giving them sufficient range to reach the Far East from Bordeaux without refuelling. However, they had to be refuelled at sea during the homeward voyage, because during that, even some of their fuel tanks would be employed as stowage space.

This unusual trading operation started with the arrival at Singapore of two Italian officers and about 30 soldiers, who established a liaison office housed in the Italian gun-boat *Eritrea*, which had reached Japan from the Red Sea in March 1941 and Singapore on 14 June 1943.[44]

Only five of the seven converted submarines effectively left Bordeaux in May and June 1943 for their logistic mission. *Cappellini* (Lt Cdr Walter Auconi), *Giuliani* (Lt Cdr Mario Tei) and *Torelli* (Lt Enrico Groppallo), although attacked by enemy planes in the Atlantic, reached Singapore safely in July and in August. However, after sailing in May and June, *Tazzoli* (Lt Cdr Giuseppe Gaito) and *Barbarigo* (Lt Umberto De Julio) disappeared at sea together with their entire crews. They were probably sunk by mines.[45]

The two remaining converted submarines, *Bagnolini* and *Finzi*, did not even manage to leave Bordeaux before the Italian armistice of 8 September. They were then seized by the Germans, who handed them over to the so-called Social-Fascist Republic (R.S.I.). This government - formed by Mussolini himself after the armistice in opposition to the King's government led by Marshal Badoglio - remained in control of central and northern Italy, as well as of Betasom, where Captain Enzo Grossi was still in command.[46]

The three Italian submarines which had already reached Singapore were likewise seized by the Japanese on 8 September and handed over to the German Navy. In particular, *Giuliani* was recommissioned as U-It.23 before being sunk off Sumatra by the British submarine *Tally Ho* on 14 February 1944. *Cappellini* and *Torelli* were respectively named U-It.24 and U-It.25 by the Germans, but were again seized by the Japanese after the German surrender in May 1945 and classified as I.503 and I.504 respectively in the Imperial Japanese Navy. Both survived the war, but were captured by the Americans and scuttled off Kobe, respectively on 15 and 16 April 1946.[47]

Unlike the submarines, the gunboat *Eritrea* escaped from Singapore and managed to avoid the Japanese chase before reaching the British base of Colombo in Ceylon.

As already mentioned, the only Betasom submarine not selected for conversion into an underwater cargo carrier was *Cagni* (Lt Cdr Giuseppe Roselli Lorenzini). This boat was nevertheless also ordered to reach Singapore and to load rubber and tin there, but not to relinquish its armament and its offensive capacity. Leaving Bordeaux on 29 June 1943, it reached the central Atlantic, and on 25 July - the very day Mussolini was dismissed by the King of Italy - it damaged but did not sink the British armed merchant cruiser *Asturias*. During this action Roselli Lorenzini mistook his target for an aircraft carrier - yet another over-optimistic assessment, all too frequent in the Italian Navy - and even believed he had sunk it.

On 6 September, while *Cagni* was crossing the Indian Ocean, Betasom ordered Roselli Lorenzini to stop his mission. Three days later the submarine reached the British base of Durban. This was certainly due to the armistice between Italy and the Allies, which had been secretly signed on 3 September and was officially declared five days later.[48]

These circumstances are nevertheless of some interest, because the orders sent to Roselli Lorenzini were not at all consistent with the official and still accepted statement, according to which the top level Italian politicians consciously kept the military chiefs in the dark about the armistice, right up to its proclamation on 8 September.[49] It is therefore quite certain that, even though this story deals with political rather than military matters, we are faced with another of Italy's many unsolved secrets.

This chapter concludes with some revised statistical data about Italian involvement in the Battle of the Atlantic. The following data has been accepted by the Ufficio Storico della Marina Militare (the Historical Department of the Italian Navy) and will be published in a forthcoming publication by the same Department. Tables Two and Three thus represent an up-to-date contribution to the knowledge of this subject.[50]

In total, 32 Italian submarines were employed in the Atlantic for more than three years, sinking 109 merchant vessels aggregating 593,864 gross tons, and damaging four more enemy or neutral cargoes and a British destroyer. Half this submarine force, namely 16 boats, was lost.

TABLE 1:
ITALIAN SUBMARINES AND THEIR EMPLOYMENT IN THE ATLANTIC

SUBMARINE	DATE OF ARRIVAL AT BORDEAUX	FATE
MALASPINA	4 September 1940	Sunk in central-eastern Atlantic between 8 September and 18 November 1941
BARBARIGO	8 September 1940	Sunk in central-eastern Atlantic between 16 June and 31 August 1943.
DANDOLO	10 September 1940	Returned to Italy in July 1941
MARCONI	28 September 1940	Sunk in central-eastern Atlantic between 28 October and 4 December 1941
FINZI	29 September 1940	Seized by the Germans at Bordeaux on 8 September 1943
BAGNOLINI	30 September 1940	Seized by the Germans at

EMO	3 October 1940	Bordeaux on 8 September 1943 Returned to Italy in September 1941
TARANTINI	5 October 1940	Sunk off Bordeaux on 15 December 1940
TORELLI	5 October 1940	Seized by the Japanese at Singapore on 8 September 1943
FAA' DI BRUNO	5 October 1940	Sunk off Ireland between 31 October 1940 and 5 January 1941
OTARIA	6 October 1940	Returned to Italy in September 1941
BARACCA	6 October 1940	Sunk in the Gulf of Biscay on 8 September 1941
GIULIANI	6 October 1940	Seized by the Japanese at Singapore on 8 September 1943
GLAUCO	22 October 1940	Sunk at 250 miles west of Gibraltar on 27 June 1941
CALVI	23 October 1940	Sunk in central Atlantic on 15 July 1942
TAZZOLI	24 October 1940	Sunk probably in the Gulf of Biscay between 17 May and 31 August 1943
ARGO	24 October 1940	Returned to Italy in October 1941
DA VINCI	31 October 1940	Sunk at 300 miles south-west of Cape Finisterre on 23 May 1943
VENIERO	2 November 1940	Returned to Italy August 1941
NANI	4 November 1940	Sunk off Ireland between 3 January and 20 February 1941
CAPPELLINI	5 November 1940	Seized by the Japanese at Sabang on 8 September 1943
MOROSINI	28 November 1940	Sunk in the Gulf of Biscay between 8 August and 10 September 1942
MARCELLO	2 December 1940	Sunk off Ireland between 7 February and 6 April 1941
BIANCHI	18 December 1940	Sunk in the Gulf of Biscay on 5 July 1941
BRIN	18 December 1940	Returned to Italy in September 1941
VELELLA	25 December 1940	Returned to Italy in August 1941
MOCENIGO	26 December 1940	Returned to Italy in August 1941
GUGLIELMOTTI	6 May 1941	Returned to Italy in October 1941
ARCHIMEDE	7 May 1941	Sunk off the Brazilian coast on 15 April 1941
FERRARIS	9 May 1941	Sunk at 300 miles west of Gibraltar on 25 October 1941
PERLA	20 May 1941	Returned to Italy in October 1941
CAGNI	20 February 1943	Arrived at Durban on 9 September 1943 after the Italian armistice

TABLE 2:
MERCHANT SHIPS SUNK BY ITALIAN SUBMARINES
IN THE ATLANTIC

DATE	NAME AND NATIONALITY OF THE MERCHANT SHIP	POSITION	ATTACKER AND CAPTAIN
1940			
August			
12	BRITISH FAME (GB)	37°44' N 22° 56' W	MALASPINA (Leoni)
26	ILVINGTON COURT (GB)	37°14'N, 21°52'W	DANDOLO (Boris)
September			
14	SAINT AGNES (GB)	41°27'N, 21°50'W	EMO (Liannaza)
18	CABO TORTOSA (SP)	Off Oporto	BAGNOLINI (Tosoni Pittoni)
19	ALMIRANTE JOSE DE CARANZA (SP)	16 miles NW of Cabo Villano	MARCONI (Chialamberto)
October			
1	AGHIOS NICOLAOS (GR)	40°00'N, 16°55'W	BARACCA (Bertarelli)
5	KINGSTON SAPPHIRE (GB)	Off Cape Spartel	NANI (Polizzi)
12	ORAO (YU)	35°34'N, 10°35'W	TAZZOLI (Raccanelli)
15	KABALO (B)	32°00'N, 31°20'W	CAPPELLINI (Todaro)
27	MEGGIE (S)	60 miles E of Azores	NANI (Polizzi)
November			
9	VIGALAND (S)	55°41'N, 18°24'W	MARCONI (Chialamberto)
18	LILIAN MOLLER (GB)	57°00'N, 17°12'W	BARACCA (Bartarelli)
December			
5	SILVERPINE (GB)	54°14'N, 18°08'W	ARGO (Crepas)
18	ANASTASSIA (GR)	54°24'N, 19°04'W	VENIERO (Petroni)
19	AMICUS (GB)	54°10'N, 15°50'W	BAGNOLINI (Tosoni Pittoni)
20	CARLTON (GB)	54°30'N, 18°30'W	CALVI (Caridi)
21	MANGEN (S)	40°45'N, 16°50'W	MOCENIGO (Agostini)
27	ARDANBHAN (GB)	59°16'N, 20°27'W	TAZZOLI (Raccanelli)

1941

January

5 SHAKESPEARE (GB)	18°05'N, 21°10'W	CAPPELLINI (Todaro)
14 EUMAEUS (GB)	08°55'N, 15°03'W	CAPPELLINI (Todaro)
15 NEMEA (GR)	52°33'N, 24°13'W	TORELLI (Longobardo)
15 BRASK (N)	52°45'N, 23°59'W	TORELLI (Longobardo)
16 NICOLAOS FILINIS (GR)	53°16'N, 4°12'W	TORELLI (Longobardo)
20 PORTUGAL(B)	50°10'N, 19°08'W	MARCELLO (Teppati)
28 URLA (GB)	54°54'N, 19°06'W	TORELLI (Longobardo)
31 PIZARRO (GB)	50°00'N, 19°40'W	DANDOLO (Boris)

February

14 BELCREST (GB)	55°16'N, 19°00'W	BIANCHI (Giovannini)
24 LINARIA (GB)	61°00'N, 25°08'W	BIANCHI (Giovannini)
27 BALTISTAN (GB)	51°52'N, 19°55'W	BIANCHI (Giovannini)

March

14 WESTERN CHIEF (GB)	58°52'N, 21°13'W	EMO (Lorenzini)
24 AGNESE MAERSK (GB)	49°00'N, 22°55'W	VENIERO (Petroni)

April

15 AURILLAC (GB)	37°09'N, 18°42'W	TAZZOLI (Fecia di Cossato)

May

7 FERNLANE (N)	10°02'N, 20°17'W	TAZZOLI (Fecia di Cossato)
.9 ALFRED OLSEN (N)	02°59'N, 20°26'W	TAZZOLI (Fecia di Cossato)
20 STARCROSS (GB)	51°45'N, 20°26'W	OTARIA (Vocatura)
30 CAIRNDALE (GB)	170 miles WSW of Cape Trafalgar	MARCONI (Pollina)

June

1	EXPORTADOR PRIMEIRO (P)	137 miles SW of Cape Saint Vincent	MARCONI (Pollina)
6	BARON LOVAT (GB)	35°34'N, 11°30'W	MARCONI (Pollina)
6	TABERG (S)	35°36'N, 11°12'W	MARCONI (Pollina)
13	DJURDJURA (GB)	38°53'N, 23°11'W	BRIN (Longanesi)
13	EIRINI KYRIAKADES (GR)	38°53'N, 23°11'W	BRIN (Longanesi)
28	AURIS (GB)	34°27'N, 11°57W	DA VINCI (Calda)

July

14	RUPERT DE LARRINAGA (GB)	36°18'N, 21°11'W	MOROSINI (Fraternale)
15	NIKOKLIS (GR)	33°51'N, 21°31'W	MALASPINA (Prini)
15	LADY SOMERS (GB)	36°00'N, 21°00'W	MOROSINI (Fraternale)
17	GUELMA (GB)	30°44'N, 17°33'W	MALASPINA (Prini)
21	IDA KNUDSEN (N)	34°34'N, 13°14'W	TORELLI (De Giacomo)
25	MACON (GB)	32°48'N, 26"12'W	BARBARIGO (Murzi)
26	HORN SHELL (GB)	33°23'N, 22° 18'W	BARBARIGO (Murzi)

August

14	SUD (YU)	44°00'N, 17°41'W	MARCONI (Pollina)
19	SILDRA (N)	05°30'N, 12°50'W	TAZZOLI (Fecia di Cossato)

1942

January

23	NAVEMAR (SP)	36°48'N, 15°26'W	BARBARIGO (Grossi)

February

20	SCOTTISH STAR (GB)	13°24'N, 49°36'W	DA VINCI (Longanesi)
25	CABEDELLO (BR)	16'08'N, 49°05'W	DA VINCI (Longanesi)
26	ESSO COPENHAGEN (PA)	10°32'N, 53°20'W	TORELLI (De Giacomo)
28	EVERASMA (LT)	17°00'N, 48°05'W	DA VINCI (Longanesi)

March

6	ASTREA (NL)	29°12'N, 64°29'W	TAZZOLI (Fecia di Cossato)
6	MELPOMENE (GB)	23°35'N, 62°39'W	FINZI (Giudice)
7	TONSBERGFJORD (N)	31°22'N, 68°05'W	TAZZOLI (Fecia di Cossato)
7	SKANE (S)	20°50'N, 62°05'W	FINZI (Giudice)
9	MONTEVIDEO (UR)	29°13'N, 69°35'W	TAZZOLI (Fecia di Cossato)
10	CHARLES RACINE (NJ)	23°10'N, 60°28'W	FINZI (Giudice)
11	CYGNET (PA)	5 miles E of S.Salvador	TAZZOLI (Fecia di Cossato)
12	STANGARTH (GB)	22°00'N, 65°00'W	MOROSINI (Fraternale)
13	DAYTONIAN (GB)	26°33'N, 74°43'W	TAZZOLI (Fecia di Cossato)
15	ATHELQUEEN (GB)	26°50'N, 75°40'W	TAZZOLI (Fecia di Cossato)
16	OSCILLA (NL)	19°15'N, 60°25'W	MOROSINI (Fraternale)
23	PEDER BOGEN (GB)	24°41'N, 57°44'W	MOROSINI (Fraternale)
29	TREDINNICK (GB)	11°46'N, 43°18'W	CALVI (Olivieri)
31	T.C. McCOBB (USA)	07°10'N, 45°20'W	CALVI (Olivieri)

April

8	EUGENE V.R. THAYER (USA)	02°12'S, 39°55'W	CALVI (Olivieri)
11	BALKIS (N)	02°30'S, 38°00'W	CALVI (Olivieri)
12	BEN BRUSH (PA)	04°32'S, 35°03'W	CALVI (0livieri)

May

19	TISNAREN (S)	03°38'N, 32°01'W	CAPPELLINI (Revedin)
28	CHALBURY (GB)	06°22'S, 29°44'W	BARBARIGO (Grossi)
31	DINSDALE (GB)	00°45'S, 20°50'W	CAPPELLINI (Revedin)

June

2	REINE MARIE STEWART(PA)	07°16'N, 13°20'W	DA VINCI (Longanesi)
7	CHILE (GB)	04°17'N, 13°48'W	DA VINCI (Longanesi)
10	ALIOTH (NL)	00°08'N, 18°52'W	DA VINCI (Longanesi)

13	CLAN MACQUAVIE (GB)	05°30'N, 23°30'W	DA VINCI (Longanesi)
15	CARDINA (PA)	04°45'N. 40°55'W	ARCHIMEDE (Gazzana)
30	TYSA (NL)	25°33'N, 57°53'W	MOROSINI (D'Alessandro)

August

2	KASTOR (GR)	11°06'N, 59°05'W	TAZZOLI (Fecia di Cossato)
6	HAVSTEN (N)	11°18'N, 54°45'W	TAZZOLI (Fecia di Cossato)
10	MEDON (GB)	09°26'N, 38°28'W	GIULIANI (Bruno)
13	CALIFORNIA (USA)	09°21'N, 34°35'W	GIULIANI (Bruno)
14	SYLVIA DE LARRINAGA (GB)	10°49'N, 33°35'W	GIULIANI (Bruno)

October

9	ORONSAY (GB)	04°29'N, 20°52'W	ARCHIMEDE (Saccardo)

November

2	EMPIRE ZEAL (GB)	00°30'N, 30°45'W	DA VINCI (Gazzana)
3	DAGOMBA (GB)	02°30'N, 19°00'W	CAGNI (Liannazza)
4	ANDREAS (GR)	02°00'S, 30°30'W	DA VINCI (Gazzana)
10	MARCUS WHITMAN (USA)	05°40'S, 32°41'W	DA VINCI (Gazzana)
11	VEERHAVEN (NL)	03°51'N, 29°22'W	DA VINCI (Gazzana)
29	ARGO (GR)	34°53'S, 17°54'E	CAGNI (Liannazza)

December

12	EMPIRE HAWK (GB)	05°56'N, 39°50'W	TAZZOLI (Fecia di Cossato)
12	OMBILIN (NL)	07°25'N, 39°19'W	TAZZOLI (Fecia di Cossato)
21	QUEEN CITY (GB)	00°49'N, 41°43'W	TAZZOLI (Fecia di Cossato)
25	DONNA AURORA (USA)	02°02'S, 35°17'W	TAZZOLI (Fecia di Cossato)

1943

February

24	MONTE IGUELDO (SP)	04°46'S, 31°55'W	BARBARIGO (Rigoli)

March

2	AFFONSO PENNA (BR)	16°14'S, 36°03'W	BARBARIGO (Rigoli)
3	STAG HOUND (USA)	16°44'S, 36°33'W	BARBARIGO (Rigoli)
14	EMPRESS OF CANADA (GB)	01°13'S, 09°7'W	DA VINCI (Gazzana)
19	LULWORTH HILL (GB)	10°10'S, 01°00'W	DA VINCI (Gazzana)
28	GRANIC0S (GR)	03°41'N, 15°15'W	FINZI (Rossetto)
30	CELTIC STAR (GB)	04°16'N, 17°44'W	FINZI (Rossetto)

April

17	SEMBILAN (NL)	31°30'S, 33°30'E	DA VINCI (Gazzana)
18	MANAAR (GB)	30°59'S, 33°00'E	DA VINCI (Gazzana)
21	JOHN DRAYTON (USA)	33°10'S, 34°50'E	DA VINCI (Gazzana)
25	DORYSSA (GB)	37°03'S, 24°03'E	DA VINCI (Gazzana)

TABLE 3: SHIPS DAMAGED BY ITALIAN SUBMARINES IN THE ATLANTIC

DATE	NAME AND NATIONALITY OF THE MERCHANT SHIP	POSITION	ATTACKER AND CAPTAIN
1940			
August			
21	HERMES (NL)	36°57'N, 13°15'W	DANDOLO (Boris)
December			
1	HMCS SAGUENAY (Canadian destroyer)	54°40'N, 15°50'W	ARGO (Crepas)
1942			
May			
18	COMMANDANTE LYRA (BR)	02°59'S, 34°10'W	BARBARIGO (Grossi)
October			
10	NEA HELLAS (GR)	04°05'N, 20°15'W	ARCHIMEDE (Saccardo)
1943			
July			
25	ASTURIAS (GB)	06°40'N, 21°00'W	CAGNI (Lorenzini)

Notes

1.   M. Gabriele and G. Friz, *La flotta come strumento di politica nei primi decenni
     dello Stato unitario italiano*, Ufficio Storico della Marina Militare, Roma 1973, pp.
     95-102 and pp. 263-281; M. Gabriele and G.Friz, *La politica navale italiana dal
     1885 al 1915*, Ufficio Storico della Marina Militare, Roma 1982, pp. 111-9.
2.   Historical Archive of the Italian Navy (A.U.S.M.M), Section O.A.: *Ufficio Piani di
     guerra, Studio sulla preparazione, promemoria sul programma anno XVII e
     seguenti*, January 1939.
3.   Italian Foreign Office, *Documenti diplomatici italiani (DDI)*, 8 section, vol.XIII,
     appendix IV, pp. 433-8.
4.   G. Schreiber, *Revisionismus und Weltmachstreben. Marinefuhrung und deutch-
     italienische Beziehungen 1919-1944*, Deutsche Verlags-Anstalt, Stuttgart 1982, pp.
     174-181.
5.   G. Giorgernini, *Da Matapan al Golfo Persico*, Mondadori, Milano 1989, p. 414.
6.   G. Ciano, *Diario 1937-1943*, Rizzoli, Milano 1980, p. 353.
7.   A.U.S.M.M., class *Betasom*, item number B/1: *Costituzione gruppo sommergibili
     atlantici* and class *Marina germanica in Italia*, item number 1/4.
8.   *Fuehrer Conferences on Naval Affairs 1939-1945*, pp. 120-121.
9.   Ufficio Storico della Marina Militare (Historical Department of the Italian Navy),
     La Marina italiana nella seconda guerra mondiale, vol.XIII: *I sommergibili negli
     Oceani*, Roma 1963, pp. 55-60.
10. A.U.S.M.M., class *Betasom*, item numbers B/1 and B/5. The name *Betasom* arose
     from Beta, second letter of the Greek alphabet that also was the initial letter of
     Bordeaùx, and Som, the abbreviation of the Italian word *sommergibile*, namely
     'submarine'.
11. *Fuehrer Conferences on Naval Affairs 1939-1945*, p. 133.
12. J. Rohwer, *Axis submarine successes 1939-1945*, pp. 24-27.
13. The eighth merchant vessel hoisted a Belgian flag. See the table above at the end of
     this paper.
14. A. Santoni, *Guerra segreta sugli Oceani: l'ULTRA britannico e i corsari tedeschi*,
     Mursia, Milano 1984, pp. 20-21.
15. C. De Risio, *Quota periscopio: cento anni di sommergibili italiani*, Uffico
     Documentazione e Attivita Promozionali della Marina, Roma 1990, pp. 59-60.
16. A. De Toro, *La costituzione di Betasom nelle relazioni navali italo-tedesche, 1939-
     1940*, in *Bollettino d'Archivio dell'Ufficio Storico della Marina Militare*, Roma,
     September 1991, pp. 188-194.
17. Ufficio Storico della Marina Militare, *La Marina italiana nella seconda guerra
     mondiale*, XIII, pp. 131-134.
18. C. De Risio, *Quota periscopio: cento anni di sommergibili italiani*, p. 128.
19. A.U.S.M.M., class F, item number B: *Convegno italogermanico di Merano, 13-14
     febbraio 1941*.
20. A. Flamigni, A. Turrini and T. Marcon, *Sommergibili italiani. Cento anni di vita*

tra storia e leggenda, special issue of *Rivista Marittima*, Roma 1990, p. 132.

21. A. Santoni and F. Mattesini, *La partecipazione tedesca alla guerra aeronavale nel Mediterraneo (1940-1945)*, Dell'Ateneo & Bizzarri, Roma 1980, pp. 597-600.

22. A. Santoni, *Il vero traditore: il ruolo documentato di ULTRA nella guerra del Mediterraneo*. Mursia, Milano 1981, pp. 91-2. German edition of the same book: *Ultra siegt im Mittelmeer*, Bernard und Graefe, Koblenz 1985. p. 103.

23. Ufficio Storico della Marina Militare, *Navi militari perdute* Roma 1969, pp. 50-6.

24. A. Santoni, *Guerra segreta sugli Oceani: l'ULTRA britannico e i corsari tedeschi*, pp. 73-75 and Public Record Office, Kew Gardens (P.R.O.), class DEFE 3, item number 68: decrypts ZIP/ZTPG/17893 of 20 November 1941 and item number 69: decrypt ZIP/ZTPG/18094 of 21 November 1941.

25. F. Mattesini, *La prima spedizione dei sommergibili italiani nelle acque americane*, in *Il Giornale d'Italia*, Roma, 28 January 1984.

26. *Ibid.* and Ufficio Storico della Marina Militare, *I sommergibili italiani 1895-1971*, Roma 1971, *passim.*

27. A.U.S.M.M., class *Sommergibili 1940-1943*, files *Giuliani* and *Calvi.*

28. *British vessels lost at sea 1914-1918 and 1939-1945: Merchant ships lost in the Second World War*, p. 41.

29. G. Raiola, *Uomini dell'Atlantico*, Longanesi, Milano 1973, pp. 166-168.

30. F. Mattesini, *Attivita e successi del sommergibile oceanico Da Vinci*, in *Il Giornale d'Italia*, Roma, 11 October 1984. According to some sources, which unfortunately do not distinguish between gross tons and tons of displacement, the most successful American submarine was the USS *Flasher*, which sank a total of 100,231 tons, while the top score among the British boats belongs to HMS *Upholder*, with a score of 99,314 tons, and the *I-27* came out as the most efficient Japanese submarine, sinking 72,406 tons.

31. F. Mattesini, *L'ultima missione del sommergibile Da Vinci*, in *Bollettino dell'Ufficio Storico dell Marina Militare*, March-June 1989, pp. 133-161.

32. A. Santoni, *Da Lissa alle Falkland: storia e politica navale dell'eta contemporanea*, Mursia, Milano 1987, p. 257.

33. A.U.S.M.M., class *Sommergibili 1940-1943*, file *Barbarigo*, May 1942.

34. *Ibid.* and Ufficio Storico della Marina Militare, *La Marina italiana nella seconda guerra mondiale*, XII, pp. 258-9.

35. See, for example, the special bulletin nr. 721, issued by the Italian Supreme Command on 22 May 1942. Ref. Ufficio Storico dello Stato Maggiore Esercito (Historical Department of the Italian Army), *Bollettini di guerra del Commando Supremo, 1940-1943*, Roma 1973, p. 389.

36. Ufficio Storico dello Stato Maggiore Esercito, *Bollettini di guerra del Comando Supremo, 1940-1943*, p.450: special bulletin nr. 863 of 6 October 1942.

37. A. Trizzino, *Sopr di noi l'Oceano*, Longanesi, Milano 1962, pp. 194-215.

38. See, for example, the official year-book *Almanacco navale italiano*, published by the Italian Department of the Navy, and above all the issue of 1943, where the USS *California* class and the USS *Maryland* class were still shown with their old lattice

masts (pp. 531-535) and where the alleged successes of *Barbarigo* against two American battleships were emphasized (p. 519).

39. Ufficio Storico della Marina Militare, *La Marina italiana nella seconda guerra mondiale*, XIII, pp. 261-274 and 298-300.

40. *Ibid.*, pp. 261-262 and G. Rocca, *Fucilate gli ammiragli: la tragedia della Marina italiana nella seconda guerra mondiale*, Mondadori, Milano 1987, p. 185

41. The British corvette HMS *Petunia* displaced 925 tons, while *Mississippi* officially displaced 33,000 tons. See Lenton and Colledge, *Warships of World War II*, pp. 201-8; Silverstone, *U.S Warships of World War II*, p. 20.

42. Ufficio Storico della Marina Militare, *La Marina italiana nella seconda guerra mondiale*, XIII p. 311.

43. *Ibid.*, XIII, pp. 332-3 and Ufficio Storico della Marina Militare, *I sommergibili italiani, 1895-1971*, pp. 245-270.

44. Ufficio Storico della Marina Militare, *La Marina italiana nella seconda guerra mondiale*, vol X: *Le operazioni in Africa orientale*, Roma 1961, pp. 125-133.

45. Ufficio Storico della Marina Militare, *Navi militari perdute*, pp. 66-67.

46. S. Nesi, *Decima flottiglia nostra: I mezzi d'assalto della Marina italiana al Sud e al Nord dopo l'armistizio*, Mursia, Milano 1986, p. 54.

47. Jentschura et al, *Warships of the Imperial Japanese Navy, 1869-1945*, p. 183.

48. G. Bernadi, *La Marina, gli armistizi e il trattato di pace*, Ufficio Storico della Marina Militare, Roma 1979, pp. 50-71.

49. *Ibid.*, p.64. For a review of these circumstances see F. Mattesini, *Il giallo dell' 8 settembre*, in *Il Giornale d'Italia*, Roma 30 June 1986.

50. F. Mattesini, *I sommergibili di Betasom 1940-1943*. Ufficio Storico della Marina Militare, next issue.

19

Allied Co-operation

by Philip Lundeberg

In the winter of 1917-18, evidently before reports of the Treaty of Brest-Litovsk had reached Western Europe, the American artist Henry Reuterdahl completed an enlistment poster that colourfully evoked Allied co-operation during the Great War. Buoyantly entitled 'All Together', his canvas depicted six seagoing Allies, linked in comradeship, ranged against a dreadnought background. Centre-stage was afforded to a stalwart British tar, who looked expectantly to an exuberant Yankee bluejacket, the pair joined in turn by a Tsarist sailor and a French matelot, flanked finally by a salty Italian and a somewhat enigmatic Japanese seaman.[1] Reuterdahl, who had served as an artist/correspondent on the world cruise of Theodore Roosevelt's Great White Fleet, clearly possessed international perspective, subtly suggesting in this canvas the regional division of operational responsibilities then employed by the Allies against the Central Powers.[2] However imminent may have been the Tsarist regime's collapse, however remote Reuterdahl's canvas may have been from the grim realities of the Eastern and Western Fronts, or indeed from the harsh experience of Allied naval and merchant ship crews under the lash of unrestricted U-boat warfare, the American's naive poster nevertheless embodied a basic fact that appears astonishing in the perspective of WWII. Three years after the Kaiser's armies had launched their ill-fated march on Paris, all of the principal Allied navies (and indeed those of the Central Powers) still mustered relatively intact squadrons of dreadnoughts and supporting vessels, each backed by long-established bases and training establishments, located in home territories or those of an Allied partner. Herein must lie a clue - a needed perspective if you will - to any brief and selective appreciation of Allied naval co-operation a generation later during successive stages of the second Battle of the Atlantic.

This model of Allied naval co-operation in WWI was well within the professional experience of many Western naval leaders, even as the dismemberment of Czechoslovakia and mounting German demands on Poland revealed fully the failure of international collective security arrangements under the League of Nations. Great Britain's war plans, approved by the Board of Admiralty on 30 January 1939, envisaged hostilities not only with Germany but also Italy, England's erstwhile ally; nor did they blink the possibility of eventual intervention with the Axis powers by Japan, the Royal Navy's traditional Far Eastern protégé. Plans for renewed co-operation with the French Navy had been substantially advanced during Anglo-French naval staff conferences at London in spring 1939, parallel to RAF talks with French Air Force leaders. Included in this pre-war naval *entente* were agreements on geographical disposition of the fleets at the outset of hostilities, co-ordination of areas of command and the establishment of convoy routes and escorting procedures.[3] It was confirmed at London that French naval forces, with major bases in southern France and North Africa, would undertake prime responsibility for the western Mediterranean, thereby permitting greater British commitment to the eastern Mediterranean. As for the Atlantic, the French agreed to maintain a *'force de raid'* (two new battleships, an aircraft carrier, three cruisers and 10 destroyers) for operations from Brest against enemy surface raiders anticipated in the Eastern Atlantic, while committing 10 additional destroyers to the Channel patrol. Broadly consistent with Anglo-French naval dispositions throughout WWI, the 1939 agreement thus again allocated prime responsibility in the North Atlantic, Norwegian Sea and North Sea to the RN, taking maximum advantage of its long-established bases on the south, west and north-east coasts of the British Isles.[4]

Across the Atlantic, meanwhile, the administration of President Franklin D. Roosevelt, deeply disturbed by events both on the Continent and in the Far East, had initiated exploratory discussions with the British Admiralty, first in January 1938, when Captain Royal E. Ingersoll, a communications specialist in WWI and currently Director of War Plans in the Office of the Chief of Naval Operations, visited London to explore means of Anglo-American co-operation, in view of the increasing likelihood that both powers would become involved in war with Japan. As personally directed by the President prior to his departure, Ingersoll discussed with the Admiralty War Plans Division the necessary arrangements regarding command relationships, communications, liaison officers and the preparation of codes and ciphers - all matters of daily relevance to Ingersoll in his subsequent role as wartime commander of the US Atlantic Fleet.[5] Ensuing events in Europe, notably the triumph of Franco in the Spanish Civil War and the adherence of Portugal as well as Spain to the Anti-Comintern Pact, raised concern at the US State Department over possible Fascist penetration of Latin America and resulted during 1938-39 in a thorough re-examination of Western Hemisphere defence plans by the Army and Navy Joint Planning Committee. The estimate of the world situation, developed by that Committee's staff, produced during 1939-41 what Tracy B. Kittredge has identified as 'the basic strategic concepts of the United States military forces which were later to be accepted as the fundamental strategy of United Nations forces in World War II'.[6]

Following the conclusion of the Anglo-French naval agreements at London early in 1939, the Admiralty dispatched Commander T. C. Hampton, RN, of the Plans Division to Washington in May for exploratory discussions on Fleet dispositions in the Far East, North Atlantic and Caribbean, in the event that Britain found herself at war with both Germany and Italy. These informal conversations (involving the Chief of Naval Operations, Admiral William D. Leahy, and the head of CNO Plans Division, Rear Admiral Robert L. Ghormley) elicited Leahy's personal view that in the event of simultaneous

British confrontation with Germany, Italy and Japan, the United States would seek control of the Pacific while Allied fleets in Europe undertook primary responsibility for the Atlantic and Mediterranean. Leahy, who had commanded a troop transport in the Atlantic in WWI, anticipated that if the US entered a European conflict, American naval forces would co-operate with the RN in organizing and escorting trans-Atlantic convoys.[7]

Possessing at this juncture a one-ocean navy, the US confronted a major strategic dilemma. The outbreak of WWII in Europe, combined with heightened tension in the Far East, gave strong impetus to efforts by the Roosevelt administration to complete plans for Western hemispheric defence, including 'short of war' co-operation with European democracies prepared to oppose German expansionism.[8] Such co-operation constantly confronted strong isolationist sentiment, bi-partisan in character, in the US, a factor complicated by the approach of the 1940 Presidential election.[9] Increasing Japanese truculence made it evident, as Ernest J. King would later recall, that 'that country would enter the war at the most propitious moment'. As the American naval chieftain observed, 'we were forced to retain the major part of our naval strength in the Pacific, in spite of the unfavourable situation in Europe, reflecting the possibility of the need of our naval strength in the Atlantic'.[10]

Britain's own strategic position during the 'Phoney War' of 1939-40 did not appear as unfavourable. Able in Far Eastern waters to rely on the deterrent presence of the US fleet based in Hawaii, and on French naval superiority in the western Mediterranean, the Admiralty could confront the threat of German surface raiders and U-boats (then restricted to their North Sea havens) with reasonable prospect of success, facilitated by growing logistical and escort support from the Royal Canadian Navy in the western Atlantic. During the fateful spring of 1940, however, Britain's strategic position deteriorated rapidly, owing initially to the success of Operation Weserübung, the astonishingly swift and well co-ordinated German conquest of neutral and unprepared Denmark and Norway. Aided by decryption of Allied diplomatic and naval radio traffic, Wehrmacht contingents landed almost simultaneously on 9 April at Oslo and five strategic points on the Norwegian Sea, ranging from Kristiansand South and Stavanger (Sola Airfield) to Bergen, Trondheim and Narvik, all destined to figure in the developing Atlantic struggle.[11] Luftwaffe dive-bombers and transports, which overwhelmed half-mobilized Norse coast defences and warships, subsequently provided German naval and ground forces with decisive support against belated Anglo-French counter-landings in northern Norway. Notwithstanding severe German surface losses and the notable torpedo failures experienced by U-boats, Weserübung powerfully altered the geography of the Atlantic battle. With air and naval bases rapidly consolidated on the Norwegian Sea, Hitler's forces had achieved that major objective envisioned a generation earlier by Vice Admiral Wolfgang Wegener - namely, release from the Kriegsmarine's North Sea trap, and possession of a strategic position which not only flanked any future Allied supply effort to Soviet Arctic ports but also brought Scapa Flow into effective range of Luftwaffe bombers.[12]

The German invasion of Norway would ultimately bring both moral and material benefit to the Allied cause, the latter including a dozen surviving Norse naval vessels capable of convoy escort and minesweeping duty; some 4 million gross tons of merchant shipping (including nearly 2 million in critically needed tanker tonnage); and, usefully for the Norwegian regime in exile, that nation's gold reserves.[13]

For the moment, however, Weserübung had provided an ominous portent of impending events on the Continent. Official paralysis engendered by traditional neutrality (as well as selective fifth column activity, which had undermined Norwegian resistance) assisted Hitler's forces during their subsequent invasion of the Low Countries in May, en route to Paris and the English Channel. Those contingents of the Royal Netherlands Navy based in home waters doggedly resisted the Wehrmacht's ground and airborne advance, but suffered heavy losses under heavy Luftwaffe attacks from Rotterdam to the Zuider Zee. Even as British destroyers evacuated Queen Wilhelmina and her Government on 13 May, some 500 Dutch merchantmen, liners, trawlers and tugs, aggregating 2,750,000 gross tons, managed to clear home waters despite extensive Luftwaffe mining efforts. Like the Norwegian merchant marine, they would make a critical contribution in the widening Atlantic struggle.[14]

The Wehrmacht's subsequent advances deep into France (which by early July had resulted in establishment of German air and naval bases both on the English Channel and the Bay of Biscay) would deprive Britain, following the armistice at Compiègne, of vital support from the French Navy. The government of Paul Reynaud, prior to its resignation, had desperately sought assurances of US intervention, as a basis for continuing the struggle with French forces from North Africa. President Roosevelt, then seeking Congressional approval of his Two-Ocean Navy legislation, even as the bulk of the US fleet remained based at Pearl Harbor, found himself unprepared to provide either the 'clouds of planes' or political assurances thus urgently requested by Paris.[15]

Even more troubling for Washington than this exchange, which ended Anglo-American efforts to forestall the establishment of a collaborationist regime in France, was a broader question. How, with limited naval forces in the Atlantic, could the US deal with the possible acquisition of the British as well as the French fleet by a triumphant Reich? Under the indomitable Winston Churchill, the British Empire was committed to resisting Axis overseas expansion even if the home islands, as well as the Continental democracies, were overwhelmed by the Luftwaffe, overrun by the Wehrmacht and subdued. But the haunting question remained as to whether Churchill's regime could survive an evidently impending German invasion of southern England.[16]

Less than one year into WWII, Great Britain found itself the last bastion of European democracy, totally devoid of any major allies - a fact poignantly emphasized if we re-examine the Reuterdahl canvas of 1917. Far removed indeed were the dreadnought contingents of the US, France, Italy, Japan and the Soviet Union from Britain's vital Western Approaches. For more than a year (which would witness the tragic pre-emptive attack by the British forces against French fleet units at Mers-el-Kebir, the Luftwaffe's prolonged assault on the British Isles, and the Wehrmacht's conquest of Yugoslavia, Greece and Crete), Britain and her Dominion partners fought the battle for survival virtually alone, doggedly sustaining their vulnerable Atlantic convoy routes. With Wehrmacht divisions and air flotillas mustering in July 1940 for Operation Seelöwe, the grim drama in Western Europe approached its climax, the Battle of Britain, upon whose outcome all else depended.[17]

The relevance of that massive Luftwaffe assault to the emerging Atlantic struggle had been foretold in a perceptive estimate by Colonel Josef ('Beppo') Schmid, head of the German Air Intelligence, who had advised Marshal Göring in November 1939:

From Germany's point of view, Britain is the most dangerous of all our possible enemies. The war cannot be ended in a manner favourable to us as long as Britain has not been mastered....Operations against the British Isles should begin soon, and in as great a strength as possible....The enemy must not be allowed the time to use past experience to perfect his defences. Furthermore, economic assistance from the British and the French colonial empires and from neutrals, particularly the USA, and the encirclement of Germany, must not be permitted to come fully into operation.

Focusing on the strangulation of Britain's harbour facilities and overseas supply, Colonel Schmid urged specifically that :

The most important ports must be attacked without exception....London, Liverpool, Hull, Bristol and Glasgow. In all these ports the primary target will be shipping. As secondary targets, dockyards and warehouse installations, in particular food and oil stores and silos may be attacked. Raids must be constantly repeated - by day and by night. To achieve the maximum effect, even small formations may be usefully employed.

Warships under repair and under construction on the point of completion are also to be considered targets worthy of attention.[18]

The Battle of Britain, launched on 10 July, had remarkable relevance to the evolving Battle of the Atlantic. The Luftwaffe's initial daylight attacks on Channel and East Coast convoys were followed by massed dive bombing attacks on major south-coast ports, actions that revealed the vulnerability of the Ju-87 Stuka to RAF fighter aircraft, while confirming the Admiralty's earlier wisdom in diverting inbound ocean convoys to west coast entrepôts.[19] RAF Fighter Command's squadrons, a number of which had not yet been committed to the battle for France and the Low Countries owing to the concurrent danger of massive air attacks on London,[20] became the prime objective in subsequent Luftwaffe bombing sorties against airfields in southern England, attacks whose costly failure nevertheless focused Marshal Göring's attention even more intently on that critical, elusive element of Britain's defences.

On 28 August, Liverpool sustained its first massive aerial attack, by some 150 bombers, opening a week of damaging raids that nevertheless failed to disrupt convoy arrivals and sailings.[21] German intentions of finishing off Fighter Command, a necessary prelude for Hitler's invasion attempt, provided the central motive for ensuing massed Luftwaffe raids on metropolitan London. Confounded by heavy bomber losses and the continued vigour of Fighter Command's Spitfire and Hurricane squadrons, Göring abandoned massed formations but continued nightly raids on the British capital. Throughout, the Luftwaffe had underestimated the role of Britain's extensive radar network in the defence of that nation's airfields, seaports and inland industrial centres.

Thus ended German prospects for gaining air supremacy over Britain's vital industrial areas and major ports of discharge. Liverpool, Bristol, Birmingham and other Midlands centres sustained further attacks during and also following the Battle of Britain, but, lying beyond the effective range of German fighter planes, those embattled cities' fighter and anti-aircraft defences proved impossible for decimated German bomber squadrons to overcome. By the end of October 1940, Luftwaffe headquarters had lost the possibility of severing Britain's maritime jugular, so clearly targeted by its Intelligence chief 11 months earlier.[22]

It must be noted that Fighter Command's heroic order of battle during autumn 1940 included several squadrons of Czech, Polish and Canadian airmen, all desperately needed at a juncture when trained pilots were in shorter supply than the redoubtable Spitfires themselves. The multi-national character of Britain's armed forces that emerged in those perilous months inevitably complicated their deployment against the battle-seasoned elements of the Wehrmacht, yet, as dramatically demonstrated in Fighter Command, much was gained in the intense, nigh suicidal determination of those volunteers to maximize German losses and ultimately fight their way back to the Continent.[23]

Thus the scene shifted from Britain's still embattled cities to her vital Northwest Approaches and the growing menace of Admiral Karl Dönitz's U-boats. This threat would generate complex logistic and operational arrangements between Britain, her Dominion partners and an increasingly restive US. Space limits and a sense of balance preclude an extended account of the measures undertaken by Washington, following the outset of WWII, to provide material assistance to the Allied cause, but some brief remarks should be made.

These measures began notably with the 'cash and carry' provisions regarding arms sales, authorized under the revised Neutrality Act of 4 November 1939. Isolationist sentiment, both academic and political, remained strong in America as the Presidential campaign of 1940 approached, yet a growing concern for hemispheric security (sharply heightened by the fall of France) generated popular support for President Roosevelt's executive order in late July implementing the transfer of 50 ageing destroyers to the RN, in exchange for 99-year leases on Dominion naval and air bases ranging from British Guiana to Newfoundland.[24] Isolationism emerged only belatedly during the election campaign of 1940, and, though bitterly contested in Congress, the passage of the Lend-Lease Act of March 1941, after Roosevelt's third inauguration, was followed by additional 'short of war' measures. Seizure of Axis assets and shipping in the US was followed by actions to deny Greenland to possible use by Luftwaffe bombers as a base for air strikes against North America, including the establishment of offshore patrols by US Coast Guard cutters and construction of airfields and radio, radar and weather stations in southern Greenland.[25]

In July 1941, six weeks after the dramatic sortie of the raider battleship *Bismarck* through the Denmark Strait, President Roosevelt authorized the dispatch of US Marines to relieve British forces in Iceland. In support of this deployment, Admiral Ernest J. King (then Commander in Chief, Atlantic Fleet) established Task Force 1, charged with escorting all shipping sailing between the US and Iceland. With commitment from 27 Canadian and the three Free French escort vessels in support of the Iceland convoys, the scene was set for the encounter south-west of Reykjavik on 4 September between the American destroyer *Greer* and U-652. This event marked the Atlantic Fleet's *de facto* entry into the Battle of the Atlantic.[26]

This growing US commitment to the Allied cause, chronicled by Captain Tracy B. Kittredge from the perspective of the American Naval Mission in London, had been paralleled by rapid expansion of war production in the States, including vastly increased warship construction authorized under the Two-Ocean Navy Act of July 1941, the legislation that would provide the men-of-war that fought America's decisive battles in WWII.[27]

As earlier observed, Britain and her Dominions had borne, for more than a year, almost the entire burden of the Atlantic struggle. In September 1941 they initiated the North Russian convoys (as well as shipments via the Middle East) in support of Soviet forces fighting to contain Hitler's armies and Luftwaffe on the Eastern front.[28] How indeed may one discuss Allied co-operation during that critical year? We may profitably focus briefly on the British Isles, that indispensable terminus of the Allied convoy system in the Atlantic.

Beleaguered Britain, whose immense role is easily overlooked, had become, perforce, the citadel and rallying ground for thousands of fighting men who had escaped from the Continent. Hither had been dispatched three of the Polish Navy's most formidable destroyers, even before the outbreak of the war, to be followed subsequently by ships and men of the Norwegian, Netherlands and Free French Navies, as well as volunteers from the Belgian merchant marine. In time, additional Norse seamen, many of whom had made the North Sea passage in fishing boats, would man Norwegian merchantmen or the new British-built escorts of the *Hunt* and *Savage* classes.[29] The RAF Coastal Command, whose British-based patrols effectively drove U-boats from the Western Approaches in spring 1941, included squadrons of volunteer airmen from Czechoslovakia, Poland and Norway.[30] Doggedly hospitable amid the rubble of cities, factories and dockyards blasted in the ongoing Blitz, the British government provided quarters, victualling, equipment and training for increasing thousands of Allied soldiers, seamen and airmen arriving from the Continent or North America. Under status-of-forces agreements with the governments-in-exile in London, these forces were incorporated by national units into the British armed services, retaining their own internal leadership and discipline.[31] Through Anglo-Canadian agreements concluded in September 1939, large numbers of British, Canadian and Norwegian volunteers received flight instruction under the Commonwealth aerial training programme at RCAF bases in Canada.[32]

Meanwhile, following relocation of the RN's Western Approaches Command from Plymouth to Liverpool in February 1941, its new chief, Admiral Sir Percy Noble, carried out a thorough overhaul of Britain's anti-submarine training and convoy control arrangements, including rigorous escort group work-up at remote Tobermory and the co-ordination of navy, Coastal Command and shipping control activities in his Western Approaches Operations Room at Derby House in Liverpool. In this manner, escort vessels of the British, Canadian and exile navies were welded into tactical groups more capable of dealing with devastating new U-boat wolf-pack attacks encountered in the North Atlantic during the winter of 1940-41.[33]

The subsequent effectiveness of CINCWA headquarters in directing Atlantic convoy escort and routeing operations derived in substantial part from communications Intelligence, whose exceptional development (also by the people of this battered, beleaguered isle) must be underlined. As Olav Riste has recently observed, Norway entered WWII with no intelligence apparatus with which to evaluate the myriad of confusing indicators preceding Operation Weserübung.[34]

In contrast, Britain entered the conflict with unrivalled experience, garnered notably in the operations of the Admiralty's celebrated Room 40 during 1914-18 in decryption and analysis of German naval radio transmissions. By mid-1941, thanks to vital initial information provided by Polish cryptologists and the subsequent capture of three German naval vessels, Bletchley Park had begun producing decrypted German U-boat traffic for Admiralty Intelligence, on a sufficiently timely basis to permit effective evasive routing by CINCWA of the Atlantic convoys. While Ultra Intelligence and its sources represented one of Britain's most vital state secrets, it was shared by the Admiralty with a selected few with a need to know at Ottawa and Washington, through personal liaison that rendered far more effective those operations centres responsible for the Western Atlantic. Ultra Intelligence, generated in Britain, soon provided one of the most vital elements of Allied co-operation in the Battle of the Atlantic.[35]

Meanwhile, in the western reaches of the North Atlantic convoy route, the

Royal Canadian Navy and RCAF sought to make their own distinctive contributions to the defence of shipping proceeding eastwards to the British Isles. Those efforts had been enhanced in August 1940 at a conference between Prime Minister Mackenzie King and President Roosevelt at Ogdensburg, NY. Arranged shortly after the fall of France, this conference established a Permanent Joint Board of Defence, charged with urgent studies on material and personnel problems inherent in the air, land and sea defence of North America. Favourably received by both nations, the Ogdensburg Agreement represented not only an historic military rapprochement but indeed a defensive alliance between the parties, providing an indispensable vehicle for identifying urgent Canadian armament requirements - particularly for neighbouring Newfoundland, strategic western terminus of North Atlantic convoys.[36]

Fully appreciating the respective logistical roles of Halifax, NS, and Newfoundland's valuable harbour at St John's, the Joint Board recognized early that Canadian Army and Air Force elements were insufficient to protect the RCN operating base then developing at St John's. The Board's consideration of possible establishment of an American air base in Newfoundland proved a prelude to the bilateral Anglo-American decision, derived from the Destroyer-Naval Base Agreement of September 1940, to press rapid development by the USN of an advance convoy support base located at Argentia, near the head of Placentia Bay.[37]

On 29 January 1941, as construction got underway at Argentia, a series of secret staff discussions (not including Canada) began at Washington between British and US armed services representatives, for the purpose of shaping a global strategy in the event the US found itself 'compelled to resort to war'. Central to the resulting 'ABC-1 Staff Agreement' was the conclusion that 'Since Germany is the predominant member of the Axis powers, the Atlantic and European war is considered to be the decisive theatre'.[38] Offensive in strategic intent, by contrast to the defence-oriented Ogdensburg Agreement, this pivotal report on US-UK staff conversations proposed that, following anticipated American entry into the conflict, the US would undertake strategic direction of US, British and other associated military forces in the Western Hemisphere, excepting 'the waters and territories in which Canada assumes responsibility for the strategic direction of military forces, as may be defined in the US-Canada joint agreements'.[39] A separate Crown Colony strategically located at the mouth of the St Lawrence, Newfoundland was vital to the military security of both Canada and the US. Accordingly, the subsequently revised US-Canadian defence plan, designated ABC-22, identified the defence of Newfoundland as a common responsibility of the American and Canadian Armies and the RCAF.[40]

For the RCN, already operating under CINCWA direction as the Dominion's prime offensive force in the Northwest Atlantic, these and subsequent Anglo-American arrangements proved troubling. Since the establishment in July 1941 of its Newfoundland Escort Force, based at St John's, the navy had augmented that force with British-built destroyers and the first Canadian-built corvettes.

Though manned by inexperienced crews and lacking radar or modern anti-submarine ordnance, the force had managed to extend its convoy operations to mid-Atlantic.[41] During the secret Churchill-Roosevelt summit at Argentia that produced the historic Atlantic Charter in mid-August, however, plans were developed by Admiral Sir Percy Noble (CINCWA) and Admiral Ernest J. King (CINCLANT) for the USN to assume strategic responsibility for convoys operating between North America and a 'Mid-Ocean Meeting Point' south of Iceland.[42] Much to his chagrin, Rear Admiral L. W. Murray, RCN, Commander of the Newfoundland Escort Force, found his undermanned force under the 'co-ordinating supervision' of a non-belligerent superior, Rear Admiral Arthur Le R. Bristol, USN, the newly appointed Commander of USNOB Argentia and of the Atlantic Fleet's Support Force, operating from that base in fulfilment of American responsibilities east of Halifax. Fortunately, cordial personal relations enabled these *de facto* allied commanders to surmount these awkward command arrangements.

Murray's force continued escorting slow SC convoys between Sydney, NS, and Iceland. Murray's force also shepherded fast HX transients between Halifax and a 'Western Ocean Meeting Point' off Newfoundland, while Bristol's Support Force destroyers assumed the escort of the latter convoys from WESTOMP to their juncture with British escort groups off Iceland. By all reports, these were bitter months of hard learning for both forces, owing not least to a shortage of shipboard radar and concurrent German decryption of convoy communications.[43]

During the autumn of 1941, mounting American and British aircraft production permitted an extension of Anglo-Canadian-US shipping protection in the Atlantic. Convoy cover became available not only from RCAF patrols flying out of Newfoundland, but also from USN aircraft from Argentia - and indeed USN Catalinas, plus three Coastal Command squadrons (including Norwegian-manned No. 330) based in Iceland.[44] Following activation of the Biscay U-boat bases, Dönitz's wolf-packs had decimated North Atlantic convoys for nearly a year. They now found the tonnage war less profitable in those waters. This trend stemmed partly from the weakening of Luftwaffe reconnaissance, as German air strength shifted to the new Eastern Front, as well as Hitler's insistence on moving more U-boats to the Gibraltar approaches and Mediterranean in support of Rommel's faltering North African campaign.[45] Events even farther afield would soon alter the Atlantic situation.

In February 1942, two months after Japan's fateful attack on Pearl Harbor, Admiral Dönitz succeeded in resuming serious attrition of Allied and neutral shipping in the Atlantic. Having only relatively few U-boats, this was an astonishing feat. Long reluctant to enter the European conflict, owing in some measure to its Pacific commitments, the US had now (like Norway and the Netherlands) been thrust into the Western alliance, with its fleet strength severely diminished in the process. Unlike Oslo in 1940, Washington possessed significant Intelligence resources. Yet indications of the timing of Japan's opening moves in the Western Pacific, revealed by skilled cryptographers, were mis-managed by civil and military authorities in Washington, with catastrophic results in Hawaii and the Philippines that would reverberate in the Atlantic.[46] As Tokyo had conspicuously not communicated its intentions either to Berlin or Rome, neither Bletchley Park nor the Admiralty could glean anything from German radio intercepts that might have alerted Washington as to Japan's initial targets.[47]

First indications of a German effort to exploit the anticipated inexperience of Canadian and US coastal defence forces became apparent to the Admiralty Plotting Room late in December 1941, enabling its staff to predict the appearance of five U-boats between New York and Cape Race by 13 January.[48] Having anticipated such a coastal assault, the newly appointed C-in-C, US Fleet, Admiral King, had proposed and subsequently secured Admiralty approval of modifications to North Atlantic convoy arrangements, designed to improve the efficiency of Canadian and US escort forces. These proposals (related to plans for a series of early troop convoy sailings) included a more southerly winter routeing for mercantile convoys and the establishment of a Mid-Ocean Escort Force of British, Canadian and American escort groups that, with more extended operations by local NEF groups, could accompany fast convoys from Newfoundland directly to Ireland.[49]

The popular 'Newfie to Derry' run, destined to maximize Allied use of the more adequate replenishment facilities at Argentia and Londonderry, marked an important logistical advance. However, it had barely been established when the stunning force of the U-boat Command's Operation Paukenschlag fell upon Allied shipping off the east coast of North America. First to enter Canadian waters was U-123 (Hardegen), whose initial success in sinking nine unescorted merchantmen between Halifax and Cape Hatteras opened an offshore offensive that, to London's dismay, accounted for 45 merchantmen off Canadian shores alone in January to February. Subsequent waves of U-boats encountered air patrols and strongly escorted shipping off Nova Scotia, but the concurrent loss of unescorted merchantmen, particularly tankers, from Massachusetts Bay to Cape Hatteras had meanwhile risen alarmingly.[50]

Weak Eastern Sea Frontier air and surface forces failed to initiate coastal convoy operations, and local Civil Defence authorities neglected to darken the East Coast shoreline, creating a veritable shooting gallery for the veteran submariners selected for this operation. During the first few months of 1942, independently operating U-boats sank 82 merchantmen aggregating 491,700 gross tons in American coastal waters. This cumulative disaster generated mounting concern at the Admiralty and the new COMINCH headquarters in Washington, which both recognized that barely a dozen U-boats were operating concurrently in the Eastern Sea Frontier.[51]

Admiral King - succinctly characterized by Morison as 'a man of adamant' - inherited no Operational Intelligence Centre in Washington and was handicapped by an Operations staff at loggerheads with its Intelligence counterparts. Nevertheless, he displayed a firm grasp of basic priorities in deploying his navy's diminished assets to meet its inescapable world-wide responsibilities.[52] King's limited options were shaped not only by major American battleship losses at Pearl Harbor, but also by decisions reached at Christmas 1941 during the Arcadia Conference, urgently convened in Washington. During that first wartime summit, Churchill, Roosevelt and their military chiefs reaffirmed their earlier ABC-1 decision to give priority to the defeat of Germany. They further approved General George C. Marshall's insistence on the principle of unified Allied command in all operational theatres. COMINCH, although determined to stabilize the Pacific situation by despatching major combat reinforcements that might slow the Japanese advance toward Indonesia and Australia, had to deploy most Atlantic Fleet forces in support of a rapid commitment of American air and ground forces to the European theatre, which offered the earliest opportunity to bring relief to the hard-pressed Soviet Union.[53] Thus, coincidentally with the extension of the Mid-Ocean Escort Force's operations to Londonderry in support of North Atlantic trade convoys, King initiated American troopship movements to Ireland, providing them typically with 10 destroyers and a battleship to deal with possible surface threats.[54] In reality a resumption of the USN's primary role in WWI, King's commitment of Atlantic Fleet destroyer squadrons has been overlooked or misconstrued in critiques of the Paukenschlag debacle.[55]

These early troop deployments, urgently sought by Churchill to allay British concern about American resolve, proved costly to the Allied war effort. For COMINCH headquarters, the apparent necessity of employing the Eastern Sea Frontier's limited air and surface forces for patrol rather than convoy operations was vitiated by a mounting toll of offshore tanker sinkings. By March 1942 these losses threatened to cripple not only burgeoning American and Canadian war production, but also the tenuous fuel resources in Britain, on which the wide-ranging operations of the RN and RAF Commands depended.[56] Mounting British concern and exasperation, transmitted to Admiral King in February, was further forcefully conveyed by Churchill to Roosevelt via Harry Hopkins on 12 March. This effectively reinforced advice on the urgent necessity of convoy that had been offered to the Admiralty by the American Vice Admiral William S. Sims a quarter century earlier.

Anglo-Canadian assistance eased the escort problem, enabling COMINCH headquarters to authorize the sailing of daylight convoys between anchorages in the Eastern Sea Frontier on 1 April, utilizing a variety of local craft, reinforced shortly by the arrival of 24 British anti-submarine trawlers. East Coast merchant ship losses were effectively reduced by Canadian initiative in instituting tanker convoys, with instant results, between Trinidad and Halifax. At Admiral King's request, the Canadians began operating convoys between Boston and Halifax, employing vessels drawn from the RCN's overworked but durable Western Local Escort Force.[57] On the recommendation of CINCLANT, Sea Frontier and COMINCH representatives queried by Admiral King,

COMINCH authorized Vice Admiral Adolphus Andrews, Commander Eastern Sea Frontier, to initiate convoys between New York and Key West. This was the kernel of what developed in May 1942 into the USN's widening Interlocking Convoy System. During this painful shakedown period, in which COMINCH headquarters still lacked an Operational Intelligence Centre, the navy had benefited from earlier Canadian assistance in establishing shipping control operations by American naval port authorities. Of immense assistance was the arrival in May of the sagacious director of the Admiralty's OIC Submarine Tracking Room, Commander Roger Winn, RN, who secured King's backing in establishing a similar Tracking Room that began to co-ordinate incoming U-boat Intelligence for the Atlantic Fleet, Sea Frontiers and the Convoy and Routeing Section of COMINCH Operations Division.[58]

Subsequent extension of the USN's Interlocking Convoy System to the Caribbean and the Gulf of Mexico, necessitated by Dönitz's southward shift of U-boat operations during May-July 1942, was enhanced by improved use of available air and surface escort forces, as well as the cumulative effect of Ultra (still in partial blackout), HF/DF and other Intelligence sources made possible through the new command organization.[59]

Concurrently with this painful demonstration of Dönitz's 'tonnage warfare' strategy in the western Atlantic, the Allied war effort was imperilled by mounting losses on the storm-wracked Arctic convoy route, vital to supporting Soviet armed forces battered by the Wehrmacht's summer offensive of 1942. Here the Admiralty faced a problem far harder than the *Bismarck* episode, namely the movement of high-risk convoys round North Cape under the menace of combined attacks by U-boats, Luftwaffe bombers and fighters, and capital ships based in northern Norway. Born of Hitler's intuition of Allied landing efforts in northern Norway, those potent forces were strengthened early in 1942 by the arrival of the battleship *Tirpitz* and the heavy cruisers *Prinz Eugen* and *Admiral Scheer* in Trondheim Fjord, raising the stakes for subsequent convoys to North Russia. Air and naval units of the Soviet Northern Fleet were barely adequate to provide escort for Arctic convoys east of Bear Island, an area dominated by growing Luftwaffe squadrons, with consequent British foreboding as Churchill sought to break a growing accumulation of war supplies from North America urgently requested by Marshal Stalin.[60]

Heavy weather and some good fortune limited Allied ship losses on the Murmansk run during spring 1942. Such was the prelude for the departure of eastbound PQ17 from Iceland on 26 June, accompanied by an Anglo-American cruiser support force and covered by a powerful task force that included the battleships HMS *Duke of York* and USS *Washington* and the aircraft carrier HMS *Victorious*. On the afternoon of 4 July, having received from reconnaissance and Ultra intercepts no indication that *Tirpitz* and her consorts had moved to intercept the 33-ship convoy, the Admiralty withdrew the Home Fleet cover force from the U-boat-filled waters south-west of Spitzbergen while the cruiser force assisted PQ17 in fighting off heavy Luftwaffe attacks east of

Bear Island. The Admiralty's further decision that night to withdraw the cruiser support force and scatter the convoy proved tragically premature. The outraged merchant seamen and armed gun crews were exposed to a running massacre by German submariners and airmen. On 5 July, *Tirpitz*, *Admiral Hipper* and *Admiral Scheer* made a brief sortie. They need not have bothered. By then, 23 of the convoy's 33 merchantmen had been sunk.[61]

In grim counterpoint to continued Allied shipping losses in the Caribbean, the PQ17 disaster persuaded London to suspend further midsummer convoys to North Russia and to gamble on small flights of unescorted merchantmen. That Anglo-American naval understanding had been severely strained was reflected in Admiral King's decision to dispatch USS *Washington* and the carrier USS *Wasp* for more profitable employment in the Pacific.[62]

Allied shipping losses had meanwhile risen again in the North Atlantic, owing to continuing delay of sea-going escort production, the failure of Allied bombing operations to stem mounting U-boat construction and, in February 1942, the introduction of the German Triton cipher for Atlantic U-boat traffic. This blacked out a critical source of Ultra Intelligence virtually to the year's end.[63] American destroyer groups, heavily committed to a growing number of high-speed troop transport movements to the UK and North Africa, played a far less prominent role than British and Canadian escort groups in the defence of North Atlantic trade convoys, which sustained severe losses in mid-ocean during autumn 1942.

Notable among the successful merchant convoy operations was the eastbound passage of HX217, escorted by a British destroyer and a corvette, three Norwegian-manned corvettes and the Polish destroyer *Burza*. During the latter half of 1942, 14 eastbound Allied troop convoys transported some 35,000 Allied serviceman without loss, a mere prelude to the vast number that would find equally secure passage to Europe during 1943-45.[64] In November 1942, that early achievement (aided greatly by British-generated HF/DF fixes and limited Ultra Intelligence) was over-shadowed by the movement of some 107,000 British and US troops from England and North America to North Africa, at the outset of Operation Torch. In this, CINCWA and Atlantic Fleet headquarters had co-operated effectively in suppressing a substantial U-boat threat while co-ordinating the complex Allied task force movements to objectives stretching from French Morocco to Algeria.[65] Although forgotten by others, the subsequent safe passage of North Atlantic troop convoys and independent 'Monster' troop transports (facilitated by Bletchley Park's solution of the Triton cipher in December 1942) remains fresh in the memories of many fortunate Allied servicemen.[66]

American plans for launching cross-Channel operations in the spring of 1943, postponed by the Torch commitment, were further delayed by decisions made at the Roosevelt-Churchill summit at Casablanca in January 1943. The Wehrmacht's position at Stalingrad was becoming desperate. While projecting an Allied movement from North Africa to Sicily and Italy to relieve the Eastern

Front further, the Anglo-American pre-requisite for sustaining all operations against Hitler's 'Fortress Europe' was the defeat of the U-boat menace.[67] In January, confronted by ominous attrition of Britain's limited pool of merchant shipping and the continued lag in American merchant ship construction, Churchill felt obliged to reduce cargo shipments to the Far East sharply, in order to ease Britain's own growing import shortages. During the first three weeks of March, a calamitous rise in *convoy* sinkings raised grave doubts in the Admiralty about the continued viability of trade convoys. London thus faced a shipping crisis that threatened not only logistical support for British forces in the Mediterranean and India-Burma theatres, but the very existence of the British Isles as the indispensable base for eventual cross-Channel operations. Alerted to the emergency by Allied shipping authorities, President Roosevelt determined late in March to meet Britain's import requirements, even at the risk of retarding American troop movements.[68]

In this context, subsequent Allied success in reducing North Atlantic trade convoy losses during spring 1943 was all the more remarkable, for in March, Admiral Dönitz had no fewer than 400 U-boats in service, some 182 of which were committed to Atlantic operations.[69] During April and May, which saw upwards of 60 boats deployed in mid-Atlantic, CINCWA at times found it virtually impossible to route both trade and troop convoys clear of the Germans' constantly shifting patrol lines.

Fortunately for well-worn British and Canadian ocean escort groups, the new Commander of Western Approaches, Admiral Sir Max Horton, was now able to strengthen convoy protection in the 'Black Pit', not only with VLR air patrols but also the activation of five British 'Support Groups', one of which included the escort carrier HMS *Biter*. This last was an early manifestation of Admiral King's unrelenting emphasis on American escort carrier production.

These roving hunter groups (notably exemplified by Captain F. J. Walker's 2nd Support Group) rapidly perfected new multi-ship 'creeping' attacks that took full advantage of Ultra Intelligence, shipboard radar and HF/DF, as well as new ahead-thrown weaponry and increasingly effective ship-to-ship tactical co-ordination. When additional escort carriers, HMS *Archer* and USS *Bogue*, entered the mid-ocean battle, CINCWA was able to punch his convoys through U-boat patrol lines when necessary.[70]

More elemental factors, it must be recognized, were involved in the passage of eastbound Convoy ONS5. Early in May 1943, east of the Grand Banks, the escorts of this 43-ship convoy inflicted a staggering defeat upon a concentration of nearly 60 U-boats. Shepherded by Commander (later Vice Admiral Sir) Peter Gretton's seasoned but short-legged ocean escort, ONS5 was badly scattered by full gales in the icy waters off Cape Farewell. Reformed with difficulty by Gretton, the convoy sustained some two dozen attacks by elements of Gruppen Fink and Amsel on the foggy night of 5-6 May, losing a dozen merchantmen. However, taking full advantage of radar and aided by the arrival of a support group from St John's, the slender British escort managed to reverse the situation, repeatedly moving out to surprise approaching surfaced U-boats in the lowering fogbanks. Four stalkers were sunk and others damaged, and the battered convoy was extricated without further loss.

Confounded by a total of seven boats lost to British and Canadian air and surface escorts of ONS5, U-boat Command had sustained the single most serious reverse suffered by German submariners in the two world wars.[71] Dönitz subsequently threw four U-boat groups against a quartet of eastbound convoys, only to take such heavy additional losses from air and surface escorts that on 22 May, he was obliged to withdraw from the long-dreaded 'Black Pit'. This historic North Atlantic victory, won largely by British and Canadian forces, marked, as Roskill well observed, 'one of the decisive stages of the war; for the enemy had made his greatest effort against our Atlantic lifeline - and he had failed'.[72]

In mid-March 1943, during the Atlantic Convoy Conference held at Washington between British, Canadian and US representatives, strategic decisions had overhauled regional convoy control responsibilities and shaped Allied co-operation in the Atlantic virtually for the remainder of WWII. These arrangements effectively raised the RCN and RCAF to full partnership in the ongoing struggle against the U-boats. In accordance with a Conference recommendation subsequently adopted by the Combined Chiefs of Staff, the British and Canadian navies assumed full responsibility for the North Atlantic route, while the USN took charge of the central Atlantic, Caribbean, troop and vital West Indies-United Kingdom oil convoys. Confirming the emergence of Canada in the new Atlantic triumvirate (Reuterdahl's poster updated!) was the establishment of the Northwest Atlantic Command, headed by Rear Admiral L. W. Murray, RCN, and based in Halifax, charged with control of northern Atlantic convoys west of a new 'chop line' established at 47° longitude West. To ease US withdrawal from the North Atlantic run, it was agreed that an American escort carrier group would operate there under CINCWA direction. This arrangement provided USS *Bogue* and her consorts with invaluable hunter-killer experience, soon to be exploited in the central Atlantic.[73]

U-boat losses during spring 1943, soaring to 41 boats in May, had been compounded by a successful turn in Coastal Command's developing offensive against U-boats transiting the Bay of Biscay. Sunderlands and Wellingtons based in southern England had enjoyed only limited success during daylight patrols in the Biscay and Faeroes transit areas, owing to U-boat radar detectors and the Luftwaffe presence. With the arrival of VLR Liberators of the US Army Air Corps' new Anti-Submarine Command and the concurrent installation of centimetric radar and Leigh Lights, Air Marshal Sir John Slessor undertook night operations that brought arresting results against Dönitz's surprised transients, whose radar detection devices failed to pick up their nocturnal stalkers' new radar. In May, employing Leigh Lights on their final approaches, Slessor's airmen sank seven U-boats and damaged the same number in the Bay, when many U-boats - newly fitted with heavy anti-aircraft batteries - were encouraged to fight back if surprised while surfaced.[74] In July, U-boat Command's effort to counter the Bay blitz with group sailings of heavily armed U-boats compounded this historic tactical blunder. CINCWA headquarters had the opportunity to throw British surface Support Groups into the action, with the result that air and surface attack claimed four transients in June and 17 more by early August. Dönitz then ordered his boats to begin furtive passages under Luftwaffe air cover along the Basque coast.[75] Nevertheless, during a two-week period in the outer Biscay and Gibraltar approaches, two Liberator groups of the USAF Anti-Submarine Command, operating from Britain and French Morocco, sighted a dozen U-boats and sank six. Curiously, this notable achievement was followed barely a month later by an agreement on the control of anti-submarine aircraft hammered out by Admiral King and General Marshall that - to the undisguised consternation of Coastal Command - effectively terminated the Anti-Submarine Command's seagoing role.[76]

As a naval airman, Admiral King emphatically preferred to see the Army Air Corps' anti-submarine effort redirected against U-boat building yards and the Biscay bases, the latter of which continued to function despite frequent heavy air attacks.[77] In May 1943, in order to rationalize the USN's growing ASW commitment, both in the Atlantic and Pacific, King moved to establish an integrated anti-submarine command within his Washington headquarters and under his personal direction. Enigmatically described as Tenth Fleet, this was charged with controlling the training and allocation of air and surface ASW forces to all US Atlantic commands, acquiring and disseminating timely U-boat Intelligence to those commands, and co-ordinating scientific research and development in support of Fleet ASW operations. In constant concert with CINCWA and the Admiralty, major contributions would be made to subsequent Atlantic operations by Tenth Fleet's Convoy and Routeing Division, by the U-boat Tracking Room in its Operations Division and by the ASW Operational Research Group. The studies of this group, enhanced by the latest Allied experience, were disseminated monthly in a secret *US Fleet Anti-Submarine Bulletin*, affectionately known as the 'Yellow Peril'.[78] Future students of the Atlantic battle may wish to explore the interchange of scientific, tactical and technical information revealed in such contemporary British, Canadian and US anti-submarine literature.

The establishment of Tenth Fleet (a logical follow-up to the Atlantic Convoy Conference) enabled COMINCH headquarters to exploit more effectively the U-boat Command's decision in late May 1943 to shift its tonnage warfare effort from the North to the Central Atlantic, that major theatre recently re-confirmed as a prime area of US responsibility. With the commissioning of additional escort carriers (CVEs),[79] Admiral Royal E. Ingersoll, Commander of the Atlantic Fleet, was able to dispatch four CVE hunter-killer groups to the waters east of Bermuda, to work over a 17-boat patrol line. This, Gruppe Trutz, had been established by U-boat Command late in May to intercept eastbound troop movements and UGS trade convoys bound for the Mediterranean. Aided by

Ultra Intelligence of the U-boats' dispositions, transmitted by Commander K. A. Knowles' Tenth Fleet Tracking Room, the *Bogue*, *Card* and *Core* groups pinned down the Trutz line with Wildcat and Avenger patrols during June, sinking two boats (including the pack's incautious 'milch cow'), while transiting convoys were diverted well clear of danger.[80] During July and August, Ultra and HF/DF analysis permitted CINCLANT to release CVE groups from close convoy support to operate independently against reported U-boat concentrations, producing no fewer than eight kills by carrier-based aircraft in Dönitz's previously secure refuelling sanctuary south-west of the Azores. Taken in conjunction with concurrent U-refueller losses in Biscay, these sinkings jeopardized future U-boat operations in both the Caribbean and South Atlantic.[81] Such would be the pattern of American CVE group operations in the central Atlantic during the autumn and winter of 1943, accounting for a total of 28 U-boats by the year's end.[82]

During autumn 1943, frustrated by growing 'milch cow' losses that hamstrung anything more than nuisance operations in the Central Atlantic, U-boat Command tested the mettle of British and Canadian ocean escort groups in the North Atlantic, employing *Zaunkönig* acoustic torpedoes that, with moderate escort loss, were promptly countered by British 'Foxer' noise-making gear.[83]

Virtual closure of the North Atlantic air gap (by Canadian, British and American VLR patrol aircraft operating from Newfoundland, Greenland and Iceland, supplemented in October by successful British negotiations for bases in the Azores) now combined with US escort carrier group operations between the Azores and Cape Verde Islands to reduce the U-boat Command's only serious tonnage war options to the Indian Ocean and the North Russian convoy route. In diverse fashion, and complemented by Coastal Command's continuing Biscay patrols, British and American carrier groups would sharply limit the effectiveness of U-boat operations in those waters as well. Allied shipping - largely unescorted east of Capetown - suffered significant losses at the hands of Monsun U-boats in the Indian Ocean during summer 1943 and again at the year's close. The latter period also witnessed the beginning of further sinkings by Japanese I-boats, based on Penang. These were marked by savage atrocities against the merchantmen's defenceless survivors, events unmatched by incidents in the harsh Atlantic battle.

Mounting Indian Ocean sinkings, which exceeded Atlantic losses from June 1943 to March 1944 and again during July and August 1944, would ultimately total 102 ships of 615,791 gross tons. High as it was, that figure could well have been much higher still, had it not been for sustained American escort carrier operations between the Azores, Cape Verdes and the coast of Brazil. Assisted as usual by timely Ultra advisories (as well as the co-operation of Brazilian authorities in making airfields available for the patrol aircraft of Vice Admiral Jonas Ingram's Fourth Fleet command), American carrier groups and land-based Liberators succeeded in sinking 21 U-boats during 1944 at the cost of the escort carrier *Block Island*.[84]

Meanwhile, in the Arctic, where the Admiralty had gambled (with disappointing result) on flights of independently routed merchantmen to Murmansk and Archangel,[85] small convoys were resumed from Loch Ewe late in 1943 to take advantage of prolonged darkness and the support of strong Home Fleet contingents. In December, the appearance of these convoys at Kola Inlet indicated to Soviet authorities their allies' determination to resume major shipments of desperately needed war material. Owing to the earlier immobilization of the battleship *Tirpitz* by British midget submarines, and the success of Admiral Sir Bruce Fraser's Home Fleet support force in sinking the battleship *Scharnhorst* during its Christmas sortie against Convoy JW55B,[86] the Admiralty had temporarily eliminated the German surface threat off North Cape, permitting the deployment of carrier air cover for subsequent North Russia convoys. Luftwaffe re-deployments from the Arctic and back to Germany, necessitated by the Wehrmacht's deepening disaster on the Eastern Front, had already become apparent. In October 1943, an Anglo-American task force including HMS *Duke of York* and USS *Ranger*, operating from Scapa Flow, had carried out an intimidating attack on the German base at Bodö, sinking or damaging some 40,000 gross tons of troop transports and supply ships, and providing FdU Narvik with an ominous portent of future Arctic operations.[87]

Admiralty consideration of employing escort carriers with larger Arctic convoys had been stimulated by the visit in October of Captain Marshall R. Greer, USN, recently detached skipper of the USS *Core*. He brought valuable insight from his successful central Atlantic operations, both on the outfitting of these mass-produced warships and the operational management of their fighter-bomber air groups. Thus, in February 1944, CINCWA dispatched the escort carrier HMS *Chaser* in close support of the 42-ship eastbound Convoy JW57, which completed its passage with the loss of a single escort vessel. On returning with westbound RA57, *Chaser*'s rocket-armed Swordfish biplanes played havoc with Gruppe Werewolf, sinking three boats and damaging others. Subsequent convoys received even more generous support, including Captain F. J. Walker's finely tuned 2nd Support Group, as well as fighter-bomber aircraft operating from the accompanying British escort carriers. During 1944, 18 heavily escorted JW and RA convoys made the stormy passage between Loch Ewe and North Russian ports. With additional substantial support from Soviet forces east of Bear Island, these voyages were exceptionally successful: out of 537 vessels in transit, only nine merchantmen were lost. During that period the Narvik U-flotilla, though armed with acoustic homing torpedoes, lost 20 boats, no fewer than 13 by carrier aircraft attack.[88] Telling the heroic saga of North Russia convoys of 1941-45, Stephen Roskill would later record that in addition to *Scharnhorst* and three destroyers, 38 U-boats had been sunk in Arctic waters, at the cost of 89 Allied merchantmen and 16 warships. The figures clearly reflect the impact of carrier operations in northern waters.[89]

Occupied Norway, strongly garrisoned and heavily fortified at strategic points, remained a major preoccupation for Allied naval authorities to the very end of WWII. With the success of Operation Overlord in summer 1944 and the rapid isolation of the Biscay U-boat bases, Dönitz's deputy, Konteradmiral Eberhard Godt, was obliged to transfer surviving Atlantic boats to available ports in southern and western Norway, particularly Kristiansand South, Bergen and Trondheim. Concern that Norway might become a final redoubt of German resistance, even after the fall of Berlin, gained further dimension with the northward movement of the first Type XXI boats in early spring 1945.

Though delayed in their assembly and trials by Allied bombing of North German building yards, these high underwater speed submersibles presented a serious potential threat to shipping in British home waters and the North Atlantic.[90] Sheltered by formidable bunkers that defied bombing, Norway-based U-boats were no less difficult to detect in outward passage from the irregular coastline. Notwithstanding mounting RAF Bomber Command mine-laying operations off south-west Norway and increased patrols by British submarines and Coastal Command aircraft in the Norwegian Sea, FdU Norway managed to continue servicing and dispatching a disturbing number of snorkel-equipped boats for operations in British coastal waters.[91]

While Anglo-American plans to deal with the Type XXI threat still await full definition, a measure of Allied readiness is found in the mustering of the Atlantic Fleet's veteran escort carrier groups early in March, with NOB Argentia as their advance logistical base. Unwittingly, the U-boat Command, itself in transit to Norway, provided Vice Admiral Jonas Ingram (recently appointed CINCLANT) with an opportunity for a realistic tactical rehearsal, on the fog-bound Newfoundland Banks. Earlier erroneous reports, that the Germans contemplated vengeance strikes against American East Coast cities by conventional U-boats fitted with V-1 launchers, were heightened late in March by the departure of seven U-boats (subsequently identified through Ultra as Gruppe Seewolf) from Norwegian ports. Rather than bombarding the East Coast, their actual intent was to resume pack operations against North Atlantic convoys, in order to draw British forces from home waters. Gruppe Seewolf was methodically tracked by London, Liverpool and Washington, while British and Canadian escort groups shepherded North Atlantic convoys well clear of the U-boats' successive patrol lines. In carrying out his Operation Teardrop, which would prove the largest hunter-killer effort of the war, Admiral Ingram deployed two successive barrier forces against the slow westward advance of the unsuspecting transients. During ensuing operations the two barrier groups, each consisting of two escort carriers and a score of destroyer escorts, succeeded (despite horrendous flying conditions) in flushing six of the Seewolf boats and sinking five, all by combined-ship attack.[92] Because of the German capitulation, the potential success of such an operation, conducted in difficult weather conditions against Type XXI boats, remains one of the final intriguing questions regarding the protracted Atlantic struggle.

Doctrinal differences, notably regarding the most effective employment of land-based aircraft against the U-boat threat, had occasionally strained but, in retrospect, rarely impaired Allied co-operation during the Battle of the Atlantic. Notwithstanding protracted difficulties in securing adequate training and equipment, the dogged emergence of the Royal Canadian Navy and Air Force as full partners in the North Atlantic, has achieved scholarly recognition and provides fresh challenges for future interpretation.[93] For most ship-board participants, frequent contact with other seagoing allies proved the exception, owing to the emerging pattern of command areas. Embattled Britain, through its enlightened reception and effective re-deployment of thousands of determined fighting men from occupied Poland, Czechoslovakia, Norway, the Netherlands and France, as well as from her Dominions, had nonetheless set the tone for Allied co-operation, drawing on powerful bonds of multi-national sentiment in North America, roused by Hitler's march of conquest. In such a context, Allied leaders, aided greatly by the conciliar mechanism found in the Combined Chiefs of Staff, moved perforce and ultimately with immense mutual confidence toward the defeat of Germany, the vital strategic concept that had held the emerging alliance together. That the sources of Ultra Intelligence remained secret to the bitter end proved the most enduring proof of Allied co-operation in World War II.

Notes

1. War Poster Collection, Accession Nr. 63993-1, in Naval Section, Division of Armed Forces History, National Museum of American History, Washington D.C.
2. Reckner, *Teddy Roosevelt's Great White Fleet*, pp. 40, 53, 60, 65-70, 124 and cover illustration.
3. Roskill, *The War at Sea*, I, pp. 41-43, 50-51.
4. *Ibid.*; Auphan and Mordal, *The French Navy in World War II*, pp. 19-20.
5. Tracy B. Kittredge, 'United States-British Naval Co-operation 1939-1942', unpublished COMNAVEU historical monograph in Operational Archives Branch, Naval Historical Center, Washington D.C., pp. 50-51 and note B.
6. *Ibid.*; Simpson *Admiral Harold R Stark: Architect of Victory*, p. 13.
7. Kittredge, 'US-British Naval Co-operation', pp. 58-59; Reynolds, *Famous American Admirals*, pp. 159-160, 188-190.
8. Simpson, *Admiral Harold R Stark*, pp. 9-10; Morison, *History of United States Naval Operations in World War II* , I, pp. 13-16.
9. *Ibid.*, I, pp. xli-xlv; Jonas, *Isolationism in America. 1935-1941*, pp. vii-x, 70-77, 152-157, 256-259.
10. King *US Navy at War, 1941-1945*, p. 37.
11. Roskill, *War at Sea*, I, pp. 147-168; Sverre Steen, ed., *Norges Krig, 1940-1945* (3 vols., Oslo, 1947-1950), I, pp. 9-46, 87-163; Hinsley, *British Intelligence in the Second World War: Its Influence on Strategy and Operations*, I, 141; Michael Salewski, *Die deutsche Seekriegsleitung. 1935-1945* (3 vols, Frankfurt am Main,

1970-1975), I, pp. 175-194; Ruge, *Der Seekrieg: The German Navy's Story*, pp. 53-96.

12. *Ibid.*, p. 79; Kemp *Key to Victory*, pp. 45-57, 56-69; Churchill, *The Second World War*, I, pp. 648-650; Steen, *Norges Krig*, II, pp. 261-348.

13. *Ibid.*, I, p. 454; Jon R. Hegland, *Nortraships Flåte* (2 vols., Oslo, 1976), I, pp. 12, 28, 35; Derry, *A Short History of Norway*, pp. 246-247; Olav Riste, *London Regjeringa: Norge i Krigsalliansen, 1940-1945* (2 vols., Oslo, 1973-1979), I, pp. 20, 26.

14. Petrow, *The Bitter Years*, pp. 1-2, 9-11, 14-17, 35-36, 42-43, 60-68; Ph. M Bosscher, *De Koninklijke Marine in de Tweede Wereldoorlog* (3 vols., Franeker, 1984-1986), I, 406-407, 631-632; Divine, *Navies in Exile*, pp. 68-90, 120-127, 212-213.

15. Langer, *Our Vichy Gamble*, pp. 27- 41; Auphan and Mordal, *The French Navy in World War II*, pp. 105-108; Churchill, *Second World War*, II, pp. 183-188.

16. *Ibid.*; Simpson, *Admiral Harold R Stark*, pp. 51-52; Leutze, *Bargaining for Supremacy*, pp. 72-127.

17. Auphan and Mordal, *The French Navy in World War II*, pp. 116-139; Churchill, *Second World War*, II, pp. 231-239, 319-380; III, pp. 156-237, 268-304.

18. Wood and Dempster, *The Narrow Margin: The Battle of Britain and the Rise of Air Power, 1930-1940*, pp. 64-65; Karl Klee, 'The Battle of Britain', in Jacobsen and Rohwer, *Decisive Battles of World War II: The German View*, pp. 74-80.

19. Wood and Dempster, *Narrow Margin*, pp. 172-173; Roskill, *War at Sea*, I, pp. 321-325.

20. Jean Lecuir and Patrick Fridenson, 'L'Organisation de la Coopération aérienne franco-britannique (1935-Mai 1940)', in *Revue d'Histoire de la Deuxième Guerre Mondiale*, 19th year, Nr. 73, pp. 43-70.

21. Wood and Dempster, *Narrow Margin*, pp. 172-246; Roskill, *War at Sea*, I, pp. 256-257, 330-331.

22. For subsequent port attacks, including heavy raids on Liverpool in May 1941, see Macmillan, *The Royal Air Force in the World War*, II, p. 300; *Naval Staff History, Second World War: The Defeat of the Enemy Attack on Shipping, 1939-1945, A Study of Policy and Operations* (2 vols., London, 1957), IA, pp. 157-159; Baumbach, *The Life and Death of the Luftwaffe*, pp. 78-83.

23. Wood and Dempster, *Narrow Margin*, pp. 285-314; Whelan, *Hunters in the Sky*, pp. 114-115.

24. Compare the revisionist analysis of the 'short of war' measures found in Tansill, *Back Door to War: The Roosevelt Foreign Policy, 1933-1941*, pp. 561-566 and thereafter, with Morison, *History of United States Naval Operations in World War II*, I, pp. 27-36; Leutze, *Bargaining for Supremacy*, pp. 72-127; and Hughes and Costello, *The Battle of the Atlantic*, pp. 75-77, 98-99.

25. *Ibid.*, pp. 112-113; Jonas, *Isolationism in America*, pp. 257-258.

26. Morison, *History of United States Naval Operations in World War II*, I, pp. 58-64; Roskill, *War at Sea*, I, pp. 455-456; Schull, *The Far Distant Ships*, pp. 65, 78.

27. Kittredge, 'US-British Co-operation' *op cit.* , pp. 72-102, 190-204, 441-445.
28. Roskill, *War at Sea*, I, pp. 292-293; Loewenheim et al. *Roosevelt and Churchill: Their Secret Correspondence*, pp. 122-127, 153-156.
29. Divine, *Navies in Exile*, pp. 10-11, 40-45, 95-107, 197-200; Steen, *Norges Krig*, I, pp. 554-555, 571-611; Churchill, *Second World War*, III, pp. 4-5.
30. Slessor, *The Central Blue*, pp. 191, 517, 549; Divine, *Navies in Exile*, p. 165.
31. See Riste, *London Regjeringa*, pp. 250-256.
32. C. P. Stacey, 'Politique et opérations militaires (1939-1945)', in *Revue de la Deuxième Guerre Mondiale*, Year 26, Nr. 104, pp. 5-9; Slessor, *Central Blue*, pp. 333-334; Steen, *Norges Krig*, I, pp. 474-485.
33. Milner, *North Atlantic Run*, pp. 48-49; Roskill, *War at Sea*, I, pp. 354-360: Hughes and Costello, *Battle of the Atlantic*, pp. 132-133.
34. Olav Riste, 'A Complete Surprise: The German Invasion of Norway in 1940' in *International Commission of Military History Acta Nr. 13* (Helsinki, 1988) pp. 97-105.
35. Beesly, *Room 40: British Naval Intelligence, 1914-1918*, pp. 1-45, 307-314; Wladyslaw Kozaczuk, *Enigma* (No place: University Publications, 1985), pp. 16-68, 193-204; Beesly, *Very Special Intelligence*, pp.1-6, 92, 111-116; Hinsley, *British Intelligence*, II, pp. 177-179.
36. Stacey, *Arms, Men and Governments: The War Policies of Canada, 1939-1945*, pp. 336-354; Dzubian *Military Relations Between the United States and Canada, 1939-1945*, pp. 19-30.
37. *Ibid.*, pp. 19-49; Morison, *History of United States Naval Operations in World War II*, I, pp. 32-36.
38. *Ibid.*, I, pp. 46-49; Dzubian, *Military Relations*, pp. 103-106.
39. *Ibid.*; W. G. D. Lund, 'The Royal Canadian Navy's Quest for Autonomy in the North Atlantic, 1941-1943', in Boutilier, ed., *The RCN in Retrospect. 1910-1968*, pp.140-141.
40. *Ibid.*, pp. 141-142; Dzubian, *Military Relations*, pp. 103-106; Stacey, *Arms, Men and Governments*, pp. 349, 357-363.
41. Milner, *North Atlantic Run*, pp. 29-44; Roskill, *War at Sea*, I, p. 453; Tucker, *The Naval Service of Canada*, II, pp. 65-56.
42. Morison, *History of United States Naval Operations in World War II*, I, pp. 69-70; Schull, *Far Distant Ships*, pp. 96-97.
43. *Ibid.*; Lund, 'RCN's Quest' *op cit.*, pp. 141-143; Morison, *History of United States Naval Operations in World War II*, I, pp. 84-85; Milner, *North Atlantic Run*, pp 49-50, 58-61.
44. Steen, *Norges Krig*, I, pp. 502-520; Roskill, *War at Sea*, I, pp. 458-463.
45. *Ibid.*, I, pp. 463-464, 500, 616, 618; Dönitz, *Ten Years and Twenty Days*, pp. 153-163; Hessler *The U-Boat War in the Atlantic*, II, pp. 2-3.
46. Layton et al., *And I Was There*, pp. 280-298, 349-351.
47. Hinsley, *British Intelligence*, II, pp. 56, 75-76; Dönitz *Ten Years and Twenty Days*, p. 195; Hessler, *U-Boat War in Atlantic*, II, p. 203.

48. Beesly, *Very Special Intelligence*, pp.108-109; Hadley, *U-boats Against Canada*, pp. 53-55.

49. Morison, *History of United States Naval Operations in World War II*, I, pp 117-118; Milner, *North Atlantic Run*, pp. 90-93; Schull, *Far Distant Ships*, pp. 104-105; Love, *History of the US Navy*, II, pp. 68-69.

50. Roskill, *War at Sea*, II, pp. 94-95; Gannon, *Operation Drumbeat*, pp. 200-302.

51. *Ibid.*, pp. 265-269, 298-299; Beesly, *Very Special Intelligence*, pp. 108-109; Morison, *History of United States Naval Operations in World War II*, I, pp. 126-132, 413.

52. *Ibid.*, I, pp. 116-117; Slessor, *Central Blue*, pp. 491-494; Lewin, *Ultra Goes to War*, p. 243.

53. Pogue, *George C. Marshall*, II, pp. 260-288; Buell, *Master of Sea Power: A Biography of Fleet Admiral Ernest J. King*, pp. 161-171; Churchill, *Second World War*, III, pp. 663-691, 700-703; Simpson, *Admiral Harold R. Stark*, pp. 118-126.

54. See Tenth Fleet Convoy and Routing Files, Box 2, AT/TA Convoy Series, 1942, in Operational History Archives Branch, Naval History Centre, Washington DC; Morison, *History of United States Naval Operations in World War II*, I, pp. 118-119; Roskill, *War at Sea*, II, p. 452; Love, *The Chiefs of Naval Operations*, pp. 153-154; Churchill, *Second World War*, III, pp. 684-685, 699-704.

55. Note the statement, 'When the United States entered the war, all of the American destroyers were withdrawn immediately for service in other theatres, and by February 1942, there were only two United States Coast Guard cutters available for duty as convoy escorts'. Lund, 'RCN's Quest', p. 241. See also Gannon, *Operation Drumbeat*, pp. 175-190, 221-223, 237-240 and 338-341.

56. Schull, *Far Distant Ships*, pp. 104-105; Morison, *History of United States Naval Operations in World War II*, I, pp. 127-135.

57. *Ibid.*, I, pp. 254-255; Roskill, *War at Sea*, I, pp. 95-97; Schull, Far *Distant Ships*, pp. 105-106; Milner, *North Atlantic Run*, pp. 99-100; Gannon, *Operation Drumbeat*, pp. 196-197.

58. *Ibid.*, pp. 339-341; Beesly, *Very Special Intelligence*, pp.113-115; Hinsley, *British Intelligence*, II, pp. 55-58.

59. Morison, *History of United States Naval Operations in World War II*, I, pp. 134-135; Roskill, *War at Sea*, II, pp. 102-105.

60. *Ibid.*, II, pp. 115-120; Churchill, *Second World War*, III, pp. 203, 255-261; Golovko, *With the Red Fleet*, pp. 83-88, 96-110; Achkasov and Pavlovich, *Soviet Naval Operations in the Great Patriotic War, 1941-1945*, pp. 302-306; Hinsley, *British Intelligence*, II, pp. 199- 214.

61. *Ibid.*, II, pp. 214-223; Achkasov and Pavlovich, *Soviet Naval Operations*, pp. 306-311; Golovko, *Red Fleet*, pp. 100-109; Morison, *History of United States Naval Operations in World War II*, I, pp. 179-192; Gleichauf, *Unsung Sailors: The Naval Armed Guard in World War II*, pp. 170-206; Roskill, *War at Sea*, I, pp. 116-146; Lund and Ludlum, *PQ17 - Convoy to Hell*, pp. 66-76.

62. *Ibid.*, pp. 205-230; Lewin, *Ultra goes to War*, pp. 223-227; Golovko, *With the Red*

Fleet, pp. 123-129; Roskill, *War at Sea*, II, pp. 277-289.

63. *Ibid.*, II, pp. 199-201, 352-353; Simpson, *Admiral Harold R.. Stark*, pp. 143-145; Love, *US Navy*, pp. 65-66; Hinsley, *British Intelligence*, II, pp. 177-178.

64.   Morison, *History of United States Naval Operations in World War II*, I, pp. 318-346; Roskill, *War at Sea*, II, p. 452; III, Pt II, p. 431.

65. *Ibid.*, II, pp. 313-320, 464-466; Ruge, *Der Seekrieg*, pp. 326-327; Morison, *Naval Operations*, II, pp. 43-54, 283-284.

66. Although neither Roskill or Morison provide statistical appendices on Allied troop movements in the Atlantic for the period 1943-1945, Morison includes a narrative summary in *ibid.*, X, pp. 133-134.

67. Slessor, *Central Blue*, pp. 433-434; Pogue, *Marshall*, II, pp. 20-35; Churchill, *Second World War*, IV, pp. 648-693.

68. *Ibid.*, IV, pp. 193-203, 434-435; Robert M. Leighton, 'US Merchant Shipping and the British Import Crisis', in Greenfield, ed., *Command Decisions*, pp. 198- 233; Roskill, *War at Sea*, II, pp. 377-379; Loewenheim et al., *Roosevelt and Churchill*, pp. 262-264, 287-290, 299-306.

69. *Ibid.*, p. 322; Rohwer, *The Critical Convoy Battles of March 1943*, pp. 47-49; Hessler, *U-boat War in Atlantic*, II, pp. 101-103; Roskill, *War at Sea*, II, pp. 372-373.

70. *Ibid.*, II, pp. 367-368, 373-374; Brown, *Carrier Operations in World War II*, I, pp. 44-47; Chalmers, *Max Horton and the Western Approaches*, pp. 148-153, 184-192; Wemyss, *Walker's Groups in the Western Approaches*, pp. 73-81; Watts, *The U-boat Hunters*, pp. 139-147; Beesly, *Very Special Intelligence*, pp. 180-192.

71. Morison, *History of United States Naval Operations in World War II*, X, pp. 65-76; Hessler, *U-boat War in Atlantic*, II, pp. 104-106; Roskill, *War at Sea*, II, pp. 373-375.

72. *Ibid.*, II, pp. 375-377.

73. *Ibid.*, II, pp. 358-360; W. A. B. Douglas, 'Alliance Warfare, 1939-1945: Canada's Maritime Forces', in *Revue Internationale d'Histoire Militaire*, Nr. 54 (Ottawa, 1982), pp. 173-174, 177; Tucker, *Naval Service of Canada*, II, pp. 409-417; Morison, *History of United States Naval Operations in World War II* , X, pp. 19-20.

74. Roskill, *War at Sea*, II, p.371; Slessor, *Central Blue*, p. 475; Morison, *History of United States Naval Operations in World War II* , X, pp. 91-92; Hessler, *U-boat War in Atlantic*, III, pp. 10-14.

75. Wemyss, *Walker's Groups in the Western Approaches*, pp. 82-96; Roskill, *War at Sea*, III, Part I, pp. 19-26, 262-263, 365-366; Craven and Gate, *The Army Air Forces in World War II*, II, pp. 394-395.

76. *Ibid.*, II, pp. 396-399, 402-411; Roskill, *War at Sea*, III, Part I, pp. 20-23; Slessor, *Central Blue*, pp. 476-477, 491-507; Morison, *History of United States Naval Operations in World War II* , X, pp. 26-31.

77. King and Whitehill, *Fleet Admiral King: A Naval Record*, pp. 459-471.

78. *Ibid*, pp. 462-463, 472-474; Morison, *History of United States Naval Operations in*

World War II , X, pp. 21-26; Farago *The Tenth Fleet*, pp. 158-160, 163-173.

79. Morison, *History of United States Naval Operations in World War II*, X, pp. 32-46.

80. *Ibid.*, X, pp. 108-116; Roskill, *War at Sea*, III, Part I, pp. 19, 31-32; Hessler, *U-boat War in Atlantic*, II, pp. 18-22; Dönitz, *Ten Years and Twenty Days*, pp. 340-341.

81. *Ibid.*, pp. 416-418; Hughes and Costello, *Battle of the Atlantic*, pp. 289-290; Morison, *History of United States Naval Operations in World War II*, X, pp. 116-129.

82. *Ibid.*, X, pp. 153-157; Roskill, *War at Sea*, III, Part I., pp. 43, 365-369.

83. *Ibid.*, III, Part I, pp. 37-43, Morison, *History of United States Naval Operations in World War II* , X, pp. 135-152; Milner, *North Atlantic Run*, pp. 272-274.

84. Roskill, *War at Sea*, III, Part I, pp. 219-221, 245-246, 258-260; Morison, *History of United States Naval Operations in World War II* , X, pp. 153-177, 274-304, 371-373.

85. *Ibid.*, X, pp. 365-366; Ruge, *Der Seekrieg*, pp. 274-276; Roskill, *War at Sea*, III, Part I, pp. 288-289; III, Part II, pp. 58-59, 63, 76-80.

86. *Ibid.*, III, Part II, pp. 79-90; Ruge, *Der Seekrieg*, pp. 279-284.

87. Morison, *History of United States Naval Operations in World War II*, X, pp. 231-233; Roskill, *War at Sea*, III, Part II, pp. 270-271.

88. *Ibid.*, III, Part I, pp. 267-280, 369-372; III, Part II, pp. 252, 432-435; Brown, *Carrier Operations in World War II,* I, pp. 40-42; Wemyss, *Walker's Group in the Western Approaches*, pp. 128-132; Morison, *History of United States Naval Operations in World War II*, X, pp. 307-310.

89. *Ibid.*, X, pp. 313-315; Roskill, *War at Sea*, III, Part II, p. 26.

90. *Ibid.*, III, Part II, pp. 298-299; Webster and Frankland, *The Strategic Air Offensive Against Germany, 1939-1945*, III, pp. 273-277; Morison, *History of United States Naval Operations in World War II*, X, pp. 338-341; Hessler, *U-boat War in Atlantic*, pp. 173-174.

91. Roskill, *War at Sea*, III, Part II, pp. 178-185, 285-288.

92. Morison, *History of United States Naval Operations in World War II*, X, pp. 344-356; Philip K. Lundeberg, 'Operation Teardrop Revisited'. Paper delivered in April 1992 at annual meeting of the North American Society for Oceanic History, at Washington, D.C.

93. Slessor, *Central Blue*, pp. 490-506; King and Whitehall *Fleet Admiral King*, pp. 451-459; Love, *Chiefs of Naval Operations*, pp. 153-154, 162-163; Morison, *History of United States Naval Operations in World War II*, X, pp. 12-19, 29-31; Churchill, *Second World War,* IV, pp. 108-111, 117-120, 385; Craven and Cate, *US Army Air Force*, II, pp. 386-392; Roskill, *War at Sea*, II, pp 358-364; Milner, *North Atlantic Run*, pp. 276-277; Douglas, 'Alliance Warfare', *op cit.*,p.177. Roger Sarty and Jürgen Rohwer, 'Intelligence and the Air Forces in the Battle of the Atlantic, 1943-1945', in *International Commission of Military History Acta Nr. 13* (Helsinki, 1988), pp. 135-158.

20

Allied Land-Based Anti-Submarine Warfare

by Henry Probert

Introduction

One of the sad things about being a military historian is the regularity with which one finds that important lessons from the past appear to have been forgotten. Nowhere was this more apparent than in the realm of anti-submarine warfare between the two World Wars. In November 1918 the recently formed Royal Air Force had 37 squadrons, comprising 285 flying boats and seaplanes, and 272 landplanes engaged on anti-U-boat duties, together with 103 airships, and the role of the aircraft in convoy escort had been fully recognized by the Naval Staff. Its value lay in the simple fact that 'for fear of being betrayed by the track of their torpedoes, the U-boat commanders refrained from attack on convoys with aerial escort.'[1]

Yet just over 20 years later, on the outbreak of another war, Coastal Command could only offer 11 'general reconnaissance' squadrons (10 of them equipped with the short-range Anson) and four long-range flying boat squadrons, two of which flew obsolete Londons and Stranraers. Only its solitary Hudson squadron and two Sunderland squadrons were remotely capable of providing a useful convoy escort.[2] Moreover, the role to be played by these limited numbers of aircraft was ill-defined. Coastal Command had been told in December 1937 that it would be 'trade protection, reconnaissance and cooperation with the Royal Navy',[3] but the forms that co-operation would take were not spelled out; in particular, there was no specific mention of anti-submarine warfare, which in the light of the experience of World War I might have been expected to take high priority.

In part this reflected the RN's own view that the more efficient asdic which had recently been developed would provide an effective counter to the U-boat; Coastal Command's main task would therefore be reconnaissance over the North Sea to monitor German trade routes.[4] This was hardly the most challenging of the many tasks facing the RAF as a whole in the late 1930s, and when we consider the great emphasis being placed on the build up of Bomber and Fighter Commands, it is hardly surprising that Coastal Command was something of a Cinderella.[5] There can be no question about the overriding importance of the air defence of the United Kingdom, but whether it was right to concentrate so much effort on the bomber force will always remain a matter of deep controversy. Nevertheless, the fact remains that as the second great war against Germany approached, Coastal Command's role was not seen as of prime importance by either the RAF or the RN, and ASW was not generally envisaged as the main challenge that would affect their joint operations.

Once the war started, however, it did not take long for the Command to become U-boat-minded. The striking success of the U-boats in September 1939 showed how dangerous they were, and the intensive air patrolling carried out throughout the autumn and winter months over the North Sea showed that it was less difficult to locate submarines from the air than many had thought. Indeed, by the end of 1939, Coastal was developing an anti-U-boat offensive in its own right,[6] but unfortunately its aircraft lacked the weapons to do more than harass and frighten the enemy. Despite the conclusion reached in 1917 that the best weapon needed to attack a submarine was a 500lb bomb fused to detonate 40 feet below the surface, most of those available in 1939 were only 100lb, incapable of doing useful damage; nor was there a proper bomb-sight. What was needed was a depth charge suitable for air dropping, but this would be a while coming. In the meantime Coastal could merely soldier on.

Then in June 1940 the French Atlantic ports fell to the Germans. With the whole European coastline from the North Cape to the Pyrenees under German occupation, the U-boats were far better placed to threaten the Atlantic supply routes, and over the coming years not only Coastal Command but also Bomber Command had to be engaged in countering them. The former, working in increasingly close co-operation with the RN, soon gave first priority to the U-boat war; the latter, primarily committed to carrying the war to Germany itself by strategic bombing, often saw its anti-submarine operations as a diversion of effort and an unwelcome distraction. For much of the war, the competition between the two Commands for scarce resources of modern aircraft and equipment would cause unfortunate tensions.

Coastal Command 1940-41

By November 1940 Coastal Command had grown to 31 squadrons comprising some 450 aircraft, though only half of these had fully trained crews - a reflection of the inevitable difficulty of expanding the RAF's overall training programme as quickly as was necessary. For the longer-range operations the Sunderlands were now supplemented by Whitleys and Wellingtons, and there were several squadrons of invaluable Hudsons, but the really long-range aircraft - the Catalinas and Liberators - were still awaited.[7] Over the coming months this growing strength enabled Air Marshal Sir Frederick Bowhill, the C-in-C, to push his patrols and escorts further and further out into the Atlantic - not only from the UK but also from new bases in Iceland, Gibraltar and West Africa, where Hudsons and Sunderlands operated, and from Canada,[8] where squadrons of the Royal Canadian Air Force (directed from a joint naval/air HQ at Halifax, Nova Scotia) were able to play a steadily increasing part.

However, a major 'Gap' remained in the central Atlantic. With the U-boats achieving much success as winter approached, there was pressure for the allocation of many more aircraft. In the view of the First Lord of the Admiralty, writing on 4 November, Coastal Command was not getting its fair share and ought to have 1,000 operational aircraft. His case was seized upon by Lord Beaverbrook, Minister of Aircraft Production, in order to propose the Command's transfer to the RN as a separate Royal Naval Air Service. The ensuing debate made it clear that the key question was the allocation of scarce resources, not who controlled what; Beaverbrook's rhetoric could not stand up to the reasoned arguments of either the Air Ministry or the Admiralty, which, in paying tribute to the already excellent co-operation between Coastal Command and the RN, could point to no likely gain in resources. The argument was eventually concluded in March 1941 with a joint report which stated that Coastal Command, while remaining an integral part of the RAF, would be under the operational command of the Admiralty, exercised through the AOC-in-C. Moreover its resources would not be diverted to other services without the Admiralty's express concurrence, except as a result of a decision by the Defence Committee.[9]

Meanwhile, not waiting for the conclusion of the top-level debate, the organization of the Command structure was being changed. Its pre-war orientation towards the North Sea had been overtaken by the events of 1940 and, since the key sector was now the Western Approaches leading to the ports of Liverpool and Glasgow, it was clear that the Command's operations over that area must be directed from a joint Naval/Air headquarters. 15 Group was therefore moved from Plymouth to Derby House, where Air Vice-Marshal J. M. Robb set up shop alongside Admiral Sir Percy Noble. John Terraine observes that 'there can rarely have been more intimate and continuous inter-Service co-operation than that of the Operations Room in Derby House during the next four years.'[10] These changes were happening, let it be remembered, at a time when the UK was under heavy air attack - not least Liverpool itself.

At the same time Coastal Command was continuing to expand and by mid-1941, when Air Marshal Sir Philip Joubert succeeded Bowhill, it numbered some 40 squadrons, including its first long-range Catalinas and Liberators. The latter could spend three hours on patrol at 1,100 miles from base, compared with two hours for the Catalina at 800 miles and for the Sunderland at 600 miles.[11] The fact remained, however, that the aircraft could do little more than alarm the U-boats and cause them to submerge, for they still lacked the equipment needed to locate them precisely and the weapons with which to destroy them.

The key to location was Air-to-Surface Vessel (ASV) radar. As early as 1936 - stimulated by the success of the work on ground radar for air defence - research had been under way to develop airborne radar both for night air defence and for the detection of shipping (although this had the lower priority), and by January 1940 Dr E. G. Bowen's team had produced the first ASV equipment for installation in a squadron of Hudsons.[12] Neither this nor its successor version, however, was accurate enough to be really effective and it was clear that only centimetric wavelength radar - experimentally produced by Bowen in late 1940 - would provide the complete answer. Carried out in co-operation with the USA, the development work was a complex and lengthy process, and it was not until early 1943 that ASV III and its American equivalent began to be fitted in Coastal Command's aircraft. One of the reasons for the delay was that Bomber Command had been pressing hard for the introduction of H_2S, the land equivalent of ASV III, and there was much debate about which should receive priority - and then about which Command should be allowed first use of it, given the risk of its falling into enemy hands. In the event, although Bomber Command was given first go, the technological advantage represented by ASV III turned out to be so great that Coastal had some eight months of operational immunity before the Germans could produce an effective answer, and by then the crisis in the Battle of the Atlantic was past.[13]

There was, of course, more to the process of detection than this. In order to avoid the Allies' defences, U-boats normally remained submerged during the day, travelling fast on the surface at night; and although ASV could increasingly indicate their presence, the airmen needed actually to be able to see them in order to attack. It was Sqn Ldr H. de V. Leigh who came up with the idea of fitting a 24" searchlight beneath a Wellington and using an ASV II to direct it. The apparatus was successfully tested against a Royal Navy submarine on 4 May 1941,[14] but it was another year, after much bureacratic wrangling, before the first five aircraft were fitted with the Leigh Light and tried out operationally over the Bay of Biscay - now appreciated to be of great significance in the anti-submarine war as the transit route to and from the U-boat bases. On that first patrol Sqn Ldr J. Grewell attacked and damaged an Italian submarine, and a month later another Leigh Light Wellington scored the first kill.[15] By the end of the war 218 U-boats had been attacked in this way and 27 sunk, with 31 more damaged.[16] Moreover, as Terraine reminds us,

> It forced the boats passing through the Bay of Biscay to remain
> submerged at night as well as by day, which was not merely bad
> for the morale of the crews, but reduced their time in the
> operational area by five days or more.[17]

The weapons too were critical. The bombs available to begin with were as dangerous to the aircraft dropping them as to the U-boats, but by mid-1940 the 450lb depth charge had been modified for air use by the fitting of a streamlined nose cap and an air tail. Thinner-cased than the anti-submarine bomb, it had a higher charge-to-weight ratio and gave a greater blast effect, and its hydrostatic fuse would detonate the weapon only when it reached a set depth.[18] It was put to particularly good use a year later in one of Coastal Command's earliest and most spectacular successes. On 27 August 1941 a Hudson of 269 Squadron attacked U-570 in daylight south of Iceland, straddling it with a stick of four depth charges and so damaging it that the crew decided to surrender.[19] In these early days, it should be added, the bombsights were almost useless; the good pilots quickly recognized this and chose to rely on their own judgment, using the 'Mark One Eyeball' as their prime bombsighting mechanism.[20] As the war continued better sights were installed and the depth charges were improved: the older Amatol filling was replaced by Torpex, 30% more powerful, and more suitable detonators were fitted.[21] Then came the air-launched torpedo with an acoustic homing head - the so-called 'Mark 24 mine' - first used by the very long range (VLR) Liberators at the critical moment in May 1943.

Advances such as these were assisted by another major innovation, that of Operational Research. Bowhill, recognizing that success in the Atlantic battle would depend on the proper application of science and technology, had started the process by appointing Professor P. M. S. Blackett as his Scientific Adviser, and with Joubert's firm support Blackett quickly built up a strong Operational Research Section (ORS) which eventually included five Fellows of the Royal Society.[22] One of their first tasks was to analyse the attacks so far made by aircraft on U-boats, only 1% of which had as yet resulted in an assessment of 'definitely sunk'. Professor Williams found that in 40% of the attacks the U-boat was either on the surface or had been out of sight for less than 15 seconds, whereas the depth charges were set to explode at 100-150 feet. He deduced that a shallower setting was needed, ideally 20 feet, so work to develop a new depth charge was given top priority.[23] Another early achievement was to demonstrate that plain white paint on all side- and under-surfaces of an aircraft conferred a remarkable degree of invisibility in normal conditions of sky and cloud in northern latitudes.

As the war proceeded, the ORS scrutinized almost every aspect of the Command's activities, such as its navigational techniques, its search and attack tactics, and its maintenance and patrol scheduling. Their work was greatly assisted by a former submariner, Commander (later Captain) D. V. Peyton-Ward, the senior naval staff officer at HQ Coastal Command. He was a man who held a very special place in the memory of all who had served in Coastal, according to Sir John Slessor.[24] In 1941, he began a systematic record of

> each individual sighting and attack on U-boats as they took place, using every scrap of first-hand evidence obtainable and analysing the probable result from all the data available. Whenever possible the attacking crews came to the headquarters which enabled personal corroboration, discussion of detail and practical experience to be effected while the event was still fresh. These individual narratives were of assistance to the Admiralty Assessment Committee but their main value lay in exposing mistakes and facilitating steps for improvement in technique.[25]

Peyton-Ward stayed until the end of the war, a specialist in all aspects of the Command's war against the U-boats and working in close collaboration with the Admiralty Submarine Tracking Room.

Thus, by the second half of 1941, much was in train that would eventually help Coastal Command make its proper contribution to the destruction of the U-boats. However, more time was needed before the new aircraft, weapons and equipment would be available in sufficient quantity and the crews trained to use them to full effect. Nor did it help in the wider battle of priorities that the situation in the U-boat war now appeared less desperate than in previous years: the continuous surface escort of convoys, the introduction of support groups, and particularly the ability to re-route convoys in the light of Ultra decrypts were all paying dividends in substantially lower shipping losses. That this evasive routeing was possible was partly thanks to Coastal Command having driven the U-boats away from the focal points off the North Channel into the open ocean further west where they were beyond the range of the air patrols[26] - in Jürgen Rohwer's view, the Command's first major achievement.[27] The improvement in the situation in late 1941 was, of course, a false dawn, but it is perhaps understandable that the needs of Coastal Command were not seen as paramount by those charged with deciding how best to allocate scarce resources at a time when the war was rapidly extending. This was, however, cold comfort to the crews of Coastal Command. Sqn Ldr Terence Bulloch, one of its most able pilots, remembers their feelings when the B17s which they had ferried from the USA were handed over to Bomber Command at a time when their greater range would have been invaluable over the Atlantic.[28]

The Decisive Period

On 22 June 1941 Germany attacked the Soviet Union. This led to insistent demands from the Russians over the next three years not only for military supplies but also for a 'Second Front'. In all the debate about the allocation of resources between Bomber Command and Coastal Command, it must be remembered that for most of this time the only way in which the UK could make a visible contribution to the great battle on the Eastern Front was by the strategic bombing of the German homeland. Then on 7 December came Pearl Harbor, the attack on Malaya, and the entry of the US into the war. This vast expansion of the conflict placed a further premium on the importance of building up the strategic bombing campaign. The Americans quickly agreed that the defeat of Germany should take priority over that of Japan, and to that end were determined to join in the strategic bombing offensive against Germany as quickly as possible. It was therefore inconceivable that the War Cabinet should do other than continue the build up of Bomber Command. Although doubts were growing about what it had so far achieved, there was a conviction that the story would be very different once the new types of aircraft and equipment were available in sufficient quantity.

The start of the Far Eastern war had another consequence. In a mere three months the Japanese overran Malaya, Singapore and the Dutch East Indies, and by April 1942, with Burma almost lost as well, India, Ceylon and even

Australia were under threat. So too were the sea routes across the Indian Ocean, including those leading from the Cape to the Middle East. Consequently the Far East theatre, hitherto starved of aircraft of all kinds, had to be heavily reinforced - not least with maritime aircraft, particularly Hudsons and the invaluable long-range Catalinas. Between late October 1941 and early January 1942, Joubert had to send no fewer than 166 complete aircrews overseas, all but 21 of them from his operational squadrons,[29] and the outflow continued.

Moreover, while all this was happening, the U-boats were taking advantage of the US entry into the war to mount a highly successful offensive against Allied shipping off the American coast, an offensive which the USN was largely unprepared to meet, and not least in the air. The US had no equivalent to the RAF, and therefore no equivalent to Coastal Command. Instead its navy controlled all sea-based aircraft, including the flying boats, while its army controlled all the land-based ones. So, as Terraine points out, 'The two types so much coveted by the RAF, Consolidated's Catalinas and Liberators, both operated by Coastal Command, fell under different authorities when they were at home.' This sad state of affairs (just one of many long-running battles between the US services) was compounded by severe shortages of aircraft. After the demands of the Pacific theatres had been met, the USN had, in early 1942, only six squadrons of modern maritime aircraft to cover the whole of the West Atlantic area, and even by July that year the USN and USAAF together could provide only 319 aircraft. It is no wonder that the British had difficulty in extracting VLR aircraft from them.[30]

By early 1942, therefore, the North Atlantic picture was very different from that of late 1941, and both the RN and Coastal Command were rightly exercised about the shortage of aircraft to enable them to counter Dönitz's resurgent U-boat force. Joubert had never shared the earlier optimism: back in September he had stressed to the Air Ministry the speed with which the U-boat fleet was expanding and the danger it would pose in 1942,[31] and his views and those of the RN can be imagined when the Prime Minister suggested a month later the return of 60 Whitleys and Wellingtons to Bomber Command.[32] Nothing came of the suggestion, but Joubert was far from getting anything like what he needed, and (as Peyton-Ward wrote) he told the Air Ministry on 19 February that:

> the prospect of Coastal Command being able to work at reasonable efficiency appeared to be becoming even more and more remote. The promise of centimetric ASV-fitted Liberators had come to nothing, the one Liberator squadron (120 Squadron, formed in June 1941) was being allowed to die out and there had been a continuous change of policy with regard to this long-range aircraft.

He went on to urge the sacrifice of part of the bomber offensive by diverting a long-range aircraft such as the Lancaster. Air Chief Marshal Sir Charles Portal, Chief of the Air Staff, replied that he strongly opposed the transfer of either Liberators or Lancasters from their respective bombing roles in the Middle East and against Germany.[33] In relation to the Lancaster this statement is unsurprising: it was only just entering service, Bomber Command's main hopes were pinned on it, and Air Marshal Harris was about to become C-in-C. To refuse Liberators was another matter, even though they were being supplied by the Americans from their own slender resources with the intention that they be used as bombers.

So Joubert had to carry on as 'piggy in the middle', feeling his position rapidly becoming impossible: he was being, 'metaphorically, kicked by the Admiralty for not asking enough and blamed by the Air Ministry for demanding impossibilities',[34] and while he was given more Whitley and Wellington squadrons (which would prove invaluable over the Bay), his biggest need - for VLR aircraft - went unanswered. Then in May he was put in an even more difficult position when Harris requested his help in assembling the force for the first thousand-bomber raid on Cologne. He offered some 250 aircraft but was overruled by the Admiralty, so Harris had to turn to his own Operational Training Units to make up the numbers. One has to recognize how dangerous it would have been to risk many of Coastal Command's highly trained crews in this way, yet four weeks later, on 25-26 June - when Bremen with its U-boat yards and docks was the target for the third such attack - the Admiralty was persuaded to agree to the use of some 100 of the Command's aircraft, mainly Hudsons.

Only three days previously, the Admiralty had sent Portal a paper about the dangers to Britain's sea communications world-wide. This accepted that 'ships alone were unable to maintain command at sea' and went on to state that about 800 more aircraft were needed for the successful prosecution of the maritime war, a figure which Joubert recognized could not be achieved in competition with other priorities.[35] Harris was at this stage urging a totally opposite view, calling for concentration of all the air effort on the bombing of Germany and *inter alia* describing Coastal Command as 'merely an obstacle to victory'. Churchill, however, perceiving that the nature of the war had now changed, had no doubts about the importance of the Atlantic battle and of Coastal Command's role in it, and as 1942 moved on, the attention switched from arguments about priorities to what the Command was at last starting to achieve.

During the first half of the year, 30% of the 21 U-boat sinkings had been attributable to Allied air action, but none to Coastal; the second half saw 65 sinkings, 48% the result of air action, including 21% by Coastal.[36] The technical advances already described were at last beginning to pay dividends, and the five Iceland-based Mark I Liberators of 120 Squadron were of particular importance, making their presence felt in the 'Gap'. They were too few to provide full cover, but when they did appear they caused consternation among the U-boat crews. The name of Sqn Ldr T. Bulloch is particularly associated with these operations; the complete professional, he destroyed his first U-boat on 12 October and a second on 5 November, and together the five aircraft provided an excellent demonstration in late 1942 of just what might be achieved if a larger force could be provided. Bulloch's sortie on 7 December gives an idea of what was involved: his crew were airborne for over 16 hours, during which they spent more than seven hours with their convoy at a distance of 800 miles from base, made eight sightings of U-boats and attacked seven times.[37]

Yet while these were encouraging signs, the sheer weight of Dönitz's campaign was causing ever greater anxiety, and on 4 November the newly formed Cabinet Anti-U-boat Warfare Committee held its first meeting. In the view of the First Lord of the Admiralty, the first need was to fill the 'Gap' with some 40 VLR aircraft. The second was to provide more and longer-range patrols over the Bay of Biscay,[38] where the Leigh Light ASV II Wellingtons were now operating well at night, and where Beaufighters were countering the attempts of Ju 88s to provide cover for U-boats trying to cross in daylight. These were among the challenges facing Air Marshal Sir John Slessor when he succeeded Joubert as C-in-C on 5 February 1943.

The force Slessor took over totalled 60 squadrons, 34 of them anti-submarine units with a strength of 430 aircraft. Like the rest of the RAF by this stage of the war, Coastal Command included many units manned by men of other nations (in this case Canadians, Australians, New Zealanders, Norwegians, Poles, Czechs and Dutch), and Slessor also had operational control of three US squadrons. Of his anti-submarine squadrons, eight were flying the Sunderland, four the Catalina and 20 the shorter-range land-based aircraft - mainly Hudsons and Wellingtons, plus some Halifaxes, B17s and lower-range Liberators. The weakness still lay in the VLR Liberators; although a second squadron (No 86) had at last been formed, there were nevertheless only 14 aircraft available, operating from Iceland and the UK.[39] Describing the earlier failure to strengthen the VLR force as 'incomprehensible negligence', Rohwer points out that 32 Liberators transferred to Coastal Command in late 1942 had been used to strengthen the Bay patrols instead of being modified to VLR standard.[40] In March 1943, however, a most important step was taken: at an Allied Atlantic Convoys Conference in Washington it was decided to establish VLR squadrons of the USAAF and RCAF in Newfoundland, enabling the 'Gap' to be closed.[41] From now on the convoys would have air cover all the way across the Atlantic (and the position would be further improved six months later when a new base was established with Portuguese agreement in the Azores). The Canadian contribution was particularly important - for years the RCAF had been doing all it could to provide cover at the western end of the route but its aircraft had lacked the range. Now, when 10 Squadron, one of its most experienced, was given 15 of Coastal's relatively small allocation of Liberators,[42] it was enabled to play a key role.

It may seem surprising, looking back, that all the air forces engaged in the battle against the U-boats were not under a single command, but given the difficulties between the USN and the USAAF already referred to, and given also the importance to the former of the Pacific War, it would have been unrealistic to expect the Americans to agree to a single commander receiving the authority needed to do the job effectively. Joubert had begun thinking along such lines in autumn 1942 and Slessor certainly understood the need for it: the Atlantic was one battlefield, and there was a single enemy. He was convinced, however, that such a system would break down over, for example, the power to switch squadrons from one area to another. While recognizing the excellence of the US squadrons which did work under British operational control, he was highly critical of the American command structure and in particular of Admiral King, commenting that King's 'obsession with the Pacific and the battle of Washington cost us dear in the Battle of the Atlantic'.[43] There can be little doubt that the close working relationship that existed almost throughout between Coastal Command and the RN in the anti-submarine war had no parallel on the American side, and a unified North Atlantic command was out of the question. As Richards and Saunders observe:

> It is difficult to escape the conclusion that Admiral King and his
> staff did not view the Battle of the Atlantic in the same light as
> General Marshall viewed the invasion of Europe in 1944.[44]

Nevertheless, by the spring of 1943, the combined weight of the Allied air forces had increased to the point at which Dönitz first conceded that they were frustrating his pack attacks[45] and then, at the end of May, decided to call off his main offensive. As he noted in his War Diary, his losses had reached an intolerable level in relation to the tonnage of merchant vessels being sunk; and he added, 'The enemy air force played a decisive role in inflicting these high losses.'[46]

They amounted during May to 41 U-boats, of which 23 were sunk by air action, including 16 of them by Coastal Command.[47] In 1943 as a whole, Coastal accounted for 84.[48] But amid all the quoting of statistics, it must not be forgotten that the Allied victory came about as a result of combined effort. The RN's skilled escort groups with their sophisticated equipment, their carriers, the intelligence staffs, the VLR aircraft with their new equipment and weapons: their activities - and those of many others - all came together in one of the war's best examples of teamwork. Nevertheless the aircraft, for so long unable to do much more than inconvenience the U-boats, had now demonstrated beyond any doubt their ability to destroy them. As Churchill said, 'In anti-U-boat warfare the air weapon was now an equal partner with the surface ship.'[49]

But it should also be remembered that most of the time, the work of the maritime crews was utterly unspectacular. In Slessor's words,

This Coastal job, though less murderously expensive in casualties than some, was exacting, dangerous, and highly skilled, and far too commonly tedious and unrewarding. Many a good flight crew flew for hundreds of hours, month after month, by day and night in all weathers over the grey, desolate wastes of the Atlantic, without ever having the excitement of so much as seeing a U-boat. That was all part of the game, and what they did was as essential to victory as the breathtaking moments enjoyed by the few lucky ones who found and killed their prey.[50]

Many others echo this, reflecting on the 12-hour sorties with no automatic pilot and no navigational aids, the dreadful fatigue that could affect all members of the crew and might cause a lost U-boat sighting, the absence of glamour, the sheer tedium. It was never easy; many aircraft failed to find convoys they were tasked to protect, and their navigational difficulties were compounded by convoys misreporting their own position. Yet their mere presence was of inestimable value; just one aircraft could compel every U-boat over a wide area to submerge, and convoy morale was enormously lifted by the sight of a friendly aircraft. Many an aircrew took comfort after a long uneventful sortie from the thought that they might have kept a submarine down.[51]

The Role of Bomber Command

Hitherto I have concentrated on the work of the maritime aircraft - chiefly those of Coastal Command - in combating the U-boat. Before completing their story we need to consider the role of the RAF's other main contributors to ASW, namely Bomber Command. As early as December 1940 the bombers had devoted some of their effort to the new French U-boat bases and the airfields being used by the Focke-Wulf Kondors - 124 sorties were mounted during that month - but at that stage in the war Bomber Command's capabilities fell far short of the hopes placed on it, and, since it had to attack at night if it was to avoid unacceptable losses, it could rarely find or hit its targets with any accuracy. Yet as Churchill's Battle of the Atlantic Directive of 6 March 1941 stated, the bombers were expected to play their part:

We must take the offensive against the U-boat...wherever we can and whenever we can. The U-boat at sea must be hunted, the U-boat in the building yard or in dock must be bombed.[52]

For the rest of 1941, however, it was the German battlecruisers *Scharnhorst* and *Gneisenau* that attracted most of Bomber Command's effort against the French ports. Understandably perhaps, in view of the threat they posed, the RN considered them a more important target than the U-boats; but while some limited success was achieved, the C-in-C (Sir Richard Peirse) felt obliged to say,

'We are not designed for this purpose and we are not particularly effective in execution.'[53]

Peirse also told Joubert in July, after the latter had suggested reducing each U-boat operating base in turn to the condition in which Plymouth had been left by the Luftwaffe, that he believed his limited force was better employed against objectives in Germany. He accepted the need to attack the German warships in Brest but could not agree to include the U-boat bases.[54] Joubert returned to the fray in September, urging the importance of at least interfering with the smooth working of the Biscay bases, but the Air Ministry remained adamant, reminding him and the navy of the long-term contribution of the bomber offensive to the maritime war by its attacks on the chief German ports and on their main industrial effort.

> There seemed no justification for a return to this defensive strategy now that conditions at sea had so much improved and we were beginning to develop fully the air offensive to which we must look for winning as opposed to not losing the war.[55]

It was at this very time that the giant U-boat pens along the French coast were under construction and at their most vulnerable to blast-bombing, and it was these alarming preparations that had helped prompt Joubert's request.[56] The failure to attack them has been widely criticised. Dönitz certainly thought it a great mistake,[57] as do Rohwer and many British historians. There is little doubt that the Air Ministry was preoccupied with Germany itself (as indeed was Churchill)[58] and the Admiralty with the big warships. At the critical time the threat represented by the pens was widely under-estimated.[59] There was also the danger to French civilians (though this had to be accepted later on) and, given that night attacks would have been necessary, it is questionable whether the bombers could have been sufficiently accurate.[60] In retrospect one feels the attempt ought to have been made, but at the time there were so many other pressures and problems - not least of them the need to be seen to be supporting the Russians in face of the initial German onslaught - that the threat from the pens was largely discounted. It was a year later, in December 1942, when the U-boat danger was all too apparent, that (to his considerable displeasure) Harris was ordered to attack the U-bases. For five weeks from mid-January 1943, half his effort was turned on Lorient and St Nazaire, where almost everything was destroyed except the pens and the submarines.[61]

In Bomber Command's view, both under Harris and his predecessor, it was better to concentrate on U-boat production in Germany itself, where such attacks would form part of the main strategic offensive, and during 1941 many raids took place against the North German ports and their shipyards. They continued to feature on the target list during 1942, and in January 1943, at the same time as the offensive against the pens, Harris was specifically directed to give the construction yards high priority. Later that year, the Blohm and Voss works in Hamburg suffered considerable damage during the firestorm attacks, yet as Rohwer tells us:

> Even the heavy attacks against the German port cities of Hamburg, Bremen and Kiel in 1943 and 1944 achieved no real destruction of the building yards and damaged only relatively few boats on the slipways or in the fitting-out basins.[62]

The main delays in U-boat construction, he continues, were caused by the absence of yard-workers after heavy raids, and by damage to component factories in other cities. While U-boat production was certainly impeded by the bombing campaign up to mid-1944 it was not seriously disrupted; the main achievements of the bomber offensive lay elsewhere.

In the final stages, however, it was a different story. The Germans were now developing more advanced types of submarine - the Types XXI and XXIII - with the potential to renew Dönitz's offensive in the Atlantic, and Bomber Command, now armed with far better bombs and able to deliver them accurately, attacked the yards and disrupted the canal routes along which the major components had to be carried. To quote Rohwer again:

> These strategic attacks (in which the 8th USAAF also took part) caused major delays in the building programmes for the new types of U-boat, mainly by damaging the transportation that supplied the assembly yards with the prefabricated sections, but also by destroying new boats or damaging them beyond repair.[63]

He goes on to remind us of another Bomber Command contribution, namely its minelaying offensive in the Baltic. This delayed the training programme and helped prevent the new types of U-boat becoming operational before the end of the war. Minelaying, undertaken by both Coastal and Bomber Commands, had proceeded in North-West European waters from the earliest days of the war, and was a task which Harris strongly supported - not least since it could often be carried out at times unsuitable for bombing operations. The number of U-boats actually sunk by aircraft-laid mines was small (17 out of total losses of 722),[64] but the campaign was intended to disrupt shipping of all kinds and its effect on the U-boats - not least on the training of their crews - was just one aspect of a little publicized but immensely valuable RAF role.

Coastal Command 1943-45

By mid-1943, as we have seen, the main U-boat offensive had been successfully countered. However, as long as the war continued, the danger remained that it might be resumed. Once it was realized through Ultra that the U-boats had largely been withdrawn from the central Atlantic, much of Coastal's effort was switched to the U-boat transit routes across the Bay of Biscay, where the use of ASV III in combination with the Leigh Light and the new acoustic homing torpedo led to considerable success.[65] Ultra remained of great importance, enabling the aircraft to be concentrated where they were needed, and, since its continued security was essential, many sorties were flown merely to try to ensure that the Germans would not suspect that their Enigma had been broken.[66] So, while Dönitz continued his efforts on a more modest scale over the winter months of 1943-44, his forces were unable to interfere seriously with the great Allied build-up for the Normandy invasion, and when the landings took place in June 1944 the joint efforts of the air and naval forces to the west of the English Channel virtually prevented interference by the U-boats.

The U-boat threat to the invasion forces was judged from Ultra to be 40 boats. To oppose them Coastal Command (now under the leadership of Air Chief Marshal Sir Sholto Douglas) could muster 51 squadrons, of which 30 were concentrated in 19 Group against the submarines operating from the bases in the Bay. In the event only 35 U-boats were available, and only nine - those equipped with the newly developed schnorkel device - achieved anything at all; the rest had no chance whatever of penetrating the Allied defences, and on 10 June the surviving U-boats had to be called off.[67] The immense build-up of Allied naval/air strength, coupled with the weapons and tactics developed over the preceding years, ensured that the invasion could proceed almost unhampered - a remarkable achievement, and one which all too often goes largely unrecognized when the tale of the Normandy invasion is recounted.

Mention of the introduction of the schnorkel reminds us of the technological advances that occurred on both sides in the later stages of the war and - but for the impact of the Allied bomber offensive on German production - might have led to a large-scale resumption of the U-boat offensive. The schnorkel made radar detection by aircraft far more difficult, thus negating much of the effectiveness of aircraft as strikers of submarines, but this advantage was at first largely offset by significant operating problems.[68] The threatened introduction of new types of submarines has already been mentioned; 290 of the large Type XXIs were ordered, but only one became operational.[69] Other advances on the German side were better weapons, including anti-aircraft guns. On the Allied side the advent of the anti-submarine homing torpedo (known as the Mark 24 mine and first used in May 1943) and the sonobuoy (which enabled aircraft to detect a submerged U-boat) were important developments, but their main value lay in the post-war era, not in the Battle of the Atlantic.[70]

This chapter has concentrated mainly on the work of Coastal Command, which operated against the U-boats from the first day of the war to the last. The precise figures that indicate its achievement remain the subject of debate, as minor readjustments continue to be made in the light of modern research. The broad pattern, however, remains as stated in the official histories, including that by Richards and Saunders, and also in Slessor's *The Central Blue*.[71] Leaving aside the German and Italian submarines sunk in the Mediterranean and Indian Ocean areas, 722 were destroyed during the war in the Atlantic, Arctic and home waters, 305 of them by Allied shore-based aircraft alone and 28 more by joint action between shore-based aircraft and naval forces. Coastal Command's share of these totals was 173 and 21 respectively. Of the remainder, 52 were destroyed in bombing attacks on the ports by Bomber Command and the USAAF, 17 by air-laid mines, and most of the others by United States and Canadian maritime aircraft. It is also noteworthy that of Coastal Command's 'kills' only three occurred before the end of 1941, and 123 were achieved during 1943 and 1944.

There was, of course, a price to pay. Coastal Command's casualty list (which included the costly operations of its strike squadrons against surface shipping) came to 5,866 men, 1,630 of them from the Dominions and the European allies,[72] and of Bomber Command's far greater list a good many were attributable at least in part to the U-boat war.

Notes

1. Air Historical Branch Narrative, *The RAF in the Maritime War*, Vol 1, p.44.
2. *Ibid.*, App 5.
3. *Ibid.*, p. 209.
4. *Ibid.*, p. 221.
5. Terraine, *The Right of the Line*, p. 70.
6. Richards and Saunders, *The Royal Air Force 1939-45*, Vol 1, p. 62.
7. *Narrative*, Vol II App I.
8. Terraine, *The Right of the Line*, p. 244.
9. *Narrative*, Vol II pp. 276-285. The senior RAF representative on the committee which compiled this report was DCAS, AVM Harris, later C-in-C Bomber Command.
10. Terraine, *The U-boat Wars*, p. 305.
11. Terraine, *The Right of the Line*, p. 245.
12. Price, *Aircraft Against Submarines*, pp. 37-55.
13. Terraine, *The Right of the Line*, pp. 436-8; Webster and Frankland, *The Strategic Air Offensive Against Germany*, Vol IV, pp. 12-14.
14. Price, *Aircraft Against Submarines*, p. 64.
15. Richards and Saunders, *op. cit.* Vol 2, pp. 103-4. Great skill was needed in using the light, with very close co-operation between the pilot and the radar operator. The pilot had to descend from patrol height to 300 feet, often in bad weather, while the radar operator had to provide all the necessary bearing and range information in order to ensure that when the light was switched on the U-boat would be squarely in the beam and about one mile away. *Seek and Sink: Proceedings of RAF*

Historical Society Symposium 1992: p.83.

16. Dean, Maurice, *The RAF and Two World Wars*, p. 155.
17. Terraine, *The Right of the Line*, p. 406.
18. *Seek and Sink, op. cit.*, paper by Dr Alfred Price, p. 50.
19. Terraine, *The U-boat Wars*, p. 364.
20. *Seek and Sink, op. cit.* p. 84.
21. Richards and Saunders, Vol 2, p. 100.
22. Terraine, *The Right of the Line*, p. 402.
23. *Seek and Sink, op. cit.* Price pp. 50-1.
24. Slessor, Sir John, *The Central Blue*, p. 486.
25. *Narrative*, Vol III, p. 43. Peyton-Ward worked after the war in the Air Historical Branch, where he wrote the official narrative of the RAF in the Maritime War, itself referred to in this paper.
26. *Seek and Sink, op. cit.*, Paper by Mr Edward Thomas, p. 40.
27. *Ibid*. Paper by Professor Jurgen Rohwer, p. 66.
28. *Ibid.*, p.75.
29. *Narrative*, Vol III, p. 7, Note 4.
30. Terraine, *The U-boat Wars*, pp. 417-418.
31. *Narrative*, Vol III, p. 30.
32. *Ibid.*, p. 4.
33. *Ibid.*, pp. 10-11.
34. *Ibid.*, p. 12.
35. *Ibid.*, p. 15.
36. Terraine, *The U-boat Wars*, pp. 432-3.
37. *Ibid.*, p.506.
38. Roskill, *The War at Sea*, Vol II, pp. 88-89.
39. Slessor, *op. cit.* pp. 465-6.
40. *Seek and Sink, op. cit.*, p. 60.
41. Terraine, *The Right of the Line*, p. 442.
42. Slessor, *op. cit.*, p.499.
43. *Ibid*, pp. 488-495.
44. Richards and Saunders, *op. cit.*, Vol 3, p. 38.
45. *Seek and Sink, op. cit.*, p. 44.
46. Terraine, *The Right of the Line*, p. 449.
47. *Ibid*, p. 450.
48. Slessor, *op. cit.* p. 465.
49. Churchill, *The Second World War*, Vol V, Closing the Ring, p. 11.
50. Slessor, *op. cit.*, p. 468.
51. *Seek and Sink, op. cit.* pp. 79-83; reflections of aircrew who took part.
52. Churchill, *The Second World War*, Vol IV, The Grand Alliance, p.107.
53. Webster and Frankland, *op. cit.*, Vol I, p. 168.
54. *Narrative*, Vol III, p. 24.
55. *Ibid*, p. 31, Note 1.

56. *Ibid*, p. 24, Note 1.

57. Terraine, *The U-boat Wars*, p. 355.

58. *Seek and Sink, op. cit.*, p. 69 - comment by Air Marshal Sir Edward Chilton.

59. Richards and Saunders, op. cit., Vol I, p. 349.

60. *Seek and Sink*, op. cit., pp. 77-78.

61. Terraine, *The Right of the Line*, p. 414.

62. *Seek and Sink, op. cit.*, p. 65.

63. *Ibid.*, p. 66.

64. Richards and Saunders, *op. cit.*, Vol 3, App VI; Terraine, in *The U-boat Wars*, App G, gives the figure as 16.

65. *Seek and Sink*, op. cit., paper by Professor Rohwer, pp. 62-3.

66. Terraine, *The Right of the Line*, p. 453.

67. *Ibid*, p. 628.

68. *Seek and Sink, op. cit.*; paper by Lt Cdr W. J. R. Gardner, p. 34.

69. Terraine, *The Right of the Line*, p. 455.

70. *Seek and Sink, op. cit.*, p. 35.

71. Richards and Saunders, *op.cit.*, Vol 3 App VI; Slessor, *op.cit.*, p. 470.

72. Richards and Saunders, *op. cit.*, Vol 3, p. 276.

21

Ship-borne Air Anti-Submarine Warfare

by David Hobbs

Ship-borne air anti-submarine warfare was one of the most important developments of World War II. As the Battle of the Atlantic proved, pre-war theories on convoy protection were outdated. They had completely underestimated the value of ship-borne tactical aircraft in ASW and had consequently not pursued the development of a suitable carrier.

Between the wars, the RAF had responsibility for air ASW. The Staff openly embraced the strategic theories of Douhet and Mitchell and stated that future wars would be fought out in the air, with navies and armies sidelined. They believed that strategic bombing, aimed at the enemy's industrial heartland, would contribute directly to ASW by defeating U-boats at source. This mistaken view deserves little further comment, but makes clear why the RN had little to contribute before 1939. The Admiralty had shown interest in trade protection carriers between the wars, but had given priority to the larger carriers required for Fleet work. These Fleet Carriers took up almost all of the RN's allocation under the Washington, and subsequent naval Treaties. In 1936, DNC prepared two designs for conversion: *Winchester Castle* (20,000 tons, 631'/192.33m) and *Waipawa* (12,500 tons, 516'/157.28m). Other ships were considered, but the press of re-armament work precluded design effort. Trade protection conferences in 1937 and 1938 took the matter forward, but in January 1939, it was decided not to proceed since resources were required for 'other, more important services'

Even the outbreak of war in September 1939 failed to change this situation since, at 12 months, auxiliary carrier conversions were felt to be too long to be practical - especially since asdic, fitted in surface escorts, was felt to have effectively countered the threat posed by U-boats on the trade routes. The 1939 Fighting Instructions discounted naval embarked aviation as being of any value for ocean convoy defence, stating that 'small escort forces and evasion could be relied upon to provide sufficient security during the ocean passage'. Coastal Command and local flotillas would augment the close escort in the approaches to port. Eight years later, with the Battle behind them, the same section of the Fighting Instructions stated 'Carriers with a convoy provide a tactical air force for its defence'.

The RN that entered World War II was, doctrinally, equipped for a fleet encounter. The U-boat threat was seen as minor compared with the threat of surface raiders - a belief that was given apparent substance by early experience, with few U-boats actually at sea, and with the *Graf Spee* proving elusive in the southern oceans.

Naval Aviation, which had only come fully under Admiralty control in May 1939, was not equipped for anti-submarine warfare. Airgroups were based on seven aircraft carriers equipped and trained to 'find, fix and strike' at an enemy fleet. A/S reconnaissance was limited to visual surface search, and the only weapon was the 100lb (45.36kg) A/S bomb developed, though never tested, by the RAF. It was procured on the theory that a large number of small weapons would do better than a small number of large ones, but, with a lethal radius of only two feet, killing a submarine with it was beyond the simple visual sighting techniques of the day. This shortcoming had been perceived in the mid '30s in HMS *Courageous,* with recommendations to modify the available 450lb (204.12kg) naval depth charge for aircraft use, but nothing came of this.

War, when it came, followed the anticipated pattern. Cruisers, formed into hunting groups, some with carrier support, scoured the ocean trade routes for German shipping. Ships taken up from trade were converted for use as Armed Merchant Cruisers and Ocean Boarding Vessels. The use of carriers to provide control of the escort's third dimension was not considered a priority, although, due to a shortage of Coastal Command aircraft, Fleet Carriers were used to hunt U-boats in what would otherwise be blank sea areas. *Courageous* and *Hermes* were allocated to CINCWA, and *Ark Royal* to C-in-C Home Fleet for use in the North-West Approaches. This cocksure attitude was a waste of invaluable assets to cover independently routed ships and cost us dear. *Ark* was narrowly missed by a torpedo on 14 September; three days later, *Courageous* was sunk by torpedoes from U-29, with the loss of 518 lives and her highly trained regular air group.

After that, the carrier patrols were stopped. The lesson, learnt at such a high price, was that asdic was not infallible and that high-value units could ill afford to 'trail their coat' with hopeful patrols in dangerous waters.

The fall of France and Norway in the summer of 1940 changed everything further for the worse. Now, German aircraft (Fw-200s of KG40) could range far into the eastern Atlantic locating convoys and attacking ships with bombs. U-boats too, from bases such as Lorient, could pass more easily into the Atlantic. Unlike their predecessors in the Great War, they ranged far out into the ocean to where convoy escorts were smaller and Coastal Command simply could not reach.

It is worth pondering for a moment the shortcomings of land-based aircraft. At any one time, one maritime patrol aircraft over a convoy at, say, 500 miles from its base, probably has its successor airborne to relieve it, its predecessor airborne on its way home, and yet more crews briefing and resting, with some aircraft dismantled for routine maintenance. It would thus be quite possible for an entire squadron of 12 aircraft to be committed to a single convoy. Moreover, many serviceable aircraft failed to get airborne due to bad weather at their base; and during 1942, up to 34% of Coastal Command sorties that got airborne failed even to *find* their allocated convoy. This hardly made for the possibility of quick reaction to a sudden threat. In contrast, carrier aircraft are generally more capable and more flexible, and can be controlled and briefed by the escort commander. Being on the spot, they can respond rapidly, and can refuel and re-arm relatively quickly. Unlike their land-based counterparts, therefore, most of their air-borne time would be on patrol, not in transit. This point is worth stressing because, once realized, it brought about the resurrection of the idea that escort carriers could provide air support for convoys in the mid-Atlantic - the 'gap' no land-based aircraft could reach.

The need for embarked aircraft was first seen as a counter to German reconnaissance aircraft - Fw-200 Condors. This need was met by fighter catapult ships and then CAM ships (merchant ships fitted with a catapult to launch a single aircraft), but, if launched out of range of land, the certain loss of the fighter (and possible loss of its pilot) gave rise to a reluctance to launch in any but ideal circumstances. The escort carrier, fitted with full flying facilities, overcame this drawback and was capable of operating both fighters and A/S aircraft. Originally called Auxiliary carriers with the abbreviated prefix AVG, their title was changed in August 1942 to escort carrier (CVE), since the word 'auxiliary' implied a merchant ship, and so was widely misunderstood by senior officers. Whilst some escort carriers were converted from merchant hulls and all were based on mercantile designs, they were most definitely warships with a powerful air capability. Their cousins, the MAC-ships (Merchant Aircraft Carriers), were not and are dealt with separately later.

In August 1940, a joint naval and Coastal Command meeting was held in HMS *Titania* in Belfast. This was followed by a meeting in the Admiralty, chaired by VCNS and attended by the AOC-in-C Coastal Command. At this, it was decided *inter alia* that a new Western Approaches Command should be set up, based in Liverpool; that existing assets were being under-used; and that depth charges, not bombs, should be the principal air A/S weapons. After further discussion, the Prime Minister made his 'Battle of the Atlantic Directive' in which he gave top priority to the destruction of U-boats. Unfortunately he gave equal priority to those at sea, those in their harbour 'nests' and those in building yards. This utopian view had the effect of encouraging Bomber Command to believe it could make a meaningful contribution by bombing 'strategic' targets. In fact, this policy took resources (especially VLR aircraft) from the real battle at sea. Such widely disparate aims were not only incompatible but also showed a lack of historical awareness: as long ago as 1918 it had been realized that U-boats were best fought in the vicinity of convoys.

The Atlantic Directive did, however, make many sound changes, including (on 15 April 1941) the transfer of Coastal Command's operational control to the Admiralty; the fitting out of Fighter Catapult ships and CAM ships; the widespread fitment of ASV radar to AS Aircraft; the issue of depth charges rather than A/S bombs. It also introduced the decisions to create MAC-ships (by equipping tankers and grain ships with flight decks suitable for Swordfish TBR aircraft), and to provide escort carriers to operate fighter and A/S aircraft in support of surface escort forces in the mid-Atlantic gap.

In autumn 1940, Captain Mathew Slattery, Director of Material at the Admiralty, had proposed the fitment of the simplest possible flight deck and landing equipment to suitable merchant ships. Almost simultaneously, Rear Admiral William Halsey USN warned that suitable merchant hulls would need to be converted to augment the USN's fleet carriers for training and aircraft transport, should America be drawn into the war. The USN was, at first, cool and the Secretary of the Navy advised the Chairman of the Maritime Board against conversions as naval aircraft were 'too fast and too heavy' to operate from small decks. However, pressure from the President and a pragmatic need for flight decks tipped the balance and USS *Long Island* (AVG1) was commissioned on 2 June 1941, with 21 aircraft, a hangar and a catapult. The next six US conversions were all intended for the RN, although one, *Charger*, was retained by the US to help in the training of RN aircrew. A total of 133 Allied CVEs were built or converted - five in Britain and 128 in the USA, with 38 of the latter being lent to the RN. This was a rate of construction with which the Axis powers could not hope to compete.

By June 1941, after 20 months of war, the initial defensive period could be said to be over. Pre-war lack of appreciation of the potency of aircraft as an A/S weapon and over-estimation of asdic in surface ships forced us to pay a terrible price in shipping losses. The shift of U-boat concentrations out of range of Coastal Command obliged it to try attacking transiting boats in the Bay of Biscay whilst Bomber Command hit the harbour 'nests'. The former bore some fruit as a subsidiary measure, but the latter has been shown by post-war analysis to have been almost totally ineffective.

The first escort carrier to see operational service was HMS *Audacity* with 802 (Martlet) Squadron embarked. She was a converted German merchant ship, captured in 1940 and commissioned on 17 June 1941. On 13 September of that year she joined OG74, her first convoy, and began a short but brilliant career. Her six fighters proved that carrier-borne aircraft with a convoy could be an effective means of protection against U-boats and shore-based enemy aircraft bent on attacking. Although they were not A/S aircraft, her fighters shared in the destruction of U-131 on 17 December 1941 with Commander Walker's escort group, the first escort carrier 'kill'.

Audacity's pioneer work exerted considerable influence on the future conduct of anti-air and anti-submarine operations. She was employed exclusively on the UK-Gibraltar convoy route. Typically her fighters intercepted unknown aircraft detected by her radar and also flew A/S patrols, with two aircraft at dawn and two hours before dusk or half an hour before any major alteration of course. A/S patrols flew 10-20 miles ahead of the ship at 200 feet (60.96m); the two aircraft then turned and circled the convoy on opposite courses for two circuits. If a U-boat was sighted, it was attacked with front guns and marked with a sea marker. The aircraft then climbed to allow *Audacity* to obtain an accurate radar mark over the sea marker for escorts to home onto. The system worked well.

The safest position for the carrier was in the middle of the convoy between the two centre columns, but since she was 'sided' navigationally, she dropped back to the rear of the centre column in thick weather. It was left to the discretion of the Commanding Officer, however, to zigzag outside the convoy at night until dawn if he preferred. In that case, if possible, two escorts were to be provided.

In her last convoy, *Audacity* chose to spend the night of 21-22 December 1941 outside the convoy but, unlike the previous night, no escort could be spared. The events of 21-22 December are covered in detail in Chapters 27 and 28, but in brief, she was hit by a torpedo which flooded the engine room and caused her to settle by the stern. Simultaneously she saw a surfaced U-boat and engaged it with gunfire. Two more torpedoes then hit her, and she sank bows first 10 miles starboard of HG76. Despite her loss, though, the attackers too had taken a hammering, and in his log for 23 December 1941 Flag Officer U-boats reported that:

> ...the worst feature was the presence of the aircraft carrier. Small, fast, manoeuvrable aircraft circled the convoy continuously, so that when they were sighted, boats were repeatedly forced to submerge or withdraw. The presence of enemy aircraft also prevented any protracted shadowing or homing procedure by German aircraft. The sinking of the aircraft carrier is, therefore, of particular importance not only in this case but in every future convoy action...

No single weapon system wins a campaign or a war, but the escort carrier was clearly of critical importance in the Battle of the Atlantic. In her six-month life, *Audacity* had escorted four convoys and flew on 35 days in the process. Her aircraft reported nine U-boats, one of which was sunk with the aid of surface escorts. Twelve enemy aircraft were intercepted, five of which were shot down and three damaged. After these successes, opposition by the Ministry of War Transport to what they saw as 'misuse' of merchant hulls evaporated, and five British ships were released for conversion to escort carriers. In October 1942, HMS *Activity* was the first of these to enter service.

Having commissioned on 2 June 1941 the first US escort carrier, USS *Long Island*, actually pre-dated *Audacity* by a few days, but she was used almost exclusively as a training and ferry carrier. The first US-built CVE for the RN, HMS *Archer*, commissioned in March 1942 but was plagued with mechanical defects which limited her usefulness. This was due to the speed of conversion in yards unused to such work and, on occasion, the British personnel (often understaffed) who manned the unfamiliar machinery. *Archer* was followed into service by *Avenger*, *Biter* and *Dasher*, but such was the shortage of fleet carriers in the RN that they were used initially to support the North African landings of Operation Torch in November 1942. To all intents and purposes in 1942, no escort carrier was employed (except in its delivery voyage) in normal transatlantic convoys.

Concern at the rate at which CVEs were coming into service led in February 1942 to a re-appraisal by the Combined Chiefs of Staff of the MAC-ship concept. After some discussion about its feasibility and the type of aircraft that might be used, two grain ship conversions were ordered in June. Both would operate four Swordfish from a 410' x 62' (124. 9 x 18. 9m) flight deck. As well as providing air facilities, including a small hangar, it was still possible for the ship to carry her normal cargo. In October, 12 more conversions were ordered - six grain ships and six oil tankers. The first, a grain ship renamed *Empire MacAlpine*, sailed with ONS9 on 29 May 1943 and the last was ready at the end of June 1944. Compared to the grain ships, the tankers had a longer and better flight deck of 460' (140.21m) but no hangar, and could only operate three Swordfish. Extensive plans were drawn up for further production in both the UK and USA, but in the event only 19 were completed, of which two were Dutch-manned. (These, incidentally, were the first aircraft carriers in the Royal Netherlands Navy.) Aircraft were provided as flights of 836 Naval Air Squadron (860 RNN Sqn for the Dutch ships), home-based at RNAS *Maydown* in Northern Ireland. With a headquarters and 92 Swordfish (nicknamed 'Stringbags') divided into flights of three or four, it was easily the largest squadron in the Fleet Air Arm.

The USN decided against MAC-ships and no conversions were made in America; but their value in convoy protection is amply proved by a few simple statistics. In the two years of their service, MAC-ships collectively made 323 transatlantic crossings, escorting 217 convoys, with their aircraft making 4,177 sorties; and of all those convoys, only one was successfully attacked by U-boats. They gave vital air cover, often in appalling weather and sometimes at night, and were especially useful in filling the vacuum left by the late appearance of the CVEs. They freed the latter to form part of Convoy Support Groups, and there can be no doubt that the sight of a MAC-Ship in convoy was a boost to the morale of the convoy - and to the whole merchant navy, which came to regard them as its own. The relationship between the merchant personnel and the air crews was excellent. As described elsewhere by one of the present editors,

> Merchant sailors usually found the Royal Navy snobby, bossy and over-organized, while the Royal Navy usually saw merchant sailors as uncouth, loutish and ill-disciplined. There was, in short, every possiblity for (even likelihood of) discord; yet if ever any occurred, no one seems to remember it now - indeed, very much the opposite. ....the pilots and their assistants, being members of a young and only half-acknowledged part of the Royal Navy, knew all too well what it was like to be cold-shouldered by their stuffier colleagues. From the start they showed every respect towards their new shipmates, proudly wearing the silver 'MN' badge in their lapels, and greatly enjoying the rage that this entirely

legitimate act caused in more hide-bound naval officers ashore; and before long they hit upon another very visible method of showing their regard....The Stringbags used in the MAC-ships were painted pure white, being the best camouflage for day-flying over the sea, and were otherwise ehtirely standard Fleet Air Arm planes - except that in many flights, so great was the MN loyalty, the aircrew would paint out the words ROYAL NAVY on the fuselage of their planes and substitute MERCHANT NAVY.

In March and April 1944 some MAC-Ships were used to ferry aircraft across the Atlantic, 212 being delivered before D-Day and air crews were reduced to reinforce other squadrons. With the defeat of the U-boat in the Atlantic, some were returned to normal trading but some remained in service until May 1945 and convoys, both east- and west-bound, retained at least one in company.

Audacity's loss, when operating unescorted outside the convoy, prompted further thought on the critical problem of where best to position a carrier operating with a convoy. In January 1943, a meeting held at the Admiralty decided that the best position for a carrier, be it a CVE or a MAC, was as rear ship of the Commodore's column both by day and night. If forced to leave the convoy because of wind direction when launching, she should have a separate escort. Flying should be paced to allow a surge of effort if the convoy were directly threatened, and night flying should not normally take place unless submarine intelligence indicated the need. It was also decided that the Senior Officer of the A/S escort should be regarded as the SO of the whole escort force, regardless of the seniority of the carrier's commanding officer. US policy, in contrast, regarded the aeroplane as the chief weapon to seek and destroy U-boats and therefore placed the carrier CO in tactical charge. To further this policy, the air support groups were given considerable independence of action and were not directly controlled by the SO escort.

The delay in introducing CVEs into the North Atlantic, mentioned briefly above, was due to several factors, of which the most important was the need to use them as assault carriers in support of the North African landings. The need to fit them to operate fighters and to acceptable British standards (most notably with safety improvements to the avgas fuel system) also took time and delayed their entry into service. As it happened, the winter of 1942-43 was an unusually severe one in the Atlantic and there is little doubt that, even had CVEs gone into service earlier, their flying would have been restricted

Specific escort carrier operations give a good idea of how they operated. In March 1943 FO U-Boats launched a major offensive with 110 submarines. Thirty ships in four convoys were lost, but 12 U-boats were also sunk. Some coverage in 'the Gap' was provided by Coastal Command's VLR aircraft and some (for the first time) by USS *Bogue* and her Task Group 22. She operated eastbound in support of convoy HX228 until 10 March, when she was forced, by the fuel state of her escorts, to return. She returned westbound in support of

SC123 and flew on four days out of six. Her aircraft were Grumman Avengers and Wildcats, both immeasurably superior to their British counterparts. The Avenger - stronger, faster and indeed a generation beyond the Swordfish - had enclosed cock-pits and weapons bays. But Swordfish were all we had; such Avengers as were available to the RN under Lend-Lease arrangements were destined for use as strike aircraft in the Far East. *Bogue*'s presence certainly helped the latter convoy through U-boat concentrations, but her aircrew were still learning and their intervention was not yet decisive.

April 1943 saw the beginning of the defeat of the U-boat and, without doubt, it was aircraft - shore-based, but more especially ship-borne, escorting and supporting convoys - that tipped the scales. With the inherent mobility of carrier-based aviation, accurate intelligence could now put a support group in the right place to keep submarines down. Strategically, CVEs allowed us to sail convoys by the southern great circle routes, previously out of range of air cover. Tactically, unlike shore-based VLR aircraft, they were able to strike and re-arm within an hour or two, ready for another sortie. This latter quality was not lost on Admiral Dönitz.

April 1943 also saw the first destruction of a U-boat by an air support group, when HMS *Biter* and three destroyers of the 5th Escort Group carried out their first patrol in support of convoy ONS4. *Biter* embarked 811 Naval Air Squadron with nine Swordfish and three Martlets. She chose to remain well clear of the convoy and maintain radio silence, causing the SO Escort, who had made room inside the convoy, some concern. On 23 April, sorties were flown despite a force 7 gale. During one of them a Swordfish sighted a surfaced U-boat through snow squalls but was unable, through lack of speed, to attack it before it dived. This was the first of many occasions in daylight A/S operations when the Swordfish's slow speed proved a handicap.

On 25 April, sorties were flown to meet the SO Escort's requirements, but in the afternoon flying became more limited due to reduced visibility. At about 1830 Swordfish L sighted a U-boat on the surface, six miles from *Biter*. When taking off, lack of wind had prevented the aircraft from carrying any more than two depth charges, but it attacked with those just 20 seconds after the conning tower submerged, and dropped two sea marker flares. The destroyer *Pathfinder* homed on these while *Biter* flew off another Swordfish and closed to join the hunt herself, an aggressive but dangerous approach. A two-hour asdic hunt followed, during which *Biter* herself dropped two charges, one of which failed to explode. *Pathfinder* carried out five depth charge attacks, and U-203 surfaced violently and then sank. No merchant ship in the convoy was touched and two U-boats had been destroyed, the second by surface escorts alone - a satisfactory conclusion to the first British air support group operation.

Subsequent analysis, however, highlighted the different views of the carrier CO and SO escort on where the former should have been positioned. Their opposing views pointed to a need for more integration of air and surface tactical practice. This was resolved by the introduction of a tactical school at Liverpool under the command of CINCWA, and, almost immediately, the joint RN/RAF Anti-Submarine School at Londonderry. In the latter, escorts and support group commanders flew in naval and RAF aircraft, with airmen able to go to sea in escort ships and submarines while taking part in realistic A/S exercises.

In *Biter*'s second support operation, further fundamental lessons were learned. The captain had doubts about the usefulness of the Martlets. As a result, they had little flying practice, and two got lost, being forced to ditch some miles from the convoy HX237 - fortunately near a straggler and tug, which rescued the pilots. On 12 May, a Swordfish was launched to investigate a HF/DF bearing. Thirty minutes later, it made a sighting report, during which machine-gun fire could be heard, followed by silence. It was later learnt that the aircraft was shot down by U-230 and that on hitting the water, its depth charges exploded.

Up to this time, no consideration had been given to sending aircraft up in pairs or keeping a 'strike force' ranged on deck. After the loss of the Swordfish, both were implemented, but it was not thought desirable to use the last remaining Martlet to shoot up the submarine while a Swordfish attacked with depth charges. Forty sorties, totalling over 100 hours airborne, were flown in support of HX237.

On 13 April, CINCWA ordered *Biter* to proceed 200 miles south to support SC129, another east-bound convoy threatened by a U-boat concentration. In this case, she took up position number 53 within the convoy, but her Swordfish patrols were drastically hampered by low winds, reducing the weapon load with which they could launch. Nevertheless, SC129 came through unscathed; *Biter*'s aircraft had certainly played a great part in keeping the U-boats down. The following statistics for operations with HX237 and SC129 are of interest:

Aircraft Sorties:	67
Flying hours:	167
U-boats sighted:	9 (one by 2 aircraft)
U-boats attacked:	8 (one by 2 aircraft)
U-boats sunk or shared:	1 shared with escorts

HMS *Archer* and USS *Bogue* were also at sea with support groups in May. The latter's aircraft successfully attacked U-569 on 22 May and caused it to surrender, the first outright kill by a CVE's aircraft. Only a day later, *Archer*'s aircraft sank U-752 with 3-inch rockets, a new and effective weapon. The U-boat had been attacked by Swordfish and a Liberator with depth charges throughout the morning but at 1000, a Swordfish of 819 Naval Air Squadron was vectored onto the surfaced U-boat by *Archer*'s radar. The pilot made good use of cloud, flying at 1,500 feet (457.2m). When he judged the submarine to be on his beam, he dived and fired his eight rockets in four salvos. The first, from 800 yards (731.52m), was 150 yards (137.16m) short; the second at 400 yards (365. 76m) was 30 yards (27.43m) short of the conning tower; the third from

300 yards (274. 32m) was only 10 feet (3.05m) short and the fourth, fired at 200 yards (182.88m) hit on the waterline, 20 feet (6.10m) forward of the rudders. Each rocket had a 25lb (11.34kg) solid head and caused extensive damage, which prevented U-752 from diving. When the 20mm gun on the conning tower was manned, the Swordfish withdrew and called up a Martlet of 892 Naval Air Squadron which carried out a strafing attack, killing the submarine's captain while his boat was scuttled beneath him.

On her return, CINCWA praised *Archer*'s use of fighter direction techniques to home her aircraft onto submarine contacts, and her creation of an air plot on which HF/DF bearings of U-boat transmissions, the positions of patrolling aircraft obtained by radar and the convoy position were all used to give action information on the U-boat situation from which air A/S countermeasures could be quickly launched.

Following these first experiences of British escort carriers, certain important steps with regard to future CVE operations were agreed. They are given here in full so that they may be discussed along with other weapons and aspects of the battle.

i. Aircrew in CVEs should be overborne up to 50%. (In the event, shortage of aircrew prevented this happening).

ii. Aircraft complements to be increased to 15 TBR and six fighters (the number then carried by USS *Bogue*). Shortage of Swordfish prevented this too.

iii. YE aircraft homing beacons to be fitted as soon as possible to facilitate the return of aircraft, espcially fighters, to CVEs.

iv. Radar Type 257 Blind Approach System (BABS) to be fitted.

v. Stowage in CVEs for aircraft depth charges to be increased from 216 to 270, as on many occasions aircraft had to jettison weapons before landing on in bad conditions, and stocks could become low in protracted operations.

vi. To reduce the time lag between sighting and attack on a U-boat, Swordfish speed during the attack was to be increased from the 100 knots (184km/h) previously laid down to 130 knots (239. 46km/h).

vii. *Biter*'s policy of single aircraft not attacking a surfaced U-boat until a second aircraft or striking force of one TBR and one fighter arrived was concurred with, while 'fighting it out' remained German policy.

viii. When R/T congestion made reporting unreliable, the practice used by *Archer*'s aircraft (of changing the IFF setting to Stop 6 to indicate that a U-boat had been sighted, and to Stop 5 to show it had dived) was made standard operating procedure.

ix. A separate Western Approaches Fleet Air Arm frequency of 4340 kc/s common to TBRs and fighters was instituted, to avoid congestion on the common R/T wave. The supply of the new Battle of Atlantic Type TR1304 R/T set to CVE aircraft was expedited.

x. The fitting of Martlet/Wildcat fighters with rocket projectiles (recommended by *Archer* as likely to prove, together with its 0.5-inch guns, a deadly combination) was already being investigated, but difficulty was being found in obtaining the necessary engineering capacity to undertake such large retrospective modifications to these American aircraft.

With these measures and other tactical improvements implemented, the success of Allied anti-submarine operations in the North Atlantic caused Flag Officer U-boats to move his boats in June 1943 to attack the US North Africa convoys in positions 300-500 miles south-west of the Azores. The American CVEs *Bogue*, *Santee* and *Core* countered, and quickly made their presence felt by sinking eight U-boats between 5 June and the end of July.

The Allies now had the measure of the U-boat. The decline in shipping losses gives graphic evidence of this, only one ship being sunk in June, and that not in convoy. This trend continued for some months with U-boats widely scattered away from the North Atlantic. For this reason, the British, who continued to patrol the northern routes, did not achieve the same spectacular successes as the USN CVEs working south-west of the Azores.

Although helped by good weather, the achievements of the American CVEs were outstanding by any standard. Their operations required resolution, tactical skill and a good aircraft, the Avenger. Their success reflected the freedom of action given to US air support groups and the fact that they saw *aircraft*, not the escorts, as the principal means of attacking submarines. It is worth noting that on her first A/S patrol, USS *Core* spent over a month at sea and achieved the following statistics:

Sailed Hampton Roads		6.04.43
Returned Hampton Roads		1.07.43
Days at Sea		34
Flying hours	- Avenger	1,200
	- Wildcat	50
Average	- per day	50
	- per pilot/day	2
Attacks made		3
U-boats sunk		2 (U-487 and U-67)

In August 1943, a dispute arose over the US perception of the length of time it took the Admiralty to get CVEs into operational service after their date of completion. A letter from the Allied Anti-Submarine Survey Board to the C-in-C US Fleet even went so far as to say that, since it took 24-30 weeks for the RN to get new ships into operational service, the next seven to be completed should be reallocated to the USN. The Admiralty replied immediately that much of the perceived delay occurred in America; on average it took 1½-3 months from completion date before the ships were ready to leave Norfolk, Virginia, for the UK. The passage to the UK was lengthened for three ships by the need to ferry US aircraft to Casablanca and for others by the need to work up new squadrons prior to passage.

On arrival in the UK, CVEs were given seven weeks in dockyard hands to improve the petrol system and fit British equipment. This was followed by a 5-6 week work-up to prepare them for operational service. The ability to operate fighters as a result of the modification package had, moreover, enabled the RN to undertake extra short-notice commitments in the Mediterranean and the East Indies, to the benefit of the Allied war effort.

The congestion in British shipyards at this period was clearly not understood by the Americans. These contrary views illustrate how easily misunderstanding could occur between inter-Allied staffs working 3,000 miles apart, even in a war with modern communications. In the event, Admiralty policy proved justified. On 27 March 1943 off the Mull of Galloway, HMS *Dasher* - an unmodified US-built CVE - sank in three minutes after a devastating petrol vapour explosion. No British-built or converted carrier suffered a similar fate, whereas those of other navies did.

In fact, if modifications had been waived and the CVEs thereby come into service earlier, the RN was so short of manpower in 1944 that it would have been unable to send the ships to sea. This influenced the Admiralty to suggest to the British Admiralty delegation in Washington that it might be prudent to agree to the USN taking over five of the seven ships expected in the first months of 1944. The Admiralty were then told in confidence that the USN had manning difficulties of its own and could not take the additional carriers. The status quo was, therefore, preserved, but it is interesting to note that Allied strategy and tactics regarding CVEs were still not completely integrated.

It is not possible, in the short space available, to cover all shipborne air anti-U-boat operations in the Atlantic. I have covered their background and their initial deployments. Statistical information showing which convoys had carrier-borne air support is provided in the annex. Escort carriers and MAC-ships proved to be most valuable weapons, demonstrating their tactical dominance over the U-boat in 1944. Usually (not only in favourable weather conditions), they were able to provide a convoy with round-the-clock protection against U-boat attack and against air attack in daylight hours, the latter limitation being due to the lack of a suitable night fighter.

In assessing U-boat kills by carrier aircraft, important factors which cannot be shown statistically are that, apart from those made outright by their aircraft and those shared by them with the surface escorts, kills were often made by escorts as a result of an air sighting. Kills were, of course, by no means the sole measure of the value of the work done by CVEs or MAC-Ships. The ultimate object of carrier-borne A/S operations was the safe and timely arrival of the convoy at its destination. Frequently, when there were no kills, it was the very presence of aircraft preventing the development of the attack by a concentration of U-boats on the convoy which allowed it to continue on its way unmolested.

Both British and American experience showed that the most profitable area, and the most economical in terms of flying hours per kill for destroying U-boats, was in the vicinity of convoys and that roving killer groups unrelated to any convoy did not achieve comparable success, even when aided by Intelligence. At the same time, the very persistence with which hunter-killer groups were able to track down a suspected U-boat did obtain some results, but this was worthwhile only during periods when current U-boats tactics were to avoid attacking convoys. From a Report by the Maritime Air Defence Joint Historical Sub-Committee, it is clear that CVEs were used on a wide variety of operational tasks in 1944:

Duty	Number of Operations
Convoy Escort	64
Aircraft Ferry	42
Support of Land Operations	23
A/S Hunts	17
Anti-Shipping Strikes	20
Minelaying Strikes	9
Search for Blockade Runners	1

'Convoy escort' includes Gibraltar, North Atlantic and Russian convoys. During these, 3,237 sorties totalling 7,032 flying hours were flown, an average of 7.3 hours per day per carrier. These results were achieved in an average of 6.9 days per operation, equivalent to 67% of the total sea days. The flying period could have been considerably higher since other factors besides weather conditions limited flying. Amongst these were:

  i. Support by land-based aircraft for convoys.
  ii. The necessity to maintain W/T silence and thus reduce operations,
       especially on the Russian route.
  iii. When more than one CVE was present, alternative duties were taken.

The following table of British CVE operations in 1944 shows the comparatively high flying hours per kill. This may be attributed to the lack of U-boats operating against convoys in the North Atlantic after March 1944:

Number of operations	14
Sea days	218
Flying days as % of sea days	74%
Sorties flown	1,060
Average hours per sortie	2.15
Approximate hours flown	2,287
Kills	1 + 2 shared
Average aircraft complement per carrier	16

To summarise, the importance of aircraft in anti-submarine warfare was underestimated before 1939. Once the flexibility of carrier-based aviation was realized, escort carriers converted from merchant hull designs proved a rapid and effective means of providing tactical aircraft where they were needed, namely near convoys. The colossal capacity of American industry to build them left the Axis powers no chance of ultimate success. CVEs were felt in combat in 1942, decisive in 1943 and overwhelmingly powerful in 1944.

Appendix 1: Atlantic Convoys Escorted or Supported by British CVEs, 1943/44

Month 1943	CVE(s) - *HMS*	Convoy(s)
Jan/Feb	*Argus*	WS23/KMF8
Mar	*Attacker*	CU1
	Hunter and *Stalker*	MKF11
Apr	*Biter* and 5th Escort Group	ON178, ONS4
May	*Biter* and 5th Escort Group	HX237, SC129
	Archer and 4th Escort Group	ONS6, ON182, HX239
	Unicorn	WS30/KMF15
June	*Unicorn*	MKF15
	Biter and 1st Escort Group	HX242, ONS10
	Battler	OS49/KMS16, XK9 (Sp)
	Chaser	HX245
July	*Biter* and 1st Escort Group	SC135
	Ravager	HX248
Aug	*Hunter*	WS33/KMF22
Sept	*Tracker* and 4th Escort Group	ON203, HX258
Oct	*Hunter, Stalker, Attacker*	MKF24
	Fencer	UA3 (ss *Franconia* only), SC45
	Biter and 7th Escort Group	ON207
	Tracker and 2nd Escort Group	ON207, HX262
Nov	*Biter*, 5th and 7th Escort Groups	SC146, HX265
	Tracker and 2nd Escort Group	HX263, ON209, HX264
	Fencer	OS60/KMS34
Dec	*Fencer*	SL141/MKS32, OS61/KMS35, SL142/MKS33
	Striker	OS62/KMS36, SL143/MKS34
	Tracker	HX270

1944

Jan	*Striker*		OS63/KMS37, SL144/MKS35
Feb	*Fencer* A/S sweep with		ON223
	Striker 16th Escort Group		HX278
	Nairana A/S sweep with		OS66/KMS40, ON22, ONS28,
	Activity 2nd Escort Group		SL147/MKS40
	Pursuer (Fighter carrier)		OS67/KMS41, SL149/MKS40
	Biter, Tracker		OS68/KMS42, ONS29
	Nairana, Activity		OS69/KMS43
	Fencer		KMF29, SL149/MKS40
Mar	*Vindex*		HX283, SC155
	Nairana, Activity		MKF29
	Biter, Tracker		SL150/MKS41
	Striker		OS70/KMS44, SL152/MKS43
	Nairana		OS72/KMS46
Apr	*Biter*	A/S sweep with 7th Escort Group	OS73/KMS47
	Empress		CU19
	Nairana		SL154/MKS45
May	*Vindex* with 3rd, 5th and 9th Escort Groups on A/S Sweep and U-boat search		Various in vicinity but not directly supported.
	Hunter, Striker, Attacker		OS77/KMF51
	Nairana	A/S Sweep with 15th Escort Group	SL158/MKS49
	Emperor		SL158/MKS49
	Activity		OS78/KMS52, SL158/MKS49 and back to OS78/KMS52
June	*Activity, Campania*		SL159/MKS50, OS79/KMS53
	Hunter, Attacker		KMS52. Through Straits and in Western Mediterranean.
	Pursuer, Tracker, Emperor		Withdrew from Op CA to give fighter protection during Op Neptune in W Approaches to Channel.

	Nairana	KMF32, MKF32
	Searcher	OS80/KMS54, SL161/MKS52
	Activity	OS81/KMS55
July	*Activity*	SL162/MKS53, KMF33
	Campania	OS82/KMS56, SL163/MKS54
	Vindex, Striker	A/S Sweep off Cape Wrath with 3rd Escort Group
	Fencer	OS83/KMS57, SL166/MKS55
	Biter	OS84/KMS57
	Striker	Op Kinetic in Bay of Biscay with Force 34
Aug	*Vindex*	A/S Sweep off Iceland. No direct support of any convoy.
	Biter	SL165/MKS56
	Campania	OS85/KMS59, SL166/MKS57
	Activity	MKF33, OS86/KMS60, SL167/MKS58
	Nairana	KMF34
	Fencer	A/S Sweep with Force 32 in Op CX. No direct support of convoys
Sept	*Nairana*	MKF34
Oct	*Trumpeter, Fencer*	A/S Sweep with Force 9 in support of homeward bound N Russian convoy RA60

Appendix 2: MAC-ship Operations, 1943-45 (based on Trade Division Records)

		1943	1944	1945	Totals	
No. of						
MAC-ships	In USA	14	116	40	170	
arriving	In UK	13	100	40	153	323
Days at Sea	Out	207	1643	605	2455	
	In	171	1295	526	1992	4447

Air sorties	Out	159	1452	742	2353	
	In	123	1151	550	1824	4177
Operational	Out	332	3189	1660	5181	
flying hours	In	235	2437	1163	3835	9016
Average of						
flying hours	Total	21	26	35	27	*(overall average)*
Ship/passage						
Days when	Out	NK	436	233	669	
flying took	In	NK	327	187	514	1183
place						
% of						
flying days		NK	44	44	44	
to days in						
convoy						
Aircraft lost						
or damaged		19	74	21	114	
beyond						
onboard repair						

Air personnel lost: 1943, 1 aircrew; 1944, 1 aircrew, 2 leading airmen; 1945, 1 pilot.

Appendix 3: Representative CVEs and MAC-ships

HMS *Activity*, British CVE conversion
Displacement: 11,800 tons standard, 14,250 tons deep load
Dimensions: 512' (156.05m) loa, 492' (149.96m) flight deck, 66'5" (20.24m) beam, 25'1" (7.65m) mean deep draught
Machinery: 2 shaft diesel, 12,000BHP = 18 knots
Armament: 2x4-inch (1 twin) Mk XVI, 24x22mm Oerlikon
Aircraft: 11
Complement: 700

MV *Empire MacAlpine*, British MAC-ship
Displacement: 8,250grt
Dimensions: 459' (139.9m) loa, 413'9" (126.11m) flight deck, 62' (18.9m) beam, 28'9" (8.76m) deep draught
Machinery: 1 shaft diesel, 3,300 BHP = 12.5 knots
Armament: 2x40mm Bofors, 4x20mm Oerlikon
Aircraft: 4
Complement:107

USS *Bogue*, US CVE conversion
Displacement: 9,393 tons standard, 13,891 tons deep load
Dimensions: 495' (141.73m) loa, 442' (134.72m) flight deck, 111' (33.83m)
   beam, 23'3" (7.09m) deep draught
Machinery: 1 shaft steam turbine, 2 boilers, 8,500SHP = 16.5 knots
Armament:2x5-inch single, 4x40mm Bofors, 10x20mm Oerlikon
Aircraft: 28
Complement: 890

Appendix 4: Naval Anti-Submarine Aircraft

Fairey Swordfish: Carrier-based, 3-seater biplane used for torpedo, bombing and
   reconnaissance as well as A/S patrol. Open cockpit, no crew heating.
Span: 45'6" (13.87m)
Length: 36'4" (11.07m)
Power plant: One 750hp Bristol Pegasus XXX
Weight empty: 5,200lbs (2,358.7kg)
        loaded: 8,330lbs (3,778.5kg)
Cruising Speed: 90 knots (165 km/h)
Maximum level speed: 120 knots (220 km/h)
Armament: 1 fixed forward-firing .303" browning in fuselage, 1 Vickers K gun
   .303" hand-operated aft in cockpit, 3 Mk VII depth charges of 8x60lb
   (27.2kg) rocket projectiles under wing or up to 1x1,600lb (725.76kg) of
   bombs, mines, or a torpedo.

Grumman Avenger: Carrier-based, 3-seater torpedo, bomber and A/S strike
   aircraft. Monoplane with enclosed cockpit.
Span: 54'2" (16.51m)
Length: 40' (12.19m)
Power plant: One 1,750 hp Wright Cyclone R-2600-20
Weight empty: 10,700lb (4853.52kg)
        loaded: 16,400lb (7439.04kg)
Cruising speed: 150 knots (275 km/h)
Maximum level speed: 225 knots (415 km/h)
Armament: 2 forward-firing 0.5" Brownings in wings, 1x0.3" Browning in
   fuselage ventral position, up to 2,000lb (907.2kg) of depth charges, mines,
   bombs or torpedoes in internal bomb bay or 8x60lb (27.2kg) rocket
   projectiles underwing.

Appendix 5:'Reptile' Air Patrols (Atlantic Convoy Instructions, Article 200)

Code Word	Action by Aircraft	Occasions for Use
Cobra 'Y'	Patrol round convoy at distance of Y miles.	Normal day conditions. No outer surface screen. No indications of U-boats shadowing or U-boats known to be in vicinity, bearing unknown.
Viper	Patrol round convoy at visibility distance.	By day in conditions of poor and/or variable visibility when U-boats are known to be in vicinity. For general use at night.
Adder	Patrol ahead of convoy at distance of 8 to 12 miles. Length of patrol 30 miles (15 miles either side of centre line).	By day when attack is expected.
'X' Python 'Y'	Search on bearing indicated X for S/M detected on that bearing at Y miles. Aircraft will carry out square search round position indicated for 20 minutes using 2 miles visibility.	When S/M has been detected by D/F bearings and when its distance has been determined.
'X' Mamba	Search on bearing indicated to a depth of 30 miles and return.	When S/M has been detected by a D/F bearing but distance is uncertain.
'X' Lizard 'Y'	Search sector indicated X to a depth of Y miles.	When a special area is suspected. May be used at night.
Frog 'Y'	Patrol astern of convoy at a distance of Y miles. Length of patrol to be 2Y miles (Y miles either side of centre line.)	To detect U-boats trailing the convoy. Of particular use at dusk prior to an alteration of course by the convoy.
Alligator Port or Starboard	Patrol on side indicated at distance of 10 miles from convoy's line of advance. Length of patrol to be 20 miles (10 miles ahead and astern of beam bearing)	When circumstances render a beam patrol desirable.

Crocodile Y	Patrol ahead of convoy from beam to beam at radius Y miles (ie half a Cobra)	With fast convoys. Normal day conditions. No outer surface screen. No indications of U-boats in the vicinity.

Unpublished Sources

Naval Staff History: *The Defeat of the Enemy Attack on Shipping*, Admiralty, London, 1957.

The Development of British Naval Aviation, Volumes 1 & 2, Admiralty, London, 1956.

The RAF in Maritime War, Air Ministry, London, nd.

Secondary sources are listed in the Consolidated Bibliography

22

The Wireless War

by Jürgen Rohwer

In the Battle of the Atlantic, the value and importance of wireless communications can scarcely be overestimated. The Allied shore commands could not have controlled their vast quantities of shipping, nor routed the convoys, without the use of radio communications. Similarly, without radio communications, Admiral (later Grand Admiral) Karl Dönitz, the German Commander U-boats, could neither have received situation reports from his U-boats at sea nor sent his orders for their deployment. Of all the instruments and weapons available to either side throughout the entire campaign, wireless was indisputably the single most important one.

From their experiences in WWI, both sides were well aware of the three methods of radio intelligence-gathering, and of the dangers they might present. To avoid the first danger - that enemy intercept-stations might read open-text messages - all navies used different systems of encoding or encrypting their signals. The experience of Room 40's decryption of Germany's encoded signals in World War I had led the three services of the Wehrmacht to adopt the now famous Enigma machine, with its ingenious cipher mechanism using three of five exchangeable rotors. By the addition of three further rotors, this was also specially adapted for use by the Kriegsmarine.

Up to mid-1943, as far as the Battle of the Atlantic is concerned, the Royal Navy, and later its Allies, used a different system, with super-enciphered code-books.

The second danger came from the methods of traffic analysis. After a period of continuous observation, an enemy's radio traffic discloses the meaning of call-signs identifying units and individual ships, while communication patterns can disclose details of their order of battle. As the third and final danger, by taking bearings of the signals, high-frequency radio direction-finding (HF/DF) can provide details of the location and the movement of enemy units.

Studying the history of the Battle of the Atlantic, eight chronological phases may now be perceived. How, then, did radio communications and these three dangers influence the developments of the various phases?

The First Phase: September 1939-June 1940

During the first phase, both sides used radio-communications between shore commands and their sea-going units - armed or civilian - only to a limited extent. On the Allied side at this time, radio intelligence existed only in the form of shore-based direction-finding. Before the war, the Germans greatly feared this method. After the outbreak, therefore, the U-boats were ordered to keep radio silence at all times, except when reporting enemy contacts. To counter the direction-finding to some extent, a short-signal system was introduced. By reducing signals into only a few signal-groups, most became too brief to be intercepted. Moreover, when using the 'Home Waters' (*Heimische Gewässer*) setting, as the U-boats did, the Enigma M-3 could not be broken by the Bletchley Park cryptanalysts. In contrast, before the war the xB-Dienst - the German decryption service - had already begun solving parts of the code-books and the super-enciphering long subtracter tables of the two current British systems, the Naval Cipher No. 1 and the Naval Code. Because of the low level of radio-traffic from escort vessels, this was, however, of only limited operational use to the small number of U-boats at sea.

During the Norwegian campaign in 1940, the Seekriegsleitung received important decrypts from the xB-Dienst about the movements of the Allied forces at sea. At this stage British decrypting progress was comparatively slow, because to begin with, it was (despite the five Engima rotors given them by the Polish in 1939) impossible to reconstruct the wiring system of the three additional rotors used by the Kriegsmarine. Even the capture of rotors VI and VII when U-33 was sunk in February 1940 in the Clyde could not solve the problem. Later in April 1940 the British destroyer *Griffin* boarded the special service trawler *Schiff 26* and captured cipher documents which allowed the reconstruction of the naval indicator system and a comparison of some plain-text messages with cipher texts. But it took until June before the decrypts were available, and in July the Germans changed the indicator tables.

The Second Phase: July 1940-May 1941

The second phase was characterized by the first real 'wolf pack' operations against convoys off the North Channel, and (until the loss of the *Bismarck*) by operations of German heavy surface ships in the Atlantic. To direct the U-boats and ships against the convoys, and to re-route the convoys or to lead the hunting groups, the shore commands on both sides needed a much greater volume of radio traffic than before.

On the Allied side, radio intelligence was still only available in the form of direction-finding and traffic-analysis, but the results were somewhat disappointing: over distances of more than 200 miles, shore-based direction-finding was not exact enough to route a convoy clear of weather-reporting U-boats far out in the west. This gave the German command a sense of security - of false security, as it turned out, with bad consequences.

On the German side, the xB-Dienst suffered its first setback when, on 20 August 1940, the British changed the code-books and tables of their two cipher systems. It took several months before the xB-Dienst could again decrypt with some delay, first about one quarter, then one third and later more of the intercepted messages, part of which were used for directing U-boats to convoys.

Even when (in August 1940) the British captured the missing rotor VIII, it remained impossible to break the daily settings of the Home Waters cipher circuit, used for about 90% of the signals, without the corresponding new indicator tables. But in the spring of 1941 the situation changed dramatically in their favour. On 4 March, during a carefully planned operation against German shipping in the Lofoten Islands, a boarding party from the destroyer *Somali* captured new cipher materials from the damaged and abandoned patrol vessel *Krebs*, and an intensive cryptanalytic attack was started. This led to the solving, between 20 March and 5 April, of most of the traffic for the period 13-23 February. Between 22 April and 10 May, April's traffic was read, with the May traffic being decrypted thereafter with delays of about seven days.

Meanwhile, in a bid to capture the daily Home Waters settings, a British force of three cruisers and four destroyers were searching for the German weather observation trawler *München*, guided by taking bearings of her weather transmissions. On 7 May the trawler was surprised in fog near Jan Mayen Island, and a boarding party from the destroyer *Somali* recovered important cipher material. Two days later, during a convoy battle, the U-boat U-110 was forced to the surface. A boarding party from the destroyer *Bulldog* found a rich haul - the settings for Officer-only signals, the U-boat short-signal and weather codebooks, the grid maps for the North Atlantic and the indicator tables, as well as the daily settings for April and June. When put together with the data from *München*, this enabled Bletchley Park in June 1941 to read German traffic on a near-current basis.

This breakthrough came too late to be of use during the operations against *Bismarck* and *Prinz Eugen*. Their radio signals were transmitted in the new *Kernflotte* or *Neptun* cipher circuit. Like the *Aegir* circuit, used by the raiders, so few signals were transmitted on this that they could never be broken. But the signals *Bismarck* did send were far too long, and by taking bearings from them, the Home Fleet was finally able to intercept the ship.

The Third Phase: July-December 1941

Knowing when Enigma's new month settings would come into force, the June cipher materials were soon augmented still further. On 28 June, the weather trawler *Lauenburg* fell victim to the destroyer *Tartar*, which went alongside the sinking vessel and recovered the ciphers for July. This enabled the Admiralty's Operational Intelligence Centre to smash the entire German surface supply organization in the Atlantic. The loss of the supply ships made further surface raiding operations impossible for the time being. This, the Seekriegsleitung thought, must have had its roots in some break into their signals. An investigation concluded that probably secret papers and possibly cipher materials had been removed from the tanker *Gedania*, captured and taken to Gibraltar. By sending a prearranged key-word the Seekriegsleitung changed the indicator tables.

But the Commander U-boats was more concerned. Since April, he had allowed the distribution of daily U-boat situation reports only on a strict 'need to know' basis. He had also ordered modified settings for the U-boats using the Home Waters circuit, while simultaneously asking the Seekriegsleitung to introduce a special cipher for U-boat use only. On 16 June 1941, he began to use fixed reference points to transmit positions. When this led to some misunderstandings the method was changed (9 September) back to grid references, but by using sets of reciprocal bigram substitution tables the two letters designating the big grid squares were disguised before the clear text went to the transmission station. Furthermore, on 28 September, when two U-boats replenishing in remote Tarafal Bay were surprised by a British submarine, Dönitz insisted that U-boat radio traffic must be separated out into the special *Triton* cipher circuit. This was effected on 4 October 1941. Finally, on 24 November, he implemented an even more difficult system of disguising references, by using an *Address-buch*, which was changed often.

Nevertheless, all these measures gave only limited trouble to the British cryptanalysts. After they had begun the analytic decryption of the German daily settings on 4 August 1941, they experienced few further delays. Most of the U-boat signals were now read with average delays of two to three days, enough to allow the Submarine Tracking Room and the Trade Division to re-route the North Atlantic convoys perfectly round the U-boat patrol lines. A conservative estimate indicates that in the second half of 1941, Ultra saved about 1.5-2 million gross tons of Allied shipping from being sunk. This led to the first big crisis in the U-boat war, which might have been in the long run more decisive than the later successes of Bletchley Park.

But there was one more important consequence of Ultra during these months. The US Atlantic Fleet had extended its Neutrality Patrols in April and June, first to 30° and then to 26° West. On 19 June, U-203 reported a meeting with the US battleship *Texas*, followed by other similar reports. From decrypted signals of the Commander U-Boats, Churchill learned that, so long as he was fighting his war of conquest against the Soviet Union, Hitler wanted at all costs to avoid incidents which might bring in the US into the war. Informed of this by Churchill at the Atlantic Conference (9-12 August), President Roosevelt now allowed the US Atlantic Fleet, together with the RN, to chase German raiders, and to escort fast Allied convoys from Newfoundland to and from a Mid-Ocean Meeting Point south of Iceland. However, Roosevelt was not yet willing for US ships to operate under British command, so Churchill agreed to transfer operational control of the North Atlantic convoys in the western part of the North Atlantic to the Chief of Naval Operations in Washington, starting on 1 September 1941.

Because the US-escorted Allied convoys were so cleverly routed round the German patrol lines by the Admiralty's Ultra-based recommendations, only very few incidents occurred involving the USN and the Kriegsmarine. There was the *Greer* case, the torpedoing of the destroyer *Kearny* and the navy tanker *Salinas*, and the sinking of the destroyer *Reuben James*. Roosevelt used these to prompt his 'shoot on sight' order and to force Congress to drop the last restrictions of the Neutrality Acts, while Hitler, wishing to avoid a two-fronted war, did not react. But on one occasion he might well have been forced to. On 5 November 1941, a US Task Force consisting of two battleships, two heavy cruisers and three destroyers was in the Denmark Strait. Ultra decrypts had revealed that the pocket battleship *Admiral Scheer* was about to sortie on a new raiding operation, and - at a time when the US and Germany were still technically at peace - the Task Force was lying in wait to intercept her. What might have happened, had not engine-trouble prevented *Admiral Scheer* from proceeding to sea? Her loss (which would have been a direct result of Ultra's efficiency) might have forced Hitler to declare war four weeks before Pearl Harbor!

The Fourth Phase: January-July 1942

On 1 February 1942 the Enigma M-4 was introduced. In this machine the reflector rotor B, used since November 1937, was divided into a smaller reflector B and an additional 'Greek' rotor, 'Beta'. Instead of one period of 16,900 digits, this provided 26 different periods of that length. Even when Bletchley Park solved the problem of the interior wiring of the new Beta rotor, analytical decryption remained impossible because there was also a new indicator system and a new weather-codebook brought into use, the most important source for 'cribs'. The so-called 'big black-out' of U-boat signals began.

In the fourth phase the U-boats sank more ships off the US East Coast, in the Gulf of Mexico and the Caribbean, than in any other phase of the war. But this was not - as is often assumed - the consequence of the 'big black-out'. Even with continuing Ultra, the situation in the Western Atlantic would probably have been serious. Notwithstanding Britain's experiences with convoying collected in autumn 1941, and massive pressure from the Admiralty, it took five months for the USN to introduce the 'Interlocking Convoy System'. For the Allies, this delay was one of the most damaging failures of the USN in the whole war. With merchant ships sailing individually and unescorted, U-boats could attack easily and with little risk, and the volume of radio signals, necessary to direct convoy-battles, was greatly reduced. The Submarine Tracking Room could only estimate the number of U-boats at sea by continuing to use decrypts of the Home Waters or Hydra circuit, used by the vessels escorting the U-boats in and out of the French or Norwegian coasts. But information about the operating areas came only from sighting reports by aircraft or attacked merchantmen.

The Fifth Phase: July 1942-May 1943

When it was finally introduced, the 'Interlocking Convoy System' so drastically reduced the U-boats' sighting of targets that, in July 1942, the Commander U-boats changed his main operating area again to the North Atlantic. Now the U-boats raked in long patrol lines along the convoy routes, while on both sides of the ocean the Allies tried to route their convoys clear of assumed U-boat concentrations. Once again intense radio traffic was necessary on both sides.

While the U-boats' Triton circuit remained impervious to Bletchley Park, in Germany the xB-Dienst was able to break into the inter-Allied Naval Cipher No 3, used since June 1941 for the control of convoy operations. At the end of 1942 about 80% of the intercepted signals could be decrypted. But with this code-system, super-enciphered by long-subtracter lists, every signal had to be decrypted individually. This took so long that only about 10% of the signals were decrypted in time for operational use. Overdue decrypts could only be used for establishing the convoy schedule.

Limited as they were, these achievements by the xB-Dienst gave the U-boats sufficient support to achieve great successes against many convoys from July 1942 to March 1943. However, using a different technique, in the same period many other convoys escaped the U-boats. Based on the experiences of 1940 and an idea by Sir Robert Watson-Watt, the British developed a small automatic HF/DF set, which after some experiments became operational in 1942. A similar set was developed in the US using the experiments of the French scientists Deloraine and Busignies. From autumn 1942, most escort groups had at least one ship with an HF/DF set, which enabled them to run down a bearing of a contact signal of an U-boat, forcing the contact holder to dive and to lose contact. Indications of this technique were reported by U-boats, and could even be found in decrypts of Allied radio signals; yet despite this, German experts connected all such indications with the effects of radar. It was one of their greatest mistakes.

Even so, from the Allied point of view HF/DF was only a second-best solution; the ideal was to continue reading German signals. The opportunity came at last on 30 October 1942, in the eastern Mediterranean. Following an action there in which U-559 was forced to surface, a boarding party of the British destroyer *Panther* was able to acquire the new weather code book, the most important source for 'cribs'. This seemed less than they had been hoping for; two British sailors tried to recover the U-boat's 4-rotor Enigma machine, but went down with the sinking boat and were drowned. Moreover, the papers recovered were printed with water-soluble ink, and were damaged. But although it took Bletchley Park until 15 December, it was enough; they had the decisive break-through.

At first there were some delays and even long gaps, but from late January to early February 1943 Ultra again became a stream, allowing the Submarine Tracking Room to re-route the convoys. Against this, the xB-Dienst was able to decrypt not only the sailing telegrams of the Harbor Captain New York (giving the exact details of the composition of the east-bound convoys), but also many re-routeing signals and the Admiralty's daily U-boat situation reports. As Dönitz concentrated all available U-boats to force a decision in the North Atlantic, so it became more and more difficult for the Submarine Tracking Room to re-route the convoys clear of the rising number of patrol lines. Thus, when the key-word for the introduction of a new weather code book was decrypted on 8 March 1943, there was great fear in Bletchley Park that, without the necessary 'cribs', Triton would once again be blacked out. Immediately the whole convoy system, backbone of the Allied strategy, seemed to be imperilled. In one 10-day period alone (9-19 March 1943), no fewer than four convoys - SC121, HX228, SC122 and HX229 - lost 20% of their ships.

By concentrating all available means and using the many contact signals intercepted during the convoy battles as 'cribs', Bletchley Park was able to solve the problem by cryptanalytic methods on 20 March. This was possibly its most important single success in the whole war, for it permitted a new tactic. Hitherto Ultra had been used to avoid losses by evading the U-boats. Now it was used to concentrate the relatively few additional escorts and aircraft sent into the battle at the areas of greatest danger for the convoys, enabling the surface and air forces to fight the convoys through and to hunt located U-boats to death. In only eight weeks this tactic caused the turn of the tide. For Admiral Dönitz, instead of victory after victory, the convoy battles became defeat after defeat, with heavy losses; and on 24 May 1943 he had to recall his U-boats from the North Atlantic.

The Sixth Phase: June–August 1943

Without this new use of Ultra, many more support groups, escort carriers and Very-Long-Range (VLR) aircraft would have been necessary to bring about the turn of the tide. Because they would not have been available until many months later, additional heavy Allied shipping losses in the late spring and summer of 1943 might have seriously interfered with the build-up for the invasion of Europe. During the sixth phase of the Battle of the Atlantic, the race for advantages in cipher security and cryptanalysts again took a sharp turn in favour of the Allies. In spring 1943, when both sides were most successful in their decryption efforts, they also became most fearful about possible breaks into their systems. In Britain an investigation produced proof of a deep break-in, and on 10 June 1943 this led to the replacement of the inter-Allied Naval Cipher No. 3 and the British Naval Cipher No. 4 by the new, much improved version, Naval Cipher No. 5. A fatal black out for the xB-Dienst followed.

Simultaneously, German experts attributed the surprisingly exact location of the U-boat groups to the closing of the North Atlantic air gap by radar-equipped VLR aircraft and the new radar devices of the strengthened surface escorts. Because of this, although ciphers were improved, the improvements were too few and were insufficiently related. On 1 July 1943 a second set with the new, small C reflector and the new Greek 'Gamma' rotor was introduced, leading to a three-week black-out at Bletchley and then to further longer delays in breaking the daily settings of Triton. Bletchley's work was made much more difficult by the U-boats using many more Triton Officer-only signals, which were double-enciphered. Until September 1943, these could very often only be solved with delays of 7-14 days.

In June, Bletchley Park learned of the attempt to cover up the removal of the U-boats from the North Atlantic by a radio-deception and warned the distant regions where the Commander U-boats hoped to achieve some successes at weak spots. The USN started an Ultra-based offensive against the replenishment points west of the Azores, and RAF Coastal Command transferred a great part of its planes from the convoy routes to south-west England for a great air offensive against the U-boat routes in the Bay of Biscay.

The Seventh Phase: September 1943-May 1944

The changes between the two 'Greek' rotors caused significant problems for Bletchley Park. Their 'bombes' now had to test not only one period of 16,900 digits but often 2 x 26 x 16,900, so that the time needed was up to 52 times as great than before. The development of the 'High-Speed Bombes' in England was delayed, with the first set being ready only in June 1943. For Bletchley, this made the assignment of capacities and priorities very difficult. However, 100 High-Speed Bombes had also been ordered in the US, the first of which was ready in August. This led, in November, to the transfer of the Triton decryption to OP-20-G in Washington, thereby freeing British capacities for other cipher circuits.

These passing difficulties allowed Dönitz to achieve some surprise with the start of a new phase of convoy battles in the North Atlantic, using new weapons and equipment. But while he greatly overestimated the successes of the 'Gnat' acoustic-homing torpedoes, Ultra steadily provided from decrypted U-boat signals the technical details of the torpedo-shots, enabling the Allies to compare them with the reports of the escorts and to find the weak spots of the German weapons. This helped considerably in the development of counter-measures. In addition, from October, the faster decryption of the Triton signals caused all attempts to deploy U-boat groups in concentrated attacks against convoys to fail. In almost every way, the Allies had the measure of the old-type U-boats. These now could only be used in a holding campaign, attempting to prevent offensive operations by the enemy's strengthened anti-U-boat forces until summer 1944. At that time, it was hoped, the Battle would start again, using the new Type XXI boats to prevent an invasion of Europe.

The Eighth and Final Phase: June 1944-May 1945

In the last phase of the Battle of the Atlantic, the importance of radio intelligence diminished. Now, as they prepared to depart, the U-boats were usually notified of their operational areas only in written orders. Many U-boat captains hesitated to use wireless for fear of being D/F'd and hunted to the end. Because of this, Dönitz could receive only a limited amount of timely operational intelligence, but this meant fewer changes in orders were sent by radio. More and more frequently, signals used coded references to written orders, which the American High-Speed Bombes could not read. In December 1944 the Germans started to use separate *Sonderschlüssel* - special keys for single U-boats - which rendered the few signals that were sent practically as unbreakable as one-time pads. The experts at Bletchley Park and at OP-20-G began to fear, too, the introduction of a new off-frequency high-speed transmitter called 'Kurier', which had already been tested by some operational U-boats and could bring almost insurmountable problems of interception and decryption.

During the last months of the war, there was also some fear on the Allied side about the expected improvements to the new U-boat types XXI, XXIII and XXVI. Their capabilities were known because Japanese diplomats in Berlin sent details of them to their superiors in Tokyo, enciphered with the 'Purple' machine, which (by virtue of 'Magic' decrypts) the Americans had been able to read since September 1940. The 'mystery of the non-appearance of the Type XXI U-Boat' remained a constant worry for the Allies until the second half of March 1945. Then, the fears of a new German offensive with modern U-boats were finally laid to rest, when Magic and Ultra revealed the loss of the U-boats' Baltic training areas, and the extent of damage caused by the Allied air mine-laying campaign and heavy British air raids against Germany's building yards and interior transport system. Thus, as the Allied armies from east and west met in Berlin, World War II and the Battle of the Atlantic ended before the new U-boats could start their operations.

Summary

To sum up: If asked, 'What was the single most important factor in the outcome of the Battle of the Atlantic?', we can only reply: 'Signal intelligence.' In the first and second phases of the Battle, its role remained limited, with some advantages to the German side. In the third phase, however, it precipitated the U-boats' first major crisis, when Ultra-based routeing of the convoys saved more than 300 merchant ships from being sunk. In the fourth phase of the Battle it was unimportant and in the first part of the fifth phase, in 1942, the Germans had again some limited advantages. But then in the second part of the fifth phase, in the spring of 1943, it was positively *the* decisive factor, when it allowed the Allies an optimum deployment of their limited sea- and air forces to fight the convoys through and to bring about the turn of the tide. In the sixth and seventh phases, Ultra was instrumental in the best use of the Allies' greatly strengthened air assets. In the final phase, Ultra could not help much in the operations, but gave the necessary information to counter new German developments.

There is, however, another element which should not be overlooked in any summary of the Battle of the Atlantic. None of us, whether of the former Axis nations or the Allied, should ever forget that the results had to be fought for at sea by the thousands of men in the U-boats, the merchant ships, the escorts and the aircraft, with the ships, aircraft, sensors and weapons designed and built by countless scientists, engineers and workers in the engineering shops, the factories and the shipyards.

There were indeed a great many factors, the combination of which decided when the tide would turn in this, the longest battle of World War II. But without the cryptanalysts at Bletchley Park, and later at OP-20-G; without the Wrens, constantly at work; and without the men who translated the intelligence into operational orders, the turn of the tide in the Battle of the Atlantic might not have come until many months later. And without the Polish contributions of 1939, Bletchley Park might never have achieved the break at all. No doubt overall, a final Allied victory was never truly in doubt, because of the great difference between the armed strength and industrial capacities of the two opposing coalitions. But without signal intelligence, the war could have developed in quite another way from that which we witnessed, with even graver consequences to both sides.

23

Operational Research
in the Battle of the Atlantic

by Paul M. Sutcliffe

Introduction

Scientists and mathematicians fulfilled a number of specialist roles during the Battle of the Atlantic. Some developed equipment for their navies and air forces in order to give their colleagues in the front line the technical edge over the opposition, at least until the opposition's scientists developed a counter-measure. One of the classic battles of this type was, of course, that between radar and radar warning receivers. Other scientists provided Intelligence support to the fighting troops, both through developing the techniques of HF/DF and through the esoteric science of decryption. In both of these areas, the scientist was essentially on his own ground and no one denied his right to be there.

There was, however, a third group of scientists and mathematicians who, unlike their colleagues, had the temerity to trespass on the preserves of others. These were the operational researchers, who applied the basic principles of scientific method to the study of military operations with the aim of helping to improve their efficiency. In other words, they sought to influence the minds of senior operational commanders in order to change tactics, deployment patterns or equipment requirements.

The application of quantitative methods to the study of war was certainly not new in WWII. Lanchester had developed his famous equations over 25 years before, whilst Clausewitz was an earlier proponent of a quantitative theory of war. Indeed, there are some who claim that Alexander the Great's gathering of commanders round the fire for a rousing after-dinner tactical discussion was an early progenitor of the OR Group. Be that as it may, operational research as we recognise it today within Defence Departments had its origins in 1938 in the study of the application of the newly developed radar chain as an aid to fighter interceptions. A special group was initially set up at the Air Ministry Research Station Bawdsey, but was subsequently transferred to Fighter Command Headquarters. Other OR Groups soon followed.

Operational research was probably first brought to bear on the Battle of the Atlantic in late 1940 when a scientist was seconded from the Telecommunications Research Establishment to Coastal Command to study the operation of radar equipments. In March 1941, Professor Patrick Blackett was appointed Scientific Adviser to the Air Officer Commanding-in-Chief, Coastal Command, and became head of the newly formed Command Operational Research Section (ORS) in June 1941. The first discussions about an Admiralty OR group were held in late 1941 and Professor Blackett moved to the Admiralty in January 1942, with the title of Chief Adviser on Operational Research (CAOR). The US Navy Anti-Submarine Warfare OR Group (ASWORG) followed in March 1942 after the US entered the War, partly inspired by the British experience.

There is no evidence that U-Boat Command ever had an OR group, or its equivalent. That is not to say that quantitative methods were not applied; indeed Admiral Dönitz's criterion of effectiveness - tonnage of shipping sunk per U-boat per day at sea[1] - has all the hallmarks of the OR practitioner. However, there does not appear to have been any attempt to exploit systematically the application of scientific methods to the study of operations.

For this reason, this chapter is written essentially from the viewpoint of the Allies. It seeks to describe briefly the role played by OR groups, the type of work done and the contributions such groups made to the course of the Battle.

The Role of OR Groups

A key feature of most, if not all, of the early OR groups was the close relationship they had with very senior officers in the area they supported. For example, on his appointment to the Admiralty, Blackett worked directly to the Vice Chief of Naval Staff, with members of his staff working to individual Naval Staff Directors. In fact, as a member of the War Cabinet's Anti-U-Boat Committee, Blackett had access to the ear of Winston Churchill. Similarly, Professor C. H. Waddington, who worked in the Coastal Command ORS for most of its wartime existence, and ultimately came to lead it, stressed the paramount importance of the loyalty of a Command OR section to its Commander-in-Chief.

The function of an OR group was essentially to analyse data collected during operations in order to assess the level of performance, trends in performance and their underlying causes. From these, it was but a small step to propose ways in which performance might be improved by changing tactics or equipment. It was here, of course, that the role of operational researchers began to encroach upon that of the operational staffs, testing the tact and patience of both. There were many occasions during the Battle when the two cultures found it easy to work together, but there were also a few occasions when relations became strained.

Type of Work

Scope of Work. The various OR groups did not restrict themselves exclusively to ASW, though it did tend to dominate during the earlier years. For example, in his paper on operational research in Admiralty Headquarters in WWII, Pratt[2] lists 311 reports published during or immediately after the war by CAOR, or the Directorate of Naval Operational Research as it became in June 1944. During the period 1942-43, there were 89, of which over 60% concerned ASW. However, of the 105 reports published in 1944, only 35% were ASW-related, and in 1945 only 15%. Other subjects included mine warfare, anti-ship warfare, air operations, amphibious operations and several more.

Attacks by Aircraft on U-boats. One of the earliest and one of the most important studies undertaken was carried out by the researchers at Coastal Command ORS. Their subject was the effectiveness of aircraft attacks on U-boats.

Throughout the war, the main weapon used to attack submarines from the air was the depth charge, usually fused with a hydrostatic or time-delayed fuse so as to explode without having to make contact with the U-boat. In the first two years, Coastal Command aircraft usually attacked with depth charges fused with a one-second delay, or set for hydrostatic initiation at 100-150 feet, on the assumption that, on average, a U-boat would sight the attacking aircraft some two minutes before the instant of attack. Unfortunately, the effectiveness of these attacks was very low - barely 1% of the U-boats attacked were sunk.

During summer 1941, Professor E. J. Williams, a scientist from Coastal Command ORS, analysed the results of the operations up to August 1941. He found that in about 40% of all attacks, the U-boat was either visible at the instant of attack, or had been out of sight for less than 15 seconds. In these cases, the position of the target was accurately known, but unfortunately, a 100-foot setting on the depth charges was too great to inflict sinking damage on most of them, though it no doubt rattled the wardroom crockery. In the remaining attacks, the uncertainty in both the position and depth of the target increased rapidly with the time for which the U-boat had been dived. Thus, in these cases, even if the depth setting of 100 feet was appropriate, the inherent inaccuracy of such attacks also resulted in a very low kill probability.[3] In other words, the attack tactics could hardly have been less optimum.

The ORS strongly recommended that much shallower depth settings be used in order to maximize the lethal effect against the substantial proportion of targets whose position was accurately known. This argument was accepted and shallower settings were progressively introduced as suitable hydrostats became available. By the end of 1941, settings of a nominal 50 feet were usual, while 33-foot settings were coming into use. A 25-foot setting was coming into general service by the summer of 1942.

The analysis of attacks carried out by the ORS had also highlighted the relatively low lethal radius of the current depth charges, and their work was used to support the case for a more powerful explosive filling.[4] Torpex-filled depth charges became available from the summer of 1942.

These changes were accompanied by a steady rise in the lethality of attacks, as shown in Table 1. Note that the data refer to all attacks, including cases where the U-boat had dived. During 1942 the average lethality of attacks against surfaced U-boats had risen to 11%, but was still only 2% against fully submerged boats.[5]

TABLE 1 - INCREASING LETHALITY
OF AIR ATTACKS AGAINST U-BOATS

Period	Charge	No of Attacks	% Sunk	Seriously Damaged
Sep 39-Jun 41	-	215	1	4
Jul 41-Dec 41	50' setting	127	2	13
Jan 42-Jun 42	33' setting	79	4	19
Jul 42-Dec 42	25' setting	346	7	9
	Torpex filling			

A possible factor in this improvement may have been the gradual increase in the number of heavy aircraft, and thus in the average weight of bomb load. Some improvement was also undoubtedly due to the use of Torpex, though here the ORS could claim some credit; but there is no doubt that the majority of the improvement was due to the shallower setting, and hence directly due to the work of the operational researchers.

It is interesting to note that, according to P. M. Morse, who set up the US ASWORG in March 1942, a similar story unfolded in the US. In his memoirs[6] he describes an early study in which the operational researchers recommended a change from a 75-foot to a 30-foot setting, the shallowest possible, and notes that this change increased the lethality by a factor of about five. Unfortunately, he does not indicate whether the conclusions were reached independently of the work of the British scientists, or whether a few hints had been dropped.

Notwithstanding the significant improvements in attack effectiveness accruing from these changes, the overall lethality of aircraft was still disappointingly low and Coastal Command ORS did not rest on its laurels. Having ensured that the depth settings were optimized for the most promising targets, they then turned their attention to the question of attack accuracy in plan. A particular issue was that the number of kills achieved was substantially less than that expected from the number of straddles reported by the aircrew. Thus, either the attack accuracy was less than that claimed by pilots, or the lethal radius of a depth charge was less than that claimed by the Admiralty.[7]

On the basis of the technical evidence available, scant though it was, ORS favoured the former hypothesis, whereas the Air Staff remained loyal to their crews and favoured the latter. The matter was only resolved after cameras were fitted to aircraft to record the attack.

Analysis of the first 16 attacks recorded showed that the ORS view was in fact correct. Furthermore, it showed that there was a bias error in the attacks in that the mean point of impact of the depth charge stick was not on the U-boat's conning tower as intended, but about 60 yards ahead, largely it must be said due to the contemporary tactical procedures which were meant to compensate for U-boat movement. Adjustment of the tactics brought the mean point of impact back to where it was meant to be - on the conning tower. This change by itself probably gave about a 50% increase in lethality.[8]

Accumulation of photographic evidence allowed the ORS to carry out a more refined analysis of attack tactics and led to improvements in stick length and stick spacing. The ORS also contributed substantially to the introduction into service of the MK III Low Level Bomb Sight early in 1944. These efforts further enhanced attack effectiveness.

Once it had been recognized that attack accuracy was not as high as aircrew had thought, steps were taken to improve training. US analysts found that accuracy improved considerably with practice on a training range. It was important therefore for aircrew to obtain as much practice as possible since on-the-job training was not a practical proposition. An attack on a real U-boat was a rare event in the life of an aircrew; typically a crew would make only one such attack in every 500 or so flying hours on operational missions over the North Atlantic. It was therefore vitally important to make the most of each opportunity.

The improvement in effectiveness up to the end of 1942 has already been noted. By the end of the war, the overall lethality of air attacks by Coastal Command had risen to over 25%, nearly four times that in late 1942 and some 25 times that in the early years of the war.[9] The effectiveness of daylight attacks against surfaced U-boats had risen to over 40%. It would of course be wrong to attribute all of this improvement to the work of the operational researchers, but they undoubtedly contributed a major share.

Deterrent Effect of Aircraft. Although aircraft had only a low probability of sinking U-boats in the early war years, they were nevertheless very effective in preventing U-boats from sinking ships. An early attempt to estimate this effectiveness was made by comparing loss rates in convoys near to and far from land, making due allowance for differing U-boat density, on the grounds that air cover was frequent for the former, but rare for the latter. This analysis suggested that air cover might reduce losses by a factor of up to seven.[10] A later, more rigorous, study of convoys in early 1943 gave the rather lower figure of about three.

The main effect of the aircraft was to force the U-boats to dive to avoid attack when the aircraft were sighted. This did reduce U-boat vulnerability but, at the same time, it deprived the U-boat of its mobility and reduced its detection horizon. Thus, it was much more difficult to close a convoy to attack, or remain in contact whilst other members of a U-boat pack gathered.

Improvements in Navigation. Not all aircraft dispatched to protect convoys actually found their charges owing to navigation errors by one or other party, particularly when the aircraft were operating far from land. For example, it was found that, during the second half of 1941, only 40% of convoys that were over 600 miles from land were met. The importance of air cover led the operational researchers to seek ways of improving aircraft navigational accuracy and procedures for effecting a rendezvous. The insights and understanding derived from their analyses helped to halve the failure rate over the next twelve months. By the end of 1943, the problem had virtually been eliminated.[11]

Employment of Long-Range Aircraft. The vital role played by aircraft in reducing ship losses, particularly Very-Long-Range aircraft, led to a major confrontation between those fighting the Battle of the Atlantic and those fighting the battle over Germany, since the same types of aircraft were required by both. The great debate between the bomber lobby and the maritime lobby is too well known to warrant repetition. However, what is perhaps less well known is that the Admiralty's Chief Adviser on Operational Research - Professor Blackett - became personally involved in this debate on the use of air power. This came about when he was asked in March 1942 to comment on an appreciation of the effects of the bombing offensive against Germany. From an analysis of the known effects of the German bombing offensive against the UK, he was able to demonstrate that the Intelligence estimates of the effects of the British offensive against Germany were highly optimistic, and that the campaign up till that point had had relatively little effect on the war.[12]

Later in the autumn of 1942, when the U-boat threat to shipping was particularly menacing, Blackett's analysis was itself deployed in battle. He used it, together with an analysis of convoy operations, to compare in quantitative terms the relative contributions to the war effort of aircraft deployed on bombing, or on the anti-U-boat campaign. He showed that during its operational life as a bomber, a single aircraft would have negligible effect on Germany's war fighting capability, whereas if allocated to Coastal Command, the same aircraft would save about six ships. The loss of aircrew would also be less in the latter role. He went on to show that, if one quarter of the bomber force were transferred to the Battle of the Atlantic, one million tons of shipping a year would be saved at the current rates.[13] Although this did not result in outright victory in the inter-departmental battle, some aircraft were transferred from Bomber Command to Coastal Command and contributed to the successful campaign in 1943. Note that the effectiveness of Bomber Command operations increased substantially in later years as improved navigation and target indication techniques were introduced.

Work of Naval OR Groups. From the creation of the naval OR groups - CAOR in January 1942 and ASWORG in March 1942 - shipping protection operations came under regular and detailed scrutiny. The studies ranged from detailed analysis of particular sensors to questions of force deployment and force structure. Typical examples of the first category were the reports showing how sonar detection performance was affected by sea, swell and wind conditions and what, if any, prior warning the sonar operator had had of the presence of a U-boat, for example an HF/DF contact, a disappearing radar contact or a ship being torpedoed - a flaming datum.

Attacks by Ships on U-boats. Following the work of their maritime air colleagues, the naval operational researchers carried out studies of surface ship attack effectiveness. They too found that a substantial proportion - about 40% - of depth charges were set too deep, although most of the rest were correctly set, very few being set too shallow. Unfortunately, however, unlike aircraft attacks, there was no straightforward solution for surface ships. Their targets were submerged U-boats and the errors arose from a lack of any reliable method of determining target depth. Nevertheless, the researchers were able to demonstrate that ahead-thrown weapons with contact fuzes should improve attack effectiveness.[14]

These studies continued throughout the war and, in 1945, a comparison was made between depth charge attacks and the newer anti-submarine weapons that had been brought into service - Hedgehog and Squid. It showed that the probability of sinking a U-boat per attack was 8%, 27% and 53% respectively, broadly in line with theoretical predictions. The analysis also showed that the effectiveness of ship attacks had increased significantly during the course of the war as tactics, training and experience had improved. For example, the effectiveness of Hedgehog attacks increased by a factor of three between late 1943 and early 1945. It was also shown that co-ordinating the efforts of two or more ships in prosecuting a U-boat was proportionally much more effective than if the ships acted independently, since it resulted in more attacks being carried out. US experience suggested that the improvement factor might be as high as four. However, despite the valuable insights which these studies undoubtedly provided, the role of operational research in stimulating improvements in performance, as opposed to illustrating them, is less clear than in the case of air attacks.

Comparison of Convoys and Independents. Considerable effort was devoted to the comparison of independent shipping and convoys, and to assessment of the vulnerability of each under different circumstances. Not surprisingly, it was found that independents were significantly more vulnerable than ships in convoy. The exact ratio of loss rates varied considerably with time, place and circumstances; typically it was in the region of 2 or 10:1, but in some cases it reached 100:1.

Effects of Speed. One of the main factors affecting the loss rate of independents, apart from U-boat density, was the speed of the ship. The loss rate was found to rise sharply as speed dropped below about 13 knots. Below 10 knots, loss rates continued to rise, but less steeply than in the region of 10-13 knots.[15] Whilst the general trend of the results was perhaps not unexpected, the operational researchers were able to explain the results in terms of the speed differential between U-boat and target. They also provided a quantitative explanation of the contribution of aircraft in reducing ship losses.

This quantitative relationship between speed and loss rate was put to good use in 1943 and '44 when the effectiveness of Admiralty Net Defence for merchant ships - a form of anti-torpedo nets - came to be assessed. It was found that, if a ship had nets streamed, only 40% of those fired at were sunk, whereas the corresponding figure for those without nets was 75%. Thus, the nets would appear to reduce losses by a factor of about two. However, a significant drawback of the net defence was that it reduced ship speed by about 17% when streamed. Thus, a 14-knot ship would be reduced to about 11½ knots. In practice, this increased the inherent danger to the ship by a factor of about 3½ if the ship sailed independently, thereby more than offsetting the beneficial effects of the nets. On the other hand, an 11-knot ship would be reduced to about 9 knots, which only increased inherent risk by about 30%, so that the nets would offer some benefit. Nevertheless, the risk would still be substantially greater than that incurred if the ship sailed in convoy.

A somewhat similar effect of speed on ship losses was also found for convoys. Data on losses were compiled for slow (7 knots) SC and ONS, and fast (9½ knots) HX and ONF convoys, which roughly followed a Great Circle route during the period October 1942-May 1943. Although the proportion of convoys sighted and attacked was very similar in both cases, 50% more ships were sunk in the slow convoys. Unfortunately, as data for only two speeds were available, it was not possible to derive such general relationships as for independents, though the principle appeared to be similar.[16]

Value of Surface Escorts. Studies into the effects of aircraft in reducing ship losses have already been mentioned, but similar studies into the effectiveness of surface escorts were also carried out. It was found that the number of ships sunk per attacking U-boat was reduced by about 0.07 per escort over a wide range of escort strengths. Increasing escort strength from 6 to 12 roughly halved losses, by reducing them from 0.75 to 0.34 per U-boat.[17]

Effects of Convoy Size. More importantly, the operational researchers also discovered that the number of ships sunk per attacking U-boat was independent of the size of the convoy.[18] This immediately led to the conclusion that convoys should be as large as practicable. For example, doubling convoy size would of itself halve loss rates. Moreover, since it would allow the available escorts to be spread across a smaller number of convoys, the number of escorts per convoy could be doubled, which would roughly halve losses again. Alternatively, the escorts could be used for other purposes, such as Hunting Groups.

This conclusion was, to some extent, at odds with current Admiralty thinking, which maintained that 40 ships was about the best size for a convoy, and that 60 ships was the maximum. Nevertheless, the operational researchers were able to persuade the Admiralty of the soundness of their conclusion, and also to convince them that the problems of convoy control, and of loading and unloading were not insoluble. As a result, the policy was changed in spring 1943 and the average size of Atlantic convoys gradually grew. By the following year, convoys of nearly 200 ships were not unknown.

Other Tasks

This brief review of the work of the operational research groups has perforce been illustrative rather than comprehensive. It has made no mention of the important work done on the tactical use of radar; of the development of the theory of search and screening, which improved the tactical effectiveness of anti-submarine forces and which is still in use today, essentially unchanged; of the unglamorous but vital work on aircraft maintenance and the organisation of flying effort; on counters to use of the *Zaunkönig* anti-escort homing torpedo; and on the optimum allocation of forces to different types of operations, such as convoy escort, or transit area patrols in the Bay of Biscay or Northern Transit Area. Nevertheless, it has given some idea of the nature and scope of the role played by operational research, ranging as it did from the most detailed aspects of equipment performance to the broadest questions of strategic policy.

The Impact of Operational Research

To describe what the OR groups did during the Battle is one thing; to say what they achieved is another. There are a number of problems in trying to establish whether and, if so, how their efforts actually changed the course of the Battle.

Firstly, at this distance in time and given the highly interactive debates that took place between operational researchers and operational staffs, it is very hard to establish how far the origin and development of a particular idea was unique to one group or the other. Even in those cases where the researchers are acknowledged to have taken the lead, it could be argued in many cases that the staffs would have come to similar conclusions in due course.

Secondly, many of the improvements predicted by the researchers were of the order of tens of percent, rather than orders of magnitude. Since anti-submarine warfare is a highly probabilistic affair, relatively large data samples are needed to demonstrate beyond reasonable doubt that any particular change had the expected effect. Very often, the large samples are simply not available.

Thirdly, it was rare for one component of the complex Battle to change without other components changing separately, but concurrently. These changes might stem from the introduction of new Allied equipment, new Allied tactics, increased force levels, or new German equipment or tactics, perhaps in response to an Allied change. In practice, it is exceedingly difficult to disentangle the effects of the two or three changes all occurring at roughly the same time. In a sense, this is a cause of the second problem mentioned - the situation was not static long enough for a useful data sample to be acquired.

Fourthly, by the time that some of the researchers' efforts were bearing fruit, the Allies had already won the Battle. Thus, no matter how dramatic the potential improvement, it would have had little real impact.

Against this background, considerable caution must be exercised to avoid making exaggerated claims for the contribution of OR. Perhaps the strongest claim can be made for the work to improve the effectiveness of air attacks. In this case, there is good evidence that the changes to depth setting, aiming points and stick spacing were pushed through by the operational researchers against some resistance.[19] It is also possible to isolate the attack phase from most of the other changes that were taking place. The substantial improvements in attack effectiveness described earlier can therefore be attributed largely to OR.

The impact on the Battle is less self-evident, but some indication can be obtained from the U-boat loss rates. During the period April 1941 to March 1943, the Germans lost some 58 U-boats to air attack, excluding boats shared between aircraft and other causes. The distribution through the period was far from uniform, as shown in Table 2 below. In part, the rapid rise was due to the improvements in attack effectiveness and in part to other causes, primarily increased numbers of aircraft.

TABLE 2: U-boats Sunk By Aircraft	
Period	U-boats sunk by Aircraft Alone
Apr 41-Sep 41	0
Oct 41-Mar 42	5
Apr 42-Sep 42	15
Oct 42-Mar 43	38

Had the improvements in attack effectiveness not taken place, then far fewer U-boats would have been sunk. On the basis of the data presented in Table 1, this might have been as low as ten. The 48 additional U-boats would have sunk nearly half a million extra tons of shipping by the end of March 1943. Whilst this would not perhaps have brought Britain to her knees, it would certainly have exacerbated the shipping crisis of the winter of 1942-43. It would also have caused a few extra sleepless nights at the Admiralty, which, as things were in March 1943, was considering whether the convoy strategy could be sustained.

In other cases, the operational researchers clearly had less impact. For example, their work on the relative vulnerability of convoys and independents, though no doubt very reassuring to the Admiralty, merely reinforced the views they already held. The USN was more reluctant to adopt the convoy strategy, but it is not clear how far the work of the researchers influenced the ultimate decision.

The work on convoy size had the potential to achieve very substantial savings, but by the time it was recognized, shipping losses had declined dramatically and the pay-off was reduced in consequence. It is interesting to note that Blackett considered that the researchers had made a serious mistake in not tackling this problem as soon as the OR group was set up. He estimated that, had the policy of large convoys been adopted in spring 1942, instead of a year later, a million tons of shipping would have been saved.[20] However, this takes us into the realm of what operational research might have achieved, rather than what it did achieve.

Most of the other work carried out by the OR groups lay between these two extremes, in that it probably had some impact, but less demonstrably than that for air attacks. However, if it is assumed that the combined efforts of all the other work done achieved as much as the latter, then operational research would have saved about one million tons of shipping by mid-1943. In other words, shipping losses to U-boats would have been about 8% higher.

This number is of course somewhat conjectural - the actual achievements might have been more; they might have been less. However, the precise value is of no particular relevance. The point is that the contribution was considerable and that it was achieved by a handful of scientists armed with little more than pencils, paper and slide-rules. In anybody's currency, that looks like good value for money.

Perhaps the final word should go to Marshal of the Royal Air Force Sir John Slessor, AOC-in-C Coastal Command at the height of the Battle. In his Foreword to Professor Waddington's book on OR in World War II, he notes that a great deal of credit for the defeat of the U-boat in 1943 was due to the OR groups. He also goes on to point out that the scientist is only one part of a team, and that teamwork is the key to success in modern war. I would not argue with him on either point.

Notes

1.   Dönitz, *Ten Years and Twenty Days*
2.   Pratt, *Operational Research in Admiralty Headquarters during World War II*
3.   Waddington, *OR in World War II.*
4.   *Ibid.*
5.   *Ibid.*
6.   Morse, *In at the Beginning: A Physicist's Life.*
7.   Waddington, *op.cit.*
8.   *Ibid.*
9.   *Ibid.*
10.   Pratt, *op.cit.*
11.   Waddington, *op.cit.*

12. P. M. S. Blackett: *Recollections of Problems Studied, 1940-45*: (In Brassey's Annual 1953).
13. Pratt, *op.cit.*
14. *Ibid.*
15. *Ibid.*
16. Blackett, *op.cit.*
17. Pratt, *op.cit.*
18. Blackett, *op.cit.*
19. Waddington, *op.cit.*
20. Blackett, *op.cit.*

24

German Technical and Electronic Development

by Axel Niestlé

Introduction

In the great conflicts of recent history, World War II was probably the first in which the outcome in various theatres of operations was heavily influenced - even decisively influenced - by technical innovations. Moreover, although technical evolution did not always bring victory in battle at that time, numerous WWII developments indicated the shape of things to come, and some remain of considerable practical importance today.

The U-boat campaign against Allied maritime supply lines, to and from Great Britain, is a prime example of the impact of technical evolution. This chapter gives an overview of developments in U-boat design, and the German role in electronic warfare, including a characterization of its impact on the course of the campaign. Only those developments which were used operationally during the war are included. The huge number of technical and electronic developments projected, under construction or in the early phases of development have been excluded, because they had no influence on the conduct and the final outcome of the U-boat campaign.

Before the War

From 1935, when U-boat building recommenced, construction departments initially followed the lessons of World War I, since any future war would probably have comparable objectives. Several improvements were introduced in the fields of shipbuilding, machinery, communications and weapon technology, and the general standards of technical reliability of the individual installations were raised, but the main technical characteristics of the new U-boats remained similar to those of WWI vessels.

The electro-acoustic and electromagnetic detection of vessels were only in their infancy. Responsibility for developing and producing naval radar equipment lay with the *Nachrichtenmittelversuchsanstalt* (NVA) of the Kriegsmarine and its dependent civilian company, *Gesellschaft für Elektroakustische und Mechanische Apparate mbH* (GEMA). However, compared to the needs of the Wehrmacht, naval developments were given low priority, so by the start of the war the navy had only one general type of radar available for operational use, commonly known as the 'Seetakt' or 'GEMA' set and working on a wavelength of 81.5cm. There were several versions of this, adapted to the special requirements of the individual naval services.[1] In 1939, two sets of a version specially adapted for use on U-boats were produced, but in August of that year U-boat Command turned them down in favour of the *S-Gerät*, the German version of asdic.[2] This was because, being in an early stage of development, the radar equipment was bulky, unreliable and only gave low performance.

Apart from communications devices, underwater electronics were limited to a few passive detection sets, capable only of listening. From 1935, the multi-unit hydrophone installation (*Gruppenhorchgerät*, or GHG) was the prime underwater detection device. All U-boats carried this, with varying numbers of hydrophones, fitted at the bow around the forward hydroplanes. Its performance was superior to all Allied listening devices, although it was vulnerable to shock effects from nearby depth charge explosions. If the boat was on the seabed, the efficiency of the GHG was reduced, so in addition, the larger Type IX boats carried a small rotatable hydrophone (*KDB-Anlage*) consisting of six receivers in line, in a small rectangular frame, which was mounted on the forward upper deck. Nevertheless, at the outbreak of war in 1939, the principal means of detecting targets was still eyesight, aided by binoculars on the surface or the periscope when submerged.

Wartime Developments

Submarine Design

Both the strategic objective and the tactical concept of the campaign required the greatest possible number of U-boats. In order to achieve their mass production, U-boat construction after the outbreak of war concentrated mainly on the existing Types VII-C and IX-C. These had been selected before the war as the principal designs for the planned U-boat fleet, and, in the tactical situation prevailing in the first years of the war, they performed extremely well.

The development and assembly of new designs would have inevitably interfered with the objective of mass production. Design work was therefore confined to improvements or modifications of existing types (such as supply or long-range boats), in accordance with the demands of the Naval Operations Staff. Novel designs to counter Allied developments in anti-submarine warfare (ASW) or electronics were neither demanded by U-boat Command, nor planned, by either the Naval Operations Staff or the U-boat Department of the Naval Construction Office, until 1942. It was only when the tactical and operational limits of the existing types became clearly apparent that the German Admiralty realized the need for new development.

Although the Types VII-C and IX-C were well designed, front-line service experience showed that a large number of modifications and design improvements were necessary. Apart from its operational War Diary, every U-boat kept another detailed War Diary about the performance of its machinery and other technical installations. Copies were forwarded to the U-boat Departments of the Naval Construction Office, and training establishments, for evaluation. Several hundred (mostly minor) modifications are recorded for the Type VII-C alone. Many of these resulted from the heavy mechanical stresses upon the hull and installations as patrols in the operational areas (sometimes under very rough sea conditions) became increasingly long, with little opportunity for proper maintenance work. Many others were the result of lessons learned from battle damage, especially from depth charge attacks.

The major modifications enhancing the operational characteristics of the U-boat types in service at the outbreak of war were as follows:

- *Increase of diving depths*

During depth charge attacks, deep diving generally increased a U-boat's chances of survival. In 1941 the Naval Construction Office sought to increase the diving depth of the existing Type VII-C while avoiding major design changes. This led to the improved type VII C/41. At 21mm, the maximum thickness of its pressure hull was 2.5mm greater than that of the VII-C, and its diving depth 20% greater.[3] The theoretical collapsing depth of the new design was calculated at that time as 300 metres. However, more accurate postwar calculations corrected this to only 280 metres. Construction orders for the first series of the Type VII C/41 were given on 14 October 1941, but the first of the type (U-292) was not commissioned until 25 August 1943.

- *Shock resistance*

A U-boat's pressure hull was able to withstand very heavy shock effects, even from nearby explosions. In most instances of battle damage, it was the installations and equipment in or outside the pressure hull which suffered. A large number of U-boats were sunk, despite the pressure hull still being intact, after having been forced to surface following depth charge damage to vital internal or external installations. However, no detailed investigations concerning questions of shock resistance were conducted until the summer of 1942.

Tests with live depth charges at the end of 1942 showed that shock effects on the pressure hull plates were higher than on its frames. Because of this, the fitting of equipment directly onto the pressure hull plates was avoided wherever possible, and elastic materials or springs between seatings and installations were used to dampen shock waves. In July 1944, U-1063 (the prototype of a largely shock-protected Type VII-C/41 U-boat) was commissioned.[4]

- *The Schnorkel*

One of the U-boats' greatest weaknesses was that, in order to charge their electric batteries (used for underwater propulsion), they had to run their air-breathing diesel engines. This meant they had to surface, sometimes for prolonged periods, which in turn made them vulnerable to air attack.

To overcome this, and to enable them to use diesel propulsion while submerged at periscope depth, Hellmuth Walter - a U-boat designer and owner of a small engineering company - proposed a breathing device. During summer 1943, a reliable one was designed, which eventually became known as the schnorkel. Although widely believed to be a German invention, it was not; in

1940, the latest Dutch submarine types had a similar device fitted. The Germans knew about these from captured examples, but under the prevailing tactical conditions the Naval Construction Office considered the equipment of no great use, and ordered its removal.

A schnorkel consisted of a folding mast, housing the induction and exhaust tubes, which were connected to the normal intake and exhaust tubes leading to the diesel engine compartment. A valve (normally a float valve) was fitted on top of the induction tube, opened by gravity and closed by the buoyant action of the float when the upper end of the schnorkel was submerged. Two sorts of float valves were used: the ball float (*Kugelschwimmer*) and the ring float (*Ringschwimmer*). In April 1945 the first, much smaller and more reliable electro-pneumatic schnorkel head valves entered front-line service.

General installation of schnorkels was ordered in August 1943. However, owing to various technical and administrative difficulties, it was not until 5 February 1944 that the first front-line schnorkel-equipped U-boat (U-264) left St. Nazaire. Slow production of schnorkel equipment meant that by the time of the Allied invasion of France (6 June 1944), only 34 schnorkel-equipped U-boats had entered front-line service. By the same date, six of them had already been sunk. By the end of the war, approximately 343 U-boats of pre-war design had been fitted with a schnorkel.

- *Cut-away 'quick-diving' foredeck*

For the small Type VII U-boats, normal diving time to periscope depth was about 30 seconds. For the larger Type IX boats, times varied between 40-50 seconds. This was because the larger upper deck structure, housing up to 12 reserve torpedo stowage containers, took longer to empty of air. After a crash dive, the remaining time to reach a safe depth before the possible release of bombs was normally extremely limited. From wartime records, British operational researchers concluded that air attacks against U-boats fully or partly visible at the time of bomb release were seven times more likely to result in a kill than attacks against U-boats which had been submerged for longer than 15 seconds.[5] In other words, the Type IX U-boats were more vulnerable to air attacks than other U-boat types.

In 1944, when large numbers of reserve torpedoes were no longer needed, about 17 metres of the deck structure on the foredeck was removed, leaving only a small walkway. This reduced diving time for the Type IX-D by 12 seconds. At least 24 craft were modified in the years 1944 and 1945.[6]

- *Sea-keeping qualities*

Many small modifications were made in order to adapt the existing design to the sometimes very rough sea conditions of the open Atlantic. These included the fitting of wind- and spray-deflectors on the conning tower casing; the enlargement of the bow design of the Type VII-C; and, for U-boats operating in the Arctic theatre, the provision of defrosting equipment on vital installations.

● *Miscellaneous*

From January 1944, many U-boats were equipped with gear enabling them to refuel underwater. However, the only U-tanker equipped for that purpose (U-490) was sunk in June 1944 before having begun supply operations. The fitting of hovering equipment on U-boats started in March 1944 (e.g. on U-867, U-1017, U-1172, U-1208 and U-1278). Similarly, automatic depth-keeping gear was installed from the end of 1944 onward (e.g. on U-881 and U-1171).

To protect bridge crews against machine-gun fire during air attacks, the bridge casing was reinforced with extra steel plates after June 1942. From January 1943, the large Type IX-D2 U-cruisers were fitted with a gliding helicopter kite to extend their visual detection range in areas with less strong air surveillance.

Development of the True Submarine

Beginning in 1933, Hellmuth Walter presented the Kriegsmarine with several revolutionary U-boat designs, with a novel turbine-powered propulsion system, using hydrogen peroxide for submerged cruising. But the Naval Construction Office was no exception to the conservatism inherent in almost any Admiralty office, and they showed little interest in his ideas. During trials in 1940 using the new propulsion system, a small experimental craft (V 80) reached the then fantastic underwater speed of 26 knots. Even so, official support for this new type of U-boat remained half-hearted. At that time the Naval Construction Office's main efforts were still directed towards high-volume production of conventional boats; but when Admiral Dönitz learned about the new design, in January 1942, he repeatedly demanded the construction of a larger boat with the new underwater propulsion system, capable of operating in the Atlantic. Early in the year, four more experimental craft of larger size were ordered. However, it was not until the end of September 1942 that the German Admiralty finally realized that what they actually needed was a completely new type of U-boat. At about the same time, the Walter company was close to completing its first studies for an advanced design of a large, streamlined, high-speed U-boat, and made strong efforts to advance the project (designated Type XVIII). But the Naval Construction Office insisted on a small experimental series to test the reliability of the new propulsion system, before commencing mass production.

Under this plan, the first boats could not have entered front-line service before 1945.[7] However, in spring 1943, calculations showed that when equipped with powerful electric engines, and partly modified to fit a greatly enlarged battery pack, the advanced streamline hull design of the Type XVIII would also produce excellent underwater performance. Building plans were quickly altered to include construction of this modified design (designated Type XXI). A smaller model for coastal operations (designated Type XXIII) was similarly derived from Walter's existing Type XXII design.[8] As a result, the earlier projects for Walter U-boats were greatly reduced, in favour of the new types, which avoided the use of a powerful, yet largely untested, propulsion system. A new building scheme was also established, using prefabricated fully-equipped sections. These only required assembly in the building yards, greatly reducing the construction time. By this method, the first of the new craft was launched in April 1944, only nine months after completion of the final design plans.

Compared with the old conventionally designed 'submersibles', the new Type XXI U-boat had no fewer than nine main operational advantages:

1. The inclusion of the schnorkel equipment. By enabling submerged travel or battery recharge with diesel engines at periscope depth, this allowed continuous underwater operations and greatly reduced the efficacy of aircraft and radar as ASW instruments.

2. Maximum underwater speed was increased by 250% to 16.5 knots, allowing rapid attack and withdrawal. At this speed, sonar detection by the Allies' existing equipment was reduced, owing to the increased water turbulence at the receiving unit.

3. Submerged endurance, with electric engines, was increased by 600%, to about 490 nautical miles at minimum speed (3 knots). This markedly decreased the danger of being hunted to exhaustion.

4. The installation of an extra electric silent-running motor, for speeds up to 5 knots, made detection by listening devices almost impossible.

5. Thicker pressure hull plating and extensive use of shock-absorbing material made the design less sensitive to depth charge explosions outside of their lethal range. However, the theoretical collapsing depth of the unusual '8-shape' cross-sectioned pressure hull, originally calculated as 330 metres, was later reduced by 10%, after pressure tank tests.

6. In combination with new advanced torpedo developments, six torpedo tubes with rapid reload facilities (5 minutes for the first reload and 20 minutes for the second) gave superior fire power. Thus even individual boats were capable of inflicting massive destruction.

7. The inclusion of the latest developments in both active and passive underwater detection (for example, the enlarged passive multi-unit hydrophone set with balcony array, and the active/passive echo-ranging 'Nibelung' apparatus). These enabled submerged torpedo attacks, without the use of the periscope.

8. Standard installation of automatic depth-keeping gear and hovering equipment. These enabled submerged operation without the use of engines.

9. Greatly improved living conditions for the crew (more space, more bunks, increased storage room for all kinds of provisions, air conditioning equipment with improved ventilation, etc.). These all

helped to reduce the physical and psychological stress factors of long submerged patrols.

The first five of these points also applied to the small Type XXIII U-boat, although its maximum submerged speed, underwater endurance and diving depth were somewhat lower, because of its smaller battery capacity and weaker pressure hull construction.

After trials with the first boats, the need for numerous small modifications, together with the effects of Allied strategic bombing attacks on the main shipbuilding centres, delayed front-line operations of the new types well into 1945. From February 1945 until Germany's capitulation, six Type XXIII U-boats (U-2321, U-2322, U-2324, U-2326, U-2329 and U-2336) conducted a total of nine patrols off the British east coast. These were carried out without loss, but only four small ships totalling 7,392 grt were sunk. Moreover only two Type XXI U-boats (U-2506 and U-2511) actually left Norway for operational patrols. That was just a few days before the end of the war, and both had to return, either because of technical difficulties, or because of recall by U-boat Command at the cessation of hostilities.

Although the new types came too late to have any impact on the course of the war, their advanced design features formed the basis for all postwar submarine developments.

Electronic Warfare

The term 'Electronic Warfare' is a post-war creation, but this aspect of conflict started much earlier. WWI saw its beginning, and in WWII the interplay of new electronic means and opposing countermeasures became a decisive factor in battle. More than in other field of war, victory or defeat in electronic warfare does not depend on bravery in the face of the enemy, but on scientific genius and technical resources in the laboratories and manufacturing companies at home. Its tactical conditions may change rapidly and drastically, with the introduction of new or superior inventions. The Battle of the Atlantic is a fine example for the impact of electronics on the final outcome in war.

The Impact of Allied Surface Electronics on U-boat Tactics

In the successful campaign against the Allied trade shipping during the first half of WWII, the U-boats used were actually 'submersibles' rather then true submarines like the revolutionary 'Elektroboats' in the very last phase of the war. Conventional U-boats commonly dived only in certain tactical situations, such as withdrawal in the presence of a superior enemy force, or daylight submerged attack. Until 1943 a U-boat on a North Atlantic patrol usually travelled submerged for no more than 10% of the total distance covered. The reasons for that were of both technical and tactical origin. Their electric batteries had quite limited capacity, and so their slow underwater speed (maximum 7 knots) and low submerged endurance (80 nautical miles at 4 knots, but only 1½ hours at maximum speed) made it technically impossible to proceed submerged over large distances without repeated surfacing to recharge the batteries. Since Dönitz always tried to employ his boats economically, their transit to the operational areas had to be as swift as possible. Consequently, they only travelled proportionally more underwater in areas like the Bay of Biscay or the Northern Transit Area, which were known to be heavily defended. Once in their operational areas, the lack of Luftwaffe reconnaissance to locate enemy shipping forced them to cruise on the surface, simply to be able to see their targets. The final reason for mostly remaining on the surface was that, once aware of its presence, any possible surface target could easily out-run a submerged U-boat and escape.

Two Allied developments in the field of electronics contributed greatly to the U-boats' defeat. From the start of the war, the Allies tried to establish the positions of U-boats by radio direction finding (HF/DF, known as Huff-Duff), using shore-based stations. However, the accuracy of radio bearings decreases with distance, and thus limited their operational value in offshore areas. The introduction of ship-borne HF/DF, fitted in increasing numbers from the end of 1942 onward, enabled convoy escorts to take accurate bearings on U-boats which transmitted near convoys. The effectiveness of this was much enhanced by the German practice of abandoning radio silence completely, once contact was established with a convoy. Likewise, in darkness or in fog, the fitting of ship-borne radar (greatly improved by the development of centimetric radar) robbed the U-boats of their prime advantage, invisibility.

Once the existing types of U-boat had lost their cover of invisibility, their technical and tactical limitations became drastically apparent. While on the surface, when facing even single escorts or aircraft, their self-defensive capabilities were very low. When forced to submerge, the chances of escaping a persistent hunt by an experienced team of warships were also limited by their lack of underwater speed and endurance. Under prolonged attack, many boats were simply exhausted, and were forced to the surface only to be sunk immediately.

From summer 1942 onward, the U-boats were driven more and more into a defensive tactical position, although the period of relative success continued well into the first half of 1943. The passage through the important transit routes to the operational areas became ever more dangerous and expensive, both in terms of time and of fuel. Night-time 'wolf pack' attacks against convoys began to fail in increasing numbers, because the boats were located early by HF/DF and by ship- or air-borne radar. When this happened, they were driven off or forced to dive, thus losing contact before they reached the range to initiate a torpedo attack. Simultaneously, with the decreased ability to launch a successful attack against a defended target, the risk of surprise attacks on the boats themselves rose greatly, especially in the dark hours or bad visibility. Moreover - no doubt influenced by the enemy's unexplained new advances in detection - U-boat commanders from 1943 onward became more and more defensively minded. Dönitz repeatedly tried to counter this erosion of confidence by transmitting strong 'Reminder' messages to his commanders at sea.

Centimetric radar (which became operational in February 1943) consolidated Allied supremacy in the field of electronic detection. Combined with similar important improvements in other fields of ASW, this resulted in growing losses among U-boats. Despite all efforts to counter the situation, in summer 1944 U-boat Command was eventually forced to abandon completely the tactic of surface operations with U-boats.[9]

Only the development of the schnorkel enabled the otherwise technologically outdated U-boats to continue operations, albeit at a reduced scale and under tactically restricted conditions. Introduced in June 1944, the new policy of 'total underwater war' - i.e. no surface operations - did bring about a drastic reduction in the effectiveness of Allied radar. During the last 12 months of the war, the number of genuine schnorkel contacts was very small, because the schnorkel itself was so small. This not only made it hard for radar to 'see', but also meant that many false contacts were made, with floating rubbish or wreckage. Nor was the schnorkel the only German advance in the latter part of the war: the Allies did not have a monopoly on electronic development.

German Electronic Counter-Measures

The Kriegsmarine did not realize the Allies were using ship-borne HF/DF until June 1944, when radio Intelligence revealed its presence.[10] Throughout the period of wolf-pack surface operations in the Atlantic (until March 1944), the Allies were therefore able to use HF/DF to the full. However, since 1942 and quite separately from the discovery of ship-borne HF/DF, the Kriegsmarine's Naval Communication Experimental Section (NVK) and the Telefunken Company in Berlin had been developing a high-speed radio telegraph system, code-named 'Kurier'. This allowed one-way, short-signal communication, containing as many as seven letters in the Morse alphabet, from U-boats to a receiving station. The total communication was compressed into an elapsed time of just 452 milliseconds, with the object of making the direction of the transmitted signal much harder to detect.[11]

The first U-boats equipped with the 'Marine-Kurier' left Germany for front-line trials on 6 August 1944. Teething troubles once again prevented the system from becoming operational until the end of the war, although a large number of U-boats were equipped with the Kurier transmitter by that time. Alarmed by radio decrypts about the new system, however, British wireless and intercept experts developed a means of receiving the Kurier signals by cathode ray tube and photographing them. The prototype of a fully capable machine was ready by the beginning of April 1945.[12]

The situation in the field of radar was no better than with HF/DF. Until 1942 U-boat Command had foreseen neither the impact of radar on U-boat warfare, nor the growing extent of the role and effectiveness of aircraft in ASW. Moreover, until the summer of 1942, the Operations Division of the German

Naval Staff had no department dealing with all questions concerning radar. An almost complete lack of liaison existed between U-boat Command, the Naval Communication Division (MND) and the *Amtsgruppe Technisches Nachrichtenwesen* (NWa) of the German Admiralty, on the capabilities of Allied radar. The decisions of U-boat Command were based almost entirely on the clues from U-boat commanders' reports.[13] This all led, until the summer of 1942, to a underestimation of Allied radar development, only to be followed by an *over*estimation thereafter.

Furthermore, U-boat Command lacked the support of an objective board of scientific advisers on vital questions of U-boat warfare. Unlike on the Allied side, there was almost no operational research to investigate problems and propose scientifically based solutions. In the Battle of the Atlantic, the net result was often disastrous.

From October 1941 (when the first indication of possible airborne radar was found) until late spring 1942, all reports about the believed use of radar in Allied A/S aircraft were ignored by the Kriegsmarine's Naval Communications Division. During late spring 1942 an increase in the number of daylight attacks, and still more so of night attacks supported by strong illumination (the Leigh Light) on U-boats in the Bay of Biscay became apparent. At the request of U-boat Command, the head of the Naval Communications Division investigated the matter, concluding that the U-boats were now being located by airborne radar.[14] There are surprising reports that a Hudson aircraft, equipped with ASV Mk II, crashed in March or April 1942 in Tunisia, with the radar set reportedly being removed and handed over to German authorities.[15] Unfortunately, no precise information is available on that incident, which does not appear in German records of information about enemy location devices.

At Dönitz's Paris HQ, in a June 1942 conference about the whole electronic warfare situation, the head of the Naval Communications Division suggested three possible counter-measures against Allied radar. They were, firstly, a search receiver, to provide passive warning; secondly, a radar capable of active detection; and thirdly, some form of camouflage against electromagnetic waves.[16] Dönitz preferred the search receiver option, which offered the quickest way of giving U-boats protection. Simultaneously, work on the other counter-measures was to be intensified. For immediate action, on 24 June 1942, he ordered boats to stay submerged as long as possible during their transit through the Bay of Biscay, surfacing only to recharge batteries. Despite this, the first U-boat loss since September 1941 (when the British Biscay patrols began) occurred on 5 July 1942, when an RAF Wellington from 172 Squadron, equipped with ASV Mk II and the Leigh Light, sank the inbound U-502 as it returned from one of the most successful of all U-boat operations.

Radar

In the early years of the war, the U-boats' opening tactics were so successful that neither Dönitz nor the German Admiralty saw any need for the boats to be given radar. However, in a meeting at the German Admiralty on 22 August 1941, it was realized that radar would help the boats to search for and maintain contact with targets during darkness and bad visibility. Since no new radar had been developed, in the following month the installation of a modified version of the existing GEMA 'Seetakt' radar was ordered. This was named FuMG41G(gu) until 1942, when it was renamed FuMO 29 - FuMO being a useful abbreviation for *Funkmessortungsgerät*. The equipment was very bulky, and so could only be stored in the already cramped control room, on the forward port side. The fixed antenna, with limited arc of search of just 10° either side of dead ahead, was fitted on the upper forward side of the conning tower. Thus the craft was required to steer a full circle to make a complete search of the horizon.

By March 1942, only five Type IX C-boats (U-156, U-157, U-158, U-507 and U-509) had been fitted with this radar. By the end of the year, only about 45 more FuMO 29 sets had been installed. These were all in new boats, delivered by the Deschimag Yards in Bremen and Wesermünde (Bremerhaven), Germaniawerft Kiel, and Blohm & Voss Hamburg. Installations ceased in December 1942.

The theoretical range of detection was believed to be 9-13 km under favourable conditions, but in March 1942, during its first transfer patrol to France, experiments in U-507 revealed a range of only 5.5 km against surface vessels. Under normal night-time visibility conditions, this was even less than the range of eyesight. Moreover, the apparatus proved to be highly unreliable, being very susceptible to moisture and shock. Even had these not been the case, there was another important factor in its poor operational results, namely, that at that time no one in the U-boats was specially trained in its use.

By modifying the fixed antenna into a slightly smaller (1 x 1.4 m) rotating mirror frame aerial and giving it a higher search position (on top of a extendible rod on the port side of the bridge), it was believed that the performance would be improved. The new antenna, manually rotated left or right 180° by a flexible drive from the control room, now allowed a complete search of the horizon while maintaining course. This, the FuMO 30, incorporated the otherwise unchanged design of the FuMO 29.

The first experimental FuMO 30 was tested on the training craft U-643 in October 1942. Standard installation on newly built craft started in January 1943, followed by installation on front-line craft, firstly in France. The first sets entered operational service during March 1943.

But the equipment still suffered from the old known deficiencies, and so commanding officers did not use their radar very often, even if it was operable. Consequently, the number of successful detections of enemy vessels was negligible. Efforts to employ radar for target range measurement, in connection with the introduction of the new FAT torpedoes, proved equally unsuccessful; so on 25 October 1943, further installations were abandoned, and old sets were gradually removed during yard overhauls.

However, following his June 1942 conference with the head of the Naval

Communication Division, Dönitz had repeatedly demanded a radar capable of countering Allied developments in this field. Now it seemed that adapting Luftwaffe sets might be worthwhile. In September 1942 the FuG (*Funkmessgerät*) 202 'Lichtenstein' radar, originally designed for use by night fighters, was tested on U-468 in the Baltic, with little success. In 1943 the Luftwaffe's new 56cm-wavelength FuG 200 Hohentwiel was adapted for use on U-boats, and again tested in the Baltic (by U-743 during August), this time successfully. Still employing a manually rotated mirror aerial, similar to that of the old FuMO 30, this much smaller set could be installed in the W/T cabin. The naval version was named FuMO 61 or Hohentwiel U, and, during its trials against a 5,500grt ship, was found to have a maximum detection of 10 km. Being originally designed for search purposes only, its minimum detection range was two km, which precluded its use for torpedo fire control purposes.

Standard installation on U-boats was ordered on 25 October 1943. The first front-line U-boat (U-763) equipped with the FuMO 61 left Germany on 14 December 1943. Owing to bomb damage in the manufacturing company (Lorenz, Berlin), by 20 September 1944 only 96 sets had been or were about to be installed. However, by the end of the war the majority of front-line U-boats were fitted with the FuMO 61.

Although the Hohentwiel radar performed better than previous systems, the chances of its operational use were limited, in the last phase of the campaign, by the policy of total underwater war. Moreover, commanding officers still hesitated to use radar, fearing detection by enemy search receivers, which were never used operationally by Allied forces.

Centimetric radar was never used operationally by U-boats during the war. Two experimental sets of the navy version of the Luftwaffe's FuG 224 'Berlin' were successfully tested from the end of 1944 in U-1207 and U-1210, in the Baltic area, but because of the generally poor performance of radar in U-boats throughout the war, crews when surfaced were always obliged to depend on visual detection of the enemy.

Search Receivers

In autumn 1941, at Boulogne in France, a German electronic listening station - part of the Naval Communication Experimental Section - provided the first information about the Allies' probable use of radar in ships and aircraft.[17] It may have been because of this that, at the end of 1941, an experimental search receiver (code-named 'Berta-Anlage') was installed on the newly commissioned Type IX-C U-172. The device consisted of a wide-frequency dipole with reflector, to detect radar transmissions in the metric band, used by British ASV Mk I and Mk II sets. U-172 carried the search receiver on its first two patrols. No records or other information concerning this matter have yet been located, but it was probably intended to get confirmation of the use of radar against U-boats, which was apparently not achieved.

When the Allied use of radar against U-boats, and the resulting threat, were finally recognized by U-boat Command in June 1942, immediate steps were taken to equip U-boats with a search receiver as soon as possible. The Naval Communication Experimental Section had already finished the development of an appropriate search receiver, designated R600. Owing to the lack of production facilities in Germany, a contract for its mass production was placed with the French companies Metox and Grandin. The antenna consisted of a rather fragile vertical wooden frame aerial. It was rotated by hand, and had to be dismounted before diving. The aerial, officially named FuMB-aerial 2 'Honduras' (FuMB being short for *Funkmessbeobachtungsgerät*), became known as the 'Biscayakreuz' or Biscay Cross. The complete set, designated FuMB 2 'Metox', was effective against radar transmissions in the 0.9-3.8 metre waveband, with the radar signals being converted into audible signals monitored by headphones.

After strong efforts to advance the project, U-214 left Brest on 9 August 1942 as the first U-boat to operate with the new search receiver. From the end of that month all U-boats leaving French bases were fitted with it. This resulted in a sharp decrease of U-boat detections in the Bay of Biscay by Allied aircraft using radar. British operational researchers later calculated a 95% efficiency of the new set for early warning against ASV Mk II radar.[18] This calculation did not include seasonal effects influencing the chances of U-boat detections (which would have somewhat downgraded the assessment)[19] but after the loss of four U-boats in Biscay between 5 July and 3 September 1942, no more losses were incurred until February 1943, when airborne centimetric radar was introduced. Because the detection range of the FuMB 2 could exceed 30 km, commanding officers sometimes became confused by the numerous detections of aircraft, which were not actually heading for their craft, and subsequently some had the equipment shut down.

From March 1943 onward, the old Biscayakreuz aerial was gradually replaced by the pressure-tight FuMB antenna 3, 'Bali I'. This fixed mounted drum-shaped aerial covered the 0.7-3.2 metre wavelengths. Later, it was also mounted on the top of the schnorkel head, and became the standard aerial against metric radar until the end of the war.

After the Allies' first operational use of centimetric airborne radar, the U-boats reported a renewal of surprise attacks, without prior warning from the search receiver. At that time, for a number of reasons, leading German experts did not believe centimetric radar could be used operationally, so, in seeking to explain these surprise attacks, they followed a number of blind alleys - infra-red detection, the short-time use of radar, the possibility of gradual power reduction of radar during an approach, and other things - and were thus diverted from the real cause. Particularly confusing for the German side was a statement from a captured Allied pilot, who convinced his interrogators that Allied aircraft were homing on the known radiations from the German R600 search receiver, while using radar only occasionally for target-ranging. Because prior tests had revealed that emissions could indeed be detected up to a range of 70 km, Dönitz radioed all U-boats on 13 August 1943 to discontinue the use of their R600 receiver with immediate effect.[20] Eleven days earlier, he had ordered all boats ready to leave, to remain in port until an improved search receiver became available. This order came after extremely heavy losses had occurred since mid-July, when 10 out of 18 boats on outward transit through the Bay of Biscay had been sunk.

Properly known as FuMB 8 and code-named 'Cypern' but more commonly called W.Anz.gl or 'Wanze', the new automatic frequency scanning search receiver covering the metric band was specially developed to detect enemy radar's use of short-impulse intervals. It could use either the existing FuMB 3 antenna Bali I, or the Butterfly aerial FuMB antenna 5 'Palau'. The latter, fitted on the back of the extendible radar frame aerial, also gave rough contact bearings. U-161 left Lorient on 8 August 1943, the first U-boat to be fitted with the new receiver. When encouraging reports were received from this and following craft about unmolested transit through the Bay of Biscay, U-boat Command believed (for a short time) that the detection problem had finally been mastered. This soon proved to be wishful thinking: from 6 September, new reports about surprise attacks started to arrive. When tests revealed that the FuMB 8 also radiated slightly, Dönitz again (on 5 November) ordered its immediate abandonment. It was to be replaced by a new radiation-free model (FuMB 9 'Cypern II'), available from the same day. At about that same time a new emission-free, untuned detector adaptor (FuMB 10 'Borkum') was introduced. Using an attached impulse amplifier, it formed a wide-band receiving installation with a relative large frequency spread.[21]

The secret of centimetric radar was unravelled in December 1943, when an H2S set captured from Bomber Command was rebuilt. Tests revealed how well it could detect surfaced U-boats. Only then did the leading German electronic experts advise U-boat Command that centimetric radar was the most probable reason for the detection of U-boats, and the severe losses during the previous months.[22]

Meanwhile, on their own initiative, the Naval Communication Experimental Section and the Telefunken company had jointly developed a prototype series of a new search receiver against centimetric radar. Work on it had started after the recovery of the first British centimetric radar set from a Bomber Command aircraft, shot down near Rotterdam in February 1943. The British 9cm radar set was thereafter often named the 'Rotterdam Apparatus'. The first sets of the new receiver (FuMB 7, 'Naxos') became available in small numbers during September 1943, and were immediately installed for experimental purposes. U-849, the first boat so equipped, left Germany on 2 October 1943. However, the associated aerial (FuMB antenna 11, 'Naxos Finger') turned out to be rather insensitive, with maximum detection ranges of only 5-8 km against 9cm radar, and was also liable to mechanical breakdown. In consequence, the series of surprise attacks continued, supporting existing suspicions about other detection methods used by the Allies until centimetric radar was finally identified as the principal device. Only at the end of January 1944 did a much improved dipole aerial (FuMB antenna 24 'Cuba Ia', known as 'Fliege') with detection ranges of at least 20 km become available.

Because of a series of wrong decisions by technical and command administrations, U-boats had to operate for almost a whole year without any effective means of early warning against centimetric radar. Given the severe losses during that period, the confidence of front-line U-boat officers and men in the efficiency of their search receiver equipment was thoroughly destroyed. Repeated setbacks led to a general reluctance among commanders to rely on electronic devices, even if their use would have offered a tactical advantage.

The discovery of Allied radar working on a wavelength of 3cm in February 1944 led to the development of the FuMB 26, 'Tunis'. Based on the existing FuMB 7 with the 'Fliege' aerial, and combined with a second horn radiator aerial ('Mücke'), it was also sensitive to transmissions around the 3cm wavelength. The first such sets became available at the end of May 1944, although 3cm radar was not used in Allied A/S aircraft before October 1944. The antenna was either fixed on top of a wooden rod attached to the periscope standards or into the direction-finder loop. The aerial system had to be dismounted before the craft submerged, but maximum detection ranges in the order of 50 km were achieved.

When the policy of total underwater war came into force from June 1944, no pressure-tight aerial covering the centimetric band was available for front-line use. Only the FuMB antenna 3 'Bali I' could be attached to the head of the schnorkel. This was effective against metric radar transmissions, but Allied airborne radar was no longer using that waveband. Therefore, U-boats schnorkeling at periscope depth had to return to the visual detection of approaching aircraft, which necessitated a continuous periscope watch.

At the end of the war, a new receiver (FuMB 35, 'Athos'), together with a pressure-tight aerial for use while schnorkeling, was about to be fitted to all U-boats. It had a combined aerial for the detection of radar transmissions in the 3cm and 9cm wavebands, which was fitted on top of a extendible mast on the conning tower. A special amplifying and display unit allowed all-round search as well as continuous indication of target bearing. By the end of the war, however, only one experimental set had been installed (on U-249).

Camouflage and Decoys

In 1943 two types of radar decoys (*Funkmesstäuschungskörper* or FuMT) were developed, to give a spurious target to enemy air and surface craft which employed radar. These were the balloon decoy FuMT 1, 'Aphrodite IV', introduced in June 1943, and the floating buoy FuMT 2, 'Thetis IIc', first used in January 1944. However, both were designed to reflect radar transmissions in the metric band, and Allied tests with recovered specimens revealed hardly any response to centimetric radar. It is therefore doubtful if they had much effect on Allied anti-submarine operations.

The development of a form of camouflage against electromagnetic waves received very little attention until 1943. After a June conference on the radar problem at the German Admiralty, all such efforts were concentrated in a special research team, designated *Arbeitsgemeinschaft 'Schwarzes Uboot'*. The teams' brief was to develop for the U-boats a camouflage (code-named 'Schornsteinfeger') against the known metric radar (ASV Mk I and II). Eventually it was found that if the energy reflection of the incoming radar beam was reduced to 1% in the area of the conning tower alone, the objective was achieved. From a large number of proposals to achieve this aim, just three became important in the course of the war.

Since 1940, the Naval Communication Experimental Section, together with Dr. Bachem of the *Entwicklungsinstitut für Nachrichtenwesen in Konstanz* (ENK), had worked on a method adapting the principle of the quarter wave plate, by the use of a conducting screen for a wavelength of 1.5 metres (which was then considered to be the ASV sets' principal wavelength). During practical trials in the Baltic from September 1943 until January 1944 (with U-311, U-390, U-968 and U-708), the detection range of the airborne ASV Mk II was reduced by about 50%. However, the construction was a mechanical failure, owing to its lack of resistance against the sea. Nor was it effective against centimetric radar, so in 1944, the idea was abandoned.

After the use of centimetric radar had been finally established, work on this waveband received priority. At the end of 1943 (when, as an unrelated matter, schnorkels were introduced) a large part of the answer was provided. Under good conditions, Allied radar could still detect the schnorkel's head, but if an unprotected schnorkel was extended one metre above the surface of the sea, its theoretical detection range was already 75-80% less than the broadside detection range against a surfaced Type VII-C. All that remained was to camouflage the schnorkel head itself.

In spring 1944 the development of a electrical absorber against centimetric radar was completed. Designed by Professor J. Jaumann, in co-operation with the IG Farben Company, and designated 'Schalen-Sumpf', it became later known to the Allies as the 'Jaumann absorber'. Consisting of a hollow cylinder with a 7cm-thick wall, it was made up of seven layers of thin, semiconducting paper (cellulose acetate films) separated by layers or spacers about 9mm thick of cellular polyvinyl chloride (Igelit, US trade name Thermozote). The surface conductivity of the paper was graduated exponentially from the inside layer towards the outer. By the use of the cellular igelit, whose electrical properties resemble those of air, the constant spacing between the paper layers and the overall form of the absorber was maintained. Absorption was primarily achieved through loss in the conducting paper, and secondarily through destructive interference. The camouflage was effective over a wave band of 3-30cm. A reflection co-efficient of less than 10% in amplitude for flat plates was achieved, with a minimum of less than 1% at 9.3cm, which was the principal wavelength of Allied centimetric radar. Compared with an unprotected schnorkel head, this reduced the range of radar detection by about 65%.

However, it did have a drawback. Because of its rigid construction, it could be fitted only to the ring float schnorkel head, whereas most schnorkel-equipped U-boats were still fitted with a ball float schnorkel head. On 30 September 1944 the first two Schalen-Sümpfe units were delivered to Germaniawerft Kiel for installation. By March 1945, when production at IG Farben ceased owing to bomb damage, a total of approximately 150 sets were built, of which about 100 were actually installed on U-boats.

For the ball float schnorkels, at first a conical metal sheet construction was designed, working on the principle of deflection; but only three experimental units were tested (on U-1024, U-1060 and U-1064) during July-August 1944. This development was subsequently abandoned in favour of the Wesch absorber, named after its inventor, Professor Wesch of the Welt Post Institut (WPI) in Heidelberg. This absorber consisted of a rubber-like mat of about 1cm thickness, built up of two layers of perbunan, with a high percentage of iron powder (carbonyl iron), underlaid by a thin Oppanol-O layer. The outer perbunan layer had a waffle-like form, with rigid squares about 20mm wide. Absorption was mainly achieved by the principle of destructive interference. The absorber was produced in mats of 52cm square, and simply glued onto the metal of the schnorkel. Its flexible nature allowed the mats to be fitted to any surface of moderate curvature. The operational performance of this type of absorber was slightly less than the Schalen-Sumpf, but against 9cm radar a reduction in detection range of the order of 50% was assumed.[23]

The first U-boat fitted with a camouflaged schnorkel (a Wesch absorber) was U-991, which left Kiel for front-line service on 5 October 1944. Approximately 150 boats were equipped with the Wesch absorber by the war's end.

The development of a successful camouflage against radar was thus achieved - the Kriegsmarine's sole success in the electronic war. In the last phase of the U-boat campaign, Allied aircrews on anti-submarine patrols had to resort, once again, to simply looking for schnorkels protruding above the surface.

Underwater Electronics

In the field of surface electronics, radar became a decisive factor. Developments in underwater electronics had no such impact on the course of operations. Although the Allies improved the reliability of their asdic equipment, successful detection of a submerged U-boat remained difficult throughout the war owing to the character and unpredictable variations of the physical properties of the surrounding seawater. Even at the end of WWII, underwater electronics were only beginning to mature into a fully capable part of ASW.

Active Detection Devices

Apart from a experimental series of a combined active/passive detection set (installed on U-64, U-65, U-122, U-123 and U-124 early in the war), the only active sonar carried by U-boats of pre-war design was a small set developed for mine detection (*SN-Gerät*). Developed from the standard German sonar set (*S-Gerät*), its transducer basis was fitted at the stem between the forward torpedo tubes. Although a large number of sets were installed on all types of new boats from spring 1941 onward, the operational performance of the set was so poor that its removal was eventually ordered on 24 April 1942.[24]

When true submarines capable of continuous underwater operations were developed, the need for a new sonar set became obvious. This led to the design of the 'Nibelung' sonar set for the Type XXI U-boats. Development had begun in 1942 for intended installation on the deep-diving Type VII C/42 submarines, which, however, were cancelled in favour of the Type XXI in 1943. The new set was designed for underwater detection and ranging, to allow torpedo fire control without the requirement for visual target observation through the periscope.

With the seemingly inevitable preliminary technical problems, sets were not available until the end of 1944, well after the delivery of the first Type XXI U-boats. Immediate sea trials in the Baltic during January 1945 demonstrated the equipment's practical value. Depending on physical water conditions, initial detection ranges of 4-8 km were achieved.[25]

The intention was to equip all boats designated for front-line service with the Nibelung set, and about 80 sets were reportedly produced before Germany's capitulation, but the total number of Type XXI boats fitted with it is unknown.[26]

Passive Listening Devices

As before the war, Germany continued to rely mainly on passive detection sets, holding the lead in this field throughout the war. The performance of the existing multi-unit hydrophone installation was greatly improved by arranging the receivers (whose number was also increased) in a box at the forward end of the keel. This array was termed *Balkon*, or balcony. Detection ranges of 20 km against single ships and 100 km against convoys were recorded. Standard installation, first on Type IX boats only, started at the end of 1943. From mid-1944, Type VII C boats were also equipped with it. It was further incorporated in the design of all new U-boat types.[27]

Its limitation was that it was directional: that is, its operator would hear loudly only sounds coming from the direction to which his D/F console was adjusted. Sounds from all other directions would be heard either weakly or not at all. In order to achieve continuous close distance all-round listening for warning purposes, one receiver unit on each side of the U-boat was connected via an amplifying unit to headphones. This NHG equipment (*Nautisches Horchgerät*, or nautical listening device) was a supplementary device to the multi-unit hydrophone equipment, intended for general installation. First sets became available at the end of 1944.

The KDB hydrophone set on the forward upper deck, which from 1941 was also installed on Type VII U-boats, usually produced poor results and was eventually removed during 1942.

Camouflage and Decoys

From 1938, research in this field was mainly directed on the development of a sound-absorbing coating for U-boats, intended to neutralize asdic. This research was undertaken by a team directed by Professor Dr. Erwin Meyer of the Technical University, Berlin, under the auspices of the Naval Communication Experimental Section. By 1941 a resonant sound absorber (code-named 'Alberich', after a dwarf in German legend who possessed a helmet which made the wearer invisible) was ready for operational use. It consisted of a two-ply, 4mm-thick smooth rubber sheet, pasted onto the steel plates of the U-boat's outer hull. The inner ply was perforated with holes of 2-5mm in diameter, forming cylindrical air cavities which were able to oscillate. The larger ones acted as sound-absorbing resonators. The number and the size type of cavities per unit area was adapted to the thickness of the underlying steel plate in order to attain the highest possible absorption in the desired frequency range. During laboratory experiments, reflection factors below 10% (i.e. absorption factors higher than 90%) were obtained in the 9-18 kilocycle frequency range, which covered asdic's frequency. The absorber was designed to work best at a frequency of 15 kilocycles, a diving depth of 150 metres and a water temperature of 10°C. In 1944, when the U-boats' operational areas shifted to shallower coastal waters, the performance of the coating was optimized to smaller diving depths by adjusting the number of holes in the perforated ply.[28]

In March 1943, the absorber's operational performance was tested in full-scale sea-trials off Arendal in Norway, comparing the coated U-470 and the uncoated U-958. Similar tests were also conducted with the coated U-480 and the uncoated U-247 and U-999 in May 1944. Simultaneous measurements with the standard German sonar (S-Gerät) were made of the beam-on echo strength and background noise level at ranges between 2 and 0.3 km and various depths ranging from periscope depths down to 150 metres. The averaged echo amplitude of the coated U-boat was only 1/6 that of the uncoated U-boat, thus resulting in a reflection factor of 17% in this particular case. However, at diving depths above 100 metres, to which the absorber was adjusted, the echo amplitude of the coated U-boat scarcely exceeded the background noise level and complete protection was achieved.[29]

By the end of the war, apart from the early experimental U-boats U-67, UD-4 and U-470, a total of eight Type VII-C boats (U-480, U-485, U-486, U-1105, U-1106, U-1107, U-1304 and U-1306) and two Type XXIII boats (U-4704 and U-4708) were equipped with Alberich.

A rather simple acoustic counter-measure was a decoy code-named 'Bold', also known as the 'submarine bubble target'. This consisted of a small cylindrical wire mesh box containing calcium hydride, which gave off hydrogen bubbles when in contact with water. The container was ejected through a small tube projecting through the pressure hull. By a simple mechanism, the device maintained in a depth of 14-25 metres for a maximum of 40 minutes. Used in groups, the cluster of bubbles reflected an asdic echo and created a false target similar to a U-boat, thus allowing the boat to escape undetected. Although experienced asdic operators could distinguish between the two kinds of echo, Bold certainly proved successful in a large number of incidents.

First tests on Bold were carried out in July 1941 with U-93. From spring 1942 the installation became standard fitting to all U-boats. A modification for use in greater depths (Bold 4) was introduced in 1944, but proved less effective owing to mechanical problems.

Another sort of decoy (code-named 'Sieglinde') was designed to imitate a submerged U-boat running on its electric motor for about 30 minutes. The only front-line U-boat known to have been equipped with this type of decoy was the Type XXI U-boat, U-2511.[30]

Summary and Conclusions

Like other naval powers, Germany entered the war with submarines whose main design characteristics were similar to those of WWI. For technical and tactical reasons they generally operated on the surface, submerging only in certain tactical situations. Enemy vessels were usually located by eyesight. In the course of the war, front-line experiences led to a number of improvements in various fields, but these did not change the U-boats' general design characteristics. As long as the existing boats were successful, U-boat Command, the Naval Staff and the Naval Construction Office considered the need for new developments less important than high construction figures.

The impact of Allied developments in ASW, especially in the field of electronics, was neither foreseen nor fully realized by U-boat Command until existing U-boat types had become technologically outdated by the introduction of radar. Furthermore, following orders from Hitler (after the fall of France) to abandon any research work on projects that would not become operational within one year, by 1943 Germany had lost touch with new technological and electronic developments on the Allied side. German naval research also suffered from too loose a central control early in the war, resulting in a lack of concentration on primary objectives in the research sector. Combined with limited technical resources and insufficient numbers of qualified technical personnel, no compensation for this backlog was possible until the war's end.

Only when defeat in the Battle of the Atlantic was becoming obvious did a radical change of opinions towards novel designs and propulsion systems take place. This led to the development of the true submarine, with revolutionary technical and operational capabilities, in a remarkably short period; but, even with innovative production methods, the new U-boat types could not be produced in time to reverse the tactical situation in the U-boat campaign.

Meanwhile, efforts were made to enable the continuation of operations with existing types. To a certain extent this was achieved by the introduction of the schnorkel. However, in attempting to counter the Allied threat of radar detection, and coupled with the absence of good radar sets for themselves, the decision to concentrate mainly on passive search receivers and camouflage instead of active detection forced the U-boats into the defensive role completely. This fundamental disadvantage was even made worse by disastrous misinterpretations concerning Allied detection devices and methods. In the end, apart from the schnorkel's effective camouflage against radar (from October 1944), there were only two phases (August 1942-February 1943 and March-June 1944) when the U-boats were equipped with effective warning devices against radar detection.

However, the German design of the true submarine and advanced developments in other fields, such as underwater listening and anti-sonar camouflage, formed the basis for all postwar designs.

Notes

1. Trenkle, F, *Die deutschen Funkmeßverfahren bis 1945* (Heidelberg, 1986), p. 124.
2. Rössler, E, *Geschichte des deutschen Ubootbau* (2 vols., Koblenz, 1987), p. 327.
3. *Ibid.*, p. 234.
4. *Ibid.*, p. 255.
5. Waddington, *OR. in World War II: Operational Research against the U-boat*, p. 82.
6. Köhl, F, & Niestlé, A, *Uboottyp IX C* (Koblenz, 1990), p. 34.
7. Rössler, E, *op. cit.*, p. 298.
8. *Ibid.*, p. 338ff.
9. Befehlshaber der Unterseeboote, War Diary, 130 vols. 1939-1945. Period 15.03.44-31.03.44, entry 22.03.1944, p. 18 (*hereafter War Diary BdU*).
10. Seekriegsleitung, War Diary 1.Skl, Part A, 68 vols. 1939-1945. Vol 58, p. 774.
11. United States Technical Mission Europe (USTME) Technical Report No. 529-45: *The low frequency aspects of the 'Marinekurier' High Speed Radio Telegraph System* (New York, 1945), p. 2.
12. Hinsley, *British Intelligence in the Second World War*, Vol 3, part II, p. 852.
13. Hessler, *The U-Boat war in the Atlantic 1939-1945*, II, p. 26.
14. *Ibid.*
15. Sternhell, C. M, & Thorndike, A. M, *Antisubmarine Warfare in World War II: Operations Evaluation Report #51* (Operations Evaluation Group, Office of the Chief of Naval Operations, Navy Department, Washington DC, 1949) p. 30.
16. Giessler, H, *Der Marine-Nachrichten- und -Ortungsdienst* (München, 1971) p. 78.
17. Trenkle, F, *Die deutschen Funkstörverfahren bis 1945* (Frankfurt a. M., 1982) p. 44.
18. Waddington, *OR. in World War II*, p. 124
19. McCue, *U-Boats in the Bay of Biscay: An Essay in Operations Analysis*, p. 9.
20. War Diary BdU, *op. cit.*, period 01.08.43-15.08.43, entry 14.08.43, p. 53.
21. Rössler, E, *op. cit.*, p. 324.

22. Trenkle, F, *op.cit.,* (1982), p. 18.
23. Köhl, F, & Niestlé, A, *Uboottyp VII C* (Koblenz, 1989), p. 35.
24. Rössler, E, *Die Sonaranlagen der deutschen U-Boote* (Herford, 1991) p. 63ff.
25. *Ibid.,* p. 72f.
26. Hackmann, *Seek & Strike: Sonar, Anti-Submarine Warfare and the Royal Navy 1913-54,* p. 297.
27. Rössler, E, *op. cit.,* (1991), p. 39ff.
28. Dept. of the Navy, Navships publication 900, 164 - *Sound Absorption and Sound Absorbers in Water* (2 vols., Washington DC, 1947) p. 6.
29. *Ibid.,* p. 31.
30. Rössler, E, *op. cit.,* (1991), p. 92.

Atlantic Escorts 1939-45

by David K. Brown

Summary

In preparing for war, the Royal Navy assumed it would have to fight a continuation of the 1914-18 campaign, conducted in the Western Approaches to the United Kingdom. The early months of the war justified this approach but after France fell and the Battle spread across the Atlantic, it was realized that more ships with longer endurance and better weapon systems were needed. Although the skill of individuals on both sides remained important, the balance was swung by the rapid introduction of new technology such as HF/DF, radar, improved asdics and ahead-throwing weapons into more numerous and better-built ships.

Introduction

In 1918 the German U-boat offensive had been defeated without the help of asdic. In 1939, it was not unreasonable to assume that the hunters had a greater advantage since geographical constraints still forced the U-boats to take a long and vulnerable passage to the Western Atlantic, submarine technology had changed little (see Table 1) and there were in any case few U-boats in service. It had been appreciated that the British objective was the safe arrival of cargoes rather than sinking U-boats and that even forcing them to submerge - thereby limiting their mobility - contributed greatly to the objective. Surface raiders were seen as a greater threat than submarines, as were aircraft in coastal waters.

This chapter deals mainly with the escort vessels of the Allied navies, which sank 225 submarines. From early 1943 onwards, after the crisis of the Battle was over, aircraft took an increasing share of kills, sinking a total of 228 U-boats at sea. Asdic's ability to detect U-boats was initally over-rated, as was the ability of depth charges to destroy them. Even in good conditions, asdic's range of detection was so small that many escorts were needed to screen a convoy, and little thought had been given to the detection of submarines attacking on the surface at night.

It was a war of rapid technical development in which it was vital to identify quickly a change in enemy tactics or weapon-fit and to introduce countermeasures. The U-boat command failed repeatedly in this, failing to accept that their codes had been broken or that HF/DF could be carried on ships, and they were slow to appreciate the importance of radar. The Allies were very quick at getting new equipment into service, even if this meant that early versions were primitive. Nevertheless, the individual still counted. A very high proportion of U-boat successes were scored by a few aces, whilst Captain Walker's 2nd Escort Group was outstanding.

Part I: Build-Up to War

Lessons of World War I

· The lessons read from WWI had an important bearing on the RN's capability in the later war. First and foremost, the German attack on the Allied supply routes had been defeated; it was not the stalemate suggested by some recent writers.[1,2] Germany's twin naval objectives were to stop supplies reaching the UK, and US troops from reaching the Western Front, and they failed in both. It is likely that the loss of their best commanders was a major factor in the defeat of the U-boats in both wars - as the saying goes, 'There are old captains and bold captains but no old, bold captains.'

The main reason for the Allied victory in WWI was the introduction of the convoy system, making it more difficult for the U-boats to find targets and simultaneously concentrating escorts against the attacker. The U-boats were unable to concentrate their own attacks, probably impossible with contemporary radios. This success made the RN over-confident in its ability to counter a new offensive, despite the lack of any new measures against surface attack which, by 1918, had accounted for two-thirds of all sinkings. It should also have been noted that, in 1918, there were few sinkings in areas with air cover, often in the form of airships.

Between the Wars

Attempts were made to ban submarines or to limit the way in which they operated, but all failed. (Indeed, it is likely they were expected to.) In 1930, there was a major review of the RN's ASW capability,[3] which concluded that sloops (then being built at 2-3 a year) and the older destroyers (which were to be fitted with asdic) would be available in sufficient numbers for ocean escort. A perceived weakness in coastal escorts would be made good by asdic-fitted trawlers. A number of prototypes were converted and tried in exercises. Air attack was seen as a more serious threat to coastal traffic, so some V and W destroyers were converted to AA ships and the small *Hunt* class, with a powerful AA armament, was begun.

A few 'coastal sloops' were built but, though both beautiful and effective, they were too expensive. Instead, a vessel based on a large whale catcher, bigger and better than a trawler, was developed for coastal escort, and became famous as the *Flower*-class corvette. Later, for want of anything else, the corvettes were used as ocean escorts.

In the early '30s the potential threat from submarines was small; Germany commissioned her first overt submarine in 1935 and it was not until 1938 that their increasing numbers and capability posed a threat. Though there was little inter-war technical advance in U-boats, the speed with which WWI boats were built and their crews trained was forgotten in Britain.

TABLE 1: Submarine Technology									
Boat	Date	Dispt. Tons	L.(m)	Speed Surf	Kts. Sub.	Gun mm	Torp. no.	Tubes Dia.	Crew	Range nm
U-161	1918	820	71.6	16.8	8.6	105	6	500	39	8500/10
U-69	1939	749	67.1	17	7.6	88	5	533	44	8500/8

Operations during the Spanish Civil War showed the problems of asdic in warm waters, where density layers were important, but it seems the problems such layers would cause were not appreciated.[4]

Though there were few convoy exercises during the '30s, there were many exercises in which submarines penetrated the screen of the main fleet, scoring a high proportion of hits, despite the stringent safety precautions enforced.[5] Though there was some complacency, preparations had been made for convoys, there were just enough escort vessels and asdics were in store for the conversion of trawlers.

1939-1940

This was the war the RN had planned for, and as the figures show, the planning was sound. Up to March 1940, when the U-boats were diverted to support the Norwegian campaign, they had sunk 854,719 tons of shipping, mainly independents. In return, 17 U-boats had been sunk - a high proportion of the operational boats. The ratio of merchant ship sunk to U-boat losses (16.6) was very similar to that of 1918. The German torpedo problems, teething troubles in new submarines and their slow refits contributed to the British success.

German plans, too, were a little confused.[6] They do not seem to have intended an all-out 'sink at sight' policy, but were forced into it by over-enthusiastic commanding officers and by the impossibility of observing the Prize Rules. When war broke out they had a total of 57 submarines, of which 39 were suitable for operations. A big building programme was started and frequently increased. At first, there were too few boats at sea for 'Wolf Pack' attacks. The Germans, too, saw the war as confined to the western approaches, not realising how great was the endurance of the Type VIIs or of their crews.

Britain Alone

From August 1940, U-boats were able to use French bases. This increased their time on station by about 25%. Shorter refit times, particularly in France, helped to get more boats at sea. Despite this and the increased building programme, there were no more boats on station in the Atlantic, since more were needed for training and the operational areas had moved west, giving longer transit times, while the bad weather in the winter of 1939-40 reduced effectiveness. On the other hand the need to keep many destroyers on the east coast as a defence against invasion greatly reduced the number of available escorts. The odds swung heavily in favour of the U-boats and showed the need for a number of changes in the escort force to meet these new conditions. Operational and training aspects are not discussed here, but the most significant technical aspects then needing attention are listed below and discussed in detail in later sections of this chapter. There were five:

- the inadequate number of effective ships;
- weapons and sensors with inadequate capability against submarines running deep or on the surface;
- poor endurance;
- speed;
- seakeeping and habitability.

Part II: Quantity and Quality

Numbers of Ships

A convoy needed sufficient escorts to ensure a high probability of a U-boat being detected by asdic before reaching a firing position. The effective range of early sets varied considerably with the weather, motion of the ship, temperature etc., as well as with the skill of the operator but an average value was about 1,300 yards. From 1942, it was recognized that big convoys increased the effectiveness of the escort force, since the perimeter to be watched increased only as the square root of the number of merchant ships.

Once a submarine was detected, the aim was to force it down; sooner or later it would have to surface for air or to charge batteries and could then be destroyed. Even if the escort could not wait for the submarine to surface, the speed of the submarine was reduced from 17 knots on the surface to about 3-4 submerged (9 knots for one hour). An escort might loiter over a submerged U-boat for hours trying for a kill, after which it needed high speed to rejoin the convoy quickly - a speed which would be greater than the U-boat's surface speed.

Asdic's short range meant that large numbers of escorts were essential but the UK's resources were limited. There was a shortage of labour, particularly skilled men, which got worse as the war went on and basic materials such as steel were in short supply. Inevitably, there was conflict between the resources needed to build merchant ships and to build escorts.

Shipbuilding

The *Flower*-class corvettes were very simple ships which could be built almost anywhere: 18 yards were involved in the UK, and 16 more in Canada.[7]

TABLE 2: *Flower* orders

UK *Flowers*		Canadian *Flowers*	
Number	**Ordered**	**Number**	**Programme**
30*	July 39	64	1939-40
30	Aug 39	6	1940-41
30	Sept 39		
20*	Dec 39	Modified	
2	June 40	10	1940-41
7	Aug 40	15	1942-43
2	Oct 40	12	1943-44
1	Dec 41	-	-
1	Feb 42	-	-
2	May 42	-	-
6	July 42	-	-
151	**TOTALS**	**107**	

GRAND TOTAL 258

* Includes 2 + 6 French contracts taken over in June 1940.

There was a remarkable variation in building times both from yard to yard and in the same yard:

TABLE 3: UK *Flower*-Class Building Times in Months	
Quickest individual ship	5.0
Slowest	22.0
Best average, Smith's Dock	6.5
Worst average, Ailsa	19.0

Variations within a yard were usually the result of bombing, which also accounts for some of the variation between yards. It is interesting that later ships usually took longer than earlier ones, contrary to the usual effects of the 'learning curve'. The longer time reflects the combined effects of bombing, shortages of labour and materials and of war-weariness.

Management, labour relations, trade union practices and capital equipment were all old-fashioned. At one meeting Lithgow said that shipbuilding practices were out of date; Goodall wryly remarked in his diary for 2 June 1942, 'Satan rebuking sin!'[8] During the depression, the few men who had joined the industry were sometimes not of the highest quality, and there had been very little capital investment.[9,10] Comparison of building times with those in the USA and Canada is embarrassing, even allowing for the very real problems of blackout and the call-up for the Forces of most young men.

TABLE 4: Comparative Building Times (Months/Days)			
Nation	**Class**	**Fastest**	**Slowest**
British	*River*	7/5	24/17
Canadian	*River*	5/3	17/6
Australian	*River*	16/8	24/15
US	*Colony*	5/0	21/8
British	*Loch*	7/25	17/10
US	*Evarts*	3/3	21/20
	Buckley	1/23	13/21
British	*Flower*	4/3	20/3
Canadian	*Flower*	7/26	17/24
British	*Castle*	5/12	17/24

The *River*-class frigates were bigger than the *Flower*s and the structural style was a little more refined, but they were only slightly more difficult to build. In 1942, a large programme of *Loch*s and *Castle*s was started, the intended numbers varying from time to time, but some 120-145 *Loch*s and 70-80 *Castle*s were expected to complete by the end of 1944.[11] More detailed plans, matching hulls to individual building slips, seem to have envisaged 133 *Loch*s and 69 *Castle*s. A total of 226 sets of machinery was ordered in December 1942.

Most of the problems in this programme were foreseen at the start, but few were solved. These later classes had more complicated electrical installations (see Table 5) and it was estimated that 400 additional fitters would be needed, but few were found and many were lost to the army. Installed electrical power was a good measure of the complexity of the ship and was directly proportional to the cost. As Goodall noted on 3 April 1943, there was also a steel shortage, but, with the problems in fitting out, late delivery of hulls was welcome. Goodall said it was sticking out a mile that presently we should have these ships ready to be lifted out, but insufficient labour.

The frigates were to be built 'on American methods', i.e. pre-fabricated. The first of class was built by a traditional shipbuilder and a team of structural steel workers then prepared from it the drawings which they would need to use. Records show that the building time was reduced, although the number of man hours increased.

TABLE 5: Costs and Installed Electric Power		
Class	**Cost (£'000)**	**KW**
Flower	90	15 (15 added later)
Castle	190	105
River	240	180
Loch	300	180
Black Swan	360	190-360

Centralized outfitting yards were set up at Dalmuir for ships built on the Clyde and at Hendon Dock for the northeast coast but, mainly due to the shortage of skilled labour, they could not keep up with the delivery of hulls. By 1945, the yards were full of ships whose fitting out was delayed. However, since the Battle of the Atlantic was by then almost over, such delay was not serious.

The *Captain* class (USN 'DE') derived from BuShip studies from 1939 onwards for small destroyers which could be built quickly and cheaply.[12] These ideas had begun to crystallize when, in 1941, the RN asked for 100 escort vessels with a dual-purpose armament. As the 5in/38mm was scarce, they were armed with three 3in/50mm, even though their shell would be unlikely to penetrate a pressure hull. The RN also asked for 112 depth charges, later increased to 180, with eight throwers and a Hedgehog. A tall, open bridge of British style was also required.

Engine supply was a problem and the first class (USN *Evarts*) were fitted with four 1,500 bhp diesels, driving twin shafts through DC generators and motors in a hull 283ft 6in long with a speed of 21 knots. The next class (*Buckley*) had turbo-electric rnachinery giving 24 knots in a 306ft hull. They had 400-600 KW generating capacity and, in 1943, cost \$5.3-6.1 million. After model testing, twin rudders were fitted, giving a reduction of 25% in turning circle (see Table 11). The *Captain*s were flush-decked with considerable sheer forward to reduce wetness, and were unduly stiff, which led to rapid rolling. They entered service from the first quarter of 1943, missing the worst of the battle, but still had many successes.

TABLE 6: *Captain*s entering Service					
1943-44 quarters	1st	2nd	3rd	4th	1st
Diesel	4	2	9	15	2
Turbine	0	2	8	28	10

Marine Engineering

During the depression, with many shipyards closed, supporting industries suffered as badly or worse. Marine engineering firms capable of building turbine plants were fully occupied with major warships and there was no possibility of building the many sets needed for escorts. There seemed no alternative to the steam reciprocating engine and from 1939-45, 942 sets of 1.8 million ihp were produced.[13] It was also believed, probably wrongly, that reservists manning these ships could not cope with more advanced machinery. Later, it took only six weeks to convert such men to the advanced steam turbo electric and diesels of the *Captain*s.

Even the resources for reciprocating engines were limited and during 1943 Goodall was worried that engines and boilers were limiting factors in frigate production. The marine engineering labour force did increase, but, he noted on 20 March 1943, mainly by taking on unskilled labour.

TABLE 7: Marine Engineering Labour Force

June 1939	58,000
Jan 1940	66,000
Jan 1941	77,000
Mar 1942	85,000

Availability[14]

Initially, as many as 50% of escorts were unavailable at any one time. However, the number of escorts with the convoys could be increased quite considerably by reducing the time taken for maintenance in harbour.

TABLE 8: Percentage of escorts unavailable for operations[15]

Year	Winter/Spring	Summer/Autumn
1939	17.0	
1940	20.7	25.0
1941	8.3	19.0
1942	19.3	18.8
1943	24.0	19.0
1944	24.8	18.6
1945	24.6	
Whole war	23.3	19.3

Overall average 22%

This table shows clearly the impact of damage during the evacuations of 1940 and brings out the effect of weather damage in the winter months. The early corvettes often completed with poorly aligned crankshafts, causing early bearing failure. The older British destroyers had no intrinsic problems, but old age led to continual difficulties with leaking rivets making life unpleasant for the crew and causing problems with contaminated feed-water and fuel. The *Town* class suffered from incurable condenseritis as the tube plates were weak and not parallel, from bearing problems due to corrosion of the cast iron housing, and from leaky rivets and bridges too weak to withstand the impact of heavy seas.[16]

With either machinery fit, the *Captain* class had few maintenance problems. The reciprocating engines of the *Colony* class were troublesome, showing that it is a mistake to think that simple machinery is necessarily reliable.

Weapon Systems[17]

Underwater. At the outbreak of war, attack on a submerged submarine depended on location by asdic followed by a depth charge attack. The asdics in use were in the 121-128 series which differed little in performance, the hull outfits for the faster ships having retractable domes. In average weather conditions detection would be at about 1,300 yards with up to 2,500 yards in ideal conditions. All forms of depth charge attack suffered from a long blind period or dead time, from the time the approaching target left the asdic beam until the charges, dropped over the stern, fell to the set depth. The deeper the submarine, the longer was this dead time giving more time for evasion, a problem not fully appreciated before the war.

Depth charges had entered service in January 1917 but at first with only two per ship and the thrower was introduced in August 1917. The Mark VII charge of 1939 had a charge of 290lbs of Amatol and was thought to have a lethal radius of 30 feet. In fact, 20 feet was a more realistic figure though, even at 40 feet, the U-boat might have to surface due to damage to systems. It is worth noting that, at full speed, the U-boat could move a distance equal to the lethal radius in just three seconds.

The Mark VII charge sank at an initial rate of 7ft/sec, increasing to 10ft/sec at 250ft. It was not very effective; in the first six months of the war, 4,000 depth charge attacks produced 33 sinkings. In late 1940 the Mark VII 'heavy' was introduced which sank at 16ft/sec and had a Minol charge, lethal at 26ft and capable of inflicting severe damage at twice that range. The effectiveness of depth charge attacks was also improved by increasing the number of charges dropped in an attack from five to 10. Fourteen charge patterns were tried but the '10 pattern', with five exploding above and five below the target, was seen as the most cost-effective. The 'One Ton' depth charge, fired from a torpedo tube, was introduced in December 1942 with a 2,000lb charge, supposed to be as effective as a 10-pattern of Mk VIIs. It sank at 6ft/sec, later increased to 21ft/sec.

Attacks on deeply submerged submarines were greatly assisted by the 'Q' attachment, introduced in 1943, which could hold contact to much closer range; it was added to the earlier asdics. The 144 set, introduced in 1943, was a much more capable set with ancillary equipment making detection and classification more certain. Many of its features were incorporated into earlier sets.

The real answer to the problem of dead time lay in the ahead-throwing weapon. It must be a matter of regret that trials of such a weapon were abandoned in 1934. Wartime experience clearly showed the need, and a number of weapons were hastily devised, some of which were tried. Of these, two were selected for production and proved successful in service. The first was 'Hedgehog' which fired 24 contact-fused bombs, each weighing 65lb, in a circular pattern 40 yards in diameter, centred 200 yards ahead of the ship. The charge weight was a matter of heated debate; its over-enthusiastic inventor in DMWD proposed a mere 5lbs, but eventually constructors showed that 30lbs was the bare minimum to rupture a pressure hull.

The Hedgehog was not very successful at first, as in some cases it was badly installed and poor maintenance was a problem - excusable since few ships had received a handbook. Operators were also concerned that the bombs only exploded if they hit, and hence the shattering effect on morale of a near-miss depth charge was lost. Once these problems were overcome, faith was restored and, as Table 9 shows, the Hedgehog became a most effective weapon.

The 'Squid' was a three-barrelled mortar firing depth-fused bombs, each containing 207lbs of Minol, to a range of 275 yards where they formed a triangle with 40-yard sides. They sank at $43^1/2$ft/sec to a maximum depth of 900ft. If two Squids were fitted, the bombs were usually set to explode 60ft apart in depth. Squid was fitted in the *Loch*s (twin) and *Castle*s (single) and also in a few destroyers.

The success of Squid depended on advances in asdics. A true depth-finding set, the 147, was introduced in September 1943 which automatically set the fuses on Squid bombs. The development of these and other weapon systems is fully described by Hackmann and their success is illustrated in Table 9.

Period	Depth Charges			Hedgehog			Double Squid			Single Squid		
	Attack	Success	%	Attack	Success	%	Attack	Success	%	Attack	Success	%
1943												
2nd half	401	15	3.7	49	4	8.2						
1944												
1st half	404	30	6.5	70	10	14.3						
2nd half	98	5.5	5.6	37	13	35.1	6	2.5	*	17	4	23.5
1945	107	7.5	7	59	15.5	26.3	21	8.5	40.3	3	2	*

TABLE 9: Effectiveness of Various Weapons

The introduction of the German Naval Acoustic homing Torpedo (GNAT), first used in the torpedoing of *Lagan* on 10 September 1941, led to the introduction of a number of decoys such as Foxer. (This was well after the introduction of the US homing torpedo, FIDO, [Mk 24 'mine'] which sank U-266 on 15 May 1943.) The early decoys were clumsy and seriously interfered with the escorts' own asdic but later versions, such as Unifoxer, were less of a problem. An alternative countermeasure was to operate below the speed at which cavitation commenced, about 8 knots for a propeller in good condition.

Surface Attack. U-boat attacks on the surface in WWI were almost entirely on single, unescorted merchant ships. Only one attempt was made, in May 1918, to bring a concentration of U-boats together and this was very different from the later wolf pack tactics. The first true pack attack was on convoy HX72 in September 1940 and then, and for some time to come, the only means of detection was the human eye.

Radar began to enter service in the Atlantic very early in 1941, first the Type 286, mainly in destroyers, and initially with a fixed aerial which would only detect objects about 50 degrees either side of the bow and could detect a surfaced submarine at some 6,000 yards. The much superior centimetric 271 first entered service in *Orchis* in March 1941. By the end of the year, 50 sets were at sea. It could pick up a destroyer at 12,000 yards, a surfaced submarine at 5,000 or a periscope (with 8ft showing) at 1,300. This set was updated as the 271Q in 1942.

These early sets were perhaps even more valuable in helping escorts to maintain station when zigzagging on a dark night than in detecting submarines while the introduction of 'Talk Between Ships' radio in early 1941 also eased the problems of the escort commander. The number of first contacts by radar only exceeded visual sightings at the end of 1942 and eyesight remained important until the end of the war.

Bridges. The layout of bridges was an emotional subject, but RN opinion was unanimous in advocating open bridges and, with 30-50% of first contacts made visually (up to the end of 1942), it seems that they were correct. There was an unrecognised price to pay, primarily in exhaustion leading to impaired decision-making. The USN tended to favour enclosed bridges and gun houses.

U-boat Command relied extensively on two-way communication with boats at sea using HF radio. They believed that direction-finding from shore would be too inaccurate and that shipborne HF/DF sets were technically impossible. In fact, the first British ship set went to sea in late 1941 and fitting was rapid in 1942, leading to the sinking of U-587 on 27 March 1942. There was only a vague and inaccurate indication of range but, as more ships were fitted, cross-bearings enabled precise locations to be obtained. By 1944, HF/DF accounted for about 30% of first detections, almost as many as from asdic, and it was particularly effective against shadowers. HF/DF at sea contributed greatly to the Admiralty tracking room's knowledge of U-boat dispositions.

A surfaced U-boat was not easy to destroy. A shell would hit the tough, curved pressure hull at a very oblique angle and would usually glance off before exploding - a problem revealed during tests with captured U-boats in 1919, but subsequently forgotten. Ramming was a more certain means of sinking, and by May 1943 some 24 U-boats had been disposed of in this way. (About half had been previously disabled by depth charge attack). On average, 7-8 weeks was required to repair the ramming ship and, though this was a profitable exchange, the use of shallow-setting depth charges was encouraged as they became available.[18]

Quiet propulsion. The RN relied almost exclusively on asdic (active sonar) and hence there was little perceived need to quieten ships. The simple but efficient propeller would begin to cavitate at about 8 knots if in good condition; more usually, minor damage - nicks in the leading edge - would reduce this to about 5-6 knots. Machinery, too, was noisy. Noise, particularly cavitation, became important with the introduction of homing torpedoes in 1943. It was unfortunate that the development of hydrophones leading to passive sonar and the associated 'quiet propulsion' techniques such as pump jets and air-bubble screening were abandoned with the introduction of asdics.[19]

Part III: Ships and the Sea

'O Lord be kind, thy sea is so big and my ship so small'

Endurance

The Atlantic is big:

TABLE 10: Atlantic Distances		
New York to Liverpool	3,043	nautical miles
Halifax to Liverpool	2,485	
Panama to Liverpool	4,530	

The typical convoy had about 3,000 miles to travel, taking some 14-19 days along a route always close to a Great Circle. Escorts would travel considerably further, zigzagging and searching for contacts, and they would also use higher speeds from time to time. Refuelling at sea only came into use in 1942 and was a slow and unreliable operation compared with today's procedures. The older destroyers could not cross the Atlantic without refuelling and some other classes had only a marginal capability. The Long Range Escorts (mainly V and W conversions) lost a boiler room and a little speed to get increased fuel stowage. In many classes the need to conserve fuel limited the use of high speed.

TABLE 11: Endurance

Note that figures differ from source to source and these are nominal figures.

The actual endurance was much less.

Class	Miles @ Knots	Tons, fuel	Long-range versions	
Destroyers				
B	2440/14	390		
E	3550/14	480		
V & W	2180/14	450	2680/14	450
H	4000/14	329		
Town	2000/14	284	2780/14	390
Sloops				
Fowey	4000/14	329		
Black Swan	4710/14	425		
Frigates etc.				
Flower	3850/12	233	(5650 with WT boilers)	
Castle	7800/12	480		
River Tripl.ex	4630/14	470	6600	
River Turbine	4920/14	470	7000	
Loch	4670/14	730		
Captain DE	4670/14	197		
Captain TE	3870/14	335		

Speed

The normal submerged speed of a World War II submarine was 3-4 knots and so in the hunt, the speed of the escort vessel was unimportant. The maximum speed at which asdic could be used was about 15 knots. Speed was important to rejoin the convoy after a prolonged hunt astern, however, and it seems that it was the faster ships which were detached to kill a submarine. With convoy speeds of 7-9 knots, new Staff Requirements looked for speeds of about 25 knots, but because of the lack of engines only the destroyers and the turbine *Captains* reached such speeds. Sloops and frigates with speeds approaching 20 knots were barely adequate, and the *Flowers* were not. In particular, the *Flowers* were slower than a surfaced U-boat, an important factor during a wolf pack attack. It is interesting that because of their greater length and better form (developed at the Admiralty Experiment Works) the much bigger *Castle*-class corvettes, with the same engine as the *Flowers*, were at least half a knot faster.

Turning Circle

A small turning circle was needed for a successful depth charge attack, so that the stern could be positioned over the U-boat. The *Flowers* were outstanding, short and with a fair-sized rudder in the slipstream of the propeller. The British twin-screw ships were less good, and it is now hard to understand why there was such reluctance to use twin rudders in the *Rivers* and *Lochs*.

TABLE 12: Turning Circles.		
Class	**Diameter (yds)**	**Speed**
Flower	136	
River & Loch	330-400	12
Captain DE	280	16
Captain TE	350	16
RN destroyer	370	10
	405	15
	600	30
Town	770	15

Seakeeping

The North Atlantic is big, cold, wet, rough - sometimes very rough - corrosive, and hard when it hits you. In bad weather a ship's fighting effectiveness falls off quite quickly, mainly due to the degradation of the physical and mental abilities of the crew. Damage to the ship could also occur; asdic domes were vulnerable and some destroyers had their bridge fronts pushed in. The effectiveness of radar was greatly reduced in big waves. Similarly, surface attacks by submarines would normally be made with wind and sea astern, and periscope depth keeping was very difficult in high sea states.

Sea State	Sig, Wave Ht m Range	Mean	Wind Speed Kts Range	Mean	Probability of sea state %	Wave Period Range Most	Probable	Likely Wave L m

<table>
TABLE 13: Relationship between Wind Speed
and Size of Waves in the North Atlantic
</table>

Sea State	Sig,Wave Ht m Range	Mean	Wind Speed Kts Range	Mean	Probability of sea state %	Wave Period Range	Most Probable	Likely Wave L m
0-1	0-0.1	0.05	0-6	3	0.7	--	--	--
2	0-0.5	0.30	7-10	8.5	6.8	3.3-12.8	7.5	90
3	0.5-1.25	0.88	11-16	13.5	23.7	5.0-14.8	7.5	90
4	1.25-2.5	1.88	17-21	19	27.8	6.1-15.2	8.8	123
5	2.5-4	3.25	22-27	24.5	20.6	8.3-15.5	9.7	148
6	4-6	5.0	28-47	37.5	13.2	9.8-16.2	12.4	238
7	6-9	7.5	48-55	51.5	6.1	11.8-18.5	15	350
8	9-14	11.5	56-63	59.5	1.1	14.2-18.6	16.4	424
9	14	14	63	63	0.05	18.0-23.7	20.0	615

Note that Sea State (SS) is not the same as Beaufort number which measures wind speed.

The figures for probability of occurrence are averaged for the whole North Atlantic over the whole year. In winter, and in the more northerly areas, weather and seas are much worse, far more often.

The cause of seasickness was not fully understood in the war, but it is now recognized as primarily associated with vertical acceleration from the combined effects of pitch and heave. It is less certain, but probable, that vertical acceleration is also a prime cause of impaired judgement in those not actually vomiting.[20] A recent study by the Institute of Naval Medicine showed that, in a 200-foot ship, some 65% of the crew would be sick occasionally and 20% frequently, whilst at a length of 300 feet these figures would reduce to 50% and 15%.

The amplitude of both pitch and heave is governed mainly by length, long ships having smaller motions. Vertical acceleration will also depend on the longitudinal position as pitching will lead to high accelerations towards the ends. Conversely, the effects of motion can be reduced by placing vital spaces, such as the bridge, operations room etc. close to amidships. Sickness is also dependent on the frequency of the motion being most likely between 0.15 and 0.30 Hz (cycles/sec). More recent work (for the new *Castle* OPV) shows the *Castle* class of WWII was the shortest ship which would be effective in North Atlantic weather.

The effect of motions on the crew's fighting ability depends on the degree of acclimatisation as well as on ship size. The figures below are based on experience with the *Leander* class - at 360ft, much longer than the ships under discussion.

TABLE 14: Effect of Motions on Fighting Capability	
Sea state	% loss of capability
0-4	0
5	10
6	30
7+	95

In recent years a single parameter, Subjective Motion Magnitude (SMM), has been derived. This combines the effects of acceleration and frequency. It is found that an instantaneous value of 12 for SMM will cause the captain to alter either course or speed to reduce motions.[21]

It is also possible to 'average' SMM over the weather pattern of a whole year and over the length of the living and working spaces, an approach used in the design of the Castle-class OPV, where an average SMM of 4 was selected[22] (SMM3 as completed) compared with 5 or over for wartime corvettes. Such an approach shows that the Flowers were too short, a suggestion fully supported by many subjective accounts such as Monsarrat's The Cruel Sea.[23]

Severe pitching will cause the bow to come out of the water and, when it re-enters fast, the ship will slam. The incidence of slamming depends on section shape at the bow, speed, draught and sea state. In sea state 6, one would expect a frigate style of hull to slam at about 10 knots with a two metre draught, 15 knots with 3 metre and 25 knots with 4 metres. Slamming can damage asdic domes and even the hull. In general, slamming would be rare in corvettes, frigates and sloops at the speeds which they could maintain in sea state 6. Surprisingly, many accounts refer to the Flowers as superb sea boats and it can only be assumed that this refers to their lack of slamming.

Destroyers were longer, shallower and faster and were likely to slam quite often from sea state 5 upwards. Their highly stressed hulls would shudder and shake, a worry to both captain and crew. Rivets would be loosened, particularly in single rivetted seams, causing troublesome leaks.[24] Pitching also caused interference with the asdic, due to the rapid flow of water, full of air bubbles, past the dome.

Sailors have always said 'One hand for yourself, one hand for the ship.' More recently, it has been shown that the ability to carry out manual work, such as loading depth charges, is mainly affected by the lateral acceleration associated with rolling. Rolling is a complicated motion influenced by the size and frequency of the waves meeting the ship (which depends on course and speed), on the metacentric height and on the resistance to roll provided by bilge keels etc. Though sufficient metacentric height is needed to ensure that the ship will not capsize in extreme seas, excessive values are to be avoided. A considerable amount of experimental work had been carried out on rolling before the war though there was still much that was not understood, or at least not quantified.

A ship which is too stiff will roll to only slightly greater angles than one with a smaller metacentric height, but the roll will be much more rapid, increasing the lateral acceleration and hence making work more difficult. It is clear that the older destroyers were marginal and needed strict control of topweight and some ballasting.[25] On the other hand, the *Captain* classes were too stiff, making work on deck dangerous, and had to be taken out of service for bigger bilge keels and more topweight. The *Flowers*, too, had to be fitted with bigger bilge keels.

By today's standards, the other classes of escorts also had bilge keels which were too small. It seems to have been thought that ships always roll, that sailors are tough - and naval architects were well aware that big keels, which needed to be very strong, would reduce speed appreciably. The sloops of the *Black Swan* class had active fin stabilizers, first tried in the *Bittern* in 1936. These were quite effective, although, because control theory was undeveloped, less so than modern stabilizers.

Wetness due to green seas over the deck or from spray over the fore end of the ship could make open gun mountings and Hedgehog difficult and even dangerous to work, and would lead to exhaustion on open bridges. Adequate freeboard is the main factor in keeping ships dry, though flare in moderation, knuckles and even breakwaters can help.

Human Factors

North Atlantic escort duty in small ships was inevitably exhausting, particularly in winter. Today, it is recognized that the combat efficiency of a crew is increased if they are well fed and can rest properly when off duty, but this was not understood during the war and British ships fell well short of what was possible and desirable. There was an impression that sailors were tough and almost revelled in discomfort. In particular, it was thought that discomfort was necessary to keep men awake when on duty. It was also claimed that hammocks were more comfortable than bunks in rough weather - although there was no obvious desire among officers, most of whom had used hammocks, to give up their bunks. In addition, the traditional RN messing was unlikely to produce a balanced diet.

The early short-forecastle *Flowers* were the worst. They had bunks in the forecastle, where the motion was worst. To reach the bridge or engine room meant crossing the open well deck, inevitably getting wet in bad weather. Worse still, the galley was aft and food had to be brought along the open upper deck to the mess, getting cold, if not spilt on the way. As more equipment was added, overcrowding became worse. The following quotation sums up conditions very well.

> It was sheer unmitigated hell. She was a short fo'c'sle corvette and even getting hot food from the galley to fo'c'sle was a tremendous job. The mess decks were usually a shambles and the wear and tear on bodies and tempers was something I shall never forget. But we were young and tough and, in a sense, we gloried in our misery and made light of it all. What possible connection it had with defeating Hitler none of us bothered to ask. It was enough to

find ourselves more or less afloat the next day and the hope of
duff for pudding and a boiler clean when we reached port.[26]

Ventilation in these vessels was grossly inadequate, contributing to the high
incidence of tuberculosis, and in the first 56 ships the side was unlined. From
1940, the side was sprayed with asbestos - which would lead to the deaths of
many dockyard workers in later years. Washing and toilet equipment was crude
in quality and inadequate in quantity.

The frigates were a little better as they were bigger, reducing the vertical
accelerations, had covered access fore and aft and their later design remedied
some of the defects of the *Flowers*. But with only a little thought and some
slight increase in cost, much of this unnecessary discomfort could have been
avoided. Monsarrat[27] compares two ships which he commanded, the US-built
Colony with the *River* class on which it was based. The American ship had a
laundry, ice water in each mess, a dish washer, potato peeler, cafeteria messing,
good insulation and ventilation, an internal communication system and was still
built more quickly - and no one can suggest that USN sailors were soft.

One cannot leave the subject of human factors without re-emphasising the
importance of the aces on both sides. Men such as Walker and some other escort
commanders, and, on the other side, Kretschmer, Prien *et alia* were good
enough to distort all statistics. The difference was that escort commanders lived
to improve their skill and to pass it on, whilst U-boat aces had a short life.

Life Saving. The question of escape is closely related to habitability. Losses of
escort vessels were not unduly high, but many of their crews found sleeping
difficult in the lower mess decks and cabins with a long and tortuous route to
the upper deck and preferred to rest, if possible, close to the deck. Adequate
escape routes add greatly to peace of mind when sinking may be rapid, and men
will stay at their posts longer when they know they can get out.

Very little consideration had been given to lifesaving gear before the war.
Boats could not be lowered in time and neither they nor the Carley float gave
any protection from exposure. Just before the war, the inflatable life belt was
shown to be dangerous in tests, but was put into production without change. A
very high proportion of those who escaped from sinking ships died in the water.
Picking up survivors from the sea was a frequent task and one to which little
thought had been given.

Class	Table 15: Time to Sink				
	Time to sink (minutes)				
	Under 10	*10-20*	*20-30*	*30-60*	*60+*
Destroyer	28	12	1	1	2
Frigate	3	-	-	1	4
Sloop	2	1	1	3	3
Corvette	13	2	1	2	5

Vulnerability

WWII escorts were small ships and, in consequence, had only a limited ability to survive major damage such as a torpedo hit. Indeed, it is remarkable that so many did survive. The Battle of the Atlantic was so wide-ranging that it is difficult to say which losses are specific to that Battle. Some ships lost in the Atlantic were merely on passage and the geographical boundaries are unclear. Table 16 can only be seen as an approximation.

TABLE 16: Losses of Escort Vessels in the Atlantic[28]		
Class	RN	Allied
Destroyer	15	13
Sloop	9	-
Frigate	4	7
Corvette	7	4

The effect of various weapons is only available on a world-wide basis. The figures for the RN in Table 17 denote sunk (S), seriously damaged (SD) and slightly damaged (D).

TABLE 17: Effect of weapons														
Ship/weapon	**Shell**			**Bomb**			**Mine**			**Torp**			Total		
	S	SD	D	S	SD	D	S	SD	D	S	SD	D	S	SD	D
Destroyers	13	40	74	44	81	118	18	35	4	52	15	2	127	171	198
Other escorts	2	2	10	16	28	33	17	39	10	50	19	2	85	88	53

The figures for escorts are probably more representative of the Atlantic and show that the majority of sinkings were due to torpedo hits. It is not often realised that the main cause of sinking of smaller warships was a broken back. Broken backs accounted for 44% of destroyer losses, 40% of frigates and 21% of sloops. The destroyer, highly stressed and with a break of forecastle amidships exacerbating the stress, was most likely to break, the lower stress and deeper hull of frigates and sloops reducing the risk, but only slightly. Fire was a less serious risk; of 496 destroyers hit, only 60 reported fire, usually started by bombs.

Part IV: How Good Were They?

It is almost impossible to measure the relative effectiveness of different types of escort to the overall task of ensuring safe arrival of cargoes. It is possible to relate the secondary task of sinking U-boats by escort type, but there are so many anomalies that the results are not very meaningful.

TABLE 18: U-boat sinkings by class	
Escort category	**Total number of kills in N Atlantic**
Destroyers	
Modern	9
Inter-war A-I	39
Old (WW I)	26
Town	8
Hunt	8
Sloops	
Black Swan	28
Older	**12**
Frigates	
River	22
Loch	12
Captain	28
Colony	5
Corvettes	
Flower	38
Castle	5

These figures must be associated with the numbers of ships of each class operating in the Atlantic, as shown in Table 19. This number fluctuated rapidly and, since the Atlantic boundary is not easy to define, the numbers given are typical rather than precise.

Destroyers of all classes were fast and even the long range escort (LRE) conversions, mainly V and Ws, could still reach 25 knots with one boiler removed, but they were designed to achieve their speed on trial in sheltered waters. Their draught was inadequate to prevent slamming at operational speeds and they had insufficient freeboard to keep them dry. As built, their endurance was insufficient for Atlantic escort work but the LREs were outstanding; at the cost of six months' work their fuel stowage was increased to 450 tons and there was more living space as well. Turning circles were large, particularly in the *Towns*. Their armament, in almost all, was Hedgehog and depth charges.

TABLE 19: Escort Vessels in service in the Atlantic by class							
	Flower		River		Loch, Castle, Captain, Black Swan	Totals	
Date	RN	RCN	RN	RCN	RN	RN	RCN
1.1.41	47	13	-	-	2	49	13
1.1.42	110	67	-	-	3	113	70
1.1.43	108	70	17	9	7	132	79
1.1.44	117	79	41	25	87	245	104
1.1.45	117	88	57	47	131	305	133
7.5.45	111	95	59	61	144	316	160
3.8.45	23	4	40	42	108	151	50

The earlier pre-war sloops seem to have been generally satisfactory. The somewhat similar ex-US Coast Guard cutters suffered from poor stability and very poor subdivision. The heavy AA armament of the *Black Swans* enabled them to venture into the Bay of Biscay where they scored many successes; even though their fire control was poor, the volume of fire would put most bombers off their aim. The figures are greatly distorted by the genius of Captain Walker. (There are indications that the *Black Swans* were a prize appointment for the most skilled officers.) The *Flower* class was intended for coastal work and had many drawbacks in ocean work. They were short so that pitch and heave motions were severe, which led to a high incidence of sickness and, in all probability, of poor decision-making, while their standard of habitability was low. Inadequate bilge keels led to heavy rolling, and they were too slow either to keep up with a surfaced submarine or to return quickly to station. On the other hand, they could be built quickly and cheaply and hence were available in considerable numbers, a very important factor when the range of asdic was short. The concept of the small, cheap escort was sound in 1939, but the *Flower*s were not a good design. A ship similar to the *Castle*s of wartime or, even better, the *Castle* class OPV would have been preferable.

The *River*s (originally known as twin-screw corvettes) were bigger and a little faster, but with a similar weapon fit. It is not easy to compare the effectiveness of these classes, as kills were often shared between ships of more than one class. Table 20 compares the successes of the *River*s and *Flower*s in the RN. A kill is credited if a ship of that class participated.

TABLE 20: *Flower/River* successes						
Year	1940	1941	1942	1943	1944	1945
Average No in Atlantic	18/0	50/0	74/8	65/17	47/20	31/19
Kills		1/0	7/0	6/ 1	16/ 7	2/ 5	1/ 1
Kills per ship %	-	14/0	8/12	25/41	4/25	3/ 5
Figures shown as *Flowers/Rivers*						

Though there is an indication that the *Rivers* were appreciably more effective in sinking U-boats than the *Flowers*, it must be recognized that the bigger ships used twice as many scarce engines, cost twice as much and do not seem to have been twice as successful. By virtue of their greater numbers, it would be expected that the *Flowers* should be more effective in keeping submarines submerged. Numbers count, and as Goodall wrote: 'Moral is don't try and force cheap ships on the Navy, which, as Winston says "always travels first class"'. The *Castles* were longer than the *Flowers*, making them better seaboats and a little faster than the earlier ships, and they carried Squid, very effective even in single form.

The *Colony* class was the US version of the *Rivers*, with the usual excellent American living standards. They were however handicapped by unreliable reciprocating engines. The *Captains* were expensive ships, but their advanced machinery was very reliable and easy to operate. Once the initial problems with rolling were overcome, they were good seaboats and fast, especially the turbine ships.

The *Lochs* were outstanding, as they were the only class with 144 and 147 fire-control asdic, by far the most effective weapon system. They were rather slow, but remained the most effective anti-submarine ships well into the 1950s.

Lessons

The lessons perceived at the time were summarized in the requirement for the '1945 Sloops':[29]

* 25 knots in rough weather
* Double Squid - later Limbo
* Good turning circle
* Twin 4.5in guns
* Easy to build.

After many changes, these ships completed as the *Leopard, Salisbury* and *Whitby* classes. These were all good designs, the *Whitbys* being outstanding, and one can only agree with the committee which drafted the 1945 requirement - though they were hardly easy to build.

It is more interesting to reflect on what should have been built before the war. The *Flowers* were seen as superior to trawlers for coastal work, but a larger ship, like the *Castle*-class corvette (or better, the new OPV) would have been more effective and only a little more expensive. Since the fall of France was unexpected, the need for open ocean escorts did not seem pressing, but it would have been sensible if effort had been made available to design and build a prototype or two of a more capable ship with turbine machinery, perhaps using sets removed from the S-class on scrapping.

A ship of 1,500-2,000 tons would have reached 26-27 knots and carried 450 tons of oil. In the late 1930s such a ship would have had a *River*-class weapon fit, but a big growth margin would have been wise. It should have had a high freeboard over most of its length, a deep draught and twin rudders. It might have looked like a two-funnelled *Black Swan*. However, hindsight is easy. The staff and constructors did the best they could with very limited resources, and before the fall of France the course of the war appeared to justify their work.

Appendix

The Seakeeping Capability of World War II Escorts

In Reference 1 (below), I showed that the loss of fighting capability due to loss of human performance in various sea states could be multiplied by the probability of occurrence of a given sea state, to obtain a figure for equivalent annual 'lost days' of capability. The first table shows the figure for loss of capability agreed with the Naval Staff as representing a ship similar to the *Leander* class. The table also shows in metres the lower boundary of wave height corresponding to the sea states.

Sea state	% loss of capability	wave ht from (m)
1-4	0	
5	10	2.5
6	30	4.0
7+	95	6.0

Applying this data to WWII escorts involves a considerable number of approximations, providing results which can only be comparative and not absolute. It is assumed that loss of capability is directly proportional to vertical acceleration and that such accelerations vary linearly with wave height. The table below shows average (rms) vertical accelerations for representative classes in waves of 5.5in height as demonstrated in reference 2. It is also assumed that the modal period for all sea states is 12.4 seconds.

Class	Length Ft	m	Vert accn M/sec^2 (5.5m waves)
Flower	200	60	3.5
Castle	240	72	3.0
River, old DD	300	90	2.5
Leander	360	108	2.0

The probability of occurrence of the wave heights in the above table during an average North Atlantic year can then be found and multiplied by the percentage loss of capability to give the percent loss of days in the year. A sample calculation (for the *Leander* class) follows.

Sea State	occurrence N Atlantic	% loss capability	% equivalent days lost/year Occurrence x loss
7+	3	95	2.8
6	14	30	4.2
5	19	10	1.9
0-4	64	0	0

Similarly, for the other classes, one may list the percentage of the year lost due to the effect of ship motions on human performance.

	Days lost %
Flowers	28
Castles	21
Rivers, old destroyers	15
Leanders	9

Since these figures are highly approximate, they have been rounded to whole numbers. One more correction could be applied. In Reference 3, I compared the motions of various ships on a different basis (Averaged Subjective Motion) which showed that - due partly to hull form but mainly because living and working spaces were relatively further forward in these ships where the motion was greater - the effect of motions on crew capability was considerably greater, by about 20%, on the older ships. It would not be unreasonable to multiply the figures above by 1.2 to allow for this. However, these figures are comparative and those given above are sufficient for the purpose. Despite the many approximations involved, these figures do seem consistent with accounts of life on board World War II escorts.

References to the Appendix

My thanks are due to Dr A. R. J. M. Lloyd for considerable help in the preparation of this Appendix.

1. D. K. Brown 'The value of reducing ship motions'. *Naval Engineers Journal* ASNE, Washington, March 1985.
2. A. R. J. M. Lloyd. *Seakeeping; Ship Behaviour in Rough Weather*
3. D. K. Brown & P. D. Marshall. 'Small warships and the fishery protection task', RINA Symposium, London, March 1978.

Notes

1. Terraine, *Business in Great Waters*.
2. Tarrant, *The U-boat Offensive*.
3. Roskill, *Naval policy between the Wars*, Vol II.
4. Osborne, *Naval Actions of the Spanish Civil War*. Proceedings of Naval Meetings, World Ship Society, Kendal, 1989.
5. Simpson, *Periscope View*.
6. Showell, *U-Boat Command and the Battle of the Atlantic*.
7. Lynch, *Canada's Flowers*.
8. Goodall, Sir Stanley. (DNC) His diaries are held in the British Library and later references will be by date of entry only.
9. Peebles, *Warship Building on the Clyde*.
10. Gordon, *British Sea Power and Procurement between the Wars*.
11. Loch Class Ship's Cover, National Maritime Museum.
12. Friedman, *US Destroyers*.
13. Bean, C.W.C. The Production of Naval Machinery from 1935 to 1945. *Journal of Naval Engineering*, April 1954. (copies of this Journal, previously Classified, are held in the British Library.)
14. Wildish, Sir H. W., Some Maintenance Aspects of the Western Approaches Command during the Second World War. *Journal of Naval Engineering*, April 1950.
15. Barley, F. W. and Waters, D., *The Defeat of the Enemy Attack on Shipping*. Naval Historical Branch. [To be reprinted by Navy Records Society in 1994.]
16. Hague, *The Towns*.
17. Hackmann, *Seek and Strike*. The weapon and sensor aspects of the battle are so well covered in this book that they need only brief treatment here.
18. Brown, D. K and Pugh, P., 'Ramming', *Warship 1990*', Conway Maritime Press, London, 1990.
19. Brown, D. K., 'Revolution Manque - the Fleet that never was', *Warship* Supplement 100, World Ship Society, Kendal, 1990.
20. It is no coincidence that *nausea* derives from the Greek word for ship.
21. Lloyd, *Seakeeping; Ship Behaviour in Rough Weather*
22. Brown, D.K. and Marshall, P.D., *Small Warships in the RN and the Fishery Protection Task*, RINA Warship Symposium, London, 1978.
23. Monsarrat, *The Cruel Sea*
24. Holt, N. G. and Clemitson, F. E., 'Notes on the Behaviour of HM Ships during the War', *Transactions of the Institute of Naval Architects*, Vol 91, London, 1949'.
25. Brown D.K., Stability of RN Destroyers during World War II, *Warship Technology*, 4/1989, RINA, London.
26. Lamb, *The Corvette Navy*.
27. Monsarrat, *HM Frigate*.
28. Brown, *Warship Losses of World War II*.
29. Brown, D.K., 'The 1945 sloops', *Warship World*, 1989.

Technology and Tactics

by David Zimmerman

Technology and tactics were the interrelated dynamics that caused the Battle of the Atlantic to become the most rapidly changing campaign in the history of warfare. It has long been recognized that the development of new weapon systems and their tactical employment were crucial in protecting convoys from attack and destroying U-boats; yet the multifarious connections between tactics and technology have received little attention from historians of the campaign. Research on the Battle has tended to focus on either the operational or the technological developments. Operational historians have been content simply to add new technology to their discussions of convoy actions. These historians have provided little or no discussion on why and how the new weapon systems were developed, and have ignored any mention of the new tactical doctrine and the training programmes introduced to make use of them. The very best operational history yet published, Jürgen Rohwer's *The Critical Convoy Battles of March 1943*, offers some tantalizing but all too brief insights into what might be accomplished by examining the impact of technology on the campaign. His conclusions pertaining to the relative importance of HF/DF to short-wave radar are rather startling. Nevertheless, there has been virtually no systematic study of the utilization of any of the principle weapon systems. Studies of technology have been equally remiss by focusing on the development of weapon systems without reference to the environment in which they were used. With the exception of Rohwer and Michael Hadley, in *U-boats Against Canada*, no one has critically compared and contrasted German and Allied perceptions of the technological war, and its impact on tactics.

The few studies that have gone beyond the traditional naval or technological histories have not focused on the 'stress-point' between technological innovation and tactical deployment. Much of the recent scholarly revisionist work has been undertaken by Canadians writing on the neglected history of the Royal Canadian Navy. These works include Marc Milner's *North Atlantic Run*, Michael Hadley's *U-boats Against Canada*, and my book *The Great Naval Battle of Ottawa*. They have gone beyond the traditional studies by integrating analyses of an operational and technical nature with many of the much broader concerns of the new military history. Milner's work and mine, when read together, form the best attempt to date to combine aspects of technical and naval operations and policy as an organic whole. Their principle limitation is that they understandably concentrate on the Canadian perspective, which is, despite our bias, only a small part of a much larger picture.

What is still lacking are comprehensive studies of both the tactics and technologies employed by the Allies against the U-boats. Milner and Rohwer have centred their tactical operational analysis on what I will call the classical period of the campaign, loosely from the beginning of 1942 until the end of 1943. Very little scholarly work has been published on either the first period of the campaign, from September 1939 until the end of 1941, or the final phase, 1944-45. We know even less about anti-submarine warfare (ASW) tactical doctrine prior to the commencement of hostilities. Most of what we understand about the tactics employed in all phases of the campaign, with the exception of the classical period, can be found in the rather indifferent official histories of the campaign, and in memoirs. The former are primarily old-fashioned operational histories. Some of the latter, particularly the superb *U-boat Killer*, by Captain Donald Macintyre, provide invaluable insights into the inter-relationship of technology and tactics. Other memoirs are at best good tales of the sea, or at worst inaccurate fiction.

The absence of a comprehensive history of ASW technology leaves us with a rather unbalanced collection of works that tend to spotlight one specific type of technology, such as radar or asdic, and only one Allied navy. ASW is usually not the primary subject of these studies.[1] Often these technological histories are from the nuts-and-bolts school, telling us a great deal about the laboratory work in developing a piece of equipment. Sacrificed are examinations of technological policy-making - why was it being built - and any analysis of effectiveness of the weapon system in operational use.[2] There are also certain vital pieces of equipment that have been subject to no scrutiny whatsoever; this includes the introduction of Talk Between Ships, VHF voice radio systems.[3] Only two historians have attempted to link technology to tactics. Anthony Watts' *The U-boat Hunters*, although a brave first effort, is neither definitive nor accurate. Montgomery Meigs' *Slide Rules and Submarines* is the most comprehensive study of technology, tactics and naval policy for any single navy during the campaign. However, Meigs' work is severely flawed by his failure to assess British influence on American ASW policy and technology. Nor is his account of ASW tactics sufficiently detailed to show how technical policy influenced operational procedures.[4]

The task the conference organizers have set for me is, therefore, an impossible one. Without a detailed understanding of either the technology or tactics employed in the Atlantic, no definitive history of the relationship between tactics and technology is possible. What I will attempt to present in this chapter, therefore, is more of an outline of the direction which future research should take in order to come to grips with this extremely important historical problem. Most of what will be presented here is based more on anecdotal rather than any definitive analytical evidence; it will be up to future studies to validate the assumptions contained herein. For the purposes of the chapter I will examine the tactical technologies employed by the convoy escorts. I am deliberately omitting strategic technology - Ultra and the Y service - and aviation technology, both of which are examined in other parts of this book.. It must be noted, however, that in order to develop a complete picture of the relationship between tactics and technology in the Battle of the Atlantic, aircraft must be considered as an integral part of the convoy's defensive systems.

The Tactical Problems for the Escort Force

When the strategic defences employed by the Allied navies failed and a convoy was at risk of being intercepted by U-boats, the escort group commander had to solve several tactical problems. From a technological perspective the tactical situation in the Battle of the Atlantic was unique. The offensive and defensive capabilities of the two opponents and their goals were completely dissimilar. The technological solutions open to an escort group varied depending on the strategy and tactics employed by the U-boats, and on the resources available. Both the tactics of the U-boats and technology available to the escorts changed considerably over the course of the war. For the sake of convenience, I have divided the six years of the Battle into three periods. These approximate to the three main stages of U-boat tactics, and the Allied technological responses to them. These periods are from September 1939 to the end of 1941, 1942-43, and from 1944 until the end of war in Europe.

Typically an escort trying to sink a U-boat had to go through the following tactical phases:

Phase One - Initial detection of U-boats approaching the convoy. The earlier an escort could detect its foe, the less likely it was that the convoy would be attacked or that other U-boats would be able to gain contact.

Phase Two - Suppression of the U-boat. After the initial detection of a surfaced U-boat the escorts had then to suppress it by forcing it to dive. This deprived the U-boat of most of its manoeuvring speed and offensive capability. The principle objective of the escort was to force the U-boat to lose contact with the convoy. If possible, during the suppression phase damage was inflicted on the U-boat by gunfire, depth charges or ramming. Phase one and two were crucial if the escorts were to achieve their principal goal, namely, the safe and timely arrival of the convoy.

Phase Three - Offensive Detection. After forcing the U-boat down the escort(s) had to re-establish contact with it, using asdic or sonar. Particularly if operating alone, escorts might have to repeat phase three if phase four was inconclusive.

Phase Four - Attack of Subsurface Target. Using depth charges, Hedgehog, homing torpedoes or Squid, the escort(s) attempted to sink the U-boat or force it to the surface. Phases three and four normally had to be repeated several times if a kill was to be achieved.

Technology and the Initial Detection Phase

Each tactical phase involved the use of a different combination of technologies, which varied considerably over the course of the war. During its first two years, initial detection could only be achieved by two methods: asdic for submerged U-boats, or visual observation for those on the surface. Throughout the war asdic remained almost the only way to detect submerged U-boats, but by itself it was never an adequate system for initial detection. Its maximum range varied according to the acoustical conditions and the skills of individual operators, and even in ideal conditions, it was rarely effective at more than 1,500 metres.

In the war's first few months, it was realised that asdic was not the 'solution' to the U-boat detection problem. As the sinking of HMS *Courageous* demonstrated, strong escort screens could not safeguard single ships. Convoys, with their far larger screening diameter and generally weaker escorts, could not be completely screened from underwater attack.

The main danger to shipping came from U-boats trimmed down on the surface, making attacks at night. By staying surfaced, they could still retain the element of surprise while retaining high speed and manoeuvrability, with their low profile making detection extremely difficult. Asdic was even less useful in this situation. Donald Macintyre provides us with one of the few accounts of the problems of an escort commander in this early period:

> It was obviously useless to hope that such a scattered force would form a screen proof against U-boat attack. By zigzagging independently around its allotted position, an escort could cover a considerable territory with asdic, but on a dark night any well-handled U-boat could sneak undetected between the escorts.[5]

Escorts had to rely on their look-outs' eyes and binoculars to make their initial detection. Macintyre describes his tactics while defending convoy HX112 in March 1941:

> [After five ships had been sunk] while the convoy stayed in impeccable formation, we escorts raced about in the exasperating business of searching in vain for the almost invisible enemy. Our only hope was to sight a U-boat's tell-tale white wake, give chase to force her to dive, and so give the asdics a chance to bring our depth charges into action. Everything had to be subordinate to that end and so, with binoculars firmly wedged on a steady bearing, I put the *Walker* into a gentle curving course, thereby putting every point of the compass under a penetrating probe.

In this case Macintyre's training and skill, mixed with what he admits was a great deal of good luck, allowed him to detect Joachim Schepke's U-100.

Luck was certainly a key ingredient in this early period. Escorts had little else with which to achieve initial contact with their foe; all too often they were only aware that U-boats were attacking after they heard the sickening sound of a torpedo detonation. Many tactical schemes, such as Operation Raspberry, were then used to illuminate the convoy to aid visual detection.

Illuminating the convoy was always a calculated risk, as it could draw other U-boats into the battle. It was a desperate measure brought about by technological weaknesses which would be corrected in the second or classical period of the campaign.

From 1942, escorts were increasingly provided with two new tools for the early location of a surfaced U-boat - radar and high-frequency direction-finding. Given the U-boats' tactics and command and control arrangements, both of these new technologies were ideal for early detection.

Radar began entering service on escort vessels in the autumn of 1940. The first such set was the Type 286 (1.5-metre wavelength or UHF) which was mounted in destroyers and a few other escort vessels. These first generation small-ship radar sets operating at the 286's wavelength - including the Canadian SW1C/2C and the American SC - were usually unable to detect a U-boat running trimmed down at more than one kilometre. As a result, visual sighting frequently occurred before radar contact could be established. First generation sets, however, did play an important role in assisting the escorts in maintaining contact with the convoy, aircraft detection and for training purposes.

Short-wave (10-centimetre wavelength or S-band) radar began entering widespread service in 1942. The British Type 271 was the first effective submarine detection radar. Early versions of the set could locate a trimmed-down U-boat at ranges up to 3,000 metres. Later improved models, the 271P and 271Q, could normally detect targets at ranges up to 5,000 metres. The American SG radar was considerably more effective, with the maximum detection range often approaching 10,000 metres.

By mid-1942, HF/DF was the principal long-range tactical detection system available to the escorts. It became crucial because of the U-boats' use of high-frequency radio to report convoy sightings and weather reports to their headquarters. U-boat command needed these messages in order to direct other U-boats onto the convoy, and did not consider breaking radio silence to be a risk; the Germans believed it impossible to locate brief short-wave messages. In fact, the Admiralty radio interception system or Y service provided crucial information, enabling most convoys to be manoeuvred around U-boat patrol lines.

Tactical HF/DF sets, such as the British FH3 and FH4 and the American DAJ and DAQ, could distinguish between long-range high-frequency radio transmissions, which reflected off the ionosphere, and ground-wave signals, which could only come from a source not more than 25 kilometres away. The sets could also provide a bearing to the source. If more then one HF/DF set detected the signal, its point of origin could be accurately located. Originally HF/DF sets were mounted on destroyers and sloops, which had sufficient space to accommodate the set and the speed to range ahead to track down a contact. HF/DF equipment was also placed on rescue ships.

Although not discussed extensively in any study, the introduction of Talk Between Ship radio-telephones was similarly crucial in co-ordinating escorts during all phases of a convoy action. In place on American ships before their entry into the Atlantic battleground, Lend-Lease made available large numbers of these sets for the RN and RCN. It appears that they were universally fitted on escorts by early 1942.

When an escort group was equipped with short-wave radar and HF/DF, and convoys provided with air cover, the surfaced U-boat's cloak of invisibility was removed for good. Technological improvements, and improved training in this first tactical stage were the decisive factors in driving the U-boats from the mid-Atlantic convoy lanes in the late spring and summer of 1943.[6]

The final stage of the U-boat campaign saw them operating for extensive periods submerged, using snorkel breathing apparatus and improved battery capacity to increase greatly their underwater performance. Once again initial detection proved to be one of the crucial problems for escorts and the increasing number of support or hunter-killer groups. Very little study has been undertaken on this stage, but what studies have been done show that HF/DF and 10-centimetre radar were no longer effective in providing early warning before a U-boat strike. Late in the war, sonar was little more effective in making initial detection of a U-boat than it had been in 1939. Improvements had mainly come in the form of better training. This was more than cancelled out by the increasing number of U-boats operating in shallow waters around the British Isles, off the coast of France and in North America coastal areas. Temperature inversions, salinity changes, and wrecks on the bottom all compounded the problem of initial detection. Some new equipment such as echo sounders were used with mixed result. Other new equipment, such as bathythermography recorders, were only just being introduced when the war ended. More study is required before the effectiveness of these new techniques can be assessed.

Another area that requires more study is in the employment of 3-centimetre wavelength radar, such as the American SU set, to detect snorkels. The Admiralty believed that sets operating at this wavelength could locate the U-boats' breathing apparatus. The ideal late-war support group was thought to contain a mixture of SU-equipped American-built *Captain*-class frigates (destroyer-escorts), together with *Loch*-class frigates and/or *Castle*-class corvettes equipped with Squid/147B (see page 486 below).[7] The few modern studies of late-war support groups are in disagreement over the effectiveness of radar in the detection of snorkels.[8]

Technology and the Suppression Phase

The suppression phase was the least influenced by technological developments. When a U-boat was detected on the surface, escorts then had to force it down or sink it. The techniques for doing this did not change markedly during the course of the war. A U-boat's vulnerability to any damage, even from a small escort, meant it would usually submerge as quickly as possible once the crew were aware they had been sighted. Although not generally equipped with radar until 1944, U-boats had an advantage in detecting escorts because of the escorts' much higher silhouette.

Gunfire against a U-boat was rarely decisive in this phase. The lack of official attention placed upon improving the gun armament of escorts is noticeable in three ways: first, the reduction of main gun armament in many escort destroyers; second, the removal of destroyer central gunnery control directors in favour of 271 radar; and third, by unauthorized mountings of anti-tank guns in many escorts to provide a short-range armour-piercing weapon. Against such a small target as a U-boat, gunfire was usually inaccurate in all but the shortest ranges. Until the advent of S-band radar, this short range of detection meant that combat often occurred below the minimum range of the escorts' main armament. In these circumstances escorts were forced to rely on secondary armament which included 2-pounder pom-poms, 20mm Oerlikon guns, .50 machine guns and Lewis guns. None of these was capable of inflicting major structural damage on a U-boat, but they could have a severe shock effect on its crew. As a result, gunfire in this phase does not appear to have often caused substantial damage, but usually did force the U-boat under. If the U-boat submerged close at hand, the escort might be able to launch one depth charge attack, aimed by eye near the point where the enemy was last seen. While infrequent, these attacks could have devastating impact upon the U-boat.

Successful completion of these first two phases, detection and suppression, was the central tactical task of an escort commander in the campaign's first two periods. In the third and final period, when U-boats usually operated submerged, suppression was rarely possible or necessary. Occasionally a snorkel might be detected nearby by the visual sighting of smoke or the device itself, and by radar contact, but in the last 18 months of the war, this appears to have been a rare event, with the suppression phase becoming correspondingly unusual.

Offensive Detection and Technology

Once a surfaced U-boat had been forced down, it was necessary for the escort to re-establish contact with the target with asdic or sonar. This task was similar to making initial detection against a submerged U-boat, except that the escort now knew the approximate location of the target. This did not mean that detection was in any way guaranteed. With good asdic conditions, an experienced crew, and rapid arrival at the last observable location of a U-boat, detection could often be quickly established. Just as frequently, however, re-establishing contact could take several hours, if it occurred at all.

Gradually a series of tactical procedures was developed to cover this eventuality. These procedures gave an escort commander a search pattern designed to find a U-boat known to be in a specific area. The most effective was the block search, in which escorts manoeuvred around the last known or suspected location of the U-boat in expanding concentric circles, sweeping the entire area in which the U-boat could have manoeuvred. All this took both time and ships, commodities which were at a premium in the early part of the war. Only with the creation of support groups towards the end of 1942 could prolonged U-boat hunts be undertaken if rapid detection did not occur.

As mentioned above, it could be necessary to repeat this phase several times during the course of an attack. Loss of contact occurred because of the 'dead zone' (see below), the effect of underwater explosions on detection apparatus, and the U-boat's own manoeuvring. In shallow waters during the final period of the campaign, echo sounders were very useful in locating bottomed U-boats.

Technology and the Attack on a Subsurface Target

At the beginning of the war, the classic attack on an underwater target was carried out with depth charges guided by asdic. The basic tactical dilemma was that contact with a U-boat could be maintained only while the boat was held in the cone of the asdic beam. Until late spring 1943, the oscillators of asdic sets were fixed to project a cone of 10 degrees below the horizontal, forward from the ship. Because depth charges were dropped or fired at the stern of the escort, a dead zone was inevitably created between the loss of contact with a U-boat and the point of attack. In pre-war tests the Admiralty had assumed that U-boats would have characteristics similar to British submarines, operating at depths of no more than 110 metres. By summer 1941 it had become evident that this assumption was wrong. Several reports showed that contact with U-boats was being lost at ranges of 475 metres, indicating the target had dived to 200-225 metres. U-boats were also proving to be far more manoeuvrable than anticipated, and were frequently escaping from depth charges by rapid changes in course after asdic contact had been lost.[9] To make matters worse, the fuses of the depth charges were not designed to detonate at these depths, nor did the canisters sink quickly enough.

The responses to these unforeseen U-boat tactics were both tactical and technological. Modifications to depth charges had to come first. A depth charge with a deep-set fuse was soon introduced. (These have been described in some detail in David K. Brown's chapter.) Once it became possible to reach the deep U-boat, Captain 'Johnnie' Walker, perhaps the most innovative and successful escort group commander, developed the famous 'creeping attack'. By using two ships in a carefully co-ordinated approach, this brilliant tactical manoeuvre deftly eliminated asdic's main technological shortcoming. While remaining outside the asdic dead zone, keeping the U-boat in its cone, the first ship would guide the second to the firing position. The attacking ship would operate without its asdic and at slow speed, in order to keep the U-boat for as long as possible unaware that it was under the immediate threat of attack.

Although a brilliant improvisation, the creeping attack was only a partial solution, and was not always possible to implement successfully. It had been realized before the war that the answer to the problem of the dead zone was to launch anti-submarine weapons ahead of the escort, and by 1940 Admiralty scientists were working on several experimental devices. The Department of Miscellaneous Weapon Development, an *ad hoc* research group, was created by Sir James Somerville in the summer of that year, specifically to bring new equipment into service as quickly as possible. The first device to enter service, in January 1942, was the Hedgehog. Developed under the leadership of Commander (later Sir) Charles Goodeve, it consisted of 24 small contact bombs fired by a recoil-less spigot-mortar system at a fixed distance 300 yards ahead of the ship.[10]

Hedgehog, however, was an archetypal example of a technology that worked better in theory than in practice. It was rushed into service during 1942 without due regard to developing tactical doctrine or training procedures for its use. Donald Macintyre describes a failed Hedgehog attack made in spring 1943:

> Here was a chance to try our new killer, the Hedgehog. With Bill Ridley controlling the asdic team the steady stream of bearings and ranges coming in I conned *Hesperus* slowly into the firing range. Everything was going perfectly. Conditions were good. Contact remained firm as we crept slowly into firing range. Then Bill Ridley's voice - 'Fire.' It is with a feeling of shame that I have to record that nothing happened! A hasty check with the crew of the Hedgehog revealed the reason. Unfamiliar with our new weapon, it had not been realized that the Hedgehog bombs, which had a complicated set of safety pins to be removed one by one, would take so long to prepare. With twenty-four bombs to arm this took some time, and the crew had not had the time, between contact and the order to fire, to complete the operation. Quite rightly they did not obey the order. Our practice firings had been done with dummy bombs which were not fitted with the same safety devices, so this time lag had gone unrealized.[11]

Even when Hedgehog did function as designed, the contact fuses were particularly unpopular because they demanded greater precision then was possible in many circumstances. They also harmed morale when carefully executed attacks brought no results. Consequently, in the classical period of the U-boat war, Hedgehog was little more effective than conventional depth charge attacks, success being achieved only 7½% of the time.[12] Revamped training, and Admiralty orders requiring captains to explain their failure to use the device, doubled the success rate, but not until 1944. Still several historians have recently been critical of Hedgehog. Marc Milner has suggested to me that evidence in his forthcoming sequel to *North Atlantic Run* will show that Hedgehog was of little use against deep-diving U-boats. Individual Hedgehog charges may also have been unable to rupture the reinforced hulls of late-war U-boats.[13]

Unlike radar, asdic went through a series of gradual incremental improvements in the first four years of the war. Improvements in asdic sets certainly increased the chances of a successful attack significantly, but they have received almost no attention from operational historians. Willem Hackmann's *Seek and Strike* traces out these improvements in great detail. His work, however, fails to analyse the impact of these technological improvements on the battlefield. Generally my sense of wartime asdic improvements is that they only marginally increased the chances of initial detection. Improvements here were confined to increasing the power of oscillators and the gain of sound reception gear. Training of operators remained the crucial ingredient for improving the probability of making contact with a U-boat. However, other incremental refinements played a major factor in increasing the likelihood of an accurate attack.

Pre-war sets were gradually improved until early 1942 when the Types 144/145 series of sets were introduced. These sets, wrote Hackmann, 'heralded a new chapter in asdic thinking and [were] the first attempt to an integrated weapon system with a certain degree of automation.'[14] New features included automatic training, improved indicating equipment such as new bearing- and range-recorders which showed the correct course to steer, and a 'time to fire' device which automatically rang buzzers at the Hedgehog and depth charge stations when firing should commence. Repeaters were provided on the bridge so that the captain could more easily follow the U-boat's course.[15]

The introduction of these new sets took time, and it remains unclear how much impact they had on the Battle's second period. Little is known concerning the rate of introduction of this equipment into the escort fleets, although I have found figures for early 1944 which, if accurate, suggest that many vessels remained burdened with earlier sets until the final period of the campaign. These figures are contained in a Canadian report which compared the state of equipment in the RCN with the RN. At this late date, 18% of British corvettes still mounted Type 123 asdic, 40% had Type 127, and only 37% had the fully modern Type 145. The figures for Canadian corvettes were respectively, 37% with Type 123, 58% with Type 127, and only 3% with Type 145. In spring 1943, *Flower*-class corvettes formed the bulk of the available escorts in the mid-ocean escort groups, and it can be assumed that far fewer Type 145 sets had by then been mounted. These figures, therefore, suggest that in the case of asdic, as with Hedgehog, these technological improvements only marginally impacted on the battlefield during the second period of the campaign.

A similar picture emerges when one considered the development and introduction into service of the Q attachment. The Q device was an extra oscillator mounted on a Type 144 or 145 set to produce a vertical, wedge-shaped beam at up to 45° but 'only about 3 degrees wide on the horizontal plane'.[16] The device allowed accurate tracking of very deep U-boats much closer to the escort vessel, thus dramatically reducing the dead zone. Unfortunately it was subject to a long series of production delays and teething technical problems which greatly delayed its widespread introduction into service. As late as August 1943 only 15 had been mounted on RN escorts, and it was not until spring 1944 that the Admiralty decided that all the technical difficulties had been rectified.[17]

Thus, it was only in the final period of the campaign that technology greatly improved the success rate of attacks upon submerged U-boats. Although it is still unclear how much improvement resulted from the combination of Hedgehog and Type 144/145Q asdic, despite the shortcomings of the former, the performance of the escort forces did increase.

It was also in 1944 that the first completely integrated ASW weapon system was introduced - the Type 147B asdic and the Squid anti-submarine mortar. The Squid threw either three or six projectiles, detonated by depth fuses, ahead of the ship in a triangular pattern carefully designed to maximize the chances of a kill. Squid's partner, the 147B asdic, was the one completely new asdic set of the war. The 147B was designed to act specifically as an attack set and to work in conjunction with Type 144/145Q. The precise and narrow beam of the 147B usually followed the target, guiding weaponry only after the U-boat had been first located by the main set. New-style recorders automatically gave range and direction for steering, while the set could automatically set Squid fuses and fire them. After the war it was estimated that a well trained Squid and 147B team could achieve kills 50% of the time, nearly nine times that of depth charges and substantially more than Hedgehog.[18]

The 147B-Squid combination was a late entry into the campaign, the first successful kill being made only in August 1944.[19] The commissioning of *Loch*-class frigates and *Castle*-class corvettes brought a large number of Squid-equipped vessels into service in the RN. Neither the RCN nor the USN had this system or its equivalent in wide scale service by the end of the war.

It was at the very end of the second period of the campaign that the U-boats began using the T5 acoustical homing torpedo. This torpedo was designed to restore the initiative to the U-boats by providing them with an offensive weapon to use against escorts.[20] Although it proved highly effective, countermeasures were soon introduced - the Canadian CAT (Canadian Anti-Torpedo) and the British Foxer equipment. These devices were towed behind the escort and generated a sound designed to decoy the homing torpedo away from the stern of the ship. The superior Canadian system was based on earlier acoustical minesweeping devices, consisting of a pair of pipes which, when towed side by side, banged together to create the required sound.[21]

Such studies as have been undertaken show that generally this gear was only deployed once a U-boat had been detected, because early deployment limited the asdic's effectiveness. On the other hand, deploying it too late often meant the loss of an escort. In the final period of the campaign, timing the tactical deployment of acoustical defensive devices was therefore one of the most important decisions made by an escort group.

The Role of Technological Innovation in the Campaign

There is no doubt that the introduction of new ASW equipment was one of the decisive factors in the defeat of the U-boats. Although much has been made of the inadequacies of technology in the first period of the campaign when compared to the second, a more accurate contrast would be with the closing days of the anti-submarine campaign in WWI. Asdic, whatever its limitations, provided a reasonably practical system for the detection and destruction of submerged U-boats. This is something escorts simply did not have in 1918.

The Germans had two technological answers to asdic. Defensively, the U-boat's deep diving and manoeuvrability certainly limited the success rate of depth charge attacks. Offensively, short-wave radio allowed for a far greater concentration of U-boats onto a convoy than had been possible in 1918. When wolf-pack tactics were first used in the Atlantic outside the range of aircraft, the U-boats relied on stealth and numbers to overwhelm the often inadequate escorts.

The second period of the campaign was dominated by the introduction of centimetric radar, HF/DF equipment, and Very-Long-Range Aircraft. It was this technological trio which forced the U-boats to abandon wolf pack attacks by the end of 1943. As I have pointed out, improvements in anti-submarine weapons and asdic did not have a significant impact on this period of the campaign. The problem was two-fold: firstly, the failure to develop adequate tactical doctrine and training for the use of Hedgehog; secondly, the slow pace in introducing technological improvements such as Type 144/145 asdic and the Q-device.

In the final phase of the war the general introduction of Type 144/145Q, and the commissioning of large numbers of vessels equipped with either the Squid/147B or SU radar certainly improved the probability of a successful attack on a submerged U-boat. These advantages were more than cancelled out by the far greater difficulty of detecting submerged targets, particularly in the confusing acoustical conditions of inshore waters. However, operating individually, and in small numbers, U-boats did not possess the same strategic threat to shipping as in previous periods.

The exact importance of technology, as opposed to other factors, in determining the outcome of the Battle's critical period was in dispute even during the war. There can be no doubt that in late 1942, compared to British or British-controlled vessels, Canadian ships were far behind in mounting 271 radar and HF/DF sets. Were these technological shortcomings the chief reason for apparent failings in Canadian operational performance? The Admiralty's official position was that the main problem was a lack of training. Many

Canadian officers were not so sure. I would argue that the truth lies somewhere in the middle. Training was crucial, but training could not compensate for deficiencies in equipment. As the experience with Hedgehog illustrates, however, adequate training was vital if a new weapon system was to perform close to expectations. Training must not only be considered in terms of the correct application of tactical doctrine, but also in terms of maintenance of these highly complex pieces of equipment.

The impact of technology on tactics is little understood. What is required are far more studies of individual battles of the campaign, particularly in the first and third periods. A history of ASW tactical doctrine is crucial if we are to link technological developments to operations. Also required are studies of how the tactics of the battle influenced technological development. One of the secrets of the Allies' success was the close integration of the scientist with operational requirement, but so far the only examinations of this issue have been my own study of the atypical Canadian experience, and Meigs' nationalistic study of the American. Histories of Admiralty and USN ASW technical policy are long overdue. Case studies of the development, manufacturing, deployment and impact upon the battlefield of some of these weapon systems are also required.

For instance, the development of the Type 271 radar by scientists at the Admiralty Signal Establishment was perhaps one of the most spectacular technological accomplishments of the war. After all, the 271 was the first operational radar to utilize the cavity magnetron, and production commenced less than nine months after the project began. Yet, while we now have a good outline of its development, we still know nothing about the formation of doctrine and training procedures which allowed for the 271's successful introduction into service.[22] Still less is known about the development of ship-based HF/DF, and virtually nothing on the impact of the introduction of TBS radio.[23]

It is remarkable that, 50 years after the defeat of the U-boats' campaign against the mid-Atlantic convoys, so much about this subject remains unstudied. Both operational and technological historians must break free of their limited approaches and present a far broader perspective of the campaign. Only then will we understand how technology and tactics were interrelated in the Battle of the Atlantic.

Notes

1. See, for example, Friedman, *Naval Radar.*
2. See, for example, Hackmann, *Seek and Strike.*
3. The only account of the development of TBS is found in Howeth, *History of Communications-Electronics in the United States Navy.*
4. Meigs, *Slide Rules and Submarines: American Scientists and Subsurface Warfare*

in World War II.
5. Macintyre, *U-boat Killer*, p. 37.
6. Rohwer, *Critical Convoy Battles*, I, 1-12; 19-21. For the development of HF/DF see Hezlett, *The Electron and Seapower.*
7. Minutes of Radar U-Committee, August 1944, NAC, RG 24 8070.
8. The only studies of late war ASW operations are unpublished. See Marc Milner, *The RCN and the Offensive Against the U-Boats*, unpublished monograph, June 1986, Directorate of History Ottawa; D.M. McLean, *The Last Cruel Winter: RCN Support of Groups and the U-Boat Schnorkel Offensive*, MA Dissertation, Royal Military College of Canada, March 1992.
9. Macintyre, *U-boat Killer*, pp. 56-60.
10. Hackmann, *Seek and Strike*, pp. 306-308; 'Modernisation of Armament and Equipment', 10; Miscellaneous Weapon Development Department Admiralty, History of Department and Projects Developed 1940-1945, PRO ADM 116/454.
11. Macintyre, *U-boat Killer*, pp. 113-114.
12. Elliott, *Allied Escort Ships of World War Two.*
13. Author's conversations with Marc Milner and James Goldrick, November 1992.
14. Hackmann, *Op. cit.*, p. 272.
15. *Ibid.*; pp. 10-11.
16. *Ibid.*, p. 279.
17. Zimmerman, *The Great Naval Battle of Ottawa*, p. 130.
18. Hackmann, *Op. cit.*, pp. 280, 309.
19. Elliott, *Allied Escort Ships of World War II.*, p. 86.
20. For an account of a late second period convoy action in which T5 was used see J. Rohwer, Canada and the Wolf Packs, September 1943, in *The RCN in Transition.*
21. Zimmerman, *The Great Naval Battle of Ottawa*, p. 96.
22. For the only account of the development of Type 271 radar see K. E. B. Jay and J. D. Scott, *A History of the Development and Production of Radio and Radar part II*, 360, PRO CAB 102/641; Howse, D., *Radar at Sea*, London, Macmilan, 1993, pp. 66-71, 77-81, 83-8, 107-116.
23. The only discussion about the development of HF/DF is contained in Hezlett's *The Electron and Sea Power.*

27

The Front Line:
Convoy HG76 - The Offence

by Jan G. Heitmann

Twice within a quarter of a century, German U-boats have attacked Britain's sea communications with every means in their power. Each time they nearly succeeded in bringing the enemy's seaborne trade to a standstill. This chapter describes the passage of convoy HG76 from Gibraltar to Great Britain in December 1941. It is intended as a practical illustration, from the German point of view, of the principles, organization, tactics and technology which have been described in earlier chapters.

*

During World War I, when the British convoy system was introduced in 1917, Allied ship-losses fell with almost miraculous speed and magnitude. At the outbreak of World War II, it was evident that the same system would soon be in full operation. Thus, it was pointless for the Kriegsmarine to scatter its few U-boats singly over wide areas. Instead, the aim was to intercept convoys and destroy them by a concentrated effort. Since locating convoys in the open sea was very difficult, the U-boats were sent to areas where enemy traffic necessarily became constricted. Before the war, Vice Admiral Karl Dönitz, the *Befehlshaber der U-Boote* (BdU, or Flag Officer U-boats), had developed the tactics of controlled 'wolf pack' operations to counter the enemy convoy system. But it was not until spring 1941 that enough boats were available to start operations characterized by the group disposition, with several attacking groups drawn up simultaneously in various traffic areas, each boat having a precise task in its group.

In surface naval operations, the commander-in-chief afloat and his subordinate commanders usually know at least the rough positions and movements of their forces. For long periods, the U-boats, in contrast, were stretched over unexplored areas where enemy patrols were an uncertain factor. The task of FO U-boats was therefore to bring as many boats as possible close to the enemy convoys. When a convoy was located, each commanding officer had to act on his own initiative and responsibility. One boat would remain in visual range of the convoy while the others set course to intercept the target. Whenever possible, the shadower had to make periodical location reports. His role was vital to subsequent operations, and for him the actual attack was a secondary consideration. Indeed, if the convoy escort was strong, he was not allowed to attack until other boats were within the range of the enemy.

If contact was lost and was unlikely to be regained with the existing disposition, the other U-boats were ordered to carry out special search operations. In FO U-boats' plotting room, calculations were made on the basis of the estimated visibility and the U-boats' positions, search courses and speeds. If they were badly out of position, long-wave homing signals allowed them to set an accurate interception course. These signals were the only means of checking the U-boats' navigation.

The radio message 'Attack when darkness falls' indicated that U-boat Command had completed arrangements for the concentration of the U-boats. Individual commanders then tried to attain a suitable firing position. If the escorting ships were close to the convoy, the attack could be made from outside the convoy, but usually it was necessary to find a gap in the escort line, through which the U-boats could penetrate. Skilled commanders purposely drove into the midst of the convoy, because among the merchant ships they were protected from the escort vessels. This failed when strong escorts were able either to keep the U-boats far from the convoy, compel them to submerge or chase them from far ahead or astern. Continuous shadowing reports throughout the night were therefore required.[1]

Controlled U-boat operations depended absolutely on wireless communications. The radio signals, however, proved to be the Achilles' heel of the wolf pack tactics. The U-boats always made initial sighting reports, which could be intercepted by HF/DF, giving the enemy a clue as to which convoy was threatened and a rough estimate of the U-boats' positions. In such cases the escorts were alerted and all possible steps were taken to reinforce them. Moreover, following the capture of U-110 in May 1941, the British possessed a current version of the Enigma cipher machine. Except for short black-out periods, the ciphered operational U-boat signals were intercepted, deciphered and read by the British for the rest of the war, enabling them to re-route convoys around the wolf packs. By avoiding battles, countless ships were saved. As the Germans were unaware that the naval code had been broken, this became one of the decisive factors in the Battle, equivalent to a major victory at sea.[2]

From autumn 1940, when the RN established their convoy system, the U-boats were forced into deeper water. Since Dönitz's efforts to locate convoys in the wide Atlantic with U-boats alone remained unrewarded, he gave his most careful consideration to the question of providing the boats with air reconnaissance. Visual observation from a submarine could never be more than that permitted by the height of the conning-tower, and the U-boats naturally had very low profiles. Dönitz constantly bemoaned the lack of 'eyes' in the Atlantic. As he had foreseen, his U-boats needed the help of aircraft to overcome this problem. What he had in mind was the equivalent of Britain's Coastal Command, under his own direction and serving the interests of the U-boats exclusively. However, all air matters were controlled by the Luftwaffe. He took up the fight for the U-boat fleet's own air arm, but the Luftwaffe strongly resisted any diminution of their authority. It became apparent that, in preparing the Luftwaffe for a Continental role, its value for maritime operations had been neglected and, even had it been amenable, it could not provide any immediate assistance. Suitable types of aircraft were expected to be ready within the near future, but in the event, the production of long-range reconnaissance aircraft was insufficient. All that was available for anti-shipping purposes was a conversion, the Focke-Wulf Fw200 'Condor' airliner, which emerged as the Fw 200C in spring 1940. Dönitz continued strongly to advocate the operational subordination of a long-range air reconnaissance unit to U-boat Command for the purpose of tactical reconnaissance. Success was slow in coming, owing to friction between the Kriegsmarine and the Luftwaffe, which in the end retained complete control of the employment and training of the naval co-operation aircraft. It was not until 7 January 1941 that Hitler himself ordered the *I. Gruppe/Kampfgeschwader 40*[3] (I./KG 40) to be placed under FO U-boats' direct operational command. From Dönitz's point of view, this order marked a decisive advance in U-boat warfare, although it was only a first step in the right direction. But his confidence was misplaced and his hopes were never realized; air support for U-boats proved to be inadequate throughout the war. The Focke-Wulfs took their toll of shipping, but the practical effects of naval-air co-operation were always disappointing.[4]

Starting early in 1940, the RN ran a regular convoy service between Britain and Gibraltar. With the German occupation of France, these convoys were within easy reach of the U-boat bases on the Biscay coast and of the Luftwaffe airfield near Bordeaux, where I./KG 40 were stationed. Thus, the Gibraltar convoys were potentially the most vulnerable of all. Consisting for the most part of small freighters and escorted throughout their voyages, they had not attracted the same attention as the more important Atlantic convoys. By late 1941, the position of the Afrika Korps, dependant upon seaborne supplies from Italy, was undermined by the severe losses being inflicted on Axis convoys running between Sicily and North Africa. When it became evident that the Italian navy and air force were unable to gain control of the central Mediterranean, support from the Kriegsmarine became necessary.

At this point, the Mediterranean was regarded as the main theatre of operations. In November 1941, U-boat Command was ordered to transfer nearly the entire force of operational U-boats to the Mediterranean and the area west of Gibraltar, in order to deny the Straits of Gibraltar to British convoys. This halted U-boat activities in the main Atlantic theatre of operations, which brought the RN a welcome easement in those vital waters. Dönitz disagreed fundamentally with the new strategy. He disliked concentrating his boats in the Gibraltar area, where constant enemy patrols made the risk excessive. Besides this, the currents in the straits were complicated and, once inside the Mediterranean, the U-boats were 'in a mouse-trap'. However, though Dönitz argued vehemently against what he believed to be a grave mistake, Hitler and his military advisers did not realize that the key to the Axis problem in the Mediterranean was not the Straits of Gibraltar but Malta, with its submarine, surface, and air threats to Field Marshal Rommel's supply-routes.[5]

The British had very quickly detected the U-boats' withdrawal from the Atlantic to the new battle area. Consequently, the RN soon offered powerful opposition to their build-up in the Mediterranean and the approaches to that sea. The British position in Africa depended on their ability to keep the sea-lanes open, in order to supply the Eighth Army and Mediterranean bases. Clearly, a battle was almost inevitable. In November and December 1941, the Kriegsmarine made a strong attempt to close the Mediterranean sea-lanes. Dönitz placed his U-boats on an east-west patrol line, allowing them on moonlit nights to push eastward as far as Tarifa, or in bad weather to withdraw to the west. Little traffic was found, but increasing enemy patrols were observed at the western entrance of the straits. These compelled the boats to submerge for long periods. The last three months of 1941 marked a defeat for the U-boats, a result not attributable to British countermeasures but largely a consequence of the deployment of the U-boats in a secondary and unsuitable theatre of war. After some uneventful weeks, FO U-boats decided that the U-boats should abandon the Mediterranean search and instead attack a definite target, Convoy HG76, homeward-bound from Gibraltar.[6]

HG76 was the only convoy attacked in that December, which was a comparatively quiet month.[7] Scheduled to leave Gibraltar at the end of November, it was postponed owing to the concentration of U-boats in the area west of Gibraltar. During the second week of December, Convoy OG77 was approaching Gibraltar with one escort group, and the escort vessels destined for HG76 were temporarily released to reinforce OG77. With the south-bound convoy safe in Gibraltar harbour, HG76 was ordered to sail on the afternoon of 14 December 1941. In the words of its Commodore, this convoy had very few dull moments from the time it left Gibraltar until it arrived in the UK on 27 December.

HG76 comprised 32 merchant ships and the 36th Escort Group, which was the most powerful escort the British had yet put to sea. The Senior Officer of the escort, making his first voyage in that position, was Commander Frederic John Walker, RN. Walker had developed tactics which were based on the principle of adopting an offensive role against U-boats rather than the conventional defensive one. His escort consisted of his own ship, the sloop *Stork*, four further sloops, nine *Flower*-class corvettes and the escort carrier *Audacity*. In addition, there were the destroyers *Blankney*, *Exmoor* and *Stanley* on attachment. The ships were carrying every weapon hitherto devised to deal with attacking aircraft and submarines. The weather was fine and calm.

At 1619 on 14 December, following Intelligence reports from German agents, who had been watching all shipping movements in the area of Gibraltar very carefully, FO U-boats ordered six U-boats (U-67, U-107, U-108, U-127, U-131 and U-574) to form Gruppe Seeräuber, a wolf pack, to intercept HG76.[8] The remaining U-boats in that area were to continue their operations as ordered. At 1836 the boats of Gruppe Seeräuber were ordered to form a certain patrol line by 1500 on 15 December, assuming that contact with the convoy had not been gained previously. Until then the boats were allowed to move freely. In the same signal was included a description of the convoy, which was fairly accurate except that *Audacity* was described as the aircraft parent ship *Unicorn* and a submarine was erroneously included.

The first boat to sight the convoy was U-74 at 2105. At the same time, U-77 watched a separate formation of four ships and a small escort travelling on a westerly course at low speed in the vicinity of HG76. Both boats were ordered to use only a favourable opportunity to attack and to move off before daybreak at the latest to continue their passage. In the early hours of 15 December, U-77 fired two torpedoes on the freighter *Empire Barracuda*. Before any avoiding action could be taken, one torpedo struck forward whilst the other hit aft. Then U-77 torpedoed a tanker, which received two hits and had to stop, heeling over. Later that night, U-74 and U-77 continued their passage into the Mediterranean. Elsewhere that same night, U-108 sank the independently sailing Portuguese ship *Cassequel* while the crew of U-127 met their fate. A group of destroyers from Force H was hunting U-boats when one of them, the *Nestor* of the Royal Australian Navy, picked up a contact and destroyed U-127 off Cape St Vincent, a position far away from HG76.

These distant events did not affect the sailing of either HG76 or Gruppe Seeräuber. During the night, the pack lost contact and were unable to regain it throughout the following day. Reconnaissance missions carried out by I./KG 40 were fruitless as well.[9] In order to have more U-boats to operate against HG76, Dönitz ordered U-434 to join Gruppe Seeräuber. Starting at 1800, the pack patrolled on a north-south course at a speed of 10 knots, turning every two hours. At the same time, Gruppe Seeräuber were given a new patrol line to be taken up by 0700 on 16 December, with U-434 to extend the patrol line to the north. Intense air reconnaissance was promised for the next morning.

The next day, 16 December, passed uneventfully. At 0915 a Focke-Wulf sighted the convoy but, being low on fuel, was unable to shadow it. Thus, it was not until 1430 that U-boat Command received another signal about the exact position of HG76. Dönitz ordered the wolf pack to operate against it at full speed. Four U-boats (U-574, U-131, U-67 and U-108), which could reach the convoy before dawn, were ordered to a position forward of the estimated convoy route and to operate in equal sectors on the enemy's course, while the other boats were to operate independently.

One hour later, U-108 gained contact but was immediately forced to submerge by the escort. Later that day, the same boat observed some destroyers but was unable to sight the convoy again. Hoping that one of his boats would be able to regain contact, FO U-boats ordered them to operate independently on the estimated convoy route. A little later, Cdr Baumann (U-131) sighted some destroyers and other escort vessels. Knowing that at least two other U-boats were close by, he decided to shadow the convoy by diving from his position, then allowing the convoy to pass over him before surfacing astern. In the middle of the manoeuvre, his hydrophones broke down and when the boat rose to periscope depth, his periscope came up right in the middle of the convoy. Quickly selecting a target, Baumann prepared to fire, but the merchantman started zigzagging to adjust her position in the convoy. U-131 was forced to call off the attack and to re-submerge. Baumann then decided that his position was too dangerous for comfort and accordingly dropped back again. Allowing the convoy to pass over him, he followed at a more discreet distance. At 1938, FO U-boats signalled that even if there was no contact, Gruppe Seeräuber were to continue to operate independently on the basis of the enemy's speed of 6-7 knots. New dispositions were not intended before dawn.

On 17 December, Gruppe Seeräuber sustained their second loss. The next homing report came from Baumann in U-131, who at 0011 passed several darkened vessels. At 0055 he was in contact with two escorts, apparently the stern escort. Two hours later, he had contact with the starboard escort. At 0502 he reported that he had been driven off, but until then, he had been in contact with various escort vessels, destroyers, gunboats and large motorboats. According to his observations, the escorts mostly operated in pairs and were widely spread out. Numerous attempts to attack were unsuccessful and the convoy itself was not found.

Meanwhile, FO U-boats had signalled Gruppe Seeräuber, urging them to strive at top speed to draw near during the night and to be in front by dawn without fail. At 0615 the pack were told there would be air reconnaissance in the area from 0900 and that they were to report bearings immediately. During the forenoon, U-108 regained contact with the convoy, reporting at 0808 several clouds of smoke and at 0840 the enemy's position. She maintained contact and reported the convoy's position again at 1028 and at 1116. U-107 also reported the convoy at 1147. Both boats were able to shadow the convoy until midnight, giving running shadowing reports, and drawing in the other U-boats. Since it was likely the remaining boats of the pack would soon locate the convoy, they were ordered to act on their own initiative and responsibility.

Starting at 0900, as promised, aircraft of I./KG 40 provided air reconnaissance in the area, reinforcing the U-boats' reports with their own. FO U-boats addressed two messages to Gruppe Seeräuber during this forenoon period, instructing them not to report bearings until told to do so, and ordering the shadower, at this time U-108, to report hourly. At 1624, U-108 reported the convoy, having so far made out 13 ships and two destroyers. Half an hour later, U-boat Command ordered the pack to report position.

U-574 gained contact at about 2000 and made an abortive attack upon an escort vessel. At 2039 she signalled, reporting the convoy's position. At 2100 she made her own position report, as did U-67. Cdr Scholtz (U-108) reported at 2248, having been driven off by destroyers, and gave one last position of the convoy. He also claimed, falsely, to have torpedoed one ship. At 0210 he asked for beacon signals from the shadower.

Before daylight, 17 December, U-131 had surfaced astern and radioed for support.[10] Among those who were close enough to join in the operation were U-434 (Lt Cdr Heyda) and U-574 (Lt Gengelbach). FO U-boats and his staff plotted the convoy's probable position, course and speed, and at 0420 sent signals to four more boats of Gruppe Seeräuber, well to the north, to make maximum speed to intercept. U-434 and U-574 were directed to Baumann's position. However, U-131's reports were intercepted by the enemy. Within a few hours, signals went out warning Cdr Walker of impending attack.

Walker requested *Audacity* to carry out an anti-submarine search. Results were quickly forthcoming: at 0925, U-131 was sighted 22 miles distant on the convoy's port beam. At once, Walker headed at full speed for the position, ordering the destroyers *Exmoor*, *Blankney* and *Stanley* and the corvette *Pentstemon* to join him. When the conning-tower crew of U-131 sighted the approaching Martlet, Cdr Baumann ordered a crash-dive instead of a surface escape.[11] A few seconds later, U-131 was diving rapidly. Despite his faulty hydrophones, Baumann altered course towards the convoy, hoping to avoid any surface attack that might follow his discovery by the aircraft. *Blankney* arrived first in the U-boat's diving position, found a number of asdic echoes and started to attack with depth charges. When the other ships arrived, Walker formed his vessels for an organized search westward, assuming that the U-boat would continue in the convoy's course. While this was going on, the slower *Pentstemon*, coming up astern, picked up an asdic contact and dropped depth charges immediately. Contact was then lost with the underwater target and *Pentstemon* and *Stanley* left the area to rejoin with *Stork*.

However, *Pentstemon* had wrought better than she knew, for the depth charges had caused severe damage to U-131. Unable to hear the enemy's approach, Baumann's crew were stunned by the closeness and accuracy of the attack. The boat began to leak water, the electric motors were partially disabled and oil began to pour into the engine room from a leaking tank. The U-boat lay at an angle of 40 degrees and began to sink. Steel plates cracked, paint peeled off in blisters, the bulkheads and locker doors became jammed and warped by the tremendous pressure as the boat sank deeper. Just in time, Baumann managed to get some trim on the boat. With lights gone, the batteries spreading deadly gases, and an ominous leak near the stern, he realized that he would have to surface very soon.

He needed to put at least 15 miles between himself and the enemy escorts before he could surface and escape at maximum speed. Baumann took the boat down to nearly 180 metres and ordered full submerged speed. The U-boat crew were fortunate to be granted nearly two hours before U-131 had to resurface with less than 20 pounds of pressure left. About one hour after the boat had broken surface, it was spotted by the searching ships, which were now well out on the port bow of the convoy. At the same moment, Baumann sighted the enemy and realized the danger. U-131 sped along, trying to escape at full speed and driving her damaged engines as hard as they could go, but the enemy chased and began to close the distance. At 1212, U-boat Command received a cry for help from Baumann, who reported that he was unable to dive and was being hunted by four destroyers. Dönitz answered that assistance could not be rendered and ordered Baumann to sink his boat if there was no other way.

Walker ordered his ships to open fire independently when in range and *Stork*, *Exmoor* and *Blankney* steamed at full speed towards the U-boat, which remained on the surface. At the same time, one of *Audacity*'s fighters dived down on U-131 in order to slow down the fast-moving enemy with machine-gun fire. As Walker had hoped, U-131 did not dive. However, the U-boat returned fire on the fighter with her anti-aircraft guns. The aircraft was repeatedly hit and crashed into the sea very close to the U-boat. *Stork*, *Stanley* and *Exmoor* now opened fire on the U-boat at a range of only slightly less than seven miles, *Exmoor*'s shooting appearing to be consistently accurate. Soon, *Stanley* joined in the barrage, *Pentstemon* still being too far astern. U-131 came under concentrated and accurate gunfire, to which she could make only a feeble reply with her single gun. With shells falling close around, Baumann realized his position was hopeless. Damaged first by *Pentstemon*'s depth charges and then hit eight times by gunfire, U-131 was almost a wreck. The barrage lasted for nearly 20 minutes, when Baumann gave orders to abandon ship and to open the vents. The crew then began jumping off the conning-tower and hull into the sea.

Stork ordered the 'cease fire', but before she could reach the scene, the U-boat's bow reared upwards. At 1330, U-131 slid backwards below the surface. After recovering the body of the Martlet pilot and the 48 survivors of the U-boat, Walker's ships headed back to the convoy.

Lt Cdr Heyda (U-434) was also in the vicinity. At 1440 he reported to Dönitz that he had seen three destroyers, shell bursts, and the explosion of depth charges. He waited submerged for two hours and when he resurfaced, Baumann was nowhere to be seen.

The first round in the battle for HG76 had gone to Walker, and the sinking of the shadower brought the convoy immunity for the remainder of the day and for the ensuing night. However, five U-boats had been directed to HG76 throughout the preceding day and were now closing in from every direction. This 18 December saw FO U-boats not too confident, for he knew about the convoy's unusually powerful escort and the prevalent good weather that favoured the enemy's use of radar and asdic. The flat calm and the extreme visibility made it difficult for the U-boats to approach undetected. Manoeuvring for attack, they could be heard plainly, while their bow-waves were easily identifiable, particularly from the air. Similarly, the nights were so dark that the U-boats had to run close in to the convoy to see their targets, but were frequently unable to detect enemy escorts until it was too late to evade them unnoticed.

Unaware of the fate of U-131, Dönitz waited anxiously for homing signals from the boat. There had been none throughout the afternoon of 17 December and none all night. Lt Cdr Gelhaus in U-107 and Cdr Scholtz in U-108 had repeatedly requested beacon signals from the shadower, since they had been driven off by the escorts and had lost contact at about midnight. At 0314, hoping that the reconnaissance aircraft would be able to gain contact throughout the day, Dönitz ordered his boats to continue operations independently after dawn and to look for beacon signals from the Focke-Wulfs, which were to be in the area from about 1000. During the forenoon, Gruppe Seeräuber reported their positions by short signals, all of them intercepted and read by the enemy. At about noon, two Focke-Wulfs began to shadow the convoy, but they were intercepted and finally driven off by two of *Audacity*'s fighters. As no boat was in contact at this time, FO U-boats signalled at 1157 that these reconnaissance aircraft had reported the course of the convoy at 1000 as 280 degrees, and that the main course since the previous evening was estimated as 330 degrees by dead reckoning.

At 1219, U-boat Command assumed from D/F evidence the convoy's position at 1100 to have been in Naval Grid Square CF92. Three hours later, to help his boats further, Dönitz informed Gruppe Seeräuber that by dead reckoning, the convoy was steering up on a main course of approximately 340 degrees. At the same time, Lt Cdr Scholtz radioed that his port Diesel was unserviceable because of a breakdown of his cooler pumps. U-108 could not do more than 11 knots and repairs would take more than two hours. At 1800, Lt Cdr Gelhaus (U-107) sighted clouds of smoke and reported the convoy's course before he was compelled to submerge, being hunted by *Pentstemon* and *Convolvulus*. Dönitz immediately ordered his boats to the position reported by U-107 and by dead reckoning estimated the course of the convoy as 330 degrees, speed 6-8 knots. At 1932, U-67 sighted two escorts and Lt Cdr Müller-Stockheim launched an attack on one, which he believed to be a destroyer, but which was actually the corvette *Convolvulus*. The attack was unsuccessful, due to torpedo failure. U-67 then had to make a surface escape after a fierce counterblast from the enemy. Cdr Scholtz reported again being in contact at 2142. He assumed that the main convoy was now dispersed into three groups.

Lt Cdr Heyda (U-434), who had witnessed the shelling of U-131 from a distance, had taken over as shadower. U-434 was on the surface about 10 miles from the convoy at dawn, 18 December, checking the positions of the escorts before diving. Later, Heyda saw *Stanley*, *Blankney*, *Exmoor* and *Deptford* dead ahead through the periscope. When the U-boat broke surface at 0906, it was sighted by *Stanley* from a range of about six miles on the port beam of the convoy. *Stanley* reported to Cdr Walker and turned away at high speed to attack. *Exmoor*, *Blankney* and *Deptford* were ordered to join *Stanley*, whose asdic had been breaking down. *Stanley* closed the enemy at 24 knots, hoping to get near enough to drop depth charges with a reasonable chance of success, but she was sighted by U-434, which crash-dived to periscope depth in seconds, with *Stanley* still three miles away. U-434 fired one torpedo, which missed, and was just about to dive deeper when the enemy attacked. In the diving position, *Stanley* circled the submarine, its position betrayed by an oil-slick, and depth charged by sight and guess, marking the area.

Blankney arrived at the scene, and, picking up the asdic echo, she dropped a pattern of five depth charges set to explode at 50 metres. While *Stanley* dropped a pattern of 14 charges set to 50 and 100 metres, *Blankney* released another pattern of 10 charges. She then passed on the ranges and bearings to guide *Stanley* on to the target. Below the two ships, U-434, taking violent avoiding action, was suffering cruelly. The charges were causing damage faster than repairs could be done. The conning-tower hatch cover cracked and seawater streamed into the control room. The lights went out, the auxiliary system failed, the steering gear was put out of action and the hydrophones went dead. Even worse, the next pattern of depth charges exploded one of the boat's own torpedoes in the stern tubes. Now she began to sink rapidly, and went out of control. Heyda ordered tanks to be blown and called the panicking crew to prepare for surfacing. Forty-nine minutes after being first sighted, U-434 came to the surface, less than a mile ahead from the enemy. *Blankney* turned to ram at full speed, but was too late. The crew abandoned ship and the last came up through the conning-tower as U-434 rolled over and sank. Heyda himself, two officers and 39 men were picked up by the two destroyers and the recently arrived *Exmoor*. The escorts then rejoined the convoy. U-434 was sunk before she had given her first homing report.[12]

Within a five-day period, Gruppe Seeräuber had lost three of their boats, but 19 December saw the surviving ones striking back. At 0115 U-107 and U-574 gained contact and reported the convoy steering north. U-574 had been the third boat to contact HG76, late on 16 December. Since then, Lt Gengelbach, who was known as an able officer of the sternest character, had been staying out of visual range and doing nothing to attack the convoy. Gengelbach had witnessed the sinking of U-131 through his periscope and had slunk away to the stern of the convoy. He stayed there throughout 18 December while U-434 was being sunk and eventually decided to attack that night. At 0200 U-574 closed the convoy from ahead, dived and maintained contact by hydrophones. Shortly before 0400, Gengelbach, being unable to see any ships through the periscope, surfaced. He discovered he had miscalculated the distance and was very close to the convoy. U-574 then followed the escorts towards the convoy. A number of ships passed to starboard, followed by *Stork* and *Stanley*. U-574 tried to torpedo *Stork*, but the enemy altered course at the critical moment. A few minutes later, the moon came out for longer than usual and Gengelbach saw *Stanley* on his port bow at a range of about 1,100 metres. At the same time *Stanley* reported that a U-boat was in sight and turned to attack. Gengelbach quickly fired two torpedoes and retired at full speed on the surface. *Stanley*'s bridge personnel reported the torpedoes as passing astern, thinking that they were missing her. *Stork* and *Stanley* had already come in sight of one another, when Gengelbach's torpedoes hit, and in a blinding sheet of flame, *Stanley* blew up. There was a violent explosion and fire broke out immediately, the ship taking a list of about 70 degrees to starboard almost at once.

On seeing *Stanley* destroyed, Cdr Walker ordered 'Operation Buttercup Astern'.[13] The escorts immediately turned outwards from the convoy, firing flare rockets in an effort to illuminate the probable directions of the enemy's escape on the surface. When *Stork* was seen in pursuit, U-574 crash-dived. *Stork* moved close to the sinking *Stanley* and dropped depth charges. While turning around the wreck, Walker gained an asdic contact. He went in to the attack, releasing a pattern of 10 charges set to 15 to 50 metres. This pattern, which exploded immediately above the U-boat, was fatefully accurate. U-574, trying to escape detection by hiding from asdic in the disturbance caused by the wreck, suffered serious damage to its main electric motors. The depth charges also fractured a rib supporting the pressure hull. A short circuit caused an electrical fire in the control room and compressed-air bottles exploded. A heated argument then followed between Gengelbach and his Engineer Officer. The latter said it was imperative to surface, but Gengelbach refused. Finally he ordered the crew to put on life-saving apparatus and for the tanks to be blown. U-574 broke surface 180 metres ahead of *Stork*. As the Diesel engines were undamaged, Gengelbach hoped to escape on the surface. Walker increased to full speed and steered a collision course, but U-574 turned to port and set off in a tight circle at high speed. *Stork* followed, unable at first to get inside the U-boat's turning circle. *Stork* turned three complete circles, with U-574 turning continuously to port just inside *Stork*'s turning circle, at only two or three knots slower than the enemy sloop. Walker kept U-574 illuminated and fired at her with his 4-inch guns until they could not be sufficiently depressed to bear on the U-boat. A stripped Lewis gun fired from over the top of the bridge screen, killing many of the U-boat's conning-tower personnel at one blow. Other crew members escaped death only by jumping into the water. Realizing that their fate was sealed, Gengelbach gave the order to abandon ship. This was done and the U-boat was left circling round on its own. Eventually, the drama ended when, at 0448, U-574 was rammed just forward of the conning-tower at an angle of 20 degrees on her starboard quarter. She hung for a few seconds on *Stork*'s bow, and again on the asdic dome, then rolled over and scraped underneath the sloop until she fell away aft. There she was blasted into pieces by a pattern of five shallow-set depth charges. Only four officers and 16 men were picked up by *Stork* and the corvette *Samphire*. Lt Gengelbach was not among the survivors. He is believed to have stayed on board and gone down with his boat. The final destruction of U-574 had taken only 11 minutes.[14]

While *Stork* was destroying U-574, other dramatic events were occurring in the port column of the convoy. Cdr Scholtz (U-108) was approaching its port bow when suddenly the whole convoy sprang into brilliant light. Instructed to fire their flare rockets as soon as a ship was torpedoed, the merchant ships had set them off when they realized that *Stanley* had been sunk. In this case, rather than helping the escorts to find their target, it helped U-108 to find hers. At 0515, Scholtz put a torpedo into the leading ship of the port wing column, the 2,869-ton freighter *Ruckinge*, which was struck amidships, the blast wrecking her bridge and throwing up a dense black cloud of smoke. Just before she was hit, the torpedo was sighted but it was too late to take any avoiding action. The freighter was abandoned, but remained afloat until *Samphire* sank her with gunfire. A few minutes later, U-108 damaged another merchant ship and, with all her torpedoes gone, withdrew at full speed.

At 0559, Scholtz reported on the situation to FO U-boats. Dönitz repeated Scholtz's report to the other boats of Gruppe Seeräuber, ordering Scholtz to maintain contact and to report his experiences with the convoy. At 1259, Scholtz transmitted his appreciation and advised his comrades to keep contact with the remote escort or clouds of smoke during the day and not to worry about the air escort, because it was mostly near the convoy. During the night the U-boats should break through the groups of destroyers, which were at a distance of three to five miles all round the convoy as remote escorts. The best chance to fire was from outside the strong close escort at a distance of about 2,000 metres. Sholz suggested they should watch carefully for a pointed position on account of range and to push ahead energetically before twilight, otherwise they might be taken by surprise by the remote escort behind the convoy. Finally, he warned the other U-boats of an enemy submarine, which was apparently proceeding on cross-courses behind the convoy, looking for an opportunity to fire.

The rest of the day was relatively quiet, although enlivened by air activity. German air reconnaissance in the area started at 0900. Two fighters from *Audacity* managed to intercept two Focke-Wulfs in the morning, shooting down one and damaging the other. In the afternoon a Focke-Wulf appeared on the starboard wing of the convoy with the intention of establishing the convoy's position, course and speed and shadowing it for a night U-boat attack. The aircraft was flying very low to get below *Audacity*'s radar beam when it was sighted by *Stork*. Cdr Walker ordered *Audacity*'s aircraft up. Two Martlets intercepted and made several stern attacks on the enemy without apparent result. The Focke-Wulf tried to escape, first in the clouds and then lower over the sea, but the Martlets climbed up alternately, hunting the slower reconnaissance aircraft over the sky, until one of the fighters collided with the Focke-Wulf. While the fighter landed on *Audacity* with chunks of a wing dangling from its tail, the Focke-Wulf was shot down by the other Martlet in a determined attack. A few minutes later, U-107, operating on the port beam of the convoy, was sighted by one of *Audacity*'s aircraft. Walker ordered *Deptford*, *Marigold* and *Convolvulus* to speed away. Lt Cdr Gelhaus quickly reported the enemy's position and escaped. The escorts returned after dark, having found nothing, only to be mistaken by some of the merchant ships for U-boats.

At 1525, a Focke-Wulf reported another convoy proceeding to Gibraltar and made beacon signals for the U-boats. FO U-boats ordered Gruppe Seeräuber not to operate against this convoy but allowed them to attack if favourably situated. He still regarded HG76 as the main object of operations. However, he was deeply worried about the unusual power of the enemy escort and the weather conditions, which made it nearly impossible for his U-boats to approach the convoy undetected. Gruppe Seeräuber had lost three boats to the escorts of HG76 and one boat to *Nestor* of Force H. Dönitz therefore faced the alternatives of calling off the survivors of Gruppe Seeräuber, or sending reinforcements to them. He chose the latter, and at 1911 he ordered three U-boats, all commanded by experienced officers, to join the wolf pack: U-71 (Lt Cdr Flachsenberg), U-567 (Lt Cdr Endrass),[15] and U-751 (Lt Cdr Bigalk). Dönitz thought that these skilled commanders would be able to cope with the difficult conditions. Cdr Scholtz's appreciation and experiences were recommended as a guide to these newcomers for the operation against HG76.

The following day, 20 December, passed uneventfully, except for occasional air activity on both sides. The U-boats were not in contact that night and the first report was made by U-107 and repeated by U-boat Command at 0520, giving the convoy's position and course. FO U-boats signalled at 0726 that air reconnaissance in the area of Gruppe Seeräuber was intended that day from 1000. Air activity opened during the forenoon with the appearance of a shadowing Focke-Wulf on the starboard side of the convoy. The plane was chased by two Martlets into cloud cover and then driven away. At 0803, FO U-boats addressed the three newcomers, who had all sent their position reports in the early morning, telling them the convoy's speed of advance. At 0945 Cdr Scholtz reported the convoy in sight. Half an hour later, he made a weather report. Assuming once more the role of the shadower, Scholtz maintained contact and reported the convoy's position again at 1141, 1620, 1829 and 1915. The afternoon and the ensuing night passed without incident. At 1245, U-67 and U-107, which had gained contact in the morning, were spotted far ahead of the convoy by one of *Audacity*'s fighters and forced to submerge. At 1945, U-67 watched an enemy escort and fired three torpedoes, which again failed owing to the failure of the middle tube to fire. Two hours later, the U-boats lost contact.

Gruppe Seeräuber maintained contact with Convoy HG76, but hesitated to attack while awaiting the reinforcements. At 0803 on 21 December, the recent arrivals U-71, U-567 and U-751 were ordered to join Gruppe Seeräuber and were told that there would be air reconnaissance in the area from 1300. Lt Cdr Müller-Stockheim (U-67) was ordered to report position and weather. At 1000 he replied, giving his position and reporting on the events of the previous night. In the meantime, *Audacity*'s dawn patrol disclosed two U-boats alongside each other some 25 miles astern of the convoy. They had a plank between them and men were moving across it. They appeared to be repairing damage to the port bow of one of the boats. When approached by the aircraft, they made no attempt to dive but opened fire with a gun from the conning-tower. The Martlet came right over the top, where their guns could not bear, and dived steeply, shooting three men off the plank and forcing the rest to cease work and scramble below. The two U-boats slowly made off on the surface, steering away from the convoy. It was concluded that they had collided in the night, and were transferring the whole of one crew or a working party from one boat to the other. Reports were made to *Stork*, and Cdr Walker detached four escorts to head along the U-boats' bearings. However, a relief aircraft could find no trace of either boat, and the surface force never gained contact.[16] At noon, U-108 and U-67 reported the position of the convoy, which was steering a north-westerly course and was guarded by fighters of the air escort. U-108 was ordered to send beacon signals for U-567. U-67 was in contact again at 1253, but lost contact one hour later, and was then forced under water by an enemy aircraft and depth charged by a destroyer. At 1452, Scholtz signalled that he had lost contact in the meantime and that he was pressing on. Lt Cdr Endrass (U-567), who benefited from U-108's beacon signals, sighted the convoy again at 1514 and reported to U-boat Command on the situation. Endrass was then ordered himself to send beacon signals for U-71.

Dönitz knew that the worst feature in this battle was the presence of the aircraft carrier *Audacity*, for her small aircraft circled the convoy continuously, so that when the convoy was sighted, the U-boats were repeatedly compelled to submerge or to withdraw. The enemy fighters also prevented any protracted shadowing or homing procedure by the Focke-Wulf reconnaissance aircraft. Therefore the sinking of *Audacity* was of particular importance, both for the reconnaissance aircraft and the U-boats. Dönitz designated her a prime target for Gruppe Seeräuber and, at 1830, ordered his boats to sink the carrier first, if they found the opportunity.

The night of 21-22 December brought success in a series of sinkings. At 1945, in sight of one another, U-71 and U-567 were both approaching the rear ship in the line of the convoy's centre column. Forty-five minutes later, U-567 torpedoed and sank the Norwegian 3,324-ton freighter *Annavore*, which was loaded with iron ore. The torpedo struck on her port side amidships, and the ship went down like a stone, disappearing within one minute and leaving only four survivors. While the escort vessels were performing their Buttercup operation, another late arrival, Lt Cdr Bigalk (U-751), heard screw noises in his listening instruments, which he assumed to be coming from the convoy.[17] He surfaced and, only a few minutes later, saw the outlines of some destroyers and the convoy. Approaching the convoy carefully, Bigalk discovered a number of destroyers. Furthest to the left, he saw a long, dark shadow, surrounded by several destroyers. Suddenly the shadow turned away sharply, and at the same moment the whole area was as light as day. This was the moment when *Annavore* was struck and a mock battle commenced astern, both events followed by a wild firing of tracer bullets. The destroyers took course for the tracer bullets and the long shadow zigzagged first eastward, then northward, presumably to get away from the convoy. Bigalk thought at first that it was a tanker, but, in the light of the tracer bullets, quickly realized that it was an aircraft carrier.

His boat then came to a favourable position for attack. Bigalk took aim at the long, dark shape, silhouetted against the distant lights and zigzagging independently, well clear of the convoy. At 2036 he fired a salvo of four torpedoes, one of which hit *Audacity* on the port side of the engine room, flooding it, cutting off the lights and bringing the ship to a standstill. The ship described a semicircle to port, then stopped, unable to manoeuvre. As there was no apparent damage, Bigalk assumed that his torpedo had smashed her steering gear and her propeller. Then he saw *Convolvulus* and *Marigold*, which were sent off to starboard where the carrier listed badly 10 miles away. As he knew that he needed at least two more torpedoes to send the carrier to the bottom, Bigalk turned a short distance off to load new torpedoes. At 2130 he watched *Pentstemon* searching for survivors and decided to launch his second attack as soon as possible.

Because U-751 had left port only a few days previously, her forward compartment down below was terrifically crowded with provisions and all sorts of things necessary for an operational cruise. Thus, it was not until 2140 that the torpedo tubes were reported clear for action. Outside, the water was phosphorescing and to avoid being detected by the aircraft carrier, by either sight or sound, the U-boat could only proceed at a crawling pace. Bigalk approached so closely that no torpedo could possibly miss and then, at 2155, put two more torpedoes into the carrier. The first hit forward, 20 metres behind the stem. The second struck amidships, causing a great column of fire. Moments later, a vast explosion was seen to blow off the whole fore-part of the ship. Bigalk presumed that ammunition or aviation fuel had been hit. A third torpedo, fired at 2157, passed the carrier and produced no effect. When he saw *Marigold* and *Convolvulus* proceeding straight to his position, Bigalk decided to turn away and not to make further attempts to get at the convoy. As he left the scene, the carrier's forecastle was already flooded and the deck was turning upwards. A rain of depth charges was dropped on the boat, but she was able to get away; and 10 minutes later, *Audacity* sank by the bows. At 2307 U-751 returned to *Audacity*'s last position, but the carrier had already vanished from the surface. Bigalk therefore had good reason to report her as being most probably sunk. FO U-boats, who apparently could not believe that the marked enemy of both I./KG 40 and the U-boats had been put out of action, signalled other members of Gruppe Seeräuber to report evidence, if the sinking of an aircraft carrier had been observed. He also asked Bigalk to signal the basis for his assumption that the victim was a carrier, and what superstructure he had observed. Bigalk answered that the ship had a continuous flight deck without superstructure, with the stem and stern raking. He then described the attack. This account persuaded Dönitz that Bigalk's claim was valid, and he signalled his congratulations.

While the search for *Audacity*'s survivors was going on, U-567 approached Convoy HG76 from its port side and tried to get through to the columns of merchant ships. At about 2245, Lt Cdr Endrass selected his target. At the very moment when U-567 was preparing for attack, she was detected and illuminated by *Deptford*. As soon as Endrass saw the escort and realized that he had been discovered, he turned away and crash-dived, trying to escape submerged. *Deptford* and *Stork* immediately began depth charge attacks on the U-boat, starting with a 10-charge pattern set to 35 and 75 metres. During the second attack, contact was lost. The U-boat appeared to have gone deep. No signs of oil or wreckage could be seen, but eight minutes after the third run, carried out with five charges set to 130 metres, a double underwater explosion occurred. U-567 had been sunk with all hands, taking down one of the most experienced and most decorated U-boat commanders. FO U-boats had to regard U-567 as lost without trace.[18]

At about 2200, U-67 sighted a formation consisting of two large shadows and seven escorts. The first silhouette was provided with a very long and flat full-length flush deck without superstructure or noticeable break. At about 1,800 metres, the target was just completely focused in the U-boat's aiming sight. The second vessel was shorter but with more freeboard, a long flush forecastle, a flat bridge and thick funnel close together in the forward part of the stern third of the ship's length. Lt Cdr Müller-Stockheim assumed that the targets were a catapult ship and an aircraft parent ship. At 2223 he made two fruitless attacks on the pair of shadows. His approach was apparently heard by the enemy and the disproportionately strong escort immediately launched an attack. U-67 crash-dived, endured depth-charging and was finally driven off. Later, she moved to eliminate an oil-trace and to repair slight damage suffered during the depth charge attack.

The following day, 22 December, passed without grave incident. No U-boats reported contact during the forenoon, so at 1307 FO U-boats again had to give them some help and signalled the estimated convoy position. At 1409 U-71 reported the convoy on a westerly course. Lt Cdr Folkers (U-125), who had left St. Nazaire the day before, westbound, ran into the convoy and reported smoke and escort vessels in sight. He was then driven under water by enemy aircraft, and at 1817 was called off and ordered to continue his passage. In spite of U-71's contact report, Gruppe Seeräuber did not succeed in making an attack during the ensuing night. The only attempt was made by Lt Cdr Bigalk (U-751), who at 2325 reported that he had fired a spread of four torpedoes at a group of destroyers. The torpedoes missed and the U-boat was driven off.

At noon on 23 December, HG76 was led into the Western Approaches safe area. However, the U-boats were still nearby. Three still had torpedoes, but two of the boats had been holding on to the convoy since 14 December, and were bound to be exhausted and no longer fit for operations. The weather was still too calm for them, and contact was lost in the deteriorating conditions. Five merchant ships, one destroyer and an aircraft carrier had been sunk, against the loss of five U-boats and two reconnaissance aircraft. This was the U-boat arm's highest loss so far in any single operation. It was becoming obvious that the chances of further loss were greater than the prospects of success. The time had come for FO U-boats to call off the operation. Dönitz, who realized how decisively his U-boats had been defeated, discussed the matter with his staff officers and the operation was finally abandoned. At 0618, 23 December, after a blank night, he ordered Gruppe Seeräuber to break off operations against HG76. Three boats were to commence accelerated return passage, while two were to remain at sea.

The battle for Convoy HG76 was important for several reasons. Both sides had suffered painful losses as well as notable successes. However, each classified it as a victory for the convoy escorts and a clear defeat for the wolf packs. Gruppe Seeräuber had been unable to deliver more than a few hectic attacks on a convoy with which they had been in touch for a full week. FO U-boats had anticipated a particularly strong escort for HG76, but its actual strength was a surprise. The weather, the exceptional strength of the escort and the skilful handling both of the anti-submarine forces and the air escort had combined to create a situation more than usually unfavourable for a U-boat attack. Experience had shown that because of the relatively short distance from Gibraltar to Britain, which enabled the enemy to concentrate his available forces, the Gibraltar convoys were more difficult to attack than those in the Atlantic. For this reason, operations against the Gibraltar convoys had generally been avoided unless U-boats were already in the area as a result of other operations. The worst feature for the U-boats was the presence of the aircraft carrier. Its sinking was therefore of major importance, not only in this particular case, but also in future convoy actions. Thus, the greatest lesson learnt by the RN was the necessity for continuous air cover if the attacks of wolf packs were to be defeated. However, this one isolated case was no reason for FO U-boats to make any fundamental change in his views concerning attacks on convoys in general. Subsequent events seemed to proved him right, but in fact, he was only justified in his views by the inability of the enemy to profit from the lessons learned in the fight for Convoy HG76.

Notes

1. Information about the development of German submarine tactics was obtained from the following sources: Dönitz, Karl, *Zehn Jahre und Zwanzig Tage*, Athenaeum 1958; Hessler, *The U-boat War in the Atlantic 1939-1945*; Jeschke, Hubert, *U-Boottakik*, Rombach 1972; Rohwer, Jürgen, *Die Funkführung der Deutschen U-Boote im 2. Weltkrieg*, Wehrtechnik, 9-10, 1969, pp. 324-328, 360-364.

2. The translated signals of *Gruppe Seeräuber* are in the Public Record Office (PRO), DEFE 3, Rolls 72, 73, 74.

3. This was the only long-range unit of Fw 200 capable of penetrating as far as 20 degrees west. Its working designation was I./KG 40.

4. The problem of air support for U-boats is described in: Bundesarchiv-Militararchiv (BA-MA), RM 87/17, *War Diary Befehlshaber der U-Boote* (B.d.U); Dönitz, *Zehn Jahre und Zwanzig Tage*; Hessler, *The U-boat War in the Atlantic*; Poolman, *Focke-Wulf Condor*.

5. The details about the deployment of U-boats in the Mediterranean are taken from: BA-MA, RM 87/18, *War Diary B. d. U.*; Dönitz, *Zehn Jahre und Zwanzig Tage*; Hessler, *The U-boat War in the Atlantic*; Creighton, *Convoy Commodore*.

6. The material in this section is from: BA-MA, RM 87/18 and RM 897/19, *War*

Diary B. d. U.; Dönitz, *Zehn Jahre and Zwanzig Tage*; Hessler, *The U-boat War in the Atlantic*.

7. Unless otherwise cited, the account on the course of the battle for Convoy HG76 is primarily based on the following sources: BA-MA, RM 87/19, *War Diary B.d.U.*; BA-MA, *War Diaries* of the U-boats involved; PRO, ADM 199/1489, *Analysis of U-boat Operations in the Vicinity of Convoy HG76*; PRO, ADM 199/2059, Monthly Anti-Submarine Warfare Report, January 1942; PRO, ADM 223/16, *Narrative of Convoy HG76*; PRO, ADM 237/136, *Commodore's Report HG76*; Robertson, *Walker, R.N.*

8. All times are B.S.T.

9. Meanwhile, at the instigation of the Luftwaffe, I./KG 40 had been transferred from FO U-boats to the command of *Fliegerführer Atlantik*, Lieutenant Colonel Martin Harlinghausen, a former Naval Officer who ensured smooth co-operation.

10. The material for much of the following section is from BA-MA, RM 98/338, *War Diary U-131* (reconstructed, translated extracts of British accounts of this action appended).

11. This was the British designation of the Grumman F4F-3 fighter.

12. Material on the sinking of U-434 is from BA-MA, Case 11/3 30488, *War Diary U-434* (reconstructed, translated British account of the loss appended).

13. 'Operation Buttercup' was a form of counter-attack, designed by Walker to detect and attack a U-boat.

14. The details about the sinking of U-574 are taken from: BA-MA, Case 13/3 39609, *War Diary U-574* (reconstructed).

15. Engelbert Endrass was one of the reigning top scorers of the U-boat fleet. He had been the watch officer under Günther Prien when he penetrated Scapa Flow earlier in the war.

16. There is no entry in the German records referring to this episode. A little later, *Samphire* sighted a metal tank, thought to be part of a Military Landing Craft which had been washed overboard from a ship in an OS Convoy. It is possible that the aircraft attacked a U-boat lying alongside this object and not alongside another U-boat.

17. The following account is from BA-MA, Case 15/2 30730, *War Diary U-751*.

18. Material for this section is taken from: BA-MA, Case 13/2 30603, *War Diary U-567* (reconstructed).

28

The Front Line:
Convoy HG76 - The Defence

by A. B. Sainsbury

The 10-day battle around Convoy HG76, homeward bound from Gibraltar, took place between 14-23 December 1941. It was both a first and a last: the first in which an aircraft carrier (although one of the most primitive type) was included in the escort, and the last fought before the Germans added a fourth wheel to their submarine Enigma and introduced the much more powerful Triton (Shark) cipher on 1 February 1942.

The battle coincided both with a strengthening of the U-boat forces off Gibraltar and up the Mediterranean, and with the global expansion of the war. During the previous week, Pearl Harbor had been bombed and Force Z had been destroyed. Not long before that, *Ark Royal* had been sunk, and some of her aircrew were now taking passage with HG76. Only recently, *Barham* had been destroyed in less than five minutes, torpedoed by U-331 off Sidi Barrani; and before HG76 reached home, her sister ships *Valiant* and *Queen Elizabeth* would be immobilized at Alexandria.

With the actual or functional loss of all these capital ships in so short a period, the OIC's appreciation of the state of the Battle of the Atlantic on 20 December was that the enemy's 'primary object seems, at least temporarily, to be no longer the destruction of merchant shipping'. This would have been cold comfort to HG76: the convoy had lost one merchant ship on the 18th and was to lose its second on the 21st, while the escort in its spirited defence lost both *Audacity*, its carrier and *Stanley*, an ex-USN destroyer.

In 1954 Roskill saw these hectic 10 days as 'a resounding victory, since five U-boats had been destroyed and only two merchant ships were lost.' By 1988, however, the same running battle seemed to John Winton to be no more than part of 'a very small and only temporary Allied victory in the Atlantic'. In his assessment, even that limited success came about only because of a withdrawal of the U-boats from the area, together with Bletchley Park's temporary and diminishing superiority over Enigma. How we should perceive it today we must see.

Jan Heitmann has given us a lucid and thorough account of the proceedings. I make one comment on his chapter - it deals essentially with a force of U-boats and is not restricted to HG76. We may therefore seem to return slightly different score cards: though our convoy lost only two merchantmen, he sinks five. I seek not to question his figures but only to clarify his classifications, for we reach, I think, roughly the same conclusions - that in terms of losses and the deflection of their strategy, the Germans lost that particular battle, even though the British may have lost some time in following up the implications of their victory. My intention is not to rehearse the various engagements that followed, but to reflect on some aspects of the situation, and where I cannot offer a definite opinion, to invite speculation or comment.

*

The convoy of 32 merchant ships sailed at 1700 on 14 December 1941, forming nine columns with the Commodore's pennant in the ambiguously named *Spero* (the Romans used the same word to mean both 'hope' and 'portend'). Its intended speed of advance was 7.3 knots. The Senior Officer of the escort was Commander F. J. Walker RN in *Stork*, with three other sloops, two *Hunt*-class destroyers and one ex-USN destroyer, and nine corvettes, of which some parted company at various times. Temporary reinforcements were provided when possible - for example, on 16 December by *Hesperus*, for less than a day. Two and a half years later, that same ship would take Walker's worn-out body down the Mersey here, past the Bar lightship for burial in the Bay, where (as Max Horton said, at Walker's impressive funeral service in Liverpool Cathedral) 'not dust nor the light weight of a stone, but all the sea of the Western Approaches shall be his tomb.' By then restored to his proper place in the Navy List by the grant of two years' backdated seniority, he was Captain Walker, a Companion of the Bath, and with three bars to his DSO. Now, however, he was setting off on his first sea-going command since the war began.

*

There is some doubt about the determination of the date and time of departure. The convoy was to have sailed considerably earlier. There is a reference in the Admiralty War Diary to orders sailing *Harvester* and *Havelock* on 26 November to escort OG77, refuel at Punta Delgada and return with HG76. On the 27th, FOCNA told the 19th Destroyer Flotilla (DF) that HG76 had been postponed, and that the DF was to patrol to the west of the Straits, at least 30 miles off Cape Spartel. This reflects the patrolling by 812 Squadron which began that night; but there is no mention of the 15 U-boats that were expected to transit the Straits between 27 November and 1 December. This Intelligence had been based on a decrypt of orders on 22 November to all Atlantic U-boats to concentrate in the Gibraltar area, but was misleading, because not all the boats were intended for deployment there; some were to go through, others to watch for our shipping doing the same, although not specifically for HG or OG convoys. Either way, the Admiralty was unlikely to sail a convoy against a tide of oncoming U-boats.

In preparing HG76 to sail, there was also the question of *Audacity*'s availability. She had arrived with OG76 on 11 November, needing generator repairs that could only be made in the UK, and with only one serviceable

Martlet. FOCNA declined an Admiralty suggestion that she should embark Swordfish - she would need extra wires, and there were no spare aircrew. He would therefore sail her with HG77 in late December, with a full house of five fighters. By 3 December, however, he was concerned at the congestion in his harbour and asked Their Lordships when they wanted HG76 to sail, requesting two days' notice of their intentions. This delay enabled the carrier to repair her Martlets, so on the 5th FOCNA reported that she would accompany HG76 after all. OG77, which should have crossed with HG76 northeast of the Azores, arrived undisturbed early on 13 December, and next forenoon FOCNA told the Admiralty and CINCWA that as an air raid was expected he would sail HG76 that afternoon, which he did. There is no evidence of his ever having had the promised two days' notice. But while it was not an unusually large or especially precious convoy it was, even apart from *Audacity*, unusually generously escorted. Was this to be some sort of a tiger trap, or, as Macintyre suggested, no more than a consequential strengthening due to the advent of 36 Escort Group? There is a suspicion that the Admiralty was unusually concerned.

Cdr D. W. Mackendrick, RN, was an officer whose name has been spelt in at least three different ways, including variations in the Navy List. More importantly, though, he was the first and last Commanding Officer of *Audacity*. She had been the German *Hannover*, 5,537 tons and designed for 15 knots, captured off San Domingo in 1940 and modified at Blyth by replacing two decks with a flight deck, 420 feet in length and 60 in beam. This was less than half the space of the recent *Ark Royal*'s. She had two arrester wires, a barrier, and no hangar. All maintenance had to be done in the open, whatever the weather, or be left undone. One propeller, damaged by contact with the barrier, was 'straightened on deck with the aid of blowlamps and approximately the right pitch reset' after which its aircraft successfully undertook further patrols. She was an altogether unprepossessing vessel, but her inexpensive and swift conversion provided the most convincing means of harassing not only the enemy long-range aircraft but his U-boats as well. On the three voyages in which she met FW 200 aircraft she destroyed or damaged more than did all the fighter catapult and CAM ships put together. HG76 was her fourth and last convoy, and by any standard it was a classic. In six flying days she reported eight U-boats and intercepted 4 Focke Wulfs, damaging three of them and shooting down two more.

She was torpedoed twice and sunk in the darkness of 21 December 1941. Her captain, who like one or two other perspicacious officers kept an FAA dinghy handy, got away at the end, after the surviving Martlets crashed down onto the survivors who had abandoned ship, but was drowned alongside *Pentstemon*, despite most valiant efforts to save him. His was a great loss; he was a man of very high principles and deep understanding, who had managed to turn the strange hybrid under his command into a brave and useful little ship, a pattern and example for the new ships of her type which were to come. His epitaph and hers were written by Dönitz himself:

> in HG76 the worst feature from our point of view was the
> presence of the aircraft carrier. Small, fast, manoeuvrable aircraft
> circled the convoy continuously, so that when it was sighted the
> boats were repeatedly forced to submerge or withdraw. the
> presence of enemy aircraft also prevented any protracted
> shadowing or homing by German aircraft. The sinking of the
> aircraft carrier is therefore of particular importance...

Mackendrick's seniority as a commander was dated 31 December 1937:
Walker's was six years earlier. On the previous convoy, Mackendrick had been
Senior Officer of the escort; now there was a specialist officer with his group
who was senior to him but unpractised. There is an impression (mainly, it must
be said, in the secondary sources, of which a recent one actually reverses their
seniorities) of an unusual uncertainty about their relationships. Words such as
'asked for', 'declined' and 'refused' suggest a mutually tentative approach. There
is however no trace of uncertainty in Walker's ROP. He says unequivocally that
for the preceding three nights, the carrier had proposed to operate with one
corvette

> on the starboard side of the convoy. I had reluctantly to refuse the
> corvette since I then had only four escorts immediately around the
> convoy; I also suggested that she should take station to port since
> I anticipated attack from starboard. She replied that the convoy's
> alterations to port would inconvenience her and eventually went
> off alone to starboard. I should have firmly ordered her either onto
> the port side or into the middle of the convoy. And I feel myself
> accordingly responsible for her loss...

What Walker did not know at the time was that *Audacity* had steamed away on
a straight course for 20 minutes and was only just beginning her first alteration
of course to an eight-minute zigzag when, momentarily illuminated by
inadvertent Snowflake, she was hit and lost steerage way. Captain (D) in
Liverpool concurred with Walker, adding that '*Audacity*, a most valuable ship,
should have remained within the convoy at night and it is for consideration that
the importance of this should be impressed on all Senior Officers of escorts'.
When forwarding Walker's ROP and the covering letter, Admiral Sir Percy
Noble on the other hand did not concur with his Captain (D). In his judgement,
it was correct - indeed, essential - for the carrier captain to choose where and
how to use his ship at night:

> this decision must be left to the Commanding Officer. It is
> interesting to note that during a previous attack when *Audacity*
> was in convoy, a torpedo passed 25 years astern of her, and while

she was out of convoy the merchant ship in her position was sunk....the Commanding Officer, *Stork* was in no way to blame. The Commanding Officer, *Audacity* was acting correctly in accordance with WACI Part 371.

Walker's Commander-in-Chief congratulated him and his Group, and there was an immediate DSO. He had certainly done well, and he and his Convoy Commodore, the retired Vice Admiral Sir Raymond Fitzmaurice, distinguished the voyage by their happy and easy liaison, the Commodore deploying his charges at one stage as though there had been no battle in progress. Perhaps that is one reason why only two merchantmen were lost.

Before leaving Gibraltar, Walker had been anxious to try out a drill which he had evolved to discomfort the enemy, and disarmingly called 'Buttercup', his nickname for his wife. It was appreciated that after an attack, a U-boat would remain near the wreck, using it as a bait, or else make off at comforting speed on the surface. Now he was to be 'plastered' into submerging, where his destruction would be 'considerably simplified'. Although it was some time before this drill was officially blessed, it was studied with respect and interest, and tacitly approved from the start. Another more traditional ploy was the staging of a mock battle, to distract any watching enemy vessel while the convoy did a diversionary side-step, but when first used by HG76,

> the plan was a flop for the following reasons - one of the convoy fired a Snowflake by mistake and gave away the exact position, and when the diversionary turn began, several merchant ships let off many more. I do not however think that this made much difference....I am well aware of the argument for returning any guarantee that 'Snowflake' will not be fired at exactly the wrong moment - as in HG76. Neither can one legislate for the regrettable tendency of some ships in any emergency, real or imaginary, to fire everything, drop everything and abandon ship

as had indeed been the case with one of the two lost and with *Ogmore Castle*, which 'abandoned ship incontinently' and only managed to rejoin the convoy 20 hours later, with a specially detailed escort. Captain (D) would not wear that one and Walker admitted that he realized he was reporting on what was his first convoy. But common sense was the order of the day. By dawn on 21 December he appreciated that 'the convoy was likely now to be continually shadowed and attacked whatever route it took; therefore the shorter the better' and, with the instant approval of his C-in-C, headed for home.

Even then his troubles were not over. His ship was rammed (understandably and in good faith but no less severely for all that) by *Deptford*, who did herself no good, twisting her stem. An officer who had been sunk in *Ark Royal* and was taking passage in *Stork* later recalled that to his own officers, Walker made only one comment on the ramming - 'Well, never a dull moment in this ship.' It was not his only memorable and reassuringly nonchalant remark during that voyage: on the 19th, U-574 had sunk *Stanley*. Giving immediate chase, *Stork* was trying to turn inside the surfaced U-boat. As the two went round in circles, Walker simply said, 'This is ridiculous', and proceeded to dispose of the enemy in 11 minutes.

After the attentions of *Deptford*, at first 'it was difficult not to take a somewhat gloomy view of the situation', but soon compensations occurred to him, and he went on to consider his intentions for the next night: 'there was clearly one thing not to be done, and that was to continue on another dummy course and passively await attack'. So he laid on another mock battle, this time successful - 'all went according to plan and a quietish night ensued' - and on the following morning, 22 December, the first Coastal Command Liberator arrived. This aircraft made a superb rendezvous after an 800-mile flight, and established a pattern of aggressive surveillance which kept off any further attentions by German aircraft or U-boats. This is perhaps not the place to reflect on the relations between the Navy and the Air Force, except to note that there seemed to be little to choose between England and Germany so far as interservice relations were concerned. But whatever balance is struck, however score cards may be compared, the hard fact was that nine U-boats had not managed to deliver more than two rather tepid attacks against a convoy they had been shadowing for over a week. On 23 December, Dönitz noted in his War Diary that 'The chances of losses are greater than the prospects of success....the decision has been made to break off operations'.

*

Although Hinsley was complimentary about HG76, he observed that it was only by the narrowest of margins that the U-boat campaign failed to become decisive in 1941. The main reason for this, known now to us but not then to Dönitz, was Bletchley Park's mastery of Hydra, the U-boats' first cipher. After Baker-Cresswell's pinch of U-110, the Atlantic Hydra was normally deciphered within 48 hours and reliable guidance was offered by the Admiralty 'with an assurance based on indisputable evidence', as Ronald Lewin put it. Jürgen Rohwer has gone so far as to say that in the second half of that year, the Submarine Tracking Room at the Admiralty thereby re-routed threatened shipping with such skill that about 300 vessels were spared the threat of damage or sinking; this seems to him 'more decisive to the outcome of the Battle of the Atlantic than the U-boats sunk in the convoy battles of 1943 or in the Bay offensives'.

This reminds us of Marder's dictum that provided an attacking submarine is prevented from damaging or sinking its target, it is in a sense a luxury, or at least a longer-term economy, to sink the attacker. The main aim is the traditional safe and timely arrival of the convoy, and as long as this is accomplished, it matters little - until the next time - how many thwarted or idle submarines are about. They are not much use to the enemy unless they are sinking ships; if they are not doing that, what they *are* doing is almost irrelevant. But to sink ships, they have to find, close and attack the convoy; they thus expose themselves to its escort which, using the convoy as a protected bait, has no need to go searching for them. Support as opposed to Escort groups are likewise a great luxury; again, though, they can be mobilized and deployed with little of that cavalry drama which so embarrassingly identified the exuberant but confused exponents of anti-submarine strategy early in World War II. HG76 was an elegant demonstration of this doctrine.

In the shorter period it is interesting to note that on 28 December 1941, less than a week after HG76 and its escorts had reached home waters, the Department of Military Aircraft Production had sent to its agency in Washington DC an appreciation that recent experience had justified completely their firm belief that, given enough aircraft around the convoys, the U-boats' massed attacks could be defeated in their present form. There was no doubt that this air effort could best be provided by auxiliary aircraft carriers, but a greater number would be needed than could be spared from trade; they were also extremely vulnerable. Consequently, the next best thing was to try and develop the principle that every merchant ship should carry its own aircraft. Although CAM ships fulfilled part of this objective, they were one-shotters, uneconomical in aircraft (even *Audacity* had expended an average of four Martlets per voyage) and hard on personnel in cold weather. It was therefore suggested, in an age before the helicopter, that the autogiro should be taken up as a military vehicle. It would be interesting to know more about the pursuit of that possibility. The very few in service with the RAF were committed to calibrating and developing the radar defence of the UK.

Before the experience of HG76, it had been impossible to obtain the release of additional merchant shipping for conversion to the role of auxiliary aircraft carrier. That little victory instantly secured the turnover of five hulls in British yards, and the placing of orders in the United States for the construction of six more of the type. *Activity* was the first of the five British conversions, commissioning in October 1942; *Avenger* was the first of the Americans to see service, with PQ18 that September. Thereafter 'Auxiliary' gave way to 'Escort', while the larger, purpose-built carriers were divided into Light and Fleet classes. But *Audacity* was the prototype of the little ones, and in her brief but illustrious life, she never performed better than in the context of HG76.

Primary Sources

Naval Historical Branch
Admiralty War Diary, Volumes 79 and 80.
BR 1736 British Naval Aviation, Volume II [NSH 53 (2)].

Monthly A/S Report, Volume V, pp. 16-37 - a printed version of ADM 199/1998 in the PRO.

Public Record Office
ADM 199/1998 - see above.
ADM 1/11895 Minutes of Board of Enquiry into the loss of HMS *Audacity*, 21 December 1941.
ADM 199/934 ROP by senior survivor HMS *Stanley*.
ADM 199/2099 Trade Division Summary, pp. 368-370.
ADM 199/932 Letter from C-in-C Western Approaches, covering one from Captain (D) Liverpool enclosing ROP by Commanding Officer HMS *Stork*.
ADM 223/16   Narrative of Convoy HG76, based on Ultra sources and declassified from Most Secret.

Secondary sources are listed in the Consolidated Bibliography.

Acknowledgements
I am indebted to J. D. Brown, Head of the Naval Historical Branch, for his customary hospitality and help there and for access to the papers of the late Cdr R. D. Wall, RN, who was taking passage in *Stork* having declined an invitation from *Audacity*, to Lieutenant Alan Burn, RNVR, Captain Walker's Gunnery Officer in *Starling*, and to Captain E. Palmer, RN, then First Lieutenant of *Deptford*.

29

An Allied Perspective

by W. J. R. Gardner

Introduction

One dictionary definition of perspective is 'any one of the aspects of something'.[1] This imprecision neatly sums up the problem of producing a single Allied view of such a long and large-scale campaign. It also indicates that there cannot really be such a thing as a single perspective. How could there be, with several nations involved in quite different ways? How can even one of the more involved countries - Great Britain, the United States, Canada - produce even a single national perspective? In each nation, there were many perspectives: from the highest levels of national leadership to individual sailors and airmen, and the efforts of many thousands of other men and women, whether armed or civilian.

In seeking a single coherent perspective, perhaps the metaphor of an ornate salad in a huge opaque bowl might help. The decorative parts visible on top are readily identifiable. Of course, the salad is not just the quantity or quality of its parts, but the way in which they are put together. Why in an opaque bowl? Because most large-scale events have at least one hidden part; and as a diner investigates a salad, sometimes uncovering unexpected objects, so the historian carrying out basic research can illuminate the truth that lies beneath the surface. Lastly in a successful salad comes the greatest mystery of all, the dressing, with just as many elements of its own. In this chapter, the type, number and quality of the ingredients will consist of a broad description of the largely high-level perspectives of three nations: Great Britain, the USA and Canada. One slightly more exotic ingredient - the British Cabinet Committee on Anti-U-boat Warfare - will be looked at in greater detail; and the dressing is 50 years of historical literature. *Bon appetit!*

National Perspectives

Great Britain. The Atlantic campaign lay at the heart of Britain's strategy. Although victory in the Atlantic alone would not guarantee overall success, defeat there would bring Britain's defeat everywhere. Atlantic victory was also a necessary precondition to winning the war in continental Europe. Many ringing Churchillian quotations emphasize this, and - particularly in the summer of 1941 and in the period from the late autumn of 1942 to the spring of 1943 - mark the recurring times of perceived crisis in the Battle.

But at the same time the Battle's strategically defensive nature sat a little uneasily with Churchill's pugnacious character and his predilection for 'offensive' operations and military leaders. This was almost certainly a factor in the replacement of Admiral Sir Percy Noble as Commander-in-Chief, Western Approaches in the autumn of 1942 by the more obviously aggressive Max Horton. The subsequent conduct of his command displayed differences more of style than substance. Some parallels might be drawn with the relief of Auchinleck by Montgomery in North Africa - although without the depths of acrimony present in the latter case.[2]

Another important indicator of Churchill's underlying attitude was his special relationship with Bomber Command's commander, Sir Arthur Harris. Although reinforced by the proximity of Harris's headquarters to Chequers (the prime minister's country residence), the most significant element in this was probably the fact that, for long periods of the war, the bombing attack against Germany was the only major offensive action being taken against the Third Reich. Certainly, even the almost weekly exposure that Horton had to Churchill in early 1943 does not seem to have been resulted in a relationship similar to that with Harris.

There were times, too, when it may appear that even Churchill's support for the Atlantic campaign wavered, particularly in the matter of the allocation of resources. But as well as his preference for offensive action, there were many other calls for ships and aircraft. Few people now disagree that by 1939, the British Empire was vastly over-stretched. By 1941, this was starkly clear. German advances into western and eastern Europe were at or near their fullest actual extent without any guarantee that the high-water mark had been reached. Japan, although not yet committed to action, was threatening much of the eastern Empire. The land battle in North Africa also resulted in the commitment of significant naval forces to the Mediterranean. This strategy has been criticized,[3] but in its support, account should be taken of the Mediterranean's allure for Hitler and Raeder, the German naval C-in-C until early 1943. (Dönitz, who felt no such attraction, bemoaned the detachment of submarines for the Mediterranean, which he felt would have been better employed in the Atlantic.)[4] While the British naval presence in the Mediterranean was considerable, many of the warships deployed there, from battleships to some of the destroyers (which were fast rather than long-legged), would have been of limited use for convoy protection. It is probably correct, therefore, to say that the commitment of U-boats to the Mediterranean damaged the Germans' Atlantic battle more than commitment of British naval forces damaged theirs.

The British tended to see Atlantic events as plateaux of concern punctuated by periodic crises. Sometimes these crises were not as great as they appeared, for example in mid-1941 when a frightening rise in sinkings quickly subsided. The fall was due in part to the now much-bruited cryptographic success in breaking submarine codes; in part to the lesser known, but more significant extension of the convoy system; and in part to a decrease in submarine productivity extending back over several months, indirectly brought about by British strength in the vicinity of the United Kingdom.[5] But if the British could be over-anxious, that was only natural: U-boats threatened Britain's very existence, which was never the case with either the USA or Canada. In any case, anxiety - even over-anxiety - had its positive side too, producing a strong national effort to counter the U-boat menace. From the British came the main developments in Asdic, weaponry, tactics, HF/DF and cryptography. Theirs, too, was the leading part in the organization and training of the ASW forces.

United States of America. In the USA, which came to the war relatively late, the Battle of the Atlantic was not dismissed entirely; but it was never quite as close to the forefront of national American thought as for the British. There were a number of very good reasons for this.

Firstly, while Britain was fighting but America was still at peace, full and formal American involvement in the Atlantic was impossible, not least because of domestic political opposition. Nonetheless, some very flexible definitions of neutrality were devised in that period, enabling American support on quite a large scale - particularly the escorting of convoys further and further east, and the exchange of 50 old destroyers for bases. Without it necessarily being the intention of the American higher leadership, the USA's participation short of war probably had its greatest operational impact in staying the Germans' hand both in North American waters and in the vicinity of shipping escorted by US forces. However, it could be argued that these acts were as much symbolic as practical, representing a declaration of intent - a signal that if it came to war, the Americans would support the British, notwithstanding the very strong reservations they had about helping to preserve the British Empire. Atlantic support allowed effective sustenance of the British Isles, without propping up the colonies. Canada, which since 1931 had been a self-governing dominion of equal status with Britain, did not count as a colony, and anyway was widely viewed in America as having little influence in operational matters.[6]

Secondly, even after America joined the war in December 1941, the Battle never threatened the USA (or Canada) to the same extent as it did Britain. The various crises of shipping loss - and less frequently, but much more importantly, shortfalls in delivery - that afflicted the UK, were unknown to North America. This too fostered a sense of detachment in the USA. It was not that the Atlantic campaign was considered unimportant, just that (since national survival was not at stake) it tended to occupy a less central psychological place than it did in the British case.

At the same time, the circumstances of US entry into the war, with the sudden Japanese descent on Pearl Harbor, also played a part. Even now, it is difficult for Britons to imagine the degree of shock that this engendered. After the immediate effects of the cataclysm had subsided, the demands of the Pacific war fell both absolutely and relatively on the Americans to a greater extent than the Far East did on the British. Hawaii is closer to San Francisco than Washington DC is to London: in late 1941 and throughout the war, it felt very much closer still. Despite subsequent Allied conferences that established the strategy of 'Germany first', a combination of the vast distances in the Pacific, the strategic balance of a Pacific with few and uncertain bases and its psychological proximity ensured that US Atlantic commitment was unlikely to be absolute.

Further, the USA was, if anything, less materially prepared than the British for the anti-submarine war that had developed in the Atlantic by late 1941. Not only was there a shortage of the right sort of ship, but time was wasted on setting up building programmes of small submarine chasers that were unsuitable for operations in the broad Atlantic. Although it has become a commonplace of British naval history to present the first six months of 1942 as a period of German successes brought about almost entirely by the intransigence of Admiral Ernest King, USN, this interpretation overlooks some of the real organizational and material difficulties facing the Americans at the time.[7] So, even as America was persuaded or convinced itself that East Coast convoy was necessary, the establishment of the system and its later extension to the Caribbean led to the absorption of many of the available escorts for that task. As a result, even as late as the middle of 1943 (when, in the view of most historians, the Battle was resolved), American escort forces on the main trans-Atlantic convoys were very much in third place numerically to the British and Canadians. Interestingly, much of this was supplied by an overlooked force, the US Coast Guard, whose cutters had both endurance and a relatively heavy armament.

Although, taken altogether, this might suggest that Americans were less than fully committed to the Battle, such a view would ignore their enormous material contribution. This resulted in the provision of many destroyer escorts (an American type similar to British frigates), some of which also served under other flags, and the supply of many escort carriers (although those tended to be initially allocated to other operations, such as Russian convoys and amphibious support as in Torch). Further significant help came from aircraft, both flown under US control and the notable presence of B-24 Liberators in the hands of Coastal Command, making considerable progress towards closing the mid-ocean air gap. Still more assistance came from the American ability to repair and refit both naval and merchant ships on a large scale. But most significant of all was the mass building of merchant shipping. This was on such a huge scale that the net balance of shipping loss (buildings against sinkings) was in credit as early as the second half of 1943 - that is, barely 18 months after US entry into the war. This not only made any of Dönitz's hopes for strangling the Allied effort by sinking shipping totally unrealistic,[8] but was probably also responsible in part for a shift of German strategic aim in mid-1943.[9]

In sum, therefore, although in some senses the USA had less reason than certain other participants for involvement in the Battle of the Atlantic, it nevertheless made an enormous, if somewhat hidden, contribution to the outcome.

The British-American Relationship. This subject lies at the heart of the coalition aspects of the war. Other than allowing his country to be used as the biggest land battlefield in world history, and thus relieving much of the air-land pressure in the West, Stalin made no direct contribution to the Battle of the Atlantic. Indeed, the Soviet Union's insistence on the Russian convoys could be argued as having a negative effect, absorbing assets that might also have been used in mid-Atlantic. So the most significant international relationship in this context remains that of Britain and the USA. The contribution of materiel by the USA has already been alluded to; its scale and advanced technology must be regarded as a war-winning factor of prime importance.

There were also important relationships between individuals and organizations. The debate about the strategy of Admiral King may have actually been lengthened by British attempts at navy level to rectify the problem, the Americans objecting to the British style in such attempts.[10]

Perhaps the most important single link was that between the President and the Prime Minister, or 'Former Naval Person' - the pseudonym adopted by Churchill in much of his correspondence with Roosevelt, presumably alluding to his two tenures as First Lord of the Admiralty in the two world wars. (It may also have been designed to appeal to Roosevelt, as an ex-Assistant Secretary of the Navy during the first war.) Both men were copious correspondents during the war, and used this medium as well as the several Allied conferences (both bilateral and multilateral, bringing in such allies as the USSR and Canada) to act as the backbone of what must be considered as one of the most successful politico-military alliances of history.

But when the Churchill-Roosevelt correspondence is examined, a curious phenomenon emerges.[11] Despite (or perhaps because of) the considerable naval background of the two statesmen and copious other evidence indicating their view that success in the Battle was essential to the conduct of the war, there is relatively little reference to it in the correspondence.[12] For example, in the period from the beginning of 1942 to the middle of 1943, there are only 16 references to the campaign. This might not seem unreasonable, but the period saw both the high sinkings off the US East Coast in the first half of 1942 (the 'Second Happy Time' for German submariners) and the critical battles in spring 1943, as well as an intervening period that was far from quiescent. To put this further into context, in those 18 months no fewer than 616 items of correspondence were exchanged. There is also no clear pattern of increased exchange of communication at times of perceived crisis. For example, Roosevelt notes Churchill's concern over US coastal sinkings in February 1942 and assures him of action, but this is confined to two short sentences;[13] some six weeks later, Roosevelt admits to slackness in American preparation for ASW.[14] Late in March, Churchill alludes to the problem, but only so as to introduce the point that more aircraft could be allocated to patrolling the Bay of Biscay.[15] Clearly not all concerns on this subject were confined to the correspondence. For example, Harry Hopkins was used as a conduit on at least one occasion.[16]

Nevertheless, this relative paucity of written communication on a vital topic remains a paradox in the midst of a most successful alliance.

Canada. It is an easy mistake to overlook the contribution made by Canada to the Battle of the Atlantic: its share was of considerable proportions. During much of the war, even after America's entry, only British escorts exceeded the numbers of Canadian escorts. Moreover, in terms of the size and wealth of the nation, the relative effort for Canada was colossal. None of this, however, happened without huge strain, and the forces of the RCN did not reach their full efficiency until after the crisis of the Battle had passed in mid-1943.

Because of the great efforts needed in trying to attain both adequacy of forces and proficiency of performance, Canada was never truly able to take the high-level perspectives on strategy that the other two nations discussed above were able to do. The reasons for Canada's laborious struggle for effectiveness are worth examination, as they point out the extreme difficulties facing any nation which suddenly has to create a competent force in an unfamiliar warfare discipline.

The pre-war RCN was extremely small by the standards of the other two; indeed, in the inter-war period, it even had to fight off an attempt to abolish it altogether. In Britain, because of the overestimation of the effectiveness of asdic, ASW was considered by many to be barely relevant, even detrimental, to an officer's career; but it was at least recognized and had considerable numbers of practitioners. In contrast, the Canadians had virtually no experience at all in the field. Consequently, the RCN had to undergo a far greater relative expansion than either the RN or the USN. Amongst others, Vice Admiral Sir Peter Gretton in his foreword to Marc Milner's *North Atlantic Run* has noted figures which indicate that the RCN had to expand at a rate six times more than the RN. By contrast, the Royal Australian Navy only grew at twice the RN rate.

The Canadians' problems did not stop there. Coming from such a small beginning, the challenge was great enough; but it was made much harder by the inevitable lack of specialist warfare skills, of organizational experience and of necessary equipment.[17] For example, the RCN leadership was keen to build and man destroyers. These were probably beyond the capabilities of the Canadian shipbuilding industry and consequently took longer to build, occupying shipyard space that could have been used to build the simpler and more needed corvettes for escort work. Worse, many of the scarce regular officers were occupied in standing by the destroyers whilst the escort vessels were entrusted to hastily recruited and eager but unfledged reservists. Making matters worse still, these were often moved on after one or two convoy operations, and the ship would start again with a wholly or largely new crew. Thus it was virtually impossible for these vessels to build up any degree of worthwhile expertise.

David Zimmerman, writing in *The Great Naval Battle of Ottawa*, also makes it clear that a combination of a relatively backward scientific base, a reluctance or inability to liaise with British and American research communities, together with an overweening desire to send *Canadian* equipment to sea resulted in Canadian warships being poorly equipped by comparison with their peers in the other navies. Well into the war, many Canadian corvettes still only had a magnetic rather than a gyroscopic compass. As well as being comparatively inaccurate, the magnetic compass also limited the effectiveness of their asdic. For most of the Battle (at least until mid-1943), many Canadians were left with the justifiable feeling that no sooner had they taken a progressive material or organisational step, with much effort and pain, than the British had already moved on at least another step further - and that the enemy, too, had made progress.

These problems often resulted in poor performance against U-boat packs. One of the worst single convoy actions (against SC42 in September 1941) was under Canadian escort, and in the second half of 1942 (one of the most intense phases of the war) 60 out of 80 mid-ocean losses were from convoys largely under Canadian escort.[18] Some of this lack of performance can be attributed to the fact that many of the slower convoys - which suffered disproportionately as it was easier for submarines to close them - were under Canadian protection.

For much of the most crucial part of the Battle, training for ships, far less groups, was virtually non-existent, despite the efforts of such as Cdr J. D. Prentice, the Canadian-born SOCC (Senior Officer, Canadian Corvettes) who had served 22 years with the RN. Other aspects of organization were also poor, including arrangements for leave. The culmination of many of these problems and the apparent inability of the senior management of the RCN to cope with them led to the relief of the Canadian CNS, Vice Admiral P. W. Nelles, in January 1944, although political overtones were also present.

It may seem that the Canadian participation in the Battle did little more than generate a catalogue of disaster, but actually the necessary proficiency was eventually achieved. Before then, the fundamental cause of virtually all the dilemmas was the difficulty of expanding enormously from an almost non-existent starting level.

The Anti-U-Boat Warfare Committee

This was a British committee, subordinate to the War Cabinet, which met from November 1942 to December 1943. Its life spanned the crisis period of the Battle in spring 1943, and an important perspective on British high-level attitudes and actions concerning the Battle can be gained from a short study of the committee.

But before looking at this body, it is worth giving brief consideration to what might be thought of as its predecessor, the Battle of the Atlantic Committee.[19] This met largely between March and October 1941, spanning the period of crisis in the shortfall of imports into the UK in that year.[20] The first meeting on 19 March was chaired by the Prime Minister and included representatives at ministerial level from the ministries of Supply, Admiralty, Board of Trade, Food, Transport, Shipping, Aircraft Production, Labour, Air and War. It is notable that for the first two meetings, there were no service representatives. However, from the third meeting onwards, Admiral Sir Dudley Pound (the First Sea Lord) and Air Marshal Sir Frederick Bowhill of Coastal Command were in attendance, as well as other staff members of the three service ministries; but all these were invariably noted as 'Also present'. Meanwhile the ubiquitous Professor Frederick Lindemann - noted as a personal assistant to Churchill - was usually there, but 'above the line', that is, as a full member of the committee. The only other scientific representation was a single attendance by Professor P. M. S. Blackett, then employed by Coastal Command. Others came on the basis of particular requirement, and a last category of attender was that of senior visitors from abroad. These included Menzies, prime minister of Australia; Harriman, Roosevelt's special war-aid representative in Britain; and Fraser, prime minister of New Zealand. Curiously, of these, only Fraser was above the line, but as Menzies was rather more important in Alliance and Empire matters, this is probably either secretarial inconsistency or Churchillian whim.

There is a clear pattern to the subjects discussed. They are almost entirely concerned with shipping and imports, with virtually no time devoted to the conduct of the Battle or the provision and development of weapons for the campaign. A very wide spread of matters was addressed by the committee. At one end of the spectrum, such important matters as the repair of merchant shipping features at every meeting, and the rate of imports receives almost as much attention. From the requirement stated here by Churchill (31 million tons annually of non-oil imports) and the monthly figures reported, the ebb and flow of adequacy and crisis can be plotted.[21] In 1941 it is clear that some shortfall occurred in the first four months of the year. This would have done little to allay projected fears for the rest of the year, in the context of a significant increase in U-boat numbers, although there is no indication that the latter subject was discussed by the committee. Nevertheless, for the rest of the year, the target was exceeded - sometimes by a reasonable margin - with the sole exception of November, when a deep dip to 25.8 million took place.

But although such weighty matters as this and the perennial problem of turnaround time merited much discussion, it also appeared that little if anything was beneath the attention of such a high-powered team. The supply of electricity at Avonmouth and the use of a pneumatic riveter in the Bristol area received repeated attention.[22] Perhaps the least weighty item considered was the provision of gangways at Hull, where

> the only way of leaving a ship was by one ladder from the stern,
> men were unwilling to carry on working on board during the
> 'alert' and as a solution *steps had been taken*. (My emphasis)

Almost the last item taken by the committee was altogether more apposite and dealt with the paucity of honours and awards given to the officers and men of the merchant service. Churchill rightly said that there were too few of these, and the situation should be remedied.

In sum, however, it would be true to say that the Battle of the Atlantic Committee would perhaps be better described with the name by which it was known for its first two meetings: the Import Executive. It is perhaps not surprising that this should be so. With Britain standing virtually on its own for most of the committee's existence, imported material was a subject of literally vital importance. Nevertheless, as the highest body meeting regularly which devoted itself to the Battle of the Atlantic, it not only established a precedent, but also set the method for its successor in 1942-3.

Although there is some suggestion that the Anti-U-Boat Warfare Committee was proposed in summer 1942,[23] it was not actually established until November 1942, with its first meeting taking place on the 13th of that month. For six months thereafter, until 12 May 1943, meetings were held on a weekly basis.[24] For the rest of May and June, the period was fortnightly; then for the rest of the year an approximately monthly frequency covered the gatherings of the committee. This in itself gives a fairly good indication of the perceptions of the British leadership as to the importance and the progress of the Battle. There is a close correlation between this frequency and the crisis of the Battle in the period between late 1942 and spring 1943 (weekly); the mauling taken by the U-boats in the late spring (fortnightly); the half-hearted German attempts to return to the mid-Atlantic convoy routes (monthly); and their virtual retiral from convoy warfare (cessation of meetings).

There was also a subtle change in the composition of the committee, with no formal division being made as hitherto into principals and 'also attended'. Despite this, some were present only on the basis of specific items. For example, Air Marshal Sir Arthur Harris, AOC-in-C Bomber Command, was present at the 12th meeting, in 1943, but only in order to be told to prepare comment on a single item in time for the next meeting. This he did, but did not appear in person, and he was not next seen until the 15th meeting to discuss H2S radar. There was stronger service representation too, with the Admiralty's Dudley Pound backed up by two other admirals and both Coastal Command and the Air Ministry represented. Amongst the politicians was the new Minister of Aircraft Production, Sir Stafford Cripps.[25] By now, the presence of this minister was indicative of a considerable overall improvement in British fortunes. Instead of being a member of the previous committee for the purpose of ensuring his share of the limited imports available, now his role was to advise on the options for use of the manufactured aircraft. Lindemann, by now ennobled as Baron Cherwell, and still comfortably ensconced as Personal Assistant to Churchill, re-appeared, as did Professor Blackett, now working for the Admiralty.

Again, there were to be late arrivals as well as a large and varied cast of transients. In the former category were to fall such as Averell Harriman (whose 10 attendances made him rather more than a transient) and Admiral Harold Stark, USN, Commander of US Naval Forces in the European Theatre of

Operations, whose attendance was even more frequent. This stressed the involvement and depth of contact between the USA and Britain.

Another late joiner but regular participant was Admiral Sir Max Horton, Commander-in-Chief Western Approaches, who had been appointed to his post in November 1942, at about the same time as the committee was being established. It would be tempting to connect the two events, seeing them as evidence of a harder and more aggressive British attitude, but there is no known evidence to support such an interpretation. Indeed, the committee was formed as a reaction to the perception of a worsening situation. Horton's appointment is a little more problematic. There is no suggestion of any specific act of omission or commission having precipitated the relief of his predecessor, Noble. It may have been that the growing sense of crisis attracted Churchill's attention to Western Approaches, and that he then wanted to see someone closer to his own style installed in Liverpool.[26] Horton certainly met this definition, and his arrival was marked by a certain amount of dead-wood cutting.

A clear indication of the subjects discussed by the committee is given by an index attached to the main minutes. This permits a fairly ready overview of the matters taken, although some caution must be exercised in using this index. Although it is comprehensive, and lists not only subjects, meeting(s) at which they were discussed and supporting memoranda, the heading under which items are listed is sometimes a little obscure. Thus, much of the important discussion on the size of convoys and their cycles is found under 'North America', rather than 'Convoys', where the rest of such material is located.[27]

A brief survey of matters brought to committee indicates a very high proportion of subjects that were regarded as important (and would still be considered so).[28] Fortunately, this time, there are far fewer items of apparently low intrinsic significance for such a high-level body: foremost amongst these must be the provision of binoculars. There is also a small section which deals with a combination of apparently unpursued desires, such as the need for a better weapon than warship hulls for ramming submarines; the Carl Holm torpedo defence (which supposedly did more harm to the ship it was supposed to be defending than to the enemy); and worthwhile items that look further forward. Of the latter, two particularly interesting ones were Magnetic Anomaly Detection of submarines, and a statement presciently, if prematurely, indicating interest in the helicopter as having ASW potential.[29]

There are two items of importance that do not appear at all: Ultra and HF/DF. The omission of Ultra is no surprise; despite the high security classification of the minutes,[30] the existence and workings of Sigint was kept within an even closer circle than those who attended the committee. Whilst many of them knew about Ultra, not all did, and so the subject went undiscussed, despite its importance. There are occasional references to Intelligence, which might refer to Ultra, but without naming the precise source. The lack of reference to HF/DF is less expected. Whilst its use was of great importance, often giving the first specific indication to the escort of a U-boat being present in the vicinity of a convoy, its existence was not as secret as Ultra. Although its fitting in suitable ships was proceeding well by this point in the war, it is hard to believe - observing the full sweep of the committee's purview - that it merited no attention.

Some of the important items indicate the ability of the committee to investigate and sometimes resolve matters of prime significance to the conduct of the Battle. The item that comes in for most attention is 'Merchant Ships', which takes up more than 10% of the index, and was discussed at every meeting. Specific topics include the monitoring of losses, repairs, net defences and American aspects.

The important matter of convoy size and cycle occupies much attention. It was during the span of this body that the debate on the number of ships forming each convoy was joined. Professor Blackett's operational research work had established that the larger the convoy, the safer it was likely to be. This was because, although a larger convoy required a larger sea area, the perimeter of the area did not increase by the same proportion. This in turn meant that available escorts could be used more efficiently. Experience and analysis also indicated that however large a body of U-boats was deployed and however inefficient the escort, only a certain number of sinkings resulted. The causes for this were complex, but are bound up with matters of space and time, and reflected the reality that it was rare for a submarine to be able to complete more than one attack. Blackett's postulates were thus well supported by a combination of easily comprehended theory and practical observation.

Nevertheless, these ran contrary to the instinct of most of the higher naval leadership, who felt that a larger convoy, especially if poorly protected, might lead to the destruction of even larger numbers of ships. Although their views were less well articulated than Blackett's, some evidence (such as the disaster of SC42 in autumn 1941) seemed to support them. It should also not be forgotten that the responsibilities weighed heavily on Pound, the First Sea Lord, in particular,[31] whereas Blackett had no such care. The discussion came to a head in committee, when the Admiralty reluctantly accepted that some convoys might have more than 60 ships.[32]

A related topic was convoy cycles. The continuing operations in North Africa had already increased the requirement for cargo flows. The need to build up troop numbers and material in Britain prior to re-entry into Europe would exacerbate this. If the Admiralty's preference for smaller convoys was accepted, then more convoys would be required. This in turn had implications for the escort requirement. Either more escorts would be needed - difficult to conjure up at short notice - or else the convoys (some or all of them) would have to have fewer escorts. A general reduction might lead to the degree of loss feared by the Admiralty. A selective policy would only make practical sense if some realistic means of supporting selection was available - that is, Intelligence, specifically Ultra.[33] Although by the time that most of the discussions on convoy cycles were taking place (February-May 1943) Ultra had settled in to being a reasonably reliable and timely source of information, there were still sometimes gaps which were difficult to predict.

By early March, discussion seems to have centred round proposals to shorten the then-current cycle from eight days, to six in April and five in May.[34] It was indicated that this would result in the abolition of the support groups of escorts, only recently established, as well as bringing training virtually to a halt. Both of these points are of substance, the latter especially so. One of the keys to British efficiency in the Battle, evident both at the time and in hindsight, was the insistence on thorough training. Halting or greatly reducing training might have released assets in the short term, but in the middle and longer term the effect on the campaign could have been marked and serious. Fortunately for the British, this path was not taken.

The subject of convoy cycles was to re-surface later when the difficulty of forecasting convoy size resulted in the sailing of several that were smaller than expected. In May 1943, therefore, consideration was given opening the cycle to 10 days - fewer but larger convoys. Although Maclay of the Ministry of War Transport was prepared to accept this as having little effect on the required import flow, Horton (C-in-C WA) made the practical point that too-frequent changes in the cycle would have disruptive effects on escort training and refit cycles.[35]

Even stragglers received significant attention from the committee. In March 1943, the Ministry of War Transport reported that 5.3% of all sailings became stragglers and that, of these, 1 in 15 was sunk.[36] Remedies put forward included improved seaworthiness, better stowage and securing of deck cargoes, better ballasting and that 'unsuitable types should be eliminated'.[37]

The committee was also prominent in the resolution of the conflicting priorities for bomber aircraft, where the Admiralty wished such to be involved both at sea in the Atlantic gap and against U-boats transiting the Bay of Biscay, and in attacking the Biscay U-boat bases.[38] Overall, as Michael Howard has indicated, the importance of the committee lay not so much in its ability to resolve the issue - which it could not - but in reducing it to its essential elements and in minimizing the distortions of service interests.[39]

Notwithstanding such apparent limitations, the greatest significance of this body was probably the relative ease with which important aspects of the Battle could be discussed widely, thoroughly and with such a broad range of high-level leaders of the widespread British effort. The tendency of its lineal predecessor (the Battle of the Atlantic Committee), to address matters in too much detail, appears to have been almost entirely avoided; and new war-winning techniques such as operational research were able to take their place at the table without apparent difficulty.

From our point of view today, there are also benefits for the Atlantic historian. Not only does the frequency of the meetings give an invaluable guide to the degree of concern about the Battle perceived at the highest British levels, but the subjects considered by the committee, both in minutes and memoranda, give a unique insight at primary source level into the detailed preoccupations of such decision-makers.

Six Years at Sea - 50 Years on Paper

There is a large historical literature dealing with the Battle of the Atlantic. This has played its own part in shaping current perceptions of the Battle. Sometimes this has enlightened the subject, but there has also been material which has been less useful. A review (albeit brief and selective) of such material will be helpful. The limitations imposed are that firstly, it is confined largely to works by Anglo-Saxon authors - an imprecise term that includes Britons, Americans and Canadians - with a further emphasis on British material. Some German material that has appeared in English is included. Secondly, in general, no attempt has been made to include the field of articles, learned papers and theses on the subject. This is a field of study in its own right and, being less accessible than the literature in book form, perhaps has less potential impact.

The broad classification adopted below is based largely on period, but several works cross these boundaries. There are often good reasons for this, of which probably the best example is Hinsley,[40] where an official history was much delayed by the long-kept secret of British cryptographic efforts in WWII.

Like Gaul, the 50 years have been divided into three parts. The first (which runs from the war into the mid-1950s and beyond) might be dubbed the age of official histories. This is succeeded by a period of 15-20 years dominated by secondary works, many of which are reminiscences - some by participants, others second-hand accounts. The start of the next era can be dated with more precision than anything else in this chronology. In 1974, F. W. Winterbotham published *The Ultra Secret*. In itself, the work is of almost no import in charting the history of the Battle, but it marks the beginning of a period dominated by what had previously been the hidden knowledge of Allied cryptography. Subsequent work has often attempted, naturally, to take account of this newly available knowledge; but Ultra has seemed so glamorous, one should add that much of the post-Winterbotham work has also been obsessed with it, leading to an inflated assessment of its significance. As a coda, but not yet eroding the three-part classification, it is possible that a post-Ultra period may now be starting, in which a more balanced view may be coming into sight.

The Official History Period. Official historians were set to work during and soon after the conflict. The point must be established at once that not all their works were to appear in the immediate aftermath of the war. This was for two reasons. Firstly, as with Roskill, the work took many years to compile, edit and be approved for release; moreover, in his particular case, he wrote not merely an account of the Battle, but of the RN's whole war. Thus, although spread over three volumes, he provided a very thorough account of the Battle.[41] This has stood for many years as the most authoritative British study of the subject, and probably still occupies pride of place.[42] But, operating sometimes in parallel with works such as Roskill and Morison, sometimes as predecessor and support, was another layer of works, like the naval staff histories. These have been known and available to historians now for some time, but are only just emerging into a more public forum.

First amongst these must be *The Defeat of the Enemy Attack on Shipping* by Barley and Waters, originally published in 1957 as a naval Classified Book. This dealt largely with the WWII U-boat offensive, but also touched on its predecessor in WWI, as well as making mention of other modes of shipping attack. With text, tables and graphs, the two volumes present a concise yet thorough account, largely from an Admiralty perspective, of the Battle of the Atlantic. The books' technique of interweaving narrative, topic, statistics and analysis make them still of great use. Although available for many years through the Public Record Office, this work is about to become even more accessible through publication by the Navy Records Society.

Perhaps the least known of any of this category, and the nearest to being a true primary source, is *The RAF in the Maritime War*, an 8-volume narrative compiled by Captain D. V. Peyton-Ward, a naval officer who was the naval liaison officer with Coastal Command during the war. Again available through the PRO and also the Air Historical Branch, its very size makes wider publication unlikely.

Lastly comes a work that resulted from one of the most enlightened historical decisions ever made by the Admiralty. At the end of the war, Fregattenkapitän Günther Hessler (a former U-boat captain and member of the staff of Flag Officer U-boats, and also Dönitz's son-in-law) was, in the words of J. D. Brown, 'immured in a cellar with all the seized German records and invited to get on with it while the events were fresh in his memory.' This account, largely chronological, was published by the Admiralty in three volumes over 27 years. It is now fully available from HMSO in single-volume form, and gives considerable insight into the German conduct of the campaign.

Perhaps a coda to this list should bring up two more things. Many British official histories other than Roskill's have a bearing on the Battle. It is appropriate to mention two at first: the many-authored *Grand Strategy* sets the Atlantic conflict in a wider frame and provides an excellent guide to the superstructure of higher Allied decision-making. *Merchant Shipping and the Demands of War* by C. B. A. Behrens is also invaluable in providing information on a neglected but essential dimension of the Battle. Secondly, what is probably the last contribution to the quasi-primary material such as Peyton-Ward and Hessler is provided by Jürgen Rohwer's *Axis Submarine Successes 1939-1945*. Although not first published until the 1960s, and unavailable in English until 1983,[43] it provides details of all attacks in which it is thought that hits were obtained. Although the work could probably now be revised, especially on the attribution of specific sinkings, this nevertheless remains a work of the greatest value to historians. The last chronological addition to this field, Hinsley, will be addressed in the section dealing with the post-Ultra school.

The Second Generation. The 1950s saw the beginning of a genre of work that was to last essentially into the mid-70s, but which continues (for better or worse) to the present. This was a series of generally secondary, sometimes tertiary, works dealing with particular aspects and personal accounts of the Battle. These range from useful additions to the earlier categories, to those which are barely literate and furthermore inaccurate. Sometimes, in the better ones, the personal dimension is described by the participant, as with Macintyre and Gretton - both good accounts. In other cases it is at second hand, or even posthumously, such as Chalmers on Horton and Robertson on Walker.

At its worst, some of this material makes no use of anything other than unchecked reminiscence, spiced with prejudice. At the other end of the spectrum, invaluable detail is added to the properly somewhat dry and dispassionate accounts of the first generation. Some further detail, too, can be gleaned from what are nominally works of fiction, especially Monsarrat's *The Cruel Sea* and Buchheim's *Das Boot*. Both have been criticized on the grounds of accuracy and misrepresentation of the author's actual experiences, but, more importantly, they both remain literate conveyors of the spirit of place and time.

Accounts of individual convoys also begin to appear, sometimes told directly by participants such as Gretton, often by others. Perhaps the best examples of the latter are the two works on the extremely large-scale actions against two convoys, HX229 and SC122, in March 1943. Rohwer provides a meticulously detailed account of this battle, in particular giving a good account of the work of the B-Dienst, the German naval equivalent of Bletchley Park - a subject rather neglected in the English literature. Martin Middlebrook, using a technique which he has all but made copyright, emphasizes the human aspect with some sensitivity, but fortunately devoid of sentimentality. Rohwer's book quite literally stands astride the revelation of Ultra, which will be described later. However, at this point, it is worth noting that the work was written in German before the public revelation of Ultra,[44] but the English edition (1977) takes some account of British cryptography.

After Ultra. The watershed in the Atlantic literature was created by a book which made virtually no reference to the Battle and is now generally regarded as having many inaccuracies and much misrepresentation. F. W. Winterbotham's *The Ultra Secret* (1974) did, however, introduce both public and many historians to the extensive British codebreaking activities in WWII.[45] It took some time for its effects to gather speed and these can be summarized in three ways:

* the subsequent availability of Ultra material to encourage research into its application to the Battle;
* the revelation opening the way to the writing of the much delayed Official History of British Intelligence in WWII; and
* a tendency to 'reinterpret in the light of Ultra'.

The first two of these can be regarded as almost entirely beneficial, but the last has proved of very mixed value at best. It is not surprising that such a revelation should have a profound effect on the writing of the Battle's history. That a factor of such importance in the war as a whole had apparently remained hidden for nearly 30 years, and then suddenly been revealed to an astonished world, was a major *coup de théâtre*: it was as if the demon king had delayed his entrance until rather more than halfway through the last act. Conferences and books began to be devoted to the subject and, particularly in secondary and tertiary works, the 'Ultra myth' was created, suffusing much of the post-Winterbotham literature, even if it was rarely stated in an explicit form. According to this, the British, due to their intellectual brilliance, were able to read virtually all German signal traffic for the entire war. A further unstated assumption was that the enemy was unable to access such skills.[46] Armed with this view of 'the other side of the hill', the Allies were able to use their meagre resources to best advantage, leading to the eventual defeat of the Axis powers.

The proper corrective to this new orthodoxy lay in the official history of British Intelligence, but its three volumes were not published until 1981-84,[47] well after the new interpretation had got into its stride. Though the timing was unfortunate, if inevitable, nevertheless Sir Harry Hinsley and his naval collaborator, Edward Thomas, not only set the record straight on the availability and significance of Ultra, but also often put it into context, stressing other operative factors.

A subsidiary postulate of the 'Ultra as main or only cause' school was that the literature prior to Winterbotham was obviously wrong, by its ignorance of Ultra, and thus needed revision at best and discarding at worst. The phrase 'Now Roskill will need to be rewritten' gained currency. But although there can be few worthwhile historical works that cannot bear revision, Roskill (and by implication the underpinning works of Barley and Waters, Hessler and Peyton-Ward) is not quite so needful of rewriting as would seem at first. There are two reasons for this. Firstly, although it cannot reasonably be argued that Ultra is of little significance in the Battle, it is now evident that it is only one of several major factors, whose perceived relative importance is not only difficult to disentangle, but also varies with time. What is perhaps more crucial is that all but one of the core first-generation works were written by authors who had knowledge of Ultra and understood its significance.[48] In one case, Peyton-Ward, the author was actually involved in using Ultra material during the campaign.

Despite the balance that should have returned to the literature after Hinsley, the impetus of the distortion has continued at least as late as 1991, and it would probably be optimistic to consider that it has passed. Thus we can find undue emphasis on Ultra being given by a very experienced historian, even in the face of a directly contradictory passage in Hinsley.[49] Nevertheless, some good work has emerged. As mentioned above, two Canadians have produced interesting work on the RCN (although it is fair to note that Ultra does not sit at the centre of their work). Within the Ultra field, good use has been made of the available material by such as David Syrett.[50]

More encouragingly still, there are also some tentative signs that the corner may have been turned and a more balanced approach is being taken. The best example of this (ironically, the work of a cryptographic historian) is David Kahn's *Seizing the Enigma*, which properly recognizes what should be the self-evident truth: that even Intelligence as good as Ultra is not sufficient to win battles by itself. The demon king may not be dead, but is now at least beginning to look like only one actor - albeit a distinguished one - amongst many. Thus, although a revision of Roskill is a feasible and possibly fruitful project, there are many other tasks in the history of the Battle of the Atlantic that could more usefully be undertaken.

To conclude: an Allied perspective, like a good salad, can be seen to have many ingredients, and the proof of the pudding (to mix culinary metaphors) lies as much in the blend as in the ingredients themselves. So, to pursue the comparison to the end, I hope that diners are not now suffering from indigestion, but rather have enjoyed this appetiser and will shortly be saying, 'Please, sir, can I have some more?'

Appendix 1: Anti-U-boat Warfare Committee - Subjects discussed

The following is a selective list of topics discussed by the committee as indicated by the index to its minutes. It shows the range and significance of matters brought before it, as well as giving a clear indication that the 'warfare' part of the committee's title was well merited. It is divided into three areas (*Important*, *Frequent* and *Other*) but does not include every matter raised. The main part of the chapter should also be consulted for mention of two significant omissions.

1. *Important*
A/S bombs
ASV (see also H2S and ASV)
Atlantic, Battle of - covering the air priorities debate for
    1) allocation of bombers to Coastal Command for ASW
    2) efficacy of bombing Biscay Coast bases
Bay of Biscay
Coastal Command
Convoys
Escort vessels
Fortresses (aircraft)
H2S and ASV
Imports

Leigh Lights
Liberators
Lorient
Merchant ships
North America North Atlantic
RDF (Radar)
Smoke abatement apparatus
Stragglers
U-boat bases
U-boat casualties
VLR aircraft
Weapons

2. *Frequent*
Binoculars
South Africa

3. *Others*
Azores
Banana - Air base (Indian Ocean)
Carl Holm torpedo defence
Helicopters
MAD submarine detection apparatus
Ramming of U-boats

Appendix 2: Battle of the Atlantic History:
A Selected and Classified Booklist

This appendix refers to those books mentioned directly in the last section of this chapter (*Six Years at sea - 50 Years on Paper*). In some cases, these also appear in the bibliography of the whole chapter. The classification adopted is the same as that used above; although broadly chronological, many works cross over the boundaries of time.

1. *Official Histories* (1945-mid 50s)
F. W. Barley and D. Waters - properly *Defeat of the Enemy Attack on Shipping*, 2 volumes, Admiralty, London, 1957
C. B. A. Behrens, *Merchant Shipping and the Demands of War*, HMSO, London, 1955
N. H. Gibbs, J. R. M. Butler, J. M. A. Gwyer, Michael Howard and John Ehrman, *Grand Strategy*, 6 Volumes, London, HMSO, 1956-1972
Hessler - properly *The U-boat War in the Atlantic*, 3 volumes, Admiralty, London, 1950-1977

F. H. Hinsley et al, *British Intelligence in the Second World War*, 3 volumes, HMSO, London, 1981-84

Samuel Eliot Morison, *History of the United States Naval Operations in World War* II, Volumes I and X, Little, Brown and Company, Boston, 1947 and 1956

Captain D. V. Peyton-Ward, RN, *The RAF in the Maritime War*,unpublished.

Jürgen Rohwer, *Axis Submarine Successes 1939-1945*, Cambridge, 1983 (in English)

Captain S. W. Roskill, *The War at Sea*, 3 volumes, HMSO, London, 1954-61

2. *Reminiscence and Secondary Works* (mid 50s-1974)

Lothar-Günther Buchheim, *The Boat (Das Boot)*, London, 1974.

Rear Admiral W. S. Chalmers, *Max Horton and the Western Approaches*, Hodder and Stoughton, London, 1954.

Vice Admiral Sir Peter Gretton, *Convoy Escort Commander*, Cassell, London, 1964.

Captain Donald Macintyre, *U-boat Killer*, Weidenfeld & Nicholson, London, 1956.

Martin Middlebrook, *Convoy*, Allen Lane, London, 1976.

Nicholas Monsarrat, *The Cruel Sea*, Cassell, London, 1952.

Jürgen Rohwer, *The Critical Convoy Battles of March 1943*, Ian Allan, London, 1977.

Terence Robertson, *Walker RN*, Evans Bros., London, 1956.

3. *After Winterbotham* (1974-present)

Marc Milner, *North Atlantic Run*, University of Toronto Press, 1985.

David Syrett, 'The Sinking of HMS *Firedrake* and the Battle for Convoy ON15' in *The American Neptune*, Spring 1991', pp. 105-111.

F. W. Winterbotham, *The Ultra Secret*, Weidenfeld & Nicholson, London, 1974.

David Zimmerman, *The Great Naval Battle of Ottawa*, Toronto, 1989.

4. *Post Ultra* (1991 on?)

David Kahn, *Seizing the Enigma*, Houghton, Mifflin, Boston, 1991.

Notes

1. *Collins Dictionary of the English Language*, 1979; Definition 3b.
2. There is one intriguing parallel, however. Montgomery made use of what were substantially Auchinleck's plans, even going as far as to negotiate the same delay in starting operations as had been responsible for the former's dismissal. Horton continued to use essentially the same organisation and system as his predecessor. Perhaps it all came down to the attitude of prime ministerial

confidence.

3. The most prominent current exponent of this is probably Corelli Barnett. See his 'Engage the Enemy More Closely' in the *Journal of the Royal United Services Institute*, London, Summer 1991, pp. 73-78.

4. Hessler, *The U-boat War in the Atlantic*, I, p. 92.

5. For a fuller explanation of the mid-1941 crisis and the factors operating in its resolution see W. J. R. Gardner, *The Battle of the Atlantic, 1941 - The First Turning Point*, public lecture (unpublished), International Commission for Maritime History and the Society for Nautical Research, King's College, London, 26 November 1992.

6. Milner, *North Atlantic Run*, p. 155. This refers directly to a later period, but is also likely to have been true for 1941.

7. King has an apologist in Robert Love. See his essay on King in *Men of War: Great Naval Leaders of World War II*, edited by Howarth, pp. 89-92.

8. See W. J. R. Gardner (cited as John R Gardner), *ASW Victory - Resources or Intelligence in Les Marines de Guerre Du Dreadnought au Nucléaire*, Paris, 1991, pp. 335-356.

9. *Fuehrer Conferences on Naval Affairs*, 31 May 1943.

10. Beesly's *Very Special Intelligence*, pp. 107-110, notes the attempts made by the British to persuade the Americans to set up an organization similar to the Admiralty's OIC. Although apparently successful in this instance, there is a clear exposition of the difficulties involved.

11. See *Churchill and Roosevelt: The Complete Correspondence*, edited with a commentary by Kimball (3 volumes).

12. It would be difficult to attribute this to selection on the part of the editor: not only is he a distinguished academic, but he also served in the USNR, specializing in Intelligence and retiring with the rank of captain.

13. Kimball, *Churchill and Roosevelt*, II; R-82X.

14. *Ibid.*, R-123/1.

15. *Ibid.*, C-60, para 3.

16. PRO CAB 120/409 PM to Hopkins 6 Feb 42 and 12 Mar 42. This channel of communication appears to be the most effective way of raising the topic, producing relatively rare outpourings from Roosevelt on the subject.

17. Milner's *North Atlantic Run* provides a good account of both, especially the former, but his book is improved on in the sad story of Canada's dilatory acquisition of the necessary technology by David Zimmerman's *The Great Naval Battle of Ottawa*.

18. Milner, *North Atlantic Run*, p129.

19. Minutes of meetings and other memoranda can be found in PRO CAB86/1.

20. The meetings straggled on until May 1942, but there were only two meetings in that year, reflecting either a perception that the problem had departed or, more likely, that it was impotent to deal with the then main difficulty - the American reluctance to introduce convoy.

21. PRO CAB86/1 BA(41) 9th Meeting for the requirement and appropriate periodic meetings for the reporting of imports achieved. For ease of comprehension, monthly figures have been converted into annual ones.

22. The choice was the committee's. It is not clear why this geographical location

was so favoured by their attention.

23. Michael Howard, *Grand Strategy*, Volume IV, p. 23.

24 . There was one gap on 28 April. For full details of the meetings see PRO CAB86/2. The memoranda generated by and submitted to the meetings are chronologically arranged in CAB86/3 and CAB86/4.

25. Succeeding Lord Beaverbrook. As Lord Privy Seal, Cripps chaired meetings of the Committee in Churchill's absence.

26. Horton not only displayed some superficial similarities of style to Churchill, but he even kept similar hours, often gracing his operations room with his presence well into the night.

27. This is not cross-indexing, it is either/or.

28. See Appendix 1.

29 See also p. 514 above.

30. After the first two meetings, the classification of the minutes was raised from 'Secret' to 'Most Secret', the British equivalent of the then American, and later universal 'Top Secret'.

31. Probably the best example of this occurred not in the Atlantic, but in the Battle for the Arctic convoy PQ17 in the summer of 1942. Although Pound almost certainly erred in ordering the dispersal of this convoy in the light of the (now known to be) illusory threat from the battleship *Tirpitz*, his actions indicate the seriousness with which he took his responsibilities.

32. CAB86/2 AU(43) 9th Meeting, 3 March 1943, Item 10.

33. As pointed out above, Ultra was not discussed by this committee, although knowledge of its capabilities and limitations undoubtedly informed the positions of several of the members.

34. CAB86/2 AU(43) 9th 3 March 1943 Item 10.

35. CAB86/2 AU(43) 18th 12 May 43 Item 9.

36. CAB86/3 AU(43) 92 22 Mar 43.

37. CAB86/4 AU(43) 131 of 3 May 1943.

38. Josef W Konwitz, 'Bombs, Cities and Submarines: Allied Bombing of the French Ports, 1942-1943' in *The International History Review*, XIV, 1, February 1992, pp. 23-44, makes the point that the effect of bombing Lorient - possibly successful in itself - was much mitigated by the Allied successes in sinking significant numbers of German submarines at sea in mid-1943, thus reducing the demand for support services.

39. Howard, *Grand Strategy*, IV, p.314.

40. All works referred to in this section of the paper can be found in a classified format (corresponding to the categories mentioned in this section) in Appendix 2.

41. Confusingly, three volumes in *four* parts. Coincidentally, Hinsley follows exactly the same formula, although with him there is the extra complication of further volumes on other intelligence subjects.

42. See the "Ultra period" below for a treatment of those advocating a revision of Roskill.

43. An objection much mitigated by its tabular format, which makes only limited demands on an English reader.

44. The German edition was actually published *after* the revelation of Ultra.

45. Stephen Roskill's correspondence, held at Churchill College, Cambridge, makes it very clear that many historians, especially those who had known about Ultra for many years, were severely critical of Winterbotham not only for revealing what a surprising number of people at all levels had held secret for nearly 30 years, but also because he claimed a much greater role for himself than was justified.

46. Whaley's *Codeword Barbarossa* indicates how widespread the practice was by means of a 'who was reading what' table. Jürgen Rohwer's works have also often stressed the role of German naval codebreakers.

47. The third was in two parts, curiously in the exact pattern of Roskill's *War at Sea*. There were also two other later volumes covering other matters not directly relevant to the Battle of the Atlantic.

48. Hessler obviously had no knowledge of Ultra.

49. See W. J. R. Gardner, *The Battle of the Atlantic, 1941 - the First Turning Point?* (unpublished lecture) 1992.

50. This departs from the earlier exclusion made of articles, theses etc.; but as such sound work is relatively rare, it demands inclusion. Syrett's particular strength is that he makes a distinction between Ultra material which was available during the conduct of an action - and thus which might have influenced the outcome - and material not decrypted in time, which may have aided reconstruction, but was of no tactical value.

30

The Campaign: The German Perspective

by Werner Rahn

Strategic Setting and Operational Concept

At the outbreak of war in September 1939, the German Navy found itself confronted by an enemy which was 10 times stronger and which enjoyed the additional benefit of an excellent strategic position. There were only two pocket-battleships and 26 U-boats ready for immediate operations in the Atlantic. Such weak naval forces could not be expected to decide the course of the war. Faced with this completely hopeless position, the Head of the U-boat Command, Captain (shortly to be Rear Admiral) Karl Dönitz demanded that the construction of U-boats must pushed as hard as possible in order to get 300 boats operational in the Atlantic.[1] However, Hitler did not accede since he still hoped to win Great Britain over. Apart from that, the imminent land campaign against France in the west demanded that armament efforts be concentrated on army and air force equipment.[2]

As in WWI, the starting points for the German conduct of the naval war were on the southern edge of the North Sea. It was not until the occupation of Norway in April 1940 and the fall of France shortly afterwards that the German Navy had the advantage of bases which would enable long range missions by surface and sub-surface units in the Atlantic.

In summer 1940, the C-in-C of the German Navy, Grand Admiral Erich Raeder, and his Naval Staff, the Skl, were convinced that Britain could be defeated without an invasion if Germany were to concentrate all its strength against the British sea approaches. This would destroy the enemy's will to fight and force him into a conciliatory position. But Hitler and the Naval Command moved on different planes of strategic thinking. Hitler expected a short war limited to Europe, and did not want to jeopardize the hope of better relations with Great Britain by a radical war on its economy.[3] The Skl, on the other hand, was convinced from a very early date that the conflict with the Anglo-Saxon opponent would be long and that it would have to be carried out into the Atlantic and won there above all other theatres, though that would undoubtedly bring the US into the war.

From their experience in WWI, the German Naval Command knew that the economic link between Great Britain and the North American continent was the island kingdom's vital artery. They also knew that in a war against the economy of that land so dependent on its sea lanes, Germany would, as ever, have to reckon with the opposition of the US as soon as Britain's existence became seriously threatened. This assessment was confirmed by the 'Short of War' policy followed by President Franklin D. Roosevelt until December 1941.[4]

In 1940-41, all major surface units and U-boats (the numbers of which in fact rose only slowly) were deployed against British sea lanes. However, after the spectacular loss of the battleship *Bismarck* in May 1941, Hitler involved himself in the conduct of the naval war by criticizing the employment hitherto of heavy surface units in the Atlantic. The land war on the eastern front cast its shadow over the sea war. Fearing a large-scale Allied attack against Norway in support of Russia, Hitler ordered all heavy surface units to this area.[5] Thenceforth, the German High Command followed a policy of combining naval and land warfare, but without having a joint strategic concept in which objectives and available potential were agreed under guidelines for the deployment and concentration of the national military effort.[6] From 1941, the U-boats stood alone in the struggle against British convoys which, thanks to Ultra, often escaped them. Air support was only occasionally available and then only from minor formations.

For Dönitz, the war in the Atlantic was always a war against the merchant tonnage of the allies. In his view, the strategic victory in the war at sea lay in winning the race between the sinking and building of ships: if, in the longer term, more ships could be sunk than the enemy could replace, then it would perforce lead to the weakening and final collapse of the British economy and its defences. As Dönitz wrote in his War Diary for 15 April 1942,

> The enemy powers' shipping is one large whole. It is therefore immaterial where any one ship is sunk, for it must ultimately be replaced by new construction. What counts in the long run is the preponderance of sinkings over new construction. Shipbuilding and arms production are centred in the United States, while England is the European outpost and sally port. By attacking the supply traffic - particularly the oil - in the American zone, I am striking at the root of the evil, for here the sinking of each ship is not only a loss to the enemy, but also deals a blow at the source of the his shipbuilding and war production. Without shipping the sally port cannot used for an attack on Europe.[7]

Because the Allies were steadily increasing their shipbuilding capacity, time was of the essence. Germany had to reach a critical volume of sinkings before the enemy's construction of new tonnage became equal to tonnage lost. Since the enemy was forced to replace every ship sunk with a new one, it did not matter to Dönitz where a ship was sunk. What mattered most to him was that they should be sunk where the greatest successes could be achieved for the shortest operations and the least loss of submarines. Coining a phrase for this, he called it 'the economical employment of U-boats'.[8]

From their analyses of WWI, he and his staff knew the U-boat had brought Great Britain then to the verge of defeat. They saw the introduction of convoys in 1917 as the turning-point and the main cause of the U-boats' eventual failure, since individual boats had been unable to score adequate successes against convoys. Dönitz's intention, therefore, was to succeed 'technically and tactically in meeting the concentration of ships in convoys with a concentration of U-boats'.[9] In this way, he could remove the convoy's advantage. The main problems, though, were first to *find* the convoys, and then to concentrate the available boats for attacks. This required efficient reconnaissance support by the Luftwaffe, a sufficient number of U-boats and freedom of communication. However, sea-air co-operation failed in the long run, the number of operational U-boats rose only slowly (from 27 in June 1940 to 53 in July 1941) and free communication always made an individual boat vulnerable.[10]

Dönitz planned the U-boats' deployment on the correlation between the available boats and their real success. The result was 'the effective U-boat quotient', by which U-boat Command meant the average sinking per U-boat per day for all boats at sea. Operating out of French bases from July 1940, U-boat Command was able to increase the number of boats at sea in the main operational area, westward of the British Isles. The monthly sinking rate climbed steadily from July to October, in which month the 'effective U-boat quotient' reached 920 tons. The successful operations against convoys SC7 and HX79 seemed 'to justify the principles on which the U-boat tactics and training have been developed since 1935, i.e. that U-boats in packs should attack the convoys'.[11]

However, due to the limited number of boats and their need for replenishment, U-boat Command could not maintain this attrition rate on British transport capacity. During winter 1940-41, the Atlantic weather made group attacks largely impossible. There were no convoy sightings for many weeks. Because of the Admiralty's successful re-routeing policy, the long search for convoys now began and ended mostly in failure.[12]

Frustrating Search for Convoys in 1941

Although the average number of U-boats in the Atlantic in 1941 increased from 12 in February to 36 in August, the number of ships they sank declined drastically. In July 1941, the sinking of only 17 ships totalling 61,470grt was the U-boats' worst result since May 1940. Noticing this serious discrepancy, staff officers at U-boat Command began to suspect that the U-boat positions must be known to the British, especially since German radio intelligence sometimes found that convoys at risk were suddenly ordered to change course, thereby evading the U-boat lines. The Naval Intelligence Division was asked to investigate, but U-boat Command took no immediate countermeasures.

Late in June 1941, 15 U-boats were on patrol, spread over a large sea area in the centre of the North Atlantic. Since no ship sightings were being reported, Dönitz decided in mid-July to concentrate these boats in a scouting line further to the east. On 17 July a convoy was detected by air reconnaissance, but the boats could not be used against it: the convoy was re-routed away from the outpost patrol after the British had deciphered German radio signals. A few days later, west of Ireland, the Luftwaffe and U-boats achieved effective co-operation for the first time, sinking seven ships totalling 11,303grt from convoy OG69. Dönitz believed this tactical success confirmed his training and operation principles, and considered this kind of attack the best way of inflicting serious damage on the enemy's shipping, since fewer and fewer vessels were sailing independently.[13]

In August, with Luftwaffe support, the U-boats conducted three operations southwest of the British Isles against convoys heading for Gibraltar. However, the convoys were heavily escorted and no major successes were achieved. Other searches carried out by 21 U-boats, deployed in a loose formation south and southwest of Iceland, were also largely unsuccessful. All convoys were able to evade the U-boats. Some members of Dönitz's staff suspected the British had a long-range detection device enabling them to evade the U-boats. He, however, did not consider this suspicion 'very likely', since in the good visibility prevailing at the time, the U-boats would at least have noticed the ships' mastheads, and on 21 August, 'since the formation comprised such a large number of U-boats that they would simply have had to come into some sort of contact with the enemy', he assumed that the adversary had ceased his shipping activities in this area.[14]

In his report to the Naval Staff on 22 August, describing his experiences of the most recent U-boat operations against convoys, Dönitz stated that, in view of the adversary's reinforced defences and air surveillance, it was now 'necessary to employ approximately three times as many U-boats as before in order to achieve any decisive successes in attacking convoys'. Consequently, he demanded a greater concentration of forces. The U-boats were now even less capable of performing secondary tasks 'than at a time when the absolute number of U-boats was in fact smaller, but the prospects of success and the successes themselves were greater'.[15] The Naval Staff no doubt agreed with Dönitz on this fundamental issue, but, given the critical Mediterranean situation, they already expected that U-boats would eventually have to be employed there.[16]

At the beginning of September 1941, the number of operational U-boats had increased to over 70, of which 38 were at sea operating in two groups: one southwest of Ireland and the other between Iceland and Greenland. At that time, deciphered Ultra Intelligence from U-boats' radio traffic was available to the British after, on average, 40-50 hours. From 11 September on, however, British deciphering was further impeded by the fact that the Staff of U-boat Command, ever suspicious and concerned about security, ordered an additional super-encryption for position information. For several weeks thereafter, this presented British radio intelligence with a considerable problem in locating and identifying U-boat positions.[17] Under these circumstances, the Admiralty was unable to re-route every convoy, as was illustrated by the fate of convoy SC42. On 9 September, despite following an evasive course, it was detected east of Greenland and within three days had lost 16 of its 62 ships in the war's largest convoy battle to that date. The fighting continued until 12 September, with 17

U-boats and 15 escorts involved. The escorts sank only two U-boats. This success did not blind Dönitz to the fact the 'the vast majority of the convoys....were sighted more or less accidentally', as he noted in his War Diary on 16 September. In his assessment, the reason for the failure to detect convoys was that the adversary must have learned about the close formation of U-boat groups 'through sources and methods which we have not identified yet'.[18]

Dönitz faced a dilemma, for as SC42 showed, it was exactly this close formation of U-boats which provided the best conditions for launching an intensive attack on a convoy once it had been detected. For the time being, therefore, he retained the close formation and, by taking further security measures, he tried to block the adversary's source of information. Despite these, as we know today, he failed to maintain secure communications.

On 28 September 1941, Dönitz became highly suspicious when two U-boats, which had met at a remote rendezvous arranged via radio message in a bay on the Cape Verde islands, only narrowly escaped a torpedo attack launched by a British submarine, which was itself rammed by a third U-boat involved in the incident. The coincidence was too great: Dönitz did not see 'why a British submarine should just happen to be at such a remote location in the ocean'.[19] Only two possible explanations presented themselves to him: either a compromise of the cryptographic material, or treason. He asked the Naval Staff for immediate clarification and for a general investigation into cryptographic security. In response to the questions on the security of cryptographic material, the Naval Intelligence Division's detailed investigations reached the conclusion on 20 October 1941

> that without contradiction from any of the experts who have been consulted so far for this extensive task, especially those from our own B-net control station and from among the most important experts from the High Command of the Armed Forces, the procedures based on cipher 'M' are considered to be by far the most secure methods known for ensuring the secrecy of military intelligence.[20]

No attempt was made to have cryptographic security investigated by independent scientists who were not part of the military hierarchy. The investigation was conducted by experts who, because of their official duties, had been constantly occupied with their own and the enemy's cipher systems. They were so convinced of the superiority of their own system that they had largely forfeited their objectivity, failing to consider the possibilities of technological development in the field of electronic computers. As a result, they dangerously underestimated the potential which their adversary had concentrated in his deciphering service, both in terms of manpower and material.[21] In order to consolidate cryptographic security, U-Boat Command instituted various countermeasures, including additional super-encryption of position data. Ultimately, the most important reason for British success eluded the Germans.

Although the average number of 36 U-boats at sea did not vary from August to October, the number of ships they succeeded in sinking decreased noticeably in October after having achieved marked success in the previous month. By October, the Admiralty had been able to resolve its difficulties with the new German encryption techniques and in most cases had at its disposal an overview of the situation within 26 hours, providing a nearly optimum means for re-directing convoys as necessary.

By autumn 1941, failing to solve the 'riddle of the convoys' and to achieve higher sinking rates, the U-boat Command had lost the race with time. This was a decisive step towards defeat.[22] One reason for this failure seems to lie 'in the absence of independent thinking' within the small staff of U-boat Command: 'Although Dönitz is credited with encouraging the open expression of opinion within his command, the U-boat professionals who surrounded him were built in his image and shared his convictions'. [23]

In December 1941, Germany's declaration of war against the USA altered the situation in the Atlantic. Before the U-boats were able to exploit it, however, they mounted an operation lasting several days against convoys west of Spain. This made it perfectly clear what awaited the boats when they came across a strong and well-trained defence. The convoys sailing between Gibraltar and Great Britain were not only exposed to the U-boat threat but also endangered by Fw 200 long-range aircraft operating from their bases in western France. In addition to performing their reconnaissance task, these aircraft often used their missions to launch attacks on detected convoys. The British Admiralty endeavoured to provide constant air cover, especially for these convoys. Since catapult ships could only launch one fighter for one sortie, the Admiralty here employed for the first time an escort aircraft carrier - *Audacity*, a converted captured German freighter. Besides being accompanied by this carrier, the 31-ship convoy HG76, which departed Gibraltar on 14 December, was heavily protected by 16 escort vessels. By applying both novel and tried and tested ASW tactics and by skilfully using its few aircraft, the escort managed to fend off most of the U-boat and air attacks. From a total of 11 U-boats which had located the convoy within a week, only seven came close enough to launch an attack, sinking no more than three freighters, one destroyer and the escort carrier. For their own part, the Germans lost five U-boats and four Fw 200s.

Losing *Audacity* no doubt constituted a severe setback for the British in their efforts to establish continuous air cover, but their ASW successes already indicated that in the duel of convoy operations, it was certainly possible to master the U-boat threat.[24] Among the staff of U-boat Command, the lack of success led to the pessimistic assessment that, in view of such losses, operations against convoys would have to cease. Dönitz, however, remained confident and believed that the reasons for the defeat by HG76 lay in the weather conditions, which had favoured defensive operations, and in the enemy's consolidated protection measures, in particular the employment of the escort aircraft carrier. Because of this interpretation, and because over the following months the new

Atlantic situation enabled the U-boats to a large extent to operate independently, U-boat Command derived few initial lessons from the failed operation against HG76. It remained to be seen whether and to what extent the Allied anti-submarine defences would use their success with HG76 for their own tactical training.

Long-Range Operations
in the Eastern and Southern Atlantic, 1942

Although the German Naval Staff had anticipated the United States' eventual entry into the war, they had not expected it as early as December 1941 and were caught by surprise, unprepared for a fast push by naval forces - especially U-boats - as far as the coastal waters of North America. The fight against Allied merchant tonnage in the Mediterranean and off Gibraltar during the autumn had resulted in heavy U-boat losses with only small successes. Now, the extension of operations to the whole Atlantic gave Dönitz the opportunity to concentrate his forces in areas where, in fulfilment of 'the economical employment of U-boats', a significant rise in sinkings could be expected.

This applied initially to the sea lanes along the eastern seaboard of America, which (considering the long approach of over 3,000 nautical miles) promised to be a rewarding area of operations as long as the shipping there was uncontrolled and largely unprotected, and as long as the US Navy had but little experience of anti-submarine warfare.

Dönitz's aim was to take advantage of the favourable conditions as quickly as possible. Consequently, on 9 December he applied to the Skl for the immediate deployment of 12 large Type IX B and C boats. With their great sea endurance (13,000 nm at 10 knots) and their large stock of torpedoes, they seemed particularly suited for this task. Dönitz meant to 'roll the drums', as he said in his War Diary. The Skl, however, still mindful of the critical situation in the Mediterranean, released only six U-boats for missions off the American east coast, a decision which Dönitz regretted.[25] The Skl, mindful of both the great distances and of the small number of available boats, at first saw the greatest chances of success in a 'free hunt' for single ships. As to the probable enemy reactions, they expected a swift introduction of convoys, 'so that the controlled attack on convoys will soon be the rule. Our U-boats will be gradually forced away from the American coast, out into the open Atlantic.'[26] This proved to be an overestimation of the enemy's potential and his capabilities.

Between 7 and 9 January 1942, seven medium-size Type VII U-boats arrived at the Newfoundland Bank. On 11 January, the first five of the larger Type IX boats reached the American east coast. Within a fortnight, they had sunk 15 ships totalling 97,242grt. More boats were to follow, so that between six and eight boats were operating there at any given time. Furthermore, they were reinforced by 8-10 medium-size boats of more limited cruising range.

Because replenishment at sea was not yet available, these boats could not reach beyond the Canadian seaboard off Halifax and south of Nova Scotia. By

February 1942, another group of five large boats was available; this meant that long-range operations were extended to the Caribbean. The successes of German and Italian submarines in the Atlantic alone rose from 295,776grt in January to 500,788grt in March 1942.[27] These figures underlined again the principle of 'economic use of U-boats', particularly since the losses in these areas of operations had remained extremely low.

Even after two-and-a-half months, U-boats continued to score impressive successes off the US east coast, and no vigorous countermeasures could be seen which might have reduced their prospects of success. Bearing in mind that the USN had been involved in escorting convoys since September 1941, it seems to modern eyes especially remarkable that this weakness in their own coastal waters should have prevailed for so long.

Several months passed before they were able to protect their own sea lanes. Dönitz was proud to state in his War Diary on 13 March 1942 that the enemy defences were thin, badly organized and untrained. There was no tight organization of sea traffic, nor any promptly reacting leadership. Dönitz expected convoys to be formed eventually; for the time being, however, he reckoned with no effective protection of Allied shipping in American waters. For that, the sea lanes seemed too numerous, and the chronic shortage of escort vessels was known to be still prevailing.[28] Dönitz's hopes revolved around the new U-tankers which were expected to become operational in spring 1942. They would greatly extend U-boat endurance in distant waters.[29]

After trials and training in the Baltic, the first U-tanker, U-459, reached its area of operations about 500 nm to the northeast of the Bermudas on 23 April 1942. By 5 May, it had replenished 15 boats, most of them medium-size Type VII C. For these boats, replenishment at sea was an essential prerequisite for any efficient operations on the American seaboard. Just a few figures will illustrate this: in spring 1942, boats of this type operating off Halifax could remain at sea for an average 41 days. However, boats of the very same type supplied by U-tankers achieved an average sea endurance of 62 days, and of up to 81 days if resupplied twice.[30]

From mid-June 1942, two to three U-tankers were constantly deployed in the Atlantic. They were stationed in zones of little traffic, beyond Allied air surveillance. This opened up entirely new operational perspectives for U-boat Command, both in the hitherto untouched busy waters of the Caribbean and the Gulf of Mexico, and in the North Atlantic, where a resumption of convoy battles was envisaged.

Dönitz decided to launch U-boat attacks into even more distant areas, hoping to tie down enemy defence forces as well as expecting substantial sinking figures. So, in mid-July 1942, four to six boats supported by a U-tanker began operating in the central Atlantic, off Freetown.

In summer 1942, the Skl decided to exert strategic pressure on the Allies supplies to the Middle East and on their links with India. The plan provided for a group of U-boats to arrive off South Africa without prior warning. This southward move was to be concealed for as long as possible, so as to leave the enemy with the least possible time for effective counter-measures. Beginning on 19 August, the four large Type IX U-boats and their tanker U-459 left their bases in western France.[31]

It was one of these boats, U-156, which, on the evening of 12 September, torpedoed the British troopship *Laconia* with more than 2,800 passengers and crew on board, including 1,800 Italian Prisoners of War. U-156 at once started rescue operations and broadcast a signal in clear English asking for assistance. Dönitz ordered all U-boats in the vicinity to support U-156 in its rescue operation.[32] The narrative in his memoirs, however, is not quite correct. The documents, especially the relevant War Diaries, prove that his main aim, as well as Hitler's and that of the Skl was to let the planned operation off South Africa run its scheduled course.[33]

The Admiralty had realized on 21 September that a southward movement of U-boats appeared imminent. Some defence arrangements had been organized but failed to have an effect. From 7 October, the boats, operating independently, succeeded in sinking 15 ships aggregating 108,070grt within six days. By the end of the month, the score had risen to 156,235grt or some 28% of all U-boat successes in October.[34]

Re-Starting Convoy Operations, Summer 1942

Since early 1942, attacks against convoys had been limited to snatched opportunities, usually while the U-boats were in transit across the Atlantic. This changed in July 1942, following the introduction of the convoy system in American coastal waters. Now U-boat Command was forced to shift the main field of activity back to the North Atlantic convoy routes.

Dönitz aimed to bring his U-boats into action against convoys for several consecutive days outside the range of enemy air cover. This necessitated the earliest possible detection of convoys, on one side or the other of the ocean. On any given day the boats could cover 320-370 nautical miles, whereas the convoys could only manage a maximum of 240. Dönitz used this advantage to conduct mobile operations. In ideal circumstances, a convoy, once detected, was repeatedly attacked by the same U-boat group, an operation which could last several days, depending on the weather and defence conditions. In order to be able to conduct operations over several days against convoys outside the adversary's air cover, Dönitz considered it important to detect the convoys as early as possible, at the outset of their passage, whether in the east or west Atlantic. U-boats sailing from the Reich or from western France initially attacked convoys heading from Great Britain to the Newfoundland Grand Banks area. Afterwards, they were re-supplied by U-tankers south of the North Atlantic routes, before attacking an eastbound convoy in a second operation. U-tankers had the great advantage of enabling a considerably higher number of U-boats to be available in the actual operating area, for without re-supply at sea the boats would have had to return to a base after their first operation simply to refuel.

During some convoy operations against convoys, the U-tankers followed the convoy at a distance of only 50-100 nm, so as to refuel the U-boats immediately after their attack. Until the end of 1942, Allied air power in the North Atlantic could only provide close cover for convoys known to be at risk. At selected rendezvous points, the Germans were therefore usually able to conduct their supply operations undisturbed and without any problems.

However, these prolonged operations, alternating between combat and replenishment, stretched the crews to their limits. Recognizing this, Dönitz also understood that even if a U-boat was still carrying torpedoes, the procedure could not be repeated indefinitely: 'It will only be possible to conduct two, at the most three convoy operations without the crews and the U-boats experiencing detrimental fatigue symptoms.'[35]

Success and Failure of Allied Intelligence

U-boats operating in remote areas mostly sank single ships. Accordingly, operational control consisted mostly of deploying available forces to the most promising areas, but it also involved the organization of relief and of replenishment at sea. The boats reported accomplished supply operations, sinkings and the general traffic situation only when ordered by BdU or when there was a favourable opportunity to do so. After 1 February 1942 British radio intelligence was badly affected by 'black out' in deciphering U-boat Command's Atlantic communications. The Admiralty's Operational Intelligence Centre was reduced to relying on conventional sources, such as radio direction-finding traffic analysis, aerial photography and so on. As a consequence, its situation reports were not nearly as complete and as accurate as in previous months. However, the continuous reading of the German Home Waters Enigma settings in 1942 provided regular information about the commissioning of U-boats and their number at sea at any one time. Thus, by March 1941, the Admiralty knew that the German Navy was developing supply U-boats, but it remained uncertain as to when this type would become operational. Nevertheless, the actual deployment of U-tankers was kept hidden for a long time. Although there had been factors hinting that U-boats were being replenished at sea as early as June 1942, it was only in August that PoW interrogation definitely confirmed the existence of U-tankers.[36] In this context, Hinsley mentions 'activities of an enemy refuelling network in central America based on British Honduras'.[37] It must be stressed that no German documents confirm this. Not a single U-boat is known to have refuelled from small surface vessels in the Western Hemisphere.

The Defeat of the U-boats in 1943

In autumn 1942, the U-boats in the North Atlantic had achieved a numerical strength which enabled them to form several overlapping scouting lines in order to detect and engage the convoys. At the beginning of January 1943, Dönitz had at his disposal 212 operational U-boats, of which 164 were assigned to the North Atlantic alone. Of these Atlantic boats, more than 90 were at sea on any given day, and out of these, 40 were employed in the actual operating area. A further increase was foreseeable. In view of these figures, which were largely known to the British, too, the operational advantage gained from Ultra Intelligence gradually diminished, since the convoys now had less chance to evade U-boat formations.[38]

The North Atlantic winter of 1942-43 brought with it unusually frequent storms. From 1 October 1942 to 18 February 1943, 106 days with a wind force of 7 or more were registered, as well as 10 days with a wind force of 10 or more. The average figures for the same period during the first three winters of the war were 76 and 3.7 respectively.[39] Such harsh weather conditions had a considerable impact on the conduct of the war at sea: since it was more difficult to keep the convoys together, the number of stragglers, which were always easy prey for the U-boats, increased. Since the escort vessels often had to go without replenishment at sea, they were for the most part forced to confine themselves to sailing at an economic rate of speed, which considerably impaired the duration and intensity of their ASW operations. Air cover had to be restricted, and in duels between escort vessels and U-boats, both parties came off badly. The escort vessels' sonar and radar range fell substantially because of the sea returns; but this applied equally to the U-boats' sound detectors, and, what is more, often enough the U-boats could not use their torpedoes. Yet despite extensive search movements, the U-boats hit only a few convoys in January, out of which they only managed to sink a total of 15 ships. Other U-boat successes were achieved against ships sailing independently.[40]

The Admiralty's redirection of convoys on the basis of Ultra Intelligence was sufficient for Dönitz to decide that the lack of sighting reports could no longer be attributed to the continuing bad weather alone. Instead, he presumed the adversary was conducting deliberate countermeasures based on actual knowledge of U-boat positions. Some of the British situation reports on North Atlantic U-boats (which were deciphered regularly by the German crypto-analysis service [B-Dienst] as they were radioed to British naval commanders) were almost identical to the German view of the situation. Since these could not be ascribed to the results of the adversary's air reconnaissance and radio direction finding alone, there were renewed doubts about the security of the Naval Staff's own cryptographic material.[41]

However, allied anti-submarine capabilities grew stronger month by month, both in the numbers of naval and naval air units, in weapon technology, and in tactical and operational command and control. After the last great U-boat successes of March 1943, the material and technical superiority of the Allies began to have an ever greater effect.

Failure of a Naval Weapon

In spring 1943, Dönitz and many officers in the Naval Command still believed that the only way of forcing a strategic decision in the Atlantic was to deploy more boats of the improved Type VII C, despite the fact that in summer 1942

Allied ASW had shown three alarming developments, which even Dönitz himself noticed and assessed realistically.

First of these was the fact that enemy reconnaissance aircraft and escort vessels had been fitted with precision radar equipment, resulting in frequent surprise attacks on surfaced U-boats at night and during bad visibility. In these attacks the boats were often damaged or sunk - increasingly so in the Bay of Biscay, where the British finally gained such air superiority that the passage of the boats through this area soon became the most dangerous phase of any operation.[42]

The second and no less important Allied development was that long-range air reconnaissance in the Atlantic became more and more intensive. On 3 September 1942, with deepest concern, Dönitz predicted that the day was coming when in almost all areas of the North Atlantic - the U-boats' principal battle-ground - the situation in the air would be just as bad around the convoys. This would reduce the chances of success of the U-boats to an unacceptable degree unless adequate countermeasures were taken.[43]

The third development was the Allies' own increasing experience coupled with better ASW weaponry. Once a submerged U-boat had been discovered by an experienced ASW group with asdic, its slow submerged speed did not allow drastic evasion manoeuvres. After being fixed and suffering from ever-improving ASW weapon effectiveness, there was then little chance of escape .

There were therefore clear alarms that, in the face of the enormous increase in the capabilities of U-boat detection and destruction systems, the established concept of the U-boat as a weapon system was no longer capable of promising success. The U-boat in service until then had, in fact, been only a submersible - a mobile torpedo boat with a long seagoing endurance and the ability to vanish from the surface for relatively short periods of time. Underwater, the boat was then very slow, but with fully charged batteries and at lowest creeping speed, it could remain submerged for nearly 50 hours. The exploitation of Ultra information, the growing surveillance of the Atlantic, the powerful submarine hunting groups and last but not least, offensive airborne anti-submarine operations, soon showed altogether that the previous concept of U-boat operations was doomed to failure. As a result of the the Allies' manifold defensive measures, U-boat losses reached in May 1943 such a height - 41 were sunk in that month alone - that Dönitz was forced to discontinue the North Atlantic convoy attacks, and to take his remaining boats southward to operational areas where there was less air reconnaissance. The heavy losses were out of all proportion to the successes.

Even by the end of 1942, the North Atlantic situation demanded that U-boats should be transformed from submersibles to real submarines. By then, if they were to reach their operational areas safely and without detection, they had to be able to cruise underwater continually. At the same time, however, they also had to regain their tactical superiority while fighting convoys, which would only be possible by giving them a significantly higher underwater speed. The new concept required either a completely new propulsion system which was independent of outside air or, if the conventional propulsion was to be retained, the supply of air for the Diesel engine via a snorkel. Either way, it involved a major re-orientation process.

But early in spring 1943 the German Naval Command had not yet recognized the need to effect this radical development. What Dönitz saw was first of all the tactical weakness of the former U-boat concept which resulted from the low underwater speed and the insufficient air defence capability. He therefore wanted to give the boats better attack and evasion capabilities through higher underwater speed, and better air-defence capabilities by equipping them with new sensors and weapons.

Summary

1.   The deployment of U-boats against the Allied sea lines of communication all over the whole Atlantic was the key element of German naval strategy in WWII. It was an offensive maritime strategy which, in giving up the struggle for sea control, sought to win victory solely by denying the sea to the superior Anglo-Saxon sea powers in the attrition and elimination of their transport capacity. It was a concept based solely on the performance of one weapon system which, for nearly three years, was able to avoid enemy surveillance and defences.

2.   In 1941, the U-boats' search for convoys ended mostly in failure because of the Admiralty's successful re-routeing policy. Although the average number of boats operating in the Atlantic increased from 12 in February to 38 in September, the number of ships they succeeded in sinking fell drastically. In December 1941, the German Navy had lost the race of time against an enemy whose war effort was being increasingly supported by the inexhaustible resources of the US.

3.   From December 1941, U-boat Command was able to extend long-range operations to the whole Atlantic and adjacent waters such as the Caribbean Sea and the western part of Indian Ocean. In supporting these distant operations, from April 1942 to December 1943 U-tankers and large Type XB U-boats replenished more than 480 U-boats, increasing their sea endurance by 20-30 days. The lack of Allied air surveillance anywhere outside the convoy routes facilitated the 1942 supply operations. However, by March-April 1943, the Allies had naval and naval air forces sufficient not only to protect the convoys directly, but also to operate offensively against known U-boat concentrations, such as replenishment groups.

4.   Since it was still possible to achieve considerable success with the proven U-boat types in spring 1943 and since the losses seemed still tolerable, the German Naval Command was determined to employ the existing capacities to

the full. The superior detection and weapons capability of the enemy, however, led to such high losses that in May 1943, U-boat warfare in the North Atlantic had to be broken off. If the U-boat weapon system was to have a chance of success and survival, it had to be adapted to the new combat conditions.

Secondary Sources

This chapter is mainly based on my earlier research:

1. *Long-range German U-boat Operations in 1942 and their Logistical Support by U-Tankers*, paper presented at Eighth Naval History Symposium, Annapolis, September 1987 (copyright USNI), published in German with the title *Weiträumige deutsche U-Boot-Operationen 1942/43 und ihre logistische Unterstützung durch U-Tanker*, in *Die operative Idee und ihre Grundlagen. Ausgewählte Operationen des Zweiten Weltkrieges* ed. by Militärgeschichtliches Forschungsamt, Herford, Bonn 1989, pp. 79-97.
2. *Der Seekrieg im Atlantik und Nordmeer* in: Horst Boog, Werner Rahn, Reinhard Stumpf, Bernd Wegner, *Der globale Krieg: Die Ausweitung zum Weltkrieg und der Wechsel der Initiative 1941-1943*, Stuttgart 1990, [= Das Deutsche Reich und der Zweite Weltkrieg, vol. 6] pp. 273-425.

Notes

1. Salewski, Michael, *Die deutsche Seekriegsleitung 1935-1945*, vol 1, (Frankfurt/M. 1970), pp. 128-129, and Memorandum by FO U-boat Command, 1 September 1939, *Fuehrer Conferences on Naval Affairs 1939-1945*, pp. 36-37. Apart from English language sources listed in the bibliography, note the following basic sources and literature necessary for any research into the U-boat campaign in WWII: *Lagevorträge des Oberbefehlshabers der Kriegsmarine vor Hitler 1939-1945*, ed. Gerhard Wagner, (Munich 1972); *Kriegstagebuch der Seekriegsleitung 1939-1945*, Teil A, vol. 1 (August/September 1939) - vol. 45 (Mai 1943), ed. Werner Rahn and Gerhard Schreiber with the assistance of Hansjoseph Maierhoffer, (Bonn, Herford 1988-94, and continuing).
2. See conference of Hitler with all C-in-Cs of German armed forces, 23 November 1939, *Lagevorträge*, pp. 49-55. The document is not published in *Fuehrer Conferences*. Cf. Hillgruber, Andreas, *Hitlers Strategie. Politik und Kriegführung 1940-1941*, 2nd. ed. (Munich 1982), p. 28 note 3 and p. 47 note 87.
3. Hillgruber, *Hitlers Strategie*, pp. 45-48.
4. See Rahn, Werner 'Der Seekrieg im Atlantik und Nordmeer', chapter 1, *Der globale Krieg, op.cit.*, pp. 275-297.
5. *Lagevorträge*, pp. 334-337; cf. *Fuehrer Conferences*, pp. 246-249.
6. Terraine, *The U-boat Wars*, pp. 359-362.
7. Dönitz, *Memoirs*, pp. 228-230; Hessler *The U-boat War in the Atlantic*, II, p.15-17.

8. Cf. Dönitz, *Memoirs*, pp. 196-197.
9. Rear Admiral Godt, *The War at Sea*, unpublished essay, November 1945 IN.ID. 1/GP/17, 3rd November 1945], p. 6.
10. Terraine, *The U-boat Wars*, p. 270.
11. War Diary U-boat Command, 20 October 1940, cited in Hessler *The U-boat War in the Atlantic*, I, p.52.
12. For details see Graham Rhys-Jones, 'The Riddle of the Convoys. Admiral Dönitz and the U-boat Campaign 1941', [unpublished paper] Newport, R.I., April 1992.
13. War Diary U-boat Command, 30 July 1941, BA-MA RM 87/18, pp. 19-20. Cf. Rhys-Jones, 'Riddle', pp. 33-36.
14. War Diary U-boat Command, 21 August 1941, BA-MA RM 87/18, p. 37.
15. Memo U-boat Command No. 2235, 22 Aug 1941, BA-MA RM 7/845, pp.149-50.
16. *Kriegstagebuch der Seekriegsleitung 1939-1945*, part A, Vol. 24 (Aug 1941), p. 306.
17. Hinsley, *British Intelligence in the Second World War*, p.173.
18. War Diary U-boat Command, 16 September 1941, BA-MA RM 87/18 pp. 53-54. Cf. Rhys-Jones, 'Riddle', pp. 42-46.
19. War Diary U-boat Command, 28 September 1941, *ibid.* p. 59.
20. Memo Naval Staff, Head of Naval Intelligence Division [Skl/Chef MND], 20 October 1941: 'Prüfung der operativen Geheimhaltung', BA-MA RM 7/845, pp. 187-202, quotation: p. 200.
21. Cf. Kahn, *Seizing the Enigma*, pp. 203-211.
22. Terraine, *U-boat Wars*, p. 401.
23. Rhys-Jones, 'Riddle of the Convoys', p. 64.
24. Hessler, *The U-boat War in the Atlantic*, I, pp.90-91; see also Macintyre *The Naval War Against Hitler*, p. 110 and A.J. Levine, 'Was World War II A Near-Run Thing?', *The Journal of Strategic Studies*, Vol. 8 (1985), No. 1, p. 48.
25. War Diary U-boat Command, 9 and 10 December 1941, BA-MA RM 87/19, pp. 95-100 (i.e. PG 30.301/a). Cf. Dönitz, *Memoirs*, pp. 197-198 and Salewski, *Seekriegsleitung*, vol. 1, p. 508-509.
26. Naval Staff Memo No. I Op 2190/41 12 Dec 1941: U-boots-einsatz im Atlantik, in 1. Skl KTB Part C IV, BA-MA RM 7/845, pp. 279-281, (i.e. Case GE 227/PG. 32.173).
27. Figures according to Rohwer, *Axis Submarine Successes 1939-1945*.
28. War Diary U-boat Command, 13 March 1942: Lage amerikanischer Raum, BA-MA RM 87/20, pp. 197-198 (i.e. PG 30.305a). See also Morison, *History of U.S. Naval Operations in World War II*, Vol. 1, *The Battle of the Atlantic, September 1939-May 1943*, *passim*, and T. J. Belke, 'Roll of Drums', US Naval Institute Proceedings April 1983, pp. 58-64.
29. The Type XIV U-tankers (1,688ts deplacement) carried, besides 203ts for their own needs, 439 ts of Diesel fuel as well as about 50ts of other supplies (provisions, water, engine oil, spares, etc.).
30. According to war journals of U-boats engaged off Halifax. Cf. Rössler, Eberhard, *The U-boat*, pp. 166-167.
31. See War Diary U-boat Command, 11 August 1942 with a long Skl comment, BA-MA RM 87/22, pp. 134-136 (i.e. PG. 30.310a). Cf. J. Rohwer, The U-boat War Against the Allied Supply Lines, *Decisive Battles*, pp. 275-276 and Dönitz, *Memoirs*, pp. 256-263.

32. In his Memoirs [p. 256] Dönitz says that he insisted on his decision to interrupt the South African mission in favour of the rescue operations.

33. For example see U-tanker *U-459*: *U-459* was 200 nm to the South when *Laconia* was sunk. It turned around and ran northwards for about 13 hours, thus coming within 70 nm of *U-156* before it received Dönitz's order to continue its voyage to the South. See KTB *U-459*, 12-14 September 1942, PG.30.512/4, p.7, for policy of Dönitz, the Naval Staff and Hitler see War Diary U-boat Command, 13 September 1942, BA-MA RM 87/23 and *Kriegstagebuch der Seekriegsleitung 1939-1945*, part A, Vol. 37, pp. 275-276 (13 September 1942).

34. Figures according to Rohwer, *Axis Submarine Successes*. Cf. Roskill, *The War at Sea 1939-1945*, II, p.269 and Beesly, *Very Special Intelligenc*, p.150, cf. also the German edition: *Very Special Intelligence. Geheimdienstkrieg der britischen Admiralität 1939-45*, (Berlin, Frankfurt 1978), pp. 181-182.

35. War Diary U-boat Command, 2 October 1942, BA-MA RM 87/23, pp. 120-122 (i.e. PG. 30.312a), cf. Dönitz, *Memoirs*, pp. 243-244.

36. See Beesly, *Very Special Intelligence*, pp. 144-145 and Hinsley, *British Intelligence*, II, pp. 230 and 683.

37. Hinsley, *British Intelligence*, II, p. 229.

38. *Ibid.*, p. 563.

39. Memorandum of First Sea Lord, 30 March 1943, A.U. (43) 103, PRO, CAB 86/4.

40. Hinsley, *British Intelligence*, Vol. 2, p. 679.

41. War Diary U-boat Command, 12 and 13 January 1943, BA-MA RM 87/25, U-boat War, Vol. 2, p. 88 and Hinsley, *British Intelligence*, II, p. 557.

42. Cf. Roskill, *The War at Sea 1939-1945*, II and III, *passim*.; Hinsley, *British Intelligence*, II, pp. 163-179 and pp. 525-572; Costello and Hughes, *The Battle of the Atlantic*. Cf. also Hezlet, *The Submarine and Sea Power*.

43. U-boat Command, Memo No. 3642-Al to OKM/Skl, 3 September 1942, BA-MA RM 7/2869 (i.e. PG 33349).

31

The Soviet View

by N. V. Naumov

On 24 November 1942, Churchill wrote to Stalin: 'You who have so much land may find it hard to realize that we can only live and fight in proportion to our sea communications.'[1] This was his reaction to Stalin's urgent demands for an increase in the delivery of armament, military technical equipment and strategic materials to the Soviet Union.[2] These deliveries, based on the Anglo-Soviet agreement of 16 August 1941, had been considerably reduced in summer and autumn 1942, especially after the disaster of Convoy PQ17. Soviet historians give varying reasons for this reduction. Some consider it as a result of 'the fact that in 1942, Anglo-American [ocean] communications were destroyed'.[3] The letter cited above was one of the numerous references made by Churchill about the importance to Britain of transatlantic communications, and their vulnerability. Since 21 July 1941 he had kept Stalin constantly informed about the situation and the course of the Atlantic naval operations.[4] In his own letters to Stalin, President Roosevelt also raised the matter.[5]

But Stalin - the Soviet Supreme Commander and the Head of the Soviet Government - scarcely mentioned the Battle of the Atlantic in any of his letters to the western leaders, and never in any of his public statements and published orders to the Red Army. It is almost as if he did not know, or did not want to know, that convoys with consignments for the Soviet Union went from the US across the Atlantic 'suffering attacks of the German submarine and Focke-Wulf'.[6] Even during the most bitter days and months of 1941-42, when, to retain its military might, the Soviet Union needed the Allies' support more urgently than it ever had done or would do again, Stalin showed little interest in Atlantic events, as though nothing deserving his attention ever happened there. If he seems to have missed this Battle, it is unnecessary to explain why Soviet politicians, journalists and historians did not notice it either. Because of this, Soviet representatives did not raise the subject of the Battle of the Atlantic either during the Moscow conference of the Ministers for Foreign Affairs of the USA, Soviet Union and Great Britain (19-30 October 1943), or during the Teheran conference (28 November-1 December 1943), or during the Yalta conference (4-12 February 1945).[7] Soviet official documents concerning relations with Britain and America during WWII contain not the slightest hint of the Battle.[8] It was only through brief and occasional reports in their newspapers, about the sinking of U-boats by the Allied navies, or the sinking of Allied Atlantic convoys by U-boats, that Soviet readers gained a glimpse of what was happening in the Atlantic.[9]

Stalin's estimation of the Battle cannot be separated from his global vision, his conception of WWII. The complete conception cannot be found in any of his works, but the analysis of his statements made during the war and published in the book *About the Great Patriotic War of the Soviet Union* (five editions, 1942-52) enable us to outline some basic elements of his conception.

First of all we have to say that after 22 June 1941, when Hitler invaded the Soviet Union, Stalin hardly ever used the term 'the World War' - although before then, he mentioned many times that WWII began on 1 September 1939. Following the German invasion, however, there was for him no other war in the world but the Great Patriotic War of the Soviet Union, supported by the Allied countries.[10] The military operations in Northern Africa, on the Mediterranean Sea and later in Sicily and southern Italy were the only Allied operations he spoke of.[11] Although he gave these operations quite a high appraisal in his public speeches, he considered them as auxiliary, incomparable to the scale of battles on the Soviet-German front. That, in his opinion, was the sole front on which Germany fought until June 1944. It was only after the landing in Northern France in June 1944 that 'the Allied troops carried on some offensive and forced Germany to fight on two fronts'.[12] But the Second Front was opened when decisive victories of the Red Army had already determined the war's outcome. By then, Germany's military forces had been basically defeated on the Soviet-German front. The defeat of the German Army in the battle of Moscow marked the beginning of the radical turn in the course of WWII, the battles of Stalingrad and Kursk consolidated this success, and the Soviet offensive operations that took place at the end of 1943 to 1944 completed the turn.[13] In his order of 1 May 1944, Stalin stressed that the success of the Red Army had been aided by 'our great Allies - the USA and Great Britain, who were holding firm against Germany in Italy, who were drawing away from us a considerable part of German forces, supplying us with valuable strategic materials and armaments, systematically bombing German military objects and so undermining German military power'.[14] At the same time, he advanced the thesis of 'the economic victory of the Soviet people in the Great Patriotic War',[15] which had allowed the Soviet industry to supply the Red Army with necessary amount of armament and military technical equipment.

Soviet propagandists correctly understood the double standard Stalin typically used in his evaluation of political and military events. Thus, his appreciation of the Allies' role in the defeat of Germany did not prevent them from asserting that 'the main crushing blows against the German Army had been struck and the backbone of the fascist beast had been broken on the battle-fields of the eastern front', or that 'without the Soviet Union the victory over German would never be possible'.[16]

As for the Battle of the Atlantic, the silence surrounding it during the war was broken in May 1945. In the fifth issue of the journal *The Naval Annals* (with Stalin's portrait in a Marshal's uniform on the cover), Rear Admiral Professor A. V. Tomashevich described the U-boats' Atlantic operations of 1939-1945, and British and American countermeasures. Although the author used the term 'the Battle of the Atlantic' in quotation marks, he stressed that during WWII 'the fight between the most powerful submarine force and the most powerful anti-submarine defence in the ocean took place in the Atlantic'.[17] This evaluation was the first of its kind in Soviet historiography. Eighteen months later, an article by 1st Captain N. N. Starov was published in the same journal. Starov gave a full description of the course of the Atlantic naval operations during 1939-45, describing the strength of U-boats operating in the Atlantic and their losses, together with the numbers of British and American warships participating in the anti-submarine struggle, as well as information about annual and total losses of Allied Atlantic convoys and measures taken by the Allies to reduce these losses. He also cited data about the volume of cargo transported by Allies during the 68 months of the war, and other facts which allowed readers to estimate the real scale of Atlantic operations.[18]

These in *The Naval Annals* were the first - and, for a decade, the last - attempts by Soviet military specialists to evaluate the place and importance of WWII Atlantic operations. For 10 years, until 1956, silence followed, and Soviet historians made no mention whatsoever of the Battle of the Atlantic in any historical journal, military journal, or historical textbook.

After Khrushchev's sensational revelations of Stalin's crimes at the 20th Communist Party Congress, Soviet historians began to examine subjects which under Stalin's rule had been taboo. They began to re-evaluate the history of WWII, and - among the various social, political and ideological factors that shaped the development of Soviet war history in the post-Stalin period - I would like to point out one circumstance which I believe has yet to be fully appreciated by either Soviet or western historians.

In the period 1956-65, over 100 works by American, British, German and French historians of WWII were published in the USSR.[19] This in itself was a radical departure from established practice. The discipline of history had long been ideologically monopolized and held under strict, absolute Party control. Never before had the Soviet government allowed such a powerful 'alien incursion' into any area of history, especially in the history of the war. Its official treatment had been one of the chief elements of the indoctrination of the Soviet people with the spirit of 'socialist patriotism'. This, then, was the first opportunity for Soviet readers to become acquainted with points of view that diverged radically from the official line. These books afforded Soviet readers with a relatively full view of events which, while they might have been known of, either were simply not spoken about (such as the Allied Lend-Lease effort), or about which precious little was known (such as the Battle of the Atlantic).

One of the first of these books was Samuel Eliot Morison's *The Atlantic Battle*, which came out in Russia in 1956. The Russian translation of his subsequent book *The Atlantic Battle Won* appeared three years later.[20] Both of these editions came complete with forewords and detailed notes by Soviet military historians (1st Captain E. N. Lebedev for the first book and 1st Captain L. M. Eremeev for the second). In addition, Eremeev published a critical essay of Morison's work in a collection of articles entitled *Against the Falsification of the History of the Second World War*.[21]

While conceding the worthiness of Morison's first book ('the author has collected a great deal of data, and has fully covered the American and British fleets' defence of the Atlantic seaways from German and Italian submarines'), Lebedev warned the reader to 'consider the huge methodological shortcoming common to all bourgeois historians' research on the war: a one-sided selection and analysis of the facts, leading to a falsification of the history of the Second World War'.[22] The Soviet commentaries on Morison's work accused him of the following weaknesses. To begin with, he conducted his account of the Battle of the Atlantic in isolation from the rest of the war - in particular, he ignored the situation on the Soviet-German front and exaggerated the significance of the Battle of the Atlantic to the outcome of the war. Likewise, he exaggerated the role of Allied military supplies to the Soviet Union 'in the victories of the Red Army over Hitler's Germany'.[23] According to Eremeev, all Anglo-American deliveries to the USSR during the whole was amounted to less than half of that which Britain had received through Lend-Lease in 1941-42, and, of the 75,000 transport ships which crossed the Atlantic, only 1,440 (c. 2%) went to Soviet ports.[24] E. N. Lebedev estimated the weight of all Allied supplies to the USSR to have been 4% of all Soviet military production during the war years. For Lebedev, the Battle of the Atlantic exercised 'some influence on the course of the war', but it was a 'secondary theatre of operations'; in his view, 'the fate of Europe and the world was decided on the continent'. Moreover, 'if we consider the economic and industrial resources which England and the USA expended in waging the Battle of the Atlantic, we see that this campaign was not of primary importance of the struggle against Germany and her satellites, indeed its diversion of colossal amount of resources actually weakened the Allies' strength'. The USA and Britain were only able to distract themselves so fully on the Battle because of 'the titanic struggle of the Soviet Union against the German-Fascist aggressor', which occupied the attention of the main German land and air forces, and 'significantly weakened German strength in the Battle'. Furthermore 'economic difficulties and the drafting of workers into the army, deprived the German U-boat fleet of many submarines', and 'the defeats Germany suffered on the Soviet-German front greatly undermined the morale of the German submarines; there were cases of U-boat crews surrendering, while submarine captains' resolve in the execution of attacks declined'.[25]

In his foreword to Morison's second book, Eremeev noted once again that the American historian 'has attempted to reinforce the myth that the campaign in the Atlantic was waged independently from the rest of the war, and from the decisive events on the Soviet-German front, and that the campaign played an especially important role in the victory over Germany'. Eremeev went on to dispute the appropriateness of the term 'battle'. Defining the word as a 'military action having strategic and political significance, and exercising decisive influence on the subsequent development of events', he averred that in

Morison's book, the term 'is applied to military operations which played no meaningful role in the outcome of the war'. He then went on to ask: 'Really, did the American and English struggle to protect their Atlantic seaways from German submarine lead to any large territorial changes? No....The invasion of northern France succeeded because of the concentration of German forces on the Soviet-German front, and the 'Atlantic barrier' was merely a bluff'. He concluded brusquely, 'There is no basis to speak of any 'battle' here.'[26]

However, experienced Soviet readers understood the true values and goals of these historic commentaries, and turned their attention specifically to those sections of Morison's books which had received the sharpest criticism. Here they could find out about the real scale both of operations in the Atlantic and of Lend-Lease to the USSR; about the routes Lend-Lease took; about naval and merchant marine construction in the USA and Britain during the war, and about the overall military-industrial output of these countries. These data presented a new picture of the course of the war, and of the co-operation of the anti-Hitler coalition.

In 1959, 1st Captain N. Volkov published an article entitled *The German Naval Campaign against USA-British Sea-Communication in the Second World War*. Based on data obtained from Western works, chiefly Morison's, the article included the obligatory rejoinder that 'it is impossible to agree with bourgeois historians, who seek to prove that the so-called 'Battle of the Atlantic' was decisive to the outcome of World War II'. Nevertheless, the figures presented in the article painted an impressive picture of Atlantic operations, detailing the quantities of cargo transported by Allied convoys and the strength of Allied naval and air actions against the U-boat.[27]

After the appearance of the Russian translation of Morison's books and the polemical publications which accompanied them, several points of view on the Atlantic campaign appeared in Soviet historiography.

One view simply did not recognize that the Atlantic campaign took place at all. Thus, in the atlas *World War II, 1939-1945: A Concise Military-Historical Essay* (published in 1958), and in V. R. M. Kulish's *The Second Front Operations in Western Europe in 1944-1945* (1960), no mention is made of the Battle of the Atlantic.[28] In Moscow at the international historical conference in 1965, devoted to the 20th anniversary of the end of the war, not one participant mentioned the Battle.[29] *The Second World War and Our Times* (a collection of papers prepared by the Institute of Military History under the Ministry of Defence of the USSR and the Academy of Sciences of the USSR) contained such articles as 'The Second World War and Italian aggression in the Balkans', 'Switzerland in the Expansionist Plan of Hitler's Germany', and so forth - but the Battle of the Atlantic was nowhere to be found, not even in P. Zhilin's article 'Fundamental Problems of the Study of the World War II'.[30] Similar 'obliviousness' is common to two books published in 1970 and 1989 by Colonel V. A. Sekistov, a doctor of history, and devoted to description of 'the political goals and character of military operations in Western Europe and the

Mediterranean in 1939-1945'.[31] Finally, in a book put out under the editorship of Marshal S. L. Sokolov, we read that 'the only region where British troops fought the fascists after the defeat in Europe was the African theatre of operations'.[32]

Representatives of the second point of view emphasize that, while there might have been a Battle of the Atlantic, it did not play a significant role in the course or the outcome of the war. As a rule they employ the term 'Battle of the Atlantic' only in quotation marks, and they further limit their recognition of the campaign with such statements as: 'By comparison with the destruction of fascist Germany's forces on the Soviet-German front, the sea campaign could play only a supplementary role in the outcome of World War II', or: 'The fate of the war was decided not in the African desert, not in the "foreign war" in the West, and not in the "Battle of the Atlantic", but on the Soviet-German front'.[33] At the same time, they criticise 'bourgeois military historians, who try to attach decisive significance to the "Battle of the Atlantic" or the "Battle of Britain"'[34] or who 'unreasonably exaggerate the significance of the "Battle of the Atlantic" and the British-American strategic bombing campaign against fascist Germany'.[35]

The most interesting works of all are those of the third point of view. These gave a detailed description of the fighting in the Atlantic. From 1958 on, several multi-author books on WWII appeared, which included sections devoted to the war in broader studies, such as World History, or History of the Foreign Policy of the USSR. The authors were all ranking scholars. They used western publications thoroughly, including the studies of the Battle of the Atlantic by Morison and Scorill, and other published documents and statistical data. These Soviet authors tried to place the Atlantic campaign in the context of other campaigns of the war. They gave detailed accounts of the Atlantic campaign, including facts and events about which Soviet official and popular publications had kept silent.[36] All the same, we must note that their interpretation of the Battle of the Atlantic fell into a single scheme.

Essentially, Soviet historians to this day still deny that after 22 June 1941, Germany fought on two fronts. In their view, actions up to June 1944 in the Atlantic, Africa, and the Mediterranean do not represent a second front. In 1971, V. M. Kulish expressed the opinion that Soviet historians had erroneously identified 'mutual aid between the Allies, and especially Western Allied military aid to the USSR, as constituting a Second Front. This perception has migrated from journalistic essays into textbooks and has involuntarily influenced historians. The domination of this definition of the Second Front in American and English historical literature has played no small role in keeping this trend alive.'[37]

This view can be well illustrated by the foreword to a collection of *Documents on the October 1943 Moscow Conference of Foreign Ministers of the USSR, USA and Britain*, published by the USSR Ministry of Foreign Affairs in 1978. The authors of this foreword say that 'having postponed plans for an invasion of Europe, in autumn 1942 the Allies began offensive operations in North Africa (Operation Torch). However, considering the inferiority of the Axis forces in this area, those operations cannot be considered as a Second Front, and provided no substantial aid to the Soviet Army.'[38] Similar views appear in the foreword to a collection of *Documents on Soviet-American Relations during the Second World War, 1941-1945*, issued by the USSR Ministry of Foreign Affairs in 1984. The authors distinguish between the 'opening a second front in Europe' and the simple 'opening of a second front', and they insist that operations in North Africa did not come into the former category. This campaign, they said, led only 'to a dispersion of forces in secondary theatres of operations', and 'was undertaken as "an indirect action" against Germany'.[39]

The thesis of the 'indirect' character of these Allied military operations can be found in one or another form in various Soviet publications. Allied military actions in North Africa and the Mediterranean are characterized as events 'far away from the main theatre of the war', as 'a strategy of splintering of forces', and as 'the peripheral strategy' of the Allies.[40]

While it may be admitted that 'war was waged in Africa, in the Mediterranean, in the Atlantic, and in the Pacific, it is likewise emphasized that in terms of scale, effort, and result, these campaigns cannot be compared with the great battles on the Soviet-German front, which from its outset represented the central front of the Second World War'.[41] If we follow the logic of Soviet authors, there could be no military operations on the Western front comparable to the battles on the Soviet-German front. Perhaps for this reason, if we find any description of the Battle of the Atlantic in Soviet works on the war, it is in a section devoted to such topics as 'The struggle for Atlantic Communication', 'Operations of the Imperialist Navies in the Atlantic Ocean', and so forth.[42] In the Soviet works, all the important periods of the war - including the important periods of the Battle of the Atlantic - are determined by the thesis of the decisive role of the Soviet-German front in the war's outcome.[43] Thus, in the 1976 *Soviet Military Encyclopaedia*, the entry 'Battle for the Atlantic, 1939-1945' (by K. V. Penzin) outlines three separate periods. The first (September 1939-June 1941) was marked by the expanding scale of the struggle in the Atlantic. The second (July 1941-March 1943) was characterized by 'the re-directing of the main German air and surface fleet forces towards the struggle with the USSR. This allowed the Allies to concentrate all of their forces against the enemy submarines', and by the end of this period, the balance of the battle had turned towards the Americans and British. The third period (April 1943-May 1945) was 'a radical turning point of the war in connection with the defeats of the Wehrmacht on the Soviet-German front. These defeats, combined with the Allied invasion of June 1944, sharply reduced the effectiveness of the German submarine fleet'. Giving the data on both the Allies' naval and merchant losses and the Germans' U-boat losses, the author concluded: 'Despite the distance of the Atlantic Ocean from the Soviet-German front, the course of the struggle in the Atlantic was directly dependent on the course of the Soviet-German campaign, the main front of World War II.'[44]

As for the inverse dependence - the degree to which the Soviet campaign against Germany was sustained by the Allies' Atlantic efforts - Soviet historiography of WWII has no definite position. Particularly during the first two years after Germany's invasion of the USSR, the volume of delivery from the west to the USSR depended on the state of Atlantic communication, but this fact is ignored. Academician A. M. Samsonov, author of *World War II*, emphasises that 'the problem of transatlantic communication was of vital importance for Britain', adding that 'the Allies won the Battle of the Atlantic by the middle of 1943' and that 'as a result, transatlantic lines of communication became less dangerous and the sea shipping of troops and military freight from the USA to the British Isles was constantly increasing'.[45] Works by other authors, such as *The Second World War: A Short History* (1985), give detailed information about Allied supply convoys to the USSR and acknowledge that they went not only across the North Atlantic to Murmansk and Archangel, but also brought supplies via the Persian Gulf, Iran and points further east. At the same time, though, the authors insist that 'convoys to the USSR formed a somewhat limited part of the Allies' total marine tonnage'.[46]

In *The Atlantic Battle*, Morison gave us the volume of Allied shipping to the USSR. He estimated it as 17,449,801 tonnes. Since that time (1956), Soviet works on the history of WWII (among which was the article on Lend-Lease in the *Soviet Military Encyclopaedia*) have neither disputed nor confirmed this figure. Soviet authors still maintain that all the Allies' deliveries amounted to only 4% of the total amount of Soviet military production.[47]

Soviet historians often connected - and still connect - the importance of the Battle of the Atlantic with the question of the opening of the Second Front in Europe. In Stalin's messages to Churchill and Roosevelt until the second half of 1944, this question ranked among the most urgent. He considered as possible, and insisted on, the opening of a second front in 1942 and 1943.[48] Since the latter half of the 1950s, whenever the Allies' military operations in the Mediterranean and particularly in the Atlantic ocean are discussed, Soviet historians have constantly returned to this question. In 1964, Colonel V. M. Kulish defended a thesis on the history of the Second Front in Europe. As reported in *The Military-Historical Journal*, he proved that 'even in 1942 when "the Battle of the Atlantic" was in full flood, the Allies had a real possibility to land troops and open the Second Front in Europe'.[49] Statements of the same character were expressed in a number of works published in the 1970s and '80s.[50] But this thesis rapidly places Soviet historians in a vicious circle. In order to prove the possibility of landing troops in Western Europe, one must say there was no Battle of the Atlantic - which, since the publication in the USSR of the works of Morison, Scorill and some Soviet authors, is hardly possible. If, however, Soviet historians acknowledge that the Battle of the Atlantic 'was in full flood',[51] than the possibility of the troops' landing before 1944 is at best problematic. In addition to many others, this logical contradiction is still present in Soviet historic writings. Does this mean that Soviet historians are still unable to overcome the Stalinist interpretation of the history of WWII?

Notes

1.   Perepiska Predsedatelya Soveta Ministrov SSSR c Presidentami SShA i Prem'er-Ministrami Velikobritanii vo vremya Velikoy Otechestvennoy voyny 1941-1945gg. Tom 1. Perepiska s U. Cherchillem i K. Ettli (iyul' 1941g.-noyabr' 1945g). [*Correspondence of the Chairman of the USSR Council of Ministers with US Presidents and British Prime Ministers during the Great Patriotic War 1941-1945. Vol. 1. Correspondence with W. Churchill and C. Attlee (July 1941-November 1945)*]. 2nd edn, Moscow 1986, p. 93.

2.   *Ibid.*, pp. 56, 57, 58, 59, 67, 68, 78, 83, 88.

3.   Andreyev V. I. Bor'ba na okeanskikh kommunikatsiyakh [*The Ocean Communications Battle*], Moscow 1961, p. 313.

4.   Perepiska..., tom 1 [*Correspondence..., vol. 1*], pp. 2022, 24, 26-27, 39-40, 56, 57, 63-67, 73-75, 99, 100, 102-104, 109, 110, 117-120.

5.   Perepiska..., tom 2. Perepiska s F. Ryzevel'tom i G. Trumenom (august 1941g.-dekabr'1945g.) [*Correspondence with F. Roosevelt and W. Churchill (August 1941-December 1945)*]. 2nd edn, Moscow 1986, pp. 17, 27-28, 32-33, 54-55, 66-68, 134-135.

6.   Tekst lichnogo i sekretnogo poslaniya ot g-na Cherchilya g-nu Stalinu, polucheno 21 iyulya 1941g. - Perepiska..., tom 1, s.21 [Text of the personal and secret message from Mr. Churchill received on 21 July 1941. *Correspondence,* vol. 1, p. 21].

7.   Sovetskiy Soyuz na mezhdunarodnykh konferentsiyakh perioda Velikoy Otechestvennoy voyny 1941-1945gg. Tom 1. Moskovskaya konferentsiya ministrov inostrannykh del SSSR, SShA i Velikobritanii (19-30 oktobrya 1943g.). Sbornik dokumentov. M. 1978g. Tom 2. Tegeranskaya konferentsiya rukovoditeley trekh soyuznikh derzhav SSSR, SShA i Velikobritanii (28 noyabrya-1 dekabrya 1943g.). Sbornik dokumentov. M. 1978. Tom 4. Krymskaya konferentsiya rukovoditeley trekh soyuznikh derzhav SSSR, SShA i Velikobritanii (4-11 fevralya 1945g.). Sbornik dokumentov. M. 1984. Tom 5. Konferentsiya Ob'edenennykh natsiy v San-Frantsisko (25 aprelya-26 iyunya 1945g) Sbornik dokumentov. M. 1980. Tom 6. Berlinskaya (potsdamskaya) konferentsiya rukovoditeley trekh soyuznikh derzhav - USSR, SShA i Velikobritanii (17 iyulya-2 avgusta 1945g.). M. 1980. [*The Soviet Union at International Conferences during the Great Patriotic War 1941-1945. Vol. 1. The Moscow Conference of the Foreign Ministers of the USSR, USA and Great Britain (19-30 October 1943). Collected documents.* Moscow 1978. *Vol. 2. The Tehran Conference of the Heads of State of the Three Allied Powers (USSR, USA, Great Britain) (28 November-1 December 1943). Collected documents.*

Moscow 1978. *Vol. 4. The Crimea Conference of the Heads of State of the Three Allied Powers (USSR, USA, Great Britain) (4-11 February 1945). Collected documents.* Moscow 1984. *Vol. 5. The United Nations Conference in San Francisco (25 April- 26 June 1945). Collected documents.* Moscow 1980. *Vol. 6. The Berlin (Potsdam) Conference of the Heads of State of the Three Allied Powers (USSR, USA, Great Britain) (17 July-2 August 1945).* Moscow 1980].

8. Sovetsko-amerikanskiye otnosheniya vo vremya Velikoy Otechestvennoy voyny 1941-1945gg. Dokumenty i materialy. Toma 1-2. M. 1984g. Sovetsko-angliyskiye otnosheniya vo vremya Velikoy Otechestvennoy voyny 19411945gg. Dokumenty i materialy. Toma 1-2. M. 1983. [*Soviet-American Relations during the Great Patriotic War 1941-1945. Documents and Materials. Vols. 1-2, Moscow 1984. Soviet-British Relations during the Great Patriotic War 1941-1945. Documents and Materials.* Vols. 1-2, Moscow 1983].

9. Pravda, 23 October 1941; Pravda, 2 November 1941; Pravda, 13 October 1942; Pravda, 17 November 1942; Pravda, 11 November 1943; Krasnaya Zvezda, 27 November 1943; Krasnaya Zvezda, 30 December 1943; Krasnaya Zvezda, 18 April 1944.

10. Stalin I. V. o Velikoy Otechestvennoy voyne Sovetskogo Soyuza. Izd. 5. M. 1952 [J. V. Stalin: *On the Great Patriotic War of the Soviet Union.* 5th edn, Moscow 1952], pp. 54, 98, 122, 125-126, 130, 136.

11. *Ibid.,* pp. 70-74, 98.

12. *Ibid.,* pp. 157, 63, 136, 152.

13. *Ibid.,* pp. 43-44, 110, 153-157.

14. *Ibid.,* p. 143.

15. *Ibid.,* p. 159.

16. Germaniya v tiskakh mezhdu dvumya frontami. Materialy v pomoshch' agitatoram [*Germany in the Clutches of Two Fronts. Materials for Use by Agitators*], Leningrad, Voyenizdat, 1945, p. 65.

17. Tomashevich A. V. Ispol'zovaniye podvodnikh lodok vo 2-oy mirovoy voyne [*The # Use of Submarines in the Second World War*], Morskoy Sbornik, 1945, N 5-6, pp. 79-85.

18. Starov N. N. Morskiye i okeanskiye kommunikatsii SSSR, SShA i Anglii v minuvshuyu voynu [*The Naval and Ocean Communications of the USSR, USA and Great Britain in the Last War*], Morskoy Sbornik, 1946, N 11-12, pp. 46-62.

19. Vtoraya mirovaya voyna. Materialy nauchnoy konferentsi, posvyashchennoy 20- y godovshchine pobedy nad fashistskoy Germaniyey. Kniga 2. Dvizheniye soprotivleniya v Evrope [*The Second World War. Materials of the Academic Conference devoted to the 20th Anniversary of the Victory over Fascist Germany. Book 2. The Resistance Movement in Europe*], Moscow 1966, p. 344. The majority of the books were published by the USSR Ministry of Defence publishing house (the Foreign Literature Publishing House section).

20. S. Morison. *The Battle of the Atlantic* (September 1939-May 1943). Moscow 1956. Same author, *The Battle of the Atlantic Won. May 1943-May 1945.* Moscow 1959.

21. Eremeyev L. M. Yeshche ob odnoy fal'sificatsii voyny na more./ Protiv fal'sificatsii
    istorii vtoroy mirovoy voyny [*More Concerning a Falsification of the History of the
    War at Sea/Against the Falsification of the History of the Second World War*],
    Moscow 1959, pp. 261-281.
22. Morison S. *The Battle of the Atlantic*, p. 3.
23. *Ibid.*, p. 4; Morison S. *The Battle of the Atlantic Won*, p. 12.
24. Morison S. *The Battle of the Atlantic Won*, p. 12.
25. Morison S. *The Battle of the Atlantic*, p. 5.
26. Morison S. *The Battle of the Atlantic Has Been Won*, pp. 17-18.
27. Voyenno-istoricheskiy zhurnal, 1959, N 5, pp. 32, 3150. In 1966 the author was
    sharply criticized for his article in which 'besides a series of methodological
    mistakes there was a lot of incorrect data about the total volume of freight both
    exported and imported in the USA, about the number of German submarines,
    tonnage losses etc' (*Blokada i kontrblokada*. Ed. Rear Admiral V. P. Bogolepov,
    Moscow 1966, p. 2).
28. Vtoraya mirovaya voyna 1939-1945. Kratkiy voyennoistoricheskiy ocherk [*The
    Second World War 1939-1945: A Short Military Historical Study*], Moscow 1958;
    Kulish V. M. Vtoroy front. Operatsii v Zapadnoy Evrope v 1944- 1945gg [*The
    Second Front: Operations in Western Europe in 1944-1945*], Moscow 1960.
29. Vtoraya mirovaya voyna. Materialy nauchnoy konferentsi, posvyashchennoy 20- y
    godovshchine pobedy nad fashistskoy Germaniyey [*The Second World War:
    Materials of the Academic Conference devoted to the 20th Anniversary of the
    Victory over Fascist Germany*], Books 1-3, Moscow 1966.
30. Vtoraya mirovaya voyna i sovremennost' [*The Second World War and the Present*],
    Moscow 1972, p. 819.
31. Sekistov V.A. Voyna i Politika (Voyenno-politicheskiy ocherk voyennikh deystviy v
    Zapadnoy Evrope i basseyne Sredizemnogo morya 1939-1945gg.) [*War and Politics
    (A Military-Political Study of Military Operations in Western Europe and the
    Mediterranean Sea Basin 1939-1945)*], Moscow 1970. Same author. Voyna i
    Politika. Politicheskiye tseli i kharakter voyennikh deystviy v Zapadnoy Evrope i
    basseyne Sredizemnogo morya 1939-1945gg. [*War and Politics. The Political Aims
    and Nature of Military Operations in Western Europe and the Mediterranean Sea
    Basin 1939-1945)*], Moscow 1989.
32. Vtoraya mirovaya voyna. Itogi i uroki [*The Second World War: Results and
    Lessons*], Moscow 1985, p. 64.
33. Rosko T. Eskadrennye minonostsy vo Vtoroy mirovoy voyne [*Destroyers in the
    Second World War*], Moscow 1962, p. 6.
34. Belli V. A., Penzin K. V. Boyevye deystviya v Atlantike i na Sredizemnom more
    1939-1945 [*Combat Operations in the Atlantic and the Mediterranean 1939-1945*],
    Moscow 1967, p. 4.
35. Orlov A. S., Novoselov B. N. Fakty protiv mifov: podlinnaya i mnimaya istoriya
    Vtoroy mirovoy voyny [*Facts versus Myths: the Real and Imaginary History of the
    Second World War*], Moscow 1986, p. 61.

36. Istoriya Velikoy Otechestvennoy Voyny 1941-1945 v 6 tomakh [*A History of the Great Patriotic War 1941-1945 in 6 volumes*], vol. 2, Moscow 1961, pp. 583-588; vol. 6, Moscow 1963, pp. 233-235; Vsemirnaya istoriya [*World History*], vol. 10, Moscow 1965, pp. 82, 224-225, 287; Istoriya Vtoroy mirovoy voyny v 12 tomakh [*History of the Second World War in 12 volumes*], vol. 3, Moscow 1974, pp. 51-64, 135-142; vol. 4, Moscow 1975, pp. 194-200; vol. 5, Moscow 1975, pp. 343-364; vol. 6, Moscow 1976, pp. 232-251; vol. 7, Moscow 1976, pp. 424437; vol. 8, Moscow 1977, pp. 267-273; vol. 9, Moscow 1978, pp. 335-343; vol. 10, Moscow 1979, pp. 267-273; Istoriya vneshney politiki SSSR 1917-1976 v 2-kh tomakh [*A History of the Foreign Policy of the USSR 1917-1976* in two volumes], 3rd edn, vol. 1 1917-1945, Moscow 1976, pp. 438-439; Velikaya Otechestvennnaya voyna Sovetskogo Soyuza. Kratkaya istoriya [*The Great Patriotic War of the Soviet Union: A Short History*], 3rd edn, Moscow 1984, pp. 179-180, 271; Vtoraya mirovaya voyna. Kratkaya istoriya [*The Second World War. A Short History*], Moscow 1985, pp. 170-179, 322- 335; Samsonov A. M., Vtoraya mirovaya voyna 1939-1945. Ocherk vazhneyshikh sobytiy [*The Second World War. A Study of the Major Events*], 2nd edn, Moscow 1990, pp. 320-322.

37. Kulish V. M. Istoriya vtorogo fronta [*A History of the Second Front*], Moscow 1971, pp. 9-10.

38. Sovetskiy Soyuz na mezhdunarodnykh konferentsiyakh perioda Velikoy Otechestvennoy voyny 1941-1945gg. Tom 1. Moskovskaya konferentsiya ministrov inostrannykh del SSSR, SShA i Velikobritanii (19-30 oktobrya 1943g.). Sbornik dokumentov.[*The Soviet Union at International Conferences during the Great Patriotic War 1941-1945. Vol. 1. The Moscow Conference of the Foreign Ministers of the USSR, USA and Great Britain (19-30 October 1943). Collected documents*], Moscow 1978, pp. 11, 12.

39. Sovetsko-amerikanskiye otnosheniya vo vremya Velikoy Otechestvennoy voyny 1941-1945gg. Dokumenty i materialy [*Soviet-American Relations during the Great Patriotic War 1941-1945. Documents and Materials*], vol. 1. 1941-1943, Moscow 1984, p. 18.

40. Vtoraya mirovaya voyna. Itogi i uroki [*The Second World War. Results and Lessons*], p. 63; Samsonov A. M., op. cit., pp. 282-284.

41. Velikaya Otechestvennnaya voyna Sovetskogo Soyuza 1941-1945. Kratkaya istoriya [*The Great Patriotic War of the Soviet Union. A Short History*], p. 177.

42. Vsemirnaya istoriya [*World History*], vol. 10, p. 224; Istoriya voyenno-morskogo iskusstva [*A History of the Art of Naval Warfare*], Moscow 1969, pp. 170, 322.

43. Istoriya Vtoroy mirovoy voyny v 12 tomakh [*History of the Second World War in 12 volumes*], vol. 6, 7; Sovetskiy Soyuz na mezhdunarodnykh konferentsiyakh perioda Velikoy Otechestvennoy voyny 1941-1945gg. Tom 1. Moskovskaya konferentsiya ministrov inostrannykh del SSSR, SShA i Velikobritanii (19-30 oktobrya 1943.). Sbornik dokumentov [*The Soviet Union at International Conferences during the Great Patriotic War 1941-1945. Vol. 1. The Moscow Conference of the Foreign Ministers of the USSR, USA and Great Britain (1930 October 1943). Collected*

documents], Moscow 1978, p. 12.
44. Sovetskaya Voyennaya Entsiklopediya [*Soviet Military Encyclopedia*], vol. 1, Moscow 1976, p. 481.
45. Vtoraya mirovaya voyna. Kratkaya istoriya [*The Second World War. A Short History*], p. 178.
46. Vtoraya mirovaya voyna. Kratkaya istoriya [*The Second World War. A Short History*], p. 178.
47. Sovetskaya Voyennaya Entsiklopediya [*Soviet Military Encyclopedia*], vol. 4, Moscow 1977, p. 599. In the 12-volume 'History of the Second World War' it says: 'The victory was achieved by the Soviet produced arms... Lend-lease deliveries also played their moderate part in supplying the Soviet Army. Allied aid was too small if compared to Soviet production.' (Vol. 12, p. 170).
48. Perepiska..., tom 1 [*Correspondence...*, vol. 1], pp. 72-73; vol. 2, p. 50.
49. Voyenno-istoricheskiy zhurnal 1965, N 8, p. 115.
50. Velikaya Otechestvennnaya voyna Sovetskogo Soyuza 1941-1945. Kratkaya istoriya [*The Great Patriotic War of the Soviet Union 1941-1945. A Short History*], p. 274; Vtoraya mirovaya voyna. Kratkaya istoriya [*The Second World War. A Short History*], p. 183; Samsonov A. M., Vtoraya mirovaya voyna 1939- 1945. Ocherk vazhneyshikh sobytiy [*The Second World War. A Study of the Major Events*], Moscow 1985, p. 283.
51. As mentioned in 12-volume *History of the Second World War,* 'the summer and autumn of 1942 were crucial in the fight for Atlantic communications. USA and Great Britain suffered the heaviest losses in the merchant marine tonnage' (vol. 5, p. 354).

Notes translated by J. V. Romano

32

A United States Overview

by Dean C. Allard

From the perspective of 50 years, several major issues arise in an American assessment of the Battle of the Atlantic. One issue is a key question that applies to any military campaign: namely, what was our essential strategic objective? Secondly, the role of international and inter-service politics needs to be addressed. Thirdly, an understanding of the basic factors that explained American operational effectiveness is of obvious importance. Finally, I will discuss the continuity between the threat of advanced German undersea technology at the end of WWII and the menace posed by Soviet submarines in the Cold War era.

Various definitions of the strategic objective in the Battle can be offered. Concerning the USN, however, it appears to me that the overwhelming purpose was to enable Allied land power to operate ashore in Northern Europe to defeat Nazi Germany.[1] As Russell Weigley has noted, it is typical of the American way of war to seek out and confront an enemy at the principal source of his strength. That is exactly what we did in the WWII European campaign.[2]

It is important to note that the destruction of U-boats was *not* our ultimate purpose. Indeed, the major American naval leaders, including Admirals King, Stark, and Low stated that they would be satisfied if not a single U-boat was sunk - providing our convoys safely crossed the North Atlantic.[3] Nevertheless, we must remember that in 1943 the Americans did seize the opportunity presented by Ultra Intelligence and the new hunter-killer task forces built around escort carriers to launch an effective assault on U-boats in the central Atlantic. Reflecting American pragmatism, our naval leaders set aside their long-standing belief that it was inefficient to use naval forces to seek out and destroy U-boats operating on the high seas. The success of the hunter-killer groups in 1943-44 was one of the major contributions made by the US to the destruction of the U-boat force.[4]

Did US leaders also recognize the defence and sustenance of Great Britain as a key objective? Obviously so; but that was not our first priority. To draw a somewhat fine distinction based on the hard-headed logic of our admirals, they did so because Britain was a vital ally and because the UK represented an essential base for the invasion of Northern Europe. This position is reminiscent of the USN's appreciation of the situation in WWI. At that time, Adm William Veazie Pratt (principal assistant to Adm William S. Benson, then Chief of Naval Operations) observed that the USN's key contribution in the Great War was to 'mobilize and transport America's great reserve power to the European war front.' Observing that our 'major part' was in 'getting our troops and munitions and supplies over there', he contrasted this with the 'the impelling reason of the British' which 'was protection to food and war supplies in transit.'[5] This remained true in WWII - a position illustrated very clearly by Adm King's insistence that priority must be given to the protection of US troop convoys.[6] Similarly (recalling the distinction developed in Philip Pugh's chapter), another indication of the tendency of our strategic thinkers to value military need over civil necessity was the willingness of American leaders to gamble, in spring 1944, on the well-being of the British civilian population, which faced a critically short food supply, in order to give maximum shipping support to the military needs of the Normandy operation.

If the grand strategy of the USN's WWII leaders was the same as in WWI, there was also continuity in the strategic means they adopted - namely, to hit the source of the enemy's strength. King consistently stressed that U-boats must be attacked *before* reaching the high seas.[7] In 1942, when he joined General George C. Marshall (Chief of Staff of the US Army) in championing an immediate cross-channel operation, one of his major intentions was to seize the U-boat bases in western France that were vital for the success of Germany's underseas campaign. In the same vein, King urged the targeting of U-boat bases and factories in the strategic bombing campaign. If U-boats could not be destroyed at their source, then the next best tactic was to attack them while transiting to their operating areas. The Bay of Biscay anti-submarine air offensive (enthusiastically endorsed by King and Stark in 1943) can be seen as the equivalent of the anti-submarine barriers in the North Sea and English Channel that the US urged in the previous war.[8]

The Battle of the Atlantic was a pre-eminent maritime conflict. It is something of an irony, therefore, that for the US, its ultimate effect must be measured by the success of the Western Allies in bringing their strength to bear on land. 'Maritime Strategy', a phrase that became famous in the US during the 1980s, describes this way of thinking. The term is now generally associated with the Reagan Administration's defence posture, but as Michael Palmer tells us, the tendency of American strategists to emphasize the use of naval forces to support land campaigns long antedates the decade of the 1980s.[9]

The role of international and inter-service politics in the Battle of the Atlantic is a second issue that deserves attention. Despite the pious American saying that politics stop at the water's edge, individual nations involved in coalition campaigns naturally have separate national interests, which are sometimes hard to reconcile. Further, within a given nation, each military service has its own perspective and goals. Part of the complexity of the Battle was that, even as the various Allied nations and services involved were locked in a prolonged and bitter conflict with Nazi Germany, neither their international nor their bureaucratic politics could be adjourned entirely.

The political story continues to be a subject of controversy. For example, Robert Love recently claimed that the British sought to use charges of American ineptitude during the initial U-boat blitz off the US as a pretext for establishing

British strategic control of the entire Atlantic in 1942.[10] Whether or not that charge is valid, it is possible that jockeying for international position was involved in the rather vivid British reaction to German success in Operation Paukenschlag. One can second-guess King for his refusal to initiate coastal convoys at once, even if they could only have been given under-strength escort forces or no escorts at all. However, his decision was to give priority to assuring the safety of American *troop* convoys to the UK as compared to the protection of *mercantile* convoys off the East Coast - again, the distinction between military and civil requirements. Clearly, this allocation of naval forces stripped key defences from the Eastern Seaboard.[11] The decision was well known to his British critics, and it is puzzling that they did not take it into account.

I do not propose in this paper to present a full discussion of Paukenschlag, or to defend the USN's role in that campaign. But since the operation has received considerable attention in this conference, and since I believe the subject deserves further study, let me enumerate a few questions for consideration by future researchers:

• To what extent were the reactions of King and his senior colleagues (all of whom had served as mid-grade officers in WWI) influenced by recollections of Germany's submarine offensive off the US East Coast in 1918? The consensus view on the earlier operation was that it was a German attempt to divert US attention from the critical theatre of the war in Europe. Despite German success in sinking about 100 ships and smaller craft, causing great public alarm, US naval leaders of the Great War refused to make basic changes to the deployment of their forces. Was this precedent a factor in King's outlook in 1942?[12]

• US and Allied losses off the American coast during the first six months of 1942 were considerable. In the Eastern Sea frontier alone, they amounted to about 100 merchantmen.[13] But, even if the American slaughter had continued, one can ask whether such a campaign promised any decisive strategic result - especially against a continental power such as the US, well endowed with natural resources and a sophisticated internal transportation network. In any case, to put the magnitude of those losses into perspective, one should remember that more than 2,500 Allied merchantmen were lost to enemy action throughout the war. A related and much broader question, of course, is whether Dönitz's tonnage warfare concept in general was strategically sound. Was there really any prospect that the simple sinking of merchant ships, without regard to the geographic importance of the areas in which these losses occurred, could win the war for Germany?

• To what extent was the USN inhibited in its response to Paukenschlag by the demands of the Pacific war? One must remember that the navy needed to organize and protect major troop movements into the Pacific early in 1942.[14]

Moreover, Japanese submarines were operating off the US West Coast at that time.[15] There were also real fears that the Japanese would invade Hawaii, or even the West Coast.[16] In other words, one should bear in mind that from December 1941, American naval leaders were fighting a two-ocean war. They were not able to concentrate exclusive attention on the Atlantic Coast.

But, setting aside the contentious issue of Paukenschlag, let us return to the overall political situation by referring to the influence on the Battle of the Atlantic of the Anglo-American dispute on the opening of a second front in northern Europe.

Following the British refusal to launch a cross-Channel operation in 1942, King and Marshall proposed that the US should shift its primary attention to the Pacific. That position probably was little more than a bluff. In any case, it was specifically overridden when Roosevelt directed the mounting of Operation Torch in North Africa later that year. These high-level decisions had tangible impacts on the anti-submarine campaign. For example, the deferral of a major amphibious operation in northern Europe allowed King to persuade Roosevelt to make the construction of landing craft a lower priority than the building of destroyer escorts, a class of warship essential for the defeat of the U-boat.[17] By the same token, though, the diversion of naval assets to the Torch landings in November 1942 was one factor contributing to the growing success of U-boats in the North Atlantic during the bloody winter of 1942-43.[18]

Two other examples of the major influence of international politics in the Battle can be noted. One was the decision (taken at the Atlantic Convoy Conference in Washington during March 1943) to shift strategic control of Canadian ASW forces in the Northwest Atlantic from the US to Canada herself. This was, in part, a military decision. But it also had a significant political dimension. In fact, as Marc Milner points out, by giving 'recognition of Canada's special interest in the North Atlantic', this decision was a true 'watershed' in Canadian history.[19]

The second example is provided by the North Russian convoys. These were viewed by Western naval officers as highly risky operations that diverted essential ships from more important tasks, notably the Battle of the Atlantic. For Churchill and Roosevelt, however, the convoys to Murmansk and Archangel were essential symbols of Western support for a hard-pressed Soviet ally. Hence, political requirements over-rode strategic considerations.[20]

Inter-service or bureaucratic politics - endemic in so much of military history - are also evident in the Battle. From the USN's point of view, the major story was its conflict with the Army Air Force concerning the role of land-based, long-range aircraft in the anti-submarine campaign. A significant lesson learned early in the Battle was the enormous value of these planes in detecting and deterring U-boats. The USN, which entered the war without such aircraft, initially depended on the co-operation of the Army Air Forces, using a system that roughly paralleled the maritime air support provided by the RAF's Coastal Command to the RN. But by summer 1943, it became clear that there were irreconcilable differences between the two services regarding the command and tactical employment of land-based aircraft. Understandably, ASW operations, especially convoy protection duty, were not of first importance to the Army Air Force. For the navy, however, ASW was crucial and the planes essential. Interestingly, in Germany the Luftwaffe and the Kriegsmarine faced a similar problem, which they never really solved - an inter-service rivalry that severely hampered Nazi efforts overall.[21] The same could have happened in the US, but, instead of continuing to dispute these issues, the two American services agreed to shift the army's long-range ASW aircraft to the navy. In return, the navy provided the army with replacement aircraft. With this step, an important bureaucratic conflict ended. Thereafter the USN had direct control of all of the critical assets for waging modern anti-submarine warfare.[22]

Let us turn from politics to a subject that is a more traditional aspect of the naval profession. What can one say about the tactical, organizational, and technical factors that allowed the USN to make significant contributions to the campaign against U-boats? Under the USN's strategic concept, the victory achieved by Allied armies in Western Europe was the ultimate measure of success in the Battle of the Atlantic. As noted, American naval leaders saw the destruction of U-boats as secondary in importance. Even so, out of a total of 606 German submarines sunk in action on the high seas, 132 kills were scored by forces under US operational control, which, of course, did not fully enter the war until December 1941.[23] The massive production by US shipyards and factories of the merchantmen, naval ships, aircraft and many other weapons and systems employed in the Battle must also be stressed in evaluating our overall contribution to the campaign.

Another statistic worth citing is the increased efficiency of American ASW attacks. In the first six months of 1942, only 2% resulted in U-boat sinkings. By the April-September 1944 period, however, the proportion of successful attacks increased to 24%.[24]

During and after the war, Admiral Francis S. Low (Admiral King's principal assistant for ASW) made several detailed analyses of the requirements for operational success in this field of naval warfare. Low concluded that operational training, adequate ASW force levels, and Intelligence on the location of enemy submarines were three key factors.[25] Somewhat surprisingly - considering our navy's traditional aversion both to centralization and to organizational solutions to problems - the establishment in 1943 of the central ASW command known as the Tenth Fleet (in which Low served as Chief of Staff to King) was viewed by Low and his colleagues as a vital step. Low's assessments acknowledged the important role of scientific analysis in developing effective doctrine and tactics.[26] Of course, he also enumerated the role played by a myriad of new weapons and detection systems, such as Hedgehogs, magnetic detection devices, anti-homing torpedo gear, direction finding equipment, the Leigh light, and improved radar and sonar. As was true for operational research, many of these devices were British innovations.[27] But

Low and his fellow naval officers did not subscribe to a simple materialistic explanation of the Allied success. Instead the dominant theme in their analysis was the absolutely essential need to co-ordinate all elements of the ASW problem, including capable ships, weapons, and other systems, proper allocation of forces, effective operational training, Intelligence, and scientific analysis, under the umbrella of an organization such as the USN's Tenth Fleet. In effect, the manifold facets of the ASW problem were recognized as being part of a seamless whole. Writing for the benefit of future naval leaders, Low stressed that success in subsequent campaigns depended above all on the integration of eachl of these elements under central control.

At the end of WWII, the USN could congratulate itself on its many contributions to the U-boats' defeat. Simultaneously, however, there was a sobering recognition that the more advanced underseas technology developed by Germany late in the war represented an entirely different problem. To be sure, the ASW barriers established by American naval forces engaged in Operation Teardrop (April-May 1945) were highly successful in countering the final U-boat threat in the Western Atlantic. During Teardrop, surface ships operating at the peak of their efficiency destroyed five of the six U-boats deployed by Admiral Dönitz. Nevertheless, the new snorkel boats used by Germany undercut the effectiveness of American ASW aircraft. Further, there was deep anxiety on the American side because of intelligence assessments (now known to be false) that the Germans planned to use submarine-launched rockets against East Coast cities. No effective defence against those weapons was available in 1945.[28]

In November 1949, a little more than four years after the end of WWII, Admiral Forrest P. Sherman (then Chief of Naval Operations) appointed Admiral Low to conduct another comprehensive study of Undersea Warfare. By that time, the Cold War was fully under way and the Western democracies viewed the Soviet Union as a hostile power intent on establishing hegemony in Europe. It was precisely this threat, when posed by Germany in 1939, that led to WWII. Though it now came from another quarter, it was profoundly unsettling to see the threat repeated so soon - especially when it emanated from a former ally. For naval officers, there was yet another arresting transference from Hitler's Germany to the Soviet Union. Bearing in mind the extensive Soviet exploitation at the end of the war of the human and industrial resources of the German undersea warfare organization, Low made this sobering observation in his final report of April 1950:

> All the improvements made by the Germans in submarines, weapons and mines are available to the Russians. These include snorkel, closed cycle propulsion, Types XXI and XXIII submarines, pattern running and acoustic torpedoes, guided missiles and influence mines....They have the industrial capacity and technical knowledge [to put these developments into production] if they decide to give the effort high priority. German

submarine production during World War II approached 30 boats per month and Russian shipbuilding capacity approximates that of pre-war Germany.[29]

Admiral Low then made an even more alarming statement:

The Anti-Submarine Warfare techniques and equipment in use by the US Navy at the present time, while adequate to defeat the conventional World War II-type submarine, are inadequate to deal with an advanced-type of submarine and improved weapons that the Russians can build now. Echo-ranging by sonar is still the only effective method of locating a fully submerged submarine which is running quietly. The nature of the ocean and the physics of underwater sound propagation make it appear that there is no early prospect of increasing sonar echo range in practicable equipment for surface craft sufficiently to deal with the submarine of the future.[30]

Thus, as the Battle of the Atlantic had many similarities within the American naval experience with the campaign of 1917-1918, we see that the Cold War flowed directly out of WWII. That development plus the decisive Allied victory in Europe must be viewed as the major outcomes of the Battle of the Atlantic.

Despite the fact that outright hostilities were avoided, the third ASW campaign in the Atlantic absorbed enormous American attention for more than 40 years after WWII. Those operations are not the subject of this chapter; but if they were, I believe that many of the points made here with regard to the strategic objective, the politics, and the war-fighting principles involved in the WWII Battle of the Atlantic could also apply to the Atlantic campaign of the Cold War era. It would not be the first time that we discover more continuities than discontinuities in the history of the North Atlantic community.

The views expressed in this paper are solely those of the author. They do not represent the views of the Departments of the Navy or Defense.

Notes

1. This analysis is based especially upon the following accounts: Love, *History of the US Navy*, II, pp. 64-119; 'The Battle of the Atlantic', pp. 205-26 in *The Second World War: Europe and the Mediterranean*, Buell et al.; and King and Whitehill, *Fleet Admiral King: A Naval Record*.
2. See Weigley, *The American Way of War*, pp. 312-59.

3.   See Francis S. Low's report forwarded by his memorandum of 28 Oct 1944 in the
     Papers of Ernest J. King, series XI, Box 13, Operational Archives, Naval Historical
     Center, Washington DC (hereafter cited as Low Report of 28 Oct 1944); Simpson
     Admiral Harold R. Stark, p. 194; and Love, *History of the USN*, II, pp. 66-68.

4.   Love, *History of the USN*, II, pp. 111-15; Morison *History of United States Naval
     Operations in World War II*, Vol. X , p. 363.

5.   Quoted in Dean C. Allard, 'Anglo-American Naval Differences in World War I', in
     In Defense of the Republic, eds. Skaggs and Browning, p. 245.

6.   Love, *History of the USN*, II, pp. 66-70.

7.   For World War I, see Allard, 'Anglo-American Naval Differences', pp. 248-50.
     King's stress on going to the source of the enemy's strength is indicated, for
     example, in King and Whitehill, *Fleet Admiral King*, p. 457.

8   King and Whitehill, *Fleet Admiral King*, p. 457; Simpson, *Admiral Harold R.
     Stark*, pp. 187-92; Love, *History of the USN*, II, p. 118.

9.   Palmer, *Origins of the Maritime Strategy*.

10. Love, *History of the USN*, p. 79. Other works on the dual themes of co-operation
     and competition in Anglo-American military relations during World War II include
     Leutze, *Bargaining for Supremacy: Anglo-American Naval Collaboration, 1937-
     1941*; Thorne, *Allies of a Kind: The Allies, Britain and the War Against Japan,
     1941-1945*; and Danchev, *Very Special Relationship: Field-Marshal Sir John Dill
     and the Anglo-American Alliance, 1941-1945*.

11. For balanced accounts of Operation Paukenschlag, see Love, *History of the USN*, II,
     pp. 66-70; and Van der Vat, *The Atlantic Campaign*, pp.237-48. In my opinion,
     Gannon's *Operation Drumbeat* is a partisan presentation that is not entirely
     reliable.

12. Morison, *History of the USN*, I, pp. 125-6.

13. *Ibid.*, p. 413.

14. *Ibid.*, III, p 265.

15. Clarke G. Reynolds, 'Submarine Attacks on the Pacific Coast, 1942', in *Pacific
     Historical Review*, May 1964, pp. 183-93.

16. See Conn and others, *Guarding the United States and its Outposts*; and Stephan
     Hawaii under the Rising Sun: Japan's Plan for Conquest after Pearl Harbor.

17. Love, *History of USN*, II, p. 100.

18. *Ibid.*, p. 97.

19. Milner, *North Atlantic Run*, p. 234.

20. Van der Vat, *The Atlantic Campaign*, pp. 203-04, 278-80.

21. Peter Padfield, 'Erich Raeder', p. 53, in Howarth, S, ed., *Men of War: Great Naval
     Captains of World War II*.

22. Morison, *History of the USN*, X, pp.26-31. A recent history by a serving Army
     officer, Montgomery C. Meigs, *Slide Rules and Submarines*, is of interest in giving
     a contemporary restatement of the Army's partisan views regarding the alleged
     shortcomings of the US Navy in the Battle of the Atlantic.

23. This statistic is derived from a table appearing in Admiralty Historical Section, *The
     Defeat of the Enemy Attack on Shipping 1939-1945* (London, 1957), p. 245. U-
     boats lost through bombing raids, by mines, other causes, or unknown causes are
     not included.

24. Low, Report of 28 Oct 1944, p. 9.

25. In addition to *The Defeat of the Enemy Attack on Shipping* (*op. cit.*) and Low's studies that appear as annexes to that report, see Low, 'Study of Undersea Warfare', 22 April 1950, and Low, 'Presentation to the Fifth Undersea Symposium', 15-16 May 1950, both of which are in the Command File, Operational Archives, Naval Historical Center, Washington, DC. The Top Secret annexe (now declassified) to the 22 April 1950 study stresses the vital importance of Ultra Intelligence.

26. A comprehensive account of US operations research appears in Keith R. Tidman, *The Operations Evaluation Group*.

27. For an excellent account of British-American technical co-operation in the Battle of the Atlantic, see Hackmann, *Seek and Strike*, especially pp. 250-65.

28. Morison, *History of the USN*, X, 344-56.

29. Low, 'Study of Undersea Warfare', 22 April 1950, p. 2.

30. *Ibid.*

33

The Modern View:
The Battle and Post-War British Naval Policy

by Eric Grove

The Battle of the Atlantic cast a long shadow over British naval policy in the period after World War II. Britain having come so close, for a second time, to defeat by the U-boat, it would have been surprising if the defence of shipping against submarine attack and anti-submarine warfare (ASW) in general had not been major priorities in shaping the postwar Royal Navy. Such indeed has been the case, down to this very day, but this persistent priority should not mask an equally persistent debate about what the lessons of the Battle actually were, how far they could continue to be applied in a changing technological environment and how far the direct defence of shipping should continue to dominate naval policy in a time when the foundations of traditional naval strategy were challenged - first by nuclear and thermonuclear weaponry and, more recently, by the end of the Cold War.

No Staff History of the Battle of the Atlantic was available until 1957.[1] Ironically, when Waters and Barley produced this vital work - the finest justification of the convoy system ever written - the tide was beginning to run quite strongly against basing the RN around a force primarily designed to repeat the success of the six-year Atlantic campaign. Despite the absence of a proper Staff Study, however, convoy escort had continued to be a major factor on Naval Staff thinking. Between 1945-52, with 'Defence of sea communications' declared in 1947 as one of the three 'pillars' of defence policy, the protection of shipping by direct escort with all available assets was the core of British naval strategy. Even the fleet carriers were primarily explained as escorts for future 'Pedestals' in the Mediterranean, the light fleets acting as escort carriers to close any potential Atlantic gaps. As the First Sea Lord put it in 1948, 'Planning can only proceed on something we know we must do, escort safely our convoys.'[2] Thus, immediate postwar fleet plans were dominated by building a new escort flotilla to counter the modern 'U-boat' - a term used in postwar planning for a decade or so. The anti-submarine problem had been revolutionized by the fast battery-driven U-boat and a new high-speed escort was needed as soon as possible, both by varying degrees of conversion of existing fleet destroyers and new frigate construction when it could be afforded. The latter did not occur until the stimulus of the Korean War in the 1950s.[3]

These 'U-boats' would of course be Soviet rather than German. There was certainly no underestimation of the threat posed. As the Maritime Air Defence Committee put it in October 1950, close to home the mine would once more be the main threat, but:

The principal threat to our shipping in the North Atlantic is from
the submarine torpedo. The Russians may from the outset deploy
in the Atlantic and in our focal areas roughly three times the
submarine effort which the Germans achieved in the early months
of the last war, and by virtue of the equipment which we believe
they will possess in 1954, they offer a threat equivalent to that of
the German peak effort in 1942.

Specifically, the threat was placed at six large and fast boats covering the
Atlantic as far as the equator, 11 large and slow boats covering the area down to
the Azores, and 23 smaller boats operating in the Norwegian and North seas. If
mainland Europe fell once more (as seemed likely), the Atlantic threat would
increase to 28 submarines - a fact only mitigated by the decline in shipping
requirements to sustain Britain alone.[4]

The Maritime Air Defence Committee was a major effort to work out the
dynamics of a re-play of the Battle of the Atlantic, in order to assess carrier-
versus land-based air priorities. A joint Admiralty and Air Ministry Historical
Sub-Committee was set up to inform it of the lessons of the past. This
committee was in

unanimous agreement that the vital factor in the defence of
Maritime Trade was the Convoy System. Coupled with the
provision of adequate air and surface escorts and evasive routing
based on Special Intelligence, the effectiveness of the system was
demonstrated not only in the protection of shipping but by the
number of U-boats detected and killed.

The Historical Sub-Committee was dismissive of the 'relative ineffectiveness' of
Hunter/Killer groups, mining and attacks on bases, although it was equivocal on
the effectiveness of the Bay offensive. This loophole allowed the the committee
to insist in its report that 'the successful defence of our shipping requires both
close defence of convoys and offensive operations in submarine transit areas.' It
was accepted that snorting submarines were much less vulnerable to air search
than surfaced U-boats, but the committee felt it was still worthwhile to force
submarines on transit to submerge, thus denying them mobility. Operational
research also seemed to show that useful attrition - 10% - might be inflicted. In
all, the force requirements were placed at 12 surface escorts per convoy plus two
air escorts constantly present, plus 20 ships and seven aircraft patrolling the
Northern transit areas, and (if France was once more occupied) 13 ships and
five aircraft in the Bay of Biscay. On the report's central issue, it was decided
that a dividing line of 550 miles from base gave the answer in principle. Up to
that range, land-based aircraft were more economical in the ASW task; beyond
it, carrier aircraft were best. In practice both types of air cover overlapped; land-
based aircraft could provide cover when bad weather precluded carrier

operations, while carriers, when required to give anti-air warfare (AAW) cover against reconnassance aircraft, could also provide ASW support, thus economizing on Shackletons and Neptunes.[5]

The trouble with the force requirement was that it was far too large. It was even larger than the navy's ambitious current building plans, and those (at least after Churchill resumed office in 1951) were all too clearly doomed themselves. As the Conservatives imposed their ever more radical defence review process, the Admiralty were forced onto the defensive. To maintain the ships required to fight a future Battle of the Atlantic, their Lordships had to assert that the very capacity to fight such a battle was vital to Britain's future strategy. In the new era of nuclear weapons, however, it was all too easy to argue that preparations for another Atlantic campaign were both superfluous and futile: superfluous, since nuclear-armed bombers could destroy the enemy 'at source'; futile, since the scale of destruction would mean that there would be nothing to supply.

The Admiralty naturally opposed such views and, with the help of scientists like Tizard, were able to make a convincing case for the need to maintain sea communications, both in the opening intense phase of a future global war and its succeeding 'broken-backed' phase. Nevertheless it is clear that within the Admiralty itself, the appearance on the scene of the nuclear-armed NATO carrier striking fleet concept in 1952 drastically altered the balance of naval thinking itself. The airmen had always wanted to attack enemy submarines in their bases, once the equipment was available. Now the US carriers provided that capability.

Suddenly the main role of the navy shifted from convoy protection to making a significant contribution to the Striking Fleet, with its ability to destroy the enemy in his bases. The Striking Fleet would be the main, albeit not the sole, British naval priority for the rest of the Cold War.[6]

In 1954 the scenario of a repeated Battle of the Atlantic was further eroded by the shocking news from Bikini that multi-megaton hydrogen bombs were now available in usable form. Even the then First Sea Lord, Sir Rhoderick McGrigor (who over the previous two years had fought succesfully for the 'Broken-Backed' war concept) now recognized that the game was up. Although the Admiralty were as committed as ever to maintaining command of the sea as long as it was possible and necessary in a future global war, this would have to be done in significantly new ways. McGrigor's Naval Staff mapped out a future in which a smaller fleet would use a range of new technologies to defeat what they still called the U-boat threat: long-range nuclear missiles (that would replace the RAF's bombers as the primary deterrent to war) to attack the enemy at source; long range sensors (notably passive arrays on the ocean floor) and ASW weapons that would allow smaller numbers of ships to cover wider areas of ocean. In the future, submarines would be tracked down and killed in much the same manner as aircraft were intercepted and killed by air defences.

Convoys would be steadily less important over the forthcoming decade as shipping was defended by torpedo countermeasures, interception of U-boats in transit and attacks on bases. As the fleet transformed itself into the new shape, planners could live with its current inadequacy for full-scale war, as this was deemed to be very unlikely in the short term. Indeed, if Western thermonuclear superiority deterred major Communist challenges, it would make *limited* challenges (to which the West would feel it was safe to respond) not less but more likely. Thus, what fleet there was should be increasingly orientated to what we would now call 'power projection' in Cold and 'Warm' (i.e. limited) wars.[7]

Two more factors added to the decline of the classical Atlantic convoy as the centrepiece of British naval thinking. One was the appearance of the Soviet missile-firing submarine. This caused the USN to re-orientate itself even more into the hunter-killer mode of ASW operations, withdrawing assets from convoy duties.[8] The other was the appearance of the nuclear-powered submarine (SSN), a veritable capital ship in its capacity to outmanoeuvre submerged every existing ASW asset. Just as the surest answer to the capital ship of the past had only been another capital ship, so the only sure answer to the SSN seemed to be another of its own kind; and (although it was possible to think of SSNs operating in support of convoys, like the battleships of old) their captains would prefer a more independent role, in the anti-submarine barricades already planned for waters close to enemy bases.

It is hard to underestimate the impact of the SSN on ASW: it made ASW the core warfare speciality of modern fleet operations. This seemed to be the apotheosis of the type of warfare characterized by the Atlantic battle, but it was not. Instead of being elements in the campaign to exercise command of the sea under the cover of main fleet forces, submarines and ASW forces were themselves the main fleet forces. This was bound to have an effect on the overall strategy of the ASW campaign and the place of mercantile convoy within it.

Nevertheless, convoy remained a vital part of NATO's plans to fight WWIII, however long that conflict might last.[9] In 1957, the RN made skilful use of these plans when Mountbatten's Naval Staff was embroiled with the Minister of Defence, Duncan Sandys, in his attempt to bring the Reviews of the previous five years to a logical and (from the navy's angle) a terrible conclusion. To defend itself from further cuts, it quoted a 1956 Staff Appreciation which assessed that by 1961 the Soviets might be able to deploy 88 submarines on patrol in the Atlantic, as against 63 U-boats in 1943. There would be 56 Allied A/S escorts on convoy duty as against 80 in 1943, and 268 aircraft as against 1,200 in 1943. Monthly shipping losses in 1961 were estimated as 100 as compared to 1943's 35. This was bad enough, but substantial withdrawal of British forces would make the situation catastrophic, forcing 'a frank avowal' that NATO's maritime forces 'were inadequate to counter the threat to NATO sea communications.' The Admiralty, rather slyly, did

not wish merely to point to the military results of losing control of the Atlantic, although if global war lasted for more than a very few weeks these would be disastrous. Much more important is that the Government should fully consider the political results which would flow from the NATO Council being informed that SACLANT could no longer meet his committments. There would be a clear physical and psychological weakening of NATO; and the seeds of doubt would be sown in the minds of its members whether we were serious about the Alliance.[10]

Thus was the spectre of a future Battle of the Atlantic manipulated to maintain some ASW capacity in the Atlantic.

The issuing of the Staff History also helped give convoy a new lease of life in 1957-8. Mountbatten was an enthusistic convoy supporter. Because it seemed as if the Americans were about to abandon convoy, the First Sea Lord tried to exert pro-convoy influence on his American counterpart, Arleigh Burke. He sent Burke the results of a Tactical School study showing that it was only profitable to use submarines in the transit offensive. Ships and aircraft were better placed around very large 400-ship convoys that would be supported by submarines - if problems of communication could be solved. Explosive echo-ranging using sono-buoys would give sufficient accuracy for engagement of enemy submarines with nuclear depth-charges. Guided missile ships in the screen would provide air defence. Mountbatten also sent Burke a copy of Peter Gretton's famous plea for convoy, his *Naval Review* article entitled 'Why Don't We Learn From History?'

Burke and his advisers seemed unconvinced. In their reply to the Tactical School study, Burke emphasized the importance of air strikes on submarine depot ships and the 'home nests' of the Soviet submarine fleet. In reply to Gretton, Burke clearly demonstated the classical American difference of view that resulted from the USN's different historical experience. Drawing Mountbatten's attention to the successes of the American hunter killer groups after May 1943, he argued they had obtained the majority of American kills. He also asserted that a balance had to be struck between the lessons of the past and the possibilities of new weapons. Burke's letter prompted rebuttals from the British Naval Staff who used their history to point to the dominance of escorts in making kills and the dependence of the American hunter-killer operations on special intelligence 'which is most unlikely to be available in a future war'. Mountbatten used these arguments in a reply to the CNO, maintaining that the popular conception of the hunter-killer group and patrolling aircraft sucessfully hunting down submarines was 'wholly false'. Perhaps prompted by this strong reply, the Deputy SACLANT wrote to inform Mountbatten of SACLANT's enthusiasm for a northern barrier offensive to prevent the deployment of missile submarines into the Atlantic.[11]

Mountbatten and Burke agreed to differ over the emphasis placed on convoy in maintaining sea communications in some future war. The debate was never allowed to stand in the way of an excellent naval 'Special Relationship' that both safeguarded the procurement of Britain's first SSN with its American reactor and saw the first moves to procure the Polaris missile.[12]

The Naval Staff at the Admiralty became increasingly preoccupied with the development of carrier-amphibious forces for limited contingencies east of Suez. By the early 1960s, power projection completely dominated British naval policy and the 1962 Naval Estimates described the role of the navy solely in terms of an amphibious landing.[13] This only began to change in 1966-8 with the decision to abandon large carriers, the withdrawal from East of Suez and the new emphasis on conventional operations imvolved in NATO's adoption of the Flexible Response strategy. By this time, however British thinking was more thoroughly conditioned by American-dominated NATO ideas, and much less convoy-centred than British thought had been in the 1940s and '50s. Sadly the Staff History seems to have been almost forgotten; it languished in a classified never-never land, unavailable to the interested and unread by those with more pressing preoccupations.[14]

There seems to have been little or no British dissent that the shape of a new Battle of the Atlantic should be a combination of a carrier and submarine offensive, both to support the defence of Norway and to keep the Soviet fleet (its submarines in particular) tied down in defensive operations. The reduced threat to shipping would be dealt with by barriers and convoy escorts. This remained the form of NATO's maritime strategy until the end of the Cold War

There were signs in the 1970s that the decline in Allied naval strength and the improvement of the Soviet Navy would prevent the Striking Fleet carrying out its tasks, but in its new 'Concept of Maritime Operations' (drawn up and approved in 1980-81) the principle of 'Forward Defence' was reasserted with 'Norwegian Sea' and 'Atlantic Lifelines' campaigns operating in mutual support. There was also exploration of whether new long-range passive sonar capabilities might allow, indeed enforce, changes in the way the 'Atlantic Lifelines' were defended. These sensors were of little use in the vicinity of noisy merchant ships, so, in order to find ways of applying the new technologies to shipping defence, the 1981 'Ocean Safari' exercise included experiments with 'defended lane' concepts.[15]

By 1981, the case for convoy had become seriously undermined. This culminated in the Nott defence review of that year. The 'scientific' studies upon which this was based argued that shipping should be concentrated into a 'shipping band' defended by maritime patrol aircraft. Submarines would be kept from overwhelming these defences by a barrier of aircraft and mines in the G-I-UK gap, and by forward submarine operations. Frigates equipped with the new towed-array long-range sonars would operate both in the barriers and the 'shipping band' to help maintain the underwater picture, but they would not serve as direct escorts. In the face of new long-range Soviet anti-shipping missiles, convoy was held to be a 'very fragile' concept. The result was a significant reduction in the surface fleet, a reduction only partially reversed by the fortuitous invasion and recovery of the Falklands the following year.[16]

British thinking was also affected by America's articulation of the new 'Maritime Strategy'. This was in fact based on existing Alliance thought, with its emphasis on forward operations by carriers and submarines.[17] Its more popular versions seemed to fly in the face of history, notably in the infamous 'spots diagram' when Allied losses in 1942 were blamed on the *absence* of a forward strategy! In reality, however, it was nothing more than a reassertion of traditional post-war American (and therefore Allied) thinking on the importance of maintaining the maximum possible maritime pressure on the Soviets, in order to reduce the direct threat to shipping.

The RN enthusiastically endorsed the new forward strategy with its re-emphasis on both the Striking Fleet and forward submarine roles. The main RN surface committment became the 'Anti-Submarine Warfare Striking Force' (ASWSTRIKFOR), a powerful ASW carrier and towed-array force clearing a path for the American carriers. RN SSNs would join their American fellows in penetrating Soviet SSBN 'bastions'.[18]

Although convoy seemed forgotten at times, it was not. NATO plans continued to rely on a massive sealift across the Atlantic - 3,045 shiploads of military reinforcement and resupply. Various options existed for the defence of this shipping, including convoy. One possible scenario was running independents on a southerly route to the Azores, with convoys from there to European ports. The historically-minded would have preferred a more wholehearted recognition that convoy was the only effective means of defending shipping against attack, and less use of the meaningless term 'sea lines of communication' (SLOCs); but at least by the late 1980s, in its plans to deal with a Soviet Navy that had never been more powerful, NATO had a clear and coherent maritime strategy - a strategy that could be justified in clear operational and intellectual terms.[19]

The Cold War Atlantic campaign - perhaps more properly the *third* Battle of the Atlantic - was only fought in exercises, but it was fought with some success. Victory in the Cold War has caused the disappearance of its strategic premises, most notably the Soviet threat on land and sea. Although a large Russian submarine fleet remains, political and economic realities mean that it hardly poses the threat it did a decade ago. Nevertheless, for as long as Britain and western Europe in general remain dependent on shipping, it behoves us to maintain some ASW potential as protection from the threat of submarine attack; but the nature of that threat has changed once more.

The current debate in the Ministry of Defence over the importance to be placed on ASW in today's navy is a result of this change. The expensive ASW techniques developed for the expected fleet actions of the 1980s may not be appropriate for the post-Cold War world, with its large numbers of operators of conventional submarines. Countering this expanding threat will have much in common with the dynamics of naval warfare in the second Battle of the Atlantic, the 1939-45 campaign. The lessons of the past will therefore be even more appropriate. It is thus even more crucial that we understand what the true lessons of the past are, so that we can apply them flexibly, utilizing the advantages of modern technology where applicable. What we must not do is repeat the same mistakes yet again.

Notes

1. Historical Section, Admiralty: Naval Staff History, Second World War; *The Defeat of The Enemy Attack Upon Shipping 1939-45: A study of Policy And Operations*, BR 1736(51)(1A) and (1B). A new edition is being prepared for publication by the Navy Records Society.
2. First Sea Lord's Papers, Public Record Office (PRO) ADM 205/69. See Grove, *Vanguard To Trident; British Naval Policy Since World War Two* Chapters 1 and 2 for the escort priority.
3. *Vanguard To Trident*, also Marriott, *Royal Navy Frigates Since 1945*.
4. Ministry of Defence, Maritime Air Defence Committee, PRO, DEFE 8/23. The committee reported on 23 October 1950. The quotation is from p 3 of the final report, MA (50) 50.
5. DEFE 8/23
6. Grove, *Vanguard To Trident*, Chapter 3
7. *Ibid*. See also my forthcoming chapter on McGrigor in Murfitt (Ed.), *First Sea Lords*. The key paper is in ADM 204/102 at the PRO but also see the discussion in Board Minutes and Memoranda for 1950, ADM 167/144.
8. The first signs of this in 1950 were in correspondence from British representatives in the USA in Section 8 of ADMN205/102.
9. See Sokolsky *Sea Power In The Nuclear Age*, Chapter 5.
10. Role of the Navy, D(57) 29, 15 November 1957, PRO, CAB 131/18.
11. Correspondence in First Sea Lord's Papers, ADM 205/172.
12. See the author's "Mountbatten As A Chief Of Staff" in *Aspects of British Defence and Naval Policy in the Mountbatten Era*, Mounbatten Centre of International Studies, University of Southampton, 1992.
13. Cmnd. 1629 quoted in *Vanguard To Trident*, pp. 252-3.
14. The author remembers a Maritime Tactical School study of shipping defence of the 1979-80 period whose bibliography, containing a number of published histories of the Atlantic Battle, notably ommitted BR1736!
15. Grove, *Vanguard To Trident*, pp 350-1.
16. *Ibid*. p. 351. The then MOD Scientific Adviser Sir Ronald Mason published a revealing paper on his thinking in G.Till (Ed.), *The Future Of British Sea Power* entitled "Problems of Fleet Balance".
17. For the evolution of NATO's Concept Of Maritime Operations (CONMAROPS) see my *Battle For The Fiords* Chapter 1 and *Maritime Strategy and European Security*, Chapter 4.
18. The Maritime Strategy received its classic exposition, complete with 'Spots Diagram' in the celebrated supplement to the US Naval Institute's *Proceedings* January, 1986. The Diagram was introduced over the CNO's, Admiral Watkins' signature by the CNO's Staff, against the wishes of the Strategy's original authors.
19. The best overall explanation and intellectual justification was Friedman, *The US Maritime Strategy*.

34

The Battle of the Atlantic as History
by Geoffrey Till

In studying the Battle of the Atlantic, historians must address many important issues, particularly its complexity and comprehensiveness. The essential characteristics of an Atlantic convoy illustrate all the most important issues about the campaign. The planning and preparation of a convoy usually had a decisive influence on whether its arrival was safe and timely - or not. Activity in and behind the reception port was similarly vital; and in the contribution it made to the position, preparation and use of forces ashore, the consequences of the convoy's arrival were frequently crucial too.

A typical convoy would include a great mixture of ships and a large variety of people: armed escorts surrounding merchantmen with many different types of cargoes and ultimate destinations. It was also likely to be highly international in flavour, with Britain's Allies providing many (often most) of the merchant ships and the defensive assets involved in a given operation. English-language studies of the Battle often neglect any great mention of other points of view, so it is good that this book also demonstrates the great diversity that existed on the German side, as well as discussing the Italian role in the campaign and reminding us of the French and Norwegian contributions, voluntary or involuntary, to its outcome. Moreover, this volume emphasizes how operations in the vicinity of the convoys were also only part of the story, whether for the Allies or the Axis. Hundreds, perhaps thousands of miles away, there were the strategic planners on both sides, the ship builders, Intelligence organizations, support organizations and headquarters staff who made it all possible.

The order of the preceding chapters imposes a framework which can help us make sense of the bewildering mass of material that confronts the historian of the Battle. It also reflects the various sequential stages of a typical convoy: first the preparations both distant and close at hand, whether in time or space, then the work up, the involvement of the support services, the sailing and any battle, and finally the outcome and consequences of the voyage. Taken together, all these approaches invite us to consider the Battle of the Atlantic as history.

In doing so, the first point that should be made derives from the sheer diversity of the issues addressed. The multifarious nature of the Battle illustrates the fatal weaknesses of what one might call mono-causal or uni-directional history. What happened in the Atlantic during WWII just cannot be reduced to simple explanations. This is so much the case that it seems futile, even faintly improper, to try to identify a fundamental cause of the Allies' ultimate success.

This comes out loud and clear in the discussion about the relative significance of Ultra and Operational Research[1] in determining the campaign's outcome. On the one hand it is possible to argue, as Hinsley does, that Ultra was decisive in the second half of 1941. At that time - a critical phase in the Battle - it forced the German high command to transfer 21 U-boats to the Mediterranean. It also made possible the Admiralty's system of evasive routeing which, according to Hinsley's authoritative estimate, saved 1½ million tons or about Allied 350 ships from sinking.[2] But later, in 1943, there were too many U-boats for evasive routeing anyway, and, with the aid of other factors (HF/DF, support groups, the closing of the air gap and so on), it was possible to fight the convoys through by the more 'offensive' tactics pioneered by Walker during Convoy HG76.

But the real point is that in trying to establish a single decisive truth, we move quickly and deeply into counterfactual history - that is, the business of speculating about what would have happened had this or that factor been different. We can safely conclude that without Ultra things would have been much worse, but it is risky, and probably a vain effort, to try to go that further step and speculate about how much worse. For example, it is possible to argue that without Ultra, the extra delays involved in Operation Bolero (the build-up of forces in the UK for the invasion of Europe) would have put the Normandy landings back to 1945 or even 1946. This would have allowed the Germans to develop further new submarines like the Types XXI and XXIII, together with such wonder weapons as jet aircraft, V-bombs and so on. But like all the best arguments, this cuts both ways. The extra delay could equally well have led to the nuclear bombing of Germany, in which case the Germans were probably better off losing the Battle than winning it. Counterfactual history is therefore fun, and often helps us identify the issues more clearly, but it does not provide the final answer.[3]

All this being so, the foregoing chapters should remind us of the need to resign ourselves to the inevitable fact that we historians should hope to find no more than multiple and approximate causes. In more ways than one, the Battle of the Atlantic should remind us (if we need reminding) of the value of humility. The tapestry is too big, too closely inter-woven, for bold and simple colours to be effective on their own.

Perhaps most of all, I think this volume should teach historians another and rather more fundamental lesson too: that there is strength in diversity. A proper understanding of so complex a set of issues as lies behind every convoy battle in the Atlantic campaign involves the contribution of many different types of history. The book demonstrates that there are really three equally necessary, equally valid ways of looking at the Battle of the Atlantic - firstly, the macro-industrial level; secondly, the grand strategic; and thirdly, the operational and tactical.

The Macro-Industrial Level of Analysis

The macro-industrial level of analysis focuses on the Battle not so much as a deadly competition in the destruction of ships and U-boats but, rather, as a gigantic battle of attrition and economic management between the world's two biggest industrial agglomerates. Here, the essential questions were questions about the efficient use of resources. In this perspective, the fighting war at sea was only a part of the campaign, and perhaps not the most important. Maybe the real 'war winners' are to be found elsewhere.[4] Perhaps, for instance, in

• the ruthless efficiency with which Britain reduced its need for imports from 60 million to 26 million tons a year,[5] paradoxically increasing the average health of its citizens in the process; or in
• the extent to which the effective management of shipping (its collection, loading, and disposition in harbour) helped the Allies make the best use of the shipping they had. Improved port management alone is reckoned by some to have saved the Allies three million tons by the end of 1941, during which time the Germans had only managed to sink just over two million tons.[6] The converse was also true: the Americans lost far more tonnage to inefficient loading than they did to U-boats.[7] Or perhaps the winning factor lay in
• the extraordinary success of the Allies in building ships faster than the Germans could sink them. Some of the chapters have reminded us how well the British did here, given their obvious difficulties, but the success of America's Henry J. Kaiser and his colleagues was amazing. The astonishing achievement of building a Liberty ship in 80 hours 30 minutes may have been a publicity stunt, but is best seen as a symbol of the scale of the problem the Germans were up against. It raises the question of whether, for them, the Battle of the Atlantic was essentially unwinnable. Between 1940-45 the US alone constructed nearly double the shipping tonnage that the Germans managed to sink. As early as June and July 1943 the Allies found they had a generous surplus of shipping, and as Churchill said later, 'All the rest was merely the proper application of overwhelming force.'[8]

Interesting issues arise if we consider the Battle of the Atlantic as a huge, complex competition in the management of economic and industrial resources. This is a very necessary part of a proper understanding of the Atlantic campaign, which is perhaps too often seen as a merely maritime affair. Even nomenclature might be significant here. The Churchillian term 'the Battle of the Atlantic' may inadvertently tend to turn our minds overmuch to the tactical and technical level of analysis.

But many people are made uneasy by this kind of strategic/industrial history, because if taken too far, it seems to consign the actual fighting - the death and destruction on the high seas - to the footnotes as though such elements were not particularly important in the grand scheme of things. And it is always necessary to recall that in the last analysis, wars are as much won or lost by *people* as by the blind forces of history. The Battle of the Atlantic was a searing experience for everyone who participated in it, and there are still many, many questions to be asked about it, simply as a human experience.

Surely one of the most sobering amongst these questions has to do with the motivation of the men on both sides. I would pick out the merchant seamen on the Allied side, suffering losses at a rate proportionately higher than many of the fighting services, yet consigned by their trade merely to the role of passive and almost entirely helpless victim. But time and time again, no sooner had they completed a voyage than they re-enlisted. On the other side, there is the extraordinary courage of the U-boat crews, especially towards the end of the war when they faced overwhelming odds of the sort so graphically described in the film *Das Boot* and Herbert A. Werner's book *Iron Coffins*. Their resolution appears to have been a heady mix of belief in the cause, loyalty to their shipmates, stubborn despair and hope in ultimate victory through new weapons.[9] The amazing courage they displayed to the very end is a sobering reminder that there is far more to war than building schedules. Historians of the Battle should never forget that what they analyse is not some kind of giant board game, but cruel hard war in all its horrors.

The Grand Strategic Level

The human element also comes out when one looks at the grand strategic level, when we consider the Atlantic campaign against the context of WWII as a whole. What effect did the campaign, and its particular stages, have on the conduct of operations ashore? This is such a huge topic that even a book as international as this cannot hope to cover all aspects of the matter.

For example, it cannot explore in detail the very important inter-connections between the progress of the campaign and the likelihood of American entry into the war. Were the Germans bound to lose because the more successful they were, the more likely it was that the US would intervene? However, the book does illustrate many of the connections between the Battle and the progress of the war on land. The close relationship between the war at sea and the progress of operations ashore is still a fruitful area for analysis. In summer 1943, Dönitz justified continuing the U-boat war partly on the grounds that it was a cost-effective means of diverting Allied efforts away from areas even more harmful to the German interest. If it was really true that the Allies had to devote far more resources to containing the U-boat threat than the Gemans did to mounting it, then even with an equal kill rate, the campaign still made sense. This essential point is often obscured by the tendency of many historians (and indeed of Dönitz himself) to focus on the 'tonnage war'. Such a proposition is analogous to, and as faulty as, the idea that Allied success in the Battle could be measured simply by the sinking of U-boats.

It is also as well to recall the *guerre de course* theories of the Jeune Ecole from which inter-war German theorists derived at least some of their inspiration. No 19th-Century Jeune Ecole theorist ever claimed it would be possible to cut the UK entirely off from its overseas supplies and dominions. Rather, they hoped to inflict such disruption on Britain's economy that the nation would be forced to sue for peace. It was the same for Dönitz. Sinking merchantmen was a necessary part of the strategy, but it was only a part.

This economic campaign might have shocked the British out of the war - and there are some indications that this was Hitler's expectation and preference. If not, it could have forced the British to make agonizing choices between its military effort and its civilian requirements (namely, staving off starvation). Given the dire straits to which the British economy was reduced as early as the end of 1940 through trying to balance the requirements of these competing commitments, such economic warfare was a very promising line of attack on such a maritime country as Britain. Britain's urgent need for Lend-Lease and America's multifarious economic assistance raises the issue of whether the Germans could have won, particularly before the Americans joined the war.

In particular (and to succumb once more to the seductions of counter-factual history), could the Germans have won if their policy towards the U-boat - especially their design and construction policy - had been different? Three arguments present themselves, and nearly all focus on the possibility of a strategic knock-out in the early part of the war, before the Allies' industrial muscle had time to bring about its otherwise inevitable effect. In a way, the iron law which demanded an early victory over the Soviet Union on land applied equally well to the sea. Against the western Allies too, Germany's only choice was between a quick victory or a slow defeat. These are the three arguments.

Argument 1: The Germans did not concentrate on U-boats early enough.
As Churchill himself remarked, 'The U-boat attack was our worst evil. It would have been wise for the Germans to stake all upon it.' Not surprisingly, Dönitz agreed. On 1 September 1939, he said, 'The only possibility of bringing England to her knees with the forces of our Navy lies in attacking her sea communications in the Atlantic....I therefore believe that the U-boat will always be the backbone of warfare against England.'

This argument has it that the Germans should have concentrated on building far more U-boats earlier, instead of going for the type of balanced fleet suggested by Raeder's plans and later by Plan Z. But in 1937, OKM was sceptical of the proposed wolf-pack tactics and of the value of U-boats for anti-shipping operations. Instead, thinking U-boats should work with the fleet and for the fleet, it would not give the Type VII the priority Dönitz wanted.

The fact that a Type VII U-boat cost only 4 million RM, compared to 200 million RM for *Bismarck*[10] reinforces the impression that too much was devoted to the latter and not enough to the former. For the financial cost of one *Bismarck*, 50 extra Type VIIs could have been built. As it was, the German

Navy started the war with only 57 U-boats all told, and only half of those were suited to Atlantic operations. Moreover, the number of operational U-boats dipped to 26 in June 1940, and 22 in March 1941. The U-boat fleet was therefore at its lowest ebb just at the time when it could have been most strategically decisive.

Despite early plans to build nearly 30 U-boats per month beginning in September 1939, only 13 new ones were commissioned in the first nine months of war, and only 37 new boats were built in 1939-40 - barely one third of those originally envisaged. Hitler's over-confidence in the prospects of a British surrender appears to have played some part in this curiously relaxed approach.[11] Worse still, the German Navy paid insufficient attention to the acquisition of effective torpedoes. Dönitz was understandably critical of the 'inadequate development and testing [and the] uncritical attitude by the Torpedo Experimental Establishment towards its own achievements.'[12]

The resultant shortage of U-boat numbers meant that until spring 1941, there were rarely more than a dozen boats in the Atlantic at any one time. This delayed the arrival of real wolf packs and, more generally, meant (in Marc Milner's words) that 'the German attack developed slowly enough for the British to take effective countermeasures'.[13]

It was much the same story in the air, where the Luftwaffe gave low priority to the anti-shipping war.[14] Göring devoted only one group of 40 aircraft to the Battle, with the result that on any one day, there were on average only three German aircraft over the Atlantic. In 1942, the Allies committed about 500 aircraft to the Battle of the Atlantic, perhaps ten times the German total.

Nevertheless, even with such limited resources committed to the attack, the Germans still managed to sink six million tons of shipping up to spring 1941.[15] This perhaps reinforces the impression that with an earlier and larger effort, a knockout blow might have been possible.

But, this argument runs, the error was compounded by Dönitz's reaction to it: his tendency to emphasize an increase in the *number* of his boats, rather than in their quality. Thus, more of the existing Types VII and IX boats were constructed, even though they were 'only marginally better than their World War I predecessors.'[16] For example, even though schnorkels had been devised in the Netherlands in 1940, they were not fitted to U-boats until 1943. By the time that Dönitz did concentrate on the new Types XXI and XXIII, it was already too late; the best opportunity for a knock-out blow had gone. Now the construction programme had to contend with the Allied air offensive on the one hand, and the voracious demands of the Eastern Front on the other. The Germans, in short, missed the boat.

Argument 2: German strategy was too continental
It is of course true that the exercise of continental land and air power hugely improved the strategic odds for Germany's campaign against Atlantic shipping. It put anti-shipping aircraft and U-boats much closer to their patrol areas,

effectively increasing their number and/or range, and posed a level of threat to Britain in its more local waters which (for example in summer 1940) distracted attention and escorts away from the Atlantic.

Nonetheless, there is justice in the German Navy's frequent complaint that national strategy was too 'continentalized.' According to this argument, Hitler was unwilling to give the navy its necessary priority, except briefly and typically impulsively in early 1939.[17] Perhaps this was because he was essentially a land animal, unfamiliar with the potential of sea power, particularly against a maritime power such as Britain. Perhaps it was because he thought Britain would negotiate a peace. Perhaps it was a very proper appreciation of the seriousness of the land threat from the east. Whatever the cause, the result was a continued reluctance to provide naval construction programmes with the necessary resources, and a tendency to take U-boats away from the main theatre of operations, sometimes at crucial moments, to support army objectives in the Mediterranean and the North.

For their part, the British never had any such doubt. Winning the Battle of the Atlantic for them was crucial, vital - the top priority, and they were prepared to provide everything it required. There was only one strategic dispute in Britain: not whether, but how this should be best achieved. Not even Bomber Harris ever denied the vital necessity of winning the war at sea; his argument was that a blitz on German industrial capacity was in fact the the surest way to that victory.[18]

This difference in emphasis between Germany and Great Britain was natural given the fact that Britain was a profoundly maritime nation, acutely aware of the fundamental strategic vulnerability that this implied. It was all rather nicely summed up by a children's book on the RN which appeared in 1941:

> A mere glance at the map of our far-flung Dominions is all that is required to understand why it is imperative for us to have a strong Navy. In every direction, the highways from Great Britain - the Mother Country - to our possessions abroad are across the sea. And our Navy is necessary to keep open under all circumstances the whole of the routes between England and her Dominions, so that trading ships and all other ships can move safely along them in peace and war. Keeping these sea routes open is of vital importance to us, for our population depends to a great extent upon food brought to it from overseas. If those sea-lanes were effectively closed for a few weeks and all our food imports stopped, everybody in the country would soon be reduced to a state of starvation, and our enemies know this all too well. It is the first means of defeating us an enemy attempts.[19]

But there was an offensive side to this argument as well. The fact of the matter was that the Axis powers represented 193 million people and 17% of the world's productive capacity, whereas Britain, the US and the Soviet Union together, with much less than double the number of people - 360 million - commanded over 60% of the world's industrial capacity, or nearly four times the industrial resources of the Axis. It was the sea that tied the Allies together. So if the Allies could only keep the shipping going, they would surely win the war, other things being equal.[20] Given that, the Germans should perhaps have given maximum emphasis to the anti-shipping war.

Argument 3: Germany had the wrong sort of navy
This intriguing proposition has not so far been much discussed in this book. It sounds a little traditional and Mahanist, but might still be right for all that. Its conclusion is that Raeder was right and Dönitz was wrong. The Germans lost not because they did not have enough U-boats, but because they did not have a properly balanced fleet capable of wresting control of the sea away from the British. Instead, German strategy rested on a single weapon system and a strategy of denial.[21] The real challenge would have been Admiral Raeder's Z Plan fleet. This would have provided enough powerful surface ships out on the world's oceans to force the RN to disperse its major forces to look for them, while simultaneously keeping enough forces in European waters to pose a major threat to Britain there as well. A moderate U-boat force would then be able to exploit the gaps this strategic dilemma would cause. U-boats would force the merchant ships to convoy and powerful commerce raiders would destroy the convoys.

It is important to remember that there was another Battle of the Atlantic, in which surface warships commerce raiders *were* the threat rather than U-boats. The early sinkings and disruptions brought about by such raiders and the potential effectiveness of ships like *Scharnhorst*, *Gneisenau*, *Bismarck* and *Tirpitz* (had these been able to operate at will) together show how serious this threat could have been. From this perspective, pre-war Admiralty policy towards the U-boat, often vehemently criticized, begins to look more respectable. This threat also makes it very clear why the British were determined that France's fleet should not fall into German hands along with her ports.

In the event, this threat did not materialize. German warships usually appeared on the open ocean largely as fugitives, and were extremely reluctant to take on even quite weak defensive forces. But it would certainly have been a different story if Germany had gone to war with the Z Plan fleet.

Mines were another serious threat to British shipping, and in fact sank more ships than did the U-boats. More investment there, relative to other forms of naval activity, might have paid even better dividends for the Germans. More radically still, a switch in emphasis towards land-based maritime airpower might have resulted in an even more serious threat to British shipping; it was bad in the ferocious summer of 1940, but it might have been worse. Certainly, the British Naval Staff of the late 1930s assumed that the Luftwaffe would play an important role in any attempted 'knock-out' blow against British shipping in the Thames estuary, and other British east coast ports. Here too, then, a different force structure might have resulted in a much more serious level of threat.

The Operational/Tactical Level

Turning to our third level of analysis, this concerns the tactics and the technical aspects of the convoy battle itself. Here we are concerned with 'battle history'. At this level, a whole series of detailed issues emerge concerning the relative effectiveness of this weapon or that tactic. Ultra was obviously important. The importance of airpower in making the most of the inherent limitations of the Type VIIs is hard to exaggerate. That being so, it is easy to have at least some sympathy with the argument that, on both sides, there was a tendency to give maritime airpower too little priority when compared to the other things that air forces did. But in truth, there were innumerable such issues, many of which have been raised in earlier chapters.

Some of the most interesting questions were posed when the true submarine arrived, in the shapes of the Types XXI and XXIII. Among the Allies there was widespread and long-lasting concern that contemporary ASW simply was not up to the challenge presented by these vessels. On the other hand, it was not clear that the capacity of the new Types to *find* targets had increased in parallel with their ability to sink them. Accordingly, the arrival of the true submarine would simply have signified a new stage in the defence/offence balance that had been developing and changing all the way through the campaign. The Battle of the Atlantic can be seen, pre-eminently, as a transient and highly technical battle between the back-room boys on both sides. Over and over again they produced first the weapon, or the sensor, and then its counter, and then the refinement, and then the counter and so on.

Understanding each stage requires familiarity with the nuts and bolts of history. Only this can provide the raw material for any attempt to relate technology to operations, or to assess the fascinating (but probably unanswerable) question of the relationship between, and the relative importance of, technical and tactical developments.[22]

But neither should we forget the organizational/bureaucratic approach which seeks to understand decisions in terms of the process which led to them. Command arrangements, inter-service relations, political considerations all had their part to play even at the lowest tactical and technical level. A case in point is the command relationship between Walker and Mackendrick during HG76 and its relevance to the sinking of the escort carrier *Audacity*. The close relationship between the Admiralty and Coastal Command compares well with the level of achievement of their American equivalents, and also illustrates the operational significance of such arrangements.[23]

Perhaps the only way really to analyse the relative importance of such considerations is to look at specific case studies, through detailed battle histories. Some earlier chapters reviewed HG76; the spring 1943 battles are also good examples. The melancholy story of the campaign on the United States' 'Eastern Sea Frontier' is another useful case study; and if it suggests rather different conclusions, this is because upon close consideration, each case study looks unique - and should probably be treated as such by historians. It would clearly be highly dangerous to read the results of the analysis of one battle across to another. The bewildering variety in reputable estimates of shipping and U-boat losses is a sobering reminder of how difficult it has been in the last 50 years even to agree the Battle's basic statistics. Given that, developing a consensus in battle analysis would obviously be even more challenging. The second point to emerge from considering the significance of technology in the Atlantic campaign is an obvious one. Perhaps, given their huge industrial superiority, the Allies' scientific victory was inevitable, and in the triumph of one weapon over another we should really see a symptom of the industrial odds against the U-boat. With this, though, we are getting back to the macro-industrial issues.

Conclusions

While the failure of the RN of the inter-war period to take the defence of shipping seriously may often be exaggerated, it is certainly true that the accumulated experience of WWI provided was not as well processed as it might have been. This led to the repetition of certain mistakes (most notably in the sizing of convoys) and in due course to Peter Gretton's question, 'Why Don't We Learn From History?'[24]

Historians deal with unique, unrepeatable events. It is therefore not their business to supply lessons for the present and future; but any analysis of the Battle of the Atlantic certainly tempts them to point out some of the obvious implications for later generations. By this means, historians of the Battle extend the permanent importance of their subject. It remains a subject of widespread interest, and (as some of the chapters in this book show) a sensitive subject as well.[25] Relevant lessons for today's policy-makers include the following.

• On both sides, Allied or Axis, the Battle of the Atlantic was a great international endeavour requiring the closest co-operation of many nations and all the services in preparing and posing threats and in meeting them. This applied at all levels of the campaign. Much of this volume reminds us that this kind of multi-national naval co-operation, so much the fashion these days, cannot be improvised, but on the contrary requires a good deal of time to work up, and patience to maintain. Today we are so familiar with multi-national naval co-operation in Nato, the UN or both that it is easy to forget how remarkable the level of international integration displayed in the Battle of the

Atlantic actually was. In the constant perils that attended such joint operations, the Battle still has much to teach us.

● The chapters which focused on the ability to train huge number of young conscripts and reservists to the necessary level were especially significant, reminding us that highly trained manpower is, in the modern jargon, the most effective 'force multiplier'. Weapons designers, constructors, commanders-in-chief and U-boat captains all needed to exhibit a capacity for high-level decision; merchant sailors, escort crews, airmen and submariners all demanded the best training. Over and over again, whether it was a question of Captain Walker's 2nd Escort Group or U-boat aces like Kretschmer and Prien, quality told.

● Finally, this book cannot fail to remind us, especially in Britain, of our continuing need to look to the sea, and to provide well for ourselves in all maritime needs: naval and merchant shipping, construction and perhaps above all, the training of maritime people. Being a maritime nation is, as the Battle of the Atlantic illustrates, a source not just of strength but of potentially fatal weakness too - unless we are prepared to defend our maritime characteristics in peace as well as in war.[26]

Notes

1. See preceding chapters by Rohwer and Sutcliffe.
2. See Hinsley, *British Intelligence*, II, p. 169.
3. *Ibid.* and III Pt 1, p. 51. 'What consequences would have followed if Germany had taken these developments in hand earlier, or if sbe had succeeded in prolonging war by delaying *Overlord* or checking the Allies on the Normandy beaches? It would serve no purpose to attempt to answer such questions.' See also M. Milner, 'The Battle of the Atlantic', *Journal of Strategic Studies*, March 1990.
4. These issues are all explored in Pugh's chapter above.
5. Milner, *op.cit.*, p. 46.
6. *Ibid.*, p. 47.
7. *Ibid.*, p. 52 and Pugh's chapter, *op. cit.*
8. Quoted in Terraine, *Business in Great Waters*, p. 402.
9. See preceding chapters by Lane and Topp; also Thomas, *The German Navy in the Nazi Era*, pp. 225-259; and Herbert A. Werner, *Iron Coffins*.
10. Showell, *U-boats Under the Swastika*, p. 15
11. See preceding chapter by Rössler.
12. See Dönitz, *Memoirs*, pp. 84-90.
13. Milner, *op.cit.*, pp. 47, 49.
14. See preceding chapter by Heitmann.
15. See Roskill, *The War at Sea*, I, Appendix R.
16. Showell, *U-boats under the Swastika*, p. 98.

17. Deist, *Germany and the Second World War*, Vol I. pp. 478-9.
18. See preceding chapter by Probert.
19. *Our Navy*, p. 14.
20. Gray, *The Leverage of Seapower*, p. 239.
21. See preceding chapter by Rahn.
22. See preceding chapter by Zimmermann.
23. Probert, *op.cit.*
24. Vice Admiral P. Gretton, 'Why Don't We Learn From History?', *Naval Review*, January 1958.
25. See preceding paper by Santoni.
26. I am indebted to my colleague S/Lt Andy Yeomans, RN, for his help in preparing this chapter. None of the the views expressed in it should be taken necessarily to reflect official opinion in any way.

35

The Historiography of the Battle

by Derek G. Law

The published literature and the primary archive records of the Battle of the Atlantic are extensive. Both are readily accessible, but neither is easily navigated, and the published literature continues to grow. This chapter provides some guidance through what can be a confusing quantity of material.

Archives

The official archives of the participants are housed mainly at the BundesArchiv in Freiburg; the Public Archives of Canada in Ottawa; and the Public Record Office at Kew. Other archives (often personal papers) reside in museums and universities in all countries and are not always so easy to track down. There is little to be gained by offering a potted guide to any of these archives and the varied series of classifications and guides which allow them to be used. The best way to gain access to them is through their staff. Anyone who takes the trouble to read the acknowledgements page of almost any monograph will see fulsome tributes to individuals or the staff as a whole of libraries and archives throughout the world. They remain one of the last bastions of a public service culture and are both to be cherished and used. Rather than provide a bland list of archives and their locations and opening hours, it may be more appropriate to use illustrative examples, beginning with personal archives and moving on to official records.

For some years, funded by the Leverhulme Foundation and working jointly with the University of Southampton, the Liddell Hart Centre for Military Archives (based at King's College London) has been pursuing a special project. Staff at Southampton are undertaking research on the 19th Century and King's College on the 20th, with a view to locating papers of all senior military and defence personnel and their civilian counterparts. One of the major if regrettable achievements of the project is in identifying what papers do *not* exist or survive. Results are already available on the inter-university JANET computer network and will be published in the next 12-18 months.

As a way of describing some of the locations of archives it is worth personalizing their location a little. Thus, looking at the successive commanders of Western Approaches we find that there are no papers from Admiral Dunbar-Naismith for this period, although the Imperial War Museum has some papers relating to his exploits in the Dardanelles in submarine E11 in WWI. Admiral Noble's papers are at the Churchill Archives Centre in Cambridge, although these consist of what is correctly if imprecisely described as 'two small boxes covering his correspondence from 1900 to his death in 1955'. Admiral Horton's papers are at the RN Submarine Museum at Gosport but seem to cover the period only prior to his appointment as C-in-CWA. Not surprisingly, given their location, they relate entirely to submarine matters.

If one looks at the battlefield commanders and picks famous names such as Gretton and Macintyre, the former did have papers which were promised to the National Maritime Museum, but there are no known Macintyre papers.

A move up to the High Command reveals a little more. Starting with Dudley Pound, at the Churchill Archives Centre in Cambridge we find seven boxes of letters, together with cuttings and notes for a projected biography by Donald McLachlan, while the RN Submarine Museum at Gosport has some correspondence from Pound to Horton regarding submarine construction.

Admiral Godfrey, master of intelligence and discretion, has, curiously, left more of a mark than anyone. His papers are variously at the Churchill Archives Centre, the National Maritime Museum and the Ministry of Defence's Naval Historical Library, while copies of his unpublished memoirs are at the Imperial War Museum.

This brief examination of sources of personal papers both illustrates their scarcity and makes it clear that only a very few major archives have serious collections of relevant material.[1]

With a rather different personal story, the same point can be made for the official archives. In 1940 at Fremantle, Max Shean, born in Western Australia, volunteered for naval service. After training he moved to the UK and a posting in the corvette *Bluebell*. He later had a most distinguished career in midget submarines, but of more relevance here is his experience of the Battle of the Atlantic, as told in his recent memoirs *Corvette and Submarine*.[2] He describes the battle around convoy OG71 in December 1941. Like many such night actions it was both long and confused. In this case it was also wholly succesful, in that the convoy reached port without loss, while six U-boats were sunk. The night stuck in Shean's memory. As the officer in charge of the asdic set, he effectively controlled the attacks on the U-boats. At the critical moment the asdic set failed and *Bluebell* rejoined the convoy after a suitable 'bottle' from the senior officer.[3]

Shean always wondered what had happened and recounts in his memoirs how many years late he set out to reconstruct the events of the night. This was prompted by reading Roskill's official history, which credited *Bluebell* with the sinking of U-208. A letter to the Admiralty elicited a response that this was not the case and that *Bluebell* was now credited with damaging but not sinking U-67. Shean then records his next steps, having discovered that some nine U-boats were in the area west of Gibraltar. I quote him here as a perfect example both of what records exist and of their fallibility:

> In the course of further research I twice visited the UK and consulted records at the Public Record Office at Kew, the RN Submarine Archives at Gosport and MOD (Navy) Historical Section in London. Data obtained included convoy details,

> *Bluebell's* attack report, three publications by German authors
> crediting *Bluebell* with the sinking of U-208 and an English
> translation of the War Diary of the BdU (Befelshaber der
> Unterseeboots, or U-boat Command)....I [also] obtained
> photocopies of [the] War Diaries in German [of the four nearest
> U-boats] together with the German Naval Grid Chart of the
> Atlantic.[4]

Shean spent many hours with this documentation. He might also have
mentioned the Staff Histories as well as the Reports of Proceedings of the
commanders of naval units, likewise available at the MOD Library. Given the
heat of the action, it is not surprising that little information in the reports from
the two sides found by Shean tallies exactly. How things appeared to the
participants was not necessarily how things actually were. Today, trying to work
out just what did happen, one must remember again (in Shean's words again)
that 'in failing daylight a 1,000-ton single-funnelled corvette could well be
taken for an 1,100-ton two-funnelled destroyer' and that one U-boat mistook
another for a fast motorboat.

Shean is satisfied that *Bluebell* attacked two U-boats and sank one. However
the real points I wish to make are firstly, that copious records are available;
secondly, that they are in the major public record offices; but thirdly, that they
do not answer questions or give the unchallenged facts of the war at sea. What
they do is to provide the evidence on which judgements must be made, but not
the judgements themselves.

Published Works

In this book, Jock Gardner proposes a classification of the published historical
literature into three phases.[5] I intend to follow this classification, but to
elaborate his divisions a little so as to include further categories of material. I
have also tried to complement rather than simply repeat the material in his
chapter, but like him I will largely confine my comments to works in English
and concentrate on the monograph literature. One reason for omitting reference
to areas such as academic theses is that, by and large, they do not exist. The UK
has all too few researchers on naval matters and fewer still on the modern RN.

About 100 monographs have been written specifically about the Battle and
perhaps twice as many again (notably the official histories and the many
biographies both of men and ships) contain basic material about the Battle as
part of more general accounts of the war. These are fairly fully decribed in the
bibliographic literature, whether of fact, such as Law's *Royal Navy in World
War Two* or fiction, such as Paris's *Novels of World War Two*, and only a
selection can be mentioned below.

Before the Official Histories there was a period during the war itself when
books on the Battle began to appear. Most of the publications from this period
are essentially propaganda. Some are quite eloquent, such as *Canada's War at*

Sea, which has a long essay by Stephen Leacock, or *The Saga of the San Demetrio* by F. Tennyson Jesse. War correspondents such as Maurice Brown, Leonard Gander and Quentin Reynolds told their supportive tales, while the war artists, photographers and poets displayed their truths in ways less susceptible to censorship. The government too produced various glossy publications which presented a homogenised and glossy version of what had happened. Perhaps the only one to escape this charge is Macdonald Critchley's study of shipwreck survivors which, in spare medical language, comes as close as anything to describing the horror of it all.

The official histories are mainly well known, but one might single out for mention Tucker's masterly but all too often neglected offical history of the Naval Service of Canada, which is a treasure trove of information, and Coulter's well written history of the Royal Naval Medical Service. Blake's History of Northern Ireland's role in WWII is also too often forgotten, although it contains much useful material on the escort base at Londonderry. We should further include here the official histories of shipping companies. Many, from Ben Line to Alfred Holt, had their accounts published, often written by notable historians such as Roskill or Waters, and these add yet another dimension to the picture. Perhaps the best of these is Roskill's history of the Holt fleet.

A further category might be added to Gardner's list. The 1960's saw the beginning of lists and descriptions of the protagonists and their weapons, with the start point being marked by Lenton and Colledge's still valuable *Warships of World War II*. The 1970's saw the burgeoning of these publications ranging from the densely packed and comprehensive listing of escort vessels in some 600 pages by Peter Elliott to the guides (of 50-odd pages each) to particular classes of ship, such as Preston and Raven's *Flower Class Corvettes*. This area of publication shows no sign of diminishing and continues to produce excellent work - for example Hague's guide to the *Town* Class destroyers, workhorses of the Atlantic, a publication which began life with the ever-active World Ship Society. Finally in this section one cannot overlook Rohwer and Hümmelchen's essential *Chronology of the War at Sea*, now in its second revised edition.

Gardner's other division is essentially into pre- and post- public knowlege of ULTRA. His point is fair and any reader of the steady but small trickle of general histories of the battle will recognize this division and the arguments which flow from it. The post-ULTRA period has brought a late flowering of personal reminiscences. Many participants, notably now from the lower deck, have sprung into print, frequently in what used to be called vanity publishing. As far as these books are concerned, I feel it is fairer to describe them less as vanity books and more as a form of oral history. As evidenced by their dedications, they are often an attempt by those in the autumn of their lives to record some of their experiences for grandchildren and later generations. Naturally the fallibility of human memory - especially after the passage of 50 years - poses a risk to verity, but they remain a rich and valuable source of material, and should be more actively sought by historians.

There have also been attempts to record fragments and anecdotes about the war. Under this heading, one might note particularly the consistently interesting Canadian series of anecdotal publications called *Salty Dips*, Mason's surprisingly uncritical set of American oral testimonies in *The Atlantic War Remembered* and Kenneth Poolman's *The British Sailor: Experiences of War*. An anthology of reminiscences called simply *Battle of the Atlantic* has been published to coincide with the 50th anniversary celebrations. Other works such as Barker's *Circle of Trees*, Curry's *War at Sea* and Morin Scott's *War is a Funny Business* are all examples of this genre.

It is instructive to consider the characteristics of the literature of some of the main participants other than the British. A curious feature of Battle of the Atlantic history writing is that it took Canadians some 35 years to begin seriously to address their contribution to the battle. A general history by Swettenham, the story of corvettes by James Lamb and a personal memoir by Hal Lawrence all appeared in 1979. Since then a rich flow of literature has come from Canadian publishing houses, with Milner's *North Atlantic Run* perhaps the best of them. Ken Macpherson has also worked tirelessly to produce a series of works describing the Canadian wartime fleet.

US literature has understandably tended to concentrate on the Pacific. For the Atlantic, its major focus has been on the actions of the U-boats off the east coast of America the most recent example of this group of publications being Gannon's *Operation Drumbeat*. Nor should one omit Admiral Gallery's account of how he won the Battle of the Atlantic - if not single-handedly, then perhaps with a *little* help from his friends - with the presence of the captured U-505, now resident in Chicago, bearing testimony to this.

German literature translated into English has concentrated on individual U-boat captains or their boats. Cremer and Kretschmer, Luth and Metzler have all been the subject of biographies or autobiographies. Rohwer's listing of U-boat successes and Rössler's description of U-boats are also essential reference tools, while the recent British publication of Hessler's post-war description of the Battle is close to being an official account from the German side.

Perhaps the most notable omission from all existing bibliographic lists are the Official Despatches. Over 30 naval despatches were published as Supplements to the *London Gazette* between 1947 and 1950 and a few cover such relevant matters as the *Bismarck* hunt, the destruction of raiders in the South Atlantic and the various attacks on the *Tirpitz*. They are difficult to find, except in major research libraries, but researchers have little excuse for ignoring them. At least they are available. Coastal Command likewise suffers the indignity of being ignored. Despatches were produced by Air Chief Marshals Bowhill, Joubert de la Ferté, Slessor and Douglas in 1947, but for mysterious reasons they were not declassified until November 1967. It seems unlikely that they will now be published, but can be found in the MOD Library.

Conclusion

This necessarily brief overview of the literature of the Battle of the Atlantic attempts to draw out trends rather than aim at comprehensiveness. Even so, it has been necessary to omit mention of the Armed Merchant Cruisers, of the Fleet Air Arm and Coastal Command (all of which have commendably good literature); of the minor allied navies (the Belgian, the Free French and the Norwegian) about which little has been written; and of the Dominion navies, all of which have at least some marginal claim to have participated in the Battle. The Fleet Air Arm in particular has produced perhaps the most readable and enjoyable literature of the war, but fuller reference to it will be found in published bibliographies.

Finally, one other trend might be noted. Much of the writing of history is revisionist. Characters rise and fall from grace, the judgement on the importance of battles waxes and wanes, the relative value of individuals set against the tides of history rises and falls. Yet the Battle of the Atlantic seems to be an exception. After 50 years, apart from the question of the importance of ULTRA, no one - and I include myself - has seen any serious need to attempt to alter Macintyre's judgement of 1961 in his classic history of the Battle:

> It was to the Atlantic that ships from the seven seas came, cargoes in their bellies, of value to hard-pressed England beyond any treasure horde of olden times. It was in the Atlantic, therefore, that the enemy had the best chance to deliver a mortal blow. Every phase of the war against Germany was dominated by the necessity to bring our laden ships to port and our outgoing, empty ships away. It was from overseas that the majority of the weapons, munitions and raw materials had to come, with which to rearm ourselves. ...It can fairly be said that it was in the Atlantic that the Allies could have been most surely defeated. It was there, instead, that the war was won.[6]

Notes

1. The information on locations of papers was kindly provided by Kate O' Brien, Military Archivist at the Liddell Hart Centre for Military Archives, King's College London.
2. Shean, Max, *Corvette and Submarine*.
3. *Ibid.*
4. *Ibid.*
5. Gardner, W. J. R., *The Battle of the Atlantic: An Allied Perspective*, above.
6. Macintyre, *The Battle of the Atlantic*.

Glossary

'A'	Marinekommandoamt (Naval Command Office)
AMC	Armed Merchant Cruiser
A/S, ASW	Anti-Submarine Warfare
Asdic	Allied Submarine Detecting Investigation
ASV	Air-to-Surface Vessel radar
ASWORG	Anti-Submarine Warfare Operational Research Group (US)
'B'	Allgemeines Marineamt
BA-MA	Bundesarchiv-Militararchiv (FederalArchives/ Military Archives, Freiburg)
B-Dienst	German Intelligence service (also xB-Dienst)
BdU	Befehlshaber der U-Boote (U-boat Command)
Betasom	Italian submarine flotilla and base, Bordeaux, France
Bold	submarine bubble decoy
Bombe	decrypting machine
BuNav	Bureau of Navigation (US Navy)
BuPers	Bureau of Naval Personnel (US Navy)
CAM ship	Catapult Aircraft Merchantman
CHOP line	CHange of OPerational control
CinC	Commander in Chief
CINCLANT	Commander-in-Chief Atlantic
CINCWA	Commader-in-Chief Western Approaches
COMINCH	Commander-in-Chief, US Fleet
CNO	Chief of Naval Operations (Washington, D.C.)
COTCLANT	Commander, Operational Training, Atlantic (US)
CVE	Carrier Vessel, Escort
DEMS	Defensively-Equipped Merchant Ship
DF	Destroyer Flotilla
Dipl.-Ing	DiplomIngenieur
FdU	Führer der U-boote (Chief of Submarines)
FOCNA	Flag Officer Central North Atlantic
GEMA	Gesellschaft für Elektroakustische und Mechanische Apparate mbH
GNAT	German Naval Acoustic Torpedo
grt	gross registered tons
HAS	Hauptausschuss Schiffbau (Main Committee for Ship Construction)
Hedgehog	Ship-borne ahead-thrown mortar
HF/DF	High Frequency Direction Finder (Huff-Duff)

Igewit	Ingenieurburo fur Wirtschaft und Technik GmbH
IvS	Ingenieurskantoor voor Scheepsbouw (Holland)
kn	knots
'K' Amt	Warship Construction Office (Germany)
KDB-Anlage	German hydrophone
Kptl.	Kapitanleutnant (Lieutenant Commander)
Kpt.z.S	Kapitan zur See (Captain)
KTB	Kriegstagebuch (War Diary)
LCT	Landing Craft, Tank
Lt Cdr	Lieutenant Commander
Min.Rat	Ministerialrat
Mob Plan	Mobilization Plan (Germany)
MTB	Motor Torpedo Boat
nm	nautical miles
NSA	Norwegian Shipowners' Association
Obl.z.S.	Oberleutnant zur See (Lieutenant)
OIC	Operational Intelligence Centre, Admiralty (London)
OKM	Oberkommando der Kriegsmarine (German Naval High Command)
OKW	Oberkommando der Wehrmacht (German Army High Command)
OP-20-G	US decrypting department
PRO	Public Record Office, Kew, London
Reg.	Regierungs- (Government)
ret.	retired
S-Gerät	German Asdic
Skl	Seekriegsleitung (German Naval Staff)
sm	sea miles = nautical miles
Sonar	Sound Navigation and Ranging
Squid	Ship-borne ahead-thrown mortar
Sqn Ldr	Squadron Leader
SSN	nuclear-powered submarine
WATU	Western Approaches Tactical Unit
WESTOPM	Western Ocean Meeting Point
WW	World War
Zaunkönig	German acoustic torpedo

Consolidated Bibiliography

This section gives a full bibliographic listing of all the English-language monographs cited by authors. Foreign-language works and journal articles are cited in full in the footnotes of the chapter on the first occasion when they occur. References to unpublished records and archival sources are also given in the footnotes. Where page numbers are cited in footnotes these refer to the edition of the author's own country. Here, anonymous works are cited first, followed by an alphabetical author listing. Both British and American publishers are given, where known.

Battle of the Atlantic: An Anthology of Personal Memories, Liverpool, Picton Press, 1993.

British Merchant Vessels Lost or Damaged by Enemy Action During the Second World War, London, HMSO, 1947.

British Vessels Lost at Sea, 1939-45, Cambridge, PSL, 1976 (a reprinting of *British Vessels Lost...* and *Ships of the Royal Navy: Statement of Losses*, [*q.v.*] in a single volume. There have been several editions of this title.)

Build the Ships, London, HMSO, 1946.

Canada's War at Sea, (2 vols in 1), Montreal, Beatty, 1944.

Conway's all the World's Fighting Ships 1922-1946, London, Conway, 1980; Annapolis, NIP, 1981.

Fuehrer Conferences on Naval Affair, London, Greenhill, 1990 (published in typescript by the US Navy Department in 1947 and by the Admiralty in 1949).

Lloyd's War Losses. The Second World War, vol. I, British, Allied and Neutral merchant vessels sunk or destroyed by war causes. A facsimile reprint of the original held at the Guildhall Library, City of London. London, Lloyds, 1989.

Our Navy, London, Ward Lock, 1941.

Port At War, Liverpool, Mersey Docks and Harbour Board, 1946.

Ships of the Royal Navy: Statement of Losses during the Second World War, London, HMSO, 1947

Statistical Digest of the War, London, HMSO, 1950.

The U-Boat War in the Atlantic, see Hessler, G, below.

Achkasov, V. I., and Pavlovich, N. B. *Soviet Naval Operations in the Great Patriotic War 1941-1945*, Annapolis, NIP, 1981.

Auphan, P., and Mordal, J. *The French Navy in World War II*, Annapolis, USNIP, 1959.

Baker, R. *The Terror of Tobermory: An Informal Biography of Vice Admiral Sir Gilbert Stephenson, KBE, CB, CMG*, London, W. H. Allen, 1972.

Barker, G. H. *Circle of Trees,* Braunton, Merlin, 1989.

Barker, R. *Goodnight, Sorry for Sinking You: The Story of the ss* City of Cairo, London, Collins, 1986.

Barnett, C. *Engage the Enemy More Closely: The Royal Navy in the Second World War*, London, Hodder & Stoughton, 1991.

Baumbach, W. *Broken Swastika: The Defeat of the Luftwaffe*, London, Hale, 1960; published in the United States as *The Life and Death of the Luftwaffe*, New York, Coward McCann, 1960.

Beesly, P. *Room 40: British Naval Intelligence 1914-18*, London, Hamish Hamilton,1982.

------------ *Very Special Intelligence: The Story of the Admiralty's Operational Intelligence Centre 1939-1945*, London, Hamish Hamilton,1977; New York, Doubleday, 1978.

Behrens, C. B. A. *Merchant Shipping and the Demands of War*, London, HMSO, 1955.

Blackett, P. M. S. *Recollections of Problems Studied, 1940-45* (In Brassey's Annual 1953).

Blake, J. *Northern Ireland in the Second World War*, Belfast, HMSO, 1956.

Boutilier, J. A. *The RCN in Retrospect 1910-1968*, Vancouver, University of British Columbia, 1982; see especially the chapter by W. G. D. Lund, *The RCN's Quest for Autonomy in the North Atlantic 1941-1943*.

Brown, D. K. *A Century of Naval Construction: The History of the Royal Corp of Naval Constructors 1883-1983*, London, Conway Maritime Press, 1983.

Brown, E. *Wings on My Sleeve*, London, Barker; Toronto, McClelland & Stewart, 1961.

Brown, J. D. *Carrier Operations in World War II*, 2 vols., London, Ian Allan, 1968-74.

--------------- *Warship Losses of World War II*, London, Arms & Armour, 1990

Brown, M. *We Sailed in Convoy*, London, Hutchinson, 1942.

Buchheim, L.-G. *The U-boat War*, London, Collins; New York, Knopf, 1978.

Buell, T. B. *Master of Sea Power: A Biography of Fleet Admiral Ernest J. King* Boston, Little Brown, 1980

------------- *et al. The Second World War: Europe and the Mediterranean*, Wayne, NJ, Avery Publishing, 1984.

Bunker, J. G. *Liberty Ships: the Ugly Ducklings of World War II*, Annapolis, NIP, 1972.

Burn, A. *The Fighting Captain: Frederic John Walker RN and the Battle of the Atlantic*, London, Leo Cooper, 1993.

Calvocoressi, P., and Wint, G. *Total War: Causes and Courses of the Second World War*, London, Allen Lane, 1972.

Chalmers, W. S. *Max Horton and the Western Approaches: A Biography of Admiral Sir Max Kennedy Horton, GCB, DSO*, London, Hodder & Stoughton, 1954.

Churchill, W. S. *The Second World War*, 6 vols., London, Cassell; Boston, Houghton Mifflin, 1948-53.

Conn, S. *et al. Guarding the United States and its Outposts*, Washington, GPO, 1964

Coote, J. *Submariner*, London, Leo Cooper, 1991; New York, Norton, 1992.

Costello, J., and Hughes, T. *The Battle of the Atlantic*, London, Collins; New York, Dial, 1977.

Coulter, J. L. *Royal Naval Medical Service*, 2 vols., London, HMSO, 1954-56

Craven, W. F. and Cate, J. L. *The Army Air Forces in World War II*, 7 vols., Chicago, University of Chicago Press, 1948-1958.

Creighton, K. *Convoy Commodore*, London, Kimber, 1956.

Cremer, P. *U-333: The Story of a U- Boat Ace*, Oxford, Bodley Head, 1984; published in the USA as *U-boat Commander*, Annapolis, NIP, 1984.

Critchley, M. *Shipwreck Survivors: A Medical Study*, London, Churchill, 1943.

Curry, F. *War at Sea: A Canadian Seaman on the North Atlantic*, Toronto, Lugus, 1990.

Danchev, A. *Very Special Relationship: Field-Marshal Sir John Dill and the Anglo-American Alliance, 1941-1945*, London, Brassey's, 1986.

Dean, M. *The RAF and Two World Wars*, London, Cassell, 1979.

Deist, W. *et al., Germany and the Second World War*, Oxford, Clarendon Press, 1990.

Derry, T. K. *A Short History of Norway*, 2nd ed., London, Allen & Unwin, 1968.

Des Pres, T. *The Survivor: An Anatomy of Life in the Death Camps*, New York, OUP, 1976.

Divine, A. D. *Navies in Exile*, London, New York, Murray, 1944.

Dönitz, K. *Memoirs: Ten Years and Twenty Days*, London, Weidenfeld & Nicolson; Cleveland, World Publishing, 1959.

Dziuban, S. W. *Military Relations between the United States and Canada 1939-1945*, Washington, Department of the Army, 1959.

Eade, C. (ed.) *Secret Session Speeches*, London, Cassell, 1946; published in the USA by Simon & Schuster as *Winstin Churchill's Secret Session Speeches.*

Elliott, P. *Allied Escort Ships of World War Two*, London, Macdonald & Jane's, 1977.

Farago, L. *The Tenth Fleet*, New York, Obolensky, 1962.

Fayle, C. E. *Seaborne Trade (History of the Great War)*, 3 vols., London, HMSO, 1920-24.

Fayle, C. E. *War and the Shipping Industry*, Oxford, OUP, 1927.

Foreman, S. *Shoes and Ships and Sealing-Wax*, London, HMSO, 1986.

Friedman, N. *British Carrier Aviation: the Evolution of the Ships and their Aircraft*, London, Conway; Annapolis, NIP, 1989.

---------------- *US Destroyers: An Illustrated Design History*, Annapolis, NIP, 1982.

---------------- *The US Maritime Strategy*, London, Jane's, 1988.

Gallery, D. *Twenty Million Tons under the Sea*, Chicago, Regnery, 1956; published in the UK as *We Captured a U-boat*, London, Sidgwick & Jackson, 1957.

Gander, L. *Atlantic Battle: A Personal Narrative*, London, Hutchinson, 1941.

Gannon, M. *Operation Drumbeat*, New York, Harper & Row, 1990.

German, T. *The Sea is at Our Gates: The History of the Canadian Navy* Toronto, MacCelland and Stewart, 1990.

Gibbs, N. H., Butler, J. R. M., Gwyer, J. M. A., Howard, M., and Ehrman, J. *Grand Strategy*, 6 vols., London, HMSO, 1956-76.

Gleichauf, J. F. *Unsung Sailors: The Naval Armed Guard in World War II*, Annapolis, NIP, 1990.

Golovko, A. G. *With the Red Fleet: The War Memoirs of the late Admiral Arsenil G. Golovko*, London, Putnam, 1965.

Gordon, G. A. H. *British Seapower and Procurement Between the Wars*, London, Macmillan; Annapolis, NIP, 1988.

Graham, J. G. *A MOWT in the Med.*, author, 1946.

Granatstein, J. G. L. *Canada's War: The Politics of the Mackenzie King Government*, Toronto, OUP, 1975.

Gray, C. *The Leverage of Seapower*, New York, Free Press, 1992.

Greenfield, K. R. *Command Decisions*, Washington, Department of the Army, 1960

Gretton, P. *Convoy Escort Commander*, London, Cassell, 1964.

------------- *Crisis Convoy: The Story of HX231*, London, Davies, 1974.

Grove, E. *Battle for The Fiords*, London, Ian Allan, 1991.

------------ *Maritime Strategy and European Security*, London, Brassey's, 1991.

------------ *Vanguard to Trident: British Naval Policy since World War II*, London, Bodley Head; Annapolis, NIP, 1987.

Gwyer, J. M. A. *See* Gibbs, N. H., *Grand Strategy*.

Hackmann, W. *Seek and Strike: Sonar, Anti-Submarine Warfare and the Royal Navy1914-54*, London, HMSO, 1984.

Hadley, M.L. *U-Boats Against Canada: German Submarines in Canadian Waters*, Kingston, McGill-Queens U. P.; Annapolis, NIP, 1985.

Hague, A. *Destroyers for Great Britain*, London, Greenhill, 1990.

------------- *The Towns*, Kendal, World Ship Society, 1988.

Hall, H. D. *North American Supply (History of The Second World War)* London, HMSO, 1955.

Hancock W. K., and Gowing, M. M. *British War Economy (History of The Second World War)*, London, HMSO, 1949.

Hankey, M. P. A. *Government Control in War* (Lees Knowles Lectures on Military Science. Cambridge, Cambridge University Press, 1945.

Herwig, H. H. *Politics of Frustration: The United States in German Naval Planning 1889-1941*, Boston, Little Brown, 1976.

Hessler, G. *The U-Boat War in The Atlantic 1939-1945* (German Naval History). A facsimile edition in one volume of the three volumes prepared by G. Hessler for the Admiralty, London, HMSO, 1989.

Hezlet, A. *The Submarine and Sea Power*, London, Davies; New York, Stein & Day, 1967.

Hinsley, F. H. *British Intelligence in the Second World War: Its Influence on Strategy and Operations*, 4 vols. in 5, London, HMSO, 1981-90.

Howard, M. *See* Gibbs, N. H., *Grand Strategy*.

Howarth, S. *Men of War: Great Naval Leaders of World War II*, London,Weidenfeld & Nicolson; New York, St Martins Press, 1992.

-------------- *Sea Shell: The Story of Shell's British Tanker Fleets 1892-1992* London,Thomas Reed Publications, 1992.

Hughes, T., and Costello, J. *Battle of the Atlantic*. Published in the UK as by Costello and Hughes, *qv*

Hurd, A. *Britain's Merchant Navy*, London, Odhams, 1942.

Jacobsen, H. A., and Rohwer, J. *Decisive Battles of World War II: The German View*, including Klee, K., *The Battle of Britain* and Rohwer, J., *The U-boat War Against the Allied Supply Lines*, London, Deutsch; Don Mills, Collins; New York, Putnam, 1965.

Jesse, F. T. *The Saga of the San Demetrio*, London, HMSO, 1942.

Jonas, M. *Isolationism in America 1935-1941*, Chicago, Imprint Publications, 1990.

Jones, L. *Shipbuilding in Britain: Mainly between the Two World Wars*, Cardiff, University of Wales Press, 1957.

Kahn, D. *Seizing the Enigma: The Race to Break the German U-Boat Codes, 1939-1943*, Boston, Houghton Mifflin, 1991; London, Souvenir Press, 1992.

Kemp, P. K. *Victory at Sea 1939-1945*, London, Muller, 1957; published in the USA as *Key to Victory: The Triumph of British Seapower in World War Two*, Boston, Little Brown, 1957.

Kerr, J. L. *Touching the Adventures...of Merchantmen in the Second World War* London, Harrap, 1953.

----------- and Grenville, W., *The R.N.V.R.: A Record of Achievement*, London, Harrap, 1957.

Kimball, W. F. *Churchill and Roosevelt: The Complete Correspondence*, 3 vols., Princeton, Princeton U. P., 1984.

King, E. J. *US Navy at War 1941-1945. Official Reports to the Secretary of the Navy...* Washington, US Navy Department, 1946.

------------ and Whitehall, W. *Fleet Admiral King: A Naval Record*, New York, Norton, 1952.

Koliopoulos, J. S. *Greece and the British Connection 1935-1941*, Oxford, Clarendon Press, 1977.

Lamb, J. B. *The Corvette Navy: True Stories from Canada's Atlantic War*, Toronto, Macmillan; London, Futura Publications, 1979.

Lane, F.C. *Ships for Victory: A History of Shipbuilding by the Maritime Commission in World War II*, Baltimore, Johns Hopkins U. P., 1951.

Langer, W. L. *Our Vichy Gamble*, New York, Knopf, 1947.

Lanyard *Stand by to Ram: A Stirring and Graphic Account of Dramatic Episodes in the Great Battle of the Atlantic*, London, Lockwood, 1943.

Larson, H. M., *et al., New Horizons 1927-1950:History of Standard Oil Company (New Jersey,* New York, Evanston, San Francisco, London, Standard Oil, 1971

Law, D. *The Royal Navy in World War Two: An Annotated Bibliography* London, Greenhill, 1988.

Lawrence, H. *A Bloody War*, Toronto, Macmillan, 1979.

Layton, E. T., *et.al., "And I was There": Pearl Harbor and Midway - Breaking the Secrets*, New York, Morrow, 1985.

Lemos, A. G. *The Greeks and the Sea*, London, Cassell, 1976.

Lennox-Kerr, J. *See* Kerr, J. L.

Lenton, H. T., and Colledge, J .J. *Warships of World War II*, London, Ian Allan, 1964

Leutze, J. R. *Bargaining for Supremacy: Anglo-American Naval Collaboration 1937-1941*, Chapel Hill, University of North Carolina Press, 1977.

Lewin, R. *Ultra Goes to War: The Secret Story*, London, Hutchinson; New York, McGraw Hill, 1978.

Lloyd, A. R. J. M. *Seakeeping: Ship Behaviour in Rough Weather*, Chichester, Ellis Horwood, 1989.

Loewenheim, F. L. *et. al., Roosevelt and Churchill: Their Secret Wartime Correspondence*, London, Barrie & Jenkins; New York, Saturday Review Press, 1975.

Love, R.W. *The Chiefs of Naval Operations*, Annapolis, NIP, 1980.

------------- *History of the US Navy*, 2 vols., Harrisburg, Stackpole Books, 1992.

Lund, P., and Ludlam, H. *PQ17 - Convoy to Hell: The Survivors' Story*, London, Foulsham, 1968.

Lyon, D. *The Denny List*, 4 vols, Greenwich, National Maritime Museum, 1975.

Lynch, M. *Salty Dips*, 3 vols, Ottawa, NOAC, 1983-8.

Lynch, T. G. *Canada's Flowers: History of the Corvettes of Canada*, Halifax, Nimbus, 1981.

McCance, R. A., *et al., The Hazards to Men lost at Sea, 1940-44 (MRC Special Report Series, No 291)*, London, MRC, 1956.

McCue, B. *U-boats in the Bay of Biscay*, Washington, National Defense University Press, 1990.

MacIntyre, D. *U-Boat Killer*, London, Weidenfeld & Nicolson, 1956; New York, Norton, 1957.

----------------- *The Battle of the Atlantic*, London, Batsford; New York, Macmillan, 1961

---------------- *The Naval War against Hitler*, London, Batsford; New York, Scribner, 1971.

Macmillan, N. *The Royal Air Force in the World War*, 4 vols, London, Harrap, 1942-50.

Macpherson, K. *The River Class Destroyers of the Royal Canadian Navy*, Toronto, Musson, 1985.

Marriott, L. *Royal Navy Frigates since 1945*, London, Ian Allan, 1990.

Marwick, A. *War and Social Change in the Twentieth Century: A comparative study of Britain, France, Germany, Russia and the United States*, London, Macmillan, 1974.

Mason, J. T. *The Atlantic War Remembered*, Annapolis, NIP, 1990.

Medlicott, W. N. *The Economic Blockade*, London, HMSO, 1952.

Meigs, M. C. *Slide Rules and Submarines*, Washington, National Defense University Press, 1990.

Metzler, J. *The Laughing Cow: A U-boat Captain's Story*, London, Kimber, 1955

Middlebrook, M. *Convoy: The Battles for Convoys SC122 and HX229*, London, Allen Lane, 1976

Middleton, J. *HMS King Alfred 1939-1945*, Brighton, author, 1986.

Milner, M. *North Atlantic Run: The Royal Canadian Navy and the Battle for the Convoys*, Toronto, Toronto U.P.; Annapolis, NIP, 1985.

Minns, R. *Bombers and Mash*, London, Virago, 1980.

Mitchell, W. H., and Sawyer, L. A. *Empire Ships of World War II*, 2nd ed. London, Lloyds of London Press, 1990.

Monsarrat, N. *H.M. Corvette*, London, Cassell, 1942.

----------------- *HM Frigate*, London, Cassell, 1946.

----------------- *The Cruel Sea*, London, Cassell, 1951.

Morison, S. E. *History of U.S. Naval Operations in World War II*, 15 vols, Vol. 1, The Battle of the Atlantic, September 1939-1943, and Vol. 10, The Atlantic Battle Won: May 1943-May 1945, Boston, Little Brown; London, OUP, 1947-62.

Morse, P.M. *In at the Beginning: A Physicist's Life*, Cambridge, Mass., and London, MIT Press, 1977

Moss, M., and Hume, J. R. *Shipbuilders to the World: 125 Years of Harland & Wolff*, Belfast, Blackstaff, 1986.

Mountfield, S. *Western Gateway: A History of the Mersey Docks and Harbour Board*, Liverpool, Liverpool U.P., 1965

Næss, E. D. *Autobiography of a Shipping Man*, Colchester, Seatrade, 1977.

Nielsen, R. S. *Oil Tanker Economics* (Weltschiffahrts-Archiv no. 7), Bremen, Weltschiffahrts, 1959.

Nock, O. S. *Britain's Railways at War*, London, Ian Allen, 1971.

Padfield, P. *Dönitz: The Last Führer*, London, Gollancz; New York, Harper & Row,1984.

Palmer, M. A. *Origins of the Maritime Strategy*, Washington, Naval Historical Center, 1988.

Paris, M. *The Novels of World War Two*, London, Library Association, 1990.

Payton-Smith, D. J. *Oil. A Study of War-time Policy and Administration*, London, HMSO, 1971.

Peebles, H. B. *Warship Building on the Clyde*, Edinburgh, Donald, 1987.

Petrow, D. *The Bitter Years: The Invasion and Occupation of Denmark and Norway April 1940-May 1945*, New York, Morrow, 1974.

Pogue, F.C. *George C. Marshall*, 4 vols., New York, Viking Press,1963-1987.

Poolman, K. *Focke-Wulf Condor: Scourge of the Atlantic*, London, Macdonald & Jane's, 1978

--------------- *Allied Escort Carriers of World War II in Action*, Poole, Blandford Press, 1987.

--------------- *The British Sailor: Experiences of War*, London, Arms & Armour, 1990

Postan, M. M. *British War Production*, London, HMSO, 1952.

Powell, L. H. *A Hundred Years On: History of the Liverpool Steam Ship Owners' Association, 1858-1958*, Liverpool, Liverpool Steamship Owners' Association, 1958.

Preston, A., and Raven, A. *Flower Class Corvettes (Ensign 3)*, Bivouac Books, 1973

Price, A. *Aircraft versus Submarine: The Evolution of the Anti-Submarine Aircraft 1912 to 1972*, London, Kimber, 1973.

Pugh, P. *The Cost of Seapower*, London, Conway Maritime Press, 1986.

Raeder, E. *Struggle for the Sea*, London, Kimber, 1959.

Reckner, J. R. *Teddy Roosevelt's Great White Fleet*, Annapolis, NIP, 1988.

Reynolds, C. G. *Famous American Admirals*, New York, Van Nostrand Reinhold, 1978.

Reynolds, D. *Britannia Overruled:Power and Policy in the Twentieth Century World* (US subtitle:*British Policy and World Power in the Twentieth Century)*, London, Longman, 1991; New York 1992.

Reynolds, Q. *Convoy*, New York, Random House, 1942.

Richards, D., and Saunders, H. St. G. *The Royal Air Force 1939-45*, 3 vols, London, HMSO, 1953-54.

Roberts, L. *The Canadian Merchant Navy at War*, in *Canada's War at Sea, qv.*

Robertson, T. *The Golden Horseshoe*, London, Evans, 1955: New York, Dutton, 1956.

--------------- *Walker, R.N.: The Story of Captain Frederic John Walker, CB, DSO and three bars, RN*, London, Evans, 1956: New York, Bantam, 1979.

Rohwer, J. *The Critical Convoy Battles of March 1943*, London, Ian Allan; Annapolis, NIP, 1977.

--------------- *Axis Submarine Successes 1939-1945*, Cambridge, PSL, 1983.

--------------- and Hümmelchen, G. *Chronology of the War at Sea*, 2nd ed. London, Greenhill, 1992.

Rosen, S. McK. *The Combined Boards of the Second World War: An Experiment in International Administration*, New York, Columbia UP, 1951.

Roskill, S.W. *The War At Sea, 1939-45*, 3 vols. in 4, London, 1954-61.

---------------.*Naval Policy Between the Wars*, 2 vols, London, Collins, 1976.

Rössler, E. *The U-boat: The Evolution and Technical History of German Submarines*, London, Arms & Armour Press; Annapolis, NIP, 1981.

Ruge, F. *Der Seekrieg: The German Navy's Story,* Annapolis,USNIP, 1957

Russel, J. *Britain's Food in Wartime*, Oxford, OUP, 1941.

Savage C. I. *Inland Transport*, London, HMSO, 1957.

Sawyer, L. A., and Mitchell, W. H. *The Liberty Ships: The History of the Emergency Type Cargo Ships constructed in the United States during World War II*, Newton Abbot, David & Charles; Cambridge, Cornell Maritime, 1970.

Schull, J. *The Far Distant Ships*, Ottawa, King's Printer, 1961.

Scott, J. D., and Hughes, R. *The Administration of War Production*, London, HMSO, 1955.

Scott, M. *War is a Funny Business*, Bognor Regis, Square Rigged Services, 1989.

Shaw, M. *The Dialectics of War: An Essay in the Social Theory of Total War and Peace*, London, Pluto, 1988.

Shean, M. *Corvette and Submarine*, Claremont, W. A., author, 1992

Showell, J. P. M. *U-Boat Command and the Battle of the Atlantic*, Conway Maritime Press, London, 1989.

-------------------- *U-boats Under the Swastika*, London, Ian Allan, 1973.

Silverstone, P. *US Warships of World War II*, London, Ian Allan, 1966; Garden City, Doubleday, 1970.

Simpson, B. M. *Admiral Harold R. Stark: Architect of Victory*, Columbia, SC, University of South Carolina Press, 1989.

Simpson, G. W. G. *Periscope View*, Macmillan, London, 1972.

Skaggs, D. C., and Browning, R. S. *In Defense of the Republic*, Belmont, CA, Wadsworth Publishing Co., 1991.

Slessor, J. *The Central Blue*, London, Cassell, 1956; New York, Praeger, 1957.

Sokolsky, J. J. *Sea Power in the Nuclear Age*, London and New York, Routledge, 1991.

Stacey, C. P. *Arms, Men and Governments: The War Policies of Canada 1939-1945*, Ottawa, Department of National Defence, 1970.

Stephan, J .J. *Hawaii under the Rising Sun: Japan's Plan for Conquest after Pearl Harbor*, Honolulu, University of Hawaii Press, 1984.

Sturmey, S. G. *British Shipping and World Competition*, London, Athlone Press, 1962.

Swettenham, J. *Canada's Atlantic War*, Toronto,Samuel Stevens, 1979.

Tansill, C. C. *Back Door to War: The Roosevelt Foreign Policy, 1933-1941* Chicago, Regnery, 1952.

Tarrant, V. E. *The U-Boat Offensive*, London, Arms & Armour, 1989.

Taylor, A. J. P. *English History 1914-1945*, Oxford, OUP, 1965.

Terraine, J. *The Right of the Line*, London, Hodder & Stoughton, 1985.

-------------- *Business in Great Waters: The U-boat Wars 1916-1945*, London, Leo Cooper, 1989; US title, *The U-Boat Wars*, New York, Putnam, 1989.

Terrell, E. *Admiralty Brief: The Story of Inventions that contributed to Victory in the Battle of the Atlantic*, London, Harrap, 1958.

Thetford, O. *British Naval Aircraft Since 1912*, London, Putnam, 1982.

Thomas, C. *The German Navy in the Nazi Era*, London, Unwin Hyman, 1990.

Thorne, C. G. *Allies of a Kind: The Allies, Britain and the War Against Japan, 1941-1945*, Oxford, New York, OUP, 1978.

Tidman, K. R. *The Operations Evaluation Group*, Annapolis, NIP, 1984.

Till, G. *The Future of British Sea Power*, London, Macmillan, 1984.

Tucker, G. *The Naval Service of Canada*, 2 vols, Ottawa, King's Printer, 1952.

Van der Vat, D. *The Atlantic Campaign*, London, Hodder & Stoughton; New York, Harper & Row, 1988.

Vause, J. *U-boat Ace*, Annapolis, NIP, 1990.

Waddington, C. H. *OR in World War II: Operational Research against the U-boat*, London, Elek Science, 1973.

Warner, D., and Warner, P. *Disaster in the Pacific: New Light on the Battle of Savo Island*, Annapolis, NIP, 1992.

Waters, S. D. *Ordeal at Sea: The New Zealand Shipping Company in the Second World War 1939-1945*, London, New Zealand Shipping Company, 1949

Watts, A. J. *Japanese Warships of World War II*, Ian Allan, London, 1967.

-------------- *The U-Boat Hunters*, London, Macdonald & Jane's, 1976.

Webster, C. and Frankland, N. *The Strategic Air Offensive Against Germany 1939-1945*, 4 vols, London, HMSO, 1961.

Weichold, E. *Axis Naval Policy and Operations in the Mediterranean 1939-43*, Washington, US Navy Department, 1951.

Weigley, R. F. *The American Way of War*, Bloomington, Indiana UP, 1973.

Wemyss, D. E. G. *Walker's Groups In the Western Approaches*, Liverpool, Liverpool Daily Post & Echo, 1948.

Werner, H. *Iron Coffins: A Personal Account of the German U-boat Battles of World War II*, New York, Holt Rinehart, 1969; London, Barker, 1970.

West, F. *Lifeboat Number Seven*, London, Kimber, 1960.

Whaley, B. *Codeword Barbarossa*, Cambridge, MIT, 1973.

Whelan, J. R. *Hunters in the Sky: Fighter Aces of World War II*, Washington, Regnery Gateway, 1991.

Whinney, R. *The U-boat Peril: An Anti-Submarine Commander's War*, Poole, Blandford, 1986.

Williams, M. *Captain Gilbert Roberts RN and the Anti-U-boat School*, London, Cassell, 1979.

Winterbotham, F. W. *The Ultra Secret*, London, Weidenfeld & Nicolson, 1974.

Wood, D., and Dempster, D. *The Narrow Margin: The Battle of Britain and the Rise of Air Power, 1930-1940*, London, Tristar, Washington, Smithsonian Institute, 1990 (first published by Hutchinsons in 1961).

Zimmerman, D. *The Great Naval Battle of Ottawa: How Admirals, Scientists and Politicians Impeded the Development of High Technology in Canada's Wartime Navy*, Toronto, 1989.

INDEX

NOTE: Ranks and titles are generally the highest mentioned in the text